All the
MEN
of the Bible

Books in This Series

All the
MEN
of the Bible

Herbert Lockyer

ZONDERVAN™

GRAND RAPIDS, MICHIGAN 49530 USA

ZONDERVAN™

All the Men of the Bible
Copyright © 1958 by Herbert Lockyer

Requests for information should be addressed to:

Zondervan, *Grand Rapids, Michigan 49530*

Library of Congress Catalog Card Number 58-4616

ISBN 0-310-28081-8

Printed in the United States of America

06 07 08 /DC/ 70 69 68

ABOUT THE AUTHOR

Dr. Herbert Lockyer was born in London in 1886 and held pastorates in Scotland and England for twenty-five years before coming to the United States in 1935.

In 1937 he received the honorary Doctor of Divinity degree from Northwestern Evangelical Seminary.

In 1955 he returned to England where he lived for many years. He then returned to the United States where he continued to devote time to the writing ministry until his death in November of 1984.

All poetry is but a giving of names.
Biography is the only true history:
History is the garb of biography.
                                    Thomas Carlyle

The beginning of all instruction is the study of names.
—*Antisthenes,* c. 400 B.C.

Contents

Below is a partial list of the major and familiar male characters of the Bible covered in this book, alphabetically arranged for easy reference:

The Romantic History
of Bible Names

I

The Romantic History
of Bible Names

Many readers of the Bible treat its genealogical lists as despised regions, and wonder why they form part of a divine revelation such as the Bible is. At first glance, there seems to be no point or profit in the bare enumeration of the names of men who died thousands of years ago.

Yet because the Bible is the inspired Word of God, even these uninteresting lists of names were written for our learning, and if properly studied they yield remarkable results. Many of these names describe nations, as well as men, and have therefore a priceless historical value. Consulting them, we find they often show the course taken by men in their settlement over the earth. Ancient Hebrew names, which at first sight might appear unattractive, and are passed over as unworthy of serious thought, have something about them which compels our prayerful consideration. In many cases Bible names are fragments of ancient history, revelations of divine purposes, expressions of hopes and prophecies of the future.

Every Jew kept a record of his lineage and was proud if he could claim royal or priestly descent. Joseph, for example, could boast of himself as "a son of David." The genealogical lists of Chronicles, Ezra, Nehemiah, Matthew and Luke, containing the majority of named men, prove how meticulous the Jews were in the preservation of their pedigree. It was common in almost every Jewish family to transcribe a family tree.

Josephus, the Jewish historian who lived in the time of our Lord, tells us that he could trace his ancestry back to the Maccabeans, or priest-rulers, from public registers. He also states that wherever Jews settled such registers were kept of births and marriages of the priesthood, and that registers went back some two thousand years. That the Israelites were most interested in the preservation of their pedigree can be proven by I Chronicles 9:1. The forfeit of those tribes who had lost their pedigree is seen in Ezra 2:59 and Nehemiah 7:63.

Truth taught by names is another important aspect to observe. The significance of names opens up a field of pleasant and profitable investigation to all true lovers of Scripture. While many of the names may not have been designed to be typical, they are certainly suggestive of spiritual truth, as can be seen in the names Jacob gave his sons.

11

In ancient Israel the name of a person was supposed to indicate some characteristic of that person, or be linked to circumstances, however trivial or monotonous, connected with his birth. Names and nature, as well as names and facts, were made to correspond, as can be found in the name Moses gave his son (Ex. 2:22), and the naming of Ichabod (I Sam. 4:21). As we review the suggested meanings given to the names alphabetically set forth in the following chapter, we will find that they cover many associations.

Names denote natural or personal qualities. A classic illustration of this is Abigail's plea to David for her worthless husband: "...as his name is, so is he: Nabal is his name and folly is with him" (I Sam. 25:25). Nabal means "fool." In effect then, Abigail said, "Pay no attention to my husband. He's a fool by name, and a fool by nature."

Names point to an occupation. There are many instances of these occupational names: Archippus, "governor of horses"; Asa, "physician"; Carmi, "vine-dresser."

Names bear a symbolic or prophetic feature. An instance of this is seen in the name Shear-jashub, "a remnant shall return" (Isa. 7:3). Maher-shalal-hash-baz, one of the longest names in the Bible, means "Haste ye, haste ye, to the spoil" (Isa. 8:1).

Names are fixed immediately after birth. In the choice of a name for a child, the mother usually exercised such a privilege (Gen. 19:37; 29:32). Sometimes, however, the father chose the name (Gen. 4:26; 16:15). Occasionally other interested persons came forward with a name (Ruth 4:17; Luke 1:57-63).

John the Baptist and Christ had names divinely given *before* their birth (Luke 1:13; Matt. 1:21).

Names are bestowed indifferently on men and women. Now and again a man and a woman bear the same name, for example, Abihail (Esther 2:15; I Chron. 2:29). Then persons and places have the same name. Did you know that Eden is the name of a man as well as the garden where Adam first lived, and that Bethlehem is the name of a person as well as the town where Jesus was born?

Names are connected with family relationships. A few names are taken from relatives (Luke 1:59). Ahab means "father's brother"; Ahban, "brother is son"; Ahiam, "maternal uncle." Ab means "father," so we have many names beginning with these letters, such as Abimelech ("whose father is king").

Names carry a religious relationship or significance. Sometimes a name expressed some hope or aspiration on the part of parents, as in John, meaning, "gracious gift of God." Other names (such as Samuel, meaning "God hath heard") were conceived in the spirit of prayer because they expressed religious expectation on behalf of the child. This name marks the fact that the child was born in answer to prayer.

Ancient peoples fashioned names out of the names of their gods, proved in Pan-Bel-adagal, meaning "I look to Bel," and in other heathen names in which gods are invoked. This also characterizes many Hebrew names into which the idea of God enters freely. The divine name *El*, meaning "God," is incorporated within many proper names of persons, as in Israel or Eliakim. The same is true of names containing *Jah*, or *Jeho*, as in Jahaziah and Jehoiakim. Other names extol divine sovereignty, as in Adonijah, meaning, "Jehovah is Lord."

Names are changed by God's direct intervention. Many names were not only given by God but changed by His direction: Abram to Abraham; Sarai to Sarah; Jacob to Israel; Oshea to Joshua.

Names deemed important had an acute consciousness of meaning. This fact is borne out in such names as Reuben, "see, a son"; Judah, "praise"; Joseph, "he adds." At times, given names reflect the characteristics of the parents, which the children inherited. Weak, indecisive parents were likely to coin weak, indecisive names for their children who manifested character in keeping with their names.

Names are from the vegetable world. We have many instances of names of this order: Adam, "red earth"; Elah, "oak"; Asnah, "bramble"; Shamar, "thorn."

Names are associated with natural objects in the world: Geshem, "rain"; Barak, "lightning"; Boanerges, "sons of thunder"; Adoni-Bezek, "lightning of the Lord."

Names are taken from the animal creation: Caleb, "dog"; Dan, "lion's whelp"; Shaphan, "rock-badger"; Achbor, "mouse"; Parosh, "flea."

Names, separate or double, of the same person are frequent. Some examples are: "Saul who is called Paul," "Simon Barjonas," "Simon Zelotes," "Judas Iscariot." Alongside of these double names we have those men who carry a distinguished and honorable surname.

By "surname" is meant an additional name — a name to be distinguished from the "Christian" name, the name over and above, a *sur-*, or *super*-name. As surnames, as we presently know them, were unknown among the Hebrews, the word as used in the Bible simply means the bestowal of a flattering or honorable title. Foreigners, envious of the privileges of the Jews, were eager to surname themselves by the name of Israel, that is, be enrolled as members of the Jewish nation (Isa. 44:5). God surnamed Cyrus, meaning that He gave him the honored title of "my shepherd," thereby appointing him to be His instrument for the restoration of His people (Isa. 44:28).

In the New Testament the custom of bestowing this kind of surname was becoming more widespread, for example, Simon surnamed Peter (Acts 10:5, 32); James and John surnamed Boanerges (Mark 3:17); Judas surnamed Iscariot (Luke 22:3).

Then we have names to which labels are attached indicating work or worth such as Elijah the Tishbite, Nehemiah the king's cupbearer, John the Baptist, James the Lord's brother and Luke the beloved physician.

When some of these persons experienced a changed life, why permit them to carry an appendage so suggestive of the old, worthless life? If Mary Magdalene was no longer demon-possessed, why continue to write of her, "out of whom went seven devils"? It may be that the wearers of some of these labels carried them so as not to forget the past. They were not to forget the pit from whence they had been digged (Isa. 51:1). Perhaps they were retained that those who bore them might maintain a fitting humility.

We conclude this first section of our study with two features suggested by Elsdon C. Smith, in his most enlightening book, *Story of Our Names*.

1. *The Treasure of a Name.* How true it was when Solomon declared that "a good name is rather to be chosen than great riches" (Prov. 22:1). A name is not only a person's most prominent feature to others, but his greatest treasure. The old Roman proverb states, "without a name a man is nothing." Because "a good name is better than precious ointment" (Eccl. 7:1), all who bear good names should pray for grace to live in harmony with them.

2. *The Abiding Influence of Bible Names.* Do we realize the tremendous influence of the Bible on our surnames and Christian names? It is reckoned that more than half the people of the civilized world have names originating from the Bible's vast collection.

With the publication of the Genevan Bible in 1560, the adoption of Bible names became popular. The common people, now interested in Biblical characters, had a long list of names from which to choose, and baptismal registers became records of Bible names. Elsdon C. Smith tells us that about the only Old Testament names used with any frequency before the Protestant Reformation were Adam, Elias, Samson, David, Solomon, Daniel, Joseph and Benjamin. After the Reformation the type of name changed. Because of the Puritan hatred of Roman Catholicism saints' names were avoided. Names like Elijah, Moses, Aaron, Joshua and Nathaniel became popular. English names not in the Bible were rejected as pagan. Even the longest name in the Bible, Maher-shalal-hash-baz, was often used.

Today many of our most frequently used Christian names and surnames are traceable directly to the Bible, particularly to the New Testament. Over a century ago Old Testament names were more prominent. Now *John* for a boy and *Mary* for a girl hold the lead.

The Alphabetical Order of
All Men Named in the Bible

II

The Alphabetical Order of All Men Named in The Bible

The Bible revolves around personalities and, as Augustine expressed it, "The sacred record, like a faithful mirror has no flattery in its portrait." The biographies of men outside the Bible sometimes leave us cold. The characters portrayed seem to be too ideal. Nothing is said about their faults, weaknesses and sins. But as we pursue our journey through the Scriptures, we are greatly encouraged, for here are those of like passions as ourselves.

In his arresting chapter on "Composite Portraits," in *The Joy of Bible Study*, Harrington Lees reminds us that

> ...the lives of men and women who speak to us from the pages of Scripture may be a veritable gold-mine of experience to us if we can remember the fact that they lived similar lives and triumphed—by faith, as the writer to the Hebrews reminds us—or, if they entered not into their land of promise, failed through disobedience or unbelief. All good biography is fruitful, but Scripture biography is singularly so.

The Bible is the most faithful book in the world. It tells the truth about its men and women. We have the tendency to eulogize our heroes, omitting altogether their faults. But the Bible gives us a true picture; light or shade, good or evil are depicted without apology or excuse. It is a wonderful canvas of human life. Every phase of human nature is exhibited in the portraits of the Bible gallery.

Because of the limitations of space we were not able to give a full synopsis of the Bible men biographically treated. For those who desire to follow this line of study the following suggestions may be of service.

Begin with a person whose story is briefly told. Enoch, for example, only occupies six or seven verses, yet what a story they unfold. Mastering a character like Enoch whets the appetite for the study of another who fills a larger niche in the Bible's gallery of saints.

Collect all relevant Bible passages. It is essential, with the aid of a concordance, to gather into a group all references to the person to be studied.

Analyze the character of the person. Read and reread gathered Bible material with a pencil in hand, noting particular or peculiar traits.

Set down the elements of power and success. Show how heredity or personal ability produce these elements.

Describe evidences of weakness and failure. Indicate the circumstances responsible for these.

Elaborate on victory over difficulties. There is rich material along this line in characters like Joseph, David and Paul.

Suggest various helps to success. In some Bible lives there were many paths to fame and honor.

Mark out any privileges abused. When dealing with a person such as Esau, it is easy to sketch his loss.

Depict opportunities for good neglected, or how the opportunities could have been improved.

Fill in details of the life. Recorded facts of birth, parentage, death, etc., should be mentioned.

Summarize the lessons to be learned from the life. The lives of great men remind us that we too can make our lives sublime!

Note any relation the person may have had to God or to Jesus Christ. Divine relationship shapes character and determines destiny.

Study the authors who have written on Biblical characters. Once you have undertaken personal study, there is a wide field of literature to choose from, such as the books listed in the bibliography.

It has been a painstaking yet profitable task to acquaint oneself with the thousands of named and unnamed men of the Bible. With the majority of them, it has been a mere handshake and the simple questions: "Who are you? Where were you born? What is your background?"

For the most part we have nothing but the monotony of their names. Their human history was not written for our learning. We know nothing of the facts of their families, their sorrows or songs, their tears or triumphs, their vices or virtues. In the company of others, however, we lingered longer, seeing that the Divine Artist sketched their profiles in fuller detail.

Nowhere in all the world have we such an album of human life. The Bible's portrait gallery is superb. What a mixture of character it presents! Here you will find kings and knaves, princes and paupers, the tenderhearted and the traitorous, saints and sinners, the courageous and the cowardly. Here we have men of like passions as ourselves. No wonder the Bible speaks of itself as a *mirror.* As we look at the lives of its men, pure and profane, we see ourselves.

The formidable assignment of alphabetically arranging *all* the men of the Bible appeared when it was discovered that there are well over three thousand specifically named.

How rich in biographical material the Bible is! A distinguishing feature of Holy Writ is its faithfulness in recording human life and character. What a perfect biography of humanity it is! Think of what we can learn from —

The lowly life of Mephibosheth
The tried friendship of Ittai

The holy fidelity of Nathan
The lofty courage of Benaiah
The patriarchal kindness of Barzillai
The princely courtesy of Araunah.

Then there are those men who stand out as beacons, lights, warning us of dangerous vices, such as —

Joab's deeds of blood
Ammon's intemperate passion
Absalom's base ambition
Shimei's violence and meanness
David's fatal lapses.

There are also saints at hand to encourage and guide heavenly pilgrims of every age. Think of the variety covered by the men of the Bible! We have —

Abraham for explorers
Job for merchant princes
Moses for patriots
Samuel for rulers
Elijah for reformers
Joseph for men of distinction
Daniel for the forlorn
Jeremiah for the persecuted
Caleb for the soldier
Boaz for the farmer
Amos for the lay-preacher.

Well, all the men of the Bible, from A to Z are lined up for us, so let us go out and make their acquaintance, shall we? And as we meet each one of them, may help be ours to emulate their graces but shun their failures.

A

AARON [Aâr' on]—A MOUNTAIN OF STRENGTH or ENLIGHTENED. *The son of Amran and of Jochebed* his wife, and of the family of Kohath, who was the second son of Levi, who was the third son of Jacob. Miriam was Aaron's elder sister and Moses was his junior brother by some three years. Aaron married Elisheba, daughter of Amminadab and sister of Naashon, and by her had four sons — Nadab and Abihu, Eleazar and Ithamar (Ex. 6:16–23).

The Man Who Was an Excellent Speaker

It is somewhat fitting that Aaron should not only begin the list of men under the letter A—one of the longest lists of all—but also of all the men listed alphabetically in the Bible.

The first glimpse we have of this great Bible saint is that of an eloquent speaker, and because of this fact he was chosen by God to be the prophet and spokesman of his brother Moses in his encounters with Pharaoh. The fame of his oratory was known in heaven, and recognized by God. A great orator has been defined as a good man well-skilled in speaking, and of such capacities was Aaron. When Moses protested against appearing before Pharaoh, pleading that he was not eloquent, but slow of speech and of a slow tongue (Ex. 3:10; 4:11, 12) did he refer to a defect of speech he suffered from? "Not eloquent" means, *not a man of words* and "slow of speech, and of a slow tongue" means *heavy of speech and heavy of tongue.*

There are those authorities who suggest that Moses had a stammer or lisp, a physical impediment of speech necessitating a spokesman of Aaron's ability. It would seem as if God's promise that He would be with his mouth and was able to help him overcome any disability as a speaker, bears out the thought of an actual defect of speech. This we do know, Aaron must have spoken with great power when he addressed Pharaoh on the signs and plagues of Exodus four through eleven.

Aaron plays an important part in the inauguration and development of priestly functions, all of which are prescribed in Leviticus. Among the mature males of Israel there were three classes:

From the tribes of Israel came the *warriors.*

From the tribe of Levi came the *workers.*

From the family of Aaron came the *worshipers.*

Aaron became the first high priest of Israel, and in Aaron and his sons we have a fitting type of Christ and His Church. The ministry of Aaron in connection with the Tabernacle with all of its services is referred to by the writer of the Hebrews as a figure of the true ministry of the High Priest who is Jesus.

Yet in spite of his high and holy calling, Aaron suffered from the murmurings of the people (Ex. 16:2; Num. 14:2). He was persuaded by the people to make a golden calf and was reproved by Moses for his action (Ex. 32). Aaron's penitence, however, was complete, and his service faithful. Perhaps Aaron could be placed at the head of all Old Testament penitents, for his own sins as well as for the sins of others. While Aaron was Jesus Christ in type and by imputation, he yet remains Aaron all the time, Aaron of the molten image and of many untold transgressions besides. With Moses, Aaron was excluded from the Promised Land (Num. 20:12). He died at the age of 123 years on Mount Hor, in the land of Edom, and was buried there (Num. 20).

A profitable meditation on "The Priestly Calling" could be developed along the line of the following suggestions.

I. Aaron was a type of Christ, the Great High Priest.

    A. Both were chosen of God. Christ is the only mediator between God and man.

    B. Both had to be clean, seeing they bore the vessels of the Lord. Aaron was a sinner and needed cleansing—Christ was sinless.

    C. Both are clothed—Aaron with his coat, robe and ephod; Christ robed in garments of glory and beauty.

D. Both are crowned—Aaron with his mitre, or holy crown, Christ with His many diadems.

E. Both are consecrated or set apart—Aaron was blood sprinkled and had his hands filled for the Lord (Lev. 8:24–27); Christ is sanctified forever (John 17:16, 17).

F. Both feed on the bread of consecration (cf. Lev. 22:21, 22 with John 4:32).

G. Both are blameless. No man with a blemish could come nigh to offer a sacrifice unto the Lord. Christ was holy, harmless, undefiled.

II. Aaron's sons were types of the Christian. What a precious truth the priesthood of all true believers is.

A. They had names closely associated. "Aaron and his sons" appears ten times. Aaron's sons were called *in* him. We were chosen *in* Christ from the eternal past. *Priests* because *sons*, is true in both cases.

B. They had the same calling. Aaron and his sons were priests. Christ and ourselves are priests unto God.

C. They had the same anointing. Aaron and his sons were accepted by the same blood and anointed with the same oil. Christ entered the veil by His own blood, and we enter by the same blood. Head and members alike are anointed with the same blessed Spirit.

D. They had their hands filled with the same offering, ate the same food, were under the same authority. How these aspects are likewise applicable to Christ and His own!

ABAGTHA [Ă băg' thă]—HAPPY, PROSPEROUS. *One of the seven chamberlains* or eunuchs sent by king Ahasuerus to fetch his queen, Vashti, to the banquet (Esther 1:10, 11).

ABDA [Ăb' dă]—SERVANT or WORSHIPER.
1. *Father of Adoniram,* Solomon's officer in charge of forced levy (I Kings 4:6).
2. *A chief Levite* after the exile, the son of Shemaiah or Shammua (Neh. 11:17). He is called Obadiah in I Chronicles 9:16.

ABDEEL [Ăb' de el]—SERVANT OF GOD. *The father of Shelemiah,* and one of those ordered by king Jehoiakim to arrest Jeremiah and Baruch (Jer. 36:26).

ABDI [Ăb' dī]—SERVANT OF JEHOVAH.
1. *Grandfather of Ethan,* a Merarite, and one of those set over the service of song by David (I Chron. 6:44).
2. *A son of Elam,* who had married a foreign wife (Ezra 10:26).

ABDIEL [Ăb' dĭ el]—SERVANT OF GOD. *The son of Guni,* a Gadite of Gilead (I Chron. 5:15).

ABDON [Ăb′ dŏn]—SERVILE, SERVICE or CLOUD OF JUDGMENT.

1. *A son of Hillel,* the Pirathonite, Abdon judged Israel for eight years, and because of a plurality of wives, had forty sons and thirty nephews, who rode seventy ass colts (Judg. 12:13–15). Perhaps the same as Bedan in I Samuel 12:11.

2. *A Benjamite* in Jerusalem (I Chron. 8:23).

3. *The first-born of Jehiel* from Maachah (I Chron. 8:30; 9:36).

4. *A son of Micah* sent with others by king Josiah to Huldah the prophetess to enquire of Jehovah regarding the Book of the Law found in the Temple (II Chron. 34:20). Called Achbor in II Kings 22:12. Also the name of a Levitical city in Asher (Josh. 21:30; I Chron. 6:74).

ABEDNEGO (Ă bĕd′–ne gō]—SERVANT OF NEBO or SERVANT OF LIGHT. The name given by the prince of the eunuchs of King Nebuchadnez-zar to Azariah, one of the four young princes of Judah who were car-ried away into Babylon. He was one of the three faithful Jews de-livered from the fiery furnace (Dan. 1:7; 2:49; 3). How God honored the faith and courage of these Hebrew youths!

The Man Who Defied a King

There are at least four lessons to be learned from the dauntless, defiant witness of Abed-nego and his two companions:

I. God's dearest servants are sometimes called to pass through heavy trials.

II. God is able to deliver when help seems farthest off. He does not promise to keep us free *from* trouble, but that He will be with us *in* trouble.

III. God's permitted furnace purifies, but never destroys us. As we pass through the fire, He is with us and we cannot be burned.

IV. God's children must never be ashamed of Him. No matter how adverse the situation, we must be bold and unshaken in our witness.

ABEL [Ā′ bĕl]—MEADOW, VANITY or VAPOR. *The second son of Adam and Eve* slain by his brother Cain (Gen. 4:1–15; Matt. 23:35; Heb. 11:4; 12:24).

The Man Who Was First to Die

Abel's name, meaning breath or vapor, is associated with the short-ness of his life. What was his life but a vapor? (Ps. 90 : 6; Jas. 4:14) Abel was a shepherd and a possessor of flocks and herds; Cain was a tiller of the ground. It was not occupation, however, that parted these first two brothers in the world, but their conception of what was pleasing and acceptable to God. Abel feared God and because he did, he offered to God the best of his flock. His was a sacrifice of blood and represented the surrender of a heart to God. Cain brought what he had gathered from the earth, an offering representing his own effort. Because God accepted Abel's offering and not Cain's, the angry brother slew Abel in the field. But Abel's blood cried from the ground for punishment. Abel's blood is placed alongside Christ's shed blood

(Heb. 12:24), which is better than Abel's in that his blood cried out for vengeance but the blood of Christ cries out for mercy. Abel's blood, although the blood of a righteous man (Matt. 23:35), cannot atone, but Christ's blood is ever efficacious (I John 1:7). Abel is unique among Bible men in a fourfold direction:

He was the first one of the human race to die.

He was the first person on the earth to be murdered.

He was the first man to be associated with Christ.

He was the first saint to present an offering acceptable to God.

Abel is also the name given to geographical locations (I Sam. 6:18; II Sam. 20:14).

ABIA, ABIAH [Ă bĭ' ă, Ā bĭ' ah]—JEHOVAH IS FATHER.

1. *The second son of Samuel* the prophet and judge of Israel, Abia, with his brother Joel or Vashni, judged so unworthily as to force Israel to desire a king (I Sam. 8:2; I Chron. 6:28).

2. *A son of Rehoboam* (I Chron. 3:10; Matt. 1:7). Called Abijam in I Kings 14:31; 15:6–8.

3. *The seventh son of Becher* the son of Benjamin (I Chron 7:8).

4. *A priest* in the days of David, appointed to service in the Tabernacle (Luke 1:5). Also the name of the wife of Hezron, grandson of Judah by Pharez (I Chron. 2:24). Our study of Bible men will bring out the fact that the same name is often borne by both men and women.

ABIALBON [Ā' bĭ–ăl' bŏn]—FATHER OF STRENGTH. *One of David's heroes* who came from Beth-arabah (II Sam. 23:31). He is called Abiel in I Chronicles 11:32.

ABIASAPH [Ă bĭ' a săph]—REMOVER OF REPROACH or FATHER OF GATHERING. *The third son of Korah,* first-born of Izhar, second son of Kohath (Ex. 6:24).

ABIATHAR [Ă bĭ' a thär]—FATHER OF SUPERFLUITY or EXCELLENT FATHER. *Son of Ahimelech* and the eleventh high priest in succession from Aaron (I Sam. 22:20–22; 23:6, 9).

Abiathar escaped and fled to David in the cave of Adullam when Doeg the Edomite slew his father and eighty-five priests. He went back to Jerusalem with the Ark when David fled from Absalom. He was joint high-priest with Zadok and conspired to make Adonijah king. He rebelled against David in his old age, was spared by Solomon for the sake of his first love, but dismissed from office for his treachery at the last.

ABIDA, ABIDAH [Ă bĭ' dă, Ă bĭ' dah]—FATHER OF KNOWLEDGE. *The fourth son of Midian,* the fourth son of Keturah and Abraham (Gen. 25:4; I Chron. 1:33).

ABIDAN [Ăb' i dăn]—THE FATHER JUDGETH. *A Benjamite chieftain,* the son of Gideoni and representative prince in the taking of the census (Num. 1:11; 2:22; 7:60, 65; 10:24).

ABIEL [Ă bī' el]—FATHER OF STRENGTH.
1. *Son of Zeror* and father of Ner and of Kish and grandfather of Saul, Israel's first king (I Sam. 9:1; 14:51).
2. *One of David's* heroes from Beth-arabah (I Chron. 11:32). Called Abi-albon in II Sam. 23:31.

ABIEZER [Ă bĭ ĕ' zûr]—FÁTHER OF HELP or IN HELP.
1. *The son of Hammoleketh,* who was the sister of Machir and daughter of Manasseh. Gideon belonged to this family (Josh. 17:2; Judg. 6:11; I Chron. 7:18). Perhaps the same as Jeezer (Num. 26:30).
2. *An Anethothite,* one of David's thirty-seven chief heroes, who had command of the army during the ninth month (II Sam. 23:27; I Chron. 11:28; 27:12). Also the name of a district (Judg. 6:34).

ABIGIBEON [Ă bĭ gĭb' e on]—FATHER OF GIBEON. *A descendant of Benjamin* who dwelt at Gibeon, whose family afterwards settled in Jerusalem (I Chron. 8:29).

ABIHAIL [Ăb i hā' il]—FATHER OF MIGHT.
1. *A Levite,* father of Zuriel, the chief of the Merarites in the time of Moses (Num. 3:35).
2. *The head of a family* of the tribe of Gad (I Chron. 5:14).
3. *The father of Esther,* the niece of Mordecai who became Queen of Persia in the place of Vashti (Esther 2:15; 9:29).
Abihail occurs as a woman's name two times in the Bible (I Chron. 2:29; II Chron. 11:18).

ABIHU [Ă bī' hū]—HE IS MY FATHER. *The second son of Aaron,* who was destroyed with his brother Nadab for offering strange, or unauthorized fire upon the altar (Ex. 6:23: 24:1, 9; 28:1; Lev. 10:1, 2).

ABIHUD [Ă bī' hud]—FATHER OF HONOR or OF MAJESTY. *A son of Bela,* son of Benjamin (I Chron. 8:3).

ABIJAH, ABIAH, ABIA [Ă bī' jah, Ă bī' ah, Ă bī' ă]—JEHOVAH IS MY FATHER or FATHER OF THE SEA.
1. *A son of Jeroboam* who died in his youth (I Kings 14:1).
2. *A priest in David's time* who was head of the eighth course in Temple service (I Chron. 24:10). See Abiah.
3. *Son and successor of Rehoboam* whose mother was Maachah, Absalom's daughter (II Chron. 11:20, 22; 12:16; 13; 14:1). Called Abijam in I Kings 14:31. See Abia.
4. *A priest* who sealed the covenant made by Nehemiah and the

people to serve the Lord. As further references are encountered to this act, it will be borne in mind that it represented the re-dedication of the people to the worship and work of God after their return from the Babylonian captivity.

5. *Another priest* who returned from exile. Perhaps the same person as the preceding Abijah (Neh. 12:1–4, 12–17). Also the name of the mother of Hezekiah, king of Judah (II Chron. 29:1; she is also called Abi, II Kings 18:2).

ABIJAM [Ă bĭ′ jăm]—FATHER OF LIGHT. *Rehoboam's son* (I Kings 14:31; 15:1–8). Called Abijah in II Chronicles.

ABIMAEL [Ă bĭm′ a el]—MY FATHER IS GOD. *A son of Joktan of the family of Shem* (Gen. 10:26–28; I Chron. 1:20–22).

ABIMELECH [Ă bĭm′ e lĕch]—FATHER OF THE KING.

1. *A king of Gerar* in the time of Abraham (Gen. 20; 21:22–32; 26:1–16, 26–31).

The Man Who Rebuked Another for Lying

Abimelech would have taken Sarah, Abraham's wife, into his harem, but learning that she was the wife of another, returned her uninjured. Abraham appears here in a bad light. He deceived Abimelech, but when found out was justly rebuked by the God-restrained Abimelech. Certainly the righteous should rebuke the ungodly (I Tim. 5:20), but how sad it is when the ungodly have just reason for rebuking the righteous. What a degradation it was for Abraham, then, to be rebuked by a heathen king!

Abraham sought to palliate his deception by claiming that Sarah was actually his half sister, daughter of the same father but not the same mother (Gen. 20:12, 16).

> A lie if half a truth
> Is ever the worst of lies.

Abraham was the more blameworthy because he had done the same thing before (Gen. 12) and had suffered much in the same way as upon this occasion. How grateful Abimelech was for the dream warning him of his danger! The covenant made with Abraham is somewhat significant —

I. It was proposed by Abimelech who, although knowing how Abraham had failed God, yet saw how favored he was of God (Gen. 21:22).

II. It revealed certain distrust of Abraham. Abimelech requested Abraham not to be tempted to sin in such a direction again (Gen. 21:23).

III. It was meant to secure Abraham's good will. The king desired the favor of the wandering pilgrim who had failed to act kingly. Abraham consented to the king's request (Gen. 21:24).

IV. It gave Abraham the opportunity of rebuking Abimelech. The matter of the stolen well had to be put right. Wrong had to be repudiated before a covenant could be agreed upon (Gen. 20:9; 21:23, 26).

V. It secured for Abraham the inheritance of Beer-sheba, "the well of oath," which possession the patriarch sanctified (Gen. 21:27–33).

2. *The son of Gideon* by a concubine in Shechem who belonged to a leading Canaanite family (Judg. 8:30, 31; 9; 10:1).

The Man Who Was Bramble King

This Abimelech, who made the first attempt to set up a monarchy in Israel, is known as "The Bramble King." But his violent and ill-fated reign over Israel only lasted for three years. After the death of Gideon his father, Abimelech took seventy pieces of silver from his mother's people with which he hired vain and light persons to follow him. He slew seventy persons of his father's house. Jotham, the youngest son of Gideon, who is also called Jerubbaal, hid himself and when Abimelech was proclaimed king by the men of Shechem, he revealed himself and warned the Shechemites against Abimelech in a parable about trees, from whence he received his nickname as "Bramble King." What a tragic death this would-be king of Israel suffered (Judg. 9: 53, 54)! A fitting end, surely, for one who sowed a Biblical city with salt (Judg. 9:45).

3. *Son of Abiathar,* the high priest in David's time (I Chron. 18:16). Also known as Ahimlech.

4. *A name given to Achish,* King of Gath (according to Ellicott), to whom David fled (I Sam. 21:10).

ABINADAB [Ă bĭn' a dăb]—FATHER or SOURCE OF LIBERALITY.

1. *An Israelite* of the tribe of Judah in whose house the Ark rested after its return by the Philistines (I Sam. 7:1; II Sam. 6:3, 4; I Chron. 13:7).

2. *The second son of Jesse,* the father of David (I Sam. 16:8; 17:13; I Chron. 2:13).

3. *A son of King Saul* (I Sam. 31:2; I Chron. 8:33; 9:39; 10:2). He was slain along with his father and his brother Jonathan at Gilboa.

4. *The father of one of Solomon's officers* (I Kings 4:11).

ABINOAM [Ă bĭn' o ăm]—FATHER OF PLEASANTNESS, OF BEAUTY or OF GRACE. *The father of Barak* (Judg. 4:6, 12; 5:11, 12).

ABIRAM [Ă bī' ram]—FATHER IS THE EXALTED ONE.

1. *A son of Eliab, a Reubenite* who with others conspired against Moses and Aaron in the wilderness, and who perished with his fellow-conspirators (Num. 16:1–27; 26:9).

2. *The first-born son of Hiel* the Bethelite, who began to rebuild Jericho, but who came under the curse foretold by Joshua (Josh. 6:26; I Kings 16:34).

ABISHAI, ABSHAI [Ă bĭsh' ă ī]—POSSESSOR OF ALL THAT IS DESIRABLE. *A son of David's sister Zeruiah,* and a brother of Joab and Asahel. After his numerous victories against the Philistines, he became one of David's thirty heroes (I Sam. 26:6–9;.II Sam. 2:18, 24; 3:30; 10:10, 14). He is also called Abshai (I Chron. 18:12).

ABISHALOM [Ă bĭsh' a lom]—FATHER OF PEACE. *Father of Maachah,* who was the wife of Jeroboam (I Kings 15:2, 10). Called Absalom in II Chronicles 11:20, 21.

ABISHUA [Ă bĭsh' u ă]—FATHER OF SAFETY or OF SALVATION.
1. *A son of Phinehas,* who was the grandson of Aaron (I Chron. 6:5, 50; Ezra 7:5).
2. *A son of Bela,* the son of Benjamin (I Chron. 8:4).

ABISHUR [Ăb' i shur]—FATHER OF OXEN or OF A WALL. *A son of Shammai,* who was the grandson of Jerahmeel, a Judahite (I Chron. 2:28, 29).

ABITUB [Ăb' ĭ tŭb]—FATHER or SOURCE OF GOODNESS. *A Benjamite,* son of Shahariam (I Chron. 8:11). Called Ahitub in the Common Version.

ABIUD [Ă bī' ud]—FATHER OF HONOR or OF TRUSTWORTHINESS. *A son of Zerubbabel,* and a member of the royal tribe from which Christ sprang (Matt. 1:13).

ABNER, ABINER [Ăb' nûr]—FATHER OF LIGHT. *The son of Ner,* cousin of Saul and captain of his army. Because of his relationship to the king and his force of character he exercised great influence during Saul's reign and afterwards (I Sam. 14:50, 51; 17:55, 57).

The Man Who Was Destitute of Lofty Ideals

Although Abner was the only capable person on the side of Saul and his family, he had little time for the lofty ideas of morality or religion (II Sam. 3:8, 16).

As Saul's commander-in-chief, he greatly helped his cousin to maintain his military prowess. After Saul's death, he set Ish-bosheth, Saul's son, on the throne.

As an enemy of Joab, David's general, he fought long and bravely against him, and after a severe defeat, killed Asahel in self-defense (II Sam. 2).

As a proud man, he resented most bitterly the remonstrance of Ish-bosheth, over the matter of Saul's concubines, and negotiated with David to make him king of Israel (II Sam. 3:7–22).

As an unprincipled man, he reaped what he sowed. Joab, dreading the loss of his own position, and thirsting for revenge, murdered Abner at Hebron. David gave him a public funeral, and afterwards

charged Solomon to avenge Abner's murder (II Sam. 3:26–37; I Kings
2:5, 6).

ABRAM, ABRAHAM [Ā' brăm, Ā' brặ hăm]—THE FATHER OF A
MULTITUDE. The original name of the youngest son of Terah was
Abram, meaning "father of height." Abraham was given to him when
the promise of a numerous progeny was renewed to him by God
(Gen. 11:26; 17:5, 9).

The Man Who Was God's Friend

Abraham's place in the Bible's portrait gallery is altogether unique
and unapproachable. He stands out as a landmark in the spiritual
history of the world. Chosen of God to become the father of a new
spiritual race, the file leader of a mighty host, the revelation of God
found in him one of its most important epochs. In himself, there was
not much to make him worthy of such a distinction. His choice was
all of grace.

Abraham's life is given us in detail, and we know him as we know
few men of the Bible. He was from the great and populous city of Ur,
and therefore a Gentile although he became the first Hebrew. He was
a rough, simple, venerable Bedouin-like sheep master. He uttered
no prophecy, wrote no book, sang no song, gave no laws. Yet in the
long list of Bible saints he alone is spoken of as "the father of the
faithful" and as "the friend of God" (Isa. 41:8). Let us briefly sketch
his story and character.

I.   He was born in Ur of the Chaldees, of parents who were heathen.
Little is known of him until he was seventy years old, a striking proof
that he had yielded himself to God before he left his heathen home
for the far-off land of Canaan.

II.   He received a distinct revelation from God, and of God, but
we are not told how and when. This, however, we do know: He gave
up a certainty for an uncertainty and went out not knowing whither
he went. Willingly he surrendered the seen for the unseen.

III.   He was taught the lesson of patience, of waiting upon the
Eternal God. It was many years before the promise of God was fulfilled to him—promises three in number—of a *country*, Canaan; of
posterity, as the stars of heaven; of a *spiritual seed*, through whom
all the families of the earth would be blessed.

IV.   He believed as he waited. His soul fed upon the promises of
God. He believed God in the face of long delay and also amid difficulties that seemed insuperable. This is why he is called "the father
of all them that believe."

V.   He was renowned for his active, working, living faith (Gen.
15:6). Abraham believed in God and it was counted to him for
righteousness.

VI.   He was subject to failures. His character, like the sun, had
its spots. Abraham's conduct to Hagar on two occasions, in sending
her away, is painful to remember. Then his departure from Canaan

into Egypt when the famine was on was surely not an act of faith. The falsehood which on two occasions he told with regard to Sarah his wife gives us a glimpse into a natural character somewhat cowardly, deceitful and distrustful (Gen. 12:19; 20:2).

VII. He was called to offer up special sacrifices. The first is fully described in Genesis fifteen, where the five victims offered in sacrifice to God were symbolic and typical of the whole Mosaic economy to come. Then we have the offering up of Isaac, an act of faith on Abraham's part and yet a trial of faith (Gen. 22). What a demand God made! But Abraham did not withhold his only son of promise. What God wanted was Abraham's heart, not Isaac's life. So when the knife was raised to slay Isaac, a provided substitute appeared. After this sacrifice Abraham received the testimony that he had pleased God.

The Bible offers us many types of Christ, Isaac being one of the chiefest, but Abraham is *the only type in Scripture of God the Father*. Abraham so loved God as to give up his only son, and centuries before Christ was born entered into the inner heart of John 3:16. After serving God faithfully, Abraham died when 175 years of age.

There are many profitable lessons to be gleaned from the biography of this notable man of God:

Faith has always trials. Being a Christian does not mean that trial is impossible or unnecessary. The greater the faith, the greater the trial.

Faith shines through the cloud. How the patience and meekness of Jesus are manifest through His trials! Take away Abraham's trials and where is his faith? Faith must be tried, in order that faith may live.

Faith in spite of trial glorifies God. Abraham's story is written in tears and blood, but how God was glorified by his trials of faith! Abraham's obedience of faith earned him the honor, "Abraham My friend!" Truly, there is no greater rank or greater honor than to be described thus. Yet such is our privilege if ours is the obedience of faith, for did not Jesus say, "I have called you friends"? He also said, "Ye are my friends *if* ye do whatsoever I command you."

ABSALOM [Ăb′ sa lŏm]—FATHER OF PEACE. *The third son of David by his wife Maacah, daughter of Talmai, king of Geshur. He was born of a polygamous marriage* (II Sam. 3:2, 13, 14).

The Man Whose Lovely Hair Meant His Death

What a singular fascination there is in the story of Absalom who, lacking capacity, certainly made up for it in charm! As to the story of his rebellion against David his father, such a heartless deed carries with it one of the most solemn lessons in the whole of the Bible. Let us briefly touch on some aspects of Absalom's character and conduct.

I. He was of royal descent on both sides, for his mother was a king's daughter. Undoubtedly he was heir to the throne, and the favorite, the idol of his father.

II. He was gifted with remarkable physical beauty—"no blemish in him" (II Sam. 14:25). A commanding presence, natural dignity, extraordinary graces of person made him a conspicuous figure.

III. He also possessed a charm of eloquence and persuasiveness which won him the hearts of all Israel, who felt that in him they had a God-sent champion.

IV. He had a traitorous nature. Absalom murdered his own brother (II Sam. 13:29), was guilty of designing politeness (II Sam. 15:2, 3), and conspired against his own father (II Sam. 15:13, 14).

V. He came to an untimely end (II Sam. 18:9). Having everything in his favor—a throne ready made for him, and fortune bowing at his feet to load him with favors, his life ended in tragedy. Brilliant in its beginnings, he was buried like a dog in a pit in a lonely wood, leaving a name that was execrated. What brought Absalom to his *Paradise Lost?*

A. His all-absorbing egotism. Self-aggrandizement was Absalom's sin. He had no thought, no feeling, no pity for anyone else but himself. Those around him were only of use to him as they helped him to secure his own desires and build up his own grandeur. Filial affection and generous sentiment were sacrificed on the altar of his inordinate ambition. But in trying to save his life, he lost it.

B. His was a practical godlessness. Those around Absalom recognized God, and had a religious faith giving some restraint and principle to their conduct. But the handsome, selfish, scheming Absalom had none of this feeling. He was his own master. His own will was his only law. He was destitute of principle and destitute of faith. Love, tenderness, pity, were not his traits because he had no reverence for God.

C. His glory brought about his final tragedy. Adding to the beauty of Absalom was his flowing hair forming a crown to his person which made him the delight of Israel's daughters. Being proud of his chief ornament he must have carefully attended to it. But as Absalom was pursued by Joab's men his beautiful hair was caught fast in the thick and tangled boughs of an oak tree and he could not free himself. Thus his graceful personal endowment left him a target for those who hated him and sought his death.

May such a lesson not be lost upon us! Our chief glory can become the cause of our greatest shame. Our choicest endowments and most cherished gifts can become our greatest temptations. Our gifts, like ourselves, need to be rewashed every day in the fountain of God's truth, and guarded and sanctified by prayer, if they are to be fit for the highest service.

ACHAICUS [Ă chā′ i cŭs]—BELONGING TO ACHAIA. As slaves were often named from the country of their birth, it seems probable that this member of the Church at Corinth was a slave born in Achaia

(I Cor. 16:17). Along with Stephanas and Fortunatus this Corinthian visited Paul at Philippi and refreshed his spirit.

ACHAN, ACHAR, ACHOR [Ā' chăn, Ā' chär, Ā' chôr]—TROUBLE. *The son of Carmi* of the tribe of Judah (Josh. 7; I Chron. 2:7).

The Man Who Brought Trouble to a Nation

It did not take Joshua long to discover that his defeat at Ai, after a succession of victories, was due to some transgression of the divine covenant (Josh. 7:8–12). Thus, as the result of an inquiry, Achan was exposed as the transgressor, and confessing his sin in stealing and hiding part of the spoil taken at the destruction of Jericho, was put to death in consequence. In keeping with the custom of those days, Achan was probably stoned with his immediate relatives, and their dead bodies burned—the latter making punishment more terrible in the eyes of the Israelites.

Achan was put to death in "the valley of Achor" meaning "the valley of trouble"—the valley being called atter Achan who had been the troubler of Israel (Josh. 7:25, 26). Thus in I Chronicles 2:7 Achan is spelled as Achar. But "the valley of trouble" became a "door of hope" all of which is spiritually suggestive (Isa. 65:10; Hos. 2:15).

I. Covetousness means defeat. God had forbidden anyone taking to himself the spoils of Jericho, but one man, *only one* amongst all the hosts of Israel, disobeyed and brought failure upon all. Achan's sin teaches us the oneness of the people of God. "*Israel* hath sinned" (Josh. 7:11). The whole cause of Christ can be delayed by the sin, neglect or lack of spirituality of one person (I Cor. 5:1–7; 12:12, 14, 26).

II. The whole process of sin. Along with Eve and David in their respective sins, Achan also saw, coveted and took. James expresses the rise, progress and end of sin when he says that man is "drawn away of his own lust, and enticed. Then when lust hath conceived, it bringeth forth sin: and sin, when it is finished, bringeth forth death" (Jas. 1:14, 15). The inward corruption of Achan's heart was first drawn forth by enticing objects—desire of gratification was then formed —ultimately determination to attain was fixed.

III. Prayer was rejected for action. When the most unexpected defeat of Ai came about, Joshua fell on his face before the Lord, and earnestly asked for an explanation of the reverse. But God said, "Get thee up; wherefore liest thou thus upon thy face? ...Take away the accursed thing" (Josh. 7:10, 13). God cannot hear and bless if there is sin in the camp. For often we acknowledge the greatness of our *national* sins, but fail to drag out our *personal* sins testifying against us. Once Achan was discovered and judged, Israel went forward to victory.

IV. The richness of divine mercy. When the accursed thing was removed and chastisement exercised, triumph quickly followed trouble. The valley of Achor became a door of hope. The locust-eaten years are restored. Confession and forgiveness open closed lips, quicken dormant energies and liberate power in the service of the Lord.

ACHBOR [Ăch' bôr]—A MOUSE.

1. *Father of Baal-hanan* and king of Edom (Gen. 36:38, 39; I Chron. 1:49).

2. *Son of Michaiah* and one of Josiah's messengers (II Kings 22: 12, 14). Called Abdon in II Chronicles 34:20.

3. *A Jew,* whose son *Elnathan* was sent by Jehoiakim to bring back Urijah the prophet from Egypt (Jer. 26:22; 36:12).

ACHIM [Ā' chim]—JEHOVAH WILL ESTABLISH. *An ancestor of Joseph,* husband of Mary, our Lord's mother (Matt. 1:14).

ACHISH [Ā' chish]—SERPENT CHARMER.

1. *Son of Maoch* and the king of Gath to whom David fled (I Sam. 21:10–14; 27:2–12).

2. *A king of Gath,* who reigned about forty years later than No. 1, in Solomon's time (I Kings 2:39, 40).

ADAIAH [Ăd-a ī' ah]—JEHOVAH HATH ADORNED or PLEASING TO JEHOVAH.

1. *A man of Boscath* and father of Josiah's mother (II Kings 22:1).

2. *A Levite* descended from Gershom (I Chron. 6:41–43).

3. *A son of Shimhi* the Benjamite (I Chron. 8:12–21).

4. *A Levite* of the family of Aaron, and head of a family living in Jerusalem (I Chron. 9:10–12).

5. *The father of Captain Masseiah* who helped Jehoiada put Joash on the throne of Judah (II Chron. 23:1).

6. *A son of Bani* who married a foreign wife during the exile (Ezra 10:29).

7. *Another of a different Bani family* who did the same thing (Ezra 10:34, 39).

8. *A descendant of Judah* by Perez (Neh. 11:5).

9. *A Levite* of the family of Aaron. Most likely the same person as No. 4 (Neh. 11:12).

ADALIA [Ăd a lī' ä]—THE HONOR OF IZED. *The fifth of Haman's ten sons* all of whom were hanged with their father (Esther 9:8).

ADAM [Ăd'ăm]—OF THE GROUND or TAKEN OUT OF THE RED EARTH. *The first human son of God* (Luke 3:38), and God's masterpiece and crowning work of creation.

The Man God Made

All men should be interested in the history of the first man who ever breathed, man's great ancestor, the head of the human family, the first being who trod the earth. What a beautiful world Adam found himself in with everything to make him happy, a world without sin and without sorrow! God first made, as it were, the great house of the world, then brought His tenant to occupy it. And it was not an empty house, but furnished with everything needed to make life content. There was not a single need God had not satisfied.

The Bible does not tell us how long Adam's state of blessedness and innocence lasted. But Paradise was lost through listening to the voice of the tempter. Relieved of his occupation as a gardener, Adam was condemned to make his livelihood by tilling the stubborn ground, and to eat his bread in the sweat of his face.

I.   Adam was a necessary complement to the divine plan. "There was not a man to till the ground" (Gen. 2:5). The accomplishment of God's plan required human instrumentality. God made the earth for man, and then the man for the earth.

II.   Adam was fashioned a creature of God, bearing the image of God and possessing God-like faculties (Gen. 1:27; Ps. 8:6; Eccles. 7:29).

III.   Adam was created a tripartite being, having a spirit, soul and body (Gen. 2:7; I Thess. 5:23).

IV.   Adam was alone and needed companionship to satisfy his created instincts (Gen. 2:18), thus Eve was formed.
Society, friendship and love
Gifts divinely bestowed upon man.

V.   Adam was enticed and sinned (Gen. 3:6). After the satanic tempter there came the human tempter, and the act of taking the forbidden fruit offered by Eve ruined Adam and made him our federal head in sin and death. "In Adam we die."

VI.   Adam received the promise of the Saviour. The first promise and prophecy of One, able to deal with Satan and sin was given, not to Adam, but to the one responsible for Adam's trangression (Gen. 3:15), and in the coats of skins God provided to cover the discovered nakedness of Adam and Eve we have a type of the sacrifice of the Cross. In Adam we die, but in Christ we can be made alive. The first man Adam was of the earth earthy, but the Second Man, the last Adam, was from heaven and kept His first estate of sinless perfection.

Adam was not only the name of earth's first man and the joint name of both Adam and Eve (Gen. 5:2), but also the name of a town on the east of Jordan (Josh. 3:16).

ADAR, ADDAR [Ā' där, Ăd' där]—FIRE GOD or HEIGHT. *Son of Bela* and grandson of Benjamin (I Chron. 8:3). Also the name of the twelfth month of the Jewish sacred year (Ezra 6:15), and of a city south of Judah (Josh. 15:3).

ADBEEL [Ăd' bē al]—LANGUISHING FOR GOD. *Third son of Ishmael* and grandson of Abraham (Gen. 25:13; I Chron. 1:29).

ADDI [Ăd'dī]—MY WITNESS or ADORNED. *An ancestor of Joseph*, the husband of Mary, our Lord's mother (Luke 3:28).

ADER [Ā' dûr]—A FLOCK. *A son of Beriah,* grandson of Shaharaim, a Benjamite (I Chron. 8:15). See Eder.

ADIEL [Ā'dĭ el]—ORNAMENT OF GOD.
1. *A descendant of Simeon* (I Chron. 4:36).
2. *A priest,* son of Jahzerah (I Chron. 9:12).
3. *Father of Azmaveth,* who was supervisor of David's treasuries. Perhaps the same as No. 2 (I Chron. 27:25).

ADIN [Ā' dĭn]—DELICATE or ORNAMENT.
1. *One whose family returned from exile with Zerubbabel* (Ezra 2:15; Neh. 7:20).
2. *One whose posterity came back with Ezra* (Ezra 8:6).
3. *The name of a family* sealing the Covenant (Neh. 10:14–16).

ADINA [Ăd' ĭ nă]—ORNAMENT. *A Reubenite* and one of David's military officers (I Chron. 11:42).

ADINO [Ăd' ĭ nō]—DELICATE or ORNAMENT. *An Eznite.* One of David's thirty heroes (II Sam. 23:8).

ADLAI [Ăd' la ī]—JUSTICE OF JEHOVAH or WEARY. *Father of Shaphat,* who was overseer of David's cattle in the lowlands (I Chron. 27:29).

ADMATHA [Ăd' ma thă]—GOD-GIVEN. *One of the seven princes* of Persia and Media in the reign of King Ahasuerus (Esther 1:14).

ADNA [Ăd'nă]—PLEASURE.
1. *A son of Pahath-moab* who had married a foreign wife during the exile (Ezra 10:30).
2. *A priest,* head of his father's house in the days of Joiakim (Neh. 12:12–15).

ADNAH [Ăd' nah]—PLEASURE.
1. *A Manassite* who joined David at Ziklag (I Chron. 12:20).
2. *A man of Judah* who held high military rank under Jehoshaphat (II Chron. 17:14).

ADONI-BEZEK [Ă dŏ' nĭ-bē' zek]—LORD OF LIGHTNING or OF BEZEK. *A king of Bezek,* captured by the men of Judah and Simeon and taken to Jerusalem where he was mutilated. The cutting off of his thumbs and great toes not only rendered him harmless but reminded him that man reaps what he sows (Judg. 1:5–7; Gal. 6:3).

ADONIJAH [Ăd o nī' jah]—JEHOVAH IS LORD.
1. *The fourth son of David and Haggith,* born in Hebron (II Sam 3:4). Adonijah was the victim of Oriental intrigue. After the death

of Absalom, he became the rightful heir to the throne (I Kings 2:15), but Bathsheba had other designs for her son Solomon who, when secure on the throne interpreted Adonijah's desire for Abishag as an effort to secure the kingdom. Self-preservation compelled Solomon to order Adonijah's death, a sentence carried out by Benaiah.

2. *A Levite* sent by Jehoshaphat to teach the Law (II Chron. 17:8).

3. *A chieftain* who with Nehemiah sealed the covenant (Neh. 10:14–16).

ADONIKAM [Ă dŏn' ĭ kăm]—MY LORD HAS RISEN or HAS RAISED ME.

1. *An Israelite* whose descendants returned from exile (Ezra 2:13; Neh. 7:18).

2. *Another Israelite,* whose family returned from exile with Ezra (Ezra 8:13).

ADONIRAM, ADORAM [Ăd o nī' ram, Ă dō' ram]—MY LORD IS HIGH or THE LORD OF MIGHT. *A son of Abda* and an officer over tribute during the reigns of David and Solomon (I Kings 4:6; 5:14). See also *Hadoram.*

ADONI-ZEDEK, ADONI-ZEDEC [Ă dō' nī zē' dĕc]—LORD OF JUSTICE. *A king of the Canaanites,* who was slain by Joshua (Josh. 10:1, 3). Sometimes identified as Adoni-bezek.

ADORAM [Ă dō' ram]—HIGH HONOR or STRENGTH.

1. *An officer* set over the tribute in David's time (II Sam 20:24). Perhaps the same as Adoniram.

2. *An officer* under Solomon then under Rehoboam (I Kings 12:18).

ADRAMMELECH [Ă drăm' me lĕch]—ADAR IS KING or HONOR OF THE KING. *A son of Sennacherib,* king of Assyria, who, with his brother Sharezer, slew their father in the temple of Nisroch (II Kings 19:37; Isa. 37:38). Also the name of the heathen god, Adar (II Kings 17:31).

ADRIEL [Ă' drĭ el]—HONOR OF FLOCK OF GOD. *A man of Issachar* to whom Saul gave his daughter Merab in marriage (I Sam. 18:19; II Sam. 21:8).

AENEAS [Ae' ne ăs]—PRAISE. *This name of a Trojan hero* was also the name of the paralytic healed by Peter (Acts 9:33, 34).

AGABUS [Ăg' a bŭs]—A LOCUST. *A Christian prophet* in Jerusalem who foretold a widespread famine, and also Paul's imprisonment and shackles (Acts 11:28; 21:10, 11). Some scholars see two persons of the same name in these references.

AGAG [Ā' găg]—FLAMING or WARLIKE. *The poetic name of Amalek,* slain by Samuel as a religious act (Num. 24:7; I Sam. 15:8–23). Agagite is the name given to Haman, the Jews' enemy (Esther 3:1, 10).

AGEE [Ăg′ e ē]—FUGITIVE. *The father of Shammah,* one of David's valiant men (II Sam. 23:11).

AGRIPPA [Ă grĭp′ pȧ]—ONE WHO AT HIS BIRTH CAUSES PAIN. *Great-grandson of Herod the Great.* Agrippa's father was eaten by worms. See *Herod* (Acts 25:13–26; 26). Was Agrippa almost persuaded by Paul's eloquent witness to become a Christian? Bible scholars disagree on the point. There are those who affirm that the original language indicates clearly that Agrippa interrupted Paul to warn him that he was going too far in presuming that he was admitting his argument. "Too eagerly art thou persuading thyself that thou canst make me a Christian." The R.V. of 1881 has it, "With but little persuasion thou wouldest fain make me a Christian." However, the words of Agrippa as they stand in the A.V. have formed the basis of many an earnest and powerful gospel appeal.

AGUR [Ā′ gûr]—GATHERER. *The son of Jakeh* and author of the maxims in Proverbs thirty. Many writers feel that this name is symbolical of Solomon himself.

AHAB [Ā′ hăb]—FATHER'S BROTHER.
1. *The son of Omri,* and his successor as the seventh king of Israel (I Kings 16:28–33).

The Man Who Wanted Another's Vineyard

Ahab was an able and energetic warrior. His victories over the Syrians pushed the borders of his kingdom to the border of Damascus. Great renown became his, also great wealth indicated by the ivory palace he built for himself (I Kings 21:1; 22:39). Success, however, made him greedy for still more. Not since Solomon's time had a king been so victorious as Ahab, and what was a little matter like Naboth's vineyard to one who had grasped so much? With his wealth, Ahab bought all he wanted. One tenant, however, could not be bought out. Sentiment, affection and tender memories were more to Naboth than all the king's money.

Ahab could not say "All is mine" until the vineyard on his estate was his. First of all, there was no flaw in Ahab's advances. A fair price and richer land were offered Naboth. The sin came after Naboth's refusal to sell, because of a thousand sacred ties. Ahab sinned in not entering into a poorer man's feelings. Naboth was not obstinate. His vineyard was a sacred heritage, a precious tradition. If we are to be Christlike we must be considerate of others.

Ahab's next fault was that of making an awful grievance of his disappointment. He acted like a spoiled child and in a sulky fit told of failure to secure the vineyard to Jezebel, his strong-minded wife. Ahab and Jezebel are the Macbeth and Lady Macbeth of this inspired story. Ahab played into his wife's hands, and those hands were eager to shed blood.

Points for possible expansion are:

I.   Ahab established idolatry. He was a dangerous innovator and a patron of foreign gods (I Kings 16:31–33; 21:26).

II.   He was a weak-minded man, lacking moral fiber and righteousness (I Kings 21:4).

III.   He was the tool of his cruel, avaricious wife (I Kings 21:7, 25).

IV.   His doom, along with that of Jezebel, was foretold by Elijah (I Kings 21:22) and by Micaiah (I Kings 22:28).

2.   *The name of the false prophet* who was in Babylon during the exile, and was roasted in the fire by Nebuchadnezzar (Jer. 29:21–23).

AHARAH [Ă hăr′ ah]—BROTHER OF RACH. *Third son of Benjamin* (I Chron. 8:1). See also Ahiram and Aher (Num. 26:38).

AHARHEL [Ă här′ hel]—BROTHER OF RACHEL or AFTER MIGHT. *A son of Harum,* and a founder of a family included in the tribe of Judah (I Chron. 4:8).

AHASAI, AHZAI [Ă hăs′ a ī]—MY HOLDER or PROTECTOR; CLEAR-SIGHTED. *A priest* of the family of Immer (Neh. 11:13).

AHASBAI [Ă hăs′ ba ī]—SHINING. *Father of one of David's heroes* (II Sam. 23:34).

AHASUERUS [Ă hăs ū ē′ rŭs]—KING or MIGHTY MAN.

1.   *A Persian monarch,* to whom accusations against the Jews were brought, bore this name (Ezra 4:6).

2.   *It was also the name of a Median king,* father of Darius (Dan. 9:1).

3.   *A Persian king* who became the husband of Esther (Esther 1:2, 19).

The Man Whose Sleeplessness Saved a Nation

Two years after Queen Vashti was deposed, Esther the Jewess, and the ward of Mordecai, became the wife of Ahasuerus, and queen in Vashti's place. Two years after Esther's enthronement, wicked Haman prevailed upon the king to order the destruction of all the Jews in his empire, but the plan backfired. The king had a sleepless night, and robbed of slumber called for records carefully preserved in the royal archives. Reading of the plot to end his life, and of how Mordecai had informed the king, Ahasuerus felt that Mordecai was worthy of honor and reward. That sleepless night resulted in Mordecai's promotion to high office, the exposure of Haman's dark and devilish plot, the preservation of the Jewish nation and the hanging of Haman and his sons on the gallows Haman had prepared for Mordecai.

A character study on Ahasuerus could be worked out on his sensuality, fickleness, lack of forethought, despotism and cruelty.

AHAZ [Ā' hăz]—JEHOVAH HATH SEIZED or SUSTAINS.

1. *A Benjamite* of the family of Saul (I Chron. 8:35, 36; 9:41, 42).

2. *The son of Jotham,* king of Judah and father of Hezekiah, Ahaz became the eleventh king of Judah and reigned for sixteen years (II Kings 16). He is called Achaz in Matthew 1:9. An Assyrian inscription gives the name of the king as Jehoahaz. But the abbreviation Ahaz was commonly used and was found on the seal ring of one of his courtiers. Perhaps the consistent omission of the first part of the name Jeho, meaning "Jehovah" was deliberate because of the abhorrent apostasy of Ahaz.

The Man Who Rejected a Message of Hope

Let it not be forgotten that it was to king Ahaz that Isaiah's first evangelistic announcement was made in the promise of Emmanuel. The prophet sent a message to terrified Ahaz, but he would not turn to God and trust His deliverance. In order to help restore the faith of the wavering king, Isaiah urged Ahaz to ask for a sign from Jehovah, but he refused and in rejecting the message of hope, forfeited his soul.

It is interesting to observe that Ahaz came between two good men — between his father, Jotham, and his son, Hezekiah.

Summarizing the chief aspects of the reign of Ahaz we note his:

I.   Pursuit of the religious policy of Jehoram (II Kings 8:18); of Ahaziah (II Kings 8:27); of Joash (II Chron. 24:18). The religious vices of Ahaz were possible because of a corrupt church and a corrupt state (Isa. 1:4, 13).

II. Rejection of David's way to tread Jeroboam's way. This bad ruler exceeded the idolatry of his time by burning his children in the fire (II Chron. 28:3). Ahaz did honor to the gods of Assyria who were reckoned to be more powerful than Jehovah. The terrible slaughter of one hundred twenty thousand valiant men of Judah had no salutary effect upon Ahaz (II Chron. 28:6).

AHAZIAH [Ā ha zī' ah]—JEHOVAH HOLDS or POSSESSES.

1. *A son of Ahab,* the Ahaziah of Israel—its eighth king who reigned for only two years. He followed the religious policy of his idolatrous father. He died as the result of a fall from the palace window (I Kings 22:49, 51; II Kings 1:2; I Chron. 3:11; II Chron. 20:35, 37).

2. *A son of Jehoram* or Joram, the Ahaziah of Judah who was Judah's fifth king, and who reigned for only one year. He is also known as Jehoahaz and Azariah. Since his wife was a daughter of Ahab and Jezebel, it is not to be wondered at that he was a Baal worshiper (II Kings 8:24–29; 9:16–29; 10:13; 12:18; 13:1; 14:13; II Chron. 22).

AHBAN [Äh' băn]—BROTHER OF INTELLIGENCE. *Son of Abishur,* a Judahite of the house of Jerahmeel (I Chron. 2:29).

AHER [Ā' hûr]—ONE THAT IS BEHIND or ANOTHER. *A Benjamite,* perhaps the same as Ahiram (I Chron. 7:12).

AHI [Ā' hī]—MY BROTHER or BROTHER OF JEHOVAH.
1. *Chief of the Gadites* in Gilead (I Chron. 5:15).
2. *Son of Shamer,* an Israelite of the tribe of Asher (I Chron. 7:34).

AHIAH [Ă hī' ah]—JEHOVAH IS MY BROTHER.
1. *The son of Ahitub* and grandson of Phinehas, son of Eli (I Sam. 14:3).
2. *One of Solomon's scribes* (I Kings 4:3).
3. *A descendant of Benjamin* (I Chron. 8:7). See also Ahijah.

AHIAM [Ă hī' am]—A MOTHER'S BROTHER. *The son of Sharar* the Hararite (the Sacar of I Chron. 11:35), and one of David's heroes (II Sam. 23:33; I Chron. 11:35).

AHIAN [Ă hī' an]—FRATERNAL, BROTHER OF DAY, or BROTHERLY. *Son of Shemidah,* a Manassachite (I Chron. 7:19).

AHIEZER [Ă hī ĕ' zûr]—BROTHER OF HELP.
1. *The son of Ammishaddai,* and head of the tribe of Dan, in the wilderness (Num. 1:12; 2:25; 7:66–71; 10:25).
2. *A son of Shemaah* and a Danite chief who joined David at Ziklag (I Chron. 12:3).

AHIHUD [Ă hī' hud]—BROTHER OF HONOR, OF MAJESTY, or OF MYSTERY.
1. *A prince of Asher,* who was appointed to help in the division of the land (Num. 34:27).
2. *A Benjamite* of the family of Ehud (I Chron. 8:7).

AHIJAH (Ă hī' jah]—A BROTHER IN JEHOVAH.
1. *A prophet* belonging to Shiloh, who foretold to Jeroboam the revolt of the ten tribes. This Ahijah was the champion of the rights of the people in the face of the oppression of Solomon and Rehoboam and led the revolt that rent the kingdom of David asunder (I Kings 11:26–12:20).
2. *Father of Baasha,* king of Israel who conspired against Nadab son of Jeroboam and reigned in his stead (I Kings 15:27, 33; 21:22; II Kings 9:9).
3. *Son of Jerahmeel,* a Judahite (I Chron. 2:25).
4. *A Pelonite,* and one of David's thirty heroes (I Chron. 11:36).
5. *A Levite* who had charge of the Tabernacle treasures (I Chron. 26:20).
6. *A Levite* who, with Nehemiah, sealed the covenant (Neh. 10:26).

AHIKAM [Ă hī' kam]—MY BROTHER HATH RISEN or APPEARED. *Son*

of Shaphan, and a prince of Judah and an officer in Josiah's court
(II Kings 22:12, 14; 25:22; Jer. 26:24).

AHILUD [A hī' lud]—A BROTHER OF ONE BORN.
1. *The father of Jehoshaphat,* the recorder under David and Solomon (II Sam. 8:16; 20:24; I Kings 4:3; I Chron. 18:15).
2. *Father of Baana,* one of Solomon's twelve purveyors (I Kings 4:12).

AHIMAAZ [Ă hĭm' a ăz]—A RASCAL, POWERFUL BROTHER or MY BROTHER IS COUNSELOR.
1. *Father of Ahinoam,* Saul's wife (I Sam. 14:50).
2. *A son of Zadok* the priest, who kept David informed of Absalom's revolt (II Sam. 15:27, 36; 17:17, 20).
3. *One of Solomon's officers,* responsible for the monthly supply of victuals for the royal household (I Kings 4:15).

AHIMAN [Ă hī' man]—BROTHER OF MAN or BROTHER OF A GIFT.
1. *A son of Anak,* who lived in Hebron and who was destroyed by Judah (Num. 13:22; Josh. 15:14; Judg. 1:10).
2. *A Levite porter* who had charge of the gate of the Temple through which the king passed (I Chron. 9:17).

AHIMELECH [Ă hĭm' e lĕch]—BROTHER OF THE KING or MY BROTHER IS KING.
1. *A son of Ahitub* and chief at Nob, who was slain for assisting David when he fled from Saul (I Sam. 21:1–8; 22:9–20; 23:6; 30:7).
2. *A Hittite officer* and follower of David (I Sam. 26:6).
3. *The son of Abiathar* the priest who escaped slaughter at Nob (II Sam. 8:17; I Chron. 18:16; 24:6). Some writers feel that the names of Abiathar and Ahimelech in these verses have been transposed.

AHIMOTH [Ă hī' mŏth]—BROTHER OF DEATH. *Son of Elkanah,* descended from Kohath son of Levi (I Chron. 6:25).

AHINADAB [Ă hĭn' a dăb]—BROTHER OF LIBERALITY. *Son of Iddo* and one of Solomon's purveyors in Mahanaim (I Kings 4:14).

AHIO [Ă hī' ō]—FRATERNAL or HIS BROTHER.
1. *A son of Abinadab* and brother of Uzzah. It was in Abinadab's house that the Ark of God rested for twenty years after its return by the Philistines (II Sam. 6:3, 4; I Chron. 13:7).
2. *A son of Elpaal,* a Benjamite (I Chron. 8:14).
3. *A son of Jehiel* by his wife Maachah and an ancestor of Saul (I Chron. 8:31; 9:37).

AHIRA [Ă hī' ră]—BROTHER OF EVIL. *A son of Enan* and head of the tribe of Naphtali during the wilderness journey (Num. 1:15; 2:29; 7:78, 83; 10:27).

AHIRAM [Ă hǐ' ram]—EXALTED BROTHER. *A Benjamite* of the Ahiramites (Num. 26:38). Called Ehi in Genesis 46:21, and supposed to be the Aher of I Chronicles 7:12.

AHISAMACH [Ă hǐs' a măch]—BROTHER OF SUPPORT. *Father of Aholiab* the craftsman, a Danite (Ex. 31:6; 35:34; 38:23).

AHISHAHAR [Ă hǐsh' a här]—BROTHER OF THE DAWN. *Son of Bilhan* and grandson of Jediael (I Chron. 7:10).

AHISHAR [Ă hǐ' shär]—BROTHER OF SONG or OF A SINGER. *An official* over Solomon's household (I Kings 4:6).

AHITHOPHEL [Ă hǐth' o phĕl]—BROTHER OF FOLLY. *One of David's privy counselors* and father of one of David's heroes, a Gilonite (II Sam. 15:12–34; 16:15–23; 17).

The Man Who Was Noted for His Advice

There was no one who could hold a candle to Ahithophel in his day as an able and famous politician. His counsel "was as if a man had inquired at the oracle of God" (II Sam. 16:23). Such counsel was a proverb in Israel in David's time. Matthew Henry speaks of him as "a politic, thinking man and one that had a clear head, and a great compass of thought." Perhaps David and Ahithophel had been friends from their boyhood up and are before us in Psalms such as 41:9; 55:13, 14.

Ahithophel, the wise and trusted counselor, however, was found unfaithful because he also thought of himself, and not of David. Ahithophel joined Absalom and advised the prince to take his father's harem (II Sam. 15:12; 16:21). He advised pursuit of the fugitive monarch, but Hushai, another counselor, thwarted this move (II Sam. 17:11)). Ahithophel was so disgusted over the collapse of his influence, for he could foresee that the insurrection against David was doomed to failure, that he went home a crestfallen man and set his affairs in order and hanged himself (II Sam. 17:23).

AHITUB (Ă hǐ' tub]—BROTHER OF BENEVOLENCE or FATHER OF GOODNESS.

1. *A son of Phinehas* and grandson of Eli (I Sam. 14:3; 22:9, 11, 12, 20).

2. *A son of Amariah* and father of Zadok the priest (II Sam. 8:17; I Chron. 6:11, 12). Perhaps the same as No. 1.

3. *A priest* and ruler of the House of God in Nehemiah's time (I Chron. 9:11; Neh. 11:11).

AHLAI [Äh' lai]—JEHOVAH IS STAYING. *Father of one of David's thirty heroes* (I Chron. 11:41). Also the name of *a daughter of Sheshan* (I Chron. 2:31).

AHOAH [Ā hō ah]—A BROTHER'S NEED. *Son of Bela,* a Benjamite, and founder of a family (I Chron. 8:4).

AHOLIAB [Ā hǒ' li ăb], AHOLAH [Ā ho' lah], AHOLIBAH [Ā hǒl-ĭ bah], AHOLIBAMAH [Ā hŏl i bā' mah]—A TENT. These names in the A.V. are also given in the R.V. as Oholah - her own tent; Oholiab - a father's tent; Oholibah - my tent is in her; Oholibamah - tent of high place.
1. *A Danite,* appointed by God to work with Bezaleel in the erection of the Tabernacle (Ex. 31:6; 35:34; 36:1, 2; 38:23).
2. *A chief* who sprang from Esau (Gen. 36:41; I Chron. 1:52).

AHUMAI [Ā hŭ' ma ī]—BROTHER OF WATER. *Son of Jahath* and a descendant of Judah (I Chron. 4:2).

AHUZAM [Ā hŭ' zam]—POSSESSION or A HOLDING FAST. *A son of Ashur,* of the family of Hezron (I Chron. 4:5, 6).

AHUZZATH [Ā hŭz' zath]—POSSESSION or HOLDING FAST. *A friend of Abimelech,* king of the Philistines in Isaac's time (Gen. 26:26).

AIAH, AJAH [Ā ī' ah, Ā' jah]—A VULTURE or BIRD OF PREY.
1. *A son of Zebeon,* the Horite (Gen. 36:24; I Chron. 1:40).
2. *The father of Rizpah,* Saul's concubine (II Sam. 3:7; 21:8, 10, 11).

AKAN [Ā'kăn]—ACUTE OR TWISTED. *Son of Ezer,* grandson of Seir the Horite (Gen. 36:27; I Chron. 1:42). Also called Jakan.

AKKUB [Ăk'kŭb]—CUNNING, ARTFUL or LAIN IN WAIT.
1. *A son of Elioenai,* of the family of David (I Chron. 3:24).
2. *A porter* in the second temple (I Chron. 9:17; Neh. 11:19; 12:25), and founder of family of hereditary porters (Ezra 2:42; Neh. 7:45).
3. *The chief of a family* of the Nethinims who came to Jerusalem after the exile (Ezra 2:45).
4. *A priest* employed by Ezra to expound the Law to the people (Neh. 8:7).

ALAMETH [Ăl' a mĕth]—YOUTHFUL VIGOR. *Son of Becher* and grandson of Benjamin (I Chron. 7:8).

ALEMETH [Ăl' e mĕth]—HIDING PLACE or COVERING. *A descendant of Jonathan,* son of Saul (1 Chron. 8:36; 9:42). Also the name of a Levitical city (I Chron. 6:60).

ALEXANDER [Ăl ĕx ăn' dûr]—DEFENDER, HELPER OF MEN or ONE WHO TURNS AWAY EVIL.

1. *The son of Simon the Cyrenian* who was compelled to carry the cross of Christ (Mark 15:21).

2. *A leading man in Jerusalem* when Peter and John were tried there (Acts 4:6).

3. *A convert of Paul's* who was present at the Ephesian tumult. Perhaps the same as No. 1 (Acts 19:33).

4. *A convert to Christianity* who became an apostate (I Tim. 1:20). Perhaps the same as No. 6.

5. *Alexander the Great,* king of Macedonia, who followed his father Philip and who also brought the Jews into contact with Greek literature and life. He is described though not named in Daniel 2:39 and 6:6.

6. *The coppersmith* who opposed Paul (II Tim. 4:14). This Ephesian Jew was likely the same as the one who corrupted the faith, not from ignorance but deliberately in opposition to his judgment. Dr. Alexander Whyte deals with No. 4 and No. 6 as the same person.

ALIAH [Ă lī' ah]—SUBLIMITY. *A duke of Edom,* descended from Esau, who is called Alvah in the Vulgate (Gen. 36:40; I Chron. 1:51). See Alvah.

ALIAN [Ă lī' an]—SUBLIME. *A son of Shobal* and descendant of Seir (Gen. 36:23; I Chron. 1:40). Called Alvan in Genesis 36:23.

ALLON [Ăl' lŏn]—AN OAK. *A Simeonite* descended from Shemaiah (I Chron. 4:37). Also the name of a city near Kadesh (Josh. 19:33).

ALMODAD [Ăl mō' dăd]—THE AGITATOR. *The oldest son of Joktan,* of the family of Shem (Gen. 10:26; I Chron. 1:20).

ALPHAEUS [Ăl phē' us]—TRANSIENT, CHIEF OR A THOUSAND.

1. *The father of Levi* or Matthew the Apostle (Mark 2:14).

2. *The father of James,* one of the twelve apostles (Matt. 10:3; Mark 3:18; Luke 6:15; Acts 1:13). Sometimes identified as the same person in No. 1 and also as Cleophas.

ALVAH [Ăl' vah]—SUBLIMITY or HIGH. *A duke of Edom* descended from Esau (Gen. 36:40; I Chron. 1:51). See Aliah.

ALVAN [Ăl' van]—SUBLIME. *Son of Shobal,* a Horite (Gen. 36:23; I Chron. 1:40). Called Alian in I Chronicles 1:40; Alvah in Genesis 36:40; Aliah in I Chronicles 1:51).

AMAL [Ā' măl]—LABOR or SORROW. *Son of Helem,* an Asherite (I Chron. 7:35).

AMALEK [Ăm' a lĕk]—WARLIKE or DWELLER IN THE VALE. *Son of*

Eliphaz and grandson of Esau and founder of a tribal family known as the Amalekites (Gen. 36:12, 16; Ex. 17; I Chron. 1:36). Amalek appears to have separated from his brethren and true to his name, became the head of a warlike tribe. Balaam described him as "the first of the nations" (Num. 24:20).

AMARIAH [Ăm a rī′ ah]—JEHOVAH HATH SAID or PROMISED.
1. *A son of Meraioth,* a priest descended from Phinehas (I Chron. 6:7, 52).
2. *The son of Azariah,* a high priest in Solomon's time (I Chron. 6:11).
3. *A descendant of Kohath,* son of Levi (I Chron. 23:19; 24:23).
4. *Chief priest* of Jehoshaphat's time (II Chron. 19:11).
5. *A Levite* appointed by Hezekiah to distribute tithes and offerings (II Chron. 31:15).
6. *A man of the family of Bani* who married a foreign wife (Ezra 10:42).
7. *A priest* who signed the covenant (Neh. 10:3; 12:2, 13).
8. *A descendant of Judah* by Perez (Neh. 11:4).
9. *An ancestor of Zephaniah* the prophet in Josiah's time (Zeph. 1:1).

AMASA [Ăm′ a să]—BURDEN-BEARER.
1. *The son of David's half-sister Abigail* whom Absalom made captain of his rebel army (II Sam. 17:25; 19:13; 20). Amasa was completely defeated by his cousin Joab in the forest of Ephraim (II Sam. 18:6–8). David not only forgave Amasa but gave him Joab's place (II Sam. 19:13). Joab treacherously slew him (II Sam. 20:9–12).
2. *The name of an Ephraimite* who with others resisted the bringing into Samaria the Jews Ahaz had made prisoners (II Chron. 28:12).

AMASAI [Ă măs′ a ī]—BURDENSOME.
1. *A descendant of Kohath,* son of Levi (I Chron. 6:25; II Chron. 29:12).
2. *A chieftain* who joined David at Ziklag and became one of his captains (I Chron. 12:18). Perhaps the same as Amasa, No. 1.
3. *A Levite* who helped in the return of the Ark from the house of Obed-edom (I Chron. 15:24).

AMASHAI [Ă măsh′ a ī]—CARRYING SPOIL or BURDEN-BEARER. *A priest,* son of Azareel who lived in Jerusalem at Nehemiah's request (Neh. 11:13). Also called Amashsai.

AMASIAH [Ăm a sī′ ah]—JEHOVAH IS STRONG. *A son of Zichri,* one of Jehoshaphat's commanders (II Chron. 17:16).

AMAZIAH [Ăm a zī′ ah]—JEHOVAH HAS STRENGTH.

1. *Son of Joash or Jehoash,* king of Judah. Amaziah came to the throne after the assassination of his father. The writer of II Kings gives him unqualified praise for his religious acts (II Kings 14), but in Chronicles he is accused of gross apostasy (II Chron. 25:14).

2. *The priest at Bethel* who opposed the prophet Amos in the matter of idol-worship (Amos 7:10).

3. *A man of the tribe of Simeon* (I Chron. 4:34).

4. *A Levite* descended from Merari (I Chron. 6:45).

AMI [Ā' mī]—THE BEGINNING. *The head of a family* of Solomon's servants, whose descendants returned with Zerubbabel from exile (Ezra 2:57). He is called Amon, meaning "steadfast" in Nehemiah 7:59.

AMINADAB [Ă mĭn' a dăb]—THE KINSMAN IS GENEROUS. *Son of Aram* (or Ram), who was the son of Esrom, ancestor of our Lord (Matt. 1:4; Luke 3:33).

AMITTAI [Ă mĭt' ta ī]—TRUE or TRUTHFUL. *The father of the prophet Jonah* (II Kings 14:25; Jonah 1:1).

AMMIEL [Ăm' mĭ el]—A DEVOTED ALLY or KINSMAN OF GOD.

1. *The son of Gemalli* and spy of the tribe of Dan sent out by Moses (Num. 13:12).

2. *The father of Machir,* of Lo-debar (II Sam. 9:4, 5; 17:27).

3. *The father of Bath-sheba,* one of David's wives (I Chron. 3:5).

4. *The sixth son of Obed-edom* who, with his family, was associated with the Tabernacle porters (I Chron. 26:5).

AMMIHUD [Ăm mī' hŭd]—MAN OF PRAISEWORTHINESS or MY PEOPLE IS HONORABLE.

1. *The father of Elishama,* chief of Ephraim (Num. 1:10; 2:18; 7:48).

2. *A man of Simeon* and father of Shemuel (Num. 34:20).

3. *A Naphtalite* whose son, Pedahel, also assisted in the division of the land (Num. 34:28).

4. *Father of Talmai* and king of Geshur. Absalom fled to Talmai after he slew his brother Ammon (II Sam. 13:37).

5. *Son of Omri,* father of Uthai (I Chron. 9:4).

AMMIHUR [Ăm mī' hŭr]—MY PEOPLE IS NOBLE. *Father of Talmai* (II Sam. 13:37). Same as (4) above. "R" is found in Hebrew text, though pronounced traditionally as "Ammihud."

AMMINADAB [Ăm mĭn' a dăb]—MY PEOPLE IS WILLING or MY KINSMAN IS GENEROUS.

1. *A Levite,* Aaron's father-in-law (Ex. 6:23).

2. *A prince* of Judah (Num. 1:7; 2:3; 7:12, 17; 10:14; Ruth 4:19, 20).

3. *A son of Kohath,* son of Levi (I Chron. 6:22). Perhaps the same as No. 1.
4. *A Kohathite* who assisted in the return of the Ark from the house of Obed-edom (I Chron. 15:10, 11).

AMMINADIB [Ăm′ mi nā′ dib]—MY PEOPLE IS LIBERAL or PRINCELY. Someone famous for the chariots provided for King Solomon (S. of Sol. 6:12). Perhaps it is not a proper name.

AMMISHADDAI [Ăm mī shăd′ da ī]—AN ALLY IS THE ALMIGHTY. *Father of Ahiezer,* captain of the tribe of Dan in Moses′ time (Num. 1:12; 2:25; 7:66, 71; 10:25).

AMMIZABAD [Ăm mĭz′ a băd]—THE KINSMAN HATH ENDOWED. *Son of Benaiah,* third of David′s captains (I Chron. 27:6).

AMMON [Ăm′ mŏn]—PERTAINING TO THE NATION. *The younger son of Lot* by his younger daughter, born in a cave near Zoar, and ancestor of the Ammonites (Gen. 19:38; Num. 21:24). See Ben-amni.

AMNON [Ăm′ nŏn]—FAITHFUL or TUTELAGE.
1. *The eldest son of David* by Ahinoam the Jezreelitess, he was slain by Absalom (II Sam. 3:2; 13).
2. *The son of Shimon,* of the tribe of Judah (I Chron. 4:20).

AMOK [Ā′ mok]—DEEP. *A chief of priests* who returned with Zerubbabel from exile (Neh. 12:7, 20).

AMON [Ā′ mon]—SECURITY or A WORKMAN.
1. *Governor* of the city of Samaria under Ahab (I Kings 22: 26; II Chron. 18:25).
2. *Son of Manasseh,* and fifteenth king of Judah, who reigned for two years (II Kings 21:18–25).
3. *One of the clan* known as "Solomon′s servants" (Neh. 7:59). Called Ami in Ezra 2:57.
4. *A son of Manasses,* and an ancestor of Christ (Matt. 1:10). Amon is also the name of an Egyptian sun-god.

AMOS [Ā′ mos]—BURDEN-BEARER or ONE WITH A BURDEN.
1. *This prophet of "judgment,"* which is the key word of the book he wrote, was a citizen of Tekoa, west of the Dead Sea (Amos 1:1; 7:8–16; 8:2).

The Man Who Was a Dresser of Sycamore Trees

Although he was one of the oldest of the prophets, we know little about Amos save what he himself tells us. He does not appear to have belonged to any rank or influence. The opposite is the case, seeing he styles himself a herdsman (Amos 7:14). He was no "professional prophet, speaking for a living." Amos did not belong to the order of the prophets, nor had he been educated in the school of the prophets. The prophetic office was thrust upon him (Amos 7:14, 15). When the call came he exchanged the life of a shepherd and cultivator of sycamore trees for that of a prophet.

The desert life of Amos exercised great formative influences upon him. With time to think and pray, he was qualified to form clear judgments. The art of the seer is not cultivated in crowds.

Contemporary with Hosea, Amos prophesied in the days of Uzziah, king of Judah and in the time of Jeroboam. Most of the prophets confined their message in the main to Israel, but to Amos, Israel was only one of the nations. He took in a whole range of various nationalities and indicted them for their sins and proclaimed the judgment of God alike upon nations and individuals.

Amos pronounced judgment upon the oppression of the poor, commercial dishonesty, selfish indulgence and idolatrous worship, and was the first prophet to predict the captivity of Israel, and to announce God's rejection of His chosen people. The great lessons of the Book of Amos are:

I. Sin is sin in all its blackness, against the bright background of God's grace.

II. Mere ritual is not pleasing to God. The very worship of Israel was sin (Amos 4:4, 5; 5:21–24). Israel thought of God as a vain monarch, pleased with gifts and empty phrases. Amos had nothing but utter contempt for forms of religion that did not disturb one's conscience or change one's life.

III. The greatest perils, both of nations and men, lie not in poverty, but in prosperity.

IV. God's dealings with men are for their discipline, not their doom. Discipline, however, if unheeded, only hastens doom and determines destiny. Thus Amos is rightly called "the prophet of divine law."

2. *An ancestor of Joseph*, husband of Mary, our Lord's mother (Luke 3:25).

AMOZ [Ā' mŏz]—STRONG or BRASS. *The father of the prophet Isaiah*, a Judahite, who must be carefully distinguished from Amos (II Kings 19:2, 20; Isa. 1:1).

AMPLIATUS, AMPLIAS [Ăm' plĭ as]—ENLARGED. *A convert of Paul's* who lived in Rome and to whom the apostle sent a greeting (Rom. 16:8). This name, a common slave designation, is found inscribed in the catacombs.

AMRAM [Ăm' răm]—EXALTED PEOPLE or INEXPERIENCE.
1. *A grandson of Levi*, son of Kohath and father of Aaron, Moses and Miriam. Amram died at 137 years of age (Ex. 6:18, 20).

2. *A son of Bani,* who married a foreign wife during the exile (Ezra 10:34).

3. *A son of Dishon* and grandson of Anah (I Chron. 1:41). This name should be Hamram or Hamran.

AMRAPHEL [Ăm′ ra phĕl]—POWERFUL PEOPLE. *The king of Shinar,* ally of Chedorlaomer, in Abraham's time (Gen. 14:1, 9).

AMZI [Ăm′ zī]—ROBUST or MY STRENGTH.
1. *A descendant of Merari,* who was a son of Levi, and progenitor of Ethan, whom David set over the service of song (I Chron. 6:46).
2. *Ancestor of Adaiah,* a priest of the course in the second Temple (Neh. 11:12).

ANAH [Ā′ nah]—FRUITFUL IN GRAPES or ANSWERING.
1. *A son of Seir* the Horite, and one of the chiefs of the land (Gen. 36:20, 29; I Chron. 1:38).
2. *A son of Zibeon,* son of Seir (Gen. 36: 24; I Chron. 1:40, 41). Also the name of a daughter of Zibeon (Gen. 36: 2, 14).

ANAIAH [Ăn a ī′ ah]—JEHOVAH HATH ANSWERED.
1. *A prince or priest* who assisted in the reading of the law to the people (Neh. 8:4).
2. *A Jew* who, with Nehemiah, sealed the covenant (Neh. 10:22).

ANAK [Ā′ năk]—GIANT, OR LONG-NECKED OR ORNAMENT. *Son of Arba,* and ancestor of the Anakims (Num. 13:22, 28, 33). See also Anakim (Deut. 1:28).

ANAN [Ā′ nan]—HE BECLOUDS or COVERS. *A returned exile* who acted with Nehemiah in the sealing of the covenant (Neh. 10:26).

ANANI [Ăn ā′ nī]—COVERED WITH GOD. *A son of Elioenai,* of the family of David (I Chron. 3:24).

ANANIAH [Ăn a nī′ ah]—JEHOVAH IS A PROTECTOR. *The father of Maaseiah* and grandfather of Azariah (Neh. 3:23).

ANANIAS [Ăn a nī′ as]—JEHOVAH IS GRACIOUS. This name is the Greek form of Hananiah, meaning, "Jehovah hath been gracious" from the Aramaic, meaning, "beautiful."
1. *The disciple* who conspired with his wife to deceive the apostles in regard to the value obtained for their property (Acts 5:1-6).
The Man Who Kept Back Part of the Price
How opposite Aquila and Priscilla are Ananias and Sapphira, both of whom agreed to a dishonest transaction! They were not compelled to sell their property but because of a recognized custom among the

early Christian fraternity of having one common fund to draw upon, these two disciples wanted to maintain the appearance of self-denying liberality. There was no harm in keeping back part of the price—they might have kept back *all*. Their evil consisted in pretending to give *all*. Their lying was combined with hypocrisy. A *certain* part was retained, likely the greater part which would look more like the whole.

Peter, supernaturally endowed to detect and expose the fraud of Ananias and Sapphira, was their instrument of sudden death. Punishment was:

I.   Prompt — it followed immediately the committal of sin.

II.   Decisive — it marked the magnitude of sin.

III.   Conspicuous — it was before many witnesses.

IV.   Divine — it was not an act of Peter who simply reproved the two who, united in crime, were not separated in death (Ps. 19:13). It was God who punished them.

2.   *A godly disciple of Damascus* to whom was made known the conversion of Saul of Tarsus (Acts 9:10–17; 22:12), and who baptized Saul.

3.   *The high priest* anointed by Herod (Acts 23:2; 24:1).

ANATH [Ā′ năth]—ANSWER OR A GRANTING. *Father of Shamgar*, third judge after Joshua (Judg. 3: 31; 5:6).

ANATHOTH [Ăn′ a thŏth]—ANSWERED PRAYERS.
1.   *The eighth of the nine sons of Becher,* son of Benjamin (I Chron. 7:8).
2.   *Head and representative* of the men of Anathoth who added his seal to the covenant (Neh. 10:19). Also name of a Levitical city, now known as Anata (Josh. 21:18).

ANDREW [Ăn′ drew]—MANLINESS. *Brother of Simon Peter*, and one of the twelve apostles (Matt. 4:18; 10:2).

The Man Who was the First Missionary

Because he brought his own brother to the newly found Messiah, Andrew earned the distinction of being the first missionary of the cause of Christ (John 1:41). Andrew belonged to Bethsaida of Galilee —was a disciple of John the Baptist—attached himself to Christ with whom he enjoyed a special friendship (Mark 13:3; John 1:35–37). He was ever prompt to help (John 6:8, 9; 12:21, 22). After Christ's ascension, Andrew preached in Jerusalem. Tradition has it that he was crucified because of his rebuke of Aegeas for obstinate adherence to idolatry. He was nailed to a cross in the form of an X, hence the name *St. Andrew's Cross*. Lessons to be learned from Andrew are:

I.   It is only in true discipleship that rest can be found.

II.   If we cannot perform more conspicuous service we can yet serve the Lord. Although Peter was the spiritual father of the Pentecost converts, Andrew was their spiritual grandfather.

III.   We must discover our own gift and the gift in others and guide such into right channels of service.

IV.   If we are Christ's ours will be the passion to lead others to Him.

ANDRONICUS [Ăn drō nī′ cus]—CONQUERER or CONQUERING MEN. *A Jewish believer,* once a fellow-prisoner of Paul to whom the apostle sent a greeting (Rom. 16:7).

ANER [Ā′ nûr]—WATERFALL or AFFLICTION. *A brother of Mamre,* the Amorite, Abraham's ally in battle (Gen. 14:13, 24). Also the name of a Levitical city in Manasseh (I Chron. 6:70), now known as Anim.

ANIAM [Ā′ ni ăm]—SIGHING OF THE PEOPLE. *A son of Shemidah,* a Manassehite (I Chron. 7:19).

ANNAS [Ăn′ nas]—GRACE OF JEHOVAH. *A Jewish high priest,* the son of Seth, appointed to office in his thirty-seventh year by Quirinus, and who was in office when John the Baptist began his ministry (Luke 3:2; John 18:13, 24; Acts 4:6). Annas was an astute and powerful ecclesiastical statesman, who took part not only in the trial of Jesus, but also in those of Peter and John.

ANTIPAS [Ăn′ tĭ păs]—LIKENESS OF HIS FATHER.
1. See *Herod,* No. 3. Name is an abbreviation of Antipater.
2. *The believer at Pergamos* in Asia Minor who sealed his witness with his blood (Rev. 2:12, 13).

ANTOTHIJAH [Ăn to thī′ jah]—ANSWER OF JEHOVAH. *A son of Shashak,* a Benjamite (I Chron. 8:24).

ANUB [Ā′ nub]—STRONG or HIGH. *A son of Coz,* descendant of Caleb and Hur (I Chron. 4:8).

APELLES [Ă pĕl′ lēs]—I SEPARATE or EXCLUDE. *An approved Christian* at Rome to whom Paul sent a greeting (Rom. 16:10). A typical Jewish name. Apelles is yet found among the dependants of the Emperor. "Approved" means that this disciple's fidelity to Christ had been tried and had stood the test. Apelles had proved his faith. Weymouth translates it—"Greetings to Apelles—that veteran believer."

APHIAH [Ă phī′ ah]—REVIVIFIED or STRIVING. *One of Saul's ancestors* (I Sam. 9:1).

APHSES [Ăph′ sēs]—THE DISPERSED. *A Levite chief* of the eighteenth of the twenty-four courses in the service of the Temple (I Chron. 24:15).

APOLLOS [Ă pŏl′ los]—A DESTROYER or YOUTHFUL GOD OF MUSIC. *An eloquent and learned Jew* born at Alexandria and deeply versed in Old Testament Scriptures (Acts 18:24; 19:1; I Cor. 1:12; 3:4–6, 22; 4:6; 16:12; Titus 3:13).

The Man Whose Influence Was Enriched

This educated, cultured Alexandrian Jew was an orator and an efficient worker in the Church who knew only the baptism of John (Acts 18:24, 25). The influence of Apollos was ample and varied and, under Aquila and Priscilla, was heightened and enriched.

I. His was the influence of eloquence (Acts 18:24). Apollos wielded an ever powerful instrument of blessing—a consecrated eloquence.

II. His was the influence of exposition. Apollos was mighty in the Scriptures (Acts 18:26). What a tribute it is to be mighty in the mightiest of books!

III. His was the influence of spiritual knowledge. Apollos taught by word of mouth the things of the Lord.

IV. His was the influence of fervency. Apollos was also "fervent in spirit" (Acts 18:25). "A lively, affectionate preacher," as Matthew Henry calls him.

V. His was the influence of accuracy. Apollos taught "carefully" or "accurately" the truth of Christ (Acts 18:25 RV). Incorrectness in teaching is detrimental to all concerned.

VI. His was the influence of courage. Apollos spoke "boldly." He had no hesitation in his tone. Courage flashed in his eyes (Acts 18:26).

Yet with all his excellent gifts and goodly influence, Apollos had a distinct limitation. He knew that Christ was coming, but his was only a partial Christianity. Yet what he knew and taught profoundly impressed many in the synagogue. Under the tuition of Aquila and Priscilla, two deeply taught believers, Apollos was led into a deeper understanding of the truth. Instructed in the way of the Lord, Apollos went out to expound the truth more fully and accurately and thereafter became an unashamed herald of the Christian faith especially among the Jews (Acts 18:28).

Later on, Apollos became an apostle and one of Paul's trusted friends and companions, and remained active in his ministry during Paul's life (I Cor. 16:12; Titus 3:13). So effective a preacher did he become that some of the Corinthians put him before both Peter and Paul. Martin Luther hazarded the guess that Apollos was the writer of the Epistle to the Hebrews.

APPAIM [Ăp′ pa ĭm]—FACE or PRESENCE. *Son of Nadah,* of the family of Hezron (I Chron. 2:30, 31).

AQUILA [Ăq′ uĭ lä]—EAGLE. *A Jew whom Paul found at Corinth* on his arrival from Athens (Acts 18:2, 18, 26; Rom. 16:3; I Cor. 16:19; II Tim. 4:19).

The Man Who Is Always Linked with His Wife

A characteristic feature of Aquila and Priscilla is that their names are always mentioned together. In the truest sense they were "no more twain but one." They were one in their common interest in Christ, and all they accomplished together in the name of the Lord was the result of that perfect unity of spiritual nature, of purpose and of aim.

I.   By occupation they were tent-makers. Perhaps it was because Paul followed the same trade that he was attracted to them when he went to Corinth from Athens.

II.   By their oneness in spiritual things they were hospitable. Being in full sympathy with Paul's message they willingly received him unto their house, and he remained with them for a year and a half. What blessed times of fellowship the three of them must have had!

III.   By their faithfulness they encouraged the saints. Paul tells us that these two devoted people were willing to "lay down their own necks" for the apostle. What they did for Paul earned the gratitude of all the churches.

IV.   By their spiritual insight, Apollos and many other saints were helped. They had a "church in their house" and because of their spiritual quality and knowledge of Scripture many were blessed.

A fact that cannot escape our notice is that Priscilla is usually named first in the references to Aquila and herself. Perhaps this most "noble Roman lady" became a Christian before her husband. Maybe she was a more active worker than her husband! Chrysostom says that it was Priscilla's careful expositions of the way of God that proved so helpful to Apollos. Together, Aquila and Priscilla are a pertinent example for Christian husbands and wives.

ARA [Ā' rǎ]—STRONG. *Son of Jether*, of the tribe of Asher (I Chron. 7:38).

ARAD [Ā' rǎd]—FUGITIVE.
1.   *The Canaanite king* who attacked the Israelites near Mount Hor and was defeated (Num. 21:1; 33:40).
2.   *Son of Beriah,* a Benjamite and one of the principal men of Aijalon (I Chron. 8:15). Also the name of a town south of Judah (Josh. 12:14).

ARAH [Ā' rah]—WAYFARER.
1.   *A son of Ulla,* an Asherite (I Chron. 7:39).
2.   *The father of a family* that returned from exile (Ezra 2:5; Neh. 7:10). Perhaps the same person as No. 1.
3.   *A Jew* whose granddaughter became the wife of Tobiah the Ammonite (Neh. 6:18).

ARAM [Ā' rǎm]—EXALTED.
1.   *A son of Shem* (Gen. 10:22, 23; I Chron. 1:17).
2.   *Son of Kemuel,* Abraham's nephew (Gen. 22:21).
3.   *Son of Shamer,* of the tribe of Asher (I Chron. 7:34; Matt. 1:3, 4,

Luke 3:33). Also the name used of the whole country of Syria (Num. 23:7), and of the hill country north of Canaan (I Chron. 2:23).

ARAN [Ā' răn]—A WILD GOAT or FIRMNESS. *Son of Dishan,* the Horite, a descendant of Esau (Gen. 36:28; I Chron. 1:42).

ARAUNAH [Ă rau' nah]—JEHOVAH IS FIRM. *The Jebusite* who owned a threshing floor on Mount Moriah, which David purchased in order to erect an altar. Because of his sin in numbering the people, the land was smitten with a plague. When the plague was stayed, David presented a costly offering to the Lord (II Sam. 24:16–24). Called Ornan in I Chronicles 21:15.

ARBA [Är' ba]—THE CROUCHER or STRENGTH OF BAAL. *The father of Anak,* so named because he was the father of the city which bore his name. Kirjath-arba, later Hebron, was a chief seat of the Anakims (Josh. 14:15; 15:13; 21:11).

ARCHELAUS [Är chĕ lā' us]—PEOPLE'S CHIEF. *A son of Herod the Great* (Matt. 2:22). See Herod.

ARCHIPPUS [Är chĭp' pus]—MASTER OF THE HORSE. *A Christian at Colosse* conspicuous as a champion of the Gospel — a close friend of Philemon — an office-bearer in the Church (Col. 4:17; Philem. 2). Because of the spiritual atmosphere of Colosse (Rev. 3:14–19), it is not surprising to find Paul exhorting his fellow-soldiers to maintain his zeal and fidelity.

ARD [Ärd]—DESCENT.
1. *A son of Benjamin,* and founder of the Ardites (Gen. 46:21).
2. *A son of Bela,* son of Benjamin (Num. 26:40). Called Addar in I Chronicles 8:3.

ARDON [Är' dŏn]—DESCENDANT. *A son of Caleb,* son of Hezron, a Judahite (I Chron. 2:18).

ARELI [Ă rē' lī]—VALIANT or HEROIC. *A son of Gad* and founder of the tribal family, the Arelites (Gen. 46:16; Num. 26:17).

ARETAS [Är' e tăs]—PLEASING or VIRTUOUS. *Father-in-law of Herod the Tetrarch,* whose deputy sought to apprehend Paul at Damascus (II Cor. 11:32).

ARGOB [Är' gŏb]—HEAP OF STONES or STRONG. *A man assassinated* along with Pekahiah, king of Israel, by Pekah who aspired to the throne (II Kings 15:25). Also the name of the kingdom of Og in Bashan (Deut. 3:4, 13, 14).

ARIDAI [Ă rĭd′ a ī] probably GIFT OF THE PLOUGH or THE BULL. *The ninth of Haman's sons,* hanged along with his father and brothers (Esther 9:9).

ARIDATHA [Ă rĭd′ a thă]—GREAT BIRTH. *The sixth son of Haman* who suffered the death of hanging at the hands of the Jews (Esther 9:8).

ARIEH [Ă rī′ eh]—LION OF JEHOVAH. *A companion of Argob,* and assassinated along with him by Pekah, son of Remaliah (II Kings 15:25).

ARIEL [Ă′ rĭ el]—LION OF GOD or GOD'S ALTAR-HEARTH.
1. *A chief of the Jews* whom Ezra sent with others to Iddo at Casiphia (Ezra 8:16, 17).
2. *The name of a Moabite* whose two sons were slain by Benaiah (II Sam. 23:20; I Chron. 11:22). Also the symbolic name of Jerusalem (Isa. 29:1–7).

ARIOCH [Ă′ rĭ och]—LION-LIKE or SERVANT OF THE MOON-GOD.
1. *The king of Ellasar* in Syria and confederate with Chedorlaomer (Gen. 14:1, 4).
2. *Captain of the king's guard* at Babylon under Nebuchadnezzar (Dan. 2:14–25).

ARISAI [Ă rĭs′ a ī]—MEANING OBSCURE. *The eighth son of Haman* the Agagite who was hanged with the rest of the male members of the family (Esther 9:9).

ARISTARCHUS [Ăr ĭs tär′ chus]—THE BEST RULER. *A Macedonian of Thessalonica* and one of Paul's travel-companions. This convert from Judaism is spoken of as Paul's "fellow-prisoner," implying imprisonment for the Gospel's sake (Acts 19:29; 20:4; 27:2; Col. 4:10; Philem. 24).

ARISTOBULUS [Ăr ĭs to bū lus]—THE BEST COUNSELOR. *A Christian in Rome,* whose household Paul greeted. Tradition says that he was one of the seventy disciples and that he preached in Britain (Rom. 16:10).

ARMONI [Ăr mō′ nī]—PERTAINING TO THE PALACE. *A son of Saul* by the concubine Rizpah. He was slain by the Gibeonites to satisfy justice (II Sam. 21:8–11).

ARNAN [Ăr′ nan]—STRONG or AGILE. *A descendant of David* and founder of a tribal family (I Chron. 3:21).

ARNI [Ăr′ nī]—REJOICING. *An ancestor of Jesus Christ* (Luke 3:33). This spelling is given in the R.V. Called Aram and Ram. (See Ruth 4:19; I Chron. 2:9, 10; Matt. 1:3, 4).

AROD [Ā′rŏd]—POSTERITY. *A son of Gad* and founder of the Arodi or Arodites (Gen. 46:16; Num. 26:17).

ARPHAXAD, ARPACHSHAD [Är phăx′ ad]—ONE THAT RELEASES. *The third son of Shem,* and a remote ancestor of Abraham (Gen. 10: 22, 24; 11:10–13; I Chron. 1:17, 24; Luke 3:36).

ARTAXERXES [Är tăx ûrx′ ēs]—POSSESSOR OF AN EXALTED KINGDOM. In his concordance, Young distinguishes three of the Persian kings bearing this name.

1. *The Longimanus of secular history.* It was during the seventh year of the reign of this Persian king that Ezra went up to Jerusalem (Ezra 7:1–21; 8:1; Neh. 2:1; 5:14; 13:6).

2. *The Cambyses of secular history,* another Persian king who reigned in Ezra's time (Ezra 4:7–23).

3. *The king of Persia* who reigned around the time of Darius (Ezra 6:14).

ARTEMAS [Är′ te mäs]—WHOLE or SOUND. Another meaning of this name is "gift of Artemas," Artemas being the Greek goddess of hunting. Paul's companion at Nicopolis, whom the apostle used to send a message to Titus (Titus 3:12).

ARZA [Är′ză]—FIRM or DELIGHT. *The steward of king Elah's* house in Tirzah (I Kings 16:9).

ASA [Ā′ să]—PHYSICIAN.

1. *The third king of Judah* who succeeded Abijah. He was the great-grandson of Solomon (I Kings 15; II Chron. 14–16). He was an ancestor of Jesus Christ (Matt. 1:7, 8).

The Man Who Was Good and Right

Asa is a marvel. In spite of the fact that his father was a sinful man and his mother a heathen woman, he yet shines forth as one of Judah's most godly kings. He is praised for his religious zeal which led him to reform the worship of the people. Because of his devotion to God he deposed his idolatrous mother—an astonishing act for an oriental.

Asa's heart toward God was like David's and such was the secret of his godliness in a foul environment. He is spoken of as doing "that which was good and right in the eyes of the Lord, his God." Some people are presumptuous enough to settle what is good and right in their own eyes. Asa, however, did not invent a goodness or righteousness he could adapt to his own convenience and ambition. He only wanted what was good and right in God's sight.

I. Asa prayed before battle. He did not shrink from war with the Ethiopians. Before meeting the foe he met God. "Lord, it is nothing with Thee to help."

II. Asa began upon a good foundation. It took courage and Asa "took courage, and put away the abominable idols." Our idols of fortune, fashion, popularity, self-indulgence, must be severely dealt with if we desire God's best. We can only be right with God and with one another when we are right about our little gods, and man-made idols.

III. Asa was victorious. Being right with God, Asa was honored of Him. His foes surrendered for they saw that his God was with him.

IV. Asa was impartial. The grandeur of this good king is seen in that he would not even allow his mother to keep an idol. So he ruthlessly destroyed the little royal shrine. What was wrong for the subject was also wrong for the queen. Thus horrible abominations had to be abolished. No wonder when Asa died, his people sorely missed and mourned him!

2. *A Levite,* son of Elkanah and head of a family of Netophathites (I Chron. 9:16).

ASAHEL [Ā' sa hĕl]—GOD HATH MADE or GOD IS DOER.

1. *A Levite* sent by Jehoshaphat to teach the law to the people in Judah (II Chron. 17:8).

2. *A Levite* Hezekiah employed as an officer of the offerings, tithes and dedicated things (II Chron. 31:13).

3. *Father of a certain Jonathan,* appointed by Ezra to take a census of those Jews who had married foreign wives while in exile (Ezra 10:15).

4. *The youngest son of Zeruiah,* David's sister, and the brother of Joab and Abishai. He was slain by Abner unwillingly (II Sam. 2:18–32; 3:27, 30; 23:24; I Chron. 2:16; 11:26; 27:7).

The Man Who Died in His Boots

Conspicuous among those of David's brethren and those of his father's house who came to him while hiding in the cave of Adullam were the three sons of Zeruiah his sister, Joab, Abishai and Asahel. Asahel was the favorite among the three. Little is recorded of him beyond his activity and the manner of his death.

I. He was famous for his swiftness of foot. Speed was a much valued gift in ancient times.

II. He was near the top of David's thirty heroes. Courage made him a conspicuous fighter.

III. He was a commander of a division in David's army. He had proved himself worthy of position.

IV. He believed in persistence. He persisted in following Abner, the captain of Saul's host in the battle that began by the pool of Gibeon. Abner was unwilling to slay him, knowing how he was beloved. He seems to have struck Asahel at last only in self-defense.

V. He dies for his ambition. Asahel would aim at nothing less than the glory of slaying Saul's general, and he was slain himself instead. Thus he died in harness or as we have put it, in his boots.

ASAHIAH [Ā sa hī' ah]—JEHOVAH HATH MADE. *An officer of king Josiah's* sent with others to enquire about the Law found by Shaphan (II Kings 22:12, 14; II Chron. 34:20).

ASAIAH [Ā sa ī' ah]—JEHOVAH IS DOER.
1. *A descendant of Simeon,* a Simeonite prince (I Chron. 4:36).
2. *Of the family of Haggiah* and Merari (I Chron. 6:30).
3. *Son of a Shilonite* living in Jerusalem (I Chron. 9:5).
4. *A descendant of Merari* who helped in the return of the Ark from the house of Obed-edom (I Chron. 15:6, 11). Perhaps the same person as No. 2.

ASAPH [Ā' saph]—HE THAT GATHERED or REMOVED REPROACH.
1. *Father of Joah* who was the recorder to Hezekiah (II Kings 18:18, 37; II Chron. 29:13; Isa. 36:3, 22).
2. *Son of Berechiah* of the Gershonite family appointed by David over the service of song and by Solomon in the Temple services (I Chron. 6:39; 15:17, 19). David called this Asaph "the seer" (II Chron. 29:30).
3. *A Levite,* whose posterity lived in Jersusalem after the exile (I Chron. 9:15).
4. *A descendant of Kohath,* son of Levi, whose descendants were tabernacle porters in David's time (I Chron. 26:1).
5. *The keeper of the king's park* in Palestine under the king of Persia (Neh. 2:8).

ASAREEL, ASAREL [Ā sā' re el]—GOD IS JOINED. *A son of Jehallelel,* a descendant of Judah through Caleb the spy (I Chron. 4:16).

ASARELAH, ASHARELAH—[Ăs a rē' lah]—UPRIGHT TOWARD GOD. *A son of Asaph*—No. 2 above (I Chron. 25:2). Perhaps the Azareel of I Chronicles 25:18. Also known as Jesharelah in I Chronicles 25:14.

ASHBEA [Ăsh bē' ă]—MAN OF BAAL or LET ME CALL AS WITNESS. *A descendant of Shelah,* a Judahite who wrought in fine linen (I Chron. 4:21).

ASHBEL [Ăsh' bĕl]—MAN OF BAAL. *The second son of Benjamin* and father of a tribal family known as the Ashbelites (Gen. 46:21; Num. 26:38; I Chron. 8:1).

ASHCHENAZ, ASHKENAZ [Ăsh' che năz, Ăsh' ke năz]—A FIRE THAT SPREADS. *Eldest son of Gomer* (Gen. 10:3; I Chron. 1:6; see Jer. 51·27).

ASHER [Ăsh' ûr]—HAPPY. *The eighth son of Jacob* and second of Zilpah, Leah's maid and progenitor of a tribe (Gen 30·13. 35:26; 49:20; Deut. 33:24, 25). The New Testament form is Aser (Luke 2:36;

Rev. 7:6). Asher was the founder of the Asherites (Num. 1:13; Judg. 1:32). Also the name of a town east of Shechem (Josh. 17:7).

The Man with Shoes of Iron and Brass

In the blessings of Jacob and Moses, Asher is described as being not only acceptable to his brethren, but as one blessed of God with royal dainties or bountiful supplies. Of all the tribes of Israel the tribe of Asher has the least eventful history. It never produced a great warrior, judge, king or counselor. The land of Asher was as uneventful as the tribe itself. No great battles were fought there in Israel's time.

I.   Asher and his bounties. Asher was the tribe of rich pastures. Asher dwelt in the midst of plenty and being willing to share what he had, was most acceptable to his brethren. Dipping the foot in oil may refer to the olive-trees, so plentiful in that thickly wooded part of Palestine. Acre, the port and town given to Asher, has been regarded as the key of Palestine, and as oil has been recently discovered near by, perhaps the fatness of the prophecies of Jacob and Moses is about to be realized to the full.

II.   Asher and his female representative. No other tribe of Israel is represented in Scripture by a woman. One member of the tribe, a widow, represents the individual history of the tribe. "One Anna, a prophetess, the daughter of Phanuel, of the tribe of Asher" (Luke 2: 36–38). It was Anna who confessed Christ, at His birth, on the part of Israel.

III.   Asher and his love of ease. The chief defect in the character of Asher was his unwillingness to drive out the Canaanites. He was content to dwell among them. The command was to utterly drive them out and make no terms with them. "Live and let live," seems to have been Asher's policy. Asher's rich bounties had an enervating effect upon the tribe. The people were conspicuous by their absence during the war with Sisera (Judg. 5:17). Apart from Anna, none of the tribe appear to have been eminent for prowess or piety. Prosperity resulted in ease and declension.

IV.   Asher and the promise of endurance. Completing the blessing of Moses was a wonderful promise of endurance for the days of pilgrimage. "Thy shoes shall be iron and brass, and as thy days so shall thy strength be." The words for shoes and strength are peculiar to this verse, and are found nowhere else in the Bible. Many guesses have been made as to the true meaning of these words. Such a promise was well understood by those who, as they journeyed through the great and terrible wilderness had raiment that waxed not old upon them and feet that did not swell. Anna is a fitting illustration of the promised endurance, seeing that she was long past eighty years of age when she saw the Saviour.

ASHPENAZ [Ăsh' pe năz]—HORSE'S NOSE. The prince of the eunuchs at Babylon during the reign of Nebuchadnezzar (Dan. 1:3).

ASHUR [Ăsh' ŭr]—FREEMAN. *A son of Hezron,* son of Pharez (I Chron. 2:24; 4:5), and founder of the tribe of Ashurites (II Sam. 2:9).

ASHVATH [Ăsh' văth]—WROUGHT. *A son of Japhlet,* an Asherite (I Chron. 7:33).

ASIEL [Ā' sǐ el]—GOD HATH MADE. *Great-grandfather of Jehu* a Simeonite (I Chron. 4:35).

ASNAH [Ăs' nah]—A BRAMBLE or DWELLER IN THE THORNBUSH. *A Nethinim,* whose descendants returned from the Babylonian captivity with Zerubbabel (Ezra 2:50).

ASNAPPER [Ăs năp' pûr]—ASNAP THE GREAT. *High Assyrian dignitary* called "great and noble" who settled various foreign tribes in Samaria (Ezra 4:10). See Esar-haddon.

ASPATHA [Ăs' pa thă]—HORSE-GIVEN. *The third son of Haman,* the Jews' enemy who was hanged with his father and brothers (Esther 9:7).

ASRIEL, ASHRIEL [Ăs' rǐ el, Ăsh' rǐ el]—VOW OF GOD or GOD IS JOINED.
1. *A son of Gilead* (Num. 26:31; Josh. 17:1, 2).
2. *A son of Manasseh* (I Chron. 7:14).

ASSHUR, ASSUR [Ăs' shur]—LEVEL PLAIN.
1. *Likely a descendant of Ham,* the builder of Nineveh, or of Assyria itself (Gen. 10:11).
2. *A son of Shem* and brother of Elam (Gen. 10:22; I Chron. 1:17).

ASSHURIM [Ăs shu' rim]—MIGHTY ONES. *A son of Dedan,* or his descendants (Gen. 25:3).

ASSIR [Ăs' sǐr]—CAPTIVE.
1. *A son of Korah* who was the grandson of Kohath (Ex. 6:24; I Chron. 6:22).
2. *A son of Ebiasaph* and grandson of Elkanah (I Chron. 6:23, 37).
3. *A son of Jeconiah,* son of Jehoiakim (I Chron. 3:17).

ASYNCRITUS [Ă sўn' cri-tŭs]—INCOMPARABLE. *A Christian in Rome* to whom Paul sends a salutation (Rom. 16:14).

ATER [Ā' tûr]—BOUND or SHUT.
1. *The ancestor of an exiled family* (Ezra 2:16; Neh. 7:21).
2. *Ancestor of a family of gatekeepers* who returned from exile with Zerubbabel (Ezra 2:42; Neh. 7:45).
3. *The chief of the people* who, with Nehemiah, sealed the covenant (Neh. 10:17).

ATHAIAH [Ăth a ĭ' ah]—JEHOVAH IS HELPER. *The son of Uzziah* a Judahite in Nehemiah's time (Neh. 11:4).

ATHALIAH [Ăth a lī' ah]—JEHOVAH IS STRONG or HATH AFFLICTED.
1. *A son of Jeroham,* a Benjamite (I Chron. 8:26).
2. *The father of Jeshiah,* a returned exile (Ezra 8:7). Also the name of the wife of Jehoram, king of Judah (II Kings 8:26).

ATHLAI [Ăth' laī]—JEHOVAH IS STRONG. *A son of Bebai* who put away his foreign wife (Ezra 10:28).

ATTAI [Ăt' taī]—SEASONABLE or OPPORTUNE.
1. *Grandson of Sheshan,* a Jerahmeelite (I Chron. 2:35, 36).
2. *A Gadite* who joined David at Ziklag (I Chron. 12:11).
3. *A son of Rehoboam,* son of Solomon (II Chron. 11:20).

AUGUSTUS [Ŏu gŭs' tus]—SACRED OR KINGLY. *Name of the Caesar* who became Emperor of Rome after the death of his uncle, Julius Caesar (Luke 2:1; Acts 25:21, 25; 27:1).

AZALIAH [Ăz a lī' ah]—JEHOVAH IS NOBLE or HATH SPARED. *Father of Shapham* the scribe (II Kings 22:3; II Chron. 34:8).

AZANIAH [Ăz a nī' ah]—JEHOVAH IS HEARER or HATH GIVEN EAR. *A Levite,* father of Jeshua, whose son signed the covenant (Neh. 10:9).

AZARAEL, AZAREEL [Ă zăr' a el, Ă zăr' e el]—GOD IS A HELPER.
1. *An Aaronite* who joined David at Ziklag (I Chron. 12:6).
2. *A priest,* responsible for the service of his sons in David's time (I Chron. 25:18). Perhaps the Asarelah the son of Asaph.
3. *A Danite prince* in David's time (I Chron. 27:22).
4. *A son of Bani* who married a foreign wife during the exile (Ezra 10:41).
5. *A priest of the family of Immer* (Neh. 11:13; 12:36).

AZARIAH [Ăz a rī' ah]—JEHOVAH IS KEEPER or HATH HELPED. The fact that there are almost thirty men bearing the name of Azariah is proof that it was a common name in Hebrew, especially in the family of Eleazar, whose name has a similar meaning, and is almost identical with Ezra, Zerahiah and Seraiah. See also Azariahu and Zacharias.
1. *The son of Zadok* and a descendant of David's high priest (I Kings 4:2).
2. *The son of Nathan,* ruler of Solomon's officers (I Kings 4:5).
3. *The son of Amaziah,* who was made king of Judah after his father (II Kings 14:21; 15:1-27; I Chron. 3:12).
4. *A man of Judah,* of the family of Zerah and of the house of Ethan (I Chron. 2:8).

5. *The son of Jehu* and grandson of Obed, a Judahite (I Chron. 2:38,39).

6. *A son of Ahimaz* and grandson of Zadok (I Chron. 6:9).

7. *A son of Johanan* and grandson of No. 6 who served in Solomon's time (I Chron. 6:10, 11).

8. *A son of Hilkiah,* and father of Seraiah the high priest in Josiah's reign (I Chron. 6:13, 14; 9:11; Ezra 7:1).

9. *A Levite of the family of Kohath* and an ancestor of Samuel the prophet (I Chron. 6:36).

10. *A prophet,* son of Obed, he encouraged Asa to persevere in his national religious revival (II Chron. 15:1).

11. *A son of king Jehoshaphat* (II Chron. 21:2).

12. *Another son of the above* (II Chron. 21:2).

13. *Son of Jehoram* (II Chron. 22:6).

14. *The son of Jehoram* and a captain who assisted in the overthrow of Athaliah and the elevation of Joash to the throne of Judah (II Chron. 23:1).

15. *The son of Obed* who also assisted in the above task (II Chron. 23:1).

16. *The high priest* who hindered Uzziah from burning incense on the altar (II Chron. 26:17, 20).

17. *The son of Johanan* and a chief of the tribe of Ephraim (II Chron. 28:12).

18. *The father of Joel* and a Kohathite (II Chron. 29:12). He assisted in the purification of the Temple in Hezekiah's time.

19. *The son of Jehalelel,* a Merarite who also assisted in Hezekiah's revival (II Chron. 29:12).

20. *The chief priest* of the house of Zadok in King Hezekiah's time (II Chron. 31:10, 13).

21. *The son of Meraioth,* and an ancestor of Ezra (Ezra 7:3).

22. *The son of Maaseiah,* of the family of Ananiah, who repaired a portion of the wall of Jerusalem (Neh. 3:23, 24).

23. *An Israelite who returned with Zerubbabel* (Neh. 7:7). Name also given as Seraiah.

24. *One of the priests* who explained the Law to the people as Ezra read it. Perhaps the same person as No. 22 (Neh. 8:7).

25. *Another priest* who sealed the covenant (Neh. 10:2).

26. *A prince of Judah* who joined in the procession with Nehemiah (Neh. 12:33).

27. *A son of Hoshaiah* and an opponent of Jeremiah whom he charged with false prophecies (Jer. 43:2).

28. *The Hebrew and original name of Abed-nego,* who with Daniel and others was carried away captive to Babylon (Dan. 1:6, 7, 11, 19; 2:17).

AZAZ [Ā′ zăz]—STRONG. *Father of a Reubenite chief* in Jeroboam's time (I Chron. 5:8).

AZAZIAH [Ăz a zī′ ah]—JEHOVAH IS STRONG.
1. *A Levite harpist* who assisted in the musical service when the Ark returned from the house of Obed-edom (I Chron. 15:21).
2. *Father of Hoshea* the prince of Ephraim in David's time (I Chron. 27:20).
3. *A Levite overseer* of dedicated things in the Temple in Hezekiah's reign (II Chron. 31:13).

AZBUK [Ăz′ bŭk]—PARDON. *The father of Nehemiah*—not the governor of the same name—who repaired a portion of the wall (Neh. 3:16).

AZEL, AZAL [Ā′ zĕl, Ā′zăl]—NOBLE. *A Benjamite* and a descendant of Jonathan, Saul's son (I Chron. 8:37, 38; 9:43, 44). Also the name of a hamlet (Zech. 14:5).

AZGAD [Ăz′ găd]—WORSHIP, SUPPLICATION or STRONG OF FORTUNE.
1. *Founder of a family* that returned with Ezra and Zerubbabel (Ezra 2:12; Neh. 7:17).
2. *One who returned from exile with Ezra* (8:12).
3. *A chief of a family of Jews* who sealed the covenant (Neh. 10:15).

AZIEL [Ā′ zĭ′ el]—GOD IS MIGHT. *A Levite* who assisted in the choral service of the Tabernacle (I Chron. 15:20). Called Jaaziel in I Chronicles 15:18.

AZIZA [Ă zī′ ză]—ROBUST or STRONG. *A son of Zattu* who married a foreign wife while in exile (Ezra 10:27).

AZMAVETH [Ăz′ ma vĕth]—DEATH IS STRONG or COUNSEL.
1. *One of David's thirty heroes* (II Sam. 23:31; I Chron. 11:33).
2. *A son of Jehoada* (also called Jarah), and descendant of Saul (I Chron. 8:36; 9:42).
3. *A Benjamite* whose two sons joined David at Ziklag (I Chron. 12:3).
4. *One of David's treasury officers* (I Chron. 27:25). Also the name of a village (Neh. 12:29). Now called Hizmeh.

AZOR [Ā′ zôr]—HELPER. *Great-grandson of Zorobabel* and an ancestor of Jesus Christ (Matt. 1:13, 14).

AZRIEL [Ăz′ rĭ el]—HELP OF GOD or GOD IS HELPER.
1. *A chief man of the half tribe of Manasseh* (I Chron. 5:24).

2. *Father of Jerimoth,* ruler of Naphtali in David's time (I Chron. 27:19).

3. *Father of Seraiah* of Jeremiah's time (Jer. 36:26).

AZRIKAM [Ăz' rĭ kăm]—MY HELP HATH RISEN.
1. *A son of Neariah* of the family of David (I Chron. 3:23).
2. *A son of Azel,* of the family of Saul (I Chron. 8:38; 9:44).
3. *A Levite,* and a descendant of Merari (I Chron. 9:14; Neh. 11:15).
4. *The governor of the palace* under King Ahaz (II Chron. 28:7).

AZUR, AZZUR [Ā' zur, Ăz' zŭr]—HELPER.
1. *Father of Jaazaniah,* a prince seen in vision (Ezek. 11:1).
2. *One of those who sealed the covenant* (Neh. 10:17).
3. *Father of Hananiah who withstood Jeremiah* (Jer. 28:1).

AZZAN [Ăz' zan]—STRONG or SHARP. *The father of Paltiel,* a prince of Issachar, who assisted in the portion of the land (Num. 34:26).

B

BAAL [Bā' al]—POSSESSOR or CONTROLLER.
1. *A Reubenite* of the house of Joel who lived before the captivity of the tribes (I Chron. 5:5, 6).
2. *A Benjamite,* son of King Saul's ancestor Jehiel (I Chron. 8:30; 9:35, 36, 39). Also the name of the male deity of the Phoenicians and Canaanites, as Ashtoreth was their chief female deity. Baal is likewise the name of a village of Simeon (Num. 22:41; I Chron. 4:33).

BAAL-HANAN [Bā' al-hā' nan]—THE LORD IS GRACIOUS.
1. *Son of Achbor* and the seventh of the Edomite kings (Gen. 36:38, 39; I Chron. 1:49, 50).
2. *A custodian* of the olive and sycamore trees in David's time (I Chron. 27:28).

BAALIS [Bā' al ĭs]—LORD OF JOY or RULES. *The king of the Ammonites* who reigned after Nebuchadnezzar's capture of Jerusalem (Jer. 40:14).

BAANA, BAANAH [Bā' a nă, Bā' a nah]—SON OF GRIEF or AFFLICTION.
1. *The son of Ahilud* and one of Solomon's purveyors in Jezreel (I Kings 4:12).
2. *The son of Hushai* and another of Solomon's purveyors responsible for Asher (I Kings 4:16).

3. *The father of Zadok*, who returned from exile with Zerubbabel and who helped to repair the wall (Neh. 3:4).

BAANAH [Bā' a nah]—SON OF GRIEF.
1. *The father of Heleb*, one of David's thirty heroes (II Sam. 23:29; I Chron. 11:30).
2. *A captain of Ish-bosheth's army* and one of his murderers (II Sam. 4:5–12).
3. *One who returned from exile with Zerubbabel* (Ezra 2:2; Neh. 7:7; 10:27).

BAASEIAH [Bā' a sē' iah]—JEHOVAH IS BOLD. *A Levite*, descendant of Gershom and ancestor of Asaph the musician (I Chron. 6:40).

BAASHA [Bā' a shǎ]—BOLDNESS, OFFENSIVE or HE WHO LAYS WASTE. *The son of Ahijah*, of the tribe of Issachar who obtained the throne of Israel by usurpation. He conspired against Nadab the son of Jeroboam I, and slew all his heirs. Baasha died in his bed after reigning for twenty-four years, and his dynasty was extinguished two years after his death (I Kings 15:27—16:13; II Chron. 16:1-6; Jer. 41:9).

BAKBAKKAR [Băk băk' kar]—DILIGENT SEARCHER. *A Levite* who returned from exile (I Chron. 9:15).

BAKBUK [Băk' buk]—A FLAGON or HOLLOW. *One of the Nethinims* who returned from exile (Ezra 2:51; Neh. 7:53).

BAKBUKIAH [Băk bŭk ĭ' ah]—WASTED BY JEHOVAH or EFFUSION OF JEHOVAH.
1. *A Levite of Asaph's family*, resident of Jerusalem who held high office after the exile (Neh. 11:17; 12:9).
2. *One of the Temple porters* (Neh. 12:25). Perhaps these are the same person.

BALAAM [Bā' laam]—A PILGRIM, DEVOURING or LORD OF THE PEOPLE. *A diviner*, son of Beor and resident of the town of Pethor (Num. 22; 23; 24; Deut. 23:4).

The Man Who Heard an Ass Speak

Peter, Jude and John deal with Balaam as a historical presence (II Pet. 2:15; Jude 11; Rev. 2:14).

In Balaam we have a fitting yet tragic illustration of our Lord's teaching about the light in us being darkness. Balaam had a *head* full of light but a *heart* that was dark—and great was the darkness! This man of Mesopotamia, counted a prophet, yet followed the unholy practice of Eastern soothsayers.

Balak the king, greatly alarmed because of the Israelites swarming the Plains of Moab, sent for Balaam to pronounce a curse upon the people of God so that he would have nothing more to fear. Balaam refused and declared that all who blessed Israel would be blessed. Balak sent for Balaam again and again, tempting him with bribes but Balaam remained firm. In a further approach of Balak, Balaam was more cautious in his refusal. Instead of saying with Daniel, "Thy gifts be to thyself and give thy rewards to another," Balaam caught the bait held out and proved that he loved the wages of unrighteousness.

Balak's messengers were not immediately dismissed. Balaam asked for time to consult God as to what he should do. The line of duty, however, was perfectly clear. There was no need to pray. God allowed Balaam to go, but he did not carry divine approval with him. Sometimes God punishes us by allowing us to have our own way. Thus Balaam started to Balak but did not reach him. Suddenly the ass he was riding stopped and could not be induced to proceed. God's angel was before him although Balaam could not see him standing in the way with his drawn sword. Then the ass, the most stupid of all beasts, was made to speak and reprove one of the wisest of men. Awestruck at what had happened and trembling with fear, Balaam confessed, "I have sinned." Balaam must have known that his whole conduct was displeasing to God and that he had been wilfully blind.

Back Balaam went and with a great parade built seven altars and offered bullocks and rams on every altar. But God was not pleased with such offerings. Yet God employed Balaam for His own purposes, for He put into his mouth some of the most blessed and glorious words spoken concerning His people Israel. With his heart turned towards the eternal world Balaam wanted to die the death of a righteous man, but his end was far from righteous. He died in a general massacre and we have no record of his repentance. He died in his sins.

Clearly evident are the lessons to be learned from this renowned man who was self-willed (Num. 22:5–22); saved from death by a beast (Num. 22:33); double-minded in that he was eloquent in prophecy but presumptuous in seeking to alter the divine plan (Num. 23; 24); a failure in his mission (Num. 24:10); an evil counselor (Num. 31:16); overcome by the besetting sin of avarice (II Pet. 2:13):

The clearest knowledge without grace is worthless.

The presence of any sin is ruinous, especially covetousness.

The most pious wishes are sometimes vain. The road to hell can be paved with good resolutions.

To die well one must live well.

BALADAN [Băl′ a dăn]—HAVING POWER, or A SON HE HATH GIVEN. *The father of Berodach-baladan,* king of Babylon in Hezekiah's time (II Kings 20:12; Isa. 39:1).

BALAK, BALAC [Bā′ lăk, Bā′ lăc]—WASTER, EMPTYING or DESTROYS. *The King of Moab,* and son of Zipper who hired Balaam to curse Israel when, toward the end of their wilderness journeyings they were in

Balak's territory (Num. 22; 23; 24; Judg. 11:25; Micah 6:5). Like Balaam, Balak also lives to the end of the Bible. *Balac* is the Greek form of Balak (Rev. 2:14). Revealing the superstition of the human mind, Balak had recourse to supernatural help and sought out Balaam, the soothsayer of Pethor—a man of divination with power to bless and curse, the Simon Magus of his day. How deceived Balak was when he thought he could sow the air with curses which would work where his sword could not reach!

BANI [Bā′ nī]—BUILT or POSTERITY.

1. *The Gadite,* and one of David's thirty heroes (II Sam. 23:36).

2. *The son of Shamer,* an Aaronite (I Chron. 6:46).

3. *The father of Imri,* a Judahite through Pharez (I Chron. 9:4).

4. *Father of a family* that returned with other captives from Babylon (Ezra 2:10; 10:29). Called Binnui in Nehemiah 7:15).

5. *One whose descendants had married foreign wives* during the exile (Ezra 10:34).

6. *A descendant of No. 5* who also had married a foreign wife (Ezra 10:38).

7. *A Levite,* father of Rehum who repaired part of the city wall (Neh. 3:17; 8:7).

8. *A Levite* who regulated the devotions of the people after Ezra read and expounded the Law (Neh. 9:4, 5; 10:13).

9. *A chieftain* who sealed the covenant (Neh. 10:14).

10. *A Levite* whose son was overseer of the Levites after the exile. Perhaps the same person as No. 7 or No. 8 (Neh. 11:22).

BARABBAS [Bā răb′ bas]—SON OF A FATHER or SON OF RETURN. *The notable prisoner,* committed to prison for robbery and murder, but preferred to Christ (Matt. 27:16–26).

The Man Who Had a Substitute

Barabbas should have died for his crimes but Jesus occupied his cross, along with the two other thieves. What a night Barabbas must have spent before Christ was selected in his place! The thief and murderer had visions of a terrible death. All the torture of crucifixion came up before him. Then as the light of morning looked in through the bars of his prison he hears the march of soldiers coming to take him out to his horrible death.

Can we not imagine how stupefied he must have been when he heard the officer of the guard say, "Barabbas you are free. Another is to die in your stead"? When Barabbas came to himself and realized how true the news was, out he went, grateful to the One condemned to die as his substitute. A just and holy Man to die in the place of a thief and murderer? Yes, Barabbas was saved at such a cost. What a picture of divine grace this substitutionary death presents! Thereafter, whenever Barabbas thought of Christ, he could say, "He died for me."

BARACHEL [Băr′ a chĕl]—GOD HAS BLESSED. *Father of Elihu,* one of Job's friends (Job 32:2, 6).

BARAK [Bā′ răk]—LIGHTNING or THUNDER. *The son of Abinoam,* a Naphtalite, who, with Deborah, defeated Sisera the leader of the Canaanites (Judg. 4:6; Heb. 11:32).

The Man Whose Bravery a Woman Inspired

In the deliverance of Israel, Deborah, and not Barak, is placed first. It is not Barak and Deborah. Barak said to Deborah, "If thou wilt go with me," and she answered, "I will go with thee." Thus at the word of Deborah, Barak led his men to battle and completely routed the enemy. Pursuing Sisera, Barak discovered he had been slain by a woman. The glory of victory that day did not go to Barak but to Deborah, his guiding spirit, and to Jael, who slew the enemy's leader.

Do we have here a hint beforehand of how the seed of the woman should bruise the serpent's head? It was by the nails and the workman's hammer that our salvation was actually wrought. The nail that pierced the feet of the Saviour pierced the serpent's head.

BARIAH [Bā rī′ ah]—FUGITIVE. *A son of Shemaiah,* of the family of David (I Chron. 3:22).

BAR-JESUS [Băr-jĕ′ zus]—SON OF JOSHUA. *The name of the false prophet,* a Jew, otherwise known as Elymas, who opposed Paul and Barnabas at Paphos (Acts 13:6). In Paul's judgment upon this false prophet there is a play upon words. Elymas was full of deceit and not of wisdom: Bar-jesus meaning, "son of Jesus" had become "a son of the devil" (Acts 13:6; Phil. 3:2).

BAR-JONA [Băr-jō′ nă]—SON OF JOHANAN or JOHN. *The surname of Simon Peter* (Matt. 16:17).

BARKOS [Băr′ kŏs]—PARTLY-COLORED. *One of the Nethinims,* whose descendants returned from exile (Ezra 2:53; Neh. 7:55).

BARNABAS [Băr′ na băs]—SON OF PROPHECY or CONSOLATION. *Surname of Joses,* Paul's companion in several of his missionary journeys (Acts 4:36; 9:27).

The Man Renowned for His Winsomeness

The features of this lovable man stand out in bold relief.

I. His magnificent generosity. The first recorded deed of this Levite of Cyprus was the selling of his property and the grateful sacrifice of the money secured to the common fund of the first Christian community (Acts. 4:36). The Church has many on her ancient roll who knew what it was to be baptized with the baptism of Barnabas. His exuberant generosity inspired them to surrender their all.

II. His impressive personality. The Lycaonians named Barnabas

Jupiter, the name of the emperor of gods in Grecian mythology (Acts 14:12). Evidently this "son of comfort" had a commanding, dignified, venerable appearance and his physical nobility added to his influence. The culture and consecration of a commendable physical personality is not to be despised. Also mentally and morally, Barnabas was a man among men.

III. His innate goodness. What triple grace this man possessed! "A good man and full of the Holy Ghost and of faith" (Acts 11:24). God-possessed, Barnabas was full of love, sympathy and faith. Vision and allegiance were his. Spirit-filled, he exuded the comfort of the Spirit. Dean Church says that Barnabas was "an earthly reflection of the Paraclete."

IV. His notable ministry. Barnabas had an inspiring influence (Acts 11:25, 26), was trustworthy (Acts 11:29, 30), was adapted to missionary work (Acts 13:2), encouraged converts (Acts 11:23), was a son of Christian prophecy in that he uttered God's messages, was a devoted toiler and self-supporting (I Cor. 9:6).

V. His lamentable contention. It is sad to realize that such a captivating man as Barnabas was a party to a quarrel. How true it is that there are "surprises of sin in holiest histories." The doleful story of the sharp contention between Paul and Barnabas is told in Acts 15: 36–39. Perhaps both good men were wrong. Paul proposed to Barnabas that they should visit the brethren in every city where they had labored. Barnabas agreed and wanted to take Mark, his nephew, with them. Paul felt that Mark, having left them once, was not fit to accompany them, so they parted. Had Paul been too resentful against Mark? Had Barnabas been too eager to urge the claims of his relative? Was one too stern, the other too easy? It is good to know that they were afterwards reconciled.

There are also hints of a certain lack of firmness in Barnabas' otherwise strong character. Writing of dissembling Jews, Paul had to say that even "Barnabas was carried away with their dissimulation" (Gal. 2:13). Barnabas, like the rest of us, had some defective qualities. There has only been one perfect Man on earth — the Saviour Barnabas loved and rejoiced to preach about.

BARSABAS, BARSABBAS [Bär' sa băs]—SON OF SABA or A SON THAT SUSPENDS THE WATER.
1. The surname of the Joseph nominated with Matthias to succeed Judas in the apostolic band (Acts 1:23).
2. The surname of the disciple sent with Silas to Antioch (Acts 15:22).

BARTHOLOMEW [Bär thŏl' o mew]—SON OF TOLMAI. One of the twelve, mentioned only in the lists of the apostles (Matt. 10:3; Mark 3:18; Luke 6:14; Acts 1:13). Bartholomew is really not a name but a patronymic. This apostle is identified as Nathanael.

BARTIMAEUS [Bär ti mae' us]—SON OF TIMAEUS or HONORABLE. *The blind beggar* Jesus healed at the gate of Jericho (Mark 10:46; Luke 18:35).

BARUCH [Bä' rōoch]—BLESSED.
1. *The son of Zabbai* who helped to rebuild the wall (Neh. 3:20; 10:6).
2. *The son of Neriah,* the son of Maaseian (Jer. 32:12–16). Jeremiah owed much to this loyal secretary who acted as his amanuensis while he was in prison: Baruch made a heavy sacrifice when he threw in his lot with Jeremiah and became his scribe.
3. *A descendant of Perez,* a returned exile (Neh. 11:5).

BARZILLAI [Bär zǐl' la ī]—MADE OF IRON or STRONG.
1. *A wealthy Gileadite of Rogelim,* numbered among the friends of David (II Sam. 17:27–29; 19:31–40; I Kings 2:7).
The Man of Invincible Charm
Barzillai the Gileadite and his family are remembered for many generations, the habitation of his son Chimham is found by Bethlehem, the city of David in the days of the captivity of the land (Jer. 41:17). What an invincible charm there is about this lovable old man! In his warm commendation of Barzillai, Alexander Whyte speaks of him as an aged, venerable, hospitable highland chief and then goes on to apply the highland characteristics of loyalty, courtesy, hospitality and passionate love of hills and valleys to this ripe old saint. This old testament character displays virtues worthy of emulation.

I. His courageous loyalty. When David sorely needed support at the time of Absalom's rebellion, Barzillai rallied to his side. Like a true man of iron, he offered David indomitable loyalty (II Sam. 17:27–29). With a hero's scorn of consequences Barzillai brought necessary provisions to the hungry, thirsty followers of David. Are we as loyal to our heavenly Monarch as Barzillai was to King David?

II. His reverence of character. Barzillai was drawn to David because of the virtues he manifested. Although David was unpopular, Barzillai knew the soul of David and that he was a man after God's own heart and that therefore he was a man after his own heart. D. L. Moody once said that "Character is what a man is in the dark." To Barzillai, David was *still* godly although a fugitive, and his great, loving heart bled for the king as, like a poor panting beast, he hid from his pursuers. Bountifully he provided David with necessary sustenance as he lay at Mahanaim (II Sam. 19:32).

III. His wide influence. Barzillai is described as a great man, with a noble seat at Rogelim, and whose noble possessions were carried with a noble humility (II Sam. 19:32). He did not squander his wealth on idle pleasures nor hoard it for selfish ends. His position, prestige and purse were beneficially used for others. David wanted to reward

Barzillai but as Professor Eadie says, "The dialogue on this occasion is one of the most lovely to be on the page of history."

Barzillai felt his services were trivial and unworthy of any recompense from David. Barzillai's son received of the king's bounty and had an inheritance with David in Jerusalem (II Sam. 19:40). When David lay on his deathbed one of his charges to Solomon was, "Show kindness to the son of Barzillai the Gileadite" (I Kings 2:7). As for Barzillai himself he felt that at his time of life there were some things not worth doing. He was dead to the delights of sense, as Matthew Henry expresses it.

IV. His beautiful old age. Although not spared the infirmities of old age (II Sam. 19:35), he retained his charm. At eighty years of age his heart of love was deep and broad. Old John Trapp says of Barzillai as he reached an honored age, "He had lost his colour but kept his sweet savour with the rose." May grace be ours to grow old gracefully and beautifully!

V. His death was contemplated. Barzillai was not afraid to face the crossing of the bar. The pathetic desire expressed to David can be rendered, "The grave is ready for me; let me go out and get ready for it" (II Sam. 19:37). At eighty, Barzillai was still the loving child of the parents with whom he desired to be buried, and his love of his kindred is to be praised. Thus as Alexander Whyte puts it, "Barzillai having shown us how to live, shows us also how to die. Barzillai dies the same devout and noble and magnanimous man he has all his days lived." If ours is grace to live well, grace will be given to die well.

2. *Father of Adriel,* husband of Merab, Saul's eldest daughter (II Sam. 21:8).

3. *A priest* whose genealogy was lost, and who married a daughter of Barzillai, David's friend (Ezra 2:61; Neh. 7:63).

BASHAN-HAVOTH-JAIR [Bā′ shăn-hā′ voth-jā′ ûr]—FRUITFUL VILLAGE OF JAIR. *A name of Jair* which he gave to Argob after its capture (Deut. 3:14).

BAVAI, BAVVAI [Băv′ a ī]—WISHES. *A son or descendant of Henadad* who helped in the repair of the wall [Neh. 3:18).

BAZLITH, BAZLUTH [Băz′ lith, Băz′ lŭth]—ASKING. *One of the Nethinims* whose descendants returned from exile (Ezra 2:52; Neh. 7:54)

BEALIAH [Bē a lī′ ah]—JEHOVAH IS LORD. *A Benjamite warrior* who joined David at Ziklag (I Chron. 12:5).

BEBAI [Bĕb′ a ī]—FATHERLY.
1. *A man whose descendants returned from exile with Zerubbabel* (Ezra 2:11; Neh. 7:16).

2. *Another whose posterity came back with Ezra.* Perhaps the same man as No. 1 (Ezra 8:11; 10:28).
3. *A chieftain* who sealed the covenant (Neh. 10:15).

BECHER [Bē′ chûr]—YOUNG CAMEL or FIRST BORN.
1. *A son of Benjamin* (Gen. 46:21; I Chron. 7:6, 8).
2. *A son of Ephraim* (Num. 26:35). Called Bered in I Chronicles 7:20.

BECHORATH [Bē chō′ rath]—FIRST BIRTH. *Son of Aphiah or Abiah,* and grandson of Becher, son of Benjamin (I Sam. 9:1).

BEDAD [Bē′ dăd]—SON OF ADAD or SEPARATION. *Father of Hadad,* king of Edom (Gen. 36:35; I Chron. 1:46).

BEDAN [Bē′ dăn]—SON OF JUDGMENT.
1. *A Hebrew judge* who ruled between Gideon and Jephthah (I Sam. 12:11). Some versions give the name as Barak.
2. *Descendant of Machir,* who was the son of Manasseh (I Chron. 7:17).

BEDEIAH [Bē dē′ iah]—SERVANT OF JEHOVAH. *A son of Bani* who married a foreign wife in exile (Ezra 10:35).

BEELIADA [Bē ĕl ī′ a dǎ]—THE LORD KNOWS. *A son of David* born in Jerusalem (I Chron. 14:7). Also called Eliada in II Samuel 5:16 and I Chronicles 3:8.

BEERA [Bē ē′ rǎ]—EXPOUNDER or A WELL. *Son of Zophah,* an Asherite of the family of Heber (I Chron. 7:37).

BEERAH [Bē ē′ rah]—EXPOUNDER. *A prince of the Reubenites* who became a captive of Tilgath-pilneser (I Chron. 5:6).

BEERI [Bē ē′ rī]—EXPOUNDER or MAN OF THE WELL.
1. *A Hittite,* father of Judith wife of Esau (Gen. 26:34).
2. *The father of Hosea* the prophet (Hosea 1:1).

BELA, BELAH [Bē′ lǎ, Bē′ lah]—DEVOURING or CONSUMPTION.
1. *The first king of Edom* the Bible mentions. His father's name was Beor (Gen. 36:32, 33; I Chron. 1:43, 44).
2. *The eldest son of Benjamin,* and founder of the family of Belaites (Gen. 46:21; Num. 26:38, 40).
3. *A son of Azaz* of the tribe of Reuben (I Chron. 5:8). Also the name of a city (Gen. 14:2, 8).

BELSHAZZAR [Bĕl shăz′ zar]—BEL PROTECT THE KING or THE LORD'S

LEADER. *The son of Nebuchadnezzar* and last of the kings of Babylon (Dan. 5; 7:1; 8:1).

The Man Whose Sacrilege Brought Judgment

The story of King Belshazzar is a short one. He bursts upon the stage, then disappears. All we know about him is told in one brief chapter. What we do know about Belshazzar is that he made a great feast to which a thousand of his lords were invited and that they drank out of the vessels of gold and silver taken from the house of God as they toasted their heathen gods. Drunkenness was a prevailing vice in all ranks of the Babylonians. Belshazzar, who feared neither God nor man, manifested his vanity, profaneness and pride in the sacrilegious use of the holy vessels, and in the midst of the drunken orgy, a hidden hand writing out mysterious words interrupted their godless mirth.

Although he could not decipher the writing on the wall, Belshazzar's conscience somehow interpreted the words over against the candlestick. Terror gripped him because he felt the message spelled his doom. His own wise men failed to read the writing, so Daniel was brought in and informed the king of its significance, and that night Belshazzar, king of Babylon, was slain. The army of Darius ransacked the palace and quickly mingled the king's blood with the wine in the banqueting hall.

BELTESHAZZAR [Bĕl te shaz′ zar]—BEL PROTECT HIS LIFE or THE LORD'S LEADER. *The name given to youthful Daniel* by the prince of Nebuchadnezzar's eunuchs (Dan. 1:7; 2:26; 4; 10:1).

BENAIAH [Bē nā′ iah]—JEHOVAH HATH BUILT or IS INTELLIGENT.
1. *A Levite,* son of Jehoiada of Kabzeel in Judah, whose father was a priest, and one of David's heroes (II Sam. 8:18; 20:23; 23:20, 23; I Kings 1).

The Man of Dauntless Courage

I.   Benaiah was inspired by a noble ambition. He came of a noble ancestry, whose forefathers had left their impress upon the history of the nation. *Born* well, Benaiah sought to *live* well. Absalom became a traitor to his godly father and broke his heart. The sons of priestly Eli lived in sin and died in disgrace. Benaiah, privileged with the example of godly parentage, looked upon life as a challenge to personal and individual responsibility.

II.   He was fearless in his destruction of Israel's foes. Born in an age of warfare, when youths were valiant in fight and middle-aged men were veterans, Benaiah had been valiant in many a campaign against hostile nations. This grandson of a valiant man of Kabzeel had many mighty deeds to his credit (I Chron. 11:22–25 RV). Three glimpses are given of Benaiah's bravery. He confronted two lionhearted men of Moab—giants among their fellows—either of whom would have been more than a match for any ordinary soldier; but Benaiah took them both on and was the victor. Then he attacked the Egyptian of "great stature" but although this dark-skinned giant carried a spear "like a weaver's beam" Benaiah met him with an ordinary staff and left the field victorious.

Benaiah's next exploit finds him attacking not "lionhearted men" but an actual lion that had alarmed the people. A pit was dug to trap the marauding lion, and snow fell and hid the trap in a most effective way. The lion fell into the pit and vainly tried to extricate itself. Benaiah, the hero who had vanquished a giant and conquered two lion-hearted Moabites, descended the pit on a snowy day and single-handed slew the lion. No wonder David, who also had slain a lion, gave Benaiah the chief place among the favored three. A greater than Benaiah dealt a death blow at our three great foes — the world, the flesh, the devil.

2. *Another of David's valiant men* from Pirathon (II Sam. 23:30; I Chron. 11:31; 27:14).

3. *The head of a Simeonite family* (I Chron. 4:36).

4. *One of David's priests* in Jerusalem (I Chron. 15:18, 24; 16:5, 6).

5. *The father of one of David's counselors* (I Chron. 27:34).

6. *The grandfather of Jahaziel* (II Chron. 20:14).

7. *A Levite overseer* of Temple offerings in Hezekiah's time (II Chron. 31:13).

8. *One of the family of Parosh* (Ezra 10:25).

9. *A son of Pahath-moab* (Ezra 10:30).

10. *A son of Bani* (Ezra 10:35).

11. *A son of Nebo* (Ezra 10:43).

12. *Father of Pelatiah*, a Judahite prince (Ezek. 11:1, 13).

BEN-AMMI [Bĕn-Ăm' mĭ]—SON OF MY PEOPLE. *The son whom Lot's youngest daughter bore* to him and from whom the Ammonite tribe sprang (Gen. 19:38).

BEN-DEKAR [Bĕn dĕ' kär]—SON OF DEKAR. *Solomon's purveyor in* Bethshemesh (I Kings 4:9).

BEN-GEBER [Bĕn gĕ' bûr]—SON OF GEBER. *Solomon's purveyor in Ramoth-gilead* (I Kings 4:13).

BEN-HADAD [Bĕn hä' dăd]—SON OF THE GOD HADAH.

1. *Benhadad I*, son of Tabrimon of Damascus. This king of Syria made a league with Asa, king of Judah, to invade Israel (I Kings 15: 18, 20; II Chron. 16:2, 4).

2. *Benhadad II*, the son of No. 1 who was an able general and statesman and who reigned in the time of Ahab king of Israel. He was assassinated by the usurper Hazael (I Kings 20; II Kings 6:24; 8:7, 9).

3. *Benhadad III*, the son of Hazael who suffered heavy defeats from the Assyrians (II Kings 13:2, 24, 25; Amos 1:4). The name is also the general title of the kings of Damascus (Jer. 49:27).

BEN-HAIL [Bĕn hā' il]–SON OF MIGHT OR VALIANT. *A prince of Judah* sent by Jehoshaphat to teach the cities (II Chron. 17:7).

BEN-HANAN [Bĕn hā' nan]–SON OF KIND ONE or VERY GRACIOUS. *A son of Shimon,* registered with the tribe of Judah (I Chron. 4:20).

BEN-HESED [Bĕn hē' sed]–SON OF BENEVOLENCE. *Solomon's purveyor* in Aruboth (I Kings 4:10).

BEN-HUR [Bĕn hûr']–SON OF HUR. *Another of Solomon's purveyors* in Mount Ephraim (I Kings 4:8).

BENINU [Bĕn' Ĭ nū]–OUR SON or POSTERITY. *A Levite* who, with Nehemiah, sealed the covenant (Neh. 10:13).

BENJAMIN [Bĕn' ja mĭn]–SON OF THE RIGHT HAND.
1. *The youngest son of Jacob* and the only one born in Canaan; founder of a tribal family. His mother, Rachel, who died in giving birth to Benjamin, named him with her last breath Benoni "son of sorrow." Jacob changed the name to Benjamin (Gen. 35:18, 24).

The Man Beloved of Jehovah

The prophecy of Jacob regarding Benjamin is short and easily verified. Personal courage and martial temperament, a characteristic of the Benjamites throughout history, are before us in Benjamin as a ravening wolf devouring the prey and dividing the spoil. Benjamin was the last, the bravest and the best-beloved tribe of all the tribes of Israel, the center of the affections of the whole family, and the dwelling place of the beloved of the Lord (Deut. 33:12).

Some Benjamites of the Bible are the second of the Judges, Ehud, Saul, the first of Israel's kings and Saul of Tarsus, who was "not a whit behind the chiefest of the apostles." Although "the smallest of the tribes" (I Sam. 9:21), Benjamin was not to be despised. Christ came from a small village. In the division of the land, as Joshua records it, Jerusalem was assigned to Benjamin (Josh. 18:28)— a fact referred to by the psalmist, "There is little Benjamin their ruler." Between the shoulders of Benjamin, the God of Israel caused His name to dwell. In Benjamin He "covered Israel all the day long."

The tribe of Benjamin, as the seat of God's love, ought to be the meeting place for all Israel; Jerusalem is so, in a figure. It has open gates for all the tribes of Israel.

2. *A son or descendant of Harim* who put away his foreign wife (Ezra 10:32).

3. *A son of Bilhan* and a great-grandson of Benjamin (I Chron. 7:10).

4. *One who took part in the repair of the wall* (Neh. 3:23).

5. *Another who did the same* (Neh. 12:34). Also the name of one of the gates of Jerusalem (Jer. 20:2; 37:13; 38:7; Zech. 14:10).

BENO [Bĕ' nō]—HIS SON. *A descendant of Merari* through Jaaziah (I Chron. 24:26, 27).

BEN-ONI [Bĕn ō' nī]—SON OF MY SORROW. *The name Rachel gave to her second son.* See Benjamin (Gen. 35:18).

BEN-ZOHETH [Bĕn-Zō' hĕth]—CORPULENT or STRONG. *A son of Ishi,* a Judahite (I Chron. 4:20).

BEOR [Bĕ' ôr]—SHEPHERD, A TORCH or BURNING.
1. *The father of Bela* the first king of Edom (Gen. 36:32; I Chron. 1:43).
2. *The father of Balaam* the prophet (Num. 22:5). Also known as Bosor (II Pet. 2:15).

BERA [Bĕ' rǎ]—GIFT or EXCELLENCE. *A King of Sodom* defeated by Chedorlaomer (Gen. 14:2).

BERACHAH [Bĕr' a chah]—BLESSING. *One of Saul's brethren* who joined David at Ziklag (I Chron. 12:3). Also the name of "the valley of blessing" (II Chron. 20:26). The modern name is Bereikut.

BERAIAH [Bĕr a ī' ah]—JEHOVAH HATH CREATED. *A son of Shimhi,* a Benjamite (I Chron. 8:13, 21).

BERECHIAH, BERACHIAH [Bĕr e chī' ah, Bĕr a chī' ah]—JEHOVAH IS BLESSING or BENDING THE KNEE.
1. *The father of Asaph* the chief singer, descendant of Gershon (I Chron. 6:39; 15:17).
2. *A son of Zerubbabel* (I Chron. 3:20).
3. *The son of Asa* who lived near Jerusalem (I Chron. 9:16).
4. *A Levite doorkeeper* of the Tabernacle (I Chron. 15:23).
5. *An Ephraimite* in Pekah's time (II Chron. 28:12).
6. *Father of Mershullam* who assisted in the repair of the wall of Jerusalem (Neh. 3:4, 30; 6:18).
7. *Father of the prophet Zechariah* (Zech. 1:1, 7). Called Barachias in Matthew 23:35, meaning, "who bends the knee to God."

BERED [Bĕ' red]—SEED, PLACE or HAIL. *An Ephraimite,* perhaps the same as Becher (I Chron. 7:20). Also name of place in South Canaan (Gen. 16:14).

BERI [Bĕ' rī]—EXPOUNDER or MAN OF THE WELL. *A son of Zophah,* an Asherite (I Chron. 7:36).

BERIAH [Bĕ rī' ah]—UNFORTUNATE or IN EVIL.
1. *A son of Asher* (Gen. 46:17; Num. 26:44, 45; I Chron. 7:31).
2. *A son of Ephraim* (I Chron. 7:23).

3. *A son of Elpaal,* a Benjamite (I Chron. 8:13, 16).
4. *Son of the Levite Shimei* (I Chron. 23:10, 11).

BERODACH-BALADAN [Bē rŏ′ dăch-băl′ a dăn]—BOLD. *A king of Babylon* (II Kings 20:12; Isa. 39:1). See Merodach-baladan.

BESAI [Bĕ′ saī]—TREADING DOWN. *One of the Nethinims* who returned from exile (Ezra 2:49; Neh. 7:52).

BESODEIAH (Bĕs o dĕ′ iah] FAMILIAR WITH JEHOVAH. *Father of Meshullam* who helped to repair the old gate (Neh. 3:6).

BETH-GADER [Bĕth-gā′ dur]—WALLED PLACE. *A descendant of Caleb,* son of Hur (I Chron. 2:51).

BETHLEHEM [Bĕth′ lĕ hĕm]—HOUSE OF BREAD. *A descendant of Caleb,* son of Hur (I Chron. 2:51, 54; 4:4). Also the name of two towns (Gen. 35:19; Josh. 19:15).

BETH RAPHA [Bĕth-rā′ phȧ]—HOUSE OF A GIANT or PLACE OF FEAR. *The son of Eshton,* grandson of Chelub (I Chron. 4:12).

BETHUEL [Bĕth ōō′ el]—ABODE OF GOD or DWELLER IN GOD. *A son of Nahor* by his wife Milcah (Gen. 22:22). Also the name of a town (I Chron. 4:30).

BETH-ZUR [Bĕth′-zûr]—PLACE OF ROCK. *The son of Maon* (I Chron. 2:45). Also the name of a city (Josh. 15:58).

BEZAI [Bĕ′ zaī]—SHINING or HIGH.
1. *One of those who sealed the covenant* (Neh. 10:18).
2. *One whose posterity* to the number of 323 returned from exile with Zerubbabel (Ezra 2:17; Neh. 7:23).

BEZALEEL [Bē zăl′ e el]—UNDER GOD'S SHADOW.
1. *The chief architect of the Tabernacle* to whom was assigned the design and execution of its works of art (Ex. 31:2; 35:30; 36: 1, 2; 38:22).

The Man Who Was a Spirit-filled Workman

Bezaleel was chiefly responsible for works of metal, wood and stone. Aholiab had charge of the textile fabric. Bezaleel, however, was chief in both departments and was the principal workman and for the accomplishment of a divinely commissioned task he received divine empowerment. Whom the Lord calls, He qualifies (I Thess. 5:24).
I. His character. Bezaleel meaning, "in the shadow of God," is suggestive of this artificer's character. Although he doubtless received the name from godly parents who knew what it was to dwell beneath the shadow of the Almighty, Bezaleel himself must have lived a life

in the will of God, and was therefore responsive when the call came.

II. His commission. Bezaleel alone had the right to devise. He was the principal workman in the erection of the Tabernacle, the pattern of which came direct from God (Ex. 25:40). The choice of Bezaleel proves that the Holy Spirit is sovereign in His work. We cannot understand why He chooses certain people for great tasks. As the wind, He blows where He listeth. His gifts are distributed severally as He *wills*.

III. His cunning. This English word as used in the Bible simply represents *skill, ability*. Thus Bezaleel was filled with all wisdom and understanding in *all manner of* workmanship. All he needed to accomplish the mind and will of God was divinely bestowed. God's commands are His enablings. "Give what Thou commandest," prayed Augustine, "then command that Thou wilt." So the Great Overseer, the Holy Spirit, possessed Bezaleel and inspired him to prepare the temporary habitation of God. In our time, the same empowering Spirit gives to "every man his work," and only that which is accomplished under the guidance of the Spirit can be pleasing to God and fit for a place in His great Temple.

2. *One of the sons of Pahath-moab* who had married a foreign wife (Ezra 10:30).

BEZER [Bĕ′ zûr]—STRONG or GOLD ONE. *A son of Zophah*, an Asherite (I Chron. 7:37).

BICHRI [Bĭch′ rī]—YOUTHFUL, FIRST-BORN or FIRST-FRUITS. *The father of the rebellious Sheba* who rose against David, descendant of Becher (II Sam. 20).

BIDKAR [Bĭd′ kär]—SERVANT OF KAR or IN SHARP PAIN. *A captain of Jehu*, who executed the sentence on Jehoram, son of Ahab (II Kings 9:25).

BIGTHA [Bĭg′ thă]—GIVEN BY FORTUNE. *One of the eunuchs or chamberlains* who served in the presence of Ahasuerus (Esther 1:10).

BIGTHAN, BIGTHANA [Bĭg′ thăn, Bĭg′ tha nă]—GIFT OF FORTUNE or GIVING MEAT. *One of the two chamberlains*, keepers of the palace door, whose plot against the king was discovered and defeated by Mordecai (Esther 2:21; 6:2).

BIGVAI [Bĭg′ va ī]—HAPPY or OF THE PEOPLE.

1. *One of the leaders* of the exiles who returned from Babylon with Zerubbabel (Ezra 2:2; Neh. 7:7).

2. *Founder of a family* of two thousand who returned from exile (Ezra 2:14; Neh. 7:19).

3. *One whose descendants returned* from exile with Ezra (Ezra 8:14).

4. *The head of a family* that with Nehemiah sealed the covenant (Neh. 10:16).

BILDAD [Bĭl' dăd]—SON OF CONTENTION, LORD ADAD or OLD FRIEND-SHIP. *One of Job's three friends,* a Shuhite, descended from Shuah, Abraham's son by Keturah (Job 2:11; 8:1; 18:1; 25:1; 42:9).

The Man Who Made a Speech

Bildad's name is an interesting study. One meaning of it is "Lord of Hadad" and "Hadad" means *to shout.* Studying the speeches of this second speaker who came to comfort Job, one can see how apt the name is, for Bildad was inclined to be loud, insistent and boisterous in his declarations.

This Shuhite, in a vehement fashion, implied as he continued the discussion opened by Eliphaz, that all the extraordinary misfortune overtaking Job were the certain proof of hidden and exceptional crimes of which Job must have been guilty. Doubtless Bildad thought his speech was rich in ideas. But he is before us as the religious dogmatist whose dogmatism vested upon human tradition. With proverbial wisdom and pious phrases, abounding throughout his discourses, Bildad sought to illustrate the principle that Job suffered because of his sin.

With philosophy, wisdom and tradition gathered from the fathers (Job 8:8), Bildad sought to convince Job of his wrongs. But the mystery of Job's sufferings was not to be unraveled in that way. The wisdom of man and tradition has its limits. What has been handed down and accepted by each succeeding generation as truth, is not necessarily so. Every man must be fully persuaded in his own mind. The mysterious dealings of God can only be revealed by God Himself. He is His own Interpreter.

BILGAH [Bĭl' gah]—CHEERFUL or BURSTING FORTH.
1. *A descendant of Aaron,* head of the fifteenth course of Tabernacle priests in David's time (I Chron. 24:14).
2. *A chief of priests* who returned from exile with Zerubbabel (Neh. 12:5, 18).

BILGAI [Bĭl' ga ī]—BURSTING FORTH or FIRST BORN. Perhaps the same person as No. 2 under Bilgah (Neh. 10:8).

BILHAN [Bĭl' han]—TENDER or BASHFUL. From the same root of Bilhah, handmaid of Laban's youngest daughter Rachel.
1. *A son of Ezer,* son of Seir the Horite (Gen. 36:27; I Chron. 1:42).
2. *A son of Jediael,* son of Benjamin (I Chron. 7:10).

BILSHAN [Bĭl'-shăn]—SEARCHER or INQUIRER. *A prince of the Jews* and companion of Zerubbabel (Ezra 2:2; Neh. 7:7).

BIMHAL [Bĭm' hăl]—SON OF CIRCUMCISION. *A son of Japhlet,* an Asherite (I Chron. 7:33).

BINEA [Bĭn′ e ă]—WANDERER. *A son of Moza* and a descendant of Jonathan, Saul's son (I Chron. 8:37; 9:43).

BINNUI [Bĭn′ nụ ī]—A BUILDING or FAMILYSHIP.
1. *Father of a Levite* who had charge of the gold and silver vessels Ezra brought back from Babylon (Ezra 8:33).
2. *A son of Pahath-moab* (Ezra 10:30).
3. *A son of Bani* (Ezra 10:38).
4. *A son of Henadad* (Neh. 3:24; 10:9).
5. *One whose descendants returned* from exile with Zerubbabel (Neh. 7:15). Called Bani in Ezra 2:10).
6. *A Levite* who returned from exile (Neh. 12:8).

BIRSHA [Bûr′ shă]—THICK or STRONG. *A king of Gomorrah* at the time of Chedorlaomer's invasion (Gen. 14:2).

BIRZAVITH [Bûr′ za vĭth]—OLIVE WELL or WOUNDS. *A grandson of Beriah* who was a son of Asher (I Chron. 7:31). Also given as Birgaith.

BISHLAM [Bĭsh′ lăm]—PEACEFUL. *An officer of Artaxerxes* in Canaan in the time of Zerubbabel's return from Babylon, who was adverse to the rebuilding of the Temple (Ezra 4:7).

BIZTHA [Bĭz′ thă]—EUNUCH. *One of the seven chamberlains* at the court of Ahasuerus (Esther 1:10).

BLASTUS [Blăs′ tus]—A SUCKER or A BUD. *A palace chamberlain* who had charge of Herod Agrippa's bedchamber (Acts 12:20).

BOANERGES [Bō a nûr′ jēs]—SONS OF RAGE or OF THUNDER. *The name given by Christ* to James and John on account of their impetuosity (Mark 3:17; Luke 9:54, 55).

BOAZ, BOOZ [Bō′ ăz, Bō′ ŏz]—STRENGTH or FLEETNESS. *The wealthy and honorable Bethlehemite,* or Judahite, who became the second husband of Ruth the Moabitess, and ancestor of David and of Christ (Ruth 2, 3, 4; Matt. 1:5). *The name of the left pillar of Solomon's* Temple was Boaz, for "in it is strength" (I Kings 7:21). Boaz was true to his name and comes before us strong in grace, integrity and purpose. As the lord of the harvest, master of servants, redeemer, bridegroom and life-giver, he is a fitting type of Christ.

BOCHERU [Bŏch′ e rōō]—YOUTH or FIRST-BORN. *Son of Azel,* a Benjamite of the family of king Saul (I Chron. 8:38; 9:44).

BOHAN [Bō′ hăn]—THUMB or STUMPY. *A son of Reuben,* after whom a stone was named as a mark of division between Judah and Benjamin (Josh. 15:6; 18:17).

BUKKI [Bŭk′kī]—MOUTH OF JEHOVAH or DEVASTATION SENT BY JEHOVAH.

1. *Son of Abishua* and father of Uzzi, fifth in descent from Aaron in the line of high priests through Phinehas (I Chron. 6:5, 51).

2. *A son of Jogli,* a prince of the tribe of Dan, entrusted with the task of dividing Canaan among the tribes of Israel (Num. 34:22).

BUKKIAH [Bŭk kī′ah]—MOUTH OF JEHOVAH. *A Levite* of the sons of Heman, and leader of the sixth band or course in the Temple service (I Chron. 25:4, 13).

BUNAH [Bŭ′nah]—UNDERSTANDING or PRUDENCE. *Son of Jerahmeel,* a Judahite (I Chron. 2:25).

BUNNI [Bŭn′nī]—MY UNDERSTANDING or BUILT.

1. *A Levite* who assisted in the teaching of the Law of Moses (Neh. 9:4).

2. *The father of Hashabiah,* another Levite (Neh. 11:15).

3. *The representative of a family* that sealed the covenant (Neh. 10:15).

BUZ [Bŭz]—CONTEMPT or DESPISED.

1. *The second son of Milcah and Nahor* the brother of Abraham and founder of a tribal family (Gen. 22:21; Job 32:2, 6).

2. *The father of Jahdo,* a Gadite (I Chron. 5:14).

BUZI [Bŭ′zī]—CONTEMNED OF JEHOVAH or MY CONTEMPT. *An Aaronite* and father of Ezekiel, the prophet and priest (Ezek. 1:3).

C

CAESAR [Cae′zar]—ONE CUT OUT. *The surname always used in the New Testament for all Roman emperors.* See Augustus, Tiberius and Claudius (Matt. 22:17, etc.). To Caesar the Jews paid tribute and it was also to him that those Jews who were Roman citizens (for example, Paul, Acts 25:10–21), had the right of appeal.

CAIAPHAS [Cā′ia phăs]—A SEARCHER or HE THAT SEEKS WITH DILIGENCE. *Joseph Caiaphas, the son-in-law of Annas,* was high priest of the Jews for eighteen years (Matt. 26:3, 57).

The Man with Sadducaean Insolence

Dr. David Smith refers to this wicked man whom the Spirit of God used to declare divine purposes as, "a man of masterful temper, with his full share of the insolence which was a Sadducaean characteristic." The Sadducees were a sect among the Jews, so called from their founder Sadoc who lived about 260 years before Christ. Their principal tenets were:

I. There is no angel, spirit or resurrection; the soul finishes with the body (Matt. 22:23; Acts 23:8).

II. There is no fate or providence—all men enjoy the most ample freedom of action—absolute power to do good or evil.

III. There is no need to follow tradition. Scripture, particularly the first five books of the Bible, must be strictly adhered to. Caiaphas, as an ardent Sadducee, figures three times in the New Testament.

A. At the raising of Lazarus. After the miracle at Bethany, the rulers were alarmed at the popularity of Jesus which the resurrection of Lazarus brought Him, and convened a meeting of the Sanhedrin to decide what should be done with Jesus. Caiaphas presided and with a high hand forced a resolution that Jesus should be put to death (John 11:49, 53).

B. At the trial of Jesus. At a further meeting of the Sanhedrin when Jesus appeared before its members and was tried and condemned, Caiaphas again displayed his character by his open determination to find Jesus guilty. Since he was the high priest, his announcements were clothed with authority, but his shameless disregard of the forms of law to bring about the death of Jesus, revealed his warped conscience (Matt. 26:57, 58; John 18:24). Yet Caiaphas used language somewhat prophetic when he said that it was expedient for one man to die for the people, and Christ did die for Jew and Gentile alike. By His death He broke down the middle wall (Eph. 2:14–18).

C. At the trial of Peter and John. Caiaphas also took part in the examination of Peter and John when called in question over the marvels of the healing of the lame man. The manifestation of God's power was so evident that Annas and Caiaphas could do nothing about the apostles (Acts 4).

CAIN [Cāin]—ACQUISITION, FABRICATION or POSSESSED. *Eldest son of Adam and Eve,* the first man to be born naturally, and founder of the family of Kenites (Kenite is called Kain in the Hebrew) (Gen. 4; Num. 24:22; Heb. 11:4; I John 3:12; Jude 11). Also the name of a town (Josh. 15:57).

The Man Who Was Earth's First Murderer

The terrible story of Cain proves how quickly man's fallen nature developed. It did not take long for his heart to become desperately wicked, and the line of Cain continued in sin. It was in such the foul sin of polygamy was first experienced.

By calling Cain was an agriculturist, but he was not happy in his calling since he did not fear God. His heart became jealous as he witnessed the happiness of his brother Abel and his favor with God.

Ultimately he yielded to his jealous feelings and slew Abel, just as the Jews for envy sought Christ's death.

Because Cain's heart was destitute of love, his sacrifice had no heart in it and was therefore miserable, worthless and unacceptable to God. "The sacrifice of the wicked is an abomination to the Lord, but the prayer of the upright is His delight." Cain was right in his *desire* to bring an offering but wrong in his *doing* (Gen. 4:3). He sought to draw near to God with the product of his own labor. Abel brought the first-born of the flock—a blood-offering—the divine acceptance of which provoked Cain's evil temper for he "was wroth." An angry look resulted in an angry deed because in a moment of ungoverned passion Cain lifted up his hand and murdered his brother, and buried his body. But although Cain tried to conceal his dastardly crime the Lord marked the spot and brought home to the murderer his foul deed.

God set a mark on Cain, but what it was Scripture does not say. Evidently it was sufficient to make him feel the wrath of God and the abhorrence of his fellowmen. Yet the punishment of Cain reveals a judgment mingled with mercy. His brand, perhaps some kind of stigma, made Cain realize the awfulness fo the sin of fratricide, but acted as a protection against the violence of the avenger of blood. The narrative seems to affirm that Cain's mark was not consigning him to perpetual punishment, but was a token of God's redemptive compassion.

CAINAN, KENAN [Cā ĭ' nan, Kē' nan]—ACQUISITION.
1. *A son of Enos,* son of Seth (Gen. 5:9–14; I Chron. 1:2; Luke 3:38).
2. *A son of Arphaxad* and father of Sala (Luke 3:36).

CALEB [Cā' leb]—BOLD, IMPETUOUS (also an animal name, meaning "dog").
1. *A son of Jephunneh,* usually so designated to distinguish him from other persons bearing the same name (Num. 13:6, 30).

The Man Who Desired a Mountain

Although Caleb was not an Israelite by birth, he was "an Israelite indeed." He was one of the chief spies sent out by Moses. He was courageous and persevered when the other spies became discouraged. He was invincible in driving out giants, completely devoted to God and vigorous in old age. Six times it is recorded of Caleb, "he hath fully followed the Lord."

His consecration was thorough. What magnificent adverbs are used to describe Caleb. He followed faithfully, wholly, fully. He never lowered his standards, but was perpetually wholehearted.

His courage was unfaltering. Giants did not disturb Caleb nor did those dastards who were ready to stone him.

His request was answered. To Caleb, whose life was woven of one piece throughout, reward crowned his faith and faithfulness. Through autumn winds and premonitions of snow, he brought forth fruit in his old age. When we come to the record of Caleb's personal inheritance in the land of Canaan we find him at eighty years of age asking of Joshua, "Now therefore give me this mountain." Caleb was a man of altitudes. He was not content with the average or the commonplace. He never thought in terms of fences or walled cities. It was the heights for Caleb, and although the mountain he wanted was filled with hostile Anakims, he refused defeat and claimed his inheritance. At long last a worthy recompense came to this noble man for "to patient faith the prize is sure."

2. The son of Hezron, a Judahite and father of Hur and grandfather of Caleb No. 1. There is some confusion about this Caleb (I Chron. 2:18, 19, 42).

3. The son of Hur the son of Caleb No. 2 (I Chron. 2:50).

CANAAN, CHANAAN [Că' năan]—LOWLAND or TRADER. *A son of Ham* and grandson of Noah (Gen. 9:18–27; I Chron. 1:8, 13), and founder of the family of Canaanites (Gen. 10:18). It is also the name of the country in which they dwelt (Gen. 11:31).

CARCAS [Cär' cas]—SEVERE or AN EAGLE. *One of seven chamberlains* who served in the presence of king Ahasuerus (Esther 1:10).

CAREAH [Că rē' ah]—BALD HEAD. *Father of Johanan,* governor of Judah in the time of Gedaliah (II Kings 25:23). Also spelled Kareah.

CARMI [Cär' mī]—VINEDRESSER, NOBLE or MY VINEYARD.
1. *Father of Achan* "who troubled Israel," a Judahite (Josh. 7:1, 18; I Chron. 2:7). Perhaps the Carmi of I Chronicles 4:1 should be Chelubai.
2. *One of the sons* of Reuben and father of the tribal family of Carmites (Gen. 46:9; Ex. 6:14; Num. 26:6; I Chron. 5:3).

CARPUS [Cär' pus]—FRUIT or THE WRIST. *A resident of Troas* with whom Paul stayed, and with whom he left the cloak he urged Timothy to bring him (II Tim. 4:13).

CARSHENA [Cär shē' nă]—SPOILER or SLENDER. *A prince of Persia* at the court of Ahasuerus (Esther 1:14).

CEPHAS [Cē' phas]—ROCK. *A surname given to Simon Peter* (John 1:42).

CHALCOL, CALCOL, [Chăl' cŏl, Căl' cŏl]—SUSTAINING or WHO NOURISHES. *A son of Zerah (called Mahol)* whose offspring were noted for their wisdom (I Kings 4:31; I Chron. 2:6).

CHEDORLAOMER [Chĕd or lā' o mûr]—SHEAF BAND or SERVANTS OF THE GOD LAGAMAR. *A king of Elam* in Abraham's time who held sovereignty of Babylon (Gen. 14).

CHELAL [Chē' lăl]—COMPLETION or COMPLETENESS. *A son of Palath-moab* who put away his foreign wife (Ezra 10:30).

CHELLUH [Chĕl' luh]—UNION. *One of the sons of Bani* who married a foreign wife (Ezra 10:35).

CHELUB [Chē' lŭb]—WICKER BASKET, BIRD'S CAGE or BOLDNESS.
1. *A brother of Shuah,* a Judahite (I Chron. 4:11).
2. *Father of Ezri,* and superintendent of the tillers of the ground in David's time (I Chron. 27:26).

CHELUBAI [Chē' lū' baī]—BINDING TOGETHER OF THE LORD. *Son of Hezron,* elsewhere called Caleb (I Chron. 2:9).

CHENAANAH [Chĕ nā' a nah]—SUBDUER or FLAT.
1. *The father of the false prophet Zedekiah* who smote Micaiah (I Kings 22:11, 20; II Chron. 18:10, 23).
2. *The brother of Ehud,* son of Bilhan, a Benjamite (I Chron. 7:10).

CHENANI [Chĕn' a nī]—FIRM or CREATOR. *A Levite* who helped bring the returned exiles into agreement about the covenant worship of God (Neh. 9:4).

CHENANIAH [Chĕn a nī' ah]—JEHOVAH IS FIRM or PREPARATION.
1. *A chief Levite* when David brought up the Ark from the house of Obed-edom (I Chron. 15:22, 27).
2. *An Izharite,* an officer of David's (I Chron. 26:29).

CHERAN [Chē' ran]—UNION or LUTE. *Son of Dishon,* the son of Seir the Horite (Gen. 36:26; I Chron. 1:41).

CHESED [Chē' sed]—A DEVIL or INCREASE. *The fourth son of Nahor,* and nephew of Abraham (Gen. 22:22).

CHILEAB [Chĭl' e ăb]—PERFECTION OF THE FATHER. *The second son of David* by Abigail (II Sam. 3:3). Called Daniel in I Chronicles 3:1.

CHILION [Chĭl' ĭ on]—WASTING AWAY or COMPLETE. *One of the two sons of Elimelech and Naomi* who married Orpah in Moab and died there (Ruth 1:2; 4:9).

CHIMHAM [Chĭm' hăm]—LONGING or PINING. *Perhaps the son of Barzillai,* the Gileadite (II Sam. 19:37–40; Jer. 41:17).

CHISLON [Chĭs' lon]—TRUST or STRONG. *The father of Elidad,* the prince of Benjamin in Moses' time who assisted in the division of the land (Num. 34:21).

CHUSHAN-RISHATHAIM [Chŭ' shan rĭsh a thā' im]—BLACKNESS OF INIQUITIES. *A king of Mesopotamia,* defeated by Othniel (Judg. 3:8–10).

CHUZA [Chŭ' ză]—MODEST. *A steward of Herod Antipas,* son of Herod the Great whose wife ministered to Christ and His disciples (Luke 8:3).

CIS [Cĭs]—SNARING. *The father of king Saul.* Cis is the Greek form of Kish (Acts 13:21).

CLAUDIUS [Clôu' dĭ ŭs]— (meaning uncertain).
1. *The successor of Caligula* as emperor (Acts 11:28; 18:2).
2. *A Roman officer,* Claudius Lysias, chief captain in Jerusalem in Paul's time (Acts 23:26).

CLEMENT [Clĕm' ĕnt]—KIND or MERCIFUL. *A Christian of Philippi* who labored with Paul (Phil. 4:3). Possibly the apostolic father with the same name (Clement of Rome).

CLEOPAS, CLOPAS [Clĕ' o păs]—THE WHOLE GLORY. *One of the two disciples* returning to Emmaus after the death of Christ, and to whom He appeared (Luke 24:18). Same as Cleophas.

CLEOPHAS [Clĕ' o phăs]—THE WHOLE GLORY. *The husband of one of the Marys* who was the halfsister of the Virgin Mary (John 19:25). Same person as Clopas.

COLHOZEH [Cŏl hŏ' zeh]—ALL-SEEING ONE or WHOLLY A SEER. *Father of Shallun* who helped repair the wall (Neh. 3:15). The Colhozeh of Nehemiah 11:5 may be the same person.

CONANIAH, CONONIAH [Cŏn a nī' ah, Cŏn o nĭ' ah]—JEHOVAH HATH ESTABLISHED or STABILITY OF THE LORD.
1. *A chief Levite* of high station in Josiah's time (II Chron. 35:9).
2. *A Levite* who had charge of tithes and offerings in Hezekiah's time (II Chron. 31:12, 13).

CORE [Cō' rē]—ICE or HARD. *The Greek form* of Korah (Jude 11).

CORNELIUS [Cŏr nē' lĭ ŭs]—THE BEAM OF THE SUN. *A converted Roman* centurion at Caesarea, a devout man (Acts 10). He was the first Gentile convert and through his conversion the door of faith was opened unto the Gentiles. Disgusted with the Gentile paganism of his day he turned to God but did not have a full understanding of the Gospel of Grace. Through Peter's ministry, Cornelius became a believer and was received into the fellowship of the Church. From this point there is no difference between Jew and Gentile. In Christ they become one (Eph. 2:18). Benevolence, prayerfulness, obedience and spiritual receptivity characterize this godly Roman centurion.

COSAM [Cō' sam]—MOST ABUNDANT. *A son of Elmodam,* and an ancestor of Jesus in the line of Joseph, husband of Mary (Luke 3:28).

COZ [Cŏz]—NIMBLE. *A descendant of Caleb* (I Chron. 4:8).

CRESCENS [Crĕs' cens]—INCREASE. *A companion of Paul* in his final imprisonment, sent by the apostle to Galatia (II Tim. 4:10). Legend has it that he was one of the seventy disciples sent fourth by Christ and that he became a bishop of Chalcedon.

CRISPUS [Crĭs' pus]—CURLED. *Ruler of the Jewish synagogue* at Corinth, and one of the few personally baptized by Paul (Acts 18:8; I Cor. 1:14).

CUSH [Cŭsh]—BLACK or ETHIOPIA.
1. *Eldest son of Ham* and grandson of Noah and founder of a tribal family (Gen. 10:6–8; I Chron. 1:8–10). Also the name of the land where the Cushites dwelt (Isa. 11:11; 18:1). Cushite is translated Ethiopian.
2. *A Benjamite,* and enemy of David. (See Fausset's dictionary).

CUSHI [Cŭ' shī]—BLACK or AN ETHIOPIAN.
1. *The messenger* who brought news to David concerning Absalom's defeat (II Sam. 18:21–32).
2. *An ancestor of Jehudi* who lived in Jeremiah's time (Jer. 36:14).
3. *The father of Zephaniah* the prophet who lived in the time of Josiah, king of Judah (Zeph. 1:1).

CYRENIUS [Cy rē' nĭ ŭs]—ONE WHO GOVERNS. *Governor of Syria* whose full name was Pablius Sulpiciua Quirnus (Luke 2:2).

CYRUS [Cy' rus]—AS MISERABLE or AN HEIR. *Cyrus, the founder of the Persian Empire,* conquered Babylon and was anointed by God to free the Jews from captivity. The prophets frequently foretold the coming of Cyrus. Isaiah, for example, mentioned him by name two hundred years before he was born (II Chron. 36:22, 23; Ezra 1:1–8; 3:7; 4:3–5; 5:13–17; 6:3–14; Isa. 44:28; 45; Dan. 1:21; 6:28; 10:1). Classical writers adorn the life and labors of Cyrus with a variety of legendary incidents for which no confirmation can be produced.

D

DALAIAH [Dăl a ĭ' ah]—JEHOVAH IS DELIVERER. *A descendant of Shechaniah* (I Chron. 3:24). Delaiah is the same name as the original.

DALPHON [Dăl' phon]—DROPPING. *The second of the ten sons of Haman,* all of whom were put to death by the Jews (Esther 9:7).

DAN [Dăn]—HE THAT JUDGES. *The fifth son of Jacob,* and first of Bilhah, Rachel's handmaid. Dan was the full brother of Naphtali and founder of a tribal family (Gen. 30:6; Ex. 31:6). The name Dan also describes the most northern city of Canaan. "Dan even to Beersheba" (II Sam. 24:15).

The Man Whose Name is Blotted Out

With our finite minds there is a mystery about Dan we cannot solve. The history of the tribe of Dan is darker than the history of any other of the twelve tribes of Israel. When we come to the sealing of the twelve tribes (Rev. 7), Dan's name is left out. The omission is absolute — the tribe is cut off from its brethren and its name blotted out. Yet we cannot be absolutely certain that the tribe of Dan is finally cut off, for in Ezekiel's glowing prophecy there is a portion for Dan (Ezek. 48:1).

The prophecy of Jacob concerning Dan carries a twofold character —"Dan shall judge his people as one of the *sceptres* of Israel." *Tribe* also means *sceptre* (Gen. 49:10). No man among the Judges did so much for Israel single-handed as Samson the great Danite.

A further thought is associated with Jacob's prophecy of Dan. "*I have waited* for thy salvation, O Lord." This is the first mention of *salvation* in Scripture. But Dan's history is adverse to the salvation predicted of him. His birth arose out of jealousy and inordinate desire. *Dan* became the Ishmael of Jacob's family. Persistent idolatry clung to the Danites from first to last. It was because Dan was likened unto a *serpent* that some of the early fathers predicted that Antichrist would come from him. "*They* are not *all Israel* which are of Israel." As there was one among the Twelve Apostles, so there was one among the Twelve Tribes who had not the seal of God. This we do know, Dan's glory as one of the sceptres of Israel with courage as a lion's whelp, is of no avail without the seal of God upon his forehead.

DANIEL [Dăn' iel]—GOD IS MY JUDGE.

1. *The second son of David,* also called Chileol (I Chron. 3:1).

2. *A son or descendant of Ithamar* who, after the return from exile, sealed the covenant (Ezra 8:2; Neh. 10:6).

3. *The celebrated Jewish prophet,* fourth of the so-called Major Prophets, of royal or noble descent. Daniel was taken to Babylon and

trained with others for the king's service (Ezek. 14:14, 20; 28:3; Dan. 1:6, 21).

The Man Who Kept His Window Open

Nothing is known of the ancestry and early life of this celebrated Jewish prophet who exercised tremendous influence in the Babylonian court, and whose name can mean: "Who in the name of God does Justice." Daniel was not a priest like Jeremiah or Ezekiel but like Isaiah he was descended from the time of Judah and was probably of royal blood (Dan. 1:3-6). A comparison of II Kings 20:17, 18 with Isaiah 29:6, 7 seems to indicate that Daniel was descended from king Hezekiah.

As a youth of the age of fifteen or thereabouts, Daniel was carried captive to Babylon (Dan. 1:1-4) in the third year of Jehoiakim. From then on his whole life was spent in exile. What Daniel was like we are not expressly told but the details given in the first chapter of his book suggest he must have been a handsome youth. There is a tradition to the effect that "he had a spare, dry, tall figure with a beautiful expression." Dr. Alexander Whyte says of Daniel: "There is always a singular lustre and nobility and stately distinction about him. There is a note of birth and breeding and aristocracy about his whole name and character." As we study his character we cannot but be impressed with his refinement, his reserve and the high sculpture of his life.

Daniel comes before us as an interpreter of dreams and of signs, a conspicuous seer, an official of kings. He lived a long and active life in the courts and councils of some of the greatest monarchs the world has known, like Nebuchadnezzar, Cyrus and Darius. Close intimacy with heaven made Daniel the courtier, statesman, man of business and prophet he was. Bishop Ken reminds us that "Daniel was one that kept his station in the greatest of revolutions, reconciling politics and religion, business and devotion, magnanimity with humility, authority with affability, conversation with retirement, Heaven and the Court, the favour of God and of the King."

The significant meaning of Daniel's name accords with the character and contents of the Book of Daniel, written by the prophet himself — the first six chapters in the *third* person, the last six in the *first* person.

As the distinguished historian of some of the most important dispensational teaching given in the Bible, Daniel's book sets forth:

A statement of God's judgment on history.

The purpose of God until the final consummation.

The vindication of righteousness.

It would take a whole book to deal with Daniel's prophetic visions of Gentile dominion and defeat. Profitable homiletical material can be used showing Daniel's self-control (Dan. 1:8; 10:3), undaunted courage (5:22, 23), constant integrity (6:4), unceasing prayerfulness (2:17, 18; 6:16), native humility (10:17) and spiritual vision (7:9, 12; 10:5, 6).

DARA [Dā′ rǎ]—BEARER. *Son of Zerah* son of Judah by Tamar (I Chron. 2:6). Sometimes identified with Darda.

DARDA [Där' dă]—A PEARL OF WISDOM. *A son of Mahol,* a Judahite celebrated for his wisdom (I Kings 4:31).

DARIUS (Då rī' us]—HE THAT INFORMS HIMSELF or A KING.

1. *The son of Hystaspes,* and king of Persia B.C. (521–485). He allowed the Jews to rebuild the Temple (Ezra 4:5, 24).

2. *Darius the Persian,* Darius Nothus and probably the last king of Persia (Neh. 12:22).

3. *Darius the Mede,* the son of Ahasuerus of the seed of the Medes. He succeeded Belshazzar as king of Babylon at sixty-two years of age (Dan. 5:31; 6:9, 25; 9:1; 11:1).

DARKON [Där' kon]—BEARER or SCATTERING. *A servant of Solomon,* whose sons were among those who returned from exile with Zerubbabel (Ezra 2:56; Neh. 7:58).

DATHAN [Dä' than]—BELONGING TO LAW or FOUNT. *A son of Eliab* the Reubenite, who with Korah a Levite, and Abiram and On, two other Reubenites, conspired against Moses and Aaron in the wilderness and were destroyed for their rebellion (Num. 16; 26:9; Deut. 11:6; Ps. 106:17).

DAVID [Dä' vid]—BELOVED. *The youngest son of the eight sons of Jesse* the Bethlehemite, the second and greatest of Israel's kings, the eloquent poet and one of the most prominent figures in the history of the world (Ruth 4:17, 22; I Sam. 16: 13).

The Man After God's Own Heart

Volumes have been written on the trials and triumphs of David, a mountain peak among Bible characters, who was carefully chosen as Israel's second king by God Himself. David's father, Jesse, was a man of no great rank who lived in the little town of Bethlehem. In his youth David was trained to tend his father's sheep. Being the youngest of the family he was not brought into public notice, yet it pleased God to raise him from a low estate and set him upon the throne. He was overlooked by the prophet Samuel, but the prophet obeyed when God said, "Arise anoint him, this is he." All we can do in this study is to offer a brief sketch of David's eventful life. We view him as:

I. A Warrior. David was courageous as a champion and a great soldier (I Sam. 17:40; II Sam. 5:7). His fight with Goliath the giant made him a marked man. He had not the training of a soldier. As yet he had not reached the years of manhood. Dressed like a poor country shepherd lad, he had no weapons save his sling. Never were two warriors more unequally matched, but when David was victorious over Goliath there was no empty boasting, no reliance upon his own powers. God gave the victory and David gave Him all the glory. He became a man of war and because of that was not allowed to build the Temple (I Chron. 28:3).

II.   As a Musician. Because he was a skilful player on the harp he found himself in the presence of the wretched king, Saul, who could only be soothed by David's music. Poetic genius made him the sweet psalmist of Israel, and no poet has been so constantly used and quoted through the ages. His majestic psalms are the masterpiece of spiritual literature.

III.   As a Saint. David was accepted as a child of God. The general trend of his life was spiritual (I Sam. 13:14; I Kings 15: 5). What other man has had the reputation of being known as a man after God's own heart? Such an expression does not refer to any remarkable goodness in David, but to him as one whom God had chosen to be the ruler of His people. He was the man according to God's special choice. His psalms of praise, worship and meditation indicate the God-ward direction of his life.

IV.   As a Sinner. David violated a divine law (Deut. 17:17; II Sam. 5:13), yielded to his gross sin in a period of ease (II Sam. 11) and was rebuked by the prophet Nathan (II Sam. 12). David stained his character by his sin against Uriah and by the deceitful way he gained this gallant soldier's wife as his own. Such a grievous sin brought the bitterest anguish of heart. David's confession was not a cold, formal acknowledgment of guilt, but a true and heartfelt humbling of himself before God and a deep cry for pardon and restoration to divine favor as psalms thirty-two and fifty-one clearly prove.

V.   As a Prophet. David had a prophetic gift given to few. He was one of those holy men of old moved by the Holy Spirit to set forth many glorious truths related to Christ as Saviour and Messiah. When we come to the New Testament we find the Psalms quoted from more often than any other part of the Old Testament.

VI.   As a Type. Not only did David prophesy about Christ, he resembled Him in many ways. For example:

Both were born in the humble town of Bethlehem.

Both were of low estate on earth, having no rank to boast of, no wealth to recommend them to the world.

Both were shepherds—the one caring for sheep, the other for souls.

Both were sorely oppressed and persecuted but opened not their mouths.

Both came to kingship. David subdued his foes and had a kingdom stretching from shore to shore. Jesus was born a King, and is to have an everlasting Kingdom.

VII.   As a Star. Does not the children's hymn urge us to be "a star in someone's sky?" David has lighted many a spiritual traveler on the way to heaven. Glory alone will reveal what his psalms meant to Christ and to His followers in all ages. Yet he is nothing compared to the Sun of Righteousness Himself. None can compare to David's greater son, the Lord Jesus Christ, who died and rose again to become our Saviour, Friend and King.

DEBIR [Dĕ' bûr]—SPEAKER. *The king of Eglon,* ally of Adoni-zedec, who joined four other kings against Joshua, but was defeated and executed by Joshua (Josh. 10:3). Also the name of a city near Hebron (Josh. 10:38).

DEDAN [Dĕ' dan]—LOW or THEIR FRIENDSHIP.
1. *A grandson of Cush* son of Ham (Gen. 10:7; I Chron. 1:9).
2. *A son of Abraham* by Keturah (Gen. 25:3; I Chron. 1:32). Also the name of a district near Edom (Jer. 25:23).

DEKAR [Dĕ' kär]—LANCE BEARER or PERFORATION. *Father of one of Solomon's purveyors* at Mahaz (I Kings 4:9).

DELAIAH [Dĕl a ī' ah]—JEHOVAH IS DELIVERER.
1. *A descendant of Aaron,* and one of David's priests (I Chron. 24:18).
2. *One of the Nethinims,* founder of a family whose genealogy had been lost (Ezra 2:60; Neh. 7:62).
3. *One who tried to dishearten Nehemiah* (Neh. 6:10).
4. *A Judahite prince,* son of Shemaiah who urged king Jehoiakim not to burn the sacred roll (Jer. 36:12, 25).
5. *A son of Elioenai* (I Chron. 3:24).

DEMAS [Dĕ' mas]—POPULAR or RULER OF PEOPLE. *A companion of Paul* during his first Roman imprisonment (Col. 4:14; Philem. 24).

The Man Who Forsook His Friend

This seems to be an indication that this native of Thessalonica was not fully trusted even when he was near to Paul (Phil. 2:20). Scripture has this against him, that he forsook Paul for this present world (II Tim. 4:10). It is amazing how a student of Comparative Anatomy can build up a whole unknown structure from one or two known bones. In the same way we can sketch the character of Demas from the few references to him in the Bible's portrait gallery.

Before he met Paul we can picture him as an agreeable young man with no particular vice. The material of his character had no rent in it. It was only shoddy throughout. Under the strong influence of Paul's personality, Demas was like a piece of soft iron, temporarily magnetized by the presence of a magnet. Becoming a disciple, he was carried away by the enthusiasm of sacrifice. He wanted to live with Paul and die with him, and have a throne and a halo among the martyred saints.

But when Demas came up to the great capital of the then known world in company with the Lord's prisoners, Paul and Epaphras, it was a different story. He was not a prisoner, and gradually the contrast between the cell and the outer world became intolerable to him. He saw the magnificent halls of the Caesars, the gorgeous homes of the rich and the glitter of a world of music, venal loves, jest and wine. Such a gay world cast its glamor over Demas, and he yielded to its charms. The prison where his friends were languishing seemed wretched alongside the music-haunted, scented, dazzling halls of Rome. Thus Paul had to write one of the most heartbreaking lines in his letters:

"Demas hath forsaken me, having loved this present world." This man of wavering impulse who surrendered the passion of sacrifice and sank in the swirling waters of the world, is a true reflection of the thought that where our love is, there we finally are.

DEMETRIUS [Dē mē′ trĭ ŭs]—BELONGING TO DEMETER. Demeter was the goddess of agriculture and rural life.

1. *The silversmith at Ephesus* who made silver models of the celebrated Temple of Diana, and who opposed Paul and incited the mob against him (Acts 19:24, 38).

2. *A believer,* well-commended by the Apostle John (III John 12). This man of God had the testimony of all men of the truth and of John also. It is one of the finest recommendations of the Gospel when a Christian impresses and attracts those around him by the reality of his or her life.

DEUEL [Deŭ′ el]—INVOCATION OF GOD or GOD IS KNOWING. *The father of Eliasaph,* a Gadite prince (Num. 1:14; 2:14; 7:42, 47). Called Reuel (friend of God) in Numbers 2:14.

DIBLAIM [Dĭb′ la ĭm]—DOUBLE EMBRACE or TWIN BALLS. *Father of Gomer wife* of Hosea the prophet (Hos. 1:3).

DIBRI [Dĭb′ rī]—ON THE PASTURE BORN or PROMISE OF THE LORD. *A Danite* whose daughter married an Egyptian and whose son was stoned for blasphemy (Lev. 24:11).

DIDYMUS [Dĭd′ ў mŭs]—A TWIN. *The surname of the apostle Thomas* (John 11:16; 20:24; 21:2).

DIKLAH [Dĭk′ lah]—PALM GROVE. *A son of Joktan* of the family of Shem (Gen. 10:27; I Chron. 1:21).

DIONYSIUS [Dī o nŷs′ ĭ ŭs]—DIVINELY TOUCHED or THE GOD OF WINE. *A member of the Athenian supreme court* at Athens who became a convert to Christianity (Acts 17:34).

DIOTREPHES [Di ŏt′ re phēs]—NOURISHED BY JUPITER. *The professed disciple* who refused to recognize the authority of John as an apostle, and who loved to have the pre-eminence (III John 9). Diotrephes tried to act like a little Caesar. Pride and self-pleasing led to the dethronement of Christ. The word "pre-eminence" occurs twice in the New Testament. Paul speaks of Christ having the "pre-eminence" (Col. 1:18). Diotrephes substituted self for Christ.

DISHAN [Dĭ' shan]—LEAPING. *The youngest son of Seir* the Horite (Gen. 36:21-30; I Chron. 1:38, 42).

DISHON [Dĭ' shon]—LEAPING.
1. *The fifth son of Seir* the Horite (Gen. 36:21, 26, 30; I Chron. 1:38).
2. *The son of Anah* and grandson of Seir (Gen. 36:25; I Chron. 1:41).

DODAI [Dŏ' da ĭ]—BELOVED OF JEHOVAH. *An Ahohite,* one of David's captains (I Chron. 27:4).

DODANIM [Dŏ' da nĭm]—A LEADER. *A descendant or race descended from Javan* the son of Japhet (Gen. 10:4; I Chron. 1:7).

DODAVAH [Dŏ' da vah]—JEHOVAH IS LOVING. *Father of the Eliezer* who prophesied about the ships (II Chron. 20:37). Also called Dod-waha.

DODO [Dŏ' dō]—LOVING.
1. *Grandfather of the judge Tolah* of the tribe of Issachar (Judg. 10:1).
2. *Father of the second of David's thirty heroes* (II Sam. 23:9; I Chron. 11:12).
3. *A man of Bethlehem,* father of Elhanan and another of David's heroes (II Sam. 23:24; I Chron. 11:26).

DOEG [Dŏ' eg]—TIMID or FEARFUL. *Chief of Saul's herdsmen,* an Edomite, who informed Saul of Ahimelech's help for David. Because of Doeg's report Ahimelech and his companions were slain (I Sam. 22:7-22).

DUMAH [Dŭ' mah]—SILENCE or RESEMBLANCE. *A son of Ishmael* son of Abraham by Hagar (Gen. 25:14; I Chron. 1:30). Also the name of two cities (Josh. 15:52; Isa. 21:11).

E

EBAL [Ē' bal]—BARE.
1. *Son of Shobal,* son of Seir the Horite (Gen. 36:23; I Chron. 1:40).
2. *A Son of Joktan,* son of Eber, grandson of Shem (I Chron. 1:22). Also the name of a mountain in Ephraim (Deut. 11:29).

EBED [Ē′ bed]—SERVANT or SLAVE.

1. *The father of Gaal,* an Ephraimite who rebelled against Abimelech when he reigned in Shechem (Judg. 9:26–35).

2. *A chief of the father's house of Adin* who returned from Babylon with fifty males under the leadership of Ezra (Ezra 8:6).

EBED-MELECH [Ē′ bed-mē ′lĕch]—SERVANT or SLAVE OF THE KING. *An Ethiopian eunuch* of the palace in Zedekiah's time who assisted Jeremiah in his release from prison (Jer. 38:7–12; 39:16).

The Man Who Was a Credit to His Class

It is said of Ebed-melech that he was an *Ethiopian* which means that he was a heathen and one of a despicable type at that time. "Can the Ethiopian change his skin?" No! But this Ethiopian had a transformed moral character, and was a triumph of grace in the clan to which he belonged. The Eastern eunuchs were a pitilessly cruel race, whose delight was to wound and vex. No clan had a worse reputation for cruelty, but here again Ebed-melech was different. He was as kind as the rest of his clan was cruel. Kitto calls him, "The benevolent Eunuch." Then he is likewise described as a *servant of the king.* Royal servants were usually a godless company. But Ebed-melech was as faithful a servant to God as he was to king Zedekiah. He loved the prophet Jeremiah and risked his own life to save the man of God.

Among the lessons to be gleaned from the record of this eunuch who was greater than his fellows are:

He was superior to his surroundings.

He put more pretentious people to shame.

He had the courage of his convictions.

He had a kind way of doing kindness.

He achieved a great service with poor instruments.

Old rags and cords! How God can use weak things for the accomplishment of His plan!

His faith in God was the secret of his noble life.

He was divinely rewarded. God is a grand Paymaster.

EBER [Ē′ bûr]—A SHOOT.

1. *A descendant of Shem* through Arphaxad, and the progenitor of various peoples (Gen. 10:21–25; 11:14–17; I Chron. 1:18–25).

2. *The head of a family in Gad* (I Chron. 5:13).

3. *A son of Elpaal* a Benjamite (I Chron. 8:12).

4. *A son of Shashak* a Benjamite (I Chron. 8:22).

5. *A priest,* head of the father's house of Amok in the days of the high priest, Joiakim (Neh. 12:20). Name is also used of the descendants of Eber (Num. 24:24) (No. 1). Heber is another spelling.

EBIASAPH [Ĕ bī′ a săph]—THE FATHER OF GATHERING. *A son of Elkanah* and a great-grandson of Korah (I Chron. 6:23, 37; 9:19). Also given as Abiasaph.

EDEN [Ē' dĕn]—DELIGHT.
1. *The son of Joah,* a Gershomite (II Chron. 29:13).
2. *A Levite* in Hezekiah's time appointed to distribute oblations (II Chron. 31:15). Also the name of man's first abode (Gen. 2:8).

EDER, EDAR [Ē' dûr, Ē' där]—A FLOCK.
1. *A son of Elpaal,* a Benjamite (I Chron. 8:15). See Ader.
2. *A son of Mushi,* a Levite of the family of Merari (I Chron. 23:23; 24:30). Also the name of two places (Gen. 35:21; Josh. 15:21).

EDOM [Ē' dom]—RED EARTH. *The elder son of Isaac,* and so named in memory of the red color of the lentil pottage for which he sold his birthright to his twin brother Jacob (Gen. 25:30; 36:1, 8, 19). See Esau. Name is also used to describe those descended from Esau, the Edomites (Gen. 36:9).

EGLON [Ĕg' lŏn]—CIRCLE or CHARIOT. *A king of Moab* who captured Jericho and who, after his long oppression of the Israelites, was slain by Ehud, son of Gera (Judg. 3:12–17). Also the name of a city near Judah (Josh. 10:3).

EHI [Ē' hī]—UNITY. *Son of Benjamin* (Gen. 46:21). Same as Ehud in I Chronicles 8:6.

EHUD [Ē' hŭd]—STRONG or UNION.
1. *The son of Bilhan,* great-grandson of Benjamin (I Chron. 7:10; 8:6).
2. *The son of Gera,* the second judge of Israel (Judg. 3:15–26; 4:1).

The Man Who Was Left-Handed

This left-handed man was a ruler in Israel, and the peculiar thing about the tribe of Benjamin to which Ehud belonged was that in it were seven hundred left-handed men. So skillful had they all become in the use of the left hand that they could sling stones at a hair's breadth and never miss.

Eglon, king of Moab, oppressor of Israel, imposed an outrageous tax upon the people, and Ehud received a divine commission to destroy the oppressor. Meeting the king in his summerhouse and saying that he had a secret message for him, Ehud, the left-handed man, put his left hand to his right side, pulled out a dagger and Eglon died. Thus for the salvation of Israel the left-handed weapon did its work. Wonderful is it not, that God can use all kinds for the fulfilment of His purpose?

EKER [Ē' kŭr]—ONE TRANSPLANTED. *Son of Ram,* a Judahite and of the household of Jerahmeel (I Chron. 2:27).

ELADAH [Ĕl′ a dah]—GOD HATH ADORNED. *A descendant of Ephraim* (I Chron. 7:20). Also given as Eleadah.

ELAH, ELA [Ē′ lah]—AN OAK or LIKE A TREE.
1. *A duke of Edom,* named from his habitation (Gen. 36:41; I Chron. 1:52).
2. *The father of one of Solomon's purveyors* (I Kings 4:18).
3. *The son and successor of Baasha,* king of Israel, who only reigned for about a year and who was killed while drunk by Zimri (I Kings 16:6–14).
4. *The father of Hoshea,* last king of Israel (II Kings 15:30; 17:1; 18:1, 9.)
5. *A son of Caleb*, son of Jephunneh (I Chron. 4:15).
6. *One of the tribe,* a Benjamite (I Chron. 9:8). Also the name of the valley where David slew Goliath (I Sam. 17:2, 19).

ELAM [Ē′ lăm]—YOUTH or HIGH.
1. *A son of Shem* and founder of the Elamites (Gen. 10:22; I Chron. 1:17; Ezra 4:9; Acts 2:9).
2. *Son of Shashak,* a Benjamite (I Chron. 8:24).
3. *Son of Meshelemiah,* a Kohathite (I Chron. 26:3).
4. *The head of a family* of 1,254 that returned from exile with Zerubbabel (Ezra 2:7; Neh. 7:12).
5. Another whose posterity returned from exile (Ezra 2:31; Neh. 7:34). Perhaps same person as No. 4.
6. *One whose descendants came back with Ezra* (Ezra 8:7).
7. *The father of Jehiel,* ancestor of Shechaniah, who confessed the trespass of marrying foreign wives (Ezra 10:2, 26).
8. *A chieftain who,* with Nehemiah, sealed the covenant (Neh. 10:14).
9. *A priest* who assisted in the dedication of the rebuilt wall (Neh. 12:42). Elam is also the name of the country inhabited by his descendants (Gen. 14:1, 9).

ELASAH, ELEASAH [Ĕl′ a sah]—GOD HATH MADE.
1. *A priest* who married a foreign wife (Ezra 10:22).
2. *The ambassador* Zedekiah sent to Nebuchadnezzar (Jer. 29:3).

ELDAAH [Ĕl′ da ah]—WHOM GOD CALLED. *A son of Midian* and descendant of Abraham (Gen. 25:4; I Chron. 1:33).

ELDAD [Ĕl′ dăd]—GOD IS A FRIEND or GOD HATH LOVED. *One of the two elders* who assisted Moses in the government of Israel (Num. 11:26, 27).

ELEAD [Ē′ le-ăd]—GOD IS WITNESS or GOD CONTINUETH. Perhaps a *son of Ephraim* who, with his brother, was killed by invaders (I Chron. 7:21).

ELEASAH, ELASAH [Ĕ′ lĕ′ a sah]—GOD HATH MADE or IS DOER.

1. *A son of Helez,* a Judahite with Egyptian blood in his veins (I Chron. 2:39, 40).

2. *A son of Rapha or Raphaiah,* a descendant of Saul and Jonathan (I Chron. 8:37; 9:43).

ELEAZAR [Ĕ le ā′zar]—GOD IS HELPER.

1. *The third son of Aaron* by Elisheba and father of Phinehas (Ex. 6:23, 25). He was consecrated a priest (Ex. 28:1) and was chief of the Levites (Num. 3:32).

2. *A son of Amminadab,* set apart to care for the Ark after its return (I Sam. 7:1).

3. *A son of Dodo,* the Ahohite, one of the three chief captains of David's army (II Sam. 23:9; I Chron. 11:12).

4. *A son of Mahli,* a Merarite, who had daughters only, who married their cousins (I Chron. 23:21, 22; 24:28).

5. *A priest* who participated in the dedication of the rebuilt wall (Neh. 12:42).

6. *A son of Phinehas,* a Levite (Ezra 8:33).

7. *A son of Eliud* and an ancestor of Christ (Matt. 1:15).

ELHANAN [Ĕl hā′ nan]—GOD HATH BEEN GENEROUS or MERCY OF GOD.

1. *A son of Jair,* who slew Lahmi the brother of Goliath (II Sam. 21:19; I Chron. 20:5).

2. *A son of Dodo* the Bethlehemite, and one of David's thirty heroes (II Sam. 23:24; I Chron. 11:26).

ELI [Ĕ′ lī]—JEHOVAH IS HIGH or MY GOD. *The high priest and judge of Israel* of the family of Ithamar (I Sam. 1–4; 14:3).

The Man Who Lacked Parental Authority

There are few Bible men in whose character we cannot find some great and glaring fault. There is usually a dead fly in the ointment, a rent in the garment, a spot on the whitest sheet. Eli was a good man whose life was pure. He loved and delighted in God's service, but was faulty in one point. He failed to exercise the proper authority of a parent over his children.

Eli belonged to the tribe of Levi, and for years acted as a judge and as High Priest in Israel. He lived at Shiloh in a dwelling adjoining the Temple for the greater portion of his life. We know little about him until he was well advanced in age. The first mention of him is when Hannah came to pour out her heart.

Eli's fault which brought sorrow upon his declining years was the conduct of his own two sons, Phinehas and Hophni, who, although lacking their father's character and qualities, were yet put into the priest's office. Their conduct disgraced their high calling and shocked the people so much that they "abhorred the offering of the Lord." While Eli warned them of their shameful ways, he did not rebuke them with the severity their evil deeds merited. He should have exercised the stern authority of a father and rebuked them as a judge. Instead Eli only mildly reasoned with his sons saying: "Why do ye such things?" But the sons disregarded such a weak and useless protest for their hearts were cold and callous and so they no longer heeded their father's feelings.

Although Eli had no power to change the hearts of his sons, he could have prevented their ministry before the Lord, but he "restrained them not." He wanted to be kind to them but it was a false and mistaken kindness. A seasonable correction would have saved them from ruin. Eli had no need to be harsh and severe, only firm and decided in the matter of obedience. Eli was twice warned that judgment would overtake him and his sons, but such warning was lost upon him. He dearly loved his sons and could not take action against them.

What a pitiable spectacle Eli presents! An old man of ninety, almost blind, waited to hear the result of the grim battle between the Israelites and the Philistines. How he trembled for his nation, his sons and also for the Ark of God which would be dishonored if it fell into enemy hands! Then the messenger came with news of the slaughter of his sinful sons and of the taking of the Ark. As Eli heard mention of the latter he fell off his seat by the side of a gate and died of a broken neck, yes, and of a broken heart! As is often the case, children bring down their father's gray hairs with sorrow to the grave.

ELIAB [Ĕ lĭ' āb]—GOD IS A FATHER.

1. *A son of Helon* and leader of the tribe of Zebulun when the census was taken in the wilderness (Num. 1:9; 2:7; 7:24, 29).

2. *A son of Pallu or Phallu,* a Reubenite, and father of Dathan and Abiram (Num. 16:1, 12; 26:8, 9; Deut. 11:6).

3. *The eldest son of Jesse* and brother of David (I Sam. 16:6; 17:13, 28). Called Elihu in I Chronicles 27:18.

4. *A Levite* in David's time who was a Tabernacle porter and musician (I Chron. 15:18, 20; 16:5).

5. *A Gadite* warrior who with others came over to David when a fugitive in the wilderness (I Chron. 12:9).

6. *An ancestor of Samuel* the prophet; a Kohathite Levite (I Chron. 6:27). Called Elihu in I Samuel 1:1 and Eliel in I Chronicles 6:34.

ELIADA [Ĕ lĭ' a dă]—GOD IS KNOWING or GOD KINDLY REGARDED.

1. *One of David's sons* (II Sam. 5:16; I Chron. 3:8).

2. *A Benjamite,* a mighty warrior who led two hundred thousand of his tribe to the army of Jehoshaphat (II Chron. 17:17).

ELIADAH [Ĕ lĭ' a dah]—GOD IS KNOWING. *The father of Rezon,* the captain of a roving band that annoyed Solomon (I Kings 11:23).

ELIAH [Ĕ lī ah]—GOD IS JEHOVAH.
1. *A son of Jeroham,* the Benjamite who was head of his tribe (I Chron. 8:27).
2. *One of the sons of Elam* who married a foreign wife (Ezra 10:26).

ELIAHBA [Ĕ lī′ ah bä]—GOD DOTH HIDE. *A Shaalbonite,* and one of David's famous guard (II Sam. 23:32; I Chron. 11:33).

ELIAKIM [Ĕ lī′ ā kĭm]—GOD IS SETTING UP or DOTH ESTABLISH.
1. *A son of Hilkiah,* successor of Shebna as master of Hezekiah's household (II Kings 18:18, 26, 37; 19:2).
2. *The original name of king Jehoiakim* (II Kings 23:34; II Chron. 36:4).
3. *A priest* who helped at the dedication of the rebuilt wall in Nehemiah's time (Neh. 12:41).
4. *The eldest son of Abiud* or Judah and father of Azor in Christ's genealogy (Matt. 1:13; Luke 3:30).

ELIAM [Ĕ lī′ am]—GOD IS ONE OF THE FAMILY or GOD'S FOUNDER OF THE PEOPLE. *The father of Bath-sheba,* wife of David (II Sam. 11:3). Called also Ammiel.

ELIAS, ELIJAH [Ĕ lī′ as, Ĕ lī′ jah]—GOD IS JEHOVAH or GOD HIMSELF.
1. *Elias is the Greek form of Elijah* (Matt. 11:14). Elijah the Tishbite is the grandest and most romantic character Israel ever produced (I Kings 17; 18; 19).

The Man Who Had No Fear of Man

No career in the Old Testament is more vividly portrayed, or has as much fascination as that of the unique character of Elijah. The New Testament attests to his greatness and reveals what an indelible impression he made upon the mind of his nation. All we know of him before his dramatic appearance can be summed up in the words: "Elijah the Tishbite, who was of the inhabitants of Gilead" (I Kings 17:1). Scripture is silent about his past history. Suddenly and with abrupt impetuosity the figure of the prophet bursts upon the scene to rebuke the godless and to reawaken and restore the nation of which he was a part. This man of iron is presented in many ways:

As a fearless, bold and dauntless reformer (I Kings 18:17–46).
As a rebuker of kings (I Kings 21:20; II Kings 1:16).
As a mighty intercessor, praying with faith and intensity (I Kings 17:20, 22; 18:36–38; Jas. 5:17).
As a man prone to discouragement (I Kings 19:4).
As one capable of fallible judgment (I Kings 19:4, 18).
As a prophet divinely honored (II Kings 2:11; Matt. 17:3).
As a performer of miracles (I Kings 19:8).
As a God-inspired prophet ready to obey and trust God (I Kings 17:1; 21:9–24; II Kings 1:2–17).

As a saint whose end was glorious (II Kings 2:1).

Both mystery and majesty are associated with Elijah, the mightiest of the prophets. His history in I Kings can be appropriately studied under five prepositions:

Before Ahab (I Kings 17:1). When God commands us to speak, no thought of peril need make us dumb.

By Cherith (I Kings 17:2–7). Faith moves on, trusting that when the first step is taken the next will be revealed.

At Zarephath (I Kings 17:10, 24). Elijah was miraculously fed on three occasions—by ravens (I Kings 17:6); by a widow (I Kings 17:9); by an angel (I Kings 19:5–8).

On Carmel (I Kings 18). Here we see the power of a fully surrendered man.

In the wilderness (I Kings 19). The overwrought prophet suffered a lapse of confidence, but was quickly restored.

Elijah, the rugged prophet, suggests John the Baptist, who came in the same spirit and power of the prophet.

Note these points of correspondence:

Their familiarity with the deserts and solitude.

Their austere manner and dress.

Their strong reproof of prevailing evils.

Their intrepid fidelity in calling all classes to repentance.

Their exposure of the wrath of a wicked king.

Their continued influence after death through disciples.

Their fruitful labors. "Many of the children of Israel did they turn to the Lord their God."

2. *A son of Harim* who married a foreign wife during the exile (Ezra 10:21).

3. *A Benjamite* and son of Jeroham, resident at Jerusalem (I Chron. 8:27 R.V.).

4. *An Israelite* induced to put away his foreign wife. (Ezra 10:26).

ELIASAPH [Ĕ lī' a săph]—GOD HATH ADDED or GOD IS GATHERED.

1. *The son of Deuel* and head of the Gadites at the census in the wilderness (Num. 1:14; 2:14; 7:42, 47; 10:20).

2. *A son of Lael,* a Levite and prince of the Gershonites during the wilderness wanderings (Num. 3:24).

ELIASHIB [Ĕ lī' a shĭb]—GOD IS REQUITER or GOD HATH RESTORED.

1. *A priest* in David's time from whom the eleventh priestly course took its name (Chron. 24:12).

2. *A son of Elioenai,* descendant of Zerubbabel, a Judahite (I Chron. 3:24).

3. *The high priest* at the time of the rebuilding of the city wall (Neh. 3:1, 20, 21; 13:4, 7, 28).

4. *A Levite and singer* who put away his foreign wife (Ezra 10: 24).

5. *A son of Zattu* who married a foreign wife (Ezra 10:27).

6. *A son of Bani* who also married a foreign wife (Ezra 10:26).

7.   *An ancestor of Johanan* who helped Ezra in the assembly of foreign wives (Ezra 10:6; Neh. 12:10, 22, 23).

ELIATHAH [Ĕ lī′ a thah]—GOD HATH COME. *A son of Heman* and a musician in David's reign (I Chron. 25:4, 27).

ELIDAD [Ĕ lī′ dăd]—GOD IS A FRIEND or GOD HATH LOVED. *A prince* of the tribe of Benjamin and a member of the commission in the division of Canaan (Num. 34:21).

ELIEL [Ĕ lī el]—GOD IS GOD.
1.   *A Levite* of the family of Kohath and an ancestor of Samuel the prophet (I Chron. 6:34).
2.   *A chief man of the half tribe of Manasseh* in Bashan (I Chron. 5:24).
3.   *A son of Shimhi* the Benjamite (I Chron. 8:20).
4.   *A son of Shashak,* A Benjamite (I Chron. 8:22).
5.   *A Mahavite* and a captain in David's army (I Chron. 11:46).
6.   *Another of David's heroes* (I Chron. 11:47).
7.   *A Gadite* who joined David at Ziklag (I Chron. 12:11). Perhaps the same person as No. 5 or 6.
8.   *A chief of Judah* in David's reign (I Chron. 15:9). Perhaps the same man as No. 5.
9.   *A chief Levite* who helped in the return of the Ark from the house of Obed-edom (I Chron. 15:11).
10.   *A Levite overseer* of tithes and offerings in Hezekiah's time (II Chron. 31:13).

ELIENAI [Ĕ lī ē′ na ī]—UNTO GOD ARE MINE EYES. *A son of Shimhi,* a Benjamite (I Chron. 8:20).

ELIEZER [Ĕ li ē zûr]—GOD IS MY HELP.
1.   *The second son of Moses* and Zipporah to whom his father gave this name as a memento of his gratitude to God (Ex. 18:4; I Chron. 23:15, 17; 26:25).
2.   *A son of Becher* and grandson of Benjamin (I Chron. 7:8).
3.   *A priest* who assisted in the return of the Ark to Jerusalem (I Chron. 15:24).
4.   *A Reubenite* ruler in David's time (I Chron. 27:16).
5.   *The prophet who rebuked Jehoshaphat* for his alliance with king Ahaziah in the Ophir expedition (II Chron. 20:37).
6.   *A chieftain* sent with others to induce many of the Israelites to return with Ezra to Jerusalem (Ezra 8:16).
7.   *A priest* who put away his foreign wife (Ezra 10:18).
8.   *A Levite* who had done the same (Ezra 10:23).
9.   *One of the sons of Harim* who had done likewise (Ezra 10:31).
10.   *An ancestor of Joseph,* husband of Mary (Luke 3:29).

11. *Abraham's chief servant,* and "son of his house," that is, one of his large household. He is named "Eliezer of Damascus" probably to distinguish him from others of the same name (Gen. 15:2; 24).

The Man Who Found a Wife for His Master

There can be little doubt that the Damascus Eliezer is the nameless servant Abraham sent to his own country and kindred to secure a bride for Isaac, his son of promise. Of the search of Eliezer, Dr. C. I. Scofield says that the entire chapter (Genesis 24) is highly typical, and then he gives us this most helpful outline:

I. Abraham—type of a certain king who would make a marriage for his son (Matt. 22:2; John 6:44).

II. The unnamed servant—type of the Holy Spirit who does not speak of or from himself, but takes of the things of the bridegroom with which to win the bride (John 16:13, 14).

III. The servant—type of the Spirit as enriching the bride with the bridegroom's gifts (I Cor. 12:7–11; Gal. 5:22).

IV. The servant—type of the Spirit as bringing the bride to the meeting with the bridegroom (Acts 13: 4; 16:6, 7; Rom. 8:11; I Thess. 4:14–17).

V. Rebekah—type of the Church, the *ecclesia,* the "called out" virgin bride of Christ (Gen. 24:16; II Cor. 11:2; Eph. 5:25–32).

VI. Isaac—type of the bridegroom "whom not having seen" the bride loves through the testimony of the unnamed servant (I Pet. 1:8).

VII. Isaac—type of the bridegroom who goes out to meet and receive His bride (Gen. 24:63; I Thess. 4:16, 17).

Points to emphasize as we peruse this beautiful chapter twenty-four with its love-quest are clearly evident:

Prayer should precede our pursuits (v. 12).

Leading depends upon living (v. 27).

The Lord is before us and with us (v. 40).

The place of privilege (v. 43 with John 4:14).

The importance of a personal decision (v. 58).

The right attitude for the reception of God's gifts (v. 63).

ELIHOENAI, ELIOENAI [Ĕ lĭ ho ĕ′ na ĭ, Ĕ lĭ o ĕ′ na ĭ]—TO JEHOVAH ARE MINE EYES.

1. *A son of Neariah* of the family of David (I Chron. 3:23, 24).

2. *The head of a family of Simeon* (I Chron. 4:36).

3. *The head of one of the families of the sons of Becher,* son of Benjamin (I Chron. 7:8).

4. *A son of Pashur,* a priest who put away his foreign wife (Ezra 10:22). Perhaps the same person as the one mentioned in Nehemiah 12:41.

5. *A son of Zattu* who married a foreign wife (Ezra 10:27).

6. *A priest,* perhaps the same person as No. 4 (Neh. 12:41).

7. *The seventh son of Meshelemiah,* the son of Kore (I Chron. 26:3). Also given as Elihoenai.

8. *A descendant of Pahath Moab* who returned with Ezra in Artaxerxes' time (Ezra 8:4).

ELIHOREPH [Ĕl ĭ hō' reph]—GOD OF HARVEST RAIN or GOD IS A REWARD. *One of king Solomon's scribes* (I Kings 4:3).

ELIHU [Ĕ lī' hū]—HE IS GOD HIMSELF.
1. *The father of Jeroham* and great-grandfather of Samuel the prophet, who also has the name of Eliel (I Sam. 1:1; I Chron. 6:34).
2. *A man of Manasseh* who joined David at Ziklag (I Chron. 12:20).
3. *A Kohathite* of the family of Korah, and a Tabernacle porter in David's time (I Chron. 26:7).
4. *A brother of David,* who became ruler over Judah (I Chron. 27:18). Also known as Eliab.
5. *The youngest of Job's friends,* the son of Barachel, a Buzite (Job 32:2–6; 34:1; 35:1; 36:1).

The Man Who Was a Self-Assertive Dogmatist

The lineage of Elihu, the fourth speaker in Job's dialogue, is given in fuller detail. He was the son of Barachel the Buzite, the kindred of Ram (Job 32:2). Buz was the brother of Uz and son of Nahor (Gen. 22:21). Buz is also mentioned along with Tema and the Arab tribes (Jer. 25:23).

Elihu's name, "God is Lord," suggests his desire to exalt the Almighty. One writer has described him as "the forerunner of Jehovah." This youthful, somewhat self-assertive speaker reaches a high level and has "a far juster and more spiritual conception" in dealing with the problem that has confronted Eliphaz, Bildad and Zophar. But he gives only half the truth, and his appeal, although so lofty and eloquent, is marred by a self-assertiveness evident from his sayings, "Great men are not always wise: neither do the aged understand judgment" (Job 32:9) and, "My words shall be the uprightness of my heart" (Job 33:3).

It is interesting to observe that Job did not reply to Elihu as he did to the other three, "Who is this that darkeneth counsel by words without knowledge?" This was Jehovah's word to Elihu, in which He lays the very charge at his feet which he had sought to bring against His servant Job (Job 34:35; 35:16).

Elihu's vindication appears to be along three lines:
I. He first of all condemns Job for his self-justification (Job 32:2; 33:8, 9).
II. He sets out to modify the doctrine of the three friends by affirming that affliction is as much a judgment upon sin as a warning of judgment to come (Job 34:10, 11).
III. He then unveils in a way completely overmastering the mind, the majesty and glory of God, the climax of which is in Job 37:5.

Elihu claimed inspiration for his presence and message (Job 32:8). Eagerness was his to speak before he did, but youth and modesty kept him back (Job 32:4–8, 18, 19). What Elihu seemed to forget was, trial can overtake the saintliest of men (I Pet. 1:7).

ELIKA [Ĕl' i kǎ]—GOD IS REJECTOR or HATH SPEWED OUT. *A Harodite,* one of David's mighty men (II Sam. 23:25).

ELIMELECH [Ĕ lĭm' e lĕch]—GOD IS KING. *The husband of Naomi* and father of Mahlon and Chilion, Ephrathites of Bethlehem-judah (Ruth 1:2, 3; 2:1, 3; 4:3–9; I Sam. 17:12).

The Man Whose Ways Contradicted His Name

It is one thing to have a good name, but a different matter altogether to have a life corresponding to that name. Elimelech's name implies that God is King, an expressive name given him by godly parents when the nation followed the Lord. But Elimelech belied the name he bore, for had he truly believed that God was King, he would have stayed in Bethlehem in spite of the prevailing famine.

But one might argue that it was a wise thing to do to leave a famine-stricken land for another land where there was plenty of food for his family. Surely that was a journey any father would undertake to save his dear ones from starvation. But Elimelech was a Jew and as such had the promise, "In the days of famine ye shall be satisfied." Had he firmly believed in the sovereignty of God, Elimelech would have remained in Bethlehem, knowing that need can never throttle God. Had he not declared that bread and water for His own would be sure? Alas, however, Elimelech did not live up to his wonderful name! In going down to Moab, he stepped out of the will of God, who had forbidden His people to have any association with the Moabites. In Moab, Elimelech and his two sons found graves. Yet such a wrong move was overruled by God, for as the result of it, Ruth the Moabitess returned to Bethlehem with Naomi, who was to become the ancestress of our blessed Lord.

ELIPHAL [Ĕl' Ĭ phăl] GOD IS JUDGE or HATH JUDGED. *The son of Ur,* and one of David's heroes (I Chron. 11:35).

ELIPHALET, ELIPHELET [Ĕ lĭph' a lĕt, Ĕ lĭph' e lĕt]—THE GOD OF DELIVERANCES or GOD IS ESCAPE.

1. *The last of David's sons* (II Sam. 5:16; I Chron. 3:8; 14:7). The names of Elphalet and Phaltiel are the same as Eliphalet.

2. *Another son of David* born after he made Jerusalem his home and center (I Chron. 3:6). Called Elpalet in I Chronicles 14:5.

3. *A son of Ahasbai,* and one of David's heroes (II Sam. 23:34).

4. *A son of Eshek* and descendant of Saul, a Benjamite (I Chron. 8:39).

5. *A leader of the sons of Adonikam* who returned from exile with Ezra (Ezra 8:13).

6. *A son of Hashum* who put away his foreign wife (Ezra 10:33).

ELIPHAZ [Ĕl' i phăz]—GOD IS FINE GOLD or GOD IS DISPENSER.

1. *A son of Esau* by Adah daughter of Elon (Gen. 36:4–16; I Chron. 1:35, 36).

2. *The chief of Job's three friends,* a descendant of Teman, son of Eliphaz from whom a part of Arabia took its name (Gen. 36:11; Job 2:11; 4:1; 15:1; 22:1; 42:7, 9; Jer. 49:20).

The Man Who Was a Religious Dogmatist

Teman was noted for its wisdom and this Temanite descendant was a law unto himself. His name means "refined gold" but his fine gold was that of self-glory and of self-opinion from which he would not budge. As a wise man he gloried in his wisdom, and represented the orthodox wisdom of his day. This wise man from the East declared that God was just and did not dispense happiness or misery in a despot fashion, committing people to what He deemed best.

Eliphaz was a religious dogmatist, basing all his deductions upon a solitary remarkable experience he had had, namely that of a spirit passing before his face, causing his hair to stand up (Job 4:12–16). As the result of this weird occasion he felt he had a message of divine justice to declare (Job 4:17–21). Thus his speeches, delivered with a sacerdotal pathos are hard, cruel and rigidly dogmatic. His folly was that he tried to press Job into the mold of his own experience.

In his first speech (Job 4, 5), Eliphaz begins by informing Job of all his affliction, namely, sin. Approaching Job in a courteous yet cold manner, Eliphaz seeks to prove that all calamity is judgment upon sin. The crux of his argument is: "Remember, I pray thee, who ever perished being innocent? or where were the righteous cut off?" (Job 4:7).

In his second speech Eliphaz reveals a spirit wounded by Job's sarcastic remarks (Job 15:2). He then proceeds to maintain his argument that Job is suffering because of his sin (Job 15:16).

In his third speech, Eliphaz definitely charges Job with sin (Job 22:5) and seeks to point out to him the pathway of restoration (Job 22:21).

ELIPHELEH [Ĕ lĭph' e leh]—JEHOVAH IS DISTINCTION or DISTINGUISHED. *A Levite singer and harpist* who had charge of the choral service when the Ark was returned (I Chron. 15:15–21). Also given as Eliphelehu.

ELISEUS Ĕl ĭ sē' us]—GOD IS SALVATION. *The Greek form of the name of Elisha* (Luke 4:27).

ELISHA [Ĕ lĭ' shă]—GOD IS SAVIOUR. *The son of Shaphat* of Abelmeholah, of the tribe of Issachar, the companion and successor of Elijah (I Kings 19:16–19; II Kings 2–13).

The Man Who Was a Model Leader

There is a striking difference between Elijah and Elisha, both of whom labored in the Northern Kingdom. Elijah's name means, *Jehovah my God* and suggests the *Law* while Elisha's name speaks of *grace—Jehovah my Saviour*.

Elisha left a peaceful occupation to become a model spiritual leader. Elijah prepared Elisha for his commission (II Kings 2:1–14), and the two became devoted to each other. Elisha's character is marked by mercy (II Kings 2:21), disinterestedness (II Kings 5) and toleration (II Kings 5:19). He earned a wonderful posthumous influence (II Kings 13:20, 21). What a victorious death was his (II Kings 13:14–19)! Summarizing the life of this prophet who spoke with the authority of an oracle of God (II Kings 3:16, 17), we see him etched as:

A man of indomitable faith (I Kings 19:20, 21; II Kings 1–18).
A man of swift action (II Kings 2:12–18).
A man of spiritual power (II Kings 2:19–22).
A man of dauntless courage (II Kings 3).
A man of deep sympathy (II Kings 4:1–7).
A man of God (II Kings 4:8–37).
A man of willing help (II Kings 4:38–41).
A man who merited blessing (II Kings 4:42–44).
A man of clear understanding (II Kings 5:1–19).
A man of force and might (II Kings 6:1–7).
A man who knew secrets (II Kings 6:8–23).
A man of remarkable foresight (II Kings 6:24–33; 7).
A man of unerring counsel (II Kings 8:1–6).
A man of tears and sorrow (II Kings 8:7–15).

Elisha suggests the ministry of Christ. On the whole, Elijah's work was destructive — he was the prophet of fire. Elisha's task was more merciful and beneficial. He had double the power of Elijah (II Kings 2:8, 9, 15), and consequently performed twice as many miracles as his former master. The following contrasts between these two prophets can be noted:

Elijah was a prophet of the wilderness;
    Elisha was a prince of the court.
Elijah had no settled home;
    Elisha enjoyed the peace of a home.
Elijah was known by his long hair and shaggy mantle;
    Elisha by his staff and bald head.
Elijah was mainly prophetical;
    Elisha's work was mainly miraculous.
Elijah's ministry was one of stern denunciation;
    Elisha's task was that of teaching and winning.
Elijah was a rebuker of kings;
    Elisha was a friend and admirer.
Elijah was a messenger of vengeance;
    Elisha was a messenger of mercy.
Elijah represented exclusiveness;
    Elisha stood for comprehension.
Elijah was fierce, fiery, energetic;

Elisha was gentle, sympathetic, simple.
Elijah was a solitary figure;
Elisha was more social.
Elijah had an extraordinary disappearance from earth;
Elisha's death was ordinary.

ELISHAH [Ĕ lī' shah]—*The eldest son of Javan,* grandson of Noah and founder of a tribal family (Gen. 10:4; I Chron. 1:7; Ezek. 27:7).

ELISHAMA [Ĕ lĭsh' a mă]—GOD IS HEARER or GOD HAS HEARD.
1. *The son of Ammihud* and prince of the Ephraimites at the outset of the wilderness sojourn (Num. 1:10; 2:18; 7:48, 53; 10:22; I Chron. 7:26).
2. *A son of David* born in Jerusalem (II Sam. 5:16; I Chron. 3:8).
3. *Another son of David,* who is also called Elishua (I Chron. 3:6).
4. *A son of Jekamiah,* a Judahite (I Chron. 2:41).
5. *Father of Nethaniah* and grandfather of Ishmael "of the seed royal" who lived at the time of the exile (II Kings 25:25; Jer. 41:1). Perhaps the same person as No. 4.
6. *A scribe or secretary to Jehoiakim* (Jer. 36:12, 20, 21).
7. *A priest* sent by Jehoshaphat to teach the people the Law (II Chron. 17:8).

ELISHAPHAT [Ĕ lĭsh' a phăt]—GOD IS JUDGE or HATH JUDGED. *One of the "captains of hundreds"* who supported Jehoiada in the revolt against Athaliah (II Chron. 23:1).

ELISHUA [Ĕl ĭ shu' ă]—GOD IS RICH or GOD IS SALVATION. *A son of David* born in Jerusalem (II Sam. 5:15; I Chron. 14:5). Likewise called Elishama in I Chronicles 3:6.

ELIUD [Ĕ lī' ud]—GOD IS MAJESTY OR GOD IS MY PRAISE. *The son of Achim* and father of Eleazar and ancestor of Christ (Matt. 1:14, 15).

ELIZAPHAN, ELZAPHAN [Ĕ lĭz' a phăn]—GOD IS PROTECTOR or HATH CONCEALED.
1. *The son of Uzziel,* chief ruler of the Kohathites when the census was taken at Sinai (Num. 3:30; I Chron. 15:8).
2. *The son of Parnach,* prince of the tribe of Zebulun in the wilderness (Num. 34:25).
3. *Ancestor of certain Levites* assisting in the revival under Hezekiah (II Chron. 29:13).

ELIZUR [Ĕ lī' zur]—GOD IS A ROCK. *The son of Shedeur,* and prince of the Reubenites who helped in the census Moses took (Num. 1:5; 2:10; 7:30, 35; 10:18).

ELKANAH [Ĕl′ kă nah]—GOD HATH CREATED or IS JEALOUS, POS-SESSING.
1. *A Levite* of the family of Kohath and brother of Assir and Abia-saph (Ex. 6:24; I Chron. 6:23).
2. *The father of the prophet Samuel,* and a descendant of No. 1 in the fifth generation (I Sam. 1:1–23; 2:11, 20; I Chron. 6:27, 34).
3. *A descendant of Levi* through Kohath (I Chron. 6:25, 36).
4. *A descendant of Kohath* (I Chron. 6:26, 35). Perhaps the same person as No. 3.
5. *An ancestor of Netophathite villagers* (I Chron. 9:16).
6. *A Korhite* who joined David at Ziklag (I Chron. 12:6).
7. *A Levite, doorkeeper* of the Ark (I Chron. 15:23). Perhaps the same as No. 6.
8. *An officer in king Ahaz′ household* and second only to the king, who was slain when Pekah invaded Judah (II Chron. 28: 7).

ELMODAM, ELMADAN [Ĕl mō′ dam]—THE GOD OF MEASURE. *The son of Er,* and ancestor of Joseph, Mary's husband (Luke 3:28).

ELNAAM [Ĕl′ na ăm]—GOD IS PLEASANT or PLEASANTNESS. *The father of David's guard,* Jeribai and Joshaviah (I Chron. 11:46).

ELNATHAN [Ĕl′ na thăn]—GOD HATH GIVEN OR IS GIVING.
1. *The father of Nehushta,* Jehoiakim's queen (II Kings 24:8; Jer. 26:22; 36:12, 25).
2. *Name of three Levites in Ezra's time* (Ezra 8:16).

ELON [Ē′ lŏn]—AN OAK or STRONG.
1. *The father of Esau's wife* (Gen. 26:34; 36:2).
2. *The second of Zebulun's three sons* (Gen. 46:14; Num. 26:26).
3. *The Zebulonite who judged Israel* for ten years (Judg. 12:11, 12). Elon is also the name of a town (Josh. 19:43; I Kings 4:9).

ELPAAL [Ĕl′ pă al]—GOD IS A REWARD or IS WORKING. *The son of Shaharaim,* a Benjamite and head of his father's house (I Chron. 8:11, 12, 18).

ELPALET [Ĕl′ pa lĕt]—GOD IS ESCAPE. *A son of David* (I Chron. 14:5). See Eliphalet (I Chron. 3:6).

ELUZAI [Ĕ lū′ za ī]—GOD IS MY STRENGTH. *A Benjamite* who joined David at Ziklag (I Chron. 12:5).

ELYMAS [Ĕl′ y̆ măs]—A MAGICIAN or A SORCERER. *The false prophet or Jewish impostor,* Bar-jesus, meaning son of Jesus or Joshua, who withstood Paul and Barnabas at Paphos in Cyprus (Acts 13:8).

ELZABAD [Ĕl' za băd]—GOD HATH ENDOWED or BESTOWED.
1. *A Gadite* who joined David at Ziklag (I Chron. 12:12).
2. *The Son of Shemaiah* and a Korhite Levite (I Chron. 26:7).

ELZAPHAN [Ĕl' za phăn]—GOD HAS CONCEALED or PROTECTED.
1. *The second son of Uzziel* and grandson of Levi (Ex. 6:22; Lev. 10:4). Called also Elizaphan.
2. *A prince of Zebulun*, who assisted in the division of Canaan (Num. 34:25).

EMMOR [Ĕm' môr]—AN ASS. *The father of Sychem* (Acts 7:16). Same as Hamor.

ENAN [Ē' nan]—HAVING EYES or A FOUNTAIN. *The father of Ahira*, of the tribe of Naphtali, who assisted in the Sinai census (Num. 1:15; 2:29; 7:78, 83; 10:27).

ENEAS [Ē' ne ăs]—I PRAISE or PRAISE OF JEHOVAH. *A man of Lydia*, healed by Peter (Acts 9:33, 34).

ENOCH, HENOCH [Ē' nŏch, Hē' nŏch]—TEACHER, INITIATED, DEDICATED.
1. *The eldest son of Cain*, who had a city called after him (Gen. 4:17, 18; I Chron. 1:3).
2. *A son of Jared*, a descendant of Seth and father of Methuselah (Gen. 5:18–23; Luke 3:37; Heb. 11:5; Jude 14).

The Man Who Was Missed

In some six verses the Bible sets forth the brief biography of this Old Testament saint—but what a biography! We know nothing of the rank or profession of Enoch. Two things of great interest characterize him, namely, his holy life on earth and his glorious exit from earth.

Enoch walked with God. Twice over we are reminded of this evident fact. The wicked are "without God." Enoch was at peace with God. Although born a child of wrath, he became a child of grace. He must have been at peace with God; two cannot walk together unless they be agreed (Amos 3:3).

Enoch enjoyed close communion with God. What a real union of hearts the repeated phrase, "walked with God" implies! What sweet hours of holy and happy intercourse God and Enoch must have had as they communed with each other. There was never a cloud between their fellowship. God was a pleasure to Enoch, and Enoch pleased God.

Enoch was separated from the world. This seventh man from Adam did not walk in the way of the sinners of his corrupt age. His character and conduct were a distinct rebuke to the godless around. Jude tells us that Enoch functioned as a prophet, declaring God's just judgment upon the unrighteousness of his time.

Enoch's life was one of progress. Walking with God implies a steady progress in his course. He did not walk for awhile and then stand still. Each day found him nearer the divine goal. In unbroken companionship with his Friend, he found himself more weaned from the world and more ripe for heaven. He did not attempt to walk alone to heaven. He walked *with* God, and as he took each step his eyes were fixed on his heavenly Companion.

Enoch had an unusually glorious end. He is the only one of the line of whom it is not said that "he died." He was not—God took him. "He was not" suggests that his friends sought for him. He was a missing person they could not trace. "God took him," which means he was translated that he should not taste death. Among the millions upon millions of men who have lived, only two out of the vast number never died—Enoch and Elijah! Andrew Bonar has the sweet suggestion that God and Enoch were in the habit of taking a long walk together every day and that one day God said to his companion, "Why go home? Come all the way with Me." Thus at 365 years of age—a year for every day of our year—God took His servant directly to heaven.

ENOS, ENOSH [Ē′ nos, Ē′ nosh]—MAN IS HIS FRAILTY. *The son of Seth* and father of Cainan, he lived for 905 years (Gen. 4:26; 5:6–10; I Chron. 1:1). He was also an ancestor of Christ (Luke 3:38). It is mentioned in connection with the birth of Enos that it was then that man began to call upon the name of the Lord. This first mention of recourse to prayer is suggestive. Men were somehow driven by sickness, frailty and dependence to cry for health and help to the invisible Creator.

EPAENETUS [Ĕ păen′ e tŭs]—LAUDABLE, WORTHY OF PRAISE. *A native of Asia or Achaia,* greeted by Paul as "my well-beloved" (Rom. 16:5).

EPAPHRAS [Ĕp′ a phrăs]—CHARMING or FOAMY. *A fellow laborer* of Paul and in some sense his fellow-prisoner (Col. 1:7; 4:12; Philem. 23.

The Man Who Was a Giant in Prayer

This Colossian is described in many ways. He was Paul's "fellow-servant" and "servant," his "fellow-prisoner," and a "faithful minister." He was also Paul's representative at Colossae where he had founded the church (Col. 1:7), and sought under Paul's advice to combat prevalent heresies there. The apostle had affection for Epaphras, who ministered unto his need and the need of others.

It is in his prayer-ministry, however, that Epaphras is conspicuous. This giant in prayer knew how to lay all before the Lord, and laboring in secret, made the saints to be perfect and complete in their *standing* through his *kneeling.* He "strove earnestly in his prayers" for the Colossians. He wrestled in prayer that they might be perfect in the perfection of Christ, and "fully assured in all the will of God."

Paul also testified to the perseverance as well as the prayers of Epaphras. He knew how to *toil* on behalf of the saints of God. He was practical as well as prayerful.

His prayers for the stability and maturity of others were numerous, continuous and strenuous. Epaphras brought to Paul at Rome a report of the Colossian Church where he had ministered in Paul's stead, an account that cheered his heart and resulted in the writing of the Colossian Epistle which Epaphras took back with him to his flock. Can we say that we are true successors of the devoted servant of God? Like him, do we know how to wrestle in agony of prayer? (Rom. 15:30). Epaphras also manifested great *zeal* or properly "great labour of anxiety" for those under his care. Too few of us are concerned about the spiritual welfare of others.

EPAPHRODITUS [Ĕ păph ro dī' tus]—LOVELY, HANDSOME, CHARMING. *A trusted messenger between Paul and the churches* (Phil. 2:25; 4:18). Epaphras is a shortened form of this common name.

The Man with a Kind Heart

How fully and fittingly Paul describes the commendable character of this kindly man who went as Paul's representative to the Philippian Church!

He was a *brother*—a term implying a spiritual relationship.

He was a *companion in labor*—their hearts beat as one in the cause they both loved.

He was a *fellow soldier*—together they endured all the hardness and discipline of daring and suffering which discipleship involves (II Tim. 3:14).

He was a *messenger* — or "apostle" as the word really is; and he was ever the Lord's messenger in the Lord's message.

He was a *sacrificial witness*. What a brief but blessed biography Paul gives us of his dear companion. He "ministered to my wants" — "longed after you all" — caused much "heaviness" because of his fatal sickness — was mercifully spared lest his death should have brought "sorrow upon sorrow" to Paul.

He *regarded not his life*. Literally he gambled his life to assist and bless the Philippians. How rich was the Early Church in leaders who were entirely abandoned to God, that through their consecrated lives their fellow-saints might be filled with all the "fulness of God"!

EPHAH [Ē' phah]—OBSCURITY or DARKNESS.

1. *A son of Jahdai,* a Judahite (I Chron. 2:47).

2. *A son of Midian,* son of Abraham by Keturah and father of a tribal family (Gen. 25:4; I Chron. 1:33; Isa. 60:6). Also the name of Caleb's concubine (I Chron. 2:46); and description of a measure (Ex. 16:36).

EPHAI [Ē' phāi]—FATIGUED or OBSCURED. *A Netophathite,* who was promised protection but was subsequently massacred by Ishmael (Jer. 40:8, 13; 41:3).

EPHER [Ē' phûr]—MULE or YOUNG CALF.
1. *The second son of Midian,* son of Abraham (Gen. 25:4; I Chron. 1:33).
2. *A son of Ezra,* a Judahite (I Chron. 4:17).
3. *A chief of the half-tribe of Manasseh* (I Chron. 5:24).

EPHLAL [Ĕph' lăl]—JUDICIOUS or JUDGING. *A descendant of Pharez.* through Jerahmeel (I Chron. 2:37).

EPHOD [Ē' phŏd]—COVERING. *The father of Hanniel,* prince of Manasseh, who assisted Joshua in the division of Canaan (Num. 34:23). Also the name of a priestly garment (Ex. 25:7).

EPHRAIM [Ē' phră Im]—DOUBLY FRUITFUL. *The second son of Joseph* by Asenath and founder of a tribal family (Gen. 41:52; Num. 1:10). Also the name of a town (II Sam. 13:23), a city (John 11:54), a gate of Jerusalem (II kings 14:13), and a wood (II Sam. 18:6).

The Man Who Represented Fruitful Pruning

In Jacob's prophetic blessing of his sons the prominent feature of Joseph's portion was that of *fruitfulness,* a prophecy receiving its fulfilment in the double tribe springing from Joseph, namely, Ephraim and Manasseh, like two branches out of the parent stem. Joseph himself was "a fruitful bough" because he had been so well pruned. The sharp knife of adversity led to the sweet fruit, and the fruitful bough ran over the wall. Ephraim and Manasseh were the heads of most fruitful tribes. The Book of Hosea, however, reveals how the blessings showered upon these tribes were ill requited.

Joseph named his second son Ephraim because as he said "God hath caused me to be fruitful in *the land of my affliction."* Here Joseph, although a Hebrew, speaks as a Gentile. Ephraim was the fruitfulness of his father in the land of Egypt as a Gentile prince, and Jacob rightly calls his seed "the fulness of the Gentiles," when he adopts him on his dying bed.

The representative man of the tribe of Ephraim is Joshua. No other like him arose afterwards in this tribe. Jeroboam, the son of Nebat, founder of the kingdom of Ephraim, was the exact opposite to Joshua in faith and conduct.

The significance of Ephraim's name must not be lost upon us. What Joseph said of him indicated that God had brought good out of evil, privilege out of pain, triumph out of tragedy. In spite of any affliction that may be ours, do we remain fruitful in every good work? To Joseph the birth of Ephraim came as luscious fruit after the severe pruning of ill-treatment, slavery and prison. See John 15:1-8.

EPHRON [Ē' phron]—STRONG or FAWN. *A son of Zohar* a Hittite, from whom Abraham purchased a field with the cave in which he buried Sarah (Gen. 23:8). Also the name of a mountain (Josh. 15:9).

ER [Ûr]—AWAKE or ON THE WATCH.
1. *The eldest son of Judah* by the daughter of Shuah the Canaanite, whose wickedness, which is not described, merited death (Gen. 38:3–7; 46:12; Num. 26:19; I Chron. 2:3).
2. *A son of Shelah,* youngest son of Judah by the above Shuah (I Chron. 4:21).
3. *An Ancestor of Christ* who lived between David and Zerubbabel (Luke 3:28).

ERAN [Ē' răn]—WATCHFUL. *A son of Ephraim's* eldest son Shuthelah and founder of a tribal family (Num. 26:36).

ERASTUS [Ē răs ' tus]—BELOVED.
1. *A Christian who assisted Paul* and whom he sent into Macedonia (Acts 19:22; II Tim. 4:20).
2. *A high official of Corinth,* a convert of Paul's (Rom. 16:23). Several authorities suggest that these two men are the same person.

ERI [Ē' rī]—MY WATCHER. *A son of Gad* and founder of a tribal family (Gen. 46:16; Num. 26:16).

ESAIAS [Ē sā' ias]—JEHOVAH HAS SAVED. *The Greek form of Isaiah* (Matt. 3:3).

ESAR-HADDON [Ē' sar-hăd' don]—VICTORIOUS or ASHUR HATH GIVEN BROTHERS. *The favorite son of Sennacherib* and one of the greatest kings of Assyria, equally eminent as a military leader and a political ruler (II Kings 19:37; Ezra 4:2; Isa. 37:38).

ESAU [Ē' sôu]—HAIRY. *The eldest son of Isaac* and twin brother of Jacob by Rebekah. His name is associated with his appearance at birth (Gen. 25:25).

The Man Who Bartered His Birthright

This cunning hunter and man of the field (Gen. 25:27) supplies us with one of the tragic biographies among the men of the Bible. He is prominent in God's portrait gallery as the man rejected of God because he had sold his birthright. Let us briefly sketch what Scripture records of "Esau, who is Edom." Had he retained his birthright we might have read "Esau, who is Israel." The wrong act, however, left a black mark upon his future history.

He was a profane person. What a terrible epitome! It is like a label fastened to Esau as he disappears from Bible history (Heb. 12:16). The work "profane" does not mean that he delighted in profanity, but that he was a man of the earth who lived for worldly things and nothing else. With many good qualities, Esau was of the earth, earthy.

He sold his birthright. As the elder son of his father, even although he came from the womb only a half-hour before his twin brother, Jacob, he was entitled by law and custom to receive twice as much as a younger son's portion, and to be regarded in due time as the head of the family. But we all know the story of how, for a mess of pottage, he bartered away his spiritual and temporal rights. The record says that Esau sold his birthright because he "despised" it. How easily some men part with the rich blessings they are heirs to!

His was a fruitless repentance. Esau lifted up his voice and cried, "Bless me, even me also, O my father!" But his repentant prayer was directed, not to God, but to Isaac. In the whole of Genesis Esau does not mention the name of God. Had Esau's repentance been Godward, what a different story we would have had! Esau only repented of *his bargain,* not of *his sin.* Such a bargain turned out to be a bad one, and he was sorry for it. Further, all Esau sought was *restitution,* not *pardon.* He had lost one blessing, and sought another.

Under grace the penitent sinner who has wasted his substance has a Saviour to turn to, and repenting of his sin, finds mercy. Esau, even with his tears, found no mercy. God was not in his thoughts, and he had therefore to abide by the consequences of what he had brought upon himself. Yet he learned his lesson, for Esau called his firstborn Eliphaz, "strength of God," and his second son Reuel, "joy of God."

ESHBAAL [Ĕsh-bā' al]—A MAN OF BAAL. *The fourth son of Saul,* the same as Ishbosheth, meaning "a man of shame" (I Chron. 8:33; 9:39).

ESHBAN [Ĕsh' ban]—INTELLIGENCE or MAN OF UNDERSTANDING. *A son of Dishon,* son of Seir the Horite (Gen. 36:26; I Chron. 1:41).

ESHCOL [Ĕsh' cŏl]—CLUSTER OF GRAPES. *One of the three Amorite brothers* who helped Abraham in his pursuit of the four kings who captured Lot (Gen. 14:13, 24). Also the name of the valley or brook of Eshcol, famous for its grapes (Num. 13:23, 24; 32:9; Deut. 1:24).

ESHEK [Ĕ' shĕk]—STRIFE or VIOLENCE. *A descendant of Saul* through Jonathan, a Benjamite (I Chron. 8:39).

ESHTEMOA, ESHTEMOH [Ĕsh te mō' ă, Ĕsh' te mōh]—OBEDIENCE. *A son of Hodiah,* a descendant of Ezra, a Maachathite. (I Chron. 4:17, 19). Also the name of a town (Josh. 15:50).

ESHTON [Ĕsh' ton]—REST. *A grandson of Chelab* through Mehir, a Judahite (I Chron. 4:11, 12).

ESLI [Ĕs′ lĭ]—GOD AT MY SIDE or JEHOVAH HATH RESERVED. *An ancestor of Christ* who lived after the captivity and likely the same person named Azaliah in the genealogy (Luke 3:25).

ESROM [Ĕs′ rom]—ENCLOSURE. *Son of Phares in Christ's genealogy* (Matt. 1:3; Luke 3:32). Possibly the same person as Hezron.

ETAM [Ē′ tăm]—WILD BEASTS′ LAIR. *A name found in the list of Judah's descendants* but likely the name of a place rather than a person (I Chron. 4:3, 32; II Chron. 11:6; Judg. 15:8).

ETHAN [Ē′ than]—ANCIENT, FIRMNESS or PERPLEXITY.
1. *The Ezrahite* renowned for his wisdom in Solomon's time (I Kings 4:31).
2. *A son of Zerah,* son of Judah (I Chron. 2:6, 8).
3. *A descendant of Gershon,* son of Levi (I Chron. 6:42).
4. *A descendant of Merari,* son of Levi (I Chron. 6:44; 15:17, 19).

ETHBAAL [Ĕth bā′ al]—WITH HIM IS BAAL or BAAL'S MAN. *A king of Sidon,* father-in-law of Ahab, who held the throne of Tyre for thirty-two years (I Kings 16:31).

ETHNAN [Ĕth′ nan]—GIFT or HIRE. *A son of Helah,* of the family of Ashur, of the family of Hezron (I Chron. 4:7).

ETHNI [Ĕth′ nĭ]—BOUNTIFUL or MY GIFT. *A Gershonite Levite* and an ancestor of Asaph whom David set over the service of song (I Chron. 6:41). Likely the same person named Jeaterai in I Chronicles 6:21.

EUBULUS [Eū bū lus]—WELL-ADVISED or PRUDENT. *A disciple* at *Rome* who, with others, saluted Timothy. [II Tim. 4:21].

EUTYCHUS [Eū′ tў chŭs]—HAPPY or FORTUNATE. *A young man of Troas* who fell asleep during Paul's long sermon, fell off his window seat, broke his neck and was taken up as dead. Paul, however, revived him (Acts 20:7–12). Dr. Alexander Whyte speaks of Eutychus as "the father of all such as fall asleep under sermons."

EVI [Ē′vĭ]—DESIRE. *One of the five kings of Midian,* slain in the war waged by Moses against the Midianites because they seduced the Israelites to licentious idolatry (Num. 31:8; Josh. 13:21).

EVIL-MERODACH [Ē′ vĭl-mē rō′ dach]—MAN OF GOD MERODACH or MARDUK. *The son and successor of Nebuchadnezzar* who reigned for some eight years. He it was who released Jehoiachin whom his father had kept imprisoned for thirty-seven years (II kings 25:27; Jer. 52:31).

EZBAI [Ĕz' ba ī]—BEAUTIFUL. *The father of one of David's thirty heroes* (I Chron. 11:37). Referred to as Paarai the Arbite in II Samuel 23:35.

EZBON [Ĕz' bŏn]—SPLENDOR.
1. *The son of Gad* and founder of a Gadite family (Gen. 46:16). Also spoken of as Ozni in Numbers 26:16.
2. *The son of Bela,* son of Benjamin, and head of his father's house (I Chron. 7:7).

EZEKIAS [Ĕz e kī' as]—JEHOVAH IS STRENGTH. *The Greek form of Hezekiah* (Matt. 1:9, 10).

EZEKIEL [Ĕ zē kĭ el]—GOD IS STRONG or THE MAN GOD STRENGTHENS. *The son of Buzi, a priest* who prophesied to the exiles by the river Chebar, and fourth of "The Greater Prophets" (Ezek. 1:3; 24:24).
The Man Who Was Every Inch a Churchman
Little is known of this man of a priestly family (Ezek. 1:3; 30:1). His father's name, Buzi, was a Gentile one (Gen. 22:21; Job 32:2, 6). Referring to himself as "a priest," Ezekiel was akin to Jeremiah who was also a prophet and a priest. Because of his priestly lineage, levitical tendencies appear in his book (Ezek. 40–46), as well as foregleams of the high priestly character of the Messiah (Ezek. 21:25; 45:22). Ezekiel is every inch a churchman, and his strong ecclesiastical characteristics pervade and give tone to his prophecies.

Ezekiel's call came in his thirtieth year (Ezek. 1:1), in the fifth year and on the fifth day of the month of king Jehoiachin's captivity (Ezek. 1, 2). With the call to service there came the impartation of the prophetic gift (Ezek. 3:22). The theme of the prophetic message he was commissioned to proclaim was the same as that of Jeremiah, namely, the downfall of Judah and Jerusalem with judgment upon foreign nations. The keynote of his book is: through tribulation into rest. Residing with a company of captives by the river Chebar (Ezek. 1:1; 8:1) he labored as "a prophet of the iron harp."

With divine authority Ezekiel dispelled illusions, denounced false prophets, declared repentance, restoration and renewal. He was a true shepherd of souls. Dr. Donald Fraser wrote of him: "Like a giant, he wrestled against Jewish degeneracy and Babylonish pride. Remote as we are from his times, we are stirred by his vivid imagination and his power of fervid denunciation and strenuous appeal. Even when the understanding is puzzled, the heart burns inwardly at the recital of Ezekiel's visions and those burdens which the Lord laid upon his spirit."

Ezekiel was happy in his home life (Ezek. 8:1). God, however, revealed to him that the desire of his eyes would die of a sudden sickness, which his wife did during the siege of Jerusalem. Although her death was a heavy blow, yet Ezekiel was not allowed to publicly weep or lament her passing. His anguish was to serve as a sign that Jerusalem would be destroyed without wailing or lamentation (Ezek. 24:15–27). After a prophetic ministry lasting for at least twenty-two years, tradition has it that Ezekiel was put to death by his fellow exiles because of his faithfulness and boldness in denouncing them for their idolatry.

Several aspects of the prophet's life can be applied with profit to ourselves:

I. He was an exile (Ezek. 1:1); so are we (Heb. 11:13; I Pet. 2:11).

II. He was an ambassador (Ezek 1:1; 2:1–6; 3:1–3); so are we (Eph. 6:20).

III. He was a watchman (Ezek. 3:17–20); so are we (Heb. 13:17).

IV. He was a sign (12:1–7); so are we (I Tim. 1:10).

EZER, EZAR [Ē′ zûr, E′ zar]—TREASURE or HELP.

1. *A son of Ephraim* slain by the inhabitants of Gath while stealing their cattle (I Chron. 7:21).

2. *A priest of Nehemiah's time* (Neh. 12:42).

3. *A man of Judah* and descendant of Hur (I Chron. 4:4). Perhaps the Ezra of I Chronicles 4:17.

4. *A valiant Gadite* who joined David at Ziklag (I Chron. 12:9).

5. *A Levite* who shared in the repair of the wall (Neh. 3:19).

6. *A son of Seir* the Horite (Gen. 36:21, 27, 30; I Chron. 1:38,42).

EZRA, EZRAH [Ĕz′ rä]—HELP or MY HELPER.

1. *The head of one of the twenty-two courses of priests* that came up from exile with Zerubbabel and Jeshua (Neh. 10:2–8; 12:1, 13). Probably the Azariah of Ezra 7:1.

2. *A descendant of Judah* through Caleb (I Chron. 4:17).

3. *The famous scribe and priest* descended from Hilkiah the high priest (Ezra 7:1–25).

The Man Who Honored Scripture

Ezra or I Esdras, as he is called in the Vulgate, was the son or grandson of Seraiah, the high priest who was slain after the taking of Jerusalem (II Kings 25:18, 21). As a priest, he was descended from Zadok and from Phinehas (Ezra 7:1–6). He was also a ready scribe (Ezra 7:6, 11, 12, 20), which occupation implied three things:

He was a student and as such had a duty to himself to study the will of God as revealed in His Word, that he might hide it in his own heart (Ezra 7:10).

He was an interpreter with a duty to his own generation in teaching his fellow exiles what he had learned. In this way he gave the "sense" of the Word (Neh. 8:2–8).

He was a copyist, which meant that this learned man had a duty to his own race in multiplying and preserving intact the very words of God (Ezra 7:10, 11).

Ezra was also an able administrator. He conducted the Jewish exiles back to Jerusalem in peace and safety, and establishing himself as their leader, reformed them with a vigorous hand. Summarizing his life and labors, we can say that this Old Testament reformer was:

I. A man of deep humility and self-denial (Ezra 7:10–15; 10:6).

II. A man of great learning with a fervent zeal for God's honor (Ezra 7:10; 8:21–23).

III. A man of great trustworthiness (Ezra 7:13, 26).

IV. A man anxious to commend his cause to others (Ezra 8:2–20).

V. A man who knew how to pray (Ezra 8:21; 10:1).

VI. A man deeply grieved over the sins of the people (Ezra 9:3; 10:6).

VII. A man who spared no pains to bring the people to repentance.

Traditional history says that it was Ezra who instituted the Great Synagogue, became its first President, settled the Canon of Jewish Scripture and began the building of synagogues in Jewish provincial towns. Ezra lived to a good old age, dying like Moses at the age of 120 years.

Ezra was a studious, prayerful ecclesiastic who set his heart to realize definite ideals:

To know the Law of Jehovah. What a passion was his to ascertain, explain and administer that Law!

To will to do the Law. Ezra not only taught the Law but urged the people to serve the Lord with heart, mouth and mind.

The key words of the Book of Ezra are Restoration, Reorganization, Reformation. The emphasis is upon the preservation of the national and religious life of the people. The leading ideas of the book are:

The Purity of Worship
The Sanctity of the Sabbath
The Power of Prayer
The Faithfulness of God
Order in Religion and Delight in Praise
Mutual help in Service
The Purity of Common life.

EZRI [Ez' rī]—GOD IS A HELP. *Overseer of laborers* who tilled David's fields (I Chron. 27:26).

F

FELIX [Fē' lĭx]—HAPPY, PROSPEROUS. *A cruel Roman governor of Judea,* appointed by the Emperor Claudius, whose freedman he was (Acts 23:24, 26; 24:2–27; 25:14). Felix is described by Tacitus as a bad and cruel governor, even though the title of "most excellent" was given to him.

The Man Who Procrastinated

As a true preacher, Paul pressed home the truth until it pricked the conscience of Felix so much so that he "trembled." He did not resent Paul's plain speaking but postponed the interview "till a more convenient season." Such a "convenient season," however, did not come, and Felix became a type of many whose consciences are stirred by the preached Word, but whose hopes of eternal security are ruined by a like procrastination. The two sworn enemies of the soul are "Yesterday" and "Tomorrow."

Yesterday slays its thousands. Past sins plunge many into darkness and despair. Priceless opportunities were trampled upon, and the harvest is past. But God says there is mercy still and free forgiveness through repentance.

Tomorrow slays its tens of thousands. Vows, promises, resolutions are never fulfilled. "Some other time," many say, when urged to repent and believe. They fail to realize that *now* is the acceptable time. How pitiful it is that the *convenient season* never dawns for them! The pathway to their hell is strewn with good resolutions, and as they cross "The Great Divide," the mocking voice cries out: "Too late! Too late!"

FESTUS [Fĕs' tus]—JOYFUL, FESTAL, PROSPEROUS. *Porcius Festus was a Roman governor of Judea* in the reign of Nero (Acts 24:27; 25; 26: 24, 32).

The Man Who Called Paul Mad

Felix, seeking to court the favor of the Jews, left Paul in prison, thinking that the Jews would compensate him for such a favor. This act was an investment in iniquity. But the Jewish complaints against Felix led to his recall by Nero, so Paul passed into the hands of Festus, Felix' successor. Festus, not knowing much about Jewish matters, brought the question of Paul's imprisonment before Agrippa who was conversant with many aspects of the Jewish religion. It perplexed Festus to know that Paul, a Jew with the utmost reverence for the Law and the worship of the Temple, was yet hated by his compatriots.

Agrippa agreed to hear Paul for himself, so we come to the apostle's masterly defense before the king and Bernice. With a wonderful vividness Paul gave a retrospective analysis of his former life and then a sketch of his present sacrificial witness to Christ as the risen, glorified Son of God. Such was the impact of Paul's remarkable appeal that Festus, the Roman governor, forgot the usual dignity of his office and burst out into a loud laugh of scorn saying: "Paul, thou art beside thyself; much learning doth make thee mad."

With characteristic calmness and with a firm control of his natural impulses so that no unguarded utterance might escape his lips, Paul answered Festus in all courtesy: "I am not mad, most noble Festus; but speak forth the words of truth and soberness." In his incomparable *Bible Characters,* Alexander Whyte says that a single word will sometimes immortalize a man. "What will you give me?" was all Judas said. So with one word Festus is as well known to us as if a whole chapter had been written about him. He said Paul was *mad*.

But the uncontrolled and unbecoming outburst of Festus did not stagger Paul. Did they not say of his Master, for whom he had suffered much "He is beside Himself"? The apostle counted it a privilege to share his Master's madness. Later on, he wrote about being a fool for His sake. He knew that no man is a true Christian who is not the world's fool (I Cor. 3:18; 4:10; II Cor. 11:23). All around us are those who have never been borne along by the enthusiasm of God, who deem the spiritual man to be mad (Hos. 9:7).

FORTUNATUS [Fôr tū nā' tus]—PROSPEROUS. *A believer from Corinth* who, with Stephanus and Achaicus, visited Paul and refreshed his spirit by their coming [I Cor. 16:17). A. J. Maclean comments that Fortunatus was probably baptized by Paul (I Cor. 1:16), and that Lightfoot felt that he may well have been alive forty years later and could therefore have been the Fortunatus mentioned by Clement in his *Epistle*. Evidently he was among the more spiritual believers in the Corinthian Church.

G

GAAL [Gā' al]—REJECTION or CONTEMPT. *A son of Ebed,* who aided the Shechemites when he organized the rising against Abimelech (Judg. 9:26–41). Gaal was defeated and driven out of Shechem, and terrible vengeance overtook the city.

GABBAI [Găb' ba ī]—INGATHERER or TAXGATHERER. *A Benjamite* who consented to live in Jerusalem after the captivity (Neh. 11:8).

GAD [Găd]—GOOD FORTUNE, A TROOP or A SEER.

1. *The seventh son of Jacob,* first-born of Zilpah, Leah's maid, and full brother of Asher. A tribe also sprang from Gad (Gen. 30:11; 35:26; 46:16; 49:19; Ex. 1:4; I Chron. 5:11; 12:14).

The Man of Enlargement

No name in all the twelve tribes of Israel is so much played upon in Jacob's blessing as the name of Gad, meaning "a troop." Invaders and robbers might try to plunder Gad but victory would be his with resultant enlargement. Jacob predicted for the tribe of Gad a time of sore conflict, yet of final conquest. "He shall overcome at last." God enabled Gad to discomfit and defeat his foes (I Chron. 5:18–22).

The men of Gad had faces like "the faces of lions," and when David needed help, the Gadites of lion-like character befriended the fugitive king. "They put to flight all them of the valleys, both of the east and of the west." These Gadite helpers of David "executed the justice of the Lord, and His judgments with Israel." Jephthah the Gileadite, of the tribe of Gad, judged Israel six years after delivering the nation from Ammonite oppression.

How fortunate Gad was to have God to enlarge him! "The place where we dwell... is too strait for us." Such an energetic, aggressive tribe could not remain static, so their inheritance was extended beyond its original limits until it covered the whole of Gilead. How loathe we are to possess our spiritual possessions! May ours be the enlargements of heart David prayed for (Ps. 119:32)! May ours also be the constant victorious Christian experience!

2. The prophet who joined David when in "the hold," and through whose advice he left it for the forest of Hareth (I Sam. 22:5; II Sam. 24:11–19; I Chron. 21:9–19; II Chron. 29:25). Gad, "the king's seer," announced God's judgment upon David for numbering the people. "The arm of flesh will fail us, we dare not trust our own." Gad the prophet advised the erection of the altar, and is also before us as an associate of the prophet Nathan.

GADDI [Găd′ dī]—BELONGING TO FORTUNE or FORTUNATE. *A son of Susi,* and a chief of Manasseh who was sent out to explore Canaan (Num. 13:11).

GADDIEL [Găd′ dĭ el]—GOD IS FORTUNE BRINGER or GOD HATH GIVEN FORTUNE. *The son of Sodi,* and a chief of Zebulun, the tribe's representative in the exploration of Canaan (Num. 13:10).

GADI [Gă′ dī]—FORTUNATE or A GADITE. *The father of king Menahem,* who killed Shallum and succeeded him as king of Israel (II Kings 15:14, 17).

GAHAM [Gă′ hăm]—BLACKNESS or FLAMING. *A son of Nahor* and his concubine Reumah (Gen. 22:24).

GAHAR [Gă′ här]—HIDING PLACE or PROSTRATION. *Head of the family of Nethinims* whose posterity returned with Zerubbabel from captivity (Ezra 2:47; Neh. 7:49).

GAIUS [Gā′ ius]—I AM GLAD. This common Roman name is shared by four men, and some writers find it difficult to differentiate between them.

1. *A companion of Paul* and native of Macedonia. He was seized in the riot at Ephesus (Acts 19:29).

2. *A man of Derbe* in Lycaonia and likewise a companion of Paul. This Gaius of Derbe (Acts 20:4) is sometimes identified as Gaius at Corinth — see next Gaius.

3. *The Corinthian converted and baptized by Paul,* and who was the apostle's host while he was in Corinth (Rom. 16:23; I Cor. 1:14).

4. *The godly man to whom John sent his third epistle* (III John 1). It is evident that the Apostle of Love had a deep affection for this saint he called "the wellbeloved." It would seem as if John had at sometime led him to Christ (III John 4). John desired the material, physical and spiritual prosperity of Gaius (III John 2, 3). The apostle also commended him for his faithful care of ministering brethren — a responsibility some seem to neglect these days (III John 5–8).

GALAL [Gā' lăl]—ROLLING OF ONE'S DAY UPON THE LORD.
1. *The name of a Levite* who returned from exile (I Chron. 9:15).
2. *Another Levite,* the son of Jeduthun who came up from exile (I Chron. 9:16; Neh. 11:17).

GALLIO [Găl' lĭ ō]—HE THAT SUCKS. *The Roman proconsul of Achia,* the elder brother of Seneca, described by Seneca as a man of extreme amiability of character (Acts 18:12, 14, 17).

The Man with a Righteous Carelessness

The antagonistic Jews of Corinth brought Paul before Gallio, charging the apostle with having persuaded men to "worship God contrary to the law" (v. 13). But when Gallio realized that Paul was not guilty of "villainy," but only of questions which the Jews as a self-administering community were competent to decide for themselves, he dismissed them, saying he "cared for none of those things," meaning questions concerning Jewish law. Because of his statement, Gallio has been crowned with a condemnation he does not deserve. His apparent carelessness proves:

I.   There are more important concerns in life than the settlement of frivolous and petty disputes.

II.   There should be that determination not to meddle needlessly in other men's affairs. It is folly to judge questions we do not understand.

III.   There should be patience, leaving trifling wrongs to arrange and compose themselves. Blessed are the peacemakers.

IV.   There should be the firm resolve to be just and impartial rather than to curry favor and win thereby a little passing popularity. Righteousness should always be placed above policy. Thus we can learn from Gallio's attitude lessons both profitable and wise.

GAMALIEL [Gå mā' lĭ el]—GOD IS RECOMPENSER OT THE GIFT OR REWARD OF GOD.
1. *A chief of Manasseh* chosen to aid in taking the census in the wilderness (Num. 1:10; 2:20; 7:54, 59; 10:23).
2. *The renowned Doctor of Jewish law* (Acts 5:34), and instructor of the apostle Paul (Acts 22:3). It may be that Paul's instruction in the Law began when he was about the age of twelve (Luke 2:42). Like his Master, Paul, as Saul of Tarsus, sat in the midst of the doctors, hearing and asking questions. These learned men sat in a high chair,

and the scholars on the floor and were thus literally at their masters' feet (see Deut. 33:3).

The Man Who Was Tolerant

Ellicott speaks of Gamaliel as one of the heroes of rabbinical history. His dramatic speech before the Council on Peter's behalf, and the part he played in the instruction of Paul mark him out a man worthy of note. Gamaliel was the son of Simeon, perhaps of Luke 2:25, and the grandson of the great Hillel, the representative of the best school of Pharisaism, the tolerant and largehearted rival of the narrow and fanatic Shammai. Through the weight of years and authority Gamaliel rose to eminence and counseled with moderation.

Being of the house and lineage of David, this cultured teacher had full sympathy with the claims of Christ, who was welcomed as the Son of David. Perhaps he was influenced to a decision for Christ through contact with a brother-teacher like Nicodemus (John 3:1, 2; 7:50, 51) and can therefore be included among the many chief rulers who secretly believed in Christ (John 12:42, 43).

Digging beneath Gamaliel's able and successful performance before the Council at Jerusalem, Alexander Whyte feels that he was only a "fluent and applauded opportunist" and warns young men against his presentation. "He was a politician, but he was not a true churchman or statesman. He was held in repute by the people; but the people were blind, and they loved to be led by blind leaders, and Gamaliel was one of them." With all his insight and lawyerlike ability, Gamaliel turned all things completely upsidedown when he sat in judgment, and gave his carefully balanced caution concerning the Son of God, comments Dr. Whyte.

Perhaps the renowned author of *Bible Characters* is right when he suggests that Gamaliel made the tremendous and irreparable mistake of approaching Jesus Christ and His cause on the side of policy, handling Him as a matter open to argument and debate. But Christ is an Ambassador of Reconciliation, and we are not permitted to sit in judgment on God, and on His message of mercy to us. Without apology Dr. Whyte pronounces Gamaliel as "a liberal long before his time. He was all for toleration, and for a free church in a free state, in an intolerant and persecuting day."

GAMUL [Gā' mŭl]—MATURED or RECOMPENSED. *A priest,* descendant of Aaron, and leader of the twenty-second course in the sanctuary service in David's time (I Chron. 24:17).

GAREB (Gā' rĕb]—REVILER or ROUGH. *One of David's worthies* (II Sam. 23:38; I Chron. 11:40). Also the name of a hill near Jerusalem (Jer. 31:39).

GASHMU [Găsh' mŭ]—CORPOREALNESS. *An influential Samaritan in Nehemiah's time* (Neh. 6:6). Perhaps the same as Geshem.

GATAM [Gā′ tam]—PUNY or BURNT VALLEY. *The fourth son of Eliphaz,* son of Esau, and one of the dukes of an Edomite clan (Gen. 36:11, 16; I Chron. 1:36).

GAZEZ [Gā′ zĕz]—SHEARER.
1. *A son of Caleb* by Ephah his concubine (I Chron. 2:46).
2. *A son of Haram,* who was another of Ephah's sons (I Chron. 2:46).

GAZZAM [Găz′ zam]—SWAGGERER or DEVOURER. *A founder of a family of Nethinims* who returned from exile with Zerubbabel (Ezra 2:48; Neh. 7:51).

GEBER [Gē′ bûr]—A HERO or STRONG.
1. *One of Solomon's twelve purveyors* for Southern Gilead (I Kings 4:13).
2. *The son of Uri,* who was over great pasture lands east of Jordan (I Kings 4:19). The two Gebers are sometimes identified as the same person.

GEDALIAH [Gĕd a lī′ ah]—JEHOVAH IS GREAT.
1. *A son of Ahikam* and grandson of Shaphan, king Josiah's secretary and Governor of Mizpah (II Kings 25:22–25; Jer. 39:14; 40:5–16; 41; 43:6). This Judean of high birth was the one who protected Jeremiah, whose views he shared, from the anti-Chaldeans. Nebuchadnezzar made him governor over "the poor people left in the land." He only ruled however, for two months. The anniversary of his treacherous murder is observed as one of the four Jewish feasts (Zech. 7:5; 8:19).
2. *A priest,* of the sons of Jeshua, who had taken a strange wife during the exile (Ezra 10:18).
3. *Grandfather of the prophet Zephaniah* (Zeph. 1:1).
4. *One of the six sons of Jeduthun,* a harper and head of the second of twenty-four companies or twelve musicians (I Chron. 25:3, 9).
5. *A son of Pashur and the prince* who caused Jeremiah to be imprisoned (Jer. 38:1, 4).

GEDOR [Gē′ dôr]—A FORTRESS.
1. *The son of Jehiel* and brother of Ner and an ancestor of king Saul (I Chron. 8:31; 9:37).
2. This name occurs in connection with two Judahite families. Penuel is called the father of Gedor, and Jered is in the same relation. The *Targum* gives both these names to Moses as coming from Jehudijah, identified as Pharaoh's daughter (I Chron. 4:4, 18). Gedor is also the name of a town or village in the tribe of Simeon (I Chron. 4:39).

GEHAZI [Gē′ hā′ zī]—DENIER or VALLEY OF VISION. *The servant of the prophet Elisha* who likely stood in the same relationship to Elisha as Elisha had done to Elijah (II Kings 4:12–36; 5:20–27; 8:4, 5).

The Man Who Was Unholy Amid Holiness

Gehazi's name, "valley of vision," is appropriate enough if we think of what he saw as to the nature of wicked men when the prophet opened his eyes. As the servant of Elisha, the man of God, Gehazi should have been a good man. But a holy man had an unholy servant. Gehazi was near, yet far distant from all that was pure and beautiful. It is possible in our time for a man to build churches, yet be a destroyer of Christian doctrine generally.

What a contrast exists between one man and another: Elisha — living a vibrant spiritual life, the grand prayer-life and faith-life; Gehazi— grubbing in the earth and seeking contentment in the dust. And these contrasts still exist.

Dinsdale T. Young enlarges upon the following features of Gehazi, the avaricious servant in this telling fashion:

I.   He was familiar with sacred things, yet a stranger to their power. Gehazi was irreligious amid religion. He lived with good men and had a knowledge of God, yet succumbed to the hardening influence of spiritual things.

II.   He had the incapacity to understand a saint. Gehazi failed to understand or appreciate both the character and conduct of Elisha.

III.   He was enslaved in his youth. Gehazi's early manhood was marred by evil thoughts, greed, deliberate lying and revolting hypocrisy. How his wrecked youth should warn the young today to remember their Creator!

IV.   He prostituted a strong and imaginative mind. The story Gehazi concocted and told to Naaman was skilfully constructed. His invention was a lie, and the cleverness in telling it revealed his depravity. How tragic when genius and gifts sell their birthright for a mess of pottage.

V.   He was successful at a fearful cost. He gained the social splendor he desired in the gold and garments Naaman gave him. But think of the price Gehazi paid. He lost his health, for he became a leper, a judgment Gehazi himself felt to be just. Gehazi also brought a blight upon his family. Instead of leaving his ill-gotten gains to his descendants, his judgment likewise fell upon his seed.

VI.   He was likely restored to Divine favor. The incident of Gehazi recounting to King Joram the great deeds of Elisha seems to suggest that he had been restored to health and usefulness. For the Gehazi of modern society there is forgiveness. Christ's blood can make the vilest clean.

GEMALLI [Gē măl' lī]—CAMEL OWNER or RIDER OF A CAMEL. *The father of Ammiel,* ruler of his tribe and one of the twelve spies sent out to explore the land (Num. 13:12).

GEMARIAH [Gĕm a rī' ah]—JEHOVAH HATH FULFILLED or ACCOMPLISHMENT OF THE LORD.

1.   *A prince,* son of Shaphan the scribe and brother of Ahikam

(Jer. 36:10–25). This scribe sought in vain to keep King Jehoiakim from burning the roll.

2. *A son of Hilkiah,* sent by King Zedekiah as ambassador to Nebuchadnezzar. He also carried a letter from Jeremiah to the captive Jews (Jer. 29:3).

GENUBATH [Gē-nū′ băth]—THEFT. *A son of Hadad* the Edomite, the fugitive prince, by the sister of Queen Tahpenes, the wife of Pharaoh, who governed Egypt toward the end of David's reign [I Kings 11:20).

GERA [Gē′ ră]—ENMITY or PILGRIMAGE. *A son or grandson of Benjamin.* The four different Geras named may be reduced to this one Gera: The Gera of Judges 3:15 indicated as the ancestor of Ehud; and the Gera of II Samuel 16:5 as the ancestor of Shimei. (See also Gen. 46:21; II Sam. 19:16, 18; I Kings 2:8; I Chron. 8:3–7).

GERSHOM [Gûr′ shŏm]—A STRANGER THERE.
1. *The first-born son of Moses* and Zipporah. He was born in Midian (Ex. 2:22; 18:3; I Chron. 23:15, 16).
2. *The eldest son of Levi,* and referred to as Gershon (Gen. 46:11; Josh. 21:6).
3. *One of the family of Phinehas,* and one of the "heads of houses" who returned with Ezra from Babylon (Ezra 8:2).
4. *Father of Jonathan,* the Levite who became priest to the Danites who settled at Laish (Judg. 18:30). The Danite tribe was guilty of the evil of setting up a graven image.

GESHAM, GESHAN [Gē′ shăm]—FIRM, STRONG. *A son of Jahdai* and descendant of Caleb (I Chron. 2:47).

GESHEM [Gē′ shem]—RAIN. *The Arabian* who along with Sanballat and Tobiah, sought to oppose the building of the wall by Nehemiah (Neh. 2:19; 6:1, 2). See Gashmu (6:6).

GETHER [Gē′ thûr]—VALE OF TRIAL. *Third of Aram's sons* (Gen. 10:23; I Chron. 1:17). The latter reference reckons him among the sons of Shem.

GEUEL [Gē ū′ el]—SALVATION OF GOD or MAJESTY OF GOD. *A son of Machi,* a prince of Gad and the representative of the Gadite tribe sent out to explore Canaan (Num. 13:15).

GIBBAR [Gĭb′ bar]—MIGHTY MAN. *A man whose children returned from captivity* with Zerubbabel (Ezra 2:20). Perhaps the Gibeon of Nehemiah 7:25.

GIBEA [Gĭb′ e ă]—HIGHLANDER. *A son of Sheva,* and grandson of Caleb (I Chron. 2:49). Perhaps this reference is more geographical than genealogical, Gibeah in Judah being meant.

GIDDALTI [Gĭd dăl′ tĭ]—I HAVE MAGNIFIED or I MAGNIFY GOD. *A son of Heman,* and one of the heads of music (I Chron. 25:4, 29).

GIDDEL [Gĭd′ del]—VERY GREAT or HE HATH MAGNIFIED.
1. *A member of the family of Nethinims* who returned from exile with Zerubbabel (Ezra 2:47; Neh. 7:49).
2. *Sons of Giddel,* Solomon's servants who also came up to Jerusalem from exile (Ezra 2:56; Neh. 7:58).

GIDEON, GEDEON [Gĭd′ e on, Gĕd′ e on]—A CUTTING DOWN, HE THAT BRUISES or GREAT WARRIOR. *A son of Joash* of the family of Abiezer, a Manassite, who lived in Ophrah and delivered Israel from Midian. He is also called Jerubbaal, and judged Israel forty years as the fifth judge (Judg. 6; 7; 8).

The Man of Might and Valor

Without doubt Gideon is among the brightest luminaries of Old Testament history. His character and call are presented in a series of tableaux. We see:

I.   Gideon at the flail. The tall, powerful young man was threshing wheat for his farmer-father when the call came to him to rise and become the deliverer of his nation. History teaches that obscurity of birth is no obstacle to noble service. It was no dishonor for Gideon to say, "My family is poor."

II.   Gideon at the altar. Although humble and industrious, Gideon was God-fearing. His own father had become an idolator but idols had to go, and Gideon vowed to remove them. No wonder they called him Jerubbaal, meaning "Discomfiter of Baal."

III.   Gideon and the fleece. Facing the great mission of his life, he had to have an assuring token that God was with him. The method he adopted was peculiar, but found favor with heaven, God condescending to grant Gideon the double sign. With the complete revelation before us in the Bible, we are not to seek supernatural signs, but take God at his Word.

IV.   Gideon at the well. How fascinating is the incident of the reduction of Gideon's army from thirty-two thousand to ten thousand, then to only three hundred. Three hundred men against the countless swarms of Midian! Yes, but the few choice, brave, active men *and God* were in the majority. God is not always on the side of big battalions.

V.   Gideon with the whip. Rough times often need and warrant rough measures. The men of Succoth and Penuel made themselves obnoxious, but with a whip fashioned out of the thorny branches off the trees, Gideon meted out to them the punishment they deserved.

VI.   Gideon in the gallery of worthies. It was no small honor to have a niche, as Gideon has, in the illustrious roll named in the eleventh chapter of Hebrews, where every name is an inspiration, and every character a miracle of grace.

Preachers desiring to continue the character-study of Gideon still further might note his humility (Judg. 6:15); caution (Judg. 6:17); spirituality (Judg. 6:24); obedience (Judg. 6:27); divine inspiration (Judg. 6:34); divine fellowship (Judg. 6:36; 7:4, 7–9); strategy (Judg. 7:16–18); tact (Judg. 8:1–3); loyalty to God (Judg. 8:23); the fact that he was weakened by his very prosperity (Judg. 8:24–31).

GIDEONI [Gĭd e ō′ nī]—A CUTTING OF or HE THAT BRUISES. *The father of Abidan*, a prince of Benjamin. He was one of the census-takers at Sinai in the time of Moses (Num. 1:11; 2:22; 7:60, 65; 10:24).

GILALAI [Gĭl′ a laī]—WEIGHTY. *A Levitical musician* who took part in the consecration of the wall of Jerusalem (Neh. 12:36).

GILEAD [Gĭl′ e ăd]—MASS OF TESTIMONY or STRONG.
1. *Father of Jephthah*, judge of Israel, and grandson of Zelophedad (Judg. 11:1, 2).
2. *Son of Machir*, and grandson of Manasseh (Num. 26:29, 30; 27:1; 36:1; Josh. 17:1–3).
3. *A chief of the family of Gad* (I Chron. 5:14). Also the name of a mountainous area in Jordan (Gen. 37:25; Judg. 7:3).

GINATH [Gī′ năth]—PROTECTION. *The father of Tibni*, who tried to dethrone Omri after the death of Zimri (I Kings 16:21, 22).

GINNETHO, GINNETHON [Gĭn′ne thō, Gĭn′ ne thŏn]—GREAT PROTECTION. *A prince or a priest* who, with Nehemiah, sealed the covenant (Neh. 12:4, 16).

GISPA, GISHPA [Gĭs′ pă]—BLANDISHMENT or ATTENTIVE. *An overseer of the Nethinims* in Nehemiah's time (Neh. 11:21).

GOG [Gŏg]—A ROOF or A MOUNTAIN.
1. *A Reubenite, and grandson of Joel* (I Chron. 5:4).
2. *A prince of Rosh, Meshech and Tubal*, and not the mystic character of Revelation 20:8–15. Who is this dominant figure Ezekiel pictures as leading a great host of Northern nations against Israel? Ezekiel 38:2, 3, 14, 16, 18; 39:1, 11 are passages to be closely studied.

The Man of the Future

Gog is mentioned as the son of Shemaiah, in the line of Reuben, as above. Here in Ezekiel Gog appears as the chief prince of Meshech and Tubal, and is foretold as being defeated and five-sixths of his army destroyed as he comes up from "the north parts" and invades "the mountains of Israel."

There are those who affirm that Gog merely represents a title of royal dignity, similar to the Egyptian word Pharaoh. It has also been suggested that as Ezekiel represents Gog as being accompanied in his invasion of the land of Israel by the Persians, Ethiopians, Libyans and others, that the term may be a general designation for all the enemies of Israel. Those who hold this theory find confirmation for it in Revelation 20:8–10 where Gog and Magog are linked together as if they were persons who seem to symbolize all the future foes of Israel. This may be the reason why various writers in the seventh century identified Gog with the Antichrist.

Historically, Gog may have been an actual ruler of a non-Semitic nation over against the north of Palestine and Asia Minor, Armenia, Syria or Scythia.

Prophetically, Gog is to be the chief prince, the fearsome force in the great Northern Confederacy in which Russia will play a prominent part.

GOLIATH [Gō lī′ ath]—THE EXILE or SOOTHSAYER. The famous giant of Gath, who defied the armies of Israel (I Sam. 17:4, 23; 21:9; 22:10; II Sam. 21:19).

The Man a Pebble Killed

The story of David and Goliath has thrilled our hearts from childhood days. How spectacular it must have been to see a stripling like David slay a massive man some ten feet high with only a pebble from the stream. Saul's proffered armor was of no use against Goliath. David had to meet the giant with the weapon he was used to. A ready-made suit was of no avail for the son of Jesse.

The religious character of the duel between Goliath and David should not be lost sight of. The giant cursed David by his gods. David went out to meet Goliath "in the name of the Lord of Hosts." But why did David take *five* stones, if his God was able to direct a single one into the forehead? Did he want to make sure that if one pebble failed, he would have four more to swing? Going over the passages we discover that Goliath had four sons, all of whom were giants, and five pebbles were needed to slay the lot of them. Thus the choice of five was an act of faith. Through God, only one pebble was needed. David went forth to meet Goliath with five pebbles and he came back with five—four in his hand and the other in Goliath's massive forehead. How God delights to use the insignificant things of life to accomplish His purpose!

GOMER [Gō′ mûr]—COMPLETION or HEAT. *The first born of Japheth* and father of Ashkenaz, Riphath, and Togarmah. Also the head of many families (Gen. 10:2, 3; I Chron. 1:5, 6; Ezek. 38:6). The eldest son of Japheth is the father of the ancient Cimmerians or as the Assyrians called them, Gimirra, who settled on the northern shores of the Baltic Sea. The modern and familiar name in English history,

Crimea, and the Cimbri of old times are derived from the Cimmerians, the immediate descendants of Gomer. Their original home appears to have been north of the Euxine, but by the seventh century they had completely conquered Cappadocia and settled there.

The Man Who Became a Nation

The Gauls and Celts of ancient times, and of more modern date, the Germans, French and British are descendants of Gomer. In the *Talmud,* Gomer is spoken of as Germani, that is, Germany. The present divided land of Germany was first called "The Land of Gomer" or *Gomerland,* and many old maps bear the name of Ashkenaz, one of the sons of Gomer. Other maps carry the name Gomer.

The major portion of Germany was never connected with the old Roman Empire. Although presently divided, with communists controlling the East, and the western powers eager to keep West Germany free from communist control, prophecy declares that "Gomer and all his bands," will be found allied to the Northern Confederacy. Owing to Germany's divided condition, European stability is endangered. With West Germany under intense Soviet pressure to refuse any military alliance with western nations, one wonders how long they can resist the determination of Russia to reunite all Germany under the "Hammer and the Sickle."

Gomer is also the name of Hosea's wife, the daughter of Diblaim, and affords another instance of the same name being used by a man and a woman (Hos. 1:3).

GUNI [Gŭ′ nī]—PROTECTED or PAINTED WITH COLORS.
1. *A son of Naphtali* and founder of a tribal family called the Gunites (Gen. 46:24; Num. 26:48; I Chron. 7:13).
2. *Father of Abdiel* and a Gadite chief (I Chron. 5:15).

H

HAAHASHTARI [Hā a hăsh′ ta rī]—THE COURIER. *A descendant of Judah* from Ashur, father of Tekoa, by his second wife Naarah (I Chron. 4:6).

HABAIAH, HOBIAH [Hā bā′ iah]—JEHOVAH HATH HIDDEN or IS PROTECTION. *The head of a priestly family* who returned from Babylonian captivity with Zerubbabel. Although claiming sacerdotal descent, the members of this priestly family failed to trace their genealogy and were therefore not allowed to serve (Ezra 2:61; Neh. 7:63).

HABAKKUK [Hā băk′ kuk]—LOVE'S EMBRACE or HE THAT EMBRACES. *The eighth of the Minor Prophets* whose parentage, birthplace and era are unrecorded (Hab. 1:1; 3:1).

The Man Who Caressed the People

Although he is not much more than a mere name to us, we know that Habakkuk was a prophet of Judah and of the tribe of Levi and of the temple singers (Hab. 3:19). He is also referred to as a prophet and the last prophet before the destruction of Jerusalem (Hab. 3:11). Rabbinical tradition makes him the son of the Shunammite woman whom Elisha restored to life (II Kings 4:16). Habakkuk prophesied the coming of the Babylonians upon Judah. This invasion took place in 606 B.C. and also in 597 B.C. and 586 B.C. "In your days" (Hab. 1:5), would indicate that he prophesied scarcely a generation before the first invasion.

In his prophecy Habakkuk was true to his name, which means "strong embrace of God," for he caressed and comforted the people as one would embrace a weeping child until its tears are dried. A modern writer suggests that his name may have contributed somewhat to the unpopularity of the prophet. "His name is against him; its coarse gutterals, falling upon the modern ears with a forbidden ring, and creating a prejudice from the beginning."

From the book Habakkuk wrote, we gather that he was the questioning prophet. He wants to know "Why?" and "How?" Answers were granted him. Why does God permit the destruction of His own people by a hand so cruel and unclean? The prophet waited patiently for an answer, and it came. The ungodly shall pass; the just shall live by faith.

Then we have a chant of derision against the Chaldeans raised by their victims — a fivefold *woe:*

I.   Their insatiable greed.
II. Their overreaching ambition.
III. Their cruel tyranny.
IV. Their shameful treatment of conquered people.
V.   Their brutal idolatry.

Then there is Habakkuk's great message of faith which gave Paul a hint of the most precious truth of the Gospel (Rom. 1:17; Gal. 3:11; Heb. 10:38) and aided the Reformation under Martin Luther, the charter of evangelical liberty.

HABAZZINIAH, HABAZINIAH [Hăb a zĭ nĭ′ ah]—MEANING UNCERTAIN. *The head of a family of Rechabites* and grandfather of Jaazariah the chief Rechabite in Jeremiah's time (Jer. 35:3).

HACHALIAH [Hăch a lĭ′ ah]—JEHOVAH IS HIDDEN. *The father of Nehemiah* the Tirshatha (Neh. 1:1; 10:1). Also the name of a hill in Judah (I Sam. 23:19; 26:3).

HACHMONI [Hăch′ mō nĭ]—THE WISE. *The father of Jehiel* who was a companion of the sons of David, and also founder of a tribal family (I Chron. 11:11; 27:32).

HADAD [Hā' dăd]—MIGHTY or FIERCENESS.

1. *A son of Bedad,* king of Edom and of the city of Avith (Gen. 36:35, 36; I Chron. 1:46, 47).

2. *An Edomite prince* of Solomon's time (I Kings 11:4–25).

3. *Eighth son of Ishmael,* and grandson of Abraham (Gen. 25:15; I Chron. 1:30). Also called Hadar.

4. *The last of the early kings* of Edom (I Chron. 1:50, 51). This is the Hadar of Genesis 36:39 who, as a child, escaped massacre under Joab, David's general.

HADADEZER, HADAREZER [Hăd ăd ē' zûr, Hăd är ē' zûr]—MIGHTY IS THE HELP, HADAR IS A HELP or BEAUTY OF ASSISTANCE. *The son of Rehob,* and king of Zobah in Syria who was defeated by David and driven across the Euphrates (II Sam. 8:3–12; I Kings 11:23). Called Hadarezer in I Chronicles 18:8 and 19:16, 19).

HADLAI [Hăd' la ī]—FRAIL or LAX. *A man of Ephraim,* father of Amasa, one of the chiefs of the tribe in the reign of Pekah (II Chron. 28:12).

HADORAM [Hā dō' ram]—HADAR IS HIGH.

1. *A son of Joktan* of the family of Shem (Gen. 10:27; I Chron. 1:21).

2. *A son of Tou,* king of Hamath in David's time (I Chron. 18:10).

3. *An officer over Rehoboam's taxes,* who was killed at the revolt of Shechem (II Chron. 10:18). Adoniram is the longer form (I Kings 4:6). See also Adoram of II Samuel 20:24.

HAGAB [Hā' găb]—A LOCUST or BENT. *Founder of a family of Nethinims* who returned with Zerubbabel to Jerusalem [Ezra 2:46). Nehemiah omits the name in his list.

HAGABAH, HAGABA [Hăg' a bah, Hăg' a bă]—A LOCUST. *Another Nethinim* who returned from captivity (Ezra 2:45; Neh. 7:48).

HAGGAI [Hăg' ga ī]—FESTAL or BORN OF A FESTIVAL DAY. *The tenth of the Minor Prophets,* and the first of those to prophesy after the captivity (Ezra 5:1; 6:14).

The Man Who Was a Messenger

All we know of Haggai is told us in the first verse of his book, where we have a description of himself and his message, which gives us a key to the whole of his ministry. Haggai was "The Lord's messenger in the Lord's message." We reject the legend that he was an angel incarnate.

His name is suggestive and may imply that he was born on a Feast Day. Another meaning is "Jehovah hath quieted." As a prophet, he was contemporary with Zechariah (Hag. 1:1; 2:1, 20; Zech. 1:1). He prophesied in the second year of the reign of Darius Hystaspes, King of Persia, sixteen years after Cyrus' decree permitting the rebuilding of the Temple. Compare Zechariah 1:1–11 with Ezra 4:24 and 5:1.

As a prophet, he preached righteousness and predicted the future. As a man, he was simple, strong in faith and bold in hope. He urged the people to work and be strong (Hag. 2:4), assuring them that when they began to build the Temple, God would begin to bless them.

The *first message* was one of stern rebuke (Hag. 1:1–11).

The *second message* was one of comfort and commendation (Hag. 1:12–15).

The *third message* was a cheering one of encouragement (Hag. 2:1–9).

The *fourth message* was an assuring one concerning cleansing and blessing (Hag. 2:10–19).

The *fifth message* was a steadying one associated with safety (Hag. 2:20–23).

Dr. Stuart Holden suggests that these five lessons can be gathered from Haggai:

I. *Danger of lapsing* into self-content, even after honest and sincere beginnings in the work of Christ.

II. That *the time for blessing is always at hand.* The people said: "The time has not come." God said: "My time is an eternal NOW." The only hindrance to blessing lies in His people.

III. In the will of God for His people — particularly in respect to the great work of building His Temple — *there is always a conjunction of precept and power, of duty and dynamic.* The promises of God are "Yea and Amen" to those who are in Christ Jesus, *walking* in Him, and *living* in Him.

IV. *The greatest of all mistakes is to leave God out in His own work.* To live in the light of His presence is to build for eternity.

V. In the work to which we pledge ourselves as God's children, *the greatest need of all is for patience.* We shall be opposed if our work is worth opposing; but the opposition of the Evil One is the opportunity to express our faith and loyalty toward God. "Our God is marching on. The best is yet to be; and we may reckon upon God."

HAGGERI [Hăg′ gē rī]—WANDERER. *The father of Mibhar,* one of David's brave men (I Chron. 11:38).

HAGGI [Hăg′ ḡī]—FESTIVE or BORN ON A FESTIVAL. *The second son of Gad* and founder of the tribal family of Haggites (Gen. 46:16; Num. 26:15).

HAGGIAH [Hăg ḡī′ ah]—FEAST OF JEHOVAH. *A descendant of Merari,* the son of Levi (I Chron. 6:30).

HAKKATAN [Hăk′ ka tăn]—THE YOUNGER or THE LITTLE ONE. *The father of Johanan* and head of a family of returning exiles with Ezra

(Ezra 8:12). The name, says Young, is simply Katan, meaning "little," with the definite article prefixed.

HAKKOZ, KOZ, COZ [Hăk′ kŏz, Kŏz, Cŏz]—THE THORN or THE NIMBLE.

1. *A descendant of Aaron* and chief of the seventh course in the sanctuary service appointed by David (I Chron. 24:10; see Koz in Ezra 2:61; Neh. 3:4, 21). This family of priests failed to prove their identity.

2. *A man of Judah* (I Chron. 4:8).

HAKUPHA [Hā kū′ phă]—INCITEMENT or BENT, CURVED. *Founder of a family of Nethinims* who returned from Babylon with Zerubbabel (Ezra 2:51; Neh. 7:53).

HALOHESH, HALLOHESH [Hā lō′ hesh, Hăl lō′ hesh]—THE WHISPERER or THE ENCHANTER.

1. *The father of Shallum* who ruled over a portion and helped to rebuild the wall (Neh. 3:12).

2. *One of the number sealing the covenant with Nehemiah* (Neh. 10:24). Some writers identify these two men as the same person.

HAM [Hăm]—HOT or DARK, COLORED, SWARTHY. *The youngest son of Noah* and father of Canaan and founder of many peoples (Gen. 5:32; 6:10; 7:13; 9:18, 22; Ps. 78:51).

The Man Whose Sin Brought a Curse

In consequence of the improper conduct of Ham when Noah was drunk, the heart of his father was set against him. Without doubt, Ham's act was the manifestation of an impure heart. Perhaps he had always been a filthy dreamer.

Because every imagination of our heart is defiled (Gen. 8:21), we are all the sons of Ham in this respect. There is none clean, no not one (Rom. 3:10, 12).

The indignation of Noah found expression in the thrice repeated curse upon Canaan, one of Ham's sons (Gen. 9:25-27). Ham himself suffered in failing to receive the blessing pronounced on his brothers, Shem and Japheth. The peoples polluted by Ham's sin (Gen. 10:15-19) inhabited the land later promised to Abraham's seed; thus the curse of servitude was fulfilled in Joshua's conquest of the Canaanites, when he made them hewers of wood and drawers of water (Josh. 9:23, 27).

The Hebrew word for Ham means "hot" and is surely prophetic of the climates that have created the blackness of the skin of the Negro, and the dark complexions of other peoples from the same stock. Egypt is called "the land of Ham" (Ps. 105:23) and the Egyptian word for "Ham" is *Kem,* meaning black and warm. From Ham we have the Egyptians, Africans, Babylonians, Philistines and Canaanites.

HAMAN [Hă′ man]—WELL DISPOSED. *The son of Hammedatha,* the chief minister of king Ahasuerus, who is called the Agagite because of his Amalekitish descent (Esther 3:1–5).

The Man Who Hated Jews

Haman, an oriental despot's favorite, had an innate passion for elevation. He never considered principle when seeking the king's honor. But Mordecai pricked Haman's bubble and would not bow to him. How could he honor an Amalekite whom God had cursed (Ex. 17: 14–16)! All of Haman's tragedy is condensed in the arrestive designation—he was the Jews' enemy. As the first great anti-semite, he came to prove that they who curse the Jews are cursed of God.

Haman, the vain and fussy courtier, the vulgar and unwise upstart, the cruel enemy of the Jews, the villain of the plot, is a name still hated by the Jews. Long ago at *The Feast of Purim,* it was customary to hang an effigy of Haman; but as the gibbet was sometimes made in the form of a cross, riots between Jews and Christians were the result, and a warning against insults to the Christian faith was issued by the Emporer Theodosius II. The Jews, however, in *The Feast of Purim* still celebrate their victory from annihilation by Haman.

HAMMATH, HEMATH [Hăm′ math, Hĕ′ math]—WARMTH or HOT SPRING. *The founder or father of the house of Rechab* (I Chron. 2:55). Also the name of a city near Tiberius famous for its hot baths (Josh. 19:35).

HAMMEDATHA [Hăm mĕd′ a thà]—GIVEN BY HOM—MOON GOD or HE THAT TROUBLETH THE LAW. *The Persian name of the father of Haman* the Agagite we have just considered (Esther 3:1, 10; 8:5; 9:10, 24).

HAMMELECH [Hăm′ me lĕch]—THE KING. *The father of Jerahmeel,* and of royal blood (Jer. 36:26; 38:6). Although given as a proper name, perhaps it should have been translated "the king" as stated in the R.V.

HAMOR, EMMOR [Hă′ mor]—AN ASS. *The prince of Shechem,* a Hivite (Gen. 33:19; 34:1–26).

HAMUEL, HAMMUEL [Hă mŭ′ el]—GOD IS A SUN or WARMTH OF GOD. *A son of Mishma,* a Simeonite, of the family of Shuah (I Chron. 4:26).

HAMUL [Hă′ mŭl]—PITY or PITIED. *The younger son of Pharez,* son of Judah by Tamar, and founder of the Hamulites (Gen. 46:12; Num. 26:21; I Chron. 2:5).

HANAMEEL, HANAMEL [Hā năm' e el]—GOD HATH PITIED, GIFT or GRACE OF GOD. *The son of Shallum* and cousin of the prophet Jeremiah (Jer. 32:7-12). See this portion on advice concerning a good investment.

HANAN [Hā' nan]—GRACIOUS or MERCIFUL.
1. *A son of Shashak* and a Benjamite chief (I Chron. 8:23).
2. *A son of Azel*, descendant of Jonathan and Saul (1 Chron. 8:38; 9:44).
3. *A son of Maachah*, one of David's heroes (I Chron. 11:43).
4. *A Nethinim* who returned from exile (Ezra 2:46; Neh. 7:49).
5. *A Levite who assisted Ezra* when he read and explained the Law (Neh. 8:7).
6. *A Levite who sealed the covenant* with Nehemiah. Perhaps the same person as No. 5 (Neh. 10:10; 13:13).
7. *A chief of the people* or a family who also sealed the covenant (Neh. 10:22).
8. *Another chief* who likewise signed the covenant (Neh. 10:26).
9. *The son of Igdaliah*, an officer in the Temple whose sons had a chamber therein (Jer. 35:4).

HANANEEL [Hâ năn' e el]—GOD IS GRACIOUS or THE MERCY OF GOD. *The builder of the tower bearing his name* near the sheepgate of Jerusalem (Neh. 3:1; 12:39; Jer. 31:38; Zech. 14:10).

HANANI [Hā nā' nī]—GRACIOUS or HE HATH SHEWED ME MERCY.
1. *One of the sons of Heman* and a head musician (I Chron. 25: 4, 25).
2. *The seer* who rebuked Asa for buying off Ben-hadad, king of Syria (II Chron. 16:7).
3. *The father of Jehu*, the seer who testified against Baasha and Jehoshaphat (I Kings 16:1, 7; II Chron. 19:2; 20:34).
4. *A priest* who had taken a foreign wife while in exile (Ezra 10:20).
5. *A brother of Nehemiah* who brought news of Jerusalem and became its governor (Neh. 1:2; 7:2).
6. *A musical priest* who assisted in the purification and dedication of the walls (Neh. 12:36).

HANANIAH [Hăn a nī' ah]—JEHOVAH IS GRACIOUS or GIFT OF THE LORD.
1. *A son of Heman*, and one of many musicians. Heman's sons were especially employed to blow horns (I Chron. 25:4, 23).
2. *A chief captain* in the army of king Uzziah (II Chron. 26:11).
3. *The father of Zedekiah*, and one of the princes during the reign of king Jehoiakim (Jer. 36:12).
4. *The son of Azur* of Gibeon whose false prophecy was withstood by the prophet Jeremiah (Jer. 28).
5. *Grandfather of Irijah*, who arrested Jeremiah on a charge of deserting to the Chaldeans (Jer. 37:13).

6. *Son of Shashak* and head of a Benjamite family (I Chron. 8:24).

7. *The Hebrew name of Shadrach,* who was of the house of David (Dan. 1:6, 7, 11, 19; 2:17).

8. *A son of Zerubbabel* and an ancestor of Christ (I Chron. 3:19, 21; Luke 3:27 R.V.).

9. *A son of Bebai* who returned from exile and put away his foreign wife (Ezra 10:28).

10. *An apothecary and priest* who helped to rebuild the wall of Jerusalem (Neh. 3:8).

11. *One associated with Hanun* in the repair of the wall (Neh. 3:30).

12. *The governor of the castle* and joint ruler with Nehemiah's brother over Jerusalem (Neh. 7:2).

13. *An individual who added his signature to the covenant* (Neh. 10:23).

14. *A priest* in the time of Jehoiakim (Neh. 12:12, 41).

HANNIEL, HANIEL [Hăn' nĭ el, Hăn' ĭ el]—FAVOR or GRACE OF GOD.

1. *A son of Ephod and prince of the Manassites,* who assisted in the division of the land (Num. 34:23).

2. *A son of Ulla,* a prince and hero of Asher (I Chron. 7:39).

HANOCH, HENOCH [Hā' nŏch, Hē nŏch]—DEDICATED.

1. *A son of Midian* and a descendant of Abraham by Keturah (Gen. 25:4; I Chron. 1:33). Also called Henoch.

2. *The eldest son of Reuben* and founder of the family of the Hanochites (Gen. 46:9; Ex. 6:14; Num. 26:5; I Chron. 5:3).

3. *The son of Jared,* a descendant of Seth (I Chron. 1:3). Called Enoch in Genesis 5:18.

HANUN [Hā' nŭn]—ENJOYING FAVOR, GRACIOUS or HE THAT RESTS.

1. *The son of Nahash,* king of the Ammonites, who resented David's message of condolence which resulted in a most disastrous war (II Sam. 10:1–4; I Chron. 19:2–6).

2. *A son of Zalaph* who assisted in the repair of a portion of the wall (Neh. 3:30).

3. *Another Jew* who, with the people of Zanoah, repaired one of the gates of the wall of Jerusalem (Neh. 3:13).

HAPPIZZEZ, APHSES [Ăph' sēs]—THE DISPERSION. *The head of the eighteenth course of priests* (I Chron. 24:15).

HARAN [Hā' ran]—ENLIGHTENED or STRONG.

1. *The third son of Terah,* younger brother of Abraham and father of Lot (Gen. 11:26–31).

2. *A Gershonite Levite* in David's time, and one of the family of Shimei (I Chron. 23:9).

3. *A son of Caleb* the spy, by his concubine, Ephah, and called Charun. His son was named Gazez (I Chron. 2: 46). Haran or its New

Testament equivalent Charrun, is also the name of the place Abram and his family emigrated to from Ur (Gen. 11:31, 32).

HARBONA, HARBONAH [Här bō′ nă, Här bō′ nah]—ASS DRIVER or THE ANGER OF HIM WHO BUILDS. *Third of the seven eunuchs* or chamberlains who served Ahasuerus, king of Persia (Esther 1:10; 7:9).

HAREPH [Hä′ reph]—EARLY BORN or PLUCKING OF. *A son of Caleb*, son of Hur and father of Beth-gader, and a Judahite chief (I Chron. 2:51). Called Hariph in Nehemiah 7:24.

HARHAIAH [Här ha ī′ ah]—JEHOVAH IS PROTECTING. *Father of the goldsmith Uzziel*, who repaired a part of the wall (Neh. 3:8).

HARHAS [Här′ has]—GLITTER or SPLENDOR. *The grandfather of Shallum*, the husband of Huldah the prophetess of king Josiah's time (II Kings 22:14).

HARHUR [Här′ hûr]—NOBILITY or DISTINCTION. *A member of the Nethinim family* who returned from exile with Zerubbabel (Ezra 2:51; Neh. 7:53).

HARIM [Hä′ rim]—CONSECRATED or SNUB-NOSED.
1. *A priest* who was in charge of the third division in the work of the sanctuary (I Chron. 24:8; Ezra 2:39; 10:21; Neh. 3:11; 7:42).
2. *A returned exile* who had married a foreign wife (Ezra 10:31).
3. *One who had signed the covenant* with Nehemiah (Neh. 10:5).
4. *Another who had signed the covenant* with Nehemiah (Neh. 10:27).
5. *Head of a priestly family* (Neh. 12:15). Perhaps the same as No. 3.

HARIPH [Hä′ riph]—EARLY BORN or AUTUMNAL RAIN. *Founder of a Jewish family* who sealed the covenant (Neh. 10:19). Called Jorah in Ezra 2:18. Some old versions have Jodah.

HARNEPHER [Här′ ne phûr]—PANTING. *A son of Zophah*, an Asherite (I Chron. 7:36).

HAROEH [Här′ o eh]—THE SEER. *A son of Shobal*, father of Kirjath-jearim, of the tribe of Judah (I Chron. 2:52). Perhaps the Reaiah of I Chronicles 4:2.

HARUM [Hä′ rum]—EXALTED or ELEVATED. *The father of Aharhel* a descendant of Coz, from Caleb son of Hur. A man of Judah (I Chron. 4:8).

HARUMAPH [Hă rụ′ maph]—FLAT OF NOSE. *The father of Jedaiah,* who helped in the repair of the gate (Neh. 3:10).

HARUZ [Hă′ ruz]—INDUSTRIOUS. *Father of Meshullemeth,* Manasseh's queen and mother of Amon, king of Judah (II Kings 21:19).

HASADIAH [Hăs a dĭ′ ah]—JEHOVAH IS KIND or HATH SHEWN KIND-NESS. *A son of Zerubbabel* and descendant of king Jehoiakim (I Chron. 3:20).

HASENUAH [Hăs e nū′ ah]—THE VIOLATED. *A Benjamite chief* whose name is actually Senuah (I Chron. 9:7).

HASHABIAH [Hăsh a bĭ′ ah]—JEHOVAH IS ASSOCIATED or HATH DEVISED.
1. *A Merarite Levite* descended through Amaziah and an ancestor of Jeduthun (I Chron. 6:45).
2. *Another Merarite Levite* and co-musician (I Chron. 9:14).
3. *The fourth of the sons of Jeduthun,* likewise a sanctuary musician (I Chron. 25:3).
4. *A descendant of Hebron,* son of Kohath, and an inspector of the country (I Chron. 26:30).
5. *A son of Kemuel,* prince of the Levites in David's time (I Chron. 27:17).
6. *A chief of the Levites,* who assisted king Josiah at his great passover feast (II Chron. 35:9).
7. *A Merarite Levite* who joined Ezra at the river of Ahava (Ezra 8:19; Neh. 10:11).
8. *A chief of the priests of the family of Kohath* (Ezra 8:24).
9. *A ruler of half of Keilah,* who helped in the repair of the wall (Neh. 3:17).
10. *A Levite* who sealed the covenant with Nehemiah. Perhaps the same person as in Nehemiah 12:24.
11. *The son of Bunni,* a Levite (Neh. 11:15).
12. *Another Levite,* the son of Mattaniah and a temple attendant (Neh. 11:22). See No. 14.
13. *A priest of the family of Hilkiah* in Joiakim's days (Neh. 12:21).
14. *A chief Levite* appointed for thanksgiving when the people returned from exile (Neh. 12:24). Perhaps the same person as No. 12.

HASHABNAH [Hă shăb′ nah]—JEHOVAH IS A FRIEND. *A chief who sealed the covenant with Nehemiah* (Neh. 10:25).

HASHABNIAH, HASHABIAH [Hăsh ab nĭ′ ah]—JEHOVAH IS A FRIEND.
1. *His son Hattush* helped to repair the wall (Neh. 3:10).

2. *One of the Levites* who by exhortation prepared the exiles for the sealing of the covenant (Neh. 9:5).

HASHBADANA, HASHBADDNA [Hăsh băd′ a nă]—REASON or THOUGHT. *One of those who stood on the left hand of Ezra* as he read the law (Neh. 8:4).

HASHEM [Hă′ shem]—ASTONISHED or SHINING. *The father of several of David's mighty men* (I Chron. 11:34).

HASHUB, HASSHUB [Hă′ shub, Hăs′ shub]—ASSOCIATED or THOUGHTFUL.
1. *Father of Shemaiah,* a descendant of Merari (I Chron. 9:14).
2. *A son of Pahath-moab* who joined others in the repair of the wall (Neh. 3:11).
3. *A Jew who repaired the wall* over against his own house (Neh. 3:23). A good place for reformation to begin.
4. *The head of a family,* joining Nehemiah in the sealing of the covenant (Neh. 10:23).

HASHUBAH [Hă shōō′ bah]—ESTEEMED or ASSOCIATION. *A son of Zerubbabel* and descendant of King Jehoiakim (I Chron. 3:20).

HASHUM [Hă′ shum]—WEALTHY or SHINING.
1. *Founder of a family* whose descendants returned with Zerubbabel (Ezra 2:19; 10:33; Neh. 7:22).
2. *A priest who stood at Ezra's side* as he read the Law to the people (Neh. 8:4).
3. *The head of a family* that sealed the covenant (Neh. 10:18).

HASRAH [Hăs′ rah]—SPLENDOR. *Same as Harhas* in II Kings 22:14 (II Chron. 34:22).

HASSENAAH, SENAAH [Hăs se nă′ ah, Sē nă′ ah]—THORNY or THE THORN HEDGE. *His sons built the Fish Gate* (Neh. 3:3). Identical with Senaah of Ezra 2:35 and Nehemiah 7:38.

HASUPHA, HASHUPHA [Hă sū′ phă, Hă shōō′ phă]—NAKEDNESS or MADE BARE. *Head of a Nethinim family* that returned from exile (Ezra 2:43; Neh. 7:46). Inaccurately stated as Hashupha.

HATACH, HATHACH [Hă′ tăch]—A GIFT. *A chamberlain eunuch* appointed by King Ahasuerus to attend Queen Esther. It was through him that Esther learned the details of Haman's plot against the Jews. He thus had his part in their deliverance (Esther 4:5–10).

HATHATH [Hă′ thăth]—BRUISED or TERROR. *A son of Othniel the Kenite and judge of Israel,* through Caleb, son of Hur (I Chron. 4:13).

HATIPHA [Hăt′ ĭ phă]—CAPTIVE. *Founder of a family of Nethinims* that returned from exile with Zerubbabel (Ezra 2:54; Neh. 7:56).

HATITA [Hăt′ ĭ tă]—EXPLORATION. *A member of the guild of porters or gatekeepers* that returned from exile (Ezra 2:42; Neh. 7:45).

HATTIL [Hăt′ til]—DECAYING or VACILLATING. *One of Solomon's servants or slaves* (Ezra 2:57; Neh. 7:59).

HATTUSH [Hăt′ tush]—CONTENDER or GATHERED TOGETHER.
1. *A man of Judah,* son of Shemiah and family of Shecaniah (I Chron. 3:22).
2. *A descendant of David* who returned with Ezra from Babylon (Ezra 8:2; Neh. 3:10; 10:4).
3. *A priest* who returned from captivity (Neh. 12:2).

HAVILAH [Hăv′ i lah]—CIRCLE.
1. *A son of Cush,* and descendant of Ham (Gen. 10:7; I Chron. 1:9).
2. *A son of Joktan* and descendant of Shem (Gen. 10:29; I Chron. 1:23). Also name of two places (Gen. 2:11; 25:18; I Sam. 15:7).

HAZAEL [Hăz′ a el]—GOD SEES or HATH SEEN. *A Syrian courtier,* anointed by Elijah as king over Syria. Hazael murdered his master and usurped the throne (I Kings 19:15, 17).

HAZAIAH [Hā zā′ iah]—JEHOVAH IS SEEING or HATH SEEN. *A man of Judah* and of the family of Shelah (Neh. 11:5).

HAZARMAVETH [Hā′ zar mā′ veth]—COURT OF DEATH. *A son of Joktan,* fifth in order from Shem (Gen. 10:26; I Chron. 1:20).

HAZIEL [Hā′ zĭ el]—VISION OF GOD or GOD IS SEEING. *A Gershonite Levite,* son of Shimei or Shimi in David's time (I Chron. 23:9).

HAZO [Hā′ zō]—VISION OR SEER. *A son of Nahor* by Milcah his wife (Gen. 22:22).

HEBER, EBER [Hē′ bûr]—FELLOWSHIP, PRODUCTION or ONE THAT PASSES.
1. *The head of a tribe of Gadites* (I Chron. 5:13).
2. *A son of Shashak,* a Benjamite (I Chron. 8:22).
3. *A son of Beriah* the son of Asher (Gen. 46:17; Num. 26:45; I Chron. 7:31, 32), and ancestor of Christ (Luke 3:35).
4. *The husband of Jael* who killed Sisera—a Kenite and descendant of Moses (Judg. 4:11, 17, 21; 5:24).
5. *A son of Ezra,* of the family of Caleb, son of Jephunneh (I Chron. 4:18).

6. *A son of Elpaal,* a Benjamite (I Chron. 8:17). For others see Eber.

HEBRON [Hē′ bron]—UNION or COMPANY.
1. *The third son of Kohath* and founder of a tribal family (Ex. 6:18; Num. 3:19; I Chron. 6:2, 18; 23:12, 19; 26:23).
2. *A son of Mareshah* and father of Korah (I Chron. 2:42, 43; 15:9).

HEGE, HEGAI [Hē′ ḡē, Hĕg′ a ī]—VENERABLE. *Chief chamberlain of king Ahasuerus,* and keeper of women (Esther 2:3, 8, 15).

HELDAI, HELEM, HELED [Hĕl′ da ī, Hē′ lem, Hē′ led]—ENDURING or DURABLE.
1. *A Netophathite,* descendant of Othniel and one of David's captains for monthly service (I Chron. 27:15).
2. *An Israelite exile* to whom special honor was given (Zech. 6:10). In verse fourteen his name appears as Helem.

HELEB, HELED [Hē′ lĕb, Hē′ led]—ENDURANCE or FAT. *The son of Baanah,* and one of David's valiant men (II Sam. 23:29). See I Chronicles 11:30 for Heled.

HELEK [Hē′ lĕk]—SMOOTHNESS or PORTION. *The second son of Gilead* and founder of the tribal family of Helekites (Num. 26:30; Josh. 17:2).

HELEM [Hē′ lem]—MANLY VIGOR or STRENGTH.
1. *An Asherite,* brother of Shamer (I Chron. 7:35). May be the Hotham of I Chronicles 7:32.
2. *Apparently the same as Heldai of Zechariah* 6:10, 14.

HELEZ [Hē′ lĕz]—STRENGTH or ALERTNESS.
1. *A Paltite or Pelonite,* and one of David's guard (II Sam. 23:23, 26; I Chron. 11:27; 27:10).
2. *A man of Judah* and son of Azariah and a descendant of the great family of Hezron (I Chron. 2:39).

HELI [Hē′ lī]—ELEVATION or ASCENDING. *The father of Joseph* the husband of Mary, mother of Christ (Luke 3:23). The Hebrew name is the same as Eli the high priest.

HELKAI (Hĕl′ ka ī)—JEHOVAH IS A PORTION. *A priest and head of his father's house* of Meraioth (Neh. 12:15). See Hilkiah.

HELON [Hē′ lon]—STRONG. *The father of Eliab* and chief of the tribe of Zebulon at the time the census was taken at Sinai (Num. 1:9; 2:7; 7:24, 29; 10:16).

HEMAM [Hē′ mam]—FAITHFUL or RAGING.

1. *A son of Lotan* the eldest son of Seir (Gen. 36:22). Given in I Chronicles 1:39 as Homam.

2. *A son of Zerah,* the son of Jacob (I Kings 4:31; I Chron. 2:6). A sage whose reputation for wisdom was high in Solomon's reign.

3. *The son of Joel* and grandson of Samuel, and of the Levite family of Korah (I Chron. 6:33; 15:17). Heman is called "the singer" or "the musician," and was the first of the three chief Levites appointed to conduct the vocal and instrumental music of the Tabernacle in David's time. Evidently Heman played the cymbal (I Chron. 25: 1-6; II Chron. 5:12; 35:15). Heman was also the writer of the most melancholy of all the Psalms (Ps. 88). It has been suggested that Heman composed it to console David during some inconsolable season. Heman is also referred to as David's "seer in the matters of God." What a responsible position that must have been!

HEMATH [Hē′ math]—WARMTH. *A person or place* (I Chron. 2:55; Amos 6:14). Variations of name are Hamath and Hammath.

HEMDAN [Hĕm′ dan]—PLEASANT or DESIRABLE. *The eldest son of Dishon,* son of Anah (Gen. 36:26). In I Chronicles 1:41 the name is given as Amram.

HEN [Hĕn]—GRACE or FAVOR. *A son of Zephaniah,* one of those whose memory was to be perpetuated by crowns laid up in the Temple (Zech. 6:14). Also called Josiah in Zechariah 6:10.

HENADAD [Hĕn′ a dăd]—FAVOR OF HADAD or HADAD IS GRACIOUS. *The head of a Levite family* who supported Zerubbabel when the foundation of the Temple was laid and who assisted in its re-building (Ezra 3:9; Neh. 3:18, 24; 10:9).

HEPHER [Hē′ phûr]—A DIGGING or A WELL.

1. *The youngest son of Gilead* and founder of the tribe of Hepherites. This Hepher was the father of Zelophedad whose daughters secured rights to their father's property (Num. 26:32; 27:1; Josh. 17:2, 3)

2. *The second son of Narah,* one of Asher's two wives (I Chron. 4:6).

3. *A Mecherathite,* one of the thirty heroes of David (I Chron. 11:36). (See Josh. 12:17; I Kings 4:10 for "the land of Hepher.")

HERESH [Hē′ resh]—WORK or SILENCE. *The head of a Levite family* and attached to the Tabernacle staff (I Chron. 9:15).

HERMAS [Hûr′ mas]—INTERPRETER or MERCURY. *A Christian in Rome* to whom Paul sent a greeting (Rom. 16:14). Hermas, a common name among slaves, was the name of the Greek god corresponding to the Roman Mercury.

HERMES [Hûr' mēs]—GAIN or MEANING AS AT HERMAS. *A Christian Greek in Rome,* possibly a slave in Caesar's household, to whom Paul sent a salutation. Lightfoot tells us that Hermes was a common slave's name (Rome 16:14).

HERMOGENES [Hûr mŏg' e nēs]—BEGOTTEN OF MERCURY or GENERATION OF LUCRE. *A companion of Paul* who, with Phygelus, deserted the apostle in a time of trial. Many of the so-called friends of Paul caused him great sorrow of heart (II Tim. 1:15).

HEROD [Hûr' od]—SON OF THE HERO or THE GLORY OF THE SKIN. Space forbids a detailed account of the genealogical table of the family of Herod. From Antipater, Governor of Idumaea, there were many branches. Elaborating on the history of the Herods, Henry S. Nash in his *Hastings Dictionary* article says that they brought into history a considerable amount of vigor and ability, and that the main interest attaching to the Herods is not concerned with their characters as individual rulers.

"They acquire dignity when they are viewed as parts of a supremely dramatic situation in universal history. The fundamental elements in the situation are two.

"The course of world-power in antiquity, and the relation between it and the political principle in the constitution of the Chosen People.

"The religious genius of Judaism, and its relation to the political elements in the experience of the Jews."

Among the many of the Herodian house, mention can be made of three, prominent in New Testament history.

1. Herod the Great. This son of Antipater had shown himself before his father's death both masterful and merciless. Because of his rule he earned the tile "Herod the Great." He is remembered for his massacre of the innocents, the murder of several of his sons and for his own appalling death. Stewart Perowne in his recent monumental study, *The Life and Times of Herod the Great,* tells us that Herod's life was as "eventful as his buildings were magnificent... His charm made him a close personal friend, first of Mark Antony, later of Augustus and Agrippa . . . Herod's greatest achievement was the building of the Temple in Jerusalem" (Matt. 2:1–22; Luke 1:5).

2. Herod Antipas, son of Herod the Great by his Samaritan wife, Matthaec. He became tetrarch of Galilee and Pernea. A man of craft, his cunning served him well. "The corroding immorality of his race shows itself in his marriage with Herodias, his brother's wife." His lust proved his undoing and also cost John the Baptist his head. Ultimately he was banished (Matt. 14:1–6; Mark 6:14–22; 8:15; Luke 3:1, 19; 8:3; 9:7, 9; 13:31; 23:7–15; Acts 4:27; 13:1).

3. The grandson of Herod the Great, and the son of Aristobulus and Bernice. He became Herod Agrippa I. Caligula gave him the governments of the tetrarchs Philip and Lysanias with other marks of royal favor. Parading as a little tin god, he was smitten with a foul disease and died in great agony (Acts 12; 23:35).

HERODION [Hē rō dǐ ŏn]—CONQUEROR OF HEROES. *A Jewish Christian in Rome,* whom Paul called a kinsman and to whom he sent a greeting. Perhaps he was a freedman of the Herods (Rom. 16:11).

HESED [Hē′ sed]—KINDNESS or PITY. *The father of one of Solomon's purveyors* in Aruboth, in Judah (I Kings 4:10).

HETH [Hĕth]—TERRIBLE. *The second son of Canaan,* ancestor of the Hittites. The wives of Esau are called "daughters of Heth" (Gen. 10:15; 23:3–20; 27:46; 49:32; I Chron. 1:13).

HEZEKI [Hĕz′ e kī]—JEHOVAH IS STRENGTH. *A son of Elpaal,* a descendant of Benjamin (I Chron. 8:17).

HEZEKIAH [Hĕz e kī′ ah]—JEHOVAH IS STRENGTH or A STRONG SUPPORT IS JEHOVAH. Also given as Hizkiah, Hizkijah, Ezekias.
1. *Son and successor of Ahaz* as king of Judah (II Kings 16: 20). He is referred to in well over one hundred references in II Kings, I and II Chronicles, Jeremiah, Hosea and Micah.

The Man Who Asked for Added Years

Hezekiah was one of the best kings who ever sat upon the throne of Judah, and is distinguished as the greatest in faith of all Judah's kings (II Kings 18:5). Sincere and devout, he was not a perfect man by any means, nor outstanding because of any brilliant gifts he possessed. This good king, however, is to be admired when one remembers his family background. Having such a wicked, apostate father as Ahaz, the wonder is that his son became the noble king he did. He had no pious training, but only a heritage of weakness in his moral fibre, for which God graciously made all fair allowance.

With Hezekiah's ascent to the throne at the age of twenty-five there began a period of religious revival in which he was encouraged by the noblest and most eloquent of the Hebrew prophets, Isaiah, who knew how to carry his religion into his politics.

I. Hezekiah was a man who prayed about the difficulties and dangers overtaking him. What faith and confidence in God he revealed when he spread Sennacherib's insolent letter before the Lord. Both Hezekiah and Isaiah defied mighty Assyria, God using one angel to slay one hundred and eighty-five thousand in the Assyrian camp.

The king knew how to pray about personal matters as well as military dangers. When smitten with a fatal illness, he turned his face to the wall and prayed. Isaiah, his friend and counselor, came to him with a message from God that he would not die but live. "I will add unto thy days fifteen years." Hezekiah asked with all his heart that he might live, and God continued his life.

But the question arises, why did Hezekiah desire the removal of his illness and the continuation of his life? What object did he have in mind? Was the king anxious to live in order to promote the glory of God, or was he actuated by some personal motive? It is apparent that Hezekiah was afraid of death and loved life in itself. Death was not the same to Hezekiah as it was to Paul, who had a desire to depart, seeing death was far better than life.

At the time of his sickness, Hezekiah had no son, and this fact possibly added to his desire to live. Three years after his recovery Manasseh was born, who became a curse upon the earth and an abomination in the sight of the Lord. Here, then, was one of the results of Hezekiah's answered prayer. It might have been better for Judah if Hezekiah had died without such an heir. Many prayers we offer are mistakes. God graciously grants our requests but "brings leanness to our souls" (Ps. 106:15). Perhaps Hezekiah's sin began in his unwillingness to go to heaven when God sent for him (II Kings 20:1-3).

II. Hezekiah's simple faith in God was the source and secret of his strength. He believed God ruled among the armies of heaven and of earth. His faith was the intuitive perception that God was near— a real Personality and not a mere tendency making for righteousness. The loss of faith is ultimately the loss of moral power. One of the main lessons of Hezekiah's life is, *Have faith in God.*

III. Hezekiah lost favor with God because of pride. After all the divine blessings showered upon him, he allowed his heart to be lifted up with pride. Vanity and self-sufficiency led the king astray. His heart became obsessed with his household treasures. He turned from God to goods. "Hezekiah rendered not again according to the benefit done unto him; for his heart was lifted up: therefore there was wrath upon him, and upon Judah and Jerusalem" (II Chron. 32:24, 25). Sin never ends with the person committing it.

The four crises Hezekiah faced were:

The crisis of choice, and he chose to forsake the idols of his father and purge the kingdom of idolatry (II Chron. 28:23, 25; II Kings 18:22).

The crisis of invasion (II Chron. 32:1-19). Prayer brought deliverance (II Chron. 32:20, 21).

The crisis of sickness. Obedience furnished the foundation of the king's prayer for healing (Isa. 38:1-5).

The crisis of prosperity. Alas, Hezekiah manifested pride when he displayed his treasures to the ungodly (Isa. 39).

2. *A son of Neariah* and a descendant of the royal house of Judah (I Chron. 3:23).

3. *An ancestor of the prophet Zephaniah* (Zeph. 1:1). Given in Common Version as Hizkiah.

4. *An exile,* descendant of Ater who returned from exile in Babylon (Ezra 2:16; Neh. 7:21).

HEZION [Hē′ zǐ on]—VISION. *The father of Tabrimon* and grandfather of Benhadad, king of Syria in Asa's time (I Kings 15:18). Perhaps the same as Rezon of I Kings 11:23.

HEZIR [Hē′ zûr]—RETURNING HOME or A SWINE.
1. *A descendant of Aaron* whose family grew and became leaders of the seventeenth monthly course in David's day (I Chron. 24:15).
2. *A chief of the people who sealed the covenant* (Neh. 10:20).

HEZRAI, HEZRO [Hĕz′ ra ī, Hĕz′ rō]—ENCLOSED or BEAUTIFUL. *A Carmelite,* one of David's mighty men (II Sam. 23:35; I Chron. 11:37).

HEZRON, ESRON [Hĕz′ rŏn]—SHUT IN, BLOOMING or DART OF JOY.
1. *A son of Pharez or Perez* and grandson of Judah and founder of a tribal family (Gen. 46:12; Num. 26:6, 21; Ruth 4:18, 19; I Chron. 2:9; 4:1).
2. *A son of Reuben* and founder of the Hezronite family (Gen. 46:9; Ex. 6:14; Num. 26:6; I Chron. 5:3). Also name of a town called Hazor (Josh. 15:23).

HIDDAI [Hǐd′ da ī]—JOYFUL or MIGHTY. *A man from Gaash,* one of David's heroes (II Sam. 23:30).

HIEL [Hǐ′ el]—GOD LIVETH or THE LIFE OF GOD. *A native of Bethel* who rebuilt Jericho and who experienced the curse pronounced upon the rebuilding of it by Joshua (I Kings 16:34).

HILKIAH [Hǐl kǐ′ ah]—PORTION OF JEHOVAH or JEHOVAH IS PROTECTION.
1. *The father of Eliakim* who was over Hezekiah's household (II Kings 18:18, 26, 37; Isa. 22:20; 36:3, 22).
2. *High priest* in king Josiah's reign (II Kings 22:4–14; 23:4, 24).
3. *A descendant of Merari,* son of Levi (I Chron. 6:45).
4. *A son of Hosah,* descendant of Merari, and a gatekeeper at the Tabernacle (I Chron. 26:11).
5. *A priest* who stood with Ezra as he read the law to the people (Neh. 8:4; 11:11; 12:7, 21).
6. *A priest of Anathoth* and father of the prophet Jeremiah and contemporary of Gemariah (Jer. 1:1).

HILLEL [Hǐl′ lel]—PRAISED GREATLY. *Father of Abdon,* of the judges of Israel. He lived in Mount Ephraim (Judg. 12:13, 15).

HINNOM [Hǐn′ nom]—GRATIS. *A person of whom nothing is known* save that he had a son whose name is not given. The valley of Hinnom was the place where human sacrifice and filth were burned (Josh. 15:8; 18:16).

HIRAH [Hī′ rah]—DESTINATION or NOBILITY. *An Adullamite,* and friend of Judah, with whom he shared a partnership in the matter of flocks (Gen. 38:1, 12).

HIRAM [Hī′ ram]—CONSECRATION.
1. *The king of Tyre,* and friend of both David and Solomon (II Sam. 5:11; I Kings 5:1, 8; II Chron. 2:11, 13).
2. *A man of eminence* and the principal architect sent by king Hiram to Solomon (I Kings 7:13, 40, 45). Also called Huram.

HIZKIAH, HEZEKIAH [Hĭz kī′ ah,   Hĕz e kī′ ah]—JEHOVAH IS STRONG. *An ancestor of Zephaniah the prophet.* In the Hebrew the name is the same as Hizkijah and Hezekiah (Zeph. 1:1) .

HIZKIJAH [Hĭz kī′ jah]—JEHOVAH IS STRONG. Perhaps Ater-hizkijah given in lists of returned exiles (Neh. 10:17).

HOBAB [Hō′ băb]—BELOVED, LOVER or FAVORED. *Either the father-in-law of Moses or the father-in-law's son.* In Numbers 10:29 he is called the son of Raguel or Reuel, who is also identified with Jethro (Num. 10:29; Judg. 4:11).

HOD [Hŏd]—GLORY or MAJESTY. *A son of Zophah,* a descendant of Asher (I Chron. 7:37).

HODAIAH [Hŏd a ī′ ah]—HONORER OF JEHOVAH. *The Hodaviah, son of Elioenai,* a descendant of the royal line of Judah from which Jesus sprang (I Chron. 3:24).

HODAVIAH [Hŏd a vī′ ah]—JEHOVAH IS HIS PRAISE.
1. *A chief of the half tribe of Manasseh,* east of Jordan (I Chron. 5:24).
2. *The son of Hasenuah,* a Benjamite (I Chron. 9:7).
3. *A Levite* and founder of the family of the Ben-hodaviah (Ezra 2:40). Called Hodevah in Nehemiah 7:43.

HODEVAH [Hō dĕ′ vah]—JEHOVAH IS HONOR. *A Levite family* that returned from captivity (Neh. 7:43).

HODIAH, HODIJAH [Hō dī′ ah, Hō dī′ jah]—SPLENDOR OF JEHOVAH.
1. *A Levite* of the time of Ezra and Nehemiah (Neh. 8:7; 9:5; 10:10, 13).
2. *A chief of the people under Nehemiah* (Neh. 10:18). Also name of wife of one Ezra, also called Jehudijah (I Chron. 4:19).

HOHAM [Hō' ham]—JEHOVAH PROTECTS THE MULTITUDE. *An Amorite king of Hebron,* who entered into league with other kings against Joshua. One of the five kings captured in the cave of Makkedah and put to death (Josh. 10:3).

HOMAM, HEMAM [Hō' mam, Hē' mam]—RAGING or DESTROYER. *Son of Lotan* and grandson of Seir (I Chron. 1:39). See Genesis 36:22 for Hemam.

HOPHNI [Hŏph' nī]—STRONG. *A son of Eli,* the high priest and judge who proved unworthy of his sacred offices (I Sam. 1:3; 2:34; 4:4, 11, 17). Hophni is always associated with his brother Phinehas. The two were partners in evil practices and brought a twice-pronounced curse upon their heads (I Sam. 2:34; 3). Both were slain at the battle of Aphek, and this coupled with the loss of the Ark, caused the death of Eli. Both sons disgraced their priestly office in a twofold way:

I.   In claiming and appropriating more than their due of the sacrifices (I Sam. 2:13–17).

II.   In their immoral actions in the Tabernacle (2:22; Amos 2:7, 8).

HORAM [Hō' ram]—ELEVATED. *A king of Gezer,* defeated and slain by Joshua (Josh. 10:33).

HORI [Hō' rī]—FREE or NOBLE.

1.   *A son of Seir,* a Horite, and founder of the "Horites" (Gen. 36:22, 29, 30).

2.   *A Simeonite* whose son Shaphat was one of the spies (Num. 13:5).

HOSAH [Hō' sah]—FLEEING FOR REFUGE. *A Levite porter* selected by David to be one of the first doorkeepers to the Ark after its return (I Chron. 16: 38; 26:10, 11, 16). Also name of a city of the tribe of Asher (Josh. 19:29).

HOSEA, OSHEA, OSEE, HOSHEA—[Hō zē' ă, Ō shē' ă, Hō shē' ă]—JEHOVAH IS HELP or SALVATION.

1.   *The son of Beeri* and first of the so-called Minor Prophets (Hosea 1:1).

The Man with a Sorrowful Heart

Little is known of Hosea's history beyond what we find in his writings. He has been called the first prophet of Grace and Israel's earliest evangelist. He was a native of the Northern Kingdom, the iniquities and idolatries of which weighed heavily on his heart. He bore the same name as that of the last king of Israel (II Kings 15:30). In Jewish tradition, he is identified with Beerah of Reuben (I Chron. 5:6). Christian tradition, however, relates him to the Hosea of the tribe of Isaachar.

The home tragedy overtaking him earned him the title of "The

Prophet of a Sorrowful Heart." Through the wrongs he suffered he came to realize the sins committed by Israel against God, and the long history of unfaithfulness to Him. The accounts of Hosea's marriage, the birth of his children and his wife's unfaithfulness and restoration make sad reading. Hosea was called to express God's message and to manifest His character.

Gomer, his wife, was immoral; hence the word of the Lord came to him amid much personal anguish; his home life was destroyed. Society was corrupt and God's law spurned, and Hosea came to see in his own suffering a reflection of what the sorrow of God must be, when Israel proved utterly unfaithful.

Three children were born to Hosea and Gomer:

I.   Jezreel, recalling the deed of blood (II Kings 10), and by it a knell was rung in the ears of Jeroboam. The name of this child was an omen of coming judgment.

II.   Lo-ruhamah, meaning, "one who never knew a father's love." This expressive name pointed to a time when, no more pitied by Jehovah, Israel would be given over to her enemies.

III.   Lo-ammi, signifying "one not belonging to me." Israel had turned from a father's love and deserved not to belong to God. Thus this third child's name prophesied the driving out of the children of Israel from their land to exile.

Gomer, the erring wife, is received back (Hos. 3:1, 2), the price of her redemption being paid by Hosea. So the prophet was not only God's messenger of grace — he reflected God's character and fore-shadowed ultimate redemption through the Messiah and Israel's re-establishment as a nation.

The four lessons we learn from the broken heart and the Book of Hosea have been fully expounded by Dr. Stuart Holden:

Anguish quickens apprehension.

Iniquity inspires moral indignation.

Suffering begets sympathy.

The divine character sanctifies human conduct.

2.   Joshua's earlier name — changed by Moses (Num. 13:8, 16). Deuteronomy 32:44 gives Hoshea.

3.   *The son of Azaziah* and prince of Ephraim in David's reign (I Chron. 27:20).

4.   *A son of Elah,* the last king of the Northern Kingdom (II Kings 15:30).

5.   *A chief under Nehemiah* who with others signed the covenant (Neh. 10:23).

Hosea is called Osee in the New Testament copy from the LXX.

HOSHAIAH [Hŏsh a ĭ' ah]—GOD HATH SAVED.

1.   *The man who led the princes of Judah* and walked behind the chorus at the dedication of the wall (Neh. 12:32).

2. *The father of Jezaniah* or Azariah, and a man of influence in Nebuchadnezzar's time (Jer. 42:1, 2).

HOSHAMA [Hŏsh' a mă]—JEHOVAH HATH HEARD. *A son of Jeconiah or Jehoiachin,* king of Judah (I Chron. 3:18).

HOTHAM, HOTHAN [Hŏ' tham, Hŏ' than]—SIGNET RING or DETERMINATION.
1. *A son of Heber* of the family of Beriah. An Asherite (I Chron. 7:32).
2. *An Aroerite,* whose two sons Shama and Jehiel were among David's heroes (I Chron. 11:44).

HOTHIR [Hŏ' thûr]—ABUNDANCE. *The thirteenth son of Heman,* David's seer and singer. A Kohathite (I Chron. 25:4, 28).

HOZAI—JEHOVAH IS SEEING. *The writer of the history of King Manasseh* (II Chron. 33:19 A.V.; also in footnote, R.V.).

HUL [Hŭl]—CIRCLE. *The second son of Aram* and grandson of Shem. A descendant of Noah (Gen. 10:23; I Chron. 1:17). Called son of Shem.

HUPHAM [Hŭ' pham]—PROTECTED or A COVERING. *A son of Benjamin* and founder of a tribal family known as the Huphamites (Num. 26:39). Name is given as Huppim in Genesis 46:21 and I Chronicles 7:12. Also expressed as Huram (I Chron. 8:5).

HUPPAH [Hŭp' pah]—A COVERING or PROTECTION. *A priest* of the thirteenth course in David's time. Either a son of Bela or of Ir or Iri, one of Bela's five sons (I Chron. 24:13). This name is given as Huppim in Genesis 46:21 and I Chronicles 7:12, 15.

HUR [Hûr]—NOBLE or SPLENDOR.
1. *The man who, with Aaron, held up the hands of Moses,* so that by the continual uplifting of the sacred staff Israel might prevail over Amalek. Jewish tradition has it that Hur was the husband of Miriam and the grandfather of Bezaleel (Ex. 17:10, 12; 24:14).
2. *A son of Caleb* the son of Hezron (Ex. 31:2; 35:30; I Chron. 2: 19, 20; II Chron. 1:5).
3. *The fourth of the five kings* of Midian slain with Balaam (Num. 31:8; Josh. 13:21).
4. *The father of one of Solomon's purveyors* in Mount Ephraim (I Kings 4:8).
5. *The father of Caleb* and eldest son of Ephratah (I Chron. 2: 50; 4:4).
6. *A son of Judah* (I Chron. 4:1).
7. *The father of Rephaiah,* who was ruler of half of Jerusalem and who assisted in the repair of the walls (Neh. 3:9).

HURAI [Hū′ raī]—A LINEN WEAVER or NOBLE. *One of David's heroes* from the brooks of Gaash (I Chron. 11:32). Also called Hiddai (II Sam. 23:30).

HURAM [Hū′ ram]—NOBLE or INGENIOUS.
1. *A Benjamite,* son of Bela (I Chron. 8:5).
2. *The king of Tyre,* called Hiram in II Samuel 5:11 and Huram in II Chronicles 2:3, 12.
3. *A Tyrian artificer* employed by Solomon (II Chron. 4:11, 16).

HURI [Hū′ rī]—LINEN WEAVER. *The father of Abihail,* a Gadite (I Chron. 5:14).

HUSHAH [Hū′ shah]—HASTE or PASSION. *A son of Ezer,* the son of Hur, a Judahite (I Chron. 4:4).

HUSHAI [Hū′ shaī]—QUICK or HASTENING. *One of David's two leading men,* an Archite (II Sam. 15:32, 37; 16:16–18; 17:5–15; I Chron. 27:33). This native of Erech was the friend and counselor of David who overthrew the counsels of Ahithophel.

HUSHAM [Hū′ sham]—HASTE or PASSION. *A king of Edom,* who succeeded Jobab. He came from the land of Teman (Gen. 36:34, 35; I Chron. 1:45, 46).

HUSHIM [Hū′shim]—OPULENT or HASTING.
1. *A son of Dan* (Gen. 46:23). Called Shusham in Numbers 26:42.
2. *The son of Aher,* a Benjamite (I Chron. 7:12). Also the name of one of the two wives of Shaharaim (I Chron. 8:8, 11).

HUZ [Hŭz]—FIRM. Also given as Uz, the *eldest son of Nahor and Milcah* (Genesis 22:21).

HYMENAEUS [Hў me nae′ us]—NUPTIAL or FROM HYMEN, THE GOD OF MARRIAGE. *A professed Christian* who had fallen into heresies, who tried to shipwreck the faith of true believers and who was excommunicated by Paul (I Tim. 1:20; II Tim. 2:17).

I

IBHAR [Ib′ här]—CHOOSER or GOD DOTH CHOOSE. *One of David's sons,* born at Jerusalem (II Sam. 5:15; I Chron. 3:6; 14:5).

IBNEIAH [Ib nē′ iah]—JEHOVAH DOTH BUILD. *The Benjamite son of Jeroham* and head of his father's house in Jerusalem (I Chron. 9:8).

IBNIJAH [Ĭb nĭ′ jah]—JEHOVAH IS BUILDER. *A Benjamite, father of Reuel,* whose family dwelt in Jerusalem (I Chron. 9:8).

IBRI [Ĭb′rī]—PASSER OVER or A HEBREW. *A son of Jaaziah,* a Merarite Levite in David's time (I Chron. 24:27).

IBSAM, JIBSAM [Ĭb′sam, Jĭb′ sam]—FRAGRANT. *A man of Issachar,* of the family of Tola (I Chron. 7:2).

IBZAN [Ĭb′ zăn]—SPLENDID or ACTIVE. *One of the minor judges* who succeeded Jephthah, and who judged Israel seven years and was buried at Bethlehem. He had thirty sons and thirty daughters whose marriages he arranged. His sixty children testified to his plurality of wives and his social importance. Jewish tradition identifies Ibzan as Boaz (Judg. 12:8, 10).

ICHABOD [Ĭ′ cha bŏd]—THE GLORY IS NOT, WHERE IS THE GLORY or INGLORIOUS. *The posthumous son of Phinehas* and grandson of Eli. His name commemorated a tragic crisis in Israel's history, namely, the great slaughter of the people, including Hophni and Phinehas, and the capture of the Ark by the Philistines. Such terrible calamity resulted in Eli's death at ninety-eight. The wife of Phinehas was so shocked over the dread news that when her child was born she called him Ichabod saying, "The glory is departed from Israel: for the ark of God is taken" (I Sam. 4:21, 22).

IDBASH [Ĭd′ băsh]—HONEY SWEET or CORPULENT. *One of the three sons of Abi-etam,* a man of Judah (I Chron. 4:3).

IDDO [Ĭd′ dō]—AFFECTIONATE, FESTAL, FAVORITE or HIS POWER.

1. *Father of Ahinadab,* and one of Solomon's purveyors at Mahanaim (I Kings 4:14).

2. *A descendant of Gershom,* son of Levi (I Chron. 6:21). Called Adaiah, and ancestor of Asaph the seer (I Chron. 6:41).

3. *A son of Zechariah* and a chief in David's time of the half tribe of Manasseh east of Jordan (I Chron. 27:21).

4. *A seer* who denounced the wrath of God against Jeroboam, the son of Nebat, and who wrote a book of visions (II Chron. 9:29; 12:15; 13:22).

5. *Grandfather of the prophet Zechariah* (Ezra 5:1; 6:14; Zech 1:1).

6. *A priest* who returned from Babylon (Neh. 12:4, 16).

7. *The chief at Casiphia* through whom Ezra obtained help. He was a Nethinim (Ezra 8:17).

8. *A man who put away his foreign wife* (Ezra 10:43). Jadau is a corruption of Iddo.

IGAL [Ĭ'găl]—DELIVERER or HE WILL VINDICATE.
1. *Son of Joseph* of the tribe of Issachar, and one of the spies sent from Kadesh to search Canaan (Num. 13:7).
2. *The son of Nathan of Zobah,* and one of David's guard (II Sam. 23:36). Called Joel, the brother of Nathan, in I Chronicles 11:38, and identical with Igeal in I Chronicles 3:22.

IGDALIAH [Ĭg da lĭ' ah]—GREAT IS JEHOVAH or GREATNESS OF THE LORD. *"A man of God,"* father of Hanan, who had a chamber in the Temple and is mentioned in connection with Jeremiah's interview with the Rechabites (Jer. 35:4).

IGEAL [Ĭğ' e äl]—DELIVERER. A son of Shemaiah and descendant of king Jeconiah (I Chron. 3:22). Originally the same as Igal.

IKKESH [Ĭk' kĕsh]—PERVERSE or SUBTLE. *Father of Ira the Tekoite,* and one of David's heroes (II Sam. 23:26; I Chron. 11:28; 27:9).

ILAI [Ĭ' laī]—ELEVATED or SUPREME. *An Ahohite* and another of David's heroes (I Chron. 11:29). Called Zalmon in II Samuel 23:28.

IMLA, IMLAH [Ĭm' lă, Ĭm' lah]—GOD DOTH FILL, FULFILLING, or PLENTITUDE.—*The Father of Michaiah,* a prophet in the days of Ahab who, along with Jehoshaphat, consulted Imla before the Ramoth-gilead expedition (I Kings 22:8, 9; II Chron. 18:7, 8).

IMMER [Ĭm' mŭr)—TALKATIVE or PROMINENT.
1. *A descendant of Aaron* and head of a family of priests (I Chron. 9:12; Ezra 2:37; 10:20; Neh. 7:40; 11:13).
2. *A priest* of the sanctuary in David's time (I Chron. 24:14).
3. *One who returned from Babylon* without a genealogy (Ezra 2:59; Neh. 7:61). Perhaps the name of a place rather than that of a person.
4. *The father of Zadok* (Neh. 3:29).
5. *A priest in Jeremiah's time* (Jer. 20:1).

IMNA [Ĭm' nă]—GOD DOTH RESTRAIN or WITHDRAWING. *A son of Helem* and an Asherite chief (I Chron. 7:35).

IMNAH [Ĭm' nah]—PROSPERITY or HE ALLOTTETH.
1. *The eldest son of Asher* and founder of a tribal family (Num. 26:44; I Chron. 7:30). Name given as Jimnah or Jimna (Gen. 46:17).
2. *A Levite, father of Kore,* in Hezekiah's reign (II Chron. 31:14).

IMRAH [Ĭm' rah]—STUBBORN or HEIGHT OF JEHOVAH. *An Asherite, son of Zophah* (I Chron. 7:36).

IMRI [Ĭm' rī]—PROJECTING or ELOQUENT.
1. *A Judahite, son of Bani* and descendant of Perez (I Chron. 9:4).
2. *Father of the Zaccur* who helped to rebuild the wall (Neh. 3:2).

IPHEDEIAH [Ĭph e dē' iah]—JEHOVAH DOTH DELIVER or REDEMPTION OF THE LORD. *A Benjamite chief,* son of Shashak (I Chron. 8:25).

IR [Ŭr]—WATCHER. *A Benjamite,* the father of Shuppim and Huppim (I Chron. 7:12). Perhaps same as Iri of I Chronicles 7:7.

IRA [Ĭ' rä]—WATCHER, WATCHFUL or CITY WATCH.
1. *A Jairite, and priest* or chief minister to David (II Sam. 20:26).
2. *The Ithrite,* and one of David's guard (II Sam. 23:38).
3. *Son of Ikkesh,* a Tekoite and another of David's guard (I Chron. 11:28, 40; 27:9).

IRAD [Ĭ' răd]—WILD ASS. *Son of Enoch* and grandson of Cain (Gen. 4:18).

IRAM [Ĭ' ram]—WATCHFUL. *A chieftain of Edom* (Gen. 36:43; I Chron. 1:54).

IRI [Ĭ'rī]—JEHOVAH IS WATCHER. *A son of Bela,* son of Benjamin (I Chron. 7:7). See Ir.

IRIJAH [Ĭ rī' jah]—GOD DOTH SEE, PROVIDE or FEAR OF THE LORD. *A captain of the guard in Jerusalem* who arrested Jeremiah on the charge of intending to desert to the Chaldeans (Jer. 37:13, 14).

IRNAHASH [Ŭr nā' hăsh]—SERPENT or MAGIC CITY. *A descendant of Chelub* from Judah through Caleb son of Hur (I Chron. 4:12). Some writers suggest this may be a city and not a person.

IRU—[Ĭ' rōō]—WATCH. *Eldest son of the celebrated Caleb,* Joshua's companion (I Chron. 4:15). Correct name may be Ir.

ISAAC [Ĭ' zaac] HE LAUGHETH or LAUGHING ONE. *The son of Abraham and Sarah,* who was born at Gerar when Abraham was one hundred years of age and Sarah was about ninety years old (Gen. 17:19, 21; 21:3–12; 22:2–9).

The Man Whose Birth Caused a Laugh

Isaac is one of the few cases in the Bible in which God selected a name for a child and announced it before he was born. In the Old Testament we have Isaac, Ishmael, Solomon, Josiah, Cyrus and Isaiah's son; in the New Testament, John the Baptist and Jesus.

Isaac's beautiful and suggestive name, "he laughed," commemorates the two laughings at the promise of God — the laughing of the father's joy and the laughing of Sarah's incredulity which soon passed into penitence and faith (Gen. 21:6). Isaac was the child of the covenant, "I will establish My covenant *with him*." To three patriarchs in succession was this covenant specifically given: to *Abraham,* as he left Chaldea (Gen. 12:3); to *Isaac,* when in Canaan during the famine (Gen. 26:4); to *Jacob,* at Bethel (Gen. 28:14). Isaac, however, was the first to inherit the covenant, and to him God gave the whole inheritance of Abraham (Gen. 24:35).

We have no record of Isaac's early life apart from the fact that he was circumcised when eight days of age (Gen. 21:4). Doubtless as a lad he became God's child in heart and life, ever mindful of the covenant he was heir to. When, according to Josephus, Isaac was twenty-five years of age, he was taken from Beer-sheba to the land of Moriah, where, as the burnt offering, Abraham presented him to God. While we have Abraham's unquestioning faith in his submission to the divine command to offer up his only son, we must not forget Isaac's supreme confidence in his father and also his willing consent to become the victim (Gen. 22:12; 26:5; Heb. 11:17). Thus in Isaac we have a type of Him who *gave Himself* for our sins. From the day of his surrender to death, Isaac became a dedicated man. "The altar sanctified the gift."

When his mother Sarah died, Isaac was a man of thirty-six, and was deeply grieved over the death of his mother. Comfort was his when he took Rebekah as his wife to help fill the vacant place in his heart. To the credit of Isaac it must be said that he was the only one of the patriarchs who had but one wife. It is also perfectly clear from the ancient idyll, one of the most beautiful in all literature, that Isaac left the choice of his wife to God. When the caravan bearing Rebekah neared home, Isaac was in the fields *meditating* or "praying," as the margin expresses it (Gen. 24:63).

For many years Isaac and Rebekah were childless, but God heard Isaac's prayers and Rebekah gave birth to twins, Jacob and Esau. Isaac seems to have outlived his wife, and died at the age of 180 (Gen. 35:28). For some fifty years Isaac was almost blind, a sad and pitiful lot for God's chosen one.

The character of Isaac, beautiful though it was in many ways, yet carried a few blots. He followed his father, Abraham, in deceitfulness when he called his wife his sister, bringing upon himself the rebuke of Abimelech. He also loved "savoury food," which should have been alien to a man so calm and still, lord of his passion and himself. Then in the matter of Esau and the blessing, Isaac surely rebelled against the Lord's purpose.

Among the commendable features of his character, mention can be made of Isaac's submission (Gen. 22:6, 9); meditation (Gen. 24:63); instinctive trust in God (Gen. 22:7, 8); deep devotion (Gen. 24:67; 25:21); peaceableness (Gen. 26:20–22); prayerfulness (Gen. 26:25); faith (Heb. 11:16, 17). "The fear of Isaac" (Gen. 31:42, 53), means the God tremblingly adored by the patriarch.

ISAIAH, ESAIAS [Ĭ zā′ iah, Ĭ za′ ias]—JEHOVAH IS HELPER or SALVA-
TION IS OF THE LORD. The name of the greatest of the Assyrian group
of prophets is synonymous with Joshua or Jesus and symbolic of his
message. Little is known of this gospel prophet, often severe in tone.
He is described as the son of Amoz, not Amos the prophet (Isa. 1:1;
2:1; 6:1; 7:3; 13:1). Some scholars suggest that Amoz was the uncle of
Uzziah which, if true, would make Isaiah the king's cousin. Evidently
Isaiah was of good family and education.

The Man of Many Parts

Isaiah's home and the scene of his labors was Jerusalem. His wife
was a prophetess (Isa. 8:3) and bore the prophet two sons, whose names
were symbolic of those aspects of the nation's history which Isaiah
enforced in his prophecies:

Shear-jashub, meaning, "a remnant shall return" (Isa. 7:3).

Maher-shalal-hash-baz, implying, "Haste ye, speed to the spoil" (Isa.
8:1-4). Often names were given for signs and wonders in Israel.

Isaiah's original call to service is unrecorded, but in chapter six we
have his vision and commission. A prophet of Judah, Isaiah ministered during the reign of Uzziah, Jotham, Ahab and Hezekiah, kings
of Judah. He comes before us as a man of many parts — a man eminently gifted and called of God as the first and chief of Israel's prophets
and poets.

I. The Writer. Isaiah wrote a history of the reign of Uzziah and
Ahaz (II Chron. 26:22; 32:32). No other Old Testament writer uses
so many beautiful and picturesque illustrations, epigrams and meta-
phors as Isaiah, who was also a poet of no mean order (Isa. 1:13; 5:18;
12:1-6; 13:3).

The book bearing his name is made up of sixty-six chapters, and
is a miniature Bible with its sixty-six books.

II. The Statesman. Isaiah was an ardent patriot, loving God and
his nation. He was a bold, true statesman, seeking no court favor.
How strongly he denounced all foreign alliances, (Isa. 7:5; 37:22)!
It is Isaiah who gives us the earliest recorded vision of world-wide
peace (Isa. 2:1-4).

III. The reformer. Like Noah, Isaiah was also a preacher of
righteousness, and exposed formalism as a bad substitute for spiritual
life and conduct (Isa. 36-39). Yet, like all the greatest contributors
to moral uplift, Isaiah, amid all his rebukes and denunciations of
evil, was truly optimistic.

IV. The Prophet. In no uncertain language Isaiah foretold the
future of Israel and Judah, and the downfall of Gentile nations. Many
of his predictions in regard to ancient nations have been fulfilled.
Then Isaiah was *The Christ-Harbinger,* prophesying the coming of
the Messianic King and Suffering Saviour. Chapter fifty-three of his
prophecy drips with the ruby blood of the Redeemer. No wonder
Jerome described Isaiah as "The Evangelical Prophet."

V. The Teacher. To perpetuate his message and influence, Isaiah formed a group of disciples to whose teaching and training he devoted himself when his public ministry seemed useless. He was not only a counselor of kings and princes, but an instructor of those who were eager for his vision. He was an orator without peer — Jerome likened him to Demosthenes. This trait must have made an impact upon those he sought to train.

VI. The Theologian. This dreamer and poet, architect and builder, prophet and statesman was also a theologian able to discourse upon the sovereignty and holiness of God with utmost clarity. What an artist with words Isaiah was! Every word from him stirs and strikes, as he expounds the lordship of Jehovah — the need of all men for cleansing — the forgiving grace of God. The prophet insisted upon reverence for God whose usual title he gave as "The Holy One of Israel." Sometimes stern in tone, he could also be tender and compassionate (Isa. 15:5; 16:9).

The time of his death is unknown. Legend has it that he was placed inside a hollow tree and sawn asunder at the command of Manasseh (Heb. 11:37).

ISCARIOT [Is cǎr′ I ot]—MAN OF KERIOTH or A MAN OF MURDER. *The designation of the traitor* is sometimes associated with *scortea*, a "leathern apron" which applied to Judas as the bearer of the bag, that is, "Judas with the apron." The Hebrew *ascara*, implies strangling (angina), given him after his death (Matt. 10:4; John 6:71 R.V.). See Judas.

ISHBAH [Ĭsh′ bah]—HE PRAISES or APPEASER. *Father of Eshtemoa*, a Judahite. It has been conjectured that he was the son of Mered by his Egyptian wife Bithiah (I Chron. 4:17).

ISHBAK [Ĭsh′ bǎk]—FREE, EMPTY or EXHAUSTED. *A Son of Abraham* by Keturah and founder of a tribal family in northern Arabia (Gen. 25:2; I Chron. 1:32).

ISHBI-BENOB [Ĭsh′ bĭ-bē′ nŏb]—DWELLER ON THE MOUNT or HE THAT PREDICTS. *A son of Rapha* and one of the four Philistines of the giant stock attacking David in battle, but slain by Abishai (II Sam. 21:16).

ISHBOSHETH [Ĭsh bō′ sheth]—A MAN OF SHAME. *One of Saul's younger sons* who was made king over Israel by Abner. He was originally called Eshbaal, "The Lord's man" but his name was changed after Saul's departure (II Sam. 2:8 with I Chron. 8:33; 9:39). Ishbosheth contested the throne of Israel with David for seven years. Ultimately he was deserted by Abner and murdered in his bed by two of his captains.

ISHI [Ĭ′ shĭ]—MY HELP or SAVING.

1. *A son of Appaim,* a descendant of Pharez son of Judah, and of the house of Jerahmeel (I Chron. 2:31).

2. *A descendant of Judah* through Caleb the spy (I Chron. 4:20).

3. *A Simeonite* whose tribe overcome the Amalekites (I Chron. 4:42).

4. *One of the heads of the half tribe of Manasseh* (I Chron. 5:24). Also the symbolic name given to God's people (Hos. 2:16).

ISHIAH, ISSHIAH, ISHIJAH [Ĭ shĭ′ ah, Is shĭ′ ah, Ĭ shĭ′ jah]— JEHOVAH EXISTS or FORGIVETH.

1. *The fifth son of Izrahiah,* and one of the tribal heads of Issachar in David's time (I Chron. 7:3).

2. *A descendant of Moses* (I Chron. 24:21).

3. *A descendant of Levi* (I Chron. 24:25).

4. *One of the Bene-Harim* who married a foreign wife (Ezra 10:31).

ISHMA [Ĭsh′ mă′—DESOLATION, DISTINCTION or ELEVATED. *One of the sons of Etam* and a descendant of Caleb the son of Hur (I Chron. 4:3).

ISHMAEL [Ĭsh′ ma el]—GOD HEARETH.

1. *The son of Abraham,* by Hagar, Sarah's Egyptian maid. Ishmael was born when Abraham was eighty-six years of age, and was circumcised when he was thirteen years of age, along with his father and his servants. He received the divine promise that he would beget twelve princes and become a great nation. He died at the age of 137 (Gen. 16:11–16; 17:18–26; 25:9–17; 28:9; 36:3). Ishmael was the founder of the tribal family called Ishmaelites, sometimes referred to as Midianites (Gen. 37:25–28).

The Man Who Became an Outcast

Ishmael, who was some fourteen years older than Isaac, was not his father's heir and did not share his father's property. Abraham was tenderly attached to Ishmael (Gen. 17:18), and the casting out of the boy and his mother by Sarah was a great grief to Abraham. Such a hard transaction was necessary to keep the inheritance unbroken for Isaac's possession. "To thee will I give it" (Gal. 3:16; 4:30). Ishmael's name is a monument of God's goodness in answering prayer. "God shall hear." What did He hear? He heard the moaning of Hagar's broken heart. God said concerning Ishmael: "I will make him a great nation" (Gen. 21:18).

The names of Ishmael's twelve sons have been preserved but there is no record of any good they achieved (Gen. 25:13–16).

Paul tells us that the record of Hagar and Ishmael is an allegory (Gal. 4:24). Hagar and Sarah represent two covenants — Jewish and Christian. Hagar represents the law, and Ishmael, because he was born of the bond woman, typifies those who are under the law. Isaac, because of his super-natural birth, represents those born anew by the Spirit of God.

The casting out of Ishmael has been productive of bitter fruit, surviving in the religion of Mohammed. The wild hearts beat on in the bosoms of those who form the Arab world. Little did Sarah know, when she persuaded Abraham to take Hagar that she was originating a rivalry which has run in the keenest strife through the ages, and which oceans of blood have not stopped.

The Moslem Arabs claim descent from Ishmael. Ishmael's mother and wife were Egyptian, which differentiates them from pure Hebrew. Arabian tribes springing from Ishmael are scattered throughout the Arabian peninsula. When Ishmael received his name, the Lord said that he would be "a wild man," or "a wild-ass man" as the Hebrew expresses it.

2. *An ancestor of Zebadiah* who was one of Jehoshaphat's judicial officers (II Chron. 19:11).

3. *A Son of Azer* and a descendant of Saul through Jonathan (I Chron. 8:38; 9:44).

4. *A son of Jehohanan* and one of the military officers associated with Jehoiada in the revolution to raise Joash to the throne (II Chron. 23:1).

5. *A son of Pashbur* and one of the priests persuaded by Ezra to put away his foreign wife (Ezra 10:22).

6. *A son of Nethaniah,* a member of the royal house of David who took part in the murder of Gedaliah. His vile conduct and character are fully described by Jeremiah (40:8–16; 41).

ISHMAIAH, ISMAIAH [Ish ma ī′ ah, Is ma ī′ ah]—JEHOVAH HEARETH.

1. *Son of Obadiah* and head of the Zebulunites in David's reign (I Chron. 27:19).

2. *A Gibeonite* who joined David at Ziklag (I Chron. 12:4).

ISHMERAI [Ish′ me raī]—GOD KEEPETH. *Son of Elpaal* and a descendant of Benjamin and chief of his tribe (I Chron. 8:18).

ISHOD [Ĭ′ shŏd]—MAN OF HONOR or MAN OF SPLENDOR. *Son of Hammoleketh,* of the tribe of Manasseh, and because of his near relationship to Gilead, an influential person (I Chron. 7:18). Proper name is Ish-dod.

ISHPAH, ISPAH [Is′pah]—BALD. *Son of Beriah,* a Benjamite (I Chron. 8:16).

ISHPAN [Ish′ păn]—FIRM or STRONG. *A son of Shashak,* a chief Benjamite (I Chron. 8:22).

ISHUAH, ISUAH [Ish' u ah, Is' u ah]—EQUAL or SELF-SATISFIED. *The second son of Asher,* who perhaps died childless, accounting for no list of heirs (Gen. 46:17; I Chron. 7:30). Called Isuah in I Chronicles 7:30.

ISHUI, ISHUAI, ISUI, JESUI, ISHVI [Ish' u ī, Ish' u aī, Is' u ī, Jĕs' u ī]—EQUALITY.
1. *The third son of Asher,* and founder of the tribal family of the Jesuites (Gen. 46:17; Num. 26:44; I Chron. 7:30).
2. *The second son of Saul* by his wife Ahinoam (I Sam. 14:49).

ISLIAH, JEZLIAH [Jĕz lī' ah]—DELIVERANCE. *A Benjamite,* son of Elpaal and descended from Shaharaim (I Chron. 8:18).

ISMACHIAH [Is ma chī ah]—JEHOVAH SUPPORTETH. *An overseer* connected with the Temple during Hezekiah's reign (II Chron. 31:13).

ISMAIAH [Is ma ī' ah]—JEHOVAH HEARS. *A Gibeonite warrior* who was over David's thirty valiant men (I Chron. 12:4).

ISPAH [Is' pah]—STRONG or HE WILL BE EMINENT. *A son of Beriah,* the Benjamite (I Chron. 8:16).

ISRAEL [Is' ra el]—HE STRIVETH WITH GOD or RULING WITH GOD. *The new name given to Jacob* at Jabbok (Gen. 32:28). The name also stands for the whole body of Jacob's descendants (Gen. 34:7; John 1:47). See Jacob.

ISSACHAR [Is' sa kar]—THERE IS HERE or REWARD.
1. *The ninth son of Jacob* and the fifth by Leah. Of Issachar as an individual not a word is recorded after his birth (Gen. 30:18; 49:14, 15; Deut. 33:18,19).

The Man Who Couched Down

The birth of Issachar was regarded by his mother as a kind of payment from the hand of God, "God hath given me my hire," said Leah, "because I have given my maiden to my husband: and she called his name Issachar" (that is, hire). In Jacob's blessing to Issachar, he is described as a "strong ass couching down between two burdens," or "between the sheep-folds." Two things are here mentioned as a *pair,* meaning they belong to each other; they are on either hand of Issachar, as necessary accompaniments to each other and to him. Between them his lot is cast.

When Israel was at war against Jabin, king of Canaan (Judg. 4), Reuben was at ease among the sheepfolds (Judg. 5:16), but the princes of Issachar fought valiantly, jeopardizing their lives unto death (Judg. 5:18). Then it is said that the children of Issachar had an understanding of the times and knew what Israel ought to do.

The strong-boned ass used with the cart, because of its capacity for bearing heavy burdens, was the apt figure used by Jacob to represent Issachar's great strength, a strength revealed on the field of battle. The love of ease, however, made the people of Issachar unwilling to use their strength at all times in the interests of their country. They *couched down* in luxury and the restfulness of a rural life. The tragedy overtaking many is their *couching down* when they ought to be rising up. Their prosperity induces indolence, and like the rich fool in the parable, they take their ease (Luke 12:19). The voice from heaven still cries, "Woe to them that are at ease in Zion" (Amos 6:1).

2. *A Levite doorkeeper* of the Tabernacle in David's time (I Chron. 26:5).

ITHAI [Ith' a ī]—BEING or EXISTING. *One of David's mighty men* (I Chron. 11:31). Called Ittai in II Samuel 23:29.

ITHAMAR [Ith' a mär]—PALM-COAST or PALM TREE. *The fourth and youngest son of Aaron* and Elisheba (Ex. 6:23; I Chron. 6:3; 24:1). His consecration, along with Aaron's other sons is noted in Exodus twenty-eight. Other historical facts regarding Ithamar are:

He was forbidden to mourn for Nadab and Abihu (Lev. 10:6).

He was forbidden to leave the tent of meeting (Lev. 10:7).

He was entrusted by Moses with priestly duties (Lev. 10:12).

He was rebuked by Moses for neglect (Lev. 10:16).

He was set over the Gershonites and Merarites in sanctuary service (Ex. 38:21; Num. 4:21-23; 7:7).

He was an ancestor of Eli (I Kings 2:27; I Chron. 24:3).

His family, in David's time, was only half the size of Eleazar's (I Chron. 24:4).

His family is represented among the returned exiles (Ezra 8:2).

ITHIEL [Ith' I el]—GOD IS or GOD IS WITH ME.

1. *A Benjamite,* the son of Jesaiah (Neh. 11:7).

2. *One of the two persons to whom Agar addressed* his discourse (Prov. 30:1. See R. V. margin).

ITHMAH [Ith' mah]—PURITY or BEREAVEMENT. *A Moabite,* and one of David's thirty heroes (I Chron. 11:46).

ITHRA [Ith' rä]—EXCELLENCE. *The father of Absalom's captain, Amasa,* and husband of Abigail (II Sam. 17:25).

ITHRAN [Ith' ran]—EXCELLENT or ABUNDANCE.

1. *A Horite,* son of Dishon or Dishan (Gen. 36:26; I Chron. 1:41).

2. *An Asherite,* son of Zophah (I Chron. 7:37) and who is thought to be identical with Jether (I Chron. 7:38).

ITHREAM [Ith' re ăm]—REMNANT or ABUNDANCE OF THE PEOPLE. *The sixth son of David,* born at Hebron. His mother was Eglah (II Sam. 3:5; I Chron. 3:3). Eglah was Michal and died giving birth to Ithream.

ITTAI [It 'ta ī]—PLOWMAN or LIVING.

1. *The Gittite leader* who, with six hundred Philistines, attached himself to David at the outbreak of Absalom's rebellion. This inhabitant of Gath was determined to follow David in all his trials. How admirable was the affirmation of his loyalty to the fugitive king: "As the Lord liveth, and as my lord the king liveth, surely in what place my lord the king shall be, whether in death or life, even there also will thy servant be" (II Sam. 15:21). Although a stranger and not of Israel, Ittai was more faithful than many who were Israelites by birth. His fidelity brought him a position of great trust (II Sam. 18:2).

2. *A Benjamite,* son of Ribai, who was one of David's heroes (II Sam. 23:29). He is called Ithai in I Chronicles 11:31.

IZHAR, IZEHAR [Iz' här, Iz' e här]—BRIGHT ONE or OLIVE OIL. *Son of Kohath,* son of Levi, and founder of a tribal family (Ex. 6:18, 21; Num. 3:19, 27). Also known as Zohar.

IZRAHIAH [Iz ra hī' ah]—JEHOVAH IS APPEARING or DOTH ARISE. *Son of Uzzi* and a grandson of Tola son of Issachar (I Chron. 7:3). See Jezrahiah.

IZRI [Iz' rī]—CREATIVE or FORMER. *A Levite son* of Jeduthun and chief of one of the Temple choirs (I Chron. 25:11). Perhaps the same person called Zeri in I Chronicles 25:3.

IZZIAH, JEZIAH [Jē zī' ah]—JEHOVAH EXALTETH. *A son of Parosh* who had married a foreign wife (Ezra 10:25).

J

When it comes to Bible names, the J's seem to have the longest list. There are over four hundred males listed under this letter; hence this section will be the longest in this study.

JAAKAN, JAKAN, AKAN [Jā' a kăn, Jā' kan, Ā' kăn]—INTELLIGENT. *A descendant of the Horites* of Mount Seir (Deut. 10:6; I Chron. 1:42). In Genesis 36:27 he is called Akan, a son of Ezer, son of Seir.

JAAKOBAH [Jā ăk' o bah]—TO JACOB or SUPPLANTING. *A Simeonite prince* and third son of Jacob (I Chron. 4:36).

JAALA, JAALAH [Jā ā' lă, Jā ā' lah]—DOE or ELEVATION. *A servant of Solomon* and founder of a tribal family. (Ezra 2:56; Neh. 7:58).

JAALAM [Jā ā' lam]—HE WILL BE HID. *A son of Esau by Aholibamah,* daughter of Anah (Gen. 36:5, 14, 18).

JAANAI, JANAI [Jā ā' naī]—JEHOVAH ANSWERS. *A Gadite chief* who dwelt in Bashan (I Chron. 5:12).

JAARE-OREGIM [Jā är e-Ŏr' e g͝ĭm]—FORESTERS or TAPESTRY OF THE WEAVERS. *The father of Elhanan,* one of David's heroes who killed the brother of the giant, Goliath (II Sam. 21:19). In I Chronicles 20:5 he is called Jair. Young says that Oregim, meaning "weavers," ought not to be a part of the name.

JAARESHIAH, JARESIAH [Jăr e sī' ah]—GOD DOTH NOURISH or PLANT. *A Benjamite, son of Jeroham* (I Chron. 8:27).

JAASAU, JAASU, JASSAI [Jā' a sau]—JEHOVAH MAKETH. *A son of Bani* induced by Ezra to put away his foreign wife (Ezra 10:37).

JAASIEL, JASIEL [Jā a' sĭ el, Jā' sĭ el]—GOD IS MAKER.
1. *One of David's mighty men,* and a Mesobaite (I Chron. 11:47).
2. *A son of Abner,* Saul's cousin (I Chron. 27:21).

JAAZANIAH [Jā ăz a nī' ah]—JEHOVAH DOTH HEARKEN.
1. *A son of a Maachathite* and a Jewish captain who swore allegiance to Gedaliah (II Kings 25:23). See Jezaniah (Jer. 40:8).
2. *A chief Rechabite,* son of a certain Jeremiah — not the prophet of that name (Jer. 35:3).
3. *A son of Shaphan,* a visionary exciting to idolatry in Ezekiel's time (Ezek 8:11).
4. *A son of Azur,* a wicked prince of Judah seen in vision by Ezekiel (Ezek. 11:1). The prophet prophesied against his counsels.

JAAZIAH [Jā a zī' ah]—GOD CONSOLETH or DETERMINES. *A son of Merari,* a Levite registered as head of his father's house in Solomon's time. He called his son Beno (I Chron. 24:26, 27).

JAAZIEL [Jā ā' zĭ el]—GOD IS DETERMINING or CONSOLING. *A Levite of the second rank* skilled in the use of the psaltery. He also had regular duty in the tent in Jerusalem (I Chron. 15:18). Called Aziel in I Chronicles 15:20.

JABAL [Jă' bal]—A RIVER, MOVING or WHICH GLIDES AWAY. *Son of the Canaanite,* Lamech, by his wife Adah. He became the father of those dwelling in tents and possessing cattle (Gen. 4:20).

JABESH [Jă' besh]—A DRY PLACE. *The father of king Shallum* who assassinated king Zechariah in order to reign in his stead (II Kings 15:10–14). Also the abbreviated name of Jabesh-gilead (I Sam. 11:1, 9).

JABEZ [Jă' bĕz]—HE MAKES SORROW or HEIGHT. *A man of Judah* named Jabez by his mother because she bore him in sorrow. He was noted for his honorable character and in his vow there is a play upon the meaning of his name (I Chron. 4:9, 10).

The Man Who Wanted a Blessing

The somewhat dreary genealogy of Judah in the opening chapters of Chronicles is enlivened by the heartfelt prayer of Jabez. Dr. Donald Fraser's beautiful comment on the passage is worthy of note:

> If the names are as rows of hard stones that fatigue us when we walk on them, all the more precious this fragrant shrub, growing among them, and casting a sweet scent around. For some cause untold, a mother bare her son with unusual grief and called him Jabez—Sorrowful; but it was God's good pleasure to turn this Benoni into a Benjamin, the Son of Sorrow into the Son of the Right Hand; and the sad-hearted mother's fear was not fulfilled, for Jabez proved more honorable than his brethren. If we inquire the reason, it was because he prayed.

He asked much and obtained much. The Lord did grant things for him, whereof, surely, Sorrowful was glad.

Jabez is also the name of a city in Judah where a family of scribes dwelt (I Chron. 2:55).

JABIN [Jă' bin]—GOD DISCERNETH or INTELLIGENT.
1. *A Canaanite,* king of Hazor in Galilee, defeated by Joshua near the Waters of Merom (Josh. 11:1–14).
2. *Another king of Canaan* who reigned at Hazor and oppressed Israel for twenty years. His army was defeated by Deborah and Barak. Probably a descendant of the first Hazor (Judg. 4; Ps. 83:9).

JACHAN, JACAN [Jă' chan]—AFFLICTING or TROUBLOUS. *A Gadite chief,* head of a father's house (I Chron. 5:13).

JACHIN [Jă' chin]—HE DOTH ESTABLISH or FOUNDING.
1. *The fourth son of Simeon* and founder of a tribal family (Gen. 46:10; Ex. 6:15; Num. 26:12). Called Jarib in I Chronicles 4:24.
2. *A priest in Jerusalem* after the captivity (I Chron. 9:10; Neh. 11:10.)
3. *A head of one of the families of the sons of Aaron* associated with the courses of the sacerdotal body (I Chron. 24:17).

Jachin is also the name of the right pillar in Solomon's temple (1 Kings 7:21; II Chron. 3:17).

JACOB [Jā′ cob]—HE THAT SUPPLANTETH or FOLLOWETH AFTER.

1. *The second son of Isaac and Rebekah,* and a twin brother of Esau. Jacob appeared a short time after Esau and is therefore called the younger brother. Isaac was sixty years old when Jacob and Esau were born.

The Man of Two Natures

Jacob is an outstanding illustration of the presence and conflict of the two natures within a believer. Similar to Dr. Jekyll and Mr. Hyde of Robert Louis Stevenson's story, Jacob is good and bad; he rises and falls, yet in spite of his failures was a chosen instrument.

Jacob's character then, is full of interest and difficulty because of its weakness and strength. His is not a life to be described by a single word as, for example, the *faith* of Abraham or the *purity* of Joseph. Jacob seemed to have a many-sided life. He was a man of *guile,* yet a man of *prayer.* Inconsistencies are everywhere. His life began with a prophetic revelation of God to his mother, but Jacob's early years were a singular mixture of good and bad—the bad being very bad.

I.   Jacob was the victim of his mother's partiality. "Rebekah loved Jacob" (Gen. 25:28). This fault must be kept in mind as we judge his character.

II.   Jacob was selfish. When his brother came in from the fields faint with hunger, Jacob would not give him food without bargaining over it.

III.   Jacob was naturally crafty and deceitful. He violated his conscience when he allowed his mother to draw him away from the path of honor and integrity. He practiced deception upon his blind father with the covering of kid skins. Then he told a deliberate lie in order to obtain a spiritual blessing. He further sinned upon most sacred ground, when he blasphemously used the name of the Lord to further his evil plans.

The thoroughness with which he carried out his mother's plan is one of the worst features in the life of this misguided son. "Had it been me," says Martin Luther, "I would have dropped the dish." It would have been better for Jacob had he dropped that dish of venison. But his proficiency in evil doing is to be despised.

In the life of this sharp trader who mended his ways, for there were two remarkable spiritual experiences in his life—at Bethel and Peniel —the preacher might find the following points suggestive: Jacob cheated (Gen. 25:29–34); deceived (Gen. 27:1–29); was compelled to flee (Gen 27:43; 28:1–5); was brought on to a higher level (Gen 28:10–22); had a romance spoiled, and was paid back in his own coin of deception (Gen. 29:15–30); was affectionate (Gen. 29:18); was industrious (Gen. 31:40); was prayerful (Gen. 32:9–12, 24–30); received a divine call to the promised land (Gen. 31); was disciplined by God through affliction (Gen. 37:28; 42:36); was a man of faith (Heb. 11:21); was blessed with sons who became the foundation of a nation. The Hebrew nation is spoken of as "the sons of Jacob" and "the children of Israel" (Gen. 48; 49; Num. 24:19).

2. *The father of Joseph,* the husband of Mary (Matt. 1:15, 16).

JADA [Jă′ dă]—WISE or KNOWING. *A son of Onam,* and grandson of Jerahmeel (I Chron. 2:28, 32).

JADAU [Jā dā′ u]—FAVORITE or FRIEND. *One of the family of Nebo* who had married a foreign wife. The correct name is Jaddai (Ezra 10:43).

JADDUA [Jăd dū′ ă]—VERY KNOWING or KNOWN.
1. *One of the Levites* who with Nehemiah sealed the covenant (Neh. 10:21).
2. *A son of Jonathan,* descendant of Jeshua the high priest, who returned from exile with Zerubbabel (Neh. 12:11, 22).

JADON [Jā′ dŏn]—HE THAT RULETH or ABIDETH. *A Meronothite* who helped in the repair of the wall of Jerusalem (Neh. 3:7). Josephus says that Jadon was the name of the man of God sent from Judah to Jeroboam (I Kings 13).

JAHATH [Jā′ hăth]—REVIVAL or GRASPING.
1. *A grandson of Judah* descended through Shobal (I Chron. 4:2).
2. *A son of Libni,* a Levite of the family of Gershom (I Chron. 6:20, 43).
3. *A son of Shimei,* a Levite of the family of Gershom (I Chron. 23:10, 11).
4. *A descendant of Kohath,* a son of Levi (I Chron. 24:22).
5. *A Merarite Levite,* an overseer of workmen engaged in the repair of the Temple in Josiah's reign (II Chron. 34:12).

JAHAZIAH [Jā hā zī′ ah]—JEHOVAH REVEALS. *One who was employed to enumerate* those who had married foreign wives during the exile (Ezra 10:15).

JAHAZIEL [Jā hā′ zĭ el]—GOD SEETH or REVEALS.
1. *A Benjamite* who joined David at Ziklag (I Chron. 12:4).
2. *A priest in David's reign* employed to sound the trumpet (I Chron. 16:6).
3. *A son of Hebron* the Kohathite (I Chron. 23:19).
4. *An Asaphite Levite* who encouraged Jehoshaphat and his army against the invading hosts of Moab (II Chron. 20:14).
5. *The ancestor of a family of exiles* who returned with Ezra from Babylon (Ezra 8:5).

JAHDAI [Jäh' da ī]—GUIDE or HE DIRECTETH. *A member of the family of Caleb* the spy (I Chron. 2:47).

JAHDIEL [Jäh' dǐ el]—UNION OF GOD or GOD MAKETH GLAD. *A leading man in the half tribe of Manasseh,* east of Jordan (I Chron. 5:24).

JAHDO [Jäh' dō]—UNION. *A Gadite,* son of Buz, and father of Jeshishai (I Chron. 5:14).

JAHLEEL [Jäh' lĕ el]—GOD WAITS or GOD DOTH GRIEVOUSLY AFFLICT. *The third son of Zebulun* and founder of a tribal family (Gen. 46:14; Num. 26:26).

JAHMAI [Jäh' ma ī]—JEHOVAH PROTECTS or LUSTY. *A son of Tola,* son of Issachar, Jacob's ninth son (I Chron. 7:2).

JAHZEEL, JAHZIEL [Jäh' zĕ el, Jäh' zǐ el]—GOD APPORTIONS or DISTRIBUTETH. *The first-born of Naphtali* the sixth son of Jacob, and his second by Bilhah. Founder of a tribal family (Gen. 46:24; Num. 26:48; I Chron. 7:13).

JAHZEIAH, JAHAZIAH [Jā hā zī' ah]—JEHOVAH SEETH. *A son of Tikvah* who opposed the proposition that the Jews should put away their foreign wives they married in captivity (Ezra 10:15; R.V. margin).

JAHZERAH [Jäh' ze rah]—JEHOVAH PROTECTS or MAY HE LEAD BACK. *A priest of the family of Immer* (I Chron. 9:12). Called Ahasai in Nehemiah 11:13.

JAIR [Jā' ur] JEHOVAH ENLIGHTENS, AROUSETH or WHO DIFFUSES LIGHT.
1. *A son of Segub* and grandson of Hezron, and reckoned with the tribe of Manasseh (Numbers 32:41; Deut. 3:14; I Chron. 2:22). Founder of a tribal family (II Sam. 20:26).
2. *A Gileadite* who judged Israel for twenty-three years, succeeding Tola in office. He may have been related to No. 1 (Judg. 10:3–5).
3. *A Benjamite* whose son, Mordecai, was Esther's cousin (Esther 2:5).
4. *The father of Elhanan,* who slew Lahmi the brother of the giant, Goliath (I Chron. 20:5). He is called Jaare-oregim in II Samuel 21:19.

JAIRUS [Jā ī' rus]—HE WILL ENLIGHTEN or DIFFUSE LIGHT. *A ruler of the synagogue* whose daughter Jesus raised from the dead (Mark 5:22; Luke 8:41).

JAKEH [Jā' keh]—PIOUS or HEARKENING. *The father of Agur,* the author of Proverbs thirty (Prov. 30:1; see R.V. margin).

JAKIM [Jā' kim]—A SETTER UP or HE RAISES UP.
1. *A son of Shimhi*, a Benjamite (I Chron. 8:19).
2. *A descendant of Aaron* and head of a family of Aaronites responsible for the twelfth of twenty-four courses of priests (I Chron. 24:12).

JALAM, JAALAM [Jā a' lām]—HIDDEN. *Chieftain of Edom.* Son of Esau by his wife Aholibamah (Gen. 36:5, 18; I Chron. 1:35).

JALON [Jā' lon]—OBSTINATE or JEHOVAH ABIDES. *A son of Ezra* registered with the tribe of Judah, a Calebite (I Chron. 4:17).

JAMBRES [Jăm' brēz]—OPPOSER or THE SEA WITH POVERTY. *One of the two Egyptian magicians* at the court of Pharaoh who sought to counteract the work of Moses (II Tim. 3:8). Mentioned along with Jannes.

JAMES [Jāmez]—SUPPLANTER.
1. *The son of Zebedee,* and the elder brother of John, and one of the Twelve (Matt. 4:21; 10:2; 17:1; Mark 1:19, 29; 3:17; 5:37; 9:2; 10:35; 41; 13:3; 14:33; Luke 5:10; 6:14; 8:51; 9:28, 54; Acts 1:13; 12:2). From the foregoing references several facts emerge:
James' father Zebedee, was a Galilean fisherman and prosperous, since he employed servants to assist in the management of his boats.
Zebedee had a house in Jerusalem and was known as a friend of the High Priest, Caiaphas, and his household. This would mark Him as a man of social position.
His mother's name was Salome, whom tradition says was a sister of the Virgin Mary, which may help to throw light upon the relation of her sons to the Master. This would also make James a cousin to Jesus after the flesh.
James worked in partnership with his father and brothers and was busy with his boats and nets when the call of Christ reached him.
His name is coupled with his brother John in the lists of the apostles, which could mean that when they were sent forth two by two, James and John would be paired. Evidently they were men of like spirit and disposition and received from Jesus the title "Sons of Thunder."
He was on terms of special intimacy with Christ, although he never attained the distinction of his brother John.
His life came to an untimely end when he was martyred by Herod Agrippa. The cup and the baptism of pain and death were his. Seventeen years passed between his call to service and his death. He was the second of the martyrs and the first of the apostles to give his life for Christ.
We have no word from his pen nor word he spoke unless Acts 4:24–30 be an exception, but James was content to be a disciple. He never sought fame, power, a great name. He had no ambition to be first.

2. *The son of Alphaeus* (Matt. 10:3; Mark 3:18; Luke 6:15; Acts 1:13). We know little of this James apart from his own name and his father's name, coming to us under the double form of Alphaeus and Clopas (John 19:25 R. V.). Evidently he did nothing that needed any record. We do know that this son of Alphaeus was called *the Little* (not *the Less*). Perhaps he was short of stature and to distinguish him from others of the same name he was known as "James the Little."

His mother was one of the devoted women who stood by the cross and visited the tomb.

He had a brother Joses, who was also a believer (Mark 15:40; 16:1; John 19:25).

Tradition says that he had been a tax-gatherer. It may be his father Alphaeus was the same Alphaeus who was the father of Levi the tax-gatherer, who became Matthew the Apostle.

3. *The Lord's brother* (Matt. 13:55; Mark 6:3; Acts 12:17; 15:13; 21:18; I Cor. 15:7; Gal. 1:19; 2:9, 12; Jas. 1:1). Acute controversy has raged around whether this James was an actual brother of Christ and also one of the Twelve.

The Man with Camel's Knees

Because of his relationship to Christ we deem it necessary to devote a little more attention to this honorable James. How exactly was he related to the Lord? There are some writers who affirm that there are only two persons by the name of James in the New Testament and that the one we are presently considering was the son of Alphaeus and Mary the sister of our Lord's mother, that is, the James under No. 2. Various explanations have been given of this third James.

He was a child of Joseph by a former marriage. Those like the Roman Catholics, who argue for the perpetual virginity of Mary, are against our Lord having any natural relatives apart from His mother.

The word "brother" or "kinsman" is used loosely, and means "cousin," according to Jewish usage. If he was a son of the virgin Mary's sister, then he would be our Lord's cousin, or "cousin-brother," as the Indians express it.

He, being the natural son of Joseph and Mary after their marriage, was actually our Lord's half-brother. The language of the passages cited under this James indicates that he had a relationship with Christ *within* rather than *without* the immediate family of Joseph and Mary. In the remonstration with Christ concerning His preaching, the whole circumstance points to James as being one of Mary's sons (Matt. 12:46–50). The facts are these:

I. He is spoken of as being among the sisters and brothers of Christ (Matt. 13:55, 56; John 2:12; 7:3, 10).

II. He was not a believer during our Lord's life. Along with the other children of Joseph and Mary, James did not accept the Messiahship of Jesus (Matt. 13:57; Luke 7:20, 21; John 7:5). There can be no doubt, however, that he did not remain unmoved by the goodness, unselfishness and example of Christ. Living with Him for almost thirty years must have left its impact upon James.

III. He was a witness of Christ's resurrection (I Cor. 15:7). It would seem as if James was won to faith by a special manifestation of the risen Lord. *Seen of James!* Paul would only know of one "James," the one often alluded to in the Acts of the Apostles. The result of that glorious sight and conversation transformed James into a disciple and a believer. It is after this experience that we find "the brethren of the Lord" joined with "the apostles" and "the women" assembled together in the upper chamber (Acts 1:14).

IV. He became a pillar of the Church at Jerusalem, rising to eminence (Acts 12:17; 15:4-34; 21:18, 19; Gal. 2:1-10).

V. He became known for his piety and was named "James the Just." Tradition has it that he was a Nazarite from his mother's womb, abstaining from strong drink and animal food and wearing linen. We are told of his strict adherence to the law (Acts 21:17-26; Gal. 2:12).

VI. He was the writer of the epistle bearing his name, which has always been attributed to "James the Just." But such was his character that he styled himself not as the *brother,* but only the *servant* or "slave" of the Lord Jesus Christ. His epistle gives us an admirable summary of practical duties incumbent upon all believers.

VII. He was a man who believed in the power of prayer, as evidenced by the space he devotes to it in his epistle. Because of his habit of always kneeling in intercession for the saints, his knees became calloused like a camel's; thus he became known as "The Man with Camel's Knees."

VIII. He was cruelly martyred by the Scribes and Pharisees, who cast him from the pinnacle of the Temple. As the fall did not kill him, his enemies stoned him, finally dispatching him with a fuller's club (see Matt. 4:5; Luke 4:9). Across from the Valley of Jehoshaphat, there is a sepulcher called "The Tomb of St. James."

4. *James,* the father of the Apostle Judas (Luke 6:16 R.V.). We have no further record of this James. Hastings states that, "the A.V. 'Judas the *brother* of James' is an impossible identification of the Apostle Judas with the author of the Epistle (Jude 1)."

JAMIN [Jā′ min]—THE RIGHT HAND or PROSPERITY.
1. *A son of Simeon* the second son of Jacob and founder of a tribal family (Gen. 46:10; Ex. 6:15; Num. 26:12; I Chron. 4:24).
2. *A man of Judah,* descendant of Hezron (I Chron. 2:27).
3. *A priest* who assisted Ezra in the reading and explanation of the law (Neh. 8:7, 8).

JAMLECH [Jăm′ lech]—JEHOVAH RULES or LET HIM CONSTITUTE A KING. *A Simeonite prince* (I Chron. 4:34).

JANNA, JANNAI [Jăn′ nă]—HE WILL ANSWER. *The father of Melchi,* and an ancestor of Christ (Luke 3:24).

JANNES [Jăn' nēs]—FULL OF PLEASURE, FAVOR or IMPOVERISHED. *One of the two Egyptian magicians* who withstood Moses (Ex. 7:11, 12, 22; 8:7, 18, 19; 9:11; II Tim. 3:8). The names of these opponents are not given in the Old Testament. Ancient Jewish writers expressed extravagant views on Jannes and Jambres, some affirming that they were the sons of Balaam, that they were drowned in the Red Sea or put to death for inciting Aaron to make the golden calf.

JAPHETH [Jā' pheth]—BEAUTY, LET HIM ENLARGE or HE THAT PERSUADES. *The second son of Noah,* born in the patriach's five hundredth year, and founder of those who spread over the north and west regions of the earth (Gen. 5:32; 6:10; 7:13). The Medians, Greeks, Romans, Russian and Gauls are referred to as descendants of Japheth. Most of the nations springing from him reappear in the endtime period under Gog (Ezek. 38; 39). For Greece see Zechariah 9:13.

JAPHIA [Jā phī' ă]—HIGH, SHINING, GLEAMING or WHICH ENLIGHTENS.
1. *A king of Lachish* captured and executed by Joshua at Gibeon (Josh. 10:3).
2. *A son of David* born at Jerusalem (II Sam. 5:15; I Chron. 3:7; 14:6). Also the name of a town near Carmel (Josh. 19:12).

JAPHLET [Jăph' let]—JEHOVAH CAUSES TO ESCAPE or MAY HE DELIVER. *An Asherite* of the family of Heber, a grandson of Beriah (I Chron. 7:32).

JARAH [Jā' rah]—HONEY or UNVEILER. *A son of Ahaz* and a descendant of King Saul (I Chron. 9:42). Called Jehoadah in I Chronicles 8:36.

JAREB [Jā' reb]—CONTENTIOUS, AVENGER or REVENGER. *A king of Assyria* (Hos. 5:13; 10:6). It is not clear whether this is a proper name or an appellation. Some old versions have "The King Avenger."

JARED, JERED [Jā' red, Jē' red]—DESCENDING or HE THAT DESCENDS. *The son of Mahalaleel* and father of Enoch (Gen. 5:15-20; I Chron. 1:2) and ancestor of Christ (Luke 3:37).

JARESIAH [Jăr e sī' ah]—JEHOVAH GIVES A COUCH. *A son of Jeroham,* a Benjamite (I Chron. 8:27).

JARHA [Jär' hă]—AN ADVERSARY. *An Egyptian slave* and husband of Ahlai, the daughter of Sheshan (I Chron. 2:34, 35).

JARIB [Jā' rib]—HE DOTH CONTEND or STRIVING.
1. *A son of Simeon* (I Chron. 4:24). Also known as Jachin (Gen. 46:10; Ex. 6:15).

2. *One of the chief men* who accompanied Ezra to Jerusalem (Ezra 8:16).

3. *A priest* who had married a foreign wife (Ezra 10:18).

JAROAH [Jā rō'ah]—NEW MOON. *A Gadite descendant* through Buz (I Chron. 5:14).

JASHEN [Jā' shen]—SHINING or SLEEPING. *The father of one of David's heroes* (II Sam. 23:32). Perhaps the Hashem of I Chronicles 11:34.

JASHOBEAM [Jā' shō' be ăm]—THE PEOPLE RETURN TO GOD.

1. *The son of Zabdiah,* a Hachmonite and one of David's mighty men (I Chron. 11:11; 27:2).

2. *A Korahite descended from Kohath,* who joined David at Ziklag (I Chron. 12:6).

JASHUB [Jăsh' ŭb]—TURNING BACK or HE RETURNS.

1. *The third of the four sons of Issachar* and founder of a tribal family (Num. 26:24; I Chron. 7:1). Perhaps the Job of Genesis 46:13.

2. *A son of Bani,* who, after his return from exile, put away his foreign wife (Ezra 10:29).

JASHUBI-LEHEM [Jăsh' u bī lē' hĕm]—BREAD RETURNS or TURNING BACK TO BETHLEHEM. *A member of the family of Shelah,* son of Judah (I Chron. 4:22).

JASON [Jā' son]—HEALING or HE THAT CARES.

1. *A believer* Paul sends greetings to and whom he called his "kinsman," that is, a fellow Hebrew Christian (Rom. 16:21).

2. *A believer in Thessalonica* who was hospitable to Paul and Silas (Acts 17:5–9). Perhaps the two Jasons are the same person.

JATHNIEL [Jăth' nĭ el]—GOD BESTOWETH GIFTS or GOD IS GIVING. *A son of Meshelemiah* of the house of Asaph, who was a gatekeeper at the Tabernacle (I Chron. 26:2; see also I Chron. 9:14).

JAVAN [Jā' văn]—SUPPLE, CLAY or HE THAT DECEIVES. *The fourth son of Japheth,* son of Noah (Gen. 10:2, 4; I Chron. 1:5, 7), and founder of descendants spreading afar (Isa. 66:19). Also the name of a city in South Arabia (Ezek. 27:13, 19). Now Yemen, or the same as Uzal.

JAZIZ [Jā' zĭz]—SHINING or HE MOVES ABOUT. *A Hagerite and overseer* of David's flocks (I Chron. 27:31).

JEATERAI [Jē ăt'e raī]— STEDFAST. *A descendant of Gershom,* son of Levi (I Chron. 6:21). Called Ethni in verse forty-one.

JEBERECHIAH [Jē bĕr e chī' ah]—JEHOVAH DOTH BLESS or IS BLESSING. *The father of Zechariah* and friend of Isaiah (Isa. 8:2).

JECAMIAH [Jĕc a mī' ah]—MEANING UNCERTAIN. *A son of Jecamiah* (I Chron. 3:18). See Jekamiah.

JECHONIAS, JECHONIAH [Jĕch o nī' as]—ESTABLISHED OF THE LORD. *An ancestor of Christ* (Matt. 1:11, 12). Greek form of King Jeconiah.

JECONIAH [Jĕc o nī' ah]—JEHOVAH DOTH ESTABLISH or PREPARATION OF THE LORD. *The next to last of the kings of Judah* (I Chron. 3:16, 17; Esther 2:6; Jer. 24:1; 27:20; 28:4; 29:2). Altered form of Jehoiachin, and called Jechonias in Matthew 1:11, 12.

JEDAIAH [Jē dā' iah]—JEHOVAH IS PRAISE or JEHOVAH KNOWETH.
1. *A descendant of Simeon* (I Chron. 4:37).
2. *A man of Harumaph* who repaired the part of the wall near his own house (Neh. 3:10).
3. *A descendant of Aaron* whose family came up from Jerusalem (I Chron. 9:10; 24:7; Ezra 2:36; Neh. 7:39).
4. *A chief of the priests* who returned with Zerubbabel (Neh. 11:10; 12:6, 19; Zech. 6:10, 14).
5. Another priest with the same history (Neh. 12:7, 21).

JEDIAEL [Jē dī' a el]—GOD KNOWETH or KNOWN OF GOD.
1. *A son of Benjamin* and founder of a family (I Chron. 7:6, 10, 11). Also called Ashbel (Num. 26:38).
2. *The son of Shimri,* and one of David's valiant men (I Chron. 11:45).
3. *A Manassite* who joined David at Ziklag (I Chron. 12:20).
4. *A son of Meshelemiah,* a descendant of Korah and doorkeeper in David's time (I Chron. 26:2).

JEDIDIAH [Jĕd ĭ dī' ah]—BELOVED OF JEHOVAH or JEHOVAH IS A FRIEND. *The name given to Solomon by Nathan* the prophet as instructed of the Lord (II Sam. 12:25). See Solomon.

JEDUTHUN [Jĕd' ụ thŭn]—A CHOIR OF PRAISE or ONE WHO GIVES PRAISE. *A Levite chief singer or musician* appointed by David, and also founder of an official musical family (I Chron. 16:41). Also known as Ethan.

JEEZER [Jē e′ zûr]—HELP. *A son of Gilead,* grandson of Manasseh (Num. 26:30). See Abiezer.

JEHALELEEL, JEHALELEL [Jē ha lē′ le el]—HE PRAISETH GOD.
1. *A descendant of Judah* through Caleb the spy and founder of a family (I Chron. 4:16).
2. *A Merarite Levite* in Hezekiah's time (II Chron. 29:12).

JEHDEIAH [Jeh dē′ iah]—UNION OF JEHOVAH or JEHOVAH INSPIRES WITH JOY.
1. *A son of Shubael* of the house of Amram (I Chron. 24:20).
2. *A Meronothite overseer* of David's asses (I Chron. 27:30).

JEHEZEKEL [Jē hĕz′ e kĕl]—GOD DOTH STRENGTHEN or GOD IS STRONG. *A descendant of Aaron* who was the head of the twentieth course of priests (I Chron. 24:16). His name is the same as Ezekiel.

JEHIAH [Jē hī′ ah]—GOD LIVETH or IS LIVING. *A Levite doorkeeper* of the ark in David's time (I Chron. 15:24).

JEHIEL [Jē hī′ el]—GOD LIVETH
1. *A Levite of the second degree* who played the psaltery (1 Chron. 15:18–20; 16:5).
2. *A Levite of the family of Gershom* and chief of the house of Laadan in David's time (I Chron. 23:8; 26:21, 22; 29:8).
3. *A son of Hachmoni* and companion of David's sons (I Chron. 27:32). Perhaps a tutor of the king's sons.
4. *A son of Jehoshaphat,* king of Judah, placed by his father over one of the fenced cities of Judah, but slain with his brother by Jehoram (II Chron. 21:2–4).
5. *A son of Heman the singer,* he aided Hezekiah in his religious reforms (II Chron. 29:14). R.V. has Jehuel.
6. *A Levite* set over the dedicated things by King Hezekiah (II Chron. 31:13).
7. *A chief priest* in Josiah's time who assisted in the reformation (II Chron. 35:8).
8. *The father of Obadiah* who returned from exile with Ezra (Ezra 8:9).
9. *The father of Shechaniah* who was the first to acknowledge the guilt of taking foreign, or non-Jewish wives (Ezra 10:2).
10. *A priest* who had taken a foreign wife (Ezra 10:21).
11. *A man of Elam's family* who had done the same thing (Ezra 10:26). See Jeiel.

JEHIELI [Jē hī′ e lī]—HE LIVES BY MERCY. *A son of Laadan* the Gershonite, set over the treasuries of the sanctuary in David's time (I Chron. 26:21, 22).

JEHIZKIAH [Jē hĭz kī' ah]—JEHOVAH IS STRONG or DOTH STRENGTHEN. *A son of Shallum,* a head of an Ephraimite tribe in the reign of Pekah who assisted in securing the release of captives (II Chron. 28:12). He was a strong supporter of the prophet Oded.

JEHOADAH, JEHOADDAH [Jē hŏ' a dah]—JEHOVAH UNVEILS or HATH ADORNED. *A son of Ahaz* and great grandson of Jonathan, Saul's son (I Chron. 8:36). Also called Jarah (I Chron. 9:42).

JEHOAHAZ, JOAHAZ [Jē hŏ' a hăz]—JEHOVAH UPHOLDS, HATH LAID HOLD or THE LORD THAT SEES.

1. *A son and successor of Jehu* and father of Joash who reigned for seven years (II Kings 10:35; 13; 14; II Chron. 25:17, 25). We know little of this king of Israel apart from the length of his reign and the low estate of his kingdom owing to Syrian aggression.

2. *The son and successor of King Jehoram* and father of King Joash, of Judah (II Chron. 21:17; 25:23). Called Ahaziah.

3. *A son of Josiah* who was deposed by Pharaoh-nechoh and who only reigned for three months (II Kings 23:30–34; II Chron. 36:1–4). Also called Shallum (I Chron. 3:15).

JEHOASH, JOAHAZ, JOASH [Jē hŏ' ăsh, Jŏ' ăsh]—JEHOVAH SUP-PORTS or HATH LAID HOLD. Here is another example of a name given to a king in each of the two lines, Israel and Judah.

1. Jehoash of Judah, *son of Ahaziah* and father of Amaziah (II Kings 11:21; 12:1–18; 14:13). When but an infant his brothers and cousins were massacred, but he was concealed until he was seven years old and then crowned as king. His preservation meant the continuation of the royal seed. Ultimately he was slain by some of his officers.

2. Jehoash of Israel, *son and successor of Jehoashaz* on the throne of Israel. He was the father of Jeroboam II (II Kings 13:10, 25; 14:8–17). See Joash. It was this king who visited Elisha when he was about to die, and wept over him as a great influence about to be lost to Israel.

JEHOHANAN, JOHANAN [Jē hō hā' nan, Jŏ' hā' nan]—JEHOVAH IS GRACIOUS.

1. *A Korathite Levite* who had charge of the sixth course of gate-keepers in David's reign (I Chron. 26:3).

2. *The second in honor of Jehoshaphat's captains,* who had two hundred eighty thousand men under him (II Chron. 17:15).

3. *The father of Ishmael,* a captain who aided Jehoiada in the revolt against Athaliah (II Chron. 23:1).

4. *A son of Bebai* who had taken a foreign wife (Ezra 10:28).

5. *A priest* who returned with Zerubbabel (Neh. 12:13).

6. *A priest or singer* who officiated at the dedication of the Jerusalem wall (Neh. 12:42).

7. *The son of Tobiah* the Ammonite (Neh. 6:18 R.V.). See Johanan.

JEHOIACHIN [Jē hoi' a chĭn]—JEHOVAH DOTH ESTABLISH. *A son of Jehoiakim,* king of Judah, who was placed on the throne by Nebuchadnezzar, but only reigned for three months. He was carried away to Babylon and remained a captive until freed from prison by Evilmerodach and given palace favors (II Kings 24:8, 12, 15; 25:27; II Chron. 36:8, 9; Jer. 52:31). Also called Coniah (see Jer. 22:24, 28; 37:1).

JEHOIADA [Jē hoi' a dă]—JEHOVAH KNOWS or KNOWLEDGE OF THE LORD.
1. *The father of Benaiah* and one of David's officers. Probably the priest and leader of the Aaronites who brought thirty-seven hundred men to David at Ziklag (II Sam. 8:18; 20:23; 23:20, 22; I Kings 1; 2; 4:4; I Chron. 11:22, 24; 12:27; 18:17; 27:5).
2. *The high priest who made Joash king,* and possibly the husband of Jehosheba, whose presence of mind saved the infant Jehoash from massacre (II Kings 11:4-17; 12:2-9; II Chron. 23; 24).
3. *A son of Beniah,* son of Jehoiada, the third of David's counselors (I Chron. 27:34).
4. *A son of Paseah,* who repaired "the old gate" (Neh. 3:6). Called Joiada in the R. V.
5. *A priest in Jerusalem* before the exile, but displaced by Zephaniah (Jer. 29:26).

JEHOIAKIM [Jē hoi' a kĭm]—JEHOVAH SETS UP. *The name given by Pharaoh-nechoh* to Eliakim son of Josiah, king of Judah, whom he made king instead of Jehoahaz. His reign of eleven years is not favorably viewed by Jeremiah (II Kings 23:34-36; 24:1-6, 19; I Chron. 3:15, 16; II Chron. 36: 4-8; Jer. 1:3; 22:18, 24).

The Man Who Was a Frivolous Egotist

Jehoiakim lacked moral sense and religious appreciation and was a man after the mold of his grandfather Manasseh. He took no interest in the reforms for which his father had worked. With his approval many heathen practices of Manasseh's reign were resumed.

The burning of the roll containing the sacred Word of God was the most remarkable scene in the history of this evil king who had no regard for God and no respect for the rights of others. He severely oppressed the people of Judah in order to maintain the pomp and extravagance of his court. Such a flagrant rejection of all that was godly and just brought Jeremiah out into the open, and he addressed the king in no uncertain terms. The king's doom was predicted. At last he was put to death by Nebuchadnezzar, and his body was left to decay, unburied, beyond the gates of Jerusalem. When we come to the line of our Saviour's ancestors there is a blank where a name should have been. "Josias," so we read (Matt. 1:11), (not Jehoiakim) begat Jechonias. The name is gone—taken out of the book of generations.

JEHOIARIB [Jē hoi′ a rĭb]—JEHOVAH DOTH CONTEND.
1. *A priest in Jerusalem* (I Chron. 9:10).
2. *The head of an Aaronite family* who shared in the charges of the sanctuary (I Chron. 24:7). See Joiarib.

JEHONADAB, JONADAB [Jē hŏn′ a dăb, Jŏn′ a dăb]—JEHOVAH IS LIBERAL.
1. *Son of Shimeah,* David's brother, and the friend of Ammon the son of David, who is described as "a very subtil man" (II Sam. 13:3, 32).
2. *Son of Rechab,* a Kenite, who composed the rules imposed upon the Rechabites (II Kings 10:15, 23).

JEHONATHAN [Jē *hŏn′ a than*] JEHOVAH HATH GIVEN. In the R. V. the English form of this name is given twice as Jonathan.
1. *Son of Uzziah* and an official appointed by David to have charge over royal treasures (I Chron. 27:25).
2. *A Levite* sent by Jehoshaphat to teach the people (II Chron. 17:8).
3. *A priest* and head of his father's house of Shemaiah in the days of the high priest Joiakim (Neh. 12:18). Called Jonathan in Nehemiah 12:35.

JEHORAM, JORAM [Jē hō′ ram, Jō′ ram]—JEHOVAH IS HIGH or EXALTED.
1. *A son of Ahab,* who became king of Israel after the brief reign of his brother Ahaziah (II Kings 1:17; 3:1, 6; 9:24; II Chron. 22:5-7). When Jehoram allied himself with Jehoshaphat, he paid tribute to the power of the king of Moab. Dr. Joseph Parker has this to say of the somewhat remarkable character of Jehoram:

> He was not an imitator of the evil of his father as to its precise form, but he had his own method of serving the devil. He superseded the arts of wickedness practiced by Ahab and Jezebel and found a way of his own of living an evil life . . . He re-established the worship of the calf, after the pattern which Jeroboam, its founder, had patronized . . . He made a kind of trick of wickedness, and knew how to give a twist to old forms.

Elisha was active during Jehoram's reign, and rebuked the king ultimately slain by Jehu.
2. *Son of Jehoshaphat,* who succeeded his father on the throne of Judah. He was married to Athaliah, daughter of Ahab and Jezebel. History does not record much of this king's life apart from the fact that he "walked in the ways of the kings of Israel" (I Kings 22:50; II Kings 1:17; 8:16; 25, 29; 12:18; II Chron. 21;16). He gave his

patronage to the worship of the Tyrian Baal. Although he knew the fate of those who had been guilty of idolatrous worship, he yet pursued his evil way. For provoking God by his idolatry, Jehoram was severely punished, and paid for his sin. He departed without any regret on the part of the people. Dishonor followed this king who died in contempt, for his body was not buried in "the sepulchers of kings."

3. *A priest sent by Jehoshaphat* with Elishama to teach the law to Judah (II Chron. 17:8).

JEHOSHAPHAT [Jē hŏsh′ a phăt]—JEHOVAH IS JUDGE.

1. *A recorder* during the reigns of David and Solomon (II Sam. 8:16; I Kings 4:3; I Chron. 18:15).

2. *One of Solomon's purveyors* (I Kings 4:17).

3. *A son of Asa,* king of Judah, who succeeded his father (I Kings 15:24; 22).

The Man with a Good Record

Because he carried out the religious reforms of his father, history gives Jehoshaphat a good name. What a beautiful expression that is " . . . he walked in the first ways of his father David"—meaning in the former or earlier ways of David, as contrasted with his later conduct. Because of his godward bent, "the Lord was with Jehoshaphat." Negatively, he "sought not after Baalim."

Here was a man who in every point was equally strong, a man of foresight, a man of reverence, a man of an honest heart, a man who felt that idolatry and true worship could not coexist in the same breast. He did not concern himself with "the doings of Israel." His was a blessed, spiritual singularity. He laid down a clear program for himself, and followed it out with patient and faithful endeavor. He did not seek riches and honor. No wonder the Lord "established the kingdom in his hand"! Points for the preacher to develop are:

I. He was one of the best kings of Judah (I Kings 15:24).

II. He had a godly father whose example he emulated (II Chron. 14:2).

III. He developed a system of religious instruction for the people (II Chron. 17:7–9).

IV. He commanded the judges to be just (II Chron. 19:6–9).

V. He trusted God for victory in a crisis (II Chron. 20).

VI. He manifested weakness in his alliance with wicked kings (I Kings 22:1–36).

4. *Son of Nimshi* and father of Jehu, who conspired against Joram, son of king Ahab (II Kings 9:2, 14).

5. *One of the priests* who assisted in bringing up the Ark from Obed-edom (I Chron. 15:24). Also the name of a valley east of Jerusalem which figures in coming judgment (Joel 3:2, 12). See also Josaphat.

JEHOSHUA [Jē hŏsh′ u ah]—JEHOVAH SAVES. *The name sometimes given to Joshua* the son of Nun (Num. 13:16; I Chron. 7:27).

JEHOZABAD [Jē hŏz' a băd]—JEHOVAH HATH ENDOWED.

1. *The son of Shomer* or Shimrith from Moab. He was among the number who slew Jehoash (II Kings 12:21; II Chron. 24:26).

2. *A Korathite porter,* son of Obed-edom (I Chron. 26:4).

3. *A Benjamite,* a high military officer under king Jehoshaphat (II Chron. 17:18).

JEHOZADAK, JOZADAK [Jē hŏz' a dăk]—JEHOVAH IS JUST. *The father of Jeshua* the high priest, and grandson of Azariah, the high priest during the exile (I Chron. 6:14, 15).

JEHU [Jē' hū]—JEHOVAH IS HE.

1. *A son of Hanani,* the prophet who denounced Baasha and his house, reproved Jehoshaphat and wrote a book (I Kings 16:1, 7, 12; II Chron. 19:2; 20:34).

2. *A son of Obed* and descendant of Hezron (I Chron. 2:38).

3. *A son of Josibiah* a Simeonite (I Chron. 4:35).

4. *A Benjamite of Anathoth* who joined David at Ziklag (I Chron. 12:3).

5. *The king of Israel,* appointed by Elijah in the place of Ahab. He is often called for brevity's sake, "The son of Nimshi." He reigned twenty-eight years (I Kings 19:16, 17).

The Man of Speed

Under Jehu there was a dynastic revolution, resulting in the overthrowing of the regnant religious establishment. "Jehu took no heed to walk in the law of the Lord" (II Kings 10:31). This king brought about no positive vital godliness, whose boasted "zeal for the Lord" (II Kings 10:16) was really zeal for Jehu.

There is one sentence revealing for us an insight into Jehu's character. "He driveth furiously." He came with all speed not merely because he was on an urgent errand, but because he was urged on by a headlong disposition, which earned him the reputation of a reckless driver among the watchmen. Jehu is thus a type of many who, in worldly and in religious matters, may be called reckless drivers. Without prudence or righteousness they plunge into matters of importance. The prodigal was a son of Nimshi in that he drove furiously when it came to living riotously in the far country.

It was also with lightning speed that Jehu destroyed Baal out of Israel, but he did his extermination in the wrong way, for the weapons of warfare are not carnal. For reasons of state policy Jehu maintained the worship of Bethel and Dan. He tried to serve God and Mammon. To Jehu, religion was only a political instrument. Hosea saw that the blood of Jezreel rested upon the house of Jehu, and that it would be avenged (Hos. 1:4).

JEHUBBAH [Jē hŭb' bah]—HIDDEN. *An Asherite* and a descendant of Shamer and of the family of Beriah (I Chron. 7:34).

JEHUCAL, JUCAL [Jē hŭ' cal, Jŭ' cal]—JEHOVAH IS ABLE. *A son of Shelemiah,* the courtier sent by king Zedekiah to entreat for the prayers of Jeremiah (Jer. 37:3; 38:1).

JEHUDI [Jē hŭ' dī]—A MAN OF JUDAH, A JEW. *An officer sent by king Jehoiakim* to ask Baruch for the roll of Jeremiah's prophecies and who read it to the princes of Judah (Jer. 36:14–23).

JEHUSH [Jē' hŭsh]—COLLECTOR. *A Benjamite* of the family of Saul (I Chron. 8:39).

JEIEL, JEHIEL, JEUEL [Jē ĭ' el, Jē hī' el]—TREASURE OF GOD, or GOD SNATCHES AWAY.
1. *A chief among the Reubenites* (I Chron. 5:7).
2. *A Benjamite,* the father of Gibeon, progenitor of Saul (I Chron. 9:35–39).
3. *A son of Hotham* and one of David's valiant men. Perhaps another Reubenite chief (I Chron. 11:44). Vulgate has Jeuel.
4. *A Levite gatekeeper and singer* in David's reign (I Chron. 15:18, 20; 16:5).
5. *A Levite* of the sons of Asaph (II Chron. 20:14).
6. *A principal scribe* who recorded the number of soldiers in king Uzziah's army (II Chron. 26:11).
7. *A Levite of the family of Elizaphan* in the time of Hezekiah (II Chron. 29:13).
8. *A Levite in the days of Josiah* of Judah (II Chron. 35:9).
9. *A son of Adonikam* who returned with Ezra. Vulgate has Jeuel (Ezra 8:13).
10. *One of the family of Nebo* who had married a foreign wife (Ezra 10:43).

JEKAMEAM [Jĕk a mē' am]—HE DOTH ASSEMBLE THE PEOPLE. *A son of Hebron,* grandson of Levi (I Chron. 23:19; 24:23).

JEKAMIAH, JECAMIAH [Jĕk a mī' ah, Jĕc a mī' ah]—JEHOVAH IS STANDING or DOTH GATHER.
1. *A man of Judah,* and a descendant through Sheshan through Jerahmeel (I Chron. 2:41).
2. *A son or descendant of king Jeconiah* (I Chron. 3:18).

JEKUTHIEL [Jē kū' thĭ el]—GOD IS MIGHTY or REVERENCE FOR GOD. *A son of Ezra,* a descendant of Caleb the spy (I Chron. 4:18).

JEMUEL [Jē mŭ' el] GOD IS LIGHT or DESIRE OF GOD. *A son of Simeon,* and founder of a tribal family (Gen. 46:10; Ex. 6:15). Called Nemuel in I Chronicles 4:24.

JEPHTHAH, JEPHTHAE [Jĕph' thah, Jĕph' tha ē]—HE DOTH OPEN or SET FREE. *A Gileadite,* illegitimate child expelled by his brother from the paternal abode. He became a Judge in Israel and delivered the people from the Ammonites. He judged Israel for six years (Judg. 11; Heb. 11:32).

The Man Who Made a Vow

While Jephthah is described as a "mighty man of valour" and one upon whom "the Spirit of the Lord" descended, he is conspicuous as a man who in all sincerity made a rash vow. He vowed a vow to be fulfilled if the Lord would deliver the Ammonites to him. As a thanksgiving to God, he said he would offer up whatever came out of his house at his return from battle. Jephthah defeated the Ammonites, and on his return, his daughter, an only child, came out to meet him. He told her of his vow and declared he could not go back upon his word. The daughter begged for two months' respite in order to go away and bewail her virginity. On her return, her father fulfilled the vow.

In those twilight, uncivilized times there was the practice of the sacrifice of human beings at times of special stress, but whether Jephthah offered up his daughter as a human sacrifice or surrendered her to perpetual virginity in fulfillment of his vow may be debatable. We do know that it was the custom for the daughters of Israel to lament the daughter of Jephthah the Gileadite for four days every year. And we can imagine how they would return softened, sobered and sanctified as the result of their act of remembrance.

For the preacher these aspects can be developed: Jephthah was an outcast (Judg. 11:1, 2); rose to leadership (Judg. 11:4–10); was moved by the Spirit (Judg. 11:29); made a rash vow (Judg. 11:30, 31); saved Israel from his foes (Judg. 11:33); kept his vow (Judg. 11:39).

JEPHUNNEH [Jē phŭn' neh]—IT WILL BE PREPARED, APPEARING or HE THAT BEHOLDS.

1. *The father of Caleb,* the representative spy from the tribe of Judah (Num. 13:6; 14:6, 30, 38; 26:65; 32:12; 34:19).

2. *An Asherite,* son of Jether (I Chron. 7:38).

JERAH [Jē' räh]—MOON or SON OF THE MOON. *A son of Joktan* of the family of Shem (Gen. 10:26; I Chron. 1:20).

JERAHMEEL [Jē räh' me el]—GOD HATH COMPASSION or IS MERCIFUL.

1. *A son of Hezron,* grandson of Judah, who had two wives and a numerous progeny (I Sam. 27:10; I Chron. 2:9, 42).

2. *A son of Kish* the Merarite (not Saul's father) (I Chron. 24:29).

3. *An officer of Jehoiakim,* king of Judah, who was sent to arrest Jeremiah and Baruch (Jer. 36:26).

JERED [Jē red]—DESCENT or FLOWING. *A Son of Ezra,* and descendant of Caleb the spy and father of the inhabitants of Gedor (I Chron. 4:18). See Jered (I Chron. 1:2).

JEREMAI [Jĕr' e maī]—JEHOVAH IS HIGH. *A Hebrew of the family of Hashum* who was persuaded to put away his foreign wife (Ezra 10:33).

JEREMIAH, JEREMY, JEREMIAS [Jĕr e mī' ah]—JEHOVAH IS HIGH or EXALTED OF GOD.

1. *An inhabitant of Libnah* whose daughter, Hamutal, was the wife of Josiah and mother of Jehoahaz (II Kings 23:31; 24:18; Jer. 52:1).

2. *A Manassehite* and head of a family (I Chron. 5:24).

3. *A Benjamite* who joined David at Ziklag (I Chron. 12:4)

4. *A Gadite* who also joined David (I Chron. 12:10).

5. *Another Gadite* who did the same (I Chron. 12:13).

6. *Son of Hilkiah,* the prophet from Anathoth in the days of Josiah and who was of the line of Abiathar (II Chron. 35:25; 36:12, 21, 22; Jer. 1:1).

The Man of Inconsolable Grief

This man who was *born* a priest but *became* a prophet by the divine call of God comes before us as one of the grandest men of Old Testament history. He was called to the prophetic office through a vision (Jer. 1:1, 4–16) and labored for some forty years. The book Jeremiah wrote gives us more details of his life, methods and work, as an Old Testament prophet, than of any other prophet. He is referred to as a son of Hilkiah, not only to distinguish him from others of the same name, but to prove that he was of priestly origin. He came from the priestly town of Anathoth, a name meaning, "answered prayers."

His call antedated his birth (Jer. 1:5), and he was consecrated to God before his birth. He was distinguished by his humility and native modesty. He felt he was a child and not mature enough to function as a prophet. With Browning he could say:

> I was not born
> Informed and fearless from the first, but shrank
> From aught which marked me out apart from men:
> I would have lived their life, and died their death
> Lost in their ranks, eluding destiny.

But Jeremiah could not elude destiny. So we have:

I. His equipment for a God-appointed task (Jer. 1:7–9).

II. His sufferings. What sorrow and anguish were his (Lam. 1:12; 3:1). He was not permitted to marry (Jer. 16:2). Solitude was at once his penalty and greatness. Then we have his sad antagonisms (Jer. 1:18; 15:16, 17, 20; 20:1–18).

III. His persecutions. These came to him from many quarters (Jer. 11:18–20; 12:6; 20:6; 26; 37; 38:13–28; 43:6). Bitter, however, were his denunciations of his foes (Jer. 11:20; 15:18; 17:18; 18:21–23).

IV. His death. Tradition has it that he was stoned to death in

Egypt by the Jews, and that when Alexander entered Egypt he rescued his bones from obscurity and buried them in Alexandria. See Hebrews 11:37.

Jeremiah's ministry was an intensely sad one and his song is in the minor key. His was a divine melancholy that made his head "waters" and his eyes a fountain of tears. The truths he had to proclaim were unwelcome and brought him enemies, but he carried out his task without fear or favor. In these days of national apostasy and international strife, the preacher could not do better than live near the Book of Jeremiah, which has, as its dominant note, true religion in heart and life, in church and nation.

7. *A priest* who sealed the covenant with Nehemiah (Neh. 10:2; 12:1, 12, 34).

8. *A descendant of Jonadab,* son of Rechab (Jer. 35: 3).

JEREMOTH, JERIMOTH [Jĕr′ e mŏth, Jĕr′ ĭ mŏth]—ELEVATION OF HEIGHTS.

1. *A son of the Benjamite Beriah* (I Chron. 8:14).
2. *One who married a foreign wife* (Ezra 10:26).
3. *Another who did the same* (Ezra 10:27).
4. *Another who did the same* (Ezra 10:36).
5. *A Levite* (I Chron. 25:22). Called Jerimoth in I Chronicles 24:30.
6. *A Naphtalite* (I Chron. 27:19). See Jerimoth.

JERIAH, JERIJAH [Jē rī′ ah]—JEHOVAH HATH FOUNDED. *A descendant of Hebron,* grandson of Levi and the chief of one of the Levitical courses in David's time (I Chron. 23:19; 24:23).

JERIBAI [Jĕr′ ĭ baī]—JEHOVAH CONTENDS or CONTENTIOUS. *A son of Elnaam* and one of David's mighty men (I Chron. 11:46).

JERIEL [Jē′ rĭ el]—FOUNDED or FOUNDATION OF GOD. *A son of Tola,* son of Issachar (I Chron. 7:2).

JERIMOTH [Jĕr′ ĭ mŏth]—HEIGHTS.

1. *A son of Bela,* son of Benjamin (I Chron. 7:7).
2. *A son of Becher,* son of Benjamin (I Chron. 7:8).
3. *A valiant man who joined David at Ziklag* (I Chron. 12:5).
4. *A son of Mushi,* grandson of Levi (I Chron. 23:23; 24:30).
5. *A son of Heman,* who assisted in the service of song (I Chron. 25:4). See Jeremoth, I Chronicles 25:22.
6. *A ruler in Naphtali in David's time* (I Chron. 27:19).
7. *A son of David* and father of Rehoboam's wife (II Chron. 11:18). Not mentioned elsewhere.

JEROBOAM [Jĕr o bō′ am]—ENLARGES, STRUGGLER FOR THE PEOPLE or THE PEOPLE HAVE BECOME NUMEROUS.

1. *The son of Nebat* from Zereda in Manasseh, who became the first king of the ten tribes of Israel. This Ephraimite, Jeroboam I, reigned for twenty-two years. His mother's name was Zeruah, who was widowed at the time of his birth. This is the Jeroboam who rebuked the unnamed prophet (I Kings 11:26–40; 12–16).

The Man Who Made Israel Sin

The dreadful description of Jeroboam tied to his name like a label, is that "he made Israel to sin." His sin — the root and fruit of it — are the chief things the Bible records of this widow's son. We are familiar with the incident of Ahijah taking Jeroboam's new garment and tearing it into twelve pieces, giving Jeroboam ten pieces and prophesying the rending of Solomon's kingdom, and the government of ten tribes of that kingdom passing into Jeroboam's hands. No wonder Solomon sought to kill him. But after the king's death and the refusal of Rehoboam to follow good advice, the kingdom split and ten tribes went with Jeroboam.

Solomon had lost his kingdom by idolatry and Jeroboam proposed to keep his ten-tribe kingdom by idolatry. So, abandoning the commandment and promise of God, Jeroboam set up golden bulls, one in Bethel and the other in Dan. People must have religion of some sort, Jeroboam reasoned, as he made the worship of the calves a part of the constitution of his kingdom. How sad it is to read that the Lord gave Israel up because of the sins of Jeroboam! The consequences of national idolatry continued, for eighteen kings sat upon the throne of Judah after his death, but not one of them gave up the golden calves. Of fifteen of them it is said that they departed not from the sin of Jeroboam. As with the kings, so with the people who continued to walk in all the sins of Jeroboam which he did (II Kings 17:22, 23).

There is no need to linger over what befell Jeroboam himself. He was warned by the man of God from Judah, but without avail. His son fell sick and died, and Jeroboam shortly after was defeated by his enemies. Then the Lord struck him and he died. Yet his name lives on with the terrible mark against it. "He made Israel to sin."

2. *A son of Joash or Jehoash the* grandfather of Jehu, who succeeded Joash as king over the ten tribes, and who reigned for forty-one years (II Kings 13:13; 14:16–29; 15:1, 8; I Chron. 5:17; Amos 1:1; 7:9–11). Both Hosea (Hos. 1:1) and Amos describe the temporary prosperity of Israel with the accompaniment of social and moral degeneracy during the reign of Jeroboam II. Under him, Israel regained the territory it lost to its hereditary enemy, Syria. The aspect of commanding interest in Jeroboam's age when materialism was in the saddle was the appearance of a man with a message. Amid the shallow optimism possessing king and people alike was the voice of Amos, the herdsman of Tekoa, saying in effect: "The grass withereth, the flower fadeth, but the word of our God shall stand forever."

Israel's prosperity ended with the death of this Jeroboam. A period of anarchy followed. Then he was succeeded by his son Zachariah, who after a reign of only six months, was murdered by Shallum who, in turn, was assassinated one month later. Think of it, three kings sat on Israel's throne in seven months! Four out of six kings succeeding Jeroboam died violent deaths. In less than fifteen years four of Israel's kings were murdered.

JEROHAM [Jĕr' o hăm]—LOVED or HE FINDETH MERCY.

1. *The father of Elkanah,* and grandfather of Samuel (I Sam. 1:1; I Chron. 6:27, 34).

2. *The head of a Benjamite family* dwelling in Jerusalem (I Chron. 8:27).

3. *A Benjamite and father of Ibneiah.* Perhaps the same as No. 2 (I Chron. 9:8).

4. *A priest, whose son, Adaiah,* lived in Jerusalem after the exile, and who was of the house of Malchijah (I Chron. 9:12; Neh. 11:12).

5. *A Benjamite of Gedor* whose two sons joined David at Ziklag (I Chron. 12:7).

6. *The father of Azareel,* prince of Dan in the reign of David (I Chron. 27:22).

7. *The father of Azariah* who aided Jehoiada in putting Joash on the throne (II Chron. 23:1).

JERUBBAAL [Jē rŭb' ba ăl]—BAAL STRIVES, LET BAAL DEFEND HIS CAUSE or CONTENDER WITH BAAL. *The name given to Gideon* by his father Joash (Judg. 6:32). See Gideon and next name.

JERUBBESHETH [Jē rŭb' be shĕth]—CONTENDER WITH IDOL or LET THE IDOL OF CONFUSION DEFEND ITSELF. *Another name given to Gideon* by those who wished to avoid pronouncing the name of Baal in the former name (II Sam. 11:21).

JESAIAH, JESHAIAH [Jē sā' iah, Jē shā' iah]—JEHOVAH IS OPULENT or HATH SAVED.

1. *A son of Hananiah* and grandson of Zerubbabel (I Chron. 3:21).

2. *A son of Jeduthun* and a musician in David's time (I Chron. 25:3, 15).

3. *A Levite,* son of Rehabiah and grandson of Eliezer, son of Moses (I Chron. 26:25).

4. *A son of Athaliah* and head of his father's house at Elam, who with seventy males returned from Babylon with Ezra (Ezra 8:7).

5. *A Merarite* included in the above seventy (Ezra 8:19).

6. *A son of Benjamin,* the father of Ithiel whose descendants dwelt in Jerusalem (Neh. 11:7).

JESHARELAH [Jē shăr' e lah]—UPRIGHT TOWARDS GOD. *A Levite* who presided over the service of song (I Chron. 25:14). See Asharelah.

JESHEBEAB [Jĕ shĕb′ e ăb]—SEAT or DWELLING OF FATHER. *A descendant of Aaron* and head of the fourteenth course of priests in sanctuary service (I Chron. 24:13).

JESHER [Jĕ′shur]—UPRIGHTNESS. *A son of Caleb,* son of Hezron (I Chron. 2:18).

JESHISHAI [Jĕ shĭsh′ a ī]—JEHOVAH IS ANCIENT. *A Gadite* and a descendant of Buz (I Chron. 5:14).

JESHOHAIAH [Jĕsh o hā′ iah]—HUMBLED BY JEHOVAH. *A Simeonite prince* (I Chron. 4:36).

JESHUA, JESHUAH [Jĕsh′ u ă, Jĕsh′ u ah]—JEHOVAH IS SALVATION or HELP.
1. *A descendant of Aaron* and priest of the sanctuary (1 Chron. 24:11; Ezra 2:36; Neh. 7:39).
2. *A Levite in Hezekiah's time* who had to do with the receipt and distribution of Temple offerings (II Chron. 31:15; Ezra 2:40; Neh. 7:43).
3. *A high priest* who returned with Zerubbabel, and the son of Jozadak, who built an altar and is also called Joshua (Ezra 2:2; 3:2–9; 4:3; 5:2; 10:18; Neh. 7:7; Zech. 3; 6:11–13).
4. *The father of Jozabad,* the Levite who was responsible for the sanctuary vessels (Ezra 8:33).
5. *A son of Pahath-moab,* whose descendants returned from exile with Zerubbabel (Ezra 2:6; Neh. 7:11).
6. *The father of Ezer* who helped to repair the wall (Neh. 3:19).
7. *A Levite* who helped Ezra read and explain the Law to the people (Neh. 8:7; 9:4, 5; 12:8, 24).
8. *The name given to Joshua* the son of Nun (Neh. 8:17).
9 *The son of Azariah,* a Levite, who with the others sealed the covenant (Neh. 10:9).
Also the name of a city of Benjamin (Neh. 11:26).

JESIAH [Jĕ sī′ ah]—JEHOVAH EXISTS.
1. *One who joined David at Ziklag* (I Chron. 12:6).
2. *A Kohathite,* descendant of Uzziel (I Chron. 23:20). Called also Isshiah.

JESIMIEL [Jĕ sĭm ĭ el]—GOD SETTETH UP. *A prince* of the tribe of Simeon (I Chron. 4:36).

JESSE [Jĕs′ se]—JEHOVAH EXISTS or FIRM. *The son of Obed* and father of David, and grandson of Boaz and Ruth, and an ancestor of Christ (Ruth 4:17, 22). Jesse had eight sons and two daughters by different wives (I Sam. 17:12–14, 25). Isaiah speaks of "the stock of Jesse," a phrase indicating that it was from Jesse the Messiah would come. The humble descent of the Messiah is contrasted with the glorious kingdom He is to have (Isa 11:1).

JESUI [Jĕs′ u ī]—JEHOVAH IS SATISFIED. *A descendant of Asher* (Num. 26:44). See Ishui. Founder of the Jesuites.

JESUS [Jĕ′zus]—JEHOVAH IS SALVATION. Jeshua, Jehoshua and Joshua are forms of the common name of Jesus. In this section we are only indicating those who, apart from Christ, are known by this name.

1. *Joshua, the military leader* (Acts 7:45; Heb. 4:8).
2. *An ancestor of Christ,* who lived about four hundred years after David (Luke 3:29).
3. *Jesus called Justus,* the Jewish Christian associated with the Apostle Paul (Col. 4:11).
4. *The Man Christ Jesus* (I Tim. 2:5). See chapter 4, page 363. See Jeshua.

JETHER, JETHRO [Jĕ′ thûr, Jĕth′ rō]—ABUNDANCE, EXCELLENCE or PRE-EMINENT.

1. *The first-born son of Gideon* and father of Amasa, Absalom's commander-in-chief (Judg 8:20; I Kings 2:5).
2. *A son of Jerahmeel,* son of Hezron (I Chron. 2:32). He died childless.
3. *An Ishmaelite,* the father of David's nephew, Amasa (I Kings 2:5, 32).
4. *A son of Ezra,* and a descendant of Caleb the spy (I Chron. 4:17).
5. *A descendant of Asher* (I Chron. 7:38).

JETHETH [Jĕ′ theth]—SUBJECTION. *A chieftain of Edom* of the family of Esau (Gen. 36:40; I Chron. 1:51).

JETHRO [Jĕth′ rō]—PRE-EMINENCE or EXCELLENCE. *The father-in-law of Moses,* and an Arab sheik and priest of Midian (Ex. 3:1, 4:18; 18:1–12). Called Reuel or Raguel meaning "friend of God" in Exodus 2:18 and Numbers 10:29, and Jether in Exodus 4:18.

JETUR [Jĕ′ tŭr]—DEFENSE or HE THAT KEEPS. *A son of Ishmael,* son of Hagar, Abraham's concubine (Gen. 25:15; I Chron. 1:31). Also the name of a tribe that sprang from Jetur (I Chron. 5:19).

JEUEL, JEIEL [Jĕ ŭ′ el, Jĕ ĭ′ el]—TREASURE OF GOD or SNATCHING AWAY.

1. *A descendant of Zerah,* son of Judah (I Chron. 9:6). His clan of six hundred lived at Jerusalem.

2. *A Levite*, descendant of Elizaphan who assisted in the reform under Hezekiah (II Chron. 20:14). Also known as Jeiel.

3. *A contemporary of Ezra* who returned from Babylon. Likewise known as Jeiel (Ezra 8:13).

JEUSH, JEHUSH [Jĕ′ ŭsh, Jĕ′ hŭsh]—HE WILL GATHER TOGETHER.
1. *A son of Esau* by his wife Aholibamah (Gen. 36:5, 18; I Chron. 1:35).
2. *A son of Bilhan* and grandson of Jediael, a Benjamite (I Chron. 7:10).
3. *A son of Shimei*, a Gershonite and head of a family (I Chron. 23:10, 11).
4. *A son of Rehoboam*, and grandson of King Solomon (II Chron. 11:19).
5. *A descendant of King Saul* (I Chron. 8:39).

JEUZ [Jĕ′ ŭz]—COUNSELOR or COUNSELING. *Son of Shaharaim* by his wife Hodesh (I Chron. 8:10).

JEZANIAH, JAAZENIAH [Jĕz a nī′ ah]—JEHOVAH DOTH HEARKEN or DETERMINE. *The captain of Jewish forces*, son of Hoshaiah, a Maacathite. Generally called Jaazeniah (Jer. 40:8; 42:1).

JEZER [Jĕ′ zûr]—FORMATION. *A son of Naphtali* and founder of a tribal family (Gen. 46:24; Num. 26:49; I Chron. 7:13).

JEZIAH [Jĕ zī′ ah]—JEHOVAH UNITES. *One of the Parosh family* who put away his foreign wife (Ezra 10:25).

JEZIEL [Jĕ′ zī el]—GOD UNITES or ASSEMBLY OF GOD. *Son of Azmaveth*, a Benjamite who, with his brother Pelet, joined David at Ziklag (I Chron. 12:3).

JEZLIAH [Jĕz lī′ ah]—JEHOVAH UNITES. *A son of Elpaal* a Benjamite (I Chron. 8:18).

JEZOAR [Jĕ zō′ar]—MEANING UNCERTAIN. *A son of Helah*, wife of Asher, a descendant of Caleb the son of Hur (I Chron. 4:7).

JEZRAHIAH [Jĕz ra hī′ ah]—JEHOVAH IS SHINING or THE LORD ARISES. *An overseer of singers* in Nehemiah's time (Neh. 12:42). See also Izrahiah (I Chron. 7:3).

JEZREEL [Jĕz′ re el]—GOD SOWS.
1. *A descendant of the father* of Etam (I Chron. 4:3).
2. *The symbolic name of Hosea* the prophet's eldest son, who was so named seeing God had avenged the blood of Jezreel (Hos. 1:4, 5).

Also symbolic name of Israel (Hos. 1:4, 11), and the name of towns (Josh. 15:56; I Kings 21:23).

JIBSAM [Jĭb' sam]—LOVELY, SWEET. *A son of Tola,* son of Issachar (I Chron. 7:2).

JIDLAPH [Jĭd' laph]—HE WEEPETH, MELTING AWAY or HE THAT DISTILS. *A son of Nahor* and Milcah (Gen. 22:22).

JIMNAH, JIMNA [Jĭm' nah, Jĭm' nă]—PROSPERITY. *The first-born son of Asher* and founder of a tribal family (Gen. 46:17; Num. 26:44). Called Imnah (I Chron. 7:30).

JOAB [Jō' ăb]—JEHOVAH IS A GOOD FATHER.
1. *A descendant of Caleb* the son of Hur, a Judahite (I Chron. 2:54).
2. *Son of Seraiah,* grandson of Kenaz, associated with valley craftsmen (I Chron. 4:13, 14).
3. *An Israelite* whose posterity went up from Babylon with Zerubbabel (Ezra 2:6; Neh. 7:11).
4. *One whose descendants went up from Babylon* with Ezra (Ezra 8:9.)
5. *The son of David's half-sister,* Zeruiah. This nephew of David became the most overbearing captain in his uncle's army (I Sam. 26:6; II Sam. 2; 13).

The Man Who Was Overambitious

Joab was the first person to be thought of in Joab's mind. His apparent devotion to David had one objective, namely that he himself should have first place. He loved self. He murdered those who stood in the way of pre-eminence as the leader of Israel's hosts (II Sam. 3:27). Alexander Whyte says, "Had it not been for David, Joab would have climbed up into the throne of Israel. . . Even the king himself was afraid of his commander-in-chief. The sovereign took his orders meekly from his subject." In his own well-read and picturesque way, Dean Stanley describes Joab aptly as the Marlborough of the empire of Israel.

W. O. E. Osterley gives us the following summary of Joab's life and labors:

I.   He was a skilled general, proven by the number of victories he gained (II Sam. 2:12–32; 10; 11:1; 12:26–29; 20:4–22; I Chron. 11:6–9).

II.   He was loyal to the house of David as his whole life of devoted service illustrates (II Sam. 12:26; 14:1; 18:20; 19:5–7).

III.   He was guilty of vindictiveness and ruthless cruelty. The treacherous and bloodthirsty acts of which Joab was guilty constitute a dark blot upon his character (II Sam. 3:22–27; 18:14; 20:9, 10; I Kings 11:16).

The tragedy is that in spite of all his abundant energy, boldness, ability, shrewdness and common sense, he never manifested any real faith in God. The nearest he came to such a faith is to be found in II Samuel 10:12, where his trust was more in "Providence" than a personal resting in the God of Israel. Full of self-confidence, ambition and selfishness, Joab never got far away from his own interests.

JOAH [Jō' ah]—JEHOVAH IS BROTHER.

1. *A son of Asaph* the recorder under King Hezekiah (II Kings 18:18, 26; Isa. 36: 3, 11, 22).

2. *Son of Zimmah* and descendant of Gershom son of Levi (I Chron. 6:21; II Chron. 29:12).

3. *A son of Obed-edom,* a Tabernacle porter (I Chron. 26:4).

4. *A son of Joahaz,* a recorder under King Josiah who helped to repair the house of the Lord (II Chron. 34:8).

JOAHAZ [Jō' a hăz]—JEHOVAH HELPS or HATH LAID HOLD OF. *Father of Joah,* King Josiah's recorder (II Chronicles 34:8). For others see Jehoahaz.

JOANNA, JOANAN [Jō Ăn' nă]—JEHOVAH HATH BEEN GRACIOUS. *The grandson of Zerubbabel,* an ancestor of Joseph, Mary's husband (Luke 3:27). Also the name of a female disciple, the wife of one of Herod's officers (Luke 8:3; 24:10). A further illustration of the same name identifying male and female.

JOASH, JEHOASH [Jō' ash, Jē hō' ăsh]—JEHOVAH SUPPORTS, IS STRONG or HASTENS TO HELP.

1. *A son of Becher,* a Benjamite (I Chron. 7:8).

2. *An officer* who had charge of David's oil-cellars (I Chron. 27:28).

3. *A son of Manasseh* and father of Gideon, of the family of Abiezer (Judg. 6:11–31; 7:14; 8:12, 32).

4. *A son of Ahab,* king of Israel (I Kings 22:26; II Chron. 18:25).

5. *A son of Ahaziah,* king of Judah (II Kings 11:2). Also called Jehoash.

6. *A son of Jehoahaz,* and grandson of Jehu (II Kings 13).

7. *A descendant of Shelah,* son of Judah (I Chron. 4:22).

8. *A Benjamite of Gibeah* who joined David at Ziklag (I Chron. 12:3).

JOATHAM [Jō' a thăm]—THE LORD IS UPRIGHT. *An ancestor of Joseph* as given by Matthew 1:9.

JOB [Jōb]—HATED, ONE EVER RETURNING TO GOD or HE THAT WEEPS.

1. *The third son of Issachar* (Gen. 46:13). Called Jashub in Numbers 26:24 and I Chronicles 7:1.

2. *A descendant of Aram,* son of Shem, dwelling in Uz, and possibly

contemporary with Abraham, and who died at the age of 240 years. References to the patriarch apart from his book are to be found in Ezekiel 14:14 and James 5:11.

The Man of Patience

This renowned Old Testament saint dwelt in the land of Uz on the borders of Idumaea. Job's portrait is clearly defined for us in his dramatic book.

I. As to his character, he was perfect and upright, feared God and eschewed evil (Job 1:1). Here we have the manward, Godward and selfward aspects of his life.

II. As to his family, he had seven sons and three daughters (Job 1:2, 18, 19).

III. As to his possessions, he was a wealthy landowner, having seven thousand sheep, three thousand camels, five hundred yoke of oxen, five hundred she asses and a large household (Job 1:3, 13–19).

IV. As to reputation, Job, who lived long before Israel with its religious, social and political organizations existed, was reckoned as the greatest of all the men of the East (Job 1:3).

V. As to his friends, candid friends, there were Eliphaz, Bildad, Zophar and Elihu (Job 2:11; 36:1).

VI. As to his foes, we have mention of the Sabeans and Chaldeans (Job 1:15, 17).

VII. As to his sufferings, he lost his property, sons and wealth. But his losses were doubly recompensed (Job 42:11–13).

VIII. As to his prayer-life, Job knew how to seek God. Thus we have restrained prayer (Job 15:4), purity of prayer (Job 16:17), empty prayer (Job 21:15), profitable prayer (Job 22:27), blessedness of prayer (Job 33:26), interceding prayer (Job 42:8), emancipating prayer (Job 42:10; see 8:5).

IX. As to his patience, the Bible presents him as our model. Faith was strained but Job emerged victorious (Job 19:1–27; Jas. 5:11).

As to the remarkable book bearing Job's name, the following summary might suffice:

Its purpose. It is not an apologetic vindication of the ways of God to man; not a philosophic proof of the doctrine of immortality; not an argumentative refutation of the so-called Hosaic doctrine of retribution; not a word of exhortation to man not to pry into the deep designs of providence, neither is it the testing and improvement of Job's piety. That is acknowledged by God and admitted by Satan to be perfect. It has been written to prove:

That God can be loved for His own sake; that goodness may be unselfish and disinterested; that the righteous can serve God for nought and trust in Him even when He seems to be an enemy.

That the painful riddle of human life is capable of a blessed solution; that the sufferings of the righteous are not necessarily due to their own sins; that the inequalities of this life are to be redressed in the life to come. Justice will be done somehow, some-time, somewhere.

But the Bible is the Book of Christ, and the great theme of Job is the mystery of the Cross: How can the sufferings of the righteous be reconciled with the justice of God? Job is a type of the righteous man, of the Nation, of the Church and of Christ Himself.

Hence we have in Job the picture of a righteous man suffering because it pleased the Lord, for a wise purpose, to bruise him. God reversed the verdict of the men who rejected him and numbered him among the transgressors.

Key Verse: 13:15. "Though he slay me, yet will I trust in him." This is an Old Testament anticipation of the cry of dereliction that came from Christ upon the Cross: "Why didst Thou forsake me?"

Key Thought: Confidence in God (Job 23:10; 27:2–6). He knoweth. In the depth of his darkness and in the agony of his suffering, Job held on to God. My Redeemer liveth.

JOBAB [Jŏ' băb]—HOWLING or TRUMPET CALL.
1. *A son of Joktan* the Shemite (Gen. 10:29; I Chron. 1:23).
2. *The second king of Edom* and son of Zerah of Bozrah (Gen. 36:33, 34; I Chron. 1:44, 45).
3. *A King of Madon,* whose city was conquered by Joshua (Josh. 11:1).
4. *A son of Shaharaim,* a Benjamite (I Chron. 8:9).
5. *A son of Elpaal,* another Benjamite (I Chron. 8:18).

JODA [Jŏ' dă]—HASTE.
1. *A Levite* also called Judah (Ezra 3:9); Hodaviah (Ezra 2:40); Hodevah (Neh. 7:43).
2. *An ancestor of Christ* who lived at the time of the exile (Luke 3:26). Also given as Juda.

JOED [Jŏ' ed]—JEHOVAH IS WITNESS. *A son of Pedaiah,* descended from Jeshiah, a Benjamite (Neh. 11:7).

JOEL [Jŏ' el]—JEHOVAH IS GOD or THE LORD IS GOD.
1. *The first-born son of Samuel* the prophet (I Sam. 8:2; I Chron. 6:33; 15:17). Called Vashni in I Chronicles 6:28.
2. *A Simeonite prince* (I Chron. 4:35).
3. *The father of Shemaiah,* a Reubenite (I Chron. 5:4, 8).
4. *A chief Gadite* (I Chron. 5:12).
5. *An ancestor of Samuel* the prophet (I Chron. 6:36).
6. *A chief man of Issachar,* descendant of Tola (I Chron. 7:3).
7. *One of David's heroes* and a brother of Nathan (I Chron. 11:38).
8. *A Gershonite in David's time* (I Chron. 15:7, 11; 23:8).
9. *Another Gershonite,* keeper of the treasures of the Lord's house (I Chron. 26:22).
10. *A prince of Manasseh* in David's reign (I Chron. 27:20).

11. *A Kohathite* who assisted Hezekiah in the cleansing of the Temple (II Chron. 29:12).

12. *One of Nebo's family* who had taken a foreign wife (Ezra 10:43).

13. *A son of Zechri,* and overseer of the Benjamites in Jerusalem (Neh. 11:9).

14. *Son of Pethuel,* and prophet in the days of Uzziah, king of Judah (Joel 1:1; Acts 2:16).

The Man Who Foresaw Pentecost

Because nothing is known of Joel beyond what the opening verse of his book states, he has been styled "The Anonymous Prophet." Scripture is silent as to his birthplace, parentage and rank. All we know is that he was a son of Pethuel, or Bethuel as the LXX expresses it. But who Pethuel is no one knows. Its meaning, however, is significant, "vision of God," and springs from a word implying "to open the eyes."

Joel was a common name among the Hebrews and is still so among the Orientals. The use of his name as "the son of Pethuel" was necessary to distinguish him from the other Joels we have considered. It would seem as if his home was in Jerusalem or its immediate neighborhood. Thus he speaks repeatedly of Zion (Joel 2:1, 15, 23; 3:16, 17, 21), the children of Zion (Joel 2:23), Judah and Jerusalem (Joel 2:32; 3:1–20), the children of Judah and Jerusalem (Joel 3:6, 8, 19).

It may be that Joel was a Jew of Jerusalem, and owing to his peculiar mention of priests, a priest-prophet himself (Joel 1:9, 10). His references to the Temple and its worship are frequent (Joel 1:9–16; 2:14, 17; 3:18). It is also likely that he lived and prophesied in the early days of Joash and Jehoida, 870–865 B.C., while the victory of Jehoshaphat was fresh in the nation's memory. For this reason he is termed "The Pioneer Prophet."

Dr. A. B. Simpson says,

> Amos begins his longer message with a direct quotation from Joel, as a sort of text for his whole book. Isaiah expands the thoughts which Joel uttered into the larger and loftier message of his pen. Peter, on the Day of Pentecost quotes the prophecy of Joel as the very foundation of the out-pouring of the Holy Spirit, which had occurred and which was to continue through the whole New Testament age. And even the great Apocalypse of John is but a larger unfolding of the promise of the Lord's coming which Joel gave in brief outline.

What is God's call to us through the Prophet Joel?

I.   There is the call to repentance (Joel 2:25–27).

II. There is the promise of refreshment (Joel 2:28, 29).

III. There is the message of deliverance (Joel 3:1).

IV. There is the secret of rest (Joel 3:17–21).

JOELAH [Jŏ′ ĕ′ lah]—GOD IS SNATCHING. *A son of Jeroham of Gedor* who joined David at Ziklag (I Chron. 12:7).

JOEZER [Jō ē′ zûr]—JEHOVAH IS HELP. *A Korhite* who joined David in Ziklag (I Chron. 12:6).

JOGLI [Jŏg' lī]—EXILED, or LED INTO EXILE. *Father of Bukki* and a Danish prince who took part in the division of the land (Num. 34:22).

JOHA [Jō' hă]—JEHOVAH IS LIVING.
1. *A son of Beriah,* grandson of Shaharaim, a Benjamite (I Chron. 8:16).
2. *A son of Shimri,* and one of David's heroes (I Chron. 11:45).

JOHANAN [Jō hā' nan]—JEHOVAH IS GRACIOUS.
1. *A son of Kareah or Careah,* chief of the "captains of the forces" who, after the fall of Jerusalem, joined Gedaliah at Mizpah (II Kings 25:23; Jer. 40:13–16).
2. *The eldest son of Josiah,* king of Judah (I Chron. 3:15).
3. *A son of Elioenai* (I Chron. 3:24).
4. *A grandson of Ahimaaz,* father of Azariah, a Levite (I Chron. 6:9, 10).
5. *A Benjamite* who joined David's valiant men at Ziklag (I Chron. 12:4).
6. *The eighth of the Gadites* who joined forces with David at Ziklag. He was made captain of David's army (I Chron. 12:12).
7. *An Ephraimite* who opposed making slaves of captives, in Ahaz' time (II Chron. 28:12). Hebrew for name here is Jehohanan.
8. *A son of Hakkatan,* of the clan of Azgad (Ezra 8:12).
9. *A priest* who, with Ezra, summoned the exiles to Jerusalem. Called Jehohanan in the Hebrew (Ezra 10:6).
10. *A son of Tobiah* the Ammonite and husband of Meshullam's daughter (Neh. 6:18).
11. *A priest in the days of Joiakim,* the grandson of Jozadak (Neh. 12:22, 23).

JOHN [Jŏhn]—JEHOVAH HATH BEEN GRACIOUS.
1. *A kinsman of Annas* the High Priest (Acts 4: 6).
2. *A son of Mary,* sister of Barnabas, and surnamed Mark (Acts 12:12, 25; 13:5, 13; 15:37). See Mark.
3. *The son of Zacharias and Elisabeth,* who appeared as the forerunner of Christ, and who was beheaded by Herod (Matt. 3:1, 4, 13).
The Man Who Was Plain But Powerful
With the appearance of John the Baptist we have the burial of the Old Dispensation and the emergence of the New. We seem to see his rugged figure standing with arms outstretched, as with one hand he takes the Old Testament, and with the other holds the New, and who, through his ministry, makes the transition from Law to Grace. He was the foreclosure of the old and the forerunner of the new. Perhaps we can helpfully gather the witness of John around these salient features:

I. His parentage. John came as the child of promise and was born in a city of Judah when his parents were old, and his mother long past conception (Luke 1:7, 13, 39). His parents were of priestly descent, his mother being a kinswoman of Mary the mother of our Lord (Luke 1:36).

II.   His ascetic affinities. John, as a man of the desert, knew what it was to practice self-denial (Matt. 3:4). A Nazarite from his birth, he developed self-reliance and spiritual strength as he communed with God in the desert solitudes he loved (Luke 1:15). He was a plain man in every way, akin to Elijah whom many took him for.

He was plain of dress. He dressed simply, his raiment consisting of camel's hair, that is, either a robe of camel's skin or cloth woven from camel's hair. What a humble habit compared with the luxurious robes of soft wool worn by the fashionable and great of his time!

He was plain of food. No sumptuous dishes for this Elijah-like prophet. It was on rough food he thrived. Vegetable honey exuding from fig-trees and palms, and edible locusts, classed among the flying, creeping things the Israelites were allowed to eat (Lev. 11:22), formed his diet (Matt. 3:4). John the Baptist could subscribe to the words of a devout Englishman of a past century:

> I shall be spare of sleep, sparer of diet, and sparest of time that, when the days for eating, drinking, clothing, and sleeping shall be no more, I may eat of my Saviour's hidden manna, drink of the new wine in my Father's kingdom, and inherit that rest which remaineth for the people of my God for ever and ever.

He was plain of speech. Living near to nature, he heard God's voice in solitude as well as in Scripture. Familiar with the Old Testament, he made frequent use of its picturesque language (Luke 3:17; Isa. 66:24; with Amos 9:6). After his sojourn in the desert, brooding over the need and peril of his time, he came forth to speak of barren trees fit only for burning—vipers fleeing before the flaming scrub. John saw in his desert surroundings much that symbolized his nation's calamity and which lent color to his solemn warnings of impending doom.

There is a great deal we would like to say about this man sent from God who had the privilege of acting as the forerunner and then as the baptizer of Jesus, who said of him that he was greater than a prophet. Space, however, forbids a full exposition of this mighty character in the Bible's portrait gallery. The preacher might be able to expand the following features: his self-denial (Matt. 3:4); courage (Matt. 3:7; 14:4); powerful preaching (Mark 1:5); humility (Mark 1:7); holiness (Mark 6:20); burning zeal (John 5:35); honor (Matt. 11:11); ministry of witness (John 10:41); preparatory work (Matt. 11:10); testimony (John 1:29–36); results (Matt. 9:14); death (Matt. 14:10), of which Spurgeon said, "John was the first Baptist Minister to lose his head through dancing."

4.   *John, the son of Zebedee and Salome,* the fisherman who became the beloved disciple, *The Apostle of Love.*

The Man Whom Jesus Loved

This younger brother of James has the rare distinction of being

known as "the disciple whom Jesus loved." The original of his name means, "whom Jehovah loves" and John's experience corresponded to his name. From the many references to this honored disciple we can gather these facts:

He was a native of Bethsaida in Galilee.

His godly parents were probably cousins of Christ, and John was their youngest son.

His mother followed Christ, ministered unto Him, was at the Cross and among those who went to anoint the body of Christ with sweet spices.

His father was a fisherman owning his own vessel and prosperous enough to hire servants.

John himself was also a successful fisherman.

He was called to discipleship while plying his nets.

He was the youngest of the disciples, the *Benjamin* among the Twelve.

He was one of the select triumvirate, Christ's inner cabinet of three, Peter and James being the other two.

He was surnamed by Christ as a son of "Boanerges" because of his prophetic zeal and resolution to witness for Christ.

He was treated by Christ with greater familiarity than the others enjoyed.

He sat next to Christ at the Last Supper.

He was intrusted with the care of the mother of Jesus.

He died when he was almost one hundred years of age.

He wrote the gospel and three epistles bearing his name, and also the Book of Revelation. How true are Wesley's words of John the Beloved:

> A Caesar's title less my envy moves
> Than to be styled the man whom Jesus loves;
> What charms, what beauties in his face did shine
> Reflected ever from the face divine.

From manifold references in the four gospels, the Acts and Revelation, the preacher can develop these traits in John's character: his natural energy (Mark 3:17); his intolerance (Mark 9:38); his vindictiveness (Luke 9:54); his ambition (Mark 10:35–37); his eagerness to learn (John 13:23; I John 2:9); his sympathy (John 19:26); his love (I John 4:7–21).

JOIADA [Joi' a dă]—JEHOVAH SETS UP or HATH KNOWN.

1. *Son of Eliashib,* whose son married the daughter of Sanballat the Horonite (Neh. 13:28). A great-grandson of Jeshua the high priest (Neh. 12:10, 11, 22; 13:28).

2. *A son of Paseah* who helped to repair the gate of Jerusalem (Neh. 3:6). Also called Jehoiada.

JOIAKIM [Joi' a kĭm]—JEHOVAH SETS UP or ESTABLISHES. *A high priest,* son of Jeshua the priest who returned with Zerubbabel (Neh. 12:10, 12, 26).

JOIARIB, JEHOIARIB [Joi' a rĭb, Jē hoi' a rĭb]—JEHOVAH DEPENDS or CONTENDS.
   1. *A descendant of Aaron,* father of Jedaiah (Neh. 11:10; 12:6, 19). See Jehoiarib.
   2. *One whom Ezra sent to Iddo* to ask for ministers for the Temple (Ezra 8:16).
   3. *A descendant of Pharez* whose family dwelt in Jerusalem (Neh. 11:5).

JOKIM [Jō' kim]—JEHOVAH SETS UP. *A descendant of Shelah,* son of Judah (I Chron. 4:22).

JOKSHAN [Jŏk' shan]—FOWLER. *A son of Abraham* by Keturah and father of Sheba (or Saba) and Dedan (Gen. 25:2, 3; I Chron. 1:32).

JOKTAN [Jŏk' tan]—LITTLE, SMALL or DISPUTE. *A son of Eber* of the family of Shem, from whom thirteen Arab tribes sprang (Gen. 10:26; I Chron. 1:19–23).

JONADAB [Jŏn' a dăb]—JEHOVAH IS LIBERAL, WHO ACTS AS A PRINCE or BOUNTEOUS.
   1. *A son of Shimeah,* David's brother (II Sam. 13:3, 5, 32, 35).
   2. *The son of Rechab,* the Kenite, whom Jehu took with him to show him his zeal for the Lord. He became head of a tribe refraining from agriculture and from wine (I Chron. 2:55; Jer. 35:6–19). See Jehonadab.

JONAH, JONA, JONAS [Jō' nah, Jō' nă, Jō' nas]—A DOVE. *The son of Amittai,* and the first Hebrew prophet, or missionary, sent to a heathen nation (II Kings 14:25; Jonah 1:1).

The Man Who Ran Away

The meaning of the prophet's name is suggestive. When first chosen, it doubtless meant to Jonah's mother gentleness and love. This son of Amittai was a citizen of Gath-hepher in Zebulun of Galilee and a subject of the Northern Kingdom. He is thus a proof of the false statement of the Pharisees about no prophet coming out of Galilee (John 7:52).

Jonah lived in the early part of the reign of Jeroboam II, and in a period when the kingdom was in a divided and abject condition. He is without doubt one of the earliest, if not the first, of the prophets whose writings are preserved to us. He is the first of a new order of prophets, appearing that he might declare God's love claims the whole world. By friend and foe Jonah has been ridiculed and tortured and treated as a myth or parable. Our Lord, however, believed him to be a historic person; so do we! For proof in this direction compare Jonah 1:7 with Matthew 12:39, 40 and Luke 11:29, 30; Jonah 3:5 with Matthew 12:41.

Jonah's mission was to Nineveh and therefore beyond the bounds of Israel, which is in perfect harmony; for whenever God brought His people into any relation with other peoples, He made Himself known to them as was the case in Egypt through Joseph and Moses; to the Philistines through the capture of the Ark; to the Assyrians by Elisha; to Nebuchadnezzar and Belshazzer by Daniel.

Within the Book of Jonah we have the most beautiful story ever told in so small a compass. In 1,328 words we are given a wealth of incident and all the dialogue needed to carry on the grand and varied action. Jonah was an isolationist, believing that salvation was for the Jews, and the Jews only. Through affliction he came to know of God's embracing love (John 3:16). Dealing with Jonah as a servant, Dr. C. I. Scofield gives us these helpful points: disobedient (Jonah 1:1–11); afflicted (Jonah 1:12–17); praying (Jonah 2:1–9); delivered (Jonah 2:10); recommissioned (Jonah 3:1–3); powerful (Jonah 3:4–10); perplexed, fainting but not forsaken (Jonah 4:1–11).

Another serviceable outline for the worker can be developed around these thoughts:

Chapter one: A disobedient prophet running *from* God and punished.

Chapter two: A praying prophet running *back* to God and delivered.

Chapter three: A faithful prophet running *with* God and rewarded.

Chapter four: An angry prophet running *ahead* of God and rebuked.

Here are other aspects to deal with: Jonah was sent to a foreign field (Jonah 1:2); sought to flee from his unwelcome task (Jonah 1:3); was overtaken in his flight (Jonah 1:4–17); found God in the depth of the sea (Ps. 139:10; Jonah 2); became a revivalist (Jonah 3); was disappointed with his own work (Jonah 3:5–10; 4:1); reveals bigotry (Jonah 4:1–3); was taught the breadth of divine mercy (Jonah 4:4–11). See below Jonas, Jona.

Jona is given as the name of the father of Peter (Matt. 16:17; John 1:42; 21:15).

JONAN, JONAM [Jō′ nan]—GOD HATH BEEN GRACIOUS. *An ancestor of Joseph,* the husband of Mary, the mother of our Lord (Luke 3:30).

JONAS, JONA [Jō′ nas, Jō′ nă]—A DOVE. *The father of the Apostle Peter.* Barjona means "son of Jona" (John 1:42; 21:15, 16, 17).

JONATHAN [Jŏn′ a than]—THE LORD GAVE.

1. *A Levite* who entered the service of Micah as "father and priest." The son of Gershom, son of Manasseh (Judg. 17:10; 18:30).

2. *Eldest son of King Saul* and close friend of David. Jonathan left one son, Mephibosheth (I Sam. 13:2, 3). With his father Jona-

than fell in battle with the Philistines and there is nothing comparable in literature to David's lament and eulogy when he heard of their death (II Sam. 1).

The Man Who Was Content To Be Second

The story of Jonathan is remarkable in that we know so much about him, yet he was never called to office. While he lived, he was known only as the eldest son of Saul. He knew he would never succeed his father as king. With true humility he could say to David, whom he loved, "I shall be next to thee." After his lamentable death he is only mentioned as the father of Mephibosheth. He is not to be found among the worthies in Hebrews eleven. Doubtless he was one not counted worthy by the world.

Jonathan personified all the Christian virtues or graces that Peter wrote about (II Pet. 1:5-7). In battle, his valour was absolutely stainless, and he acted without fear. As to the love-covenant Jonathan made with David, how rare it is to see two men loving one another as these two did. Truly, Jonathan was possessed of a heroic faith (I Sam. 14:6); undaunted courage (I Sam. 14:7-14); self-sacrificing friendship (I Sam. 18:4; 19:2).

3. *A Son of Abiathar,* a high priest in David's time (II Sam. 15:27, 36; 17:17, 20; I Kings 1:42, 43).

4. *A son of Shimea,* David's brother (II Sam. 21:21; I Chron. 20:7).

5. *Son of Jashen* and one of David's heroes (II Sam. 23:32; I Chron. 11:34).

6. *A son of Jada* and grandson of Onam (I Chron. 2:32, 33).

7. *An uncle of David* (I Chron. 27:32), who was a scribe.

8. *The father of Ebed* who returned with Ezra (Ezra 8:6).

9. *The son of Asahel,* who assisted in the matter of foreign wives (Ezra 10:15).

10. *A descendant of Jeshua* the high priest (Neh. 12:11).

11. *A priest descended from Melicu* (Neh. 12:14).

12. *A priest descended from Shemaiah* (Neh 12:35). Called Jehonathan in Nehemiah 12:18.

13. *A scribe* in whose house Jeremiah was imprisoned (Jer. 37:15, 20; 38:26).

14. *A son of Kareah* who went to Gedaliah (Jer. 40:8).

JORAH [Jō'rah, Jō'raĭ]–RAIN OF AUTUMN. A Gadite chief (I Chron. 5:13; Ezra 2:18).

JORAM [Jō'ram]–JEHOVAH IS HIGH.

1. *A son of Toi,* king of Zobah (II Sam. 8:10). Called Hadoram, meaning "Hadah is exalted" (I Chron. 18:10).

2. *A son of Jehoshaphat,* who reigned for eight years (II Kings 8:16-19; 11:2; I Chron. 3:11; Matt. 1:8). Called also Jehoram.

3. *A son of Ahab,* king of Israel, who reigned for eleven years.

With him the dynasty of Omri ceased (II Kings 8:16–29). Called also Jehoram.

4. *A Levite,* descendant of Eliezer the son of Moses (I Chron. 26:25).

5. *One of the priests sent by Jehoshaphat* to instruct the people (II Chron. 17:8).

JORIM [Jō′ rim]—HE THAT EXALTS THE LORD. *An ancestor of Jesus Christ* (Luke 3:29).

JORKOAM [Jôr′ ko ăm]—SPREADING THE PEOPLE. *A son of Raham,* and descendant of Hebron through Caleb the spy (I Chron. 2:44). Some writers have Jokdeam or Jorkeam. See Joshua 15:56 for the name of a city.

JOSAPHAT [Jŏs′ a phăt]—THE LORD JUDGES. *An ancestor of Christ* (Matt. 1:8). See Jehoshaphat.

JOSE [Jō′ se]—AID. *An ancestor of Christ through Mary* (Luke 3:29).

JOSECH [Jō′ sěch]—*An ancestor of Christ* who probably lived after the exile (Luke 3:26). K.J.V. and A.V. call him Joseph.

JOSEDECH [Jŏs′ e děch]—JEHOVAH IS RIGHTEOUS. *The father of Joshua* the high priest who helped to rebuild the altar and the temple (Hag. 1:1, 12, 14; 2:2, 4; Zech. 6:11.) Also called Jozadak (Ezra 3:2, 8; 5:2).

JOSEPH [Jō′ zeph]—MAY GOD ADD or INCREASER.

1. *Poetic description of the descendants of Joseph* the son of Jacob (Deut. 33:13).

2. *The Father of Igal,* one of the spies sent by Moses into Canaan (Num. 13:7).

3. *A son of Asaph* (I Chron. 25:2, 9).

4. *A man of the family of Bani* who had taken a foreign wife (Ezra 10:42).

5. *A priest* of the family of Shebaniah in Joaakim's time (Neh. 12:14).

6. *Ancestor of Joseph,* Mary's husband (Luke 3:24).

7. *Another ancestor of Joseph* in the same line (Luke 3:26).

8. *A more remote ancestor of Joseph,* Mary's husband (Luke 3:30).

9. *A disciple* nominated with Matthias to take the place of Judas Iscariot among the disciples. Matthias was chosen (Acts 1:23). This Joseph must have been a commendable Christian since he was nominated as an apostle.

10. *The eleventh son of Jacob* and first of Rachel, and one of the

most outstanding men of the Bible, meriting honorable mention (Gen. 30:24, 25).

The Man Whose Dream Came True

The story of this young man who went from pit to palace and from rags to riches, never loses its charm for young and old alike. It would take a book itself to fully portray all the vicissitudes and virtues of Joseph, who kept his record clean. All that we can do in our treatment of him is to suggest a few aspects of his character for development.

Joseph was a youthful dreamer and his dream came true (Gen. 37:5-9; 41:42-44).

Joseph labored as a slave, but was faithful in hard places (Gen. 39:1-6, 20-23).

Joseph enjoyed the presence of God and won the confidence of his master (Gen. 39:2, 4).

Joseph had physical beauty, but it was never a snare to him (Gen. 39:6).

Joseph resisted temptation. His godless mistress could not seduce him. Grace was his to flee youthful lusts. Thus he did not commit a "great wickedness" (Gen. 39:7-13).

Joseph was silent amid foul accusations and the appearance of guilt and unjust punishment (Gen. 39:14-20).

Joseph was unspoiled by sudden prosperity. When days of honor followed days of humiliation, he did not yield to pride (Gen. 41:14-16).

Joseph the interpreter of dreams proved that "prison walls do not a prison make." He acknowledged his dependence upon God for illumination, proving that he was not a mere dreamer but an interpreter of dreams (Gen. 40).

Joseph manifested great wisdom, brotherly love, filial devotion and utter submission to God (Gen. 43:20; 45:8, 14, 23; 47:7). He knew how to return good for evil (Gen. 50:16-21). If we cannot have all the gifts of Joseph, who is a perfect type of Christ, we can certainly covet all his graces. If we cannot have his greatness, we can certainly emulate his goodness.

R. W. Moss says, "A very high place must be given Joseph among the early founders of his race. In strength of right purpose he was second to none, whilst in graces of reverence and kindness, of insight and assurance, he became the type of a faith that is at once personal and national (Heb. 11:22), and allows neither misery nor a career of triumph to eclipse the sense of Divine destiny."

11. *The husband of Mary,* and foster-father of our Lord (Matt. 1:16-24; 2:13; Luke 1:27; 2:4-43; 3: 23; 4: 22; John 1:45; 6:42).

The Man of Wood and Nails

It is somewhat unique that two Josephs were associated with Christ, one at His birth and the other at His death. Both of these godly men gave Jesus of their best. In this section we think of Joseph the carpenter, who was present at the manger when Jesus was born, even though he was not His father. While Christ came as the Son of Man, He was never *a* son of a man.

Joseph's presence at Christ's birth witnesses to a severe test that had emerged triumphant. Mary was the pure young woman he had fallen in love with, and was about to make his wife. Yet the Child she was about to bear would not be his. Seeing her "great with child," without fanfare Joseph was minded to put her away. He never acted rashly with his espoused, although he was baffled by her condition. This serves for all time as an example of godly wisdom and tender consideration for others.

Bitterly disappointed that Mary had apparently betrayed him, yet believing, he made no haste. As a praying man he waited upon God, and his love for and patience with Mary were rewarded. God understood his mental difficulties and rewarded Joseph's conscientious attitude toward Mary by revealing His redemptive plan. God never fails those who carry their anxieties to Him. Joseph received a direct and distinct revelation from God, and at once his fears were banished, and his line of duty made clear.

Tenderly he cared for his dear one as if the Child she was bearing were his own. Overawed by the mystery of it all, that his beloved Mary had been chosen as the mother of the Lord he as a devout Jew had eagerly anticipated, we can imagine how he would superintend every detail of the Nativity.

What holy thoughts must have filled the mind of Mary's guardian. Where suspicion regarding Mary's purity once lurked, strong faith now reigned as he looked into the lovely face of Mary's Child. At last God's promises had been fulfilled and before him was the Babe through whom God's covenants would be established.

When it became necessary because of Herod's hatred to flee into Egypt, Joseph cared for Mary and her first-born Son with reverent devotion until tidings came that Herod was dead, and that they could safely return to their own land. While a shroud of secrecy covers the thirty years Christ spent at home, we can be sure of this, that between Jesus and Joseph there was an affection strong and deep.

Briefly stated, we have these glimpses of Joseph:

I. He was "a son of David" and could claim royal or priestly descent (Matt. 1:20).

II. His family belonged to Bethlehem, David's city.

III. He followed the trade of carpenter, and doubtless taught Christ how to use wood and nails (Matt. 13:55).

IV. He was a pious Israelite, faithful in all the ordinances of the Temple (Luke 2:22–24, 41, 42).

V. He was a kindly, charitable man, treating Mary gently in her time of need (Matt. 1:19; Luke 2:1–7).

VI. He was faithful in his care of Christ, and deserved to be called His "father" (Luke 2:33. John 1:45; 6:42).

VII. He never appears in the Gospels after Christ was twelve years of age and became "a son of the Law" (Luke 2:41–51), which may suggest that he died during the interval. This would explain why Jesus at His death asked John to care for His mother.

VIII.   He died, tradition says, at the age of 111 years, when Jesus was but eighteen years of age.

12. *Joseph of Arimathaea,* a secret disciple of Jesus, whose unused grave was surrendered to Jesus. Thus the One born in a virgin womb was buried in a virgin tomb (Matt. 27:57–60; Mark 15:43; Luke 23:50; John 19:38).

The Man Who Gave His Grave to Jesus

This wealthy and devout Israelite, a member of the Sanhedrin, lived in a city of Jews (Luke 23:51). It is to the provision he made for the body of Christ that Isaiah had reference when he said, "He made His grave with the rich" (Isa. 53:9). Of this renowned Joseph we discover:

1.   He was an honorable counselor (Mark 15:43). Because of his adherence to the Law and integrity of life he was a member of the governing body known as the Sanhedrin.

II.   He looked for the kingdom of God. Immersed in Old Testament Scriptures, he anticipated the reign of the promised Messiah.

III.   He was "a good man and just" (Luke 23:50, 51). As the Bible never uses words unnecessarily, there must be a distinction between "good" and "just." As a "good man" we have his own *internal* disposition — what he was in himself. As a "just man" we have his *external* conduct — what he was towards others. His just dealings were the fruit of the root of his goodness. His was the belief that knew how to behave.

IV.   He was a secret disciple (John 19:38). Joseph of Arimathaea was similar to Nicodemus in his respect for our Lord as a man, admiration for Him as a teacher, belief in Him as the Christ, and yet, till now, his lack of confessing Him before men. Dreading the hostility of his colleagues on the Sanhedrin, he kept his faith secret.

V.   He begged the body of Jesus (Matt. 27:58). As soon as Jesus was dead, Joseph hastened to Pilate for permission to inter His body. David Smith observes that when the condemnation of Jesus was over — a condemnation in which Joseph took no part — he realized how cowardly a part he had played and, stricken with shame and remorse, plucked up courage and went in to Pilate and asked for the body of Jesus. It was common for friends of the crucified to purchase their bodies, which would otherwise have been cast out as refuse, and give them decent burial (Mark 15:45).

VI.   He gave his grave to Christ (Matt. 27:59, 60). With lingering reverence Joseph paid his last respects to the One he admired, and in the hour of sorrow helped the friends and not the foes of the righteous Sufferer. Joseph had a garden close to Calvary, where he had hewn a smoothed and polished tomb in the side of the rock as his own last resting place, in which, aided by Nicodemus, he buried the linen-covered and perfumed body of Christ.

VII.   Joseph, legend tells us, was sent to Britain by Philip the Apostle, and founded the Church of Glastonbury. Medieval chroniclers delighted to tell of the staff Joseph stuck into the ground. The staff supposedly took root, brought forth leaves and flowers and became the parent of all the Glastonbury thorns from that day to this.

JOSES [Jŏ′ sēs]—HE THAT PARDONS.
1. *One of the brethren of our Lord* (Matt. 13:55; Mark 6:3). R.V. gives name as Joseph.
2. *The son of Mary,* probably the same as No. 1 (Matt. 27:56; Mark 15:40–47).
3. *The personal or natal name of Barnabas,* the companion and missionary colleague of Paul (Acts 4:36). The R.V. gives Joseph.

JOSHAH [Jŏ′ shah]—JEHOVAH IS A GIFT or UPRIGHTNESS. *A Simeonite chief,* son of Amaziah (I Chron. 4:34).

JOSHAPHAT [Jŏsh′ a phăt]—JEHOVAH JUDGES.
1. *A Mithnite,* one of David's valiant men (I Chron. 11:43).
2. *A priest,* one of the trumpeters before the Ark during its removal to Jerusalem (I Chron. 15:24). R.V. gives Jehoshaphat.

JOSHAVIAH [Jŏsh a vī′ ah]—JEHOVAH IS EQUALITY or SITTETH UPRIGHT. *One of David's heroes* (I Chron. 11:46).

JOSHBEKASHAH [Jŏsh bĕk′ a shah]—SEAT OF HARDNESS. *A son of Heman,* and David's leader of song (I Chron. 25:4, 24).

JOSHEB-BASSHEBETH, JOSHEB-BASSEBET—Given as a proper name in the R.V. of II Samuel 23:8. Probably Ish-baal, meaning "there is a Lord" or Jashobeam (I Chron. 11:11).

JOSHUA, JEHOSHUA, JEHOSHUAH, JESHUA, JESUS [Jŏsh′ u ă, Jē hŏsh′ u ă, Jĕsh′ u ă, Jē′ sus]—JEHOVAH IS SALVATION.
1. *The son of Nun* and successor of Moses and author of the book bearing his name. He is also called Hoshea (Num. 13:8, 16; Deut. 32:44).

The Man Who Was a Soldier-Saint

Joshua has been rightly called, "The first soldier consecrated by sacred history." A profitable way of studying his profile is to think of him in the following roles:

As a Son. Joshua was the son of Nun — a name meaning "prosperity, durable" — and of the tribe of Ephraim. Nothing is known of his mother. One usually finds, however, a good and gracious woman in the background of a man who reaches a position of influence and honor. Without doubt, Joshua's parents feared the God of Israel, and he continued their godly influence.

As a Slave. Born during the weary years of bondage his nation suffered in Egypt under Pharaoh, Joshua knew something of the lash

of the whip, the almost impossible task in the brick-fields, and the
deep sigh of liberty. But little did he realize that although a slave,
he would rise to become Israel's supreme leader and commander. He
had witnessed the moral and social degradation of his countrymen
brought about by the terrible idolatries of that time. Thus, when he
came to the position of leadership, his solemn commands were colored
by early experience (Josh. 24:15).

As a Soldier. Joshua was pre-eminent as a military leader who
knew how to plan campaigns, discipline his forces, use spies, but
above all, pray and trust in God. Many a general has closely studied
Joshua's conquest of Canaan and followed his strategy. Read how he
discomfited Amalek (Ex. 17:9–16)! He never stooped to pilfering and
plunder. It was as true of him as of Sir Henry Havelock, of whom it
was said, "He was every inch a soldier, and every inch a Christian."
Joshua was first of all a good soldier of the Lord whom he encountered and obeyed as Captain of the Lord's host (Josh. 5:13–15).

As a Servant. Joshua's victory over Amalek gave him the open door
of further usefulness and responsibility. That he was prepared for the
responsibilities of leadership is evidenced by the fact that because
of his unswerving loyalty and devotion, he is called "the servant of
Moses'" (Num. 11:28; Josh. 1:1).

As a Spy. Joshua, along with eleven others, was chosen to search the
land of Canaan (Num. 13:1–16). It was at this time that Moses changed
his servant's name from Oshea or Hoshea, meaning "help" to Joshua,
meaning "God's help" or "salvation." The changed name indicated
the desire of Moses to lift the thoughts of the people Godward, and
to lead them from reliance upon leaders to God's help. Along with
Caleb, Joshua brought back a faithful report of the land, which the
people rejected, and wandered thereby for forty years in the wilderness. But Joshua profited by such an experience (Josh. 2:1, 2).

As a Saviour. Moses, representing the Law, brought the people to
the border of the land, but it took a Joshua (God's salvation) to take
them into the land. Divinely commissioned for such a task, he was
probably about eighty-five years of age when he assumed command at
Shittim. What a saviour he was! How marvelously was he helped to
roll away Israel's reproach and to lead them to possess their possessions! His conquests and victories are typical of all the Lord has made
possible for His own.

As a Statesman. What magnanimity and unselfish statesmanship
Joshua revealed! Once the division of the land was completed, he
carried through the setting up of the Tabernacle, the appointing of
the cities of refuge, the arrangement of the Levitical order and service,
with the same precision and thoroughness that characterized his other
work as Israel's Premier and leader.

As a Saint. Joshua's saintliness marked him out as Moses' successor
(Deut. 34:9). What a soldier-saint he was!

He was filled with the Spirit of God (Deut. 34:9).

He enjoyed the presence of God (Josh. 1:5; 6:27).

He was indwelt by the word of God (Josh. 1:8).

He was ever obedient to the will of God (Num. 32:12; Josh. 5:14).

No wonder his death at 110 years of age was deeply mourned and his eminent service universally acknowledged! The brief but noble epitaph of the historian is eloquent with meaning, "before Joshua, the servant of the Lord." Dead, he could yet speak, for the nation continued to serve the Lord all the days of the elders that outlived Joshua (Josh. 24:3).

2. *A Beth-shemite,* and owner of a field in the days of Eli (I Sam. 6:14, 18).

3. *The Governor of Jerusalem* in the days of Josiah (II Kings 23:8).

4. *The son of Josedech* and high priest at the time of the rebuilding of the Temple (Hag. 1:1; 2:4; Zech. 3; 6:11).

JOSIAH [Jō sī ah]—THE FIRE OF THE LORD or JEHOVAH SUPPORTS. *The king of Judah* who succeeded his father Amon, when only eight years old, and one of Judah's good kings (I Kings 13:2; II Chron. 34:3).

The Man Who Sought After God

The history of Israel's later kings makes dreary reading. Says J. G. Greenhough,

> Four-fifths of them were equally deficient in brains and morals, a combina-
> tion of wickedness and folly, with nothing of the king about them but the
> name. But here and there you come upon a man amidst all these royal pup-
> pets. It is like finding a garden in a Sahara, or a jewel in a heap of sham
> trinkets and dirty stage finery. Josiah breaks a long, monotonous series of
> absolutely worthless monarchs. Before and behind him are moral waste and
> darkness. He stands out as a figure worth looking at and loving . . . Josiah's
> good reign was like a burst of brilliant sunset, before the final darkness comes on.

In a life worth studying, let us list a few incidents illustrating the noble character of Josiah.

He was left parentless at eight years of age. Josiah had a sorrowful childhood, and as a king at eight years of age, he was introduced to scenes of violence, outrage and civil war. But God was more than a Father to this fatherless boy.

He had a good and darling mother. We know nothing about the mother who undertook Josiah's training apart from her name, Jedidah, meaning, "God's darling," which she was not called for nought. She sought to make her son what she was called, "God's darling," and her labor had its sweet reward.

He sought after God at the age of sixteen. After sixteen years in the nursing hands of his good mother, Josiah turned from the ways of his father Amon and his grandfather Manasseh, and took his nobler and remoter ancestor, David, as his model. In life's fair morning, Josiah set his heart to seek the Lord.

He purged Judah and Jerusalem when he was twenty. Youth did not deter Josiah from necessary reformation. Out went all forms of idolatry. Borne along by a noble rage, he swept away the groves full of abominations. Would that the fervent zeal and righteous enthusiasm of this earnest, passionate young man might characterize more young men today!

He rebuilt the Temple when he was twenty-six. This consecrated young man saw that it was of no use destroying idols unless he had something better to replace them. Thus when his destroying fever had spent its force, Josiah began to rebuild and repair the house of God. In turning over the rubbish of the Temple, the king made a strange discovery. He came across a buried and forgotten copy of the Law, the reading of which strangely affected him. Profoundly humbled, he laid the axe to his own corruptions, and went forward to grow in wisdom and godliness.

He reigned for thirty-one years and was only thirty-nine when he died. That Josiah was beloved by his people is indicated by their deep and long-continued mourning after his death.

2. *A son of Zephaniah* who dwelt in Jerusalem in Zechariah's time (Zech. 6:10). Perhaps the Hen of verse fourteen.

JOSIBIAH [Jŏs ĭ bĭ' ah]—JEHOVAH CAUSES TO DWELL. *A Simeonite* (I Chron. 4:35). Also called Joshibiah.

JOSIPHIAH [Jŏs ĭ phĭ' ah]—JEHOVAH WILL INCREASE. *Head of the house of Shelomith* after the exile (Ezra. 8:10).

JOTHAM, JOATHAM [Jō' tham]—JEHOVAH IS UPRIGHT.
1. *The youngest son of Gideon.* He escaped from Abimelech (Judg. 9:5, 7, 21, 57).
2. *A son of Jahdai* (I Chron. 2:47).
3. *A son of Azariah* or Uzziah and king of Judah. He was the father of Ahab, king of Judah (II Kings 15:32). Little is known of this Jotham apart from his rebuilding of the Temple gates.

JOZABAD, JOSABAD [Jŏz' a băd, Jŏs' a băd]—JEHOVAH HATH BE-STOWED or ENDOWED.
1. *A Gederathite of Judah* who joined David at Ziklag (I Chron. 12:4). Also called Josabad.
2. *A man of Manasseh* who did the same (Chron. 12:20).
3. *Another Manassite* who did the same (I Chron. 12:20).
4. *A Levite,* and one of the overseers of tithes in Hezekiah's reign (II Chron. 31:13).
5. *A Levite chief* in Josiah's reign (II Chron. 35:9).
6. *A son of Jeshua,* employed in weighing the sanctuary vessels brought from Babylon (Ezra 8:33).
7. *A priest* who had married a foreign wife (Ezra 10:22).
8. *A Levite* who had also married a foreign wife (Ezra 10:23).
9. *A Levite interpreter* of the Law read by Ezra (Neh. 8:7).
10. *A chief Levite* in Jerusalem after the exile (Neh. 11:16).

JOZACHAR, JOZACAR [Jŏz' a chär]—JEHOVAH REMEMBERS. *The son of the Moabitess, Shimeath.* He slew Joash or Jehoash, king of Judah (II Kings 12:21). Erroneously called Zabad in II Chronicles 24:26.

JOZADAK [Jŏz' a dăk]—JEHOVAH IS GREAT or JUST. *A priest,* the father of Jeshua who returned from exile with Zerubbabel (Ezra 3:2, 8; 5:2; 10:18; Neh. 12:26). Called Josedech in Haggai and Zechariah. See also Jehozadak.

JUBAL [Jū' bal]—PLAYING, RAM'S HORN or A TRUMPET. *The younger son of Adah,* wife of Lamech, and the inventor of musical instruments (Gen. 4:21). Jubilee is from his name, which is used to describe the trumpet employed at the glad time of the Jewish jubilee.

JUCAL, JEHUCAL [Jŭ cal]—ABLE. *A son of Shelemiah* and prince of Judah, a deadly enemy of Jeremiah (Jer. 38:1).

JUDAH, JUDA, JODA [Jū'dah]—OBJECT OF PRAISE or PRAISE OF THE LORD. *The fourth son of Jacob by Leah,* and founder of a tribal family (Gen. 29:35; Num. 26:19–21; I Chron. 2:3–6).

The Man Who Was Praised

The character of Judah is revealed in his confession of sin before Joseph (Gen. 44:18–34). This appeal has been described as "One of the noblest pieces of natural eloquence in any literature, sacred or profane." In the last words of Jacob much is said of Judah (Gen. 49:8). We have:

I. His praise. "Thou art he whom thy brethren shall praise." The origin of his name is to be found in the gratitude of his mother at the time of his birth (Gen. 29:35). A still more distinguished mother praised the Lord for a greater Son who came from the tribe of Judah (Luke 1:46, 47).

II. His conquests. "Thy hand shall be in the neck of thine enemies." Here we have the prophecy of a conqueror, the anticipation of the figure of the lion, which was emblazoned on the flag of Judah, and was symbolic of the strength of the tribe in battle. Judah was the first tribe called to fight the Canaanites after Joshua's death (Judg. 1:1, 2) — a battle ending in victory for Judah. See also Psalm 18:40.

III. His pre-eminence. "Thy father's children shall bow down before thee." The superiority of the tribe of Judah continued almost to the end of the Old Testament and passed on to Him who has the pre-eminence in all things. Judah was first in numbers, first in territory, first in marching order, first in prowess, first in war.

IV. His regal dignity. The lion-king of the forest became the symbol of Judah, as the king of the tribes (Num. 2:3, 4). "A lion's whelp," speaks of the first energy of youth, and the early days of Judah were full of vigor and energy. How prophetic all this is of Him who came as the Lion of the tribe of Judah! The old divines said that Christ was a lamb in His death, but a lion in His resurrection. How different is His prowess from the deadly power of him who is a roaring lion!

2. *An ancestor of Kadmiel* who helped to rebuild the Temple (Ezra 3:9).

3. *A Levite* who had taken a strange wife (Ezra 10:23).

4. *A Benjamite,* son of Senuah, second in authority over Jerusalem in Nehemiah's day (Neh. 11:9).

5. *A Levite* who returned from exile with Zerubbabel (Neh. 12:8).

6. *A prince of Judah* (Neh. 12:34).

7. *A priest and musician* (Neh. 12:36).

JUDAS, JUDA, JUDE [Jū' das]—PRAISE OF THE LORD.

1. *The disciple surnamed Iscariot,* who betrayed the Master and then hanged himself. He was the only one of the Twelve who was not a Galilean. He acted as treasurer of the apostolic band (John 6:71; 12:6; 13:26, 29).

The Man Who Was Guilty of a Horrible Crime

The Gospels represent the betrayal of Christ by Judas as a horrible, diabolical crime. And it stands out as the darkest deed in human history. The word "betray" is a remarkable one meaning "to deliver up." This is what Judas did — delivered up Jesus. Yet such a dastardly action was overruled, for Jesus was delivered by the determinate counsel of God.

Judas is a strange character and everything about his choice and conduct is mysterious. Why was he chosen? All we can say in answer is in the declaration, "that the scriptures might be fulfilled" (Matt. 26:56). The greater mystery is, why did Christ choose you and me to be His followers? Think of these features:

I.   Judas' terrible crime was predicted (Ps. 109:5–8; Acts 1:16).

II. His cruel bargain was foretold (Zech. 11:12, 13).

III. He became a devil incarnate. "One of you is a devil." As Jesus became God-incarnate, Judas became the devil-incarnate.

IV. He is called "a son of perdition." Because the same designation is used of the Man of Sin, some writers feel that this grim figure will be Judas incarnate (II Thess. 2:3).

V.   He was a thief. He kept the bag which represented responsibility. Christ chose Judas as treasurer for the Twelve because of his commercial instinct and business acumen, but he prostituted his gift. His very endowment became a snare. A blessing was turned into a curse.

VI. He betrayed Christ with a kiss. The hatefulness of his crime reached its limit when he gave the enemies of Christ the symbol of affection. How wicked is the human heart—deceitful above all things!

VII. He was the recipient of divine patience. Why he persisted in following Christ we cannot say. All we can do is marvel at the love and patience of Christ as He bore with Judas for three years. He knew all along that this so-called disciple would betray Him, yet He kept the door open. Even when He met Judas after his contract with the foes of Christ, He greeted him as "friend." We would have scorned the traitor and hissed "enemy" or "traitor." Not so Christ, who is patient toward all men.

VIII. He went out to his own place (Acts 1:25). It was in self-excommunication. Christ did not excommunicate Judas — He only ratified the choice. Up to the last He gave Judas a chance to halt and turn from his wickedness. But when the die had been cast, Jesus said, "What thou doest, do quickly."

We leave our glimpse of the despicable man of the Bible with two lessons in mind:

The journey into sin gains momentum. We never know where a wrong path may end. Sin only needs opportunity to carry us to its utmost depths.

It is sadly possible to be associated with Jesus, to hear His gracious words, witness His wonderful works, yet refuse Him our heart's allegiance and be ultimately lost.

2. *Half-brother of Jesus,* brother of James and writer of the epistle known by his name (Matt. 13:55; Mark 6:3; Luke 6:16; Acts 1:13; Jude 1). See Jude.

3. *An apostle* also known as Lebbeus or Thaddeus (John 14:22).

4. *A Galilean* who stirred up sedition shortly after the birth of Christ (Acts 5:37).

5. *One with whom Paul lodged* in the street called Straight (Acts 9:11).

6. *The prophet surnamed Barsabas,* sent with Silas to Antioch (Acts 15:22, 27).

JUDE [Jūde]—PRAISE.—Jude is the English form of the name Judas. The author of the next to last book of the Bible describes himself as *a brother of James* (Jude 1). See James, No. 4. Although he calls himself "the servant of Jesus Christ," he was our Lord's brother, and like the rest of His brethren did not believe in Christ when they lived together under the same roof (Matt. 13:55; John 7:5).

His brief epistle contains an earnest warning appeal to the saints to defend the faith in an age of apostasy. Couched in vivid and picturesque language, Jude's letter was addressed to a church or circle of churches exposed to false teachers. What a message it has for our hearts in these days of modernistic teaching!

JULIUS [Jū' lǐ ŭs]—CURLY HEADED. *A centurion of Augustus' band* who conducted Paul to Rome (Acts 27:1, 3). Evidently he was kind to the apostle and treated him with all deference and respect (Acts 27:3–43; 28:16).

JUNIA, JUNIAS [Jū' niä]—BELONGING TO JUNO. *A Jewish Christian of Rome.* This kinsman and fellow prisoner of Paul became a Christian before Paul (Rom. 16:7).

JUSHAB-HESED [Jŭ' shăb-hē' sed]—LOVINGKINDNESS IS RETURNED. *A son of Zerubbabel,* of the family of David (I Chron. 3:20).

JUSTUS [Jŭs' tus]—JUST or RIGHTEOUS.
1. *A surname of Joseph or Barsabas,* the disciple who was the unsuccessful candidate for apostleship (Acts 1:23).
2. *A godly man of Corinth,* whose house was next to the synagogue and with whom Paul lodged (Acts 18:7).
3. *The surname of a Jew* called Jesus from whom Paul sent a salutation to the Colossian Church (Col. 4:11).

K

KADMIEL [Kăd' mĭ el]—GOD IS OF OLD.
1. *A Levite* and head of a tribal family which returned from Babylon with Zerubbabel (Ezra 2:40; Neh. 7:43).
2. *A Judahite* who assisted in the rebuilding of the Temple (Ezra 3:9).
3. *A Levite* who led the devotions of the people (Neh. 9:4, 5; 10:9; 12:8, 24).

KALLAI [Kăl' la ī]—JEHOVAH IS LIGHT or SWIFT. *A priest,* and head of his father's house of Sallai in the line of Joiakim the high priest (Neh. 12:20).

KAREAH, CAREAH [Kā rē' ah, Cā rē' ah]—BALD. *The father of Johanan,* a captain of the Jews when Gedaliah was governor of Jerusalem II Kings 25:23; Jer. 40:8, 13).

KEDAR [Kē'där]—POWERFUL. *One of the sons of Ishmael,* the son of Abraham and Hagar (Gen. 25:13; I Chron. 1:29). Also name of the tribe which sprang from Kedar (Ps. 120:5).

KEDEMAH [Kĕd' e mah]—EASTERN. *Youngest son of Ishmael* and head of a tribal family (Gen. 25:15; I Chron. 1:31).

KEILAH [Kēi' lah]—ENCLOSED. *A descendant of Caleb,* son of Jephunneh (I Chron. 4:19). Also the name of a city in Judah (Josh. 15:44).

KELAIAH—[Kē lā' iah]—JEHOVAH IS LIGHT. *A Levite* who had married a foreign wife (Ezra 10:23). Also called Kelita.

KELITA [Kĕl' ĭ tă]—DWARF or POVERTY.
1. *Same as Kelaiah* (Ezra 10:23), see above.
2. *A priest* who explained the Law when read by Ezra (Neh. 8:7).
3. *A Levite* who sealed the covenant made by Nehemiah (Neh. 10:10).

KEMUEL [Kĕ mū' el]—CONGREGATION OF GOD or GOD STANDS.
1. *The third son of Nahor*, Abraham's brother, and head of a branch of Aramaeans (Gen. 22:21).
2. *A prince of the tribe of Ephraim* and a commissioner for the allotment of Canaan (Num. 34:24)
3. *A Levite*, the father of Hashabiah, ruler of the Levites in David's time (I Chron. 27:17).

KENAN [Kĕ' nan]—ONE ACQUIRED or BEGOTTEN. *The son of Enosh*, the grandson of Adam (I Chron. 1:2). Called Cainan in Genesis 5:9.

KENAZ, KENEZ [Kĕ' năz]—THIS POSSESSION or HUNTING.
1. *The fourth son of Eliphaz*, the son of Esau (Gen. 36:11, 15; I Chron. 1:36).
2. *A duke of Edom*, chieftain in Mount Seir. Perhaps the same as No. 1 (Gen. 36:42; I Chron. 1:53).
3. *The brother of Caleb* the son of Jephunneh, and father of Othniel, one of Israel's judges (Josh. 15:17; Judg. 1:13; 3:9, 11; I Chron. 4:13).
4. *A grandson of Caleb* the son of Jephunneh (I Chron. 4:15). For Kenezites or Kenizzites see Genesis 15:19 and Joshua 14:6, 14.

KEROS [Kĕ' ros]—THE REED OF A WEAVER'S BEAM. *One of the Nethinims* whose descendants returned from exile with Zerubbabel (Ezra 2:44; Neh. 7:47).

KIRJATH-JEARIM [Kûr' jath-jĕ' a rĭm]—CITY OF FORESTS. The name of tribal appellation of a descendant of Caleb, son of Hur (I Chron. 2:50–53). Also name of a city of Judah (Josh. 9:17).

KISH, CIS [Kĭsh, Cĭs]—POWER or STRAW.
1. *A. Benjamite*, a son of Abiel and father of Saul, Israel's first king (I Sam. 9:1, 3; 10:11, 21). Called Cis in Acts 13:21.
2. *Son of Abi-gibeon*, a Benjamite (I Chron. 8:30; 9:36).
3. *A Levite in David's time*, of the family of Merari and the house of Mahli (I Chron. 23:21, 22; 24:29).
4. *A Levite and a Merarite* who assisted in the cleansing of the Temple in Hezekiah's time (II Chron. 29:12).
5. *A Benjamite*, ancestor of Mordecai, the cousin of Queen Esther (Esther 2:5).

KISHI [Kĭsh' ĭ]—BOW OF JEHOVAH. *A Merarite Levite*, ancestor of Ethan (I Chron. 6:44). Also called Kushaiah.

KITTIM [Kĭt' tim]—THEY THAT BRUISE. *A son of Javan*, son of Japheth (Gen. 10:4; I Chron. 1:7). His descendants covering Cyprus and the adjacent coasts and islands are called Chittim.

KOHATH [Kŏ' hath]—ASSEMBLY. *The second son of Levi* and ancestor of Moses. He died at the age of 133, and was the head of the Kohathites (Gen. 46:11; Num. 3:27, 30). The Kohathites held particular offices in sanctuary service.

KOLAIAH [Kŏl a ĭ' ah]—THE VOICE OF JEHOVAH.
1. *A Benjamite* who settled in Jerusalem after the captivity (Neh. 11:7).
2. *The father of the false prophet Ahab*, who suffered death for his false prophecies (Jer. 29:21).

KORAH, KORE, CORE [Kŏ' rah, Kŏ' rē, Cŏ' rē]—BALDNESS or ICY.
1. *A son of Esau by Aholibamah*, and founder of a tribe (Gen. 36:5, 18).
2. *A son of Eliphaz* and grandson of Esau (Gen. 36:16).
3. *A son of Hebron*, son of Mareshah, son of Caleb (I Chron. 2:43).
4. *A grandson of Kohath*, son of Levi — ancestor of sanctuary musicians (I Chron. 6:22).
5. *The son of Izhar*, the grandson of Levi, who with Dathan and Abiram conspired against Moses and Aaron (Ex. 6:21, 24; Num. 16). Jude 11 gives Core for Korah.

Korah, along with his two companions, resisted the civil authority of Moses. For refusing to appear before him as commanded, Korah, Dathan and Abiram along with their households and houses were swallowed up by the earth (Num. 16). Then there came the further revolt of Korah against Moses and Aaron, in the interests of the people at large as against the tribe of Levi. The rebels were consumed by fire from the Lord (Num. 17). There followed the opposition of Korah and 250 Levites against the monopoly of the priesthood claimed by Aaron. The "gainsaying," meaning *against the Word*, was Korah's denial of the authority of Moses as God's chosen spokesman, and intrusion into the priest's office (Jude 11).

KORE [Kŏ' rē]—A PARTRIDGE or A CRIER.
1. *A Korahite* whose son, Shallum, was a Tabernacle gatekeeper (I Chron. 9:19; 26:1, 19).
2. *A Levite*, son of Immah, set over the free will offerings in Hezekiah's time (II Chron. 31:14).

KOZ [Kŏz]—THE THORN.

1. *A priest* whose descendants returned from exile with Zerubbabel, but lost their position through inability to prove their descent (Ezra 2:61; Neh. 7:63).

2. *Ancestor of Meremoth,* who helped in the repair of the wall (Neh. 3:4, 21).

KUSHAIAH [Kōō shā' iah]—BOW OF JEHOVAH. *A Levite of the family of Merari* (I Chron. 15:17). Called Kishi in I Chronicles 6:44.

L

LAADAH [Lā' a dah]—ORDER or FESTIVAL. *A Judahite,* son of Shelah and father of the inhabitants of Mareshah (I Chron. 4:21).

LAADAN [Lā' a dăn]—WELL ORDERED or FESTIVE-BORN.
1. *A descendant of Ephraim* through his son Beriah (I Chron. 7:26).
2. *A descendant of Gershon,* the son of Levi (I Chron. 23:7, 8, 9; 26:21).

LABAN [Lā' ban] —WHITE or GLORIOUS. *The son of Bethuel and* grandson of Nahor. Laban was the brother of Rebekah and father of Rachel and Leah. He lived in Padan-aram (Gen. 24:29, 50; 27:43; 28:2, 5).

The transactions between Laban and Jacob are well known, and speak of cunning on both sides. After twenty years Laban was reluctant to part with Jacob, whose presence was an assurance of divine blessing. "In character Laban is not pleasing," says T. A. Moxon, "and seems to reflect in an exaggerated form the more repulsive traits in the character of his nephew, Jacob: yet he shows signs of generous impulses on more than one occasion, and especially at the final parting with Jacob."

LAEL [Lā' el]—DEVOTED TO GOD. *A Gershonite,* father of Eliasaph (Num. 3:24).

LAHAD [Lā' hăd]—OPPRESSED or DARK COLORED. *A son of Jahath,* great-grandson of Shobal, the son of Judah (I Chron. 4:2).

LAHMI [Läh' mī]—MY WAR or A WARRIOR. *A brother of Goliath the Gittite.* Lahmi was slain by Elhanan, the son of Jair (I Chron. 20:5).

LAISH [Lā' ish]—A LION. *A man of Gallim,* father of Phalti or Phaltiel. His son became the husband of Michal, David's wife (I Sam. 25:44; II Sam. 3:15.)

LAMECH [Lā' mech]—OVERTHROWER, A STRONG YOUNG MAN or WHO
IS STUCK.

1. *A son of Methusael* of the race of Cain, who had two wives, Adah
and Zillah. It is not difficult to trace in the moral character of Lamech
a close resemblance to Cain. We can detect the same haughty spirit,
the same self-confidence, the same disregard of human life, the same
absence of reverence for God. His address to his wives is that of one
who glories in his self-strength and vigor (Gen. 4:18, 19, 23, 24).

2. *A son of Methuselah,* and father of Noah. This antediluvian
was of the race of Seth (Gen. 5:26–31) and an ancestor of Christ
(Luke 3:36).

LAPPIDOTH, LAPIDOTH [Lăp' i dŏth]—TORCHES, ENLIGHTENED or
LIGHTENING FLASHES. *The husband of Deborah the prophetess* (Judg.
4:4). Deborah herself was "a woman of lightning flashes."

LAZARUS [Lăz' a rŭs]—GOD HATH HELPED or WITHOUT HELP.

1. *The beggar in the parable of the rich man.* This is the only
instance where Jesus gives a name to a parabolic character, and there
was an idea in early times that it was not a parable but a story from
real life (Luke 16:19–31).

2. *The brother of Mary and Martha* of Bethany whom Jesus raised
from the dead (John 11; 12:1–17).

The Man Who Lived Again

Alexander Whyte comments,

> Lazarus of Bethany comes as near to Jesus of Nazareth, both in his character,
> and in his services, and in his unparalleled experience, as mortal men ever
> come. Lazarus' name is never to be read in the new Testament till the ap-
> pointed time comes when he is to be sick, ...to die, and to be raised from
> the dead for the glory of God. Nor is his voice heard. Lazarus loved silence. He
> sought obscurity. He liked to be overlooked. He revelled in neglect...The
> very Evangelists pass over Lazarus as if he were a worm and no man...

I. He is the subject of the greatest and most startling miracle of
the gospel story.

II. He was the friend of Jesus, being loved by Him. Jesus wept
at his grave.

III. His resurrection threatened the life of Jesus. The Sanhedrin
were determined to put Him to death.

IV. His attendance at Simon's banquet excited the enthusiasm of
the people (John 12:9, 17, 18).

After his presence as an honored guest at Simon's house, Lazarus
vanishes from the gospel story. Of all men, he should have stood by
Jesus at His trial and crucifixion. Doubtless Lazarus was forced to
flee, seeing that the infuriated elders determined his death (John 12:
10, 11). With a deep affection for his Friend, Lazarus would withdraw
more for His sake than for his own. He felt his presence only increased
the Master's danger.

LEBANAH, LEBANA [Lĕb'a nah, Lĕb a nă]—POETIC DESIGNATION FOR THE MOON. *The head of a family of Nethinims who returned from exile* (Ezra 2:45; Neh. 7:48).

LEBBAEUS [Lĕb bae'us]—MAN OF HEART. *An apostle surnamed Thaddeus* (Matt. 10:3). See Thaddaeus.

LECAH [Lĕ'cah]—ADDITION. *Son of Er,* the son of Shelah, the son of Judah (I Chron. 4:21). Lecah may be the name of the place where Er dwelt.

LEHABIM [Lĕ'hā bĭm]—FLAME-COLORED. *The third son of Mizraim,* who is reckoned to be the ancestor of the Egyptian Lybians (Gen. 10:13; I Chron. 1:11).

LEMUEL [Lĕm'u el]—DEVOTED TO GOD or GOD IS BRIGHT. *The royal author of Proverbs 31:1, 4* who reproduces what his mother taught him. He has been identified as Solomon or Hezekiah. It is also suggested that the name may be a fanciful title to represent any virtuous king, invented for the purpose of conveying certain axioms.

LETUSHIM [Lĕ tŭ'shim]—OPPRESSED or STRUCK. *Son of Dedan,* grandson of Abraham by Keturah (Gen. 25:3).

LEUMMIM [Lĕ ŭm'mim]—PEOPLES or NATIONS. *Another son of Dedan* and founder of a tribe called Beni Lam (Gen. 25:3).

LEVI [Lĕ'vī]—JOINED or ADHESION.
1. *Another name for Matthew,* the one-time Roman tax-gatherer (Mark 2:14; Luke 5:27, 29). See Matthew.
2. *An ancestor of Jesus Christ* (Luke 3:24).
3. *Another ancestor of Jesus Christ* (Luke 3:29).
4. *The third son of Jacob by Leah.* Levi had three sons, and died in Egypt at the age of 137 (Gen. 29:34; 46:11; Ex. 6:16). His descendants, the Levites, had care of the sanctuary. The Book of Leviticus describes their ministry.

The Man of Isolation

Isolation is a feature in the history of Levi, quite as much as it characterizes Simeon, with whom he is paired. *The capacity to stand alone* made Simeon and Levi conspicuous among their brethren in their attack upon the Shechemites, and proved a valuable instrument for the work of the Lord. The tribe of Levi was fitted by the discipline of trial to discharge a most important duty in Israel — a duty which made Levi second in importance to none but Judah, whose *forerunner* and counterpart he was formed to be. Levi stands before Judah in the prophecies of Jacob — Judah before Levi in the blessings of Moses, the man of God.

"The true Levites," says Dr. C. H. Waller, "are the men who have been made lonely among their brethren that they may live alone with Jehovah, and so dwell as the families of others that they may unite them to the family of God."

Levi came under the ban of Jacob, who, in his prophecy set Simeon and Levi under a "curse." To the patriarch they were bad brothers.

Dr. Dinsdale Young has a telling chapter on Simeon and Levi in which he elaborates on these features:

I. They constituted an unholy brotherhood — they had a common disposition (Gen. 49:5).

II. They had unhallowed belongings (Gen. 49:5) — sinful homes and perverted instruments.

III. They drew from their father a heart-felt prayer (Gen. 49:6). Reviewing their sinful courses, the dying father prays for them.

IV. Their father uttered a righteous imprecation upon their sin. Jacob did not curse *them,* but their sin (Gen. 49:7).

V. A just judgment was pronounced upon them, "I will divide them" (Gen. 49:7). Though divided and scattered, they were not cut off from the promised land. Theirs was not the abundant entrance of others, yet they were privileged to enter.

LIBNI [Lĭb'nī]—WHITE or DISTINGUISHED.
1. *Son of Gershon* and grandson of Levi. Also founder of a tribal family (Ex. 6:17; Num. 3:18, 21; I Chron. 6:17, 20).
2. *Grandson of Merari* the son of Levi (I Chron. 6:29).

LIKHI [Lĭk' hī]—JEHOVAH IS DOCTRINE or CHARACTERIZED BY KNOWL-EDGE. *A son of Shemidah,* a Benjamite (I Chron. 7:19).

LINUS [Lī' nus]—NETS. *A Christian at Rome* from whom Paul sent greetings. (II Tim. 4:21). Early writers identify him as the first Bishop of Rome, whose episcopate lasted about twelve years.

LO-AMMI [Lŏ'-ăm' mī]—NOT MY PEOPLE. *A symbolic name given by Hosea to his son* (Hos. 1:9, 10; 2:23). See Hosea.

LOT [Lŏt]—CONCEALED or MYRRH. *The son of Haran,* Abraham's brother, who accompanied Abraham from Mesopotamia to Canaan (Gen. 11:27, 31; 12:4; 13:1).

The Man with a Worldly Mind

We deem it necessary to spend a little time with this character because we believe Lot to be a representative man. Perhaps there is no Bible figure who represents so many men of today as Lot of Sodom. Where you can find one Abraham, one Daniel or one Joshua you will find a thousand Lots.

Lot started out well. But he acquired riches and with his wealth came trouble. He and his uncle, Abraham, came out of Egypt with great possessions. Then came the strife among the herdsmen of both men. Lot could not pick a quarrel with his uncle, so he separated from him and made the greatest mistake of his life in doing so. If determined to have the well-watered plain, Lot should have asked Abraham to choose for him. But no, when he lifted up his eyes and saw the fruitful land, his decision was made.

The moments of solemn, decisive choice reveal the character of the two men involved. Lot's choice was a bad and selfish one, ending in disaster. Abraham's choice was lofty, unworldly, superior to all petty consideration. Although, as elder of the two, he had the undisputable right to precedence in the choice, Abraham behaved like the high-minded, noble-hearted gentleman he was and so left the choice to Lot. The meanness of Lot is seen in that he took the best. The crisis of that moment was decided by the tenor of Lot's life. In spite of his general righteousness, Lot must have had a vein of great selfishness within.

In one of his unique speeches — *The Subject of Salaries* — Benjamin Franklin said, "There are two passions which have a powerful influence in the affairs of men. These are *Ambition* and *Avarice*: the love of power and the love of money. Separately, each of these has great force in prompting man to action; but when united in view of the same object they have in many minds the most violent effects." It was thus that Lot became "a bad lot." In his choice *ambition* and *avarice* became one. Points to ponder are:

I.   His wealth (Gen. 13:5). Lot had a house — Abraham was content with a tent (Gen. 18:1; 19:3). Lot was no pilgrim (Heb. 11:13).

II. His choice (Gen. 13:10, 11). Lot was guided by selfishness, and pitching his tent toward Sodom was soon living in it (Gen. 14:12).

III. His righteous soul (II Pet. 2:8). Lot did many things that were inconsistent with his true character and that were dishonoring to God. He sat down with the ungodly. Yet he showed some good qualities. He entertained the angels — believed their message — endeavored to restrain the wicked Sodomites. His good, however, was mixed with evil.

IV. His loss (Gen. 19:17–28). Lot narrowly escaped judgment. He lost everything, his wife was turned into a pillar of salt, he lost his wealth, he sacrificed his influence, for the people of Sodom despised him, his relatives mocked him, his two daughters shamed him. Lot offered no prayer for Sodom and manifested no desire for the salvation of its people. His only concern was for his own safety, and angels delivered him.

LOTAN [Lŏ′ tan]—A COVERING. *Son of Seir the Horite* (Gen. 36:20, 22, 29; I Chron. 1:38, 39).

LUCIFER [Lōō′ cĭ fẽr]—THE SHINING ONE. *A name applied to the king of Babylon* by Isaiah to describe his glory and pomp (Isa. 14:12). Prophetically, a name of Satan.

LUCIUS [Lōō′ cius]—OF THE LIGHT or LUMINOUS.
1. *A Christian from Cyrene,* a teacher at Antioch (Acts 13:1).
2. *A kinsman of Paul.* Perhaps the same as No. 1 (Rom. 16:21).

LUD [Lŭd]—BENDING. *The son of Shem* and founder of descendants found in various parts (Gen. 10:22; I Chron. 1:17; Isa. 66:19; Ezek. 27:10).

LUDIM [Lōō′ dim]—BENDING. *Son of Mizraim* (Gen. 10:13; I Chron. 1:11).

LUKE, LUCAS [Lōōke, Lōō′ cas]—LIGHT-GIVING or LUMINOUS.
The Man Who Wrote the Most Beautiful Book in the World
Less is known of Luke than any other New Testament writer. This we do know, he was a Gentile and probably the brother of Titus (II Cor. 8:16; 12:18). Paul speaks of him as a "beloved physician." Luke must have been a man of some wealth, otherwise he could not have traveled with Paul as his friend and useful companion (Acts 1:1; Col. 4:14; II Tim. 4:11; Philem. 24). Tertullian said of this native of Antioch that he received his illumination from Paul.

Luke was a man of learning and knowledge, an exact observer and faithful recorder. His medical training taught him to be exact. He is in the first rank as a reliable historian, scholarly, skilful and sympathetic (Luke 1:1–3; Acts 1:1–3). His gospel is the most literary of the four. With his Greek mind he had a sense of form, a beautiful style — studied and elaborate. A poet, he was unsurpassed as a word-painter. Luke's gospel has been described as the most wonderful book ever written, the most beautiful book in the world. Above it and within it we hear the rustle of the angels' wings, the music of angels' songs.

Luke's qualifications for his great ministry were manifold. Above and beyond all else, he had the inspiration of the Holy Spirit. Then there was his long and close companionship with Paul, and Luke the follower of Paul set down in a book the Gospel which Paul loved to preach. Luke also had abundant opportunities for personal acquaintance with other apostles. His liberal education also indicated that in him God had a proper vessel for the accomplishment of His plan. The wisdom of the divine choice was justified.

Luke's mission was to proclaim Christ's humanity. His is *The Gentile Gospel,* thus he traces Christ's lineage back to Adam, and gives prominence to the sympathy and sociableness of Jesus as the Man (Luke 15:1) who came to save (Luke 19:10). As the representative of Grecian reason and culture, Luke presented Christ as the true Representative of universal man.

Luke wrote both the gospel bearing his name and the Book of Acts (Luke 1:1; Acts 1). The characteristic features of his gospel are clearly defined.

I. Its gratuitousness. It is *par excellence* the gospel of pardon and redemption (Luke 1:28; 2:40).

II. Its sympathy. Christ is before us as the Healer of broken hearts and the Sharer of our woes. Luke is the gospel of philanthropy.

III. Its joyfulness. How full of praise the Gospel of Luke is! Angelic joy is prominent (Luke 1:14; 2:10, 13; 15:7).

IV. Its thanksgiving. The Church continues the hymns of high praise Luke taught her to sing.

V. Its teaching of the holy spirit. It is profitable to gather out all Luke's references to the special missions of the Spirit (Luke 1:15, 35, 41; 2:23, 26; 3:22; 4:1).

LYSANIAS [Lĭ sā′ nĭ as]—ENDING SADNESS or DRIVES AWAY SORROW. *A tetrarch of Abilene* (Luke 3:1).

LYSIAS [Lỹ′ sĭ as]—HE WHO HAS THE POWER TO SET FREE. *Chief captain of the Roman garrison at Jerusalem,* who rescued Paul from the mob of hostile Jews (Acts 23:26; 24:7, 22).

M

MAACAH, MAACHAH [Mā′ a cah, Mā′ a chah]—COMPRESSION or OPPRESSION.

1. *Son of Nahor,* Abraham's brother (Gen. 22:24).

2. *A king of Maachah* (II Sam. 10:6).

3. *The father of Achish,* king of Gath in Solomon's time (I Kings 2:39).

4. *The father of Hanan,* one of David's mighty men (I Chron. 11:43).

5. *The father of Shephatiah,* ruler of the Simeonites in David's time (I Chron. 27:16). Also the name of several women (see II Sam. 3:3; I Chron. 2:48; 3:2; 8:29; II Chron. 11:21, 22; 15:16), and the name of a Syrian city (II Sam. 10:8).

MAADAI [Mā ăd′ aī]—JEHOVAH IS ORNAMENT or WAVERING. *One of the sons of Bani* who had married a foreign wife (Ezra 10:34).

MAADIAH [Mā a dī′ ah]—ORNAMENT OF JEHOVAH. *A chief priest* who returned from captivity (Neh. 12:5).

MAAI [Mā ā′ ī]—JEHOVAH IS COMPASSIONABLE. *A priest* who blew a trumpet at the dedication of the walls (Neh. 12:36).

MAASAI, MAASIAI [Mā ăs′ ĭ′ aī]—WORK OF JEHOVAH. *An Aaronite* whose family of Immer dwelt in Jerusalem after the captivity (I Chron. 9:12).

MAASEIAH [Mā a sě' iah]—WORK OF JEHOVAH or JEHOVAH IS A REFUGE.

1. *A Levite* who acted as a porter and also assisted in the service of praise in David's reign (I Chron. 15:18, 20).

2. *One of the captains* who co-operated with the high priest Jehoiada in placing Joash on the throne of Judah (II Chron. 23:1).

3. *An officer of king Uzziah* (II Chron. 26:11).

4. *Son of Ahaz,* king of Judah (II Chron. 28:7).

5. *The governor of Jerusalem* in Josiah's reign (II Chron. 34:8).

6. *A priest* who had married a foreign wife (Ezra 10:18).

7. *A priest of the family of Harim* who had done the same thing (Ezra 10:21).

8. *A priest of the family of Pashur* who had done the same thing (Ezra 10:22).

9. *Another of the same* (Ezra 10:30).

10. *Father of Azariah* who repaired a part of the wall of Jerusalem beside his own house (Neh. 3:23).

11. *A priest who assisted Ezra* in the reading of the Law (Neh. 8:4).

12. *A priest who explained the Law* read by Ezra (Neh. 8:7).

13. *One who sealed the covenant* (Neh. 10:25).

14. *A man of Judah,* a descendant of Pharez (Neh. 11:5).

15. *A Benjamite* whose descendants lived in Jerusalem after the exile (Neh. 11:7).

16. *A priest* who assisted at the dedication of the wall. Perhaps the same as No. 11 (Neh. 12:41).

17. *Another priest* who took part in the above ceremony (Neh. 12:42).

18. *A priest* whose son was sent by king Zedekiah to inquire of the Lord (Jer. 21:1; 29:25; 37:3).

19. *The father of a false prophet* during the Babylonian captivity (Jer. 29:21).

20. *Son of Shallum.* An officer of the temple in Jehoiakim's reign (Jer. 35:4).

21. *The grandfather of Baruch,* Jeremiah's scribe and messenger (Jer. 32:12; 51:59).

MAASIAI [Mā ăs' ĭ aī]—WORK OF JEHOVAH. *An Aaronite* whose family came to Jerusalem after the exile (I Chron. 9:12).

MAATH [Mā' ath]—WIPING AWAY. *An ancestor of Jesus* through Mary. He lived after Zerubbabel (Luke 3:26).

MAAZ [Mā' ăz]—ANGER or COUNSELOR. *A son of Ram,* the eldest son of Jerahmeel (I Chron. 2:27).

MAAZIAH [Mā a zī' ah]—STRENGTH or CONSOLATION OF JEHOVAH.

1. *A descendant of Aaron* responsible for sanctuary service in David's time (I Chron. 24:18).

2. *A priest* who on behalf of his father's house sealed the covenant (Neh. 10:8).

MACHBANNAI, MACHBANAI [Măch′ ba naī]—CLOTHED WITH A CLOAK. *A Gadite warrior* who joined David at Ziklag (I Chron. 12:13).

MACHI [Mā′ chī]—DECREASE. *A Gadite,* the father of Jeuel, one of Moses' spies (Num. 13:15).

MACHIR [Mā′ chĭr]—SOLD or SALESMAN.
1. *The only son of Manasseh* and founder of a tribe (Gen. 50:23; Num. 26:29; 27:1).
2. *A son of Ammiel,* who was kind to David (II Sam. 9:4, 5; 17:27).

MACHNADEBAI [Măch na dĕ′ baī]—GIFT OF THE NOBLE ONE. *A Jew who had taken a foreign wife* (Ezra 10:40).

MADAI [Măd′ a ī]—MIDDLE. *A son of Japheth,* whose descendants lived in Media (Gen. 10:2; I Chron. 1:5).

MADMANNAH [Măd măn′ nah]—HEAP. *A son of Caleb,* the son of Jephunneh (I Chron. 2:49). Also the name of a city of Judah (Josh. 15:31).

MAGDIEL [Măg′ dĭ el]—RENOWN or HONOR OF GOD. *A duke of Edom* descended from Esau (Gen. 36:43; I Chron. 1:54).

MAGOG [Mā′ gŏg]—EXPANSION or INCREASE OF FAMILY. *The second son of Japheth* and founder of descendants occupying Magog, or Scythia (Gen. 10:2; I Chron. 1:5; Ezek. 38:2; 39:6; Rev. 20:8). The grandson of Noah was the father of those Josephus calls the "Magogites," and those the Greeks call "Scythians." When Ezekiel used the terms Gog and Magog, he used them in a historical sense of the future, referring to the Prince of the Northern Confederacy and his scope of rule, and they are thus literally to be understood. Gog is the symbolic designation for the future head of all nations embraced within the Northern Confederacy (Ezek. 38; 39). Magog is the symbolic territory covered. When the Apostle John uses the terms it is to describe the wicked on the earth at the close of Christ's millennial reign, and is thus to be symbolically understood. Gog and Magog in the Book of Revelation are to be thought of in a *moral,* not a *geographical* sense (Rev. 20:8).

MAGOR-MISSABIB [Mā′ gôr-mĭs′ sa bĭb]—FEAR or TERROR IS ABOUT. *A prophetic name given to Pashur,* a priest and governor of the Temple who ill-treated the prophet Jeremiah (Jer. 20:3).

MAGPIASH, MAGBISH [Măg′ pĭ ăsh]—MOTH SLAYER or CLUSTER OF STARS. *One of the chiefs who with Nehemiah sealed the covenant* (Neh. 10:20).

MAGUS [Mā′ gŭs]—MAGICIAN. See *Simon Magus* (Acts 8:9).

MAHALALEEL, MAHALALEL, MALELEEL [Mā hā′ la lē el]—THE PRAISE OF GOD or GOD IS SPLENDOR.
1. *Son of Cainan,* the grandson of Seth (Gen. 5:12–17; I Chron. 1:2).
2. *One of the tribe of Judah,* of the family of Perez who lived in Jerusalem after the exile (Neh. 11:4).

MAHARAI [Mā hăr′ a ĭ]—IMPETUOUS or HASTY. *A Netophathite,* one of David's warriors (II Sam. 23:28; I Chron. 11:30; 27:13).

MAHATH [Mā′ hăth]—INSTRUMENT OF SEIZING or DISSOLUTION.
1. *A Kohathite Levite* of the line of Samuel (I Chron. 6:35; II Chron. 29:12).
2. *A Levite,* one of the overseers who cared for the tithes and offerings in Hezekiah's time (II Chron. 31:13).

MAHAZIOTH [Mā hā′ zĭ ŏth]—VISION OF SIGNIFICANCE. *One of the sons of Heman* who was responsible for the service of song in David's reign (I Chron. 25:4, 30).

MAHER-SHALAL-HASHBAZ [Mā′ hûr-shăl′ al-hăsh′ băz]—HASTEN THE SPOIL, RUSH ON THE PREY. *Symbolic name of Isaiah's son* (Isa. 8:1, 3).

MAHLAH, MAHALAH [Măh′ lah, Mā hā′ lah]—DISEASE or MILDNESS. *A Manassite* whose mother was Hammoleketh (I Chron. 7:18). Also the name of Zelophehad's daughter (Num. 26:33).

MAHLI, MAHALI [Măh′ lī, Mā′ ha lī]—SICK or WEAK.
1. *A son of Merari,* son of Levi and brother of Mushi. Also the founder of a tribal family (Ex. 6:19; Num. 3:20, 33).
2. *A Levite,* son of Mushi (I Chron. 6:47; 23:23; 24:30).

MAHLON [Măh′ lon]—SICKLY or MILD. *Elder son of Naomi,* and Ruth's first husband who died in Moab (Ruth 1:2, 5; 4:9, 10).

MAHOL [Mā′ hŏl]—DANCING or JOY. *The father of three noted wise men* in Solomon's time (I Kings 4:31).

MAHSEIAH, MAASEIAH [Mā a sē′ iah]—JEHOVAH IS A REFUGE. *Grandfather of Baruch and Seraiah* (Jer. 32:12; 51:59).

MALACHI ⌐Măl′ a chī]—MESSENGER OF JEHOVAH or MY MESSENGER.

1. *The last of the Old Testament prophets,* and author of the last book of The Minor Prophets.

The Man Who Believed in God's Electing Love

Nothing is known of Malachi save what his prophecy tells us. Ancient writers looked upon him as an angel incarnate, while a great number of Jews believed him to be Ezra the Scribe. It would seem as if he was connected with Nehemiah's work. Perhaps he prepared the way for it, helped in it and followed it up. Compare Malachi 1:8 with Nehemiah 5:15, 18, where it seems clear that he prophesied either during Nehemiah's absence in Persia (Neh. 13:6) or after Nehemiah assumed governorship. As the last of the prophets, he was the seal of all the goodly fellowship of prophets.

While Malachi's prominent message was the rebuke of the remnant and the announcement of future purging and blessing, the keynote of his book appears to be the unchangeableness of God, and His unceasing love (Mal. 1:2; 3:6). The tone of his message is expostulation blended with judgment. Yet gracious promises and assurances are interspersed like pearls gleaming against a dark background.

Features to note are the *whereins* repeated by Malachi's hearers. Against such the prophet amplifies and enforces his original charge (Mal. 1:2, 6, 7; 2:17; 3:7–9). We have:

I. The charge made against God involving an utter disregard of Him (Mal. 1:1, 2).

II. The rejection of the worship of God (Mal. 1:6–14).

III. The intense oration of His law (Mal. 2:1–9).

IV. Social wrongs and disorder in the home (Mal. 2:10, 16).

V. The blatant perversion of judgment (Mal. 2:17).

VI. Gross immorality and degradation (Mal. 3:5).

VII. Robbery in the service of the Temple (Mal. 3:7–9).

Other features to develop are:

Priestly qualifications—holiness, communion with God, usefulness and knowledge (Mal. 2:6, 7).

Ritual may be valuable. Only our capacity limits God's gifts (Mal. 3:10). Give and get (Mal. 3:12).

An ideal picture of the true gospel ministry (Mal. 2:5, 6).

The Lord's care for and interest in His people (Mal. 3:16, 18).

MALCHAM, MALCAM [Măl′ cham]—REGNANT or RULE. *Son of Shaharaim,* a Benjamite (I Chron. 8:9). Also the name of an idol of the Ammonites (Zeph. 1:5). Perhaps the same as Molech and Mileom.

MALCHIAH, MALCHIJAH [Măl chī′ ah, Măl chī′ jah]—JEHOVAH IS KING.

1. *A Gershonite,* ancestor of Asaph, a leader of the singing in David's time (I Chron. 6:40).

2. *A priest,* the father of Pashur whose family lived in Jerusalem after the exile (I Chron. 9:12; Neh. 11:12).

3. *Head of the fifth course of priests.* Perhaps the same person as No. 1 (I Chron. 24:9).

4. *A son of Parosh who had married a foreign wife* (Ezra 10:25).

5. *Another son of Parosh who had done the same* (Ezra 10:25).

6. *Another who had done the same* (Ezra 10:31).

7. *The son of Rechab,* who repaired the dung gate (Neh. 3:14).

8. *One of the sons of Harim* who helped to repair the wall (Neh. 3:11).

9. *One of the guild of goldsmiths* who helped to repair the wall (Neh. 3:31).

10. *A prince or Levite* who stood at Ezra's left hand as he read the law (Neh. 8:4).

11. *A priest* who assisted in the dedication of the wall (Neh. 10:3; 12:42).

12. *Father of Pashur* whom Zedekiah sent to Jerusalem to consult the Lord (Jer. 21:1; 38:1).

MALCHIEL [Măl′ chĭ el]—GOD IS A KING. *A son of Beriah,* son of Asher (Gen. 46:17; Num. 26:45; I Chron. 7:31). Founder of a tribal family.

MALCHIRAM [Măl chĭ′ ram]—MY KING IS EXALTED or GOD IS EXALTED. *The son of Jeconiah,* son of king Jehoiakim of Judah (I Chron. 3:18).

MALCHI-SHUA, MELCHI-SHUA [Măl′ chĭ-shū′ ă, Mĕl′ chĭ-shoō′ ă] —KING OF HELP. *The third son of Saul,* slain by the Philistines at Mount Gilboa (I Sam. 14:49; 31:2; I Chron. 10:2).

MALCHUS [Măl′ chus]—KING or COUNSELOR. *The high priest's servant* whose ear Peter cut off. He was healed by Jesus (John 18:10). Luke, the physician, is the only one who mentions the healing of the ear (Luke (22:51).

MALELEEL [Mā lĕ′ le el]—PRAISE OF GOD. *An ancestor of Christ* (Luke 3:37). See Mahalaleel.

MALLOTHI [Măl′ lo thī]—JEHOVAH IS SPEAKING or IS SPLENDID. *One of Heman's sons* responsible for the service of song (Chron. 25:4, 26).

MALLUCH [Măl′ luch]—REIGNING or COUNSELOR.

1. *A Levite* of the family of Merari, of the house of Mushi (I Chron. 6:44).

2. *A son of Bani* who had married a foreign wife (Ezra 10:29).

3. *One of the family of Harim* who had done the same (Ezra 10:32).

4. *A priest and chief of the people* who signed the Covenant (Neh. 10:4; 12:2).

5. *Another chief who had done the same* (Neh. 10:27).

MAMRE [Măm' rē]—FATNESS or VIGOR. *An Amorite chieftain,* confederate with Abraham (Gen. 14:13, 24). Also the name of a place (Gen. 13:18) now known as Rameh or Ramel.

MANAEN [Măn' a ĕn]—CONSOLER COMFORTER. *A Christian prophet or teacher* in the Church at Antioch (Acts 13:1). As an early associate or "foster-brother" of Herod the tetrarch, he is thought by some writers to have befriended Herod.

MANAHATH ([Măn' a hăth]—RESTING PLACE or REST. *A son of Shobal,* son of Seir the Horite, and founder of a tribal family (Gen. 36:23; I Chron. 1:40; 2:52, 54). Also the name of a city in Benjamin (I Chron. 8:6).

MANASSEH, MANASSES [Mā năs' seh, Mā năs' sēs]—CAUSING FORGETFULNESS.
1. *The elder son of Joseph,* who was born in Egypt and was half Hebrew and half Egyptian. He was the founder of a tribe (Gen. 41:51; Num. 1:10). Manasseh and his brother Ephraim were Jacob's Gentile descendants, since both were children of an Egyptian mother. Ephraim means "the multitude of nations," or "the fulness of the Gentiles," and was prophetic of Christ as the Saviour of the world. The tribe of Manasseh produced two out of the four Old Testament men whose faith has been thought worthy of notice in the New Testament—Gideon and Jephthah (Heb. 11:32).
2. *The grandfather of Jonathan* who, with his sons, became a priest to the tribe of Dan when they set up a graven image in Laish (Judg. 18:30). Perhaps Moses should be read for Manasseh in the verse.
3. *The son of Hezekiah* and father of Amon, king of Judah, who succeeded his father when he was only twelve years of age (II Kings 20:21; 21).

The Man Whose Policy Was Wrong

Manasseh, the prodigal king of the Old Testament, was overwhelmed by Assyrian forces and in the twenty-third year of his reign was taken as a prisoner to Babylon where he lingered for twelve years. During these years he turned to God and was restored to freedom and his kingdom. For the next twenty years left to him, he sought to undo the wrong of the past. His long reign of fifty-five years, the longest in Jewish history, closed not inauspiciously. He died a penitent, and left a son who followed his father in his sins but not in his repentance.

Gathering together what we can of Manasseh's life, it would seem that he was a man of policy:

His policy of idolatry. How he hated the first two commandments of Sinai, and reversed the reforms of his father! How exceedingly bold he was in his idolatry!

His policy of immorality. Idolatry and immorality go together, thus in rejecting God there came the worship of the Syrian Venus. This action let loose a flood of iniquity over the land of Judah.

His policy of persecution. Manasseh allowed nothing to stand in the way of license and open evil. Martyrdom became the cost of service. Idolatry was set up under the pain of death.

His policy of destruction. As far as he could, Manasseh destroyed the Word of God. Every copy found was consigned to the flames. God's truth testified too plainly against the sins of king and people. So complete was this destruction of the Word of God that when Josiah, Manasseh's grandson, came to the throne, a copy of it was found in the Temple.

But Manasseh's eyes were opened to his sinful condition and he sobbed out the misery of his helpless and craven soul. The *occasion* of his repentance was affliction. In the prison-house of Babylon he prayed. As to the *character* of his repentance, he besought the Lord and humbled himself before the God of his fathers and prayed unto Him. Penniless and penitent, his cry for mercy came from a broken heart, and God graciously received this prodigal king. Alas, however, he stopped short of being out-and-out for God! He allowed the high places of idolatry to remain. It will not be possible to doubt God's grace in heaven in the ages to come if we can but catch a glimpse of Manasseh—godly-reared, apostate, idolatrous, devilish, stricken, humbled, repentant Manasseh!

4. *One of the family of Hashum* who had married a foreign wife (Ezra 10:33).

5. *One of the family of Pahath-moab* who had done the same (Ezra 10:30).

MANASSES, MANASSEH [Mă năs′ sēz, Mă năs′ seh]—MAKING TO FORGET. *A king of Judah* (Deut. 4:43; Matt. 1:10; Rev. 7:6). See Manasseh.

MANOAH [Mă nō′ ah]—REST or QUIET. *A Danite* belonging to Zorah, and father of Samson (Judg. 13; 16:31). Manoah was a godly, hospitable man and was against any alliance with the Philistines. A divine messenger brought him word of Samson's birth. We have four glimpses of this devout worshiper of Jehovah:

His remonstrance with Samson over his Philistine marriage (Judg. 14:2, 3).

His visit with Samson to Timnah (Judg. 14:5, 6).

His presence at his son's marriage (Judg. 14:9, 10).

His death before Samson's tragic death (Judg. 16:31).

MAOCH [Mă′ ŏch]—POOR or OPPRESSION. *Father of Achish,* king of Gath, to whom David fled when persecuted by Saul (I Sam. 27:2).

MAON [Mă′ on]—HABITATION. *Son of Shammai,* of the tribe of Judah

(1 Chron. 2:45). Also the name of a city in Judah now called Main (Josh. 15:55; I Sam. 25:2). Also the name of a tribe (Judg. 10:12).

MARESHAH [Mā rē' shah]—AT THE HEAD or POSSESSION.
1. *The father of Hebron* (I Chron. 2:42).
2. *The son of Laadah* (I Chron. 4:21). Also the name of a fortified city of Judah (Josh. 15:44).

MARK, MARCUS [Märk, Mär' cus]—A LARGE HAMMER or POLITE. John Mark was *a Jew and a son of Mary,* who was a leading Christian at Jerusalem.

The Man Who Recovered Himself

Mark was the Roman surname of this young associate of the apostle, while his first name, John, was his Hebrew name. Mark was an apostle but held no official position among the original Twelve. The first time we come across "John, whose surname was Mark," it is in connection with one of the most remarkable prayer meetings ever held. Herod, who had just beheaded James, had Peter under arrest. But the many friends of "The Big Fisherman" gathered in the home of "Mary the mother of John Mark" for prayer, which the Lord wonderfully answered (Acts 12:12).

Mark's mother was a godly, well-to-do widow in Jerusalem and her house was a favorite meeting place for the saints (Acts 12:12; Col. 4:10). Her brother, Barnabas, Mark's uncle, was a wealthy Levite from the island of Cyprus (Acts 13:1–5). In Barnabas, Mark had a staunch and gifted friend and counselor (Acts 11:24). While we are not told how or when Mark became a disciple of Christ, it is evident that he owed his conversion to Peter, since the apostle speaks of him as "Marcus, my son" (I Pet. 5:13). Thereafter he became a close companion of Peter for about twelve years. Doubtless Mark had heard and seen Christ. Tradition identifies Mark as "the certain young man," who followed Christ when all His disciples forsook Him and fled (Mark 14:51).

Mark became an attendant of Paul and Barnabas when they set out on their great mission tour (Acts 13:5), and these two godly men must have had a formative influence upon the character of young Mark. However, our next glimpse of him is disappointing. In the early years of his service, Mark was guilty of vacillating (Acts 13:13; 15:38). The ploughman looked back. So full of promise, Mark failed Paul and Barnabas at a crisis and brought about a severance of friends. The fear of what lay ahead in arduous missionary enterprise moved Mark to retrace his steps (Acts 13:13; 15:38).

But Mark won his spurs again and recovered his place in apostolic esteem. The years the locusts had eaten were restored and he became a valued colleague of Paul (Col. 4:10, 11; Philem. 24). A further impressive testimony to Mark's reinstatement is found in Paul's tribute to Mark's usefulness (II Tim. 4:11). The wound was thoroughly healed.

In the eventide of his life, Peter could write affectionately of Mark (I Pet. 5:13). Tradition says that Mark became a bishop and a martyr and that his body was removed to Venice and buried there. St. Mark's of Venice is dedicated to his fragrant memory. *The Lion,* the emblem of Mark's Roman Gospel, is emblazoned on the standard of the Venetian Republic.

As the ministry of Mark was peculiarly a Gentile one, he is recognized by his Gentile name. Writing specifically for Romans, who stood for power, Mark manifests Christ's power in service. Accustomed as Mark was to the might of Rome's legions, he exhibits the soldier's rapidity of movement and readiness to repel attack, and gives us in his shortest and simplest gospel, a progressive series of victorious conflicts. Vividness, compactness, direction, circumstantial evidence characterize his gospel.

The main lessons to be learned from the life of Mark are apparent:

I.   The blessings of a godly home. The Christian Church owes much to "Mary, the mother of John Mark."

II.   Much depends upon the choice of friends. Mark's life was lived in the company of godly men such as Peter, Paul and Barnabas.

III.   The possibilities of life. A widow's son became an apostle and a great historian, and his name is upon the lips of men the world over.

IV.   The reward for faithful service. We do not read of Mark preaching a single sermon or performing even one miracle. All that is said about him is that he was a *helper of others.* Such service never fails to receive its reward.

MARSENA [Mär′ se nă]—WORTHY.   *One of the seven princes of Media* and Persia who had the right of access to the royal presence (Esther 1:14).

MASH [Măsh]—DRAWN OUT.   *A son of Aram,* son of Shem (Gen. 10:23). Given as Meshech in I Chronicles 1:17.

MASSA [Măs′ să]—BURDEN.   *A son of Ishmael* and representative of a north Arabian tribe (Gen. 25:14; I Chron. 1:30).

MATHUSALA [Mā thōō′ sa lă]—WHEN HE IS DEAD IT SHALL BE SENT (FLOOD).   *An ancestor of our Lord* (Luke 3:37). See Methuselah.

MATRI [Mā′ trī]—JEHOVAH IS WATCHING or RAIN.   *The head of a Benjamite family* to which Saul belonged (I Sam. 10:21).

MATTAN [Măt′ tan]—GIFT.

1.   *A priest of Baal* slain before the altar during the revolution which led to the overthrow of Athaliah (II Kings 11:18; II Chron. 23:17).

2.   *The father of Shephatiah,* a prince in Judah in Zedekiah's time (Jer. 38:1).

MATTANIAH [Măt ta nī' ah]—GIFT OF JEHOVAH.

1. *A brother of Jehoiakim,* made king instead of his nephew, Jehoiakim, also called Zedekiah (II Kings 24:17).

2. *A Levite,* descendant of Asaph and founder of a tribal family (I Chron. 9:15; II Chron. 20:14; Neh. 11:17, 22; 12:8, 25, 35).

3. *A son of Heman the singer* in David's time (I Chron. 25:4, 16).

4. *A descendant of Asaph* who assisted Hezekiah in the cleansing of the Temple (II Chron. 29:13).

5. *A descendant of Elam* who had married a foreign wife (Ezra 10:26).

6. *A son of Zattu* who had done the same (Ezra 10:27).

7. *One of the family of Pahath-moab* who had done the same (Ezra 10:30).

8. *A son of Bani* guilty of the same act (Ezra 10:37).

9. *A Levite* whose descendant, Hanan, was one of Nehemiah's treasurers (Neh. 13:13).

MATTATAH, MATTATHAH [Măt' ta thah]—GIFT. *A son of Hashum* who put away his foreign wife (Ezra 10:33).

MATTATHA [Măt' ta thă]—A GIFT. *A son of Nathan* and grandson of David (Luke 3:31).

MATTATHIAS, MATTITHIAH [Măt ta thī' as, Măt tĭ thī' ah]—GIFT OF JEHOVAH.

1. *The son of Amos* and ancestor of Christ (Luke 3:25).

2. *An ancestor of the above,* separated by five generations (I Chron. 9:31; 25:3; Luke 3:26).

MATTENAI [Măt te nā' ī]—BESTOWMENT or GIFT OF JEHOVAH.

1. *A son of Hashum,* probably the same as Mattatah (Ezra 10:33).

2. *A son of Bani* who had married a foreign wife (Ezra 10:37).

3. *A priest of the family of Joiarib* (Neh. 12:19).

MATTHAN [Măt' than]—A GIFT.

1. *Grandfather of Joseph,* Mary's husband (Matt. 1:15; Luke 3:24).

2. *A more remote ancestor,* called Matthat (Luke 3:29).

MATTHEW [Măt' thew]—GIFT OF JEHOVAH.
The Man Who Left All to Follow Christ
This son of Alphaeus was a Hebrew with two names, a common thing in Galilee at that time. Mark and Luke, when recording Matthew's call to discipleship, speak of him as Levi, but Matthew himself uses the name he has been loved by throughout the Christian era. In his despised occupation he was Levi, a name meaning "joined," and joined he was to the world's crooked extortionate ways and mercenary aims.

He was also joined by his vocation to a hated foreign power under whose yoke orthodox Jews chafed.

Thus Levi and his craft were so detested that the very name *publican* or *tax-gatherer* was commonly associated with *sinner* (Luke 15:1). His original name connected him with the tribe of Levi, the priestly house set aside for sanctuary service. But this Levi degraded his holy name. Whether the Lord changed the name to Matthew when He called Levi or whether the new found disciple chose it himself, we do not know. Meaning "the gift of God," Matthew's new name magnified the transforming power of Christ and indicated that Matthew was like the One who called him, a gift to Israel and to the world.

The call to service came when he was sitting at the receipt of custom (Matt. 9:9; Luke 5:27) at Capernaum, the first world center, "the Great West Trunk Road from Damascus and the Far East to the Mediterranean Sea." Matthew was a "publican," which is not to be confused with the modern usage of the term as an English innkeeper. "Publican" is from the Latin word *publicannus,* meaning the collector of Roman taxes, the gathering of which was farmed out to minor officials ready to undertake this odious duty among their countrymen. A publican's reward was that he could extort for his own benefit more than was due, so long as the extortion did not lead to revolt. This was why the publicans, as a class, were spoken of as "leeches." They gorged themselves with money in the process of gathering money for the Caesars and consequently were reckoned to be outside the pale of decent society and of the synagogue.

"Jesus of Nazareth, the carpenter's Son, knew Matthew the publican quite well," says Alexander Whyte. "Perhaps only too well. Jesus and His mother had by this time migrated from Nazareth to Capernaum. He had often been in Matthew's toll-booth with His mother's taxes, with other poor people's taxes." But the outcast was called by Christ to a better occupation, to better wealth than silver and gold, to serve a better King than Caesar. Without hesitation Matthew left all, arose and followed Christ (Luke 5:28).

To celebrate his surrender to Christ, Matthew entertained Christ and others to a feast in his own house (Matt. 9:10; Luke 5:29). This feast was a token of gratitude for his emancipation from a sordid occupation, and revealed a missionary spirit. Such an "At Home" served a threefold purpose:

I.   It was a *Jubilee Feast* to commemorate his translation into a new life. Matthew wanted all and sundry to know that he was now a new creature in Christ Jesus.

II.   It was a *Farewell Dinner* to declare his determination henceforth to follow and serve his new found King. It was his public confession of surrender to the call of Christ.

III.   It was a *Conversazione* to introduce his old associates and friends to his new found Saviour, that they too might have an opportunity of hearing His wonderful words of life. Matthew sought to make a dinner party an evangelistic service. He knew many would come to his house to meet Christ who would not go to the synagogue to hear Him. Doubtless many publicans and sinners learned that day that Christ did not despise them.

Matthew became not only an apostle but also the writer of the first gospel. He left behind an undying image of his Lord. Matthew has given us *The Galilean Gospel* –unique in every way. When he rose and left all to follow Christ, the only things Matthew took out of his old life were his pen and ink. It is well for us that he did, since he took them with him for such a good purpose.

Matthew's gospel is striking in that it alone gives us the Parables of the Kingdom. The theme of his book, known as "the Hebrew Porch of the New Testament" is *The King and His Kingdom*. Some fifty-six times he uses the word "kingdom." In his record of the life and labors of Christ, Matthew has given us the image of Christ as it fell upon his own heart.

Trained to systematic methods and well acquainted with Jewish character and religion, Matthew was fitted to commend Christ to the Jews. He appeals to the student of Old Testament literature. As a writer, he is before us as an eyewitness of the events he describes and as earwitness of the discourses he records. As to his qualifications, Matthew had a love of truth and was sensible of the mercy of God, and the misery of man. In self-effacing humility, he loses sight of himself in adoration of his Hero. It is thus that his book can be divided in this three-fold way:

The early days of the Messiah (Matt. 1–4:16).
The signs and works of the Messiah (Matt. 4:17–16:20).
The passion of the Messiah (Matt. 16:21–28:20).

MATTHIAS [Măt′ thī′ as]—GIFT OF GOD. *A disciple chosen by lot to succeed Judas Iscariot* as an apostle. He had been a follower of Jesus from the beginning of His ministry and was a witness of His resurrection (Acts 1:23, 26). Tradition says Matthias was one of the seventy (Luke 10:1).

David Smith feels that the choice of Matthias was not of God. The disciples prayed for guidance but instead of trusting for divine direction, had recourse to the superstitious practice of casting lots. The election of Matthias was set aside, Paul becoming the true successor to the vacant office. We have no record of him after his election. Tradition says that he went to Ethiopia and labored there where ultimately he was martyred.

MATTITHIAH [Măt tī thī ah]—GIFT OF JEHOVAH.
1. *A Korhite*, eldest son of Shallum, who had charge of "things made in the pans" (I Chron. 9:31).
2. *A Levite singer* and gate-keeper in David's time (I Chron. 15: 18, 21; 16:5).
3. *Son of the singer Jeduthun*, and a musician who played the harp (I Chron. 25:3, 21).

4. *A son of Nebo* who put away his foreign wife (Ezra 10:43).
5. *A prince,* priest or Levite who supported Ezra when he addressed the exiles about the Law (Neh. 8:4).

MEBUNNAI [Mē bun' naī]—BUILT UP. *A Hushathite,* one of David's heroes (II Sam. 23:27). Perhaps the Sibbecai of I Chronicles 11:29.

MEDAD [Mē' dăd]—LOVE. *An elder* who, though not present at the Tabernacle when the Spirit came upon the elders, yet received the gift (Num. 11:26, 27). See Eldad.

MEDAN [Mē' dan]—JUDGMENT. *A son of Abraham by Keturah* and brother of Midian (Gen. 25:2; I Chron. 1:32).

MEHETABEL, MEHETABEEL [Mē hĕt' a bĕl, Mē hĕt' a beel]—GOD BLESSES or IS DOING GOOD. *Father of a certain Delaiah* guilty of opposing Nehemiah in his good work (Neh. 6:10). Also the name of the wife of Hadar, eighth king of Edom (Gen. 36:39).

MEHIDA [Mē hĭ' dă, Mē hĭ' dă]—UNION or FAMOUS. *Founder of a family of Nethinims,* members of which returned from exile with Ezra (Ezra 2:52; Neh. 7:54).

MEHIR [Mē' hûr]—PRICE or DEXTERITY. *A Judahite,* a son of Chelub through Caleb son of Hur (I Chron. 4:11).

MEHUJAEL [Mē hū' ja el]—GOD IS COMBATING. *Son of Irad* and father of Methusael, of the family of Cain (Gen. 4:18).

MEHUMAN [Mē hū' man]—FAITHFUL. *One of the seven chamberlains* who served in the presence of Ahasuerus, king of Persia (Esther 1:10).

MEHUNIM, MEUNIM [Mē hū' nim, Mē ū' nim]—PLACE OF HABITATION. *One of the Nethinims* whose descendants returned from exile with Zerubbabel (Ezra 2:50; Neh. 7:52). Founder of an Arab tribe (II Chron. 26:7).

MELATIAH [Mĕl a tī' ah]—JEHOVAH HATH SET FREE. *A Gibeonite* who helped to repair the wall of the city (Neh. 3:7).

MELCHI [Mĕl' chī]—JEHOVAH IS MY KING.
1. *An ancestor of Christ* through Mary (Luke 3:24).
2. *A previous ancestor of Christ* (Luke 3:28).

MELCHISEDEC, MELCHIZEDEK [Mĕl chĭs' e dĕc, Mĕl chĭz' e dĕk] —KING OF RIGHTEOUSNESS or JUSTICE. *The priest and king of Salem,* who met Abraham and blessed him (Gen. 14:18; Ps. 110:4; Heb. 5: 6, 10; 6:20; 7:1–21). His pedigree is not recorded (Ezra 2:59, 62).

The Man Who Prefigured Christ's Priesthood

Although a mysterious figure, Melchisedec is yet a figure of great importance. His biography is short. He comes before us in history (Gen. 14); in prophecy (Ps. 110); in doctrine (Heb. 7), and prefigures Christ's priesthood. He is King of Righteousness, and King of Peace—cause and effect. Christ alone can bring us peace since He is our righteousness (Isa. 32:17). In a book consisting of genealogies, Melchisedec has no record of father, mother, birth or death. Such silence is part of the divine plan to make him typify more strikingly the mystery of Christ's birth and the eternity of His priesthood.

The priesthood of this mysterious man was not based on what he was, or on any inherited right. Christ was without father on earth as to His humanity, and without mother as to His deity. He was the only-begotten of the Father, and without pedigree as to His priesthood. The greatness of Melchisedec is seen in that Abraham gave him tithes, and was blessed of him. Christ being greater, deserves and demands our all.

In Christ we have an unchallengeable priesthood, for He was made Priest by the solemnity of a divine oath. His is also an uninterrupted priesthood, for death cannot overtake Him. His priesthood is likewise nontransferable—it cannot be delegated to anyone on earth. Christ, like Melchisedec, had in His office as Priest, no ancestor, no associate, no descendant. With the Aaronic priesthood it was different.

Tradition identifies Melchisedec as Shem, the son of Noah (Gen. 11:11), or as Philitis, the builder of the great Pyramid of Egypt.

MELCHISHUA, MALCHISHUA [Měl′ chĭ shoo′ ǎ, Mǎl′ chĭ shū′ ǎ] —KING OF HELP. *The third son of Saul* (I Sam. 14:49; 31:2; I Chron. 8: 33; 9:39; 10:2).

MELEA [Mē′ le ǎ]—FULNESS. *An ancestor of Christ,* through Mary. He lived shortly after David (Luke 3:31).

MELECH [Mē′ lech]—A KING. *A son of Micah and descendant of* Saul and Jonathan (I Chron. 8:35; 9:41).

MELICU [Měl′ ĭ cū]—COUNSELOR. *A priest in Jerusalem* in the days of Joiakim, grandson of Jozadek—called also Malluch (Neh. 12:14).

MELZAR [Měl′ zar]—THE OVERSEER or STEWARD. *One of the seven princes of Persia and Media* who had the care of Daniel and his companions (Dan. 1:11, 16).

MEMUCAN [Mē mū′ can]—IMPOVERISHED. *One of the princes at the court of Ahasuerus,* whose counsel was adverse to Vashti (Esther 1:14, 16, 21).

MENAHEM [Měn′ a hěm]—COMFORTER. *The son of Gadi* who, when news reached Tirzah that Shallum had murdered the king, went to Samaria and slew Shallum and reigned in his stead. He reigned for ten years (II Kings 15:14–23).

MENAN, MENNA [Mě′ nan]—CONSOLING or COMFORTING. *An ancestor of Christ through Mary.* He lived shortly after David's time (Luke 3:31).

MEONOTHAI [Mě ŏn′ o thāi]—JEHOVAH'S HABITATIONS. *Father of Ophrah* and descendant of Judah through Caleb, son of Hur (I Chron. 4:14).

MEPHIBOSHETH   [Mě phĭb′ o shĕth]—UTTERANCE OF BAAL or DESTROYING SHAME.

1. *A son of Rizpah,* Saul's concubine and the daughter of Aiah. David gave him up to the Gibeonites (II Sam. 21:8).

2. *The son of Jonathan,* son of Saul. Also called Meribbaal, meaning "a striver against Baal" (II Sam. 4:4; 9:6–13; 16:1, 4; 19:24–30; 21:7; I Chron. 8:34; 9:40).

The Man Who Was Lame in Both Feet

Mephibosheth was only five years old when Jonathan, his father, and Saul, his grandfather, both fell in the same battle on Mount Gilboa, and with their death their family fell from the throne. In the terror of that day of defeat and death, the nurse caught up Jonathan's child and fled with him in her arms. But in her haste she let the little prince fall, and thus Mephibosheth was lame in both feet for the rest of his life.

Preachers can find excellent material in what is said of Mephibosheth —a type of the redeemed sinner.

I.   He belonged to the royal line, but was made a cripple by a fall (II Sam. 4:4).

II.   He lived in exile from the king but was remembered because of a covenant (I Sam. 20:14, 15; II Sam. 9:3, 4).

III.   He was called into the king's presence and exalted because of the merits of another (II Sam. 9:5, 7).

IV.   He was given a glorious heritage (II Sam. 9:9).

V.   He lived a life of self-denial during the king's absence (II Sam. 19:24).

VI.   He was subject to persecution and slander (II Sam. 16:3; 19:27).

VII.   He rejoiced at the return of the king and cared little for material things (II Sam. 19:30).

MERAIAH [Měr a ī′ ah]—REVELATION OF JEHOVAH or STUBBORNNESS.

A priest, head of his father's house in the days of Joiakim after the exile (Neh. 12:12).

MERAIOTH [Mē rā' ioth]—REVELATIONS or REBELLION.
1. *A priest, son of Zerahiah,* ancestor of Azariah in Solomon's time (I Chron. 6:6, 7, 52; Ezra 7:3).
2. *A priest, son of Ahitub,* father of younger Zadok of the high priestly line (I Chron. 9:11; Neh. 11:11).
3. *Another priest* at the close of the exile (Neh. 12:15).

MERARI [Mē rā' rī]—BITTER or UNHAPPY. *The third and youngest son of Levi* and founder of one of the three Levitical families—the Merarites (Gen. 46:11; Ex. 6:16, 19; Num. 26:57).

MERED [Mē' red]—REBELLIOUS. *A son of Ezra,* descendant of Judah through Caleb, son of Jephunneh (I Chron. 4:17, 18).

MEREMOTH [Měr' e mŏth]—STRONG or ELEVATION.
1. *The son of Uriah the priest,* employed to weigh the gold and silver Ezra brought back from Babylon, and who helped to repair the city wall (Ezra 8:33; Neh. 3:4, 21).
2. *A son of Bani* who put away his foreign wife (Ezra 10:36).
3. *A priest* who, with Nehemiah, signed the covenant (Neh. 10:5; 12:3).

MERES (Mē' rēz]—WORTHY. *One of the seven princes of Persia and Media* who had access to the king's presence (Esther 1:14).

MERIB-BAAL [Měr' ib-bā' al]—CONTENDER AGAINST BAAL. *Son of Jonathan.* See Mephibosheth (I Chron. 8:34; 9:40).

MERODACH-BALADAN [Mē rŏ' dăch-băl' a dăn]—MERODACH HATH GIVEN A SON or THE SON OF DEATH. (Merodach was *a Babylonian idol*— the god of war). The king of Babylon in Hezekiah's time (Isa. 39:1). See Berodach-baladan and Evil-merodach.

MESHA [Mē' shă]—FREEDOM or RETREAT.
1. *A king of Moab,* son of Chemosh-malech (II Kings 3:4).
2. *The eldest son of Caleb,* brother of Jerahmeel (I Chron. 2:42).
3. *A Benjamite* and son of Shaharaim (I Chron. 8:8, 9).

MESHACH [Mē' shach]—AGILE or EXPEDITIOUS. The name given to Mishael, *one of Daniel's friends,* by the chief of Nebuchadnezzar's eunuchs (Dan. 1:7; 2:49; 3). With his other two companions he defied the edict of the king and was miraculously delivered from the fiery furnace.

MESHECH, MESECH [Mĕ' shech, Mē' sech]—DRAWING OUT.
1. *A son of Japheth* (Gen. 10:2; I Chron. 1:5).
2. *A son of Shem* (I Chron. 1:17). Also the name of a tribe (Ps. 120:5).

The descendants of the son of Japheth are the Mosochi. Meshech usually appears with Tubal (Ezek. 38:2, 3; 39:1). The Mosochi or Moschi were a race inhabiting a part of the country between the Black and Caspian Seas. From Moschi comes Muscovites—the natives of Russia—then Moscow, the large metropolis of European Russia. Meshech along with Tubal is mentioned as trading in slaves (Ezek. 27:13), a traffic Moscow is notoriously famous for today. Moscow is now the hub of the communist universe, and will likely be the center of authority when the Northern Confederacy is finally formed.

MESHELEMIAH [Mĕ' shĕl e mī' ah]—JEHOVAH RECOMPENSES. *A Kohathite* whose son Zechariah was a gate-keeper of the Tabernacle (I Chron. 9:21; 26:1, 2, 9). Called Shelemiah in I Chronicles 26:14. Perhaps the Meshullam of Nehemiah 12:25.

MESHEZABEEL, MESHEZABEL [Mē shĕz' a beel]—GOD SETS FREE.
1. *Father of a certain Berechiah* who helped to repair the city wall (Neh. 3:4).
2. *A person who sealed the covenant* (Neh. 10:21; 11:24).

MESHILLEMITH, MESHILLEMOTH [Mē shĭl' le mĭth, Mē shĭl' le mŏth]—RECOMPENSES.
1. *A priest* whose descendants lived in Jerusalem (I Chron. 9:12).
2. *An Ephraimite,* father of that Berechiah who urged the release of the captives brought from Judah by Pekah's army (II Chron. 28:12).
3. *A priest of the family of Immer,* whose descendant, Amashai, lived in Jerusalem (Neh. 11:13).

MESHOBAB [Mē shō' băb]—RESTORED or DELIVERED. *One of the Simeonite princes* who seized pasture lands near Gedor (I Chron. 4:34).

MESHULLAM [Mē shŭl' lam]—ASSOCIATE or A FRIEND.
1. *An ancestor of Shaphan,* the scribe of King Josiah's time (II Kings 22:3).
2. *A son of Zerubbabel* and descendant of Jeconiah, son of King Jehoiakim (I Chron. 3:19).
3. *A leading man among the Gadites* in the reign of Jothan (I Chron. 5:13).
4. *A Benjamite,* descended from Shaharaim through Elpaal (I Chron. 8:17).
5. *A Benjamite,* father of Sallu, who dwelt in Jerusalem (I Chron. 9:7; Neh. 11:7).
6. *Another Benjamite,* son of Shephathiah, also of Jerusalem (I Chron. 9:8).

7. *A priest,* son of Zadok and father of the high priest, Hilkiah, who lived in Josiah's reign (I Chron. 9:11; Neh. 11:11).

8. *A priest,* son of Mishilemith of the house of Immer (I Chron. 9:12).

9. *A Kohathite Levite* who, with others, superintended the repair of the Temple in Josiah's time (II Chron. 34:12).

10. *A chief man* who, with others, returned from exile with Ezra (Ezra 8:16).

11. *One who assisted in the numbering of those who had married foreign wives* (Ezra 10:15).

12. *A son of Bani* who had married a foreign wife (Ezra 10:29).

13. *A son of Berechiah* who helped to repair two portions of the wall (Neh. 3:4, 30; 6:18).

14. *The son of Besodeiah* who also repaired a part of the city wall (Neh. 3:6).

15. *A prince or priest* who stood beside Ezra as he read and explained the Law (Neh. 8:4).

16. *A priest* who, on behalf of his father's house, signed the covenant with Nehemiah (Neh. 10:7).

17. *A chief of the people* who also signed the covenant (Neh. 10:20).

18. *A priest* of the family of Ezra who assisted at the dedication of the wall (Neh. 12:13, 33).

19. *Another priest,* head of his father Ginnethon's house, in the days of Joiakim the priest (Neh. 12:16).

20. *A Levite,* and sanctuary porter after the exile (Neh. 12:25).

METHUSAEL, METHUSHAEL [Mē thōō′ sa el]—MAN OF GOD. *Son of Mehujael,* a descendant of Cain, and father of Lamech (Gen. 4:18).

METHUSELAH, MATHUSALA [Mē thōō′ se lah]—A MAN OF THE JAVELIN or IT SHALL BE SENT (DELUGE). *The son of Enoch,* and grandfather of Noah, who lived longer than any other man recorded in history (Gen. 5:21–27).

The Man Who Lived the Longest

The Bible represents human life as vastly prolonged before the Flood. Afterwards it grew rapidly briefer. The longevity of the antediluvian races proves that the constitution of man was different from what it is today. With the Flood a change took place so that now the duration of human life is rarely over one hundred years. No strength of constitution, temperance or vegetable diet can add years to such a limit. The instructive register of Genesis five shows that the man who lived for the shortest period lived for 365 years, and the one who lived for the longest period lived for 969 years.

The remarkable longevity served a useful purpose in that it made possible the reception and preservation of ancient traditions. Perhaps Adam lived for about 113 years after the birth of Methuselah, and Methuselah could not have been more than 369 years old when his grandson Noah was born. Thus, Noah conversed with one who had conversed with Adam and Enoch had the privilege of conversing with Adam. God knows how to preserve His truth for the guidance and sanctification of succeeding generations.

Although Methuselah, whose name was fitting for a time when the earth was full of violence, lived for almost a millennium, nothing whatever is recorded of his long life save the birth of his children. What an immense influence he could have exerted through the years if only, like his father Enoch, he had walked with God! It is not the *length* of a life that counts, but the *quality* of it.

Why did Methuselah die thirty-one years short of a millennium? Has God reserved the privilege of living for one thousand years for the millennial saints? During our Lord's millennial reign, life is to be prolonged again, so that one hundred years shall be the duration of childhood, and a grown man's ordinary age shall be in the age of a tree (Isa. 65:20, 22).

MEZAHAB [Mĕz' a hăb]—OFFSPRING OF THE SHINING ONE. *Grandfather of Mehetabel,* wife of Hadar, the eighth king of Edom (Gen. 36:39; I Chron. 1:50).

MIAMIN [Mī' a mĭn]—FORTUNATE.
1. *A son of Parosh* who had married a foreign wife [Ezra 10:25).
2. *A priest* who returned from exile with Zerubbabel (Neh. 12:5).

MIBHAR [Mĭb' här]—YOUTH or CHOICE. *A son of Haggeri* and one of David's heroes (I Chron. 11:38).

MIBSAM [Mĭb' sam]—SWEET ODOR.
1. *A son of Ishmael,* son of Hagar (Gen. 25:13; I Chron. 1:29).
2. *A son of Simeon* descended from No. 1 (I Chron. 4:25).

MIBZAR [Mĭb' zar]—A STRONGHOLD or FORTIFIED. *An Edomite chieftain,* descended from Esau (Gen. 36:42; I Chron. 1:53).

MICAH, MICHAH, MICA, MICHA [Mī' cah, Mī'chah, Mī' că, Mī' cha]—WHO IS LIKE JEHOVAH.
1. *An Ephramite* who hired a Levite to be priest to his image (Judg. 17; 18). This unworthy character brought great calamity to Israel. Dr. C. I. Scofield says of Micah's consecration of the Levite that it affords a striking illustration of apostasy. "With his entire departure from the revealed will of God concerning worship and priesthood there is yet an exaltation of false priesthood. Saying, 'Blessed be thou of Jehovah,' Micah's mother makes an idol; and Micah expects the blessing of Jehovah because he has linked the idolatry to the ancient levitical order."
2. *The head of a family of Reuben* (I Chron. 5:5).

3. *A son of Mephibosheth,* grandson of Saul (I Chron. 8:34, 35; 9:40, 41).

4. *A Levite* of the family of Asaph (I Chron. 9:15). See Micha.

5. *A son of Uzziel,* a Kohathite (I Chron. 23:20; 24:24, 25).

6. *Father of Abdon* whom Josiah sent to enquire of the Lord when the Law was found (II Chron. 34:20).

7. *The prophet surnamed the Morasthite,* and called Michaiah in the V.L. (Jer. 26:18; Mic. 1:1).

The Man of Strong Convictions

Micah prophesied during the reign of Jothan, Ahaz and Hezekiah (Mic. 1:1; Jer. 26:18). He was a younger contemporary of Hosea. He is called "the Morasthite" since he came from Moresheth Gath. Micah, unlike Isaiah, was no politician. He did not censure the habit of looking to Egypt or to Assyria for help. He denounces the depravity of the nation, and threatens the vengeance of God. Isaiah prophesied to royalty, Micah ministered to common people, the sort who heard Jesus gladly. Isaiah was a courtier; Micah, a rustic from an obscure town some twenty-five miles southwest of Jerusalem.

Micah was probably a yeoman, farming his own plot of land, and in vivid sympathy with the class to which he belonged. The land hunger of rich men, always to be deprecated, was positively dangerous to a country like Palestine with little foreign trade, relying mainly on the produce of the soil for the support of its citizens. The grasping avarice of large landholders doomed to poverty a considerable part of the population, and so Micah stands out as a preacher to the poor and oppressed. He regarded selfish luxury, joined with oppression of the poor, as the crowning sin of Judah. The people were heavily taxed, the Assyrians demanding large payments in tribute to satisfy their lavishness in their architectural magnificence. Thus Zion was built up with blood and Jerusalem with iniquity (Mic. 3:10). Because of such exaction and idolatry, Micah was called and empowered to declare the judgment of God (Mic. 3:8).

Micah was a man of strong convictions and corresponding courage, and as a true preacher, uncovered sin and pointed to the coming Christ. As a prophet he went against the stream and uttered truths the people did not want. For this he was consequently stoned—the usual lot of a faithful prophet. His cry, in essence, was:

Back to Bethlehem (Mic. 5:2). In other words, back to the Messianic hope. Back to David, who did so much for the nation, and to whom God promised He would raise up the Messiah. Back to David, the constant ideal of the monarchy. The Messiah of Israel's coming golden age would be like David.

Back to ethical righteousness (Mic. 6:8). Micah brushed aside all former ritual in favor of a righteousness given by God, and that had a heart for the need of others. It was a righteousness based upon God's salvation.

Back to the prince of peace (Mic. 4:1-3; 5:2-7). Micah heralded the message that the reign of the Messiah was Israel's only hope of peace. We know it to be the only hope of world peace. The Messianic predictions form the most significant passages in Micah.

The most outstanding incident in Micah's prophetic career was his preaching which led to the reformation under Hezekiah (Jer. 26:18). When king and people sought God and repented, He turned from the fierceness of His anger. The humble crofter of Philistia was chosen as God's messenger to the people, and the secret of his power was the fulness of the Holy Spirit (Mic. 3:8).

The book Micah wrote is characterized by deep spirituality, with a simple, but not rugged style. Sin and corruption, the sighing and agony of the people over the misrule of men in authority, the insistence on return to God, are all dealt with in no uncertain tones (Mic. 1:2; 3:1; 6:1). Broadly speaking, Micah's prophecy can be divided thus:

Chapters one, two and three — *judgment.*
Chapters four and five — *comfort.*
Chapters six and seven — *salvation.*

MICAIAH, MICHAIAH [Mĭ că' iah, Mĭ chă' iah]—WHO IS LIKE JEHOVAH. Here is a name occurring many times in the Old Testament and used of women as well as men. It is spelled in different ways. See Mica and Micah.

1. *A prophet, son of Imlah,* who foretold the fall of Ahab at Ramoth-gilead (I Kings 22:8, 9; II Chron. 18:8). There are no truer hearts to God than his. Carefully compare the three great prophets of I Kings — Ahijah, Elijah and Micaiah.

2. *The father of Achbor,* a chief officer of King Josiah (II Kings 22:12, 14).

3. *A prince of Judah* ordered by Jehoshaphat to teach the people (II Chron. 17:7).

4. *A priest of the family of Asaph* who blew a trumpet at the dedication of the wall [Neh. 12:35, 41).

5. *The son of Gemariah,* a prince of Judah in Jehoiakim's time (Jer. 36:11, 13).

Also the name of the daughter of Uriel of Gibeah. (See I Kings 15:2; II Chron. 11:20; 13:2).

MICHA [Mĭ' chă]—WHO IS LIKE JEHOVAH.
1. *Son of Mephibosheth* (II Sam. 9:12). See Micah.
2. *A Levite* (Neh. 11:17, 22). See Micah, No. 4.
3. *A Levite* who sealed the covenant (Neh. 10:11).

MICHAEL [Mĭ' chaĕl]—WHO IS LIKE GOD.
1. *An Asherite,* father of Sethur, whom Moses sent to spy the land (Num. 13:13).
2. *A Gadite,* descendant of Buz and head of his father's house (I Chron. 5:13).

3. *Another Gadite,* ancestor of the preceding (I Chron. 5:14).

4. *A Levite* of the family of Gershon and ancestor of Asaph (I Chron. 6:40).

5. *A chief man* of the tribe of Issachar of the family of Tola (I Chron. 7:3).

6. *A Benjamite* of the family of Beriah (I Chron. 8:16).

7. *A Manassite captain* who joined David at Ziklag (I Chron. 12:20).

8. *The father of Omri,* prince of Issachar in David's reign (I Chron. 27:18).

9. *A son of Jehoshaphat* (II Chron. 21:2).

10. *The father of Zebadiah* who returned from exile with Ezra (Ezra 8:8).

Also the name of the archangel who came to Daniel and is called by him "Prince of the people of Israel" (Dan. 10:13, 21; 12:1; Jude 9; Rev. 12:7).

Saul's youngest daughter, who became David's wife, was called Michal.

MICHRI [Mĭch' ri]—JEHOVAH POSSESSES or VALUABLE. *A Benjamite* and ancestor of a family in Jerusalem (I Chron. 9:8).

MIDIAN, MADIAN [Mĭd' ĭ an]—STRIFE or CONTENTION. *A son of Abraham by Keturah,* whose descendants covered many parts (Gen. 25: 2, 4; Ex. 2:15, 16; I Chron. 1:32, 33). Occasionally the Midianites are identified with the Ishmaelites (Judg. 6:33; 7:12).

MIJAMIN, MIAMIN [Mĭj' a mĭn, Mĭ' a mĭn]—ON THE RIGHT HAND or FORTUNATE.

1. *A descendant of Aaron,* of the family of the sixth of the twenty-four courses of priests (I Chron. 24:9).

2. *A priest* who, with Nehemiah, sealed the covenant (Neh. 10:7) and perhaps the trumpeter of Nehemiah 12:41. See Miamin and Miniamin.

MIKLOTH [Mĭk' loth]—RODS or STICKS.

1. *A military captain* in David's reign (I Chron. 27:4).

2. *A Benjamite* of the family of Jeiel of Gibeon (I Chron. 8:32; 9:37, 38).

MIKNEIAH [Mĭk nē' iah]—JEHOVAH IS JEALOUS or POSSESSION OF JEHOVAH. *A Levite* of the second degree and gatekeeper of the Ark. He played a harp (I Chron. 15:18, 21).

MILALAI (Mĭl a lā' ĭ]—JEHOVAH IS ELEVATED or ELOQUENT. *A Levite* who played a musical instrument at the dedication of the wall (Neh. 12:36).

MINIAMIN [Mĭn′ ĭ a mĭn]—ON THE RIGHT HAND or FORTUNATE.
1. *A Levite* in Hezekiah's time who distributed tithes and offerings (II Chron. 31:15).
2. *A priest* who returned with Zerubbabel. Also called Miamin (Neh. 12:17, 41).

MIRMA, MIRMAH [Mûr′ ma]—DECEIT or HEIGHT. *A son of Shaharaim* by his wife Hodesh (I Chron. 8:10).

MISHAEL [Mĭsh′ a el]—HIGH PLACE or WHO IS WHAT GOD IS.
1. *A son of Uzziel,* son of Kohath (Ex. 6:22; Lev. 10:4).
2. *One who stood with Ezra* when he preached to the people on the Law (Neh. 8:4).
3. *A companion of Daniel,* who is also called Meshek (Dan. 1:6, 7, 11, 19; 2:17).

MISHAM [Mĭ′ sham]—SWIFTNESS or IMPETUOUS. *A Benjamite,* a son of Elpaal, who with his brothers built Ono and Lod (I Chron. 8:12).

MISHMA [Mĭsh′ mă]—FAME or HEARING. *A son of Ishmael,* son of Hagar (Gen. 25:14; I Chron. 1:30; 4:25, 26).

MISHMANNAH [Mĭsh măn′ nah]—FATNESS or VIGOR. *A Gadite* who joined David at Ziklag (I Chron. 12:10).

MISPERETH, MISPAR, MIZPAR [Mĭs′ pe rĕth, Mĭz′ pär]—WRITING or A NARRATIVE. *One of those who returned with Zerubbabel* from captivity (Ezra 2:2). Called Mispar. The feminine form of this name is Mispereth (Neh. 7:7).

MITHREDATH [Mĭth′ re dăth]—GIVEN BY MITHRA, ANIMATING SPIRIT OF FIRE.
1. *The treasurer of Cyrus,* king of Persia, through whom the sacred vessels were restored to the Jews (Ezra 1:8).
2. *An enemy of the Jews* in the time of King Artaxerxes. He was averse to the rebuilding of the wall (Ezra 4:7).

MIZPAR [Mĭz′ pär]—FEAR or WRITING. *The chief of a tribe in the* land of Edom, who returned with Zerubbabel (Ezra 2:2).

MIZRAIM [Mĭz′ ra ĭm]—TRIBULATIONS. *The second son of Ham* and father of Ludim, whose descendants were found in Egypt (Gen. 10:6, 13; I Chron. 1:8, 11).

MIZZAH [Mĭz′ zah]—TERROR or JOY. *Son of Reuel,* son of Esau, and one of the dukes of Edom (Gen. 36:13, 17; I Chron. 1:37).

MNASON [Mnā' son]—A DILIGENT SEEKER.

The Man Who Was Loyal to the End

Described as "an old disciple," Mnason came into the life of Paul at a needy hour. Friends tried to dissuade him from going up to Jerusalem where bonds awaited him, but like his Master before him, he steadfastly set his face to go to Jerusalem. Thus this early disciple from Cyprus accompanied Paul on his last journey, and Paul lodged at his hospitable home (Acts 21:16). The figure of Mnason is drawn in the slightest possible outline "with a couple of hasty strokes of the pencil." We see him as:

I. *A disciple of old standing.* Can we not picture Paul's bountiful host as a grand old man with hoary head his crown of glory, and a serene face suggesting a kindly Christian heart within? "An honest old gentleman," Matthew Henry calls him. The R.V. speaks of him as "an early disciple," being possibly one of the converts of Peter on the Day of Pentecost. Conybeare and Howson suggest that Mnason was converted during the life of our Lord. There is a tradition that he was one of the twenty Jews sent out.

II. *Old yet still bearing.* The original meaning of "disciple" is *learner.* Thus Mnason had the honorable description of being "an old learner." Too often we associate learning with the young who, when they leave school, speak of their education as "finished." But the old man from Cyprus was not too old to learn. On the tombstone of the historian, John R. Green, is the inscription, "He died learning." Paul had been a believer for some twenty-five years when he wrote, "That I may know Him." The oldest saint, as well as the youngest Christian, needs to obey the exhortation about growing in grace and in the knowledge of our Lord and Saviour Jesus Christ.

III. *Ready for service although aged.* While Mnason was not able to undertake all of the long, arduous and perilous missionary journeys Paul faced, he could help those who were called and qualified to do so. He was content to fill a little space even though it was only to give a night's lodging for God's workers. Mnason felt it a privilege to entertain Paul and his companions. Here was one given to ungrudging hospitality, and who remained until the end of his day an effective witness to God's faithfulness.

MOAB [Mō' ab]—WATER OF A FATHER or DESIRE. *The son of Lot by his eldest daughter* (Gen. 19:37). It is best to draw a veil over such an incestuous union, testifying as it does to the corrupt influence of Sodom over Lot and his daughters. The descendants of the Moabites and Ammonites were closely related, and covered many chief places in Judah, the Salt Sea and Reuben (Gen. 36:35; Ex. 15:15; Judg. 3:28). The Israelites were commanded to have no dealings with the Moabites (Ruth 1:22; 2:2, 6; I Kings 11:1; II Chron. 24:26).

MOADIAH, MAADIAH [Mō a dī' ah, Mā a dī' ah]—FESTIVAL OF JE-

HOVAH. *A priest in Joiakim's time,* grandson of Jozadek (Neh. 12:17). See Maadiah.

MOLID [Mō' lid]—BEGETTER. *A descendant of Jerahmeel,* grandson of Pharez, son of Judah (I Chron. 2:29).

MORDECAI [Môr' de caī]—DEDICATED TO MARS, A LITTLE MAN or BITTER BRUISING.
1. *A Jew who returned from Babylon with Zerubbabel* (Ezra 2:2; Neh. 7:7).
2. *A Benjamite,* son or descendant of Jair, son of Shimei, son of Kish. He brought up Esther, his uncle's daughter, and adopted her as his own daughter after the death of her parents (Esther 2:5, 7).

The Man Who Was a Virtuous Patriot

What joy must have filled the heart of this foster-father of Esther, when he saw her elevated to the position of queen, and himself exalted to high office in the court. Exile and poverty were now past. Mordecai sat in the king's gate, and was aware of the plot on the king's life by two chamberlains. Mordecai reported the plot to the king, thus saving his life. According to Persian customs, a record of this act was carefully preserved in the royal archives (Esther 2:21–23; 6:1–3), and during a sleepless night of the king, was read. It resulted in Mordecai's consequent reward.

Mordecai may not appear as the most attractive of men. His message to Esther lacked courtesy and chivalry. Evidently he was insensible to the charms and graces of Esther which made her eligible as Vashti's successor. To the credit of Mordecai, however, it must be said that he refused to extend honor to one whom God had cursed (Ex. 17:14–16). Mordecai was of the tribe of Benjamin, and thus would not bow to Haman, who was an Amalekite and as such a direct descendant of the hereditary enemies of Israel.

Matthew Henry, quoting from the apocryphal chapters of Esther, says that Mordecai appeals to God in this manner:

> Thou knowest, Lord that it was neither in contempt nor pride, nor for any desire for glory, that I did not bow down to proud Haman, for I could have been content with good will for the salvation of Israel to kiss the soles of his feet, but I did this that I might not prefer the glory of man above the glory of God, neither will I worship any but Thee.

We cannot but admire Mordecai standing erect while the crowd of servants lay flat on their faces. While we have no record of his faith in God, yet his action proves him to have been a godly Jew who would not bow to any but God. "So did not I because of the fear of God," has to be our motto whatever fellow servants may say or do.

MOSES [Mō' zez]—DRAWN FORTH, TAKEN OUT OF THE WATER or A SON. *The youngest son of Amram and Jochebed,* of the family of Kohath (Ex. 2:10–21; Acts 7:20–38; Heb. 11:24, 25).

The Man Who Was God's Friend

The great Hebrew leader and legislator was born at the time the king of Egypt had resolved on the destruction of every newly born male child among the Israelites. The story of his rescue from the water by Pharaoh's daughter, of her adoption of him as her own son and his royal upbringing has charmed our hearts from earliest years.

It would take a volume in itself to fully expound the virtues and vicissitudes of Moses the historian, orator, leader, statesman, legislator and patriot. His greatest honor, however, was the privilege of being known as "the friend of God." What holy intimacy existed between God and this prophet so supernaturally guided and aided in his life and labors! No wonder this mighty leader of Israel was David Livingstone's favorite Bible hero!

Moses lived for 120 years, a period divided into three sections of forty years each:

The first forty years—from his birth until the flight into Midian. As Pharaoh's son, Moses learned how to be SOMEBODY.

The second forty years—from the flight into Midian to the Exodus. In desert places he learned how to become a NOBODY.

The third forty years—from the Exodus to his own exodus. As the leader of God's hosts he learned that GOD WAS EVERYBODY — the One he could speak to face to face as a man speaks to his friends.

The remarkable life of Moses can be viewed under three more aspects:

I. The moment when he turned fully to God.

II. The moment when he absolutely broke with the world. The refusal and choice of Hebrews 11:24, 25 must be carefully noted. It is not enough to refuse—we must choose. We must back up a negative with a positive.

III. The moment when between himself and God there was the sprinkled blood, the blood of atonement.

Further, Moses, the Law-giver in Israel, supplies us with a fitting type of Christ. Taken together we have these similarities which pastors can develop:

Both were preserved from the perils of infancy (Ex. 2:2–10 with Matt. 2:14, 15).

Both were tempted but had mastery over evil (Ex. 7:11 with Matt. 4:1).

Both knew what it was to fast for forty days (Ex. 34:28 with Matt. 4:2). Solitude was their strength.

Both had power to control the sea (Ex. 14:21 with Matt. 8:26).

Both fed a multitude (Ex. 16:26 with Matt. 14:20, 21).

Both had a radiant face (Ex. 34:35 with Matt. 17:2).

Both endured murmurings (Ex. 15:24 with Mark 7:2).

Both were discredited at home (Num. 12:1 with John 7:5).

Both were mighty intercessors (Ex. 32:32 with John 17).

Both spoke as the oracles of God (Deut. 18:18 with John 7:46).

Both had seventy helpers (Num. 11:16, 17 with Luke 10:1).

Both established memorials (Ex. 12:14 with Luke 22:19).

Both reappeared after death (Matt. 17:3 with Acts 1:3).

Moses gave us the first five books of the Old Testament, known as *The Pentateuch*. When Jesus said, "Moses wrote of me," He set His seal to the Mosaic authorship of these books. Moses died in the plains of Moab. At the ripe age of 120 years, while yet "his eye was not dim, nor his natural force abated," God called His faithful servant to climb Nebo's lonely mountain, where, upon its summit he was kissed to sleep by the angels and God buried him—the only man in the Bible to have God as his undertaker (Deut. 34:6).

MOZA [Mō' ză]—OFFSPRING or A GOING FORTH.

1. *A son of Caleb*, son of Jephunneh, of the family of Hezron (I Chron. 2:46).

2. *A Benjamite*, descendant of Saul and Jonathan (I Chron. 8:36, 37; 9:42, 43).

MUPPIM [Mŭp' pim]—OBSCURITIES. *A son of Benjamin*, Jacob's youngest son (Gen. 46:21).

MUSHI [Mū' shī]—DRAWN OUT. *A Levite*, son of Merari, son of Levi and founder of a tribal family (Ex. 6:19; Num. 3:20; 26:58).

N

NAAM [Nā' am]—SWEETNESS or PLEASANTNESS. *A son of the celebrated Caleb*, companion of Joshua (I Chron. 4:15).

NAAMAN [Nā' a man]—DELIGHT, PLEASANT or AGREEABLE.

1. *A son of Benjamin* and founder of a tribal family (Gen. 46:21).

2. *A son of Bela*, son of Benjamin (Num. 26:40; I Chron. 8:4).

3. *A son of Ehud*, or Abihud, grandson of Benjamin (I Chron. 8:7).

4. *A Syrian captain* in the army of Ben-hadad, king of Damascus. This able commander was cured of leprosy by Elisha the prophet (II Kings 5; Luke 4:27).

The Man Who Was Valiant But Leprous

What a blight Naaman's leprosy must have cast on his path! Successful, valiant, noble, yet a leper. His loathesome disease must have haunted him day and night. As there was no physician in Syria who could help him, he had the dread of going to the grave with his foul ailment. But God has a way of using little things to achieve His beneficent purpose. Among the captives brought from Israel to Syria was a girl chosen to act as maid to Naaman's wife. This slave maiden loved the Lord and was not ashamed to own Him. Thus when her mistress bemoaned the disease and despair of her husband, the girl sang the praises of Elisha. We can imagine how she would relate the miracles of the prophet, and, since her life was consistent with her testimony, the captive girl was believed.

With faith in the witness of the maid, Naaman went to Samaria, but felt rebuffed when Elisha would not see him, and instead sent his servant to the captain with the order: "Go wash in Jordan seven times."

How angry Naaman was to be told to wash himself in the muddy Jordan! Away he went in a rage, simply because his pride had been hurt. Elisha was indifferent to Naaman's honor and wealth, and also to the virtue of the better rivers in Damascus. But Naaman's excellent servant wanted his master cured of his dread disease, and influenced by him, Naaman obeyed the word of Elisha and was made whole. For the minister this old-time miracle bristles with forceful application.

NAARAI [Nă' a raī]—PLEASANTNESS OF JEHOVAH. *One of David's heroes* and son of Ezbai (I Chron. 11:37). He is called Paarai the Arbite in II Samuel 23:35.

NAASHON [Nă ăsh' on]—ORACLE or ONE THAT FORETELLS. *Brother of Elisheba,* Aaron's wife (Ex. 6:23). Perhaps Nahshon, the son of Amminadab.

NAASSON [Nă ăs' son]—ENCHANTER or SERPENT OF THE SUN. *An ancestor oj Jesus Christ* (Matt. 1:4; Luke 3:32).

NABAL [Nă' bal]—PROMINENCE or FOOLISH. *A wealthy but churlish sheepmaster of Maon* whose business was in Carmel (I Sam. 25; II Sam. 2:2).

The Man Who Was a Fool by Name and Nature

Nabal is a striking illustration of a man with a name indicative of his nature. When David came to Nabal asking food for his hungry men, this churlish man refused. David set out to kill Nabal but Abigail, his beautiful wife, pled for the life of her unworthy husband. What a contrast they afford! Abigail so beautiful and Nabal so bestial — The Beauty and the Beast. Pleading for Nabal's life, Abigail said to David, "As is his name, so is he. Nabal is his name and folly is with him." In effect, she said, "Pay no attention to my churlish husband. He's a fool by name and a fool by nature."

After his drunken orgy, Nabal was told of David's threat to take his life and he died of fright. David afterwards married Abigail, a woman of good understanding and who, as Edith Deen tells us in her most valuable handbook, *All the Women of the Bible,* was "the greatest influence for good and helped David to remember that he was God's anointed into whose keeping the kingdom of Israel had been entrusted."

NABOTH [Nā' bŏth]—PROMINENCE. *A Jezreelite of the tribe of Issachar,* whom Jezebel, wife of Ahab, caused to be put to death to obtain his vineyard adjoining the palace (I Kings 21; II Kings 9:21–26). For this dastardly act doom was pronounced upon Ahab and his house by Elijah. "The murder of Naboth seems to have deeply impressed the popular mind," comments W. F. Boyd, "and the deaths of Joram and Jezebel near the spot were regarded as Divine retribution on the act."

NACHON [Nă' chôn]—STROKE. *A Benjamite* at whose threshing floor Uzzah was smitten for touching the Ark (II Sam. 6:6). Also called Chidon in I Chronicles 13:9.

NACHOR [Nă' chôr]—NOBLE or BURNING. *An ancestor of Jesus Christ* (Luke 3:34).

NADAB [Nā' dăb]—OF ONE'S FREE WILL or LIBERAL.
1. *Elder son of Aaron,* destroyed by fire for offering strange fire upon the altar (Ex. 6:23; 24:1, 9). If we would worship and serve God acceptably, it must be in the way of His appointing.
2. *Son of Jeroboam I,* king of Israel. He was slain by Baasha (I Kings 14:20; 15:25, 27, 31).
3. *Great-grandson of Jerahmeel,* son of Hezron (I Chron. 2:28, 30).
4. *A Benjamite,* a son of Gibeon and Maachah (I Chron. 8:30; 9:36).

NAGGE, NAGGAI [Năg' ḡe]—SPLENDOR OF THE SUN. *An ancestor of Jesus Christ* (Luke 3:25).

NAHAM [Nā' ham]—SOLACE or CONSOLATION. *Brother of Hodiah,* wife of Ezra, and descendant of Caleb, son of Jephunneh (I Chron. 4:19).

NAHAMANI [Nā hăm' a nī]—COMFORTER or COMPASSIONATE. *A chief man who returned with Zerubbabel from Babylon* (Neh. 7:7).

NAHARAI, NAHARI [Nā hăr' a ī, Nā' ha rī]—SNORING or SNORTING ONE. *A Beerothite,* Joab's armorbearer (II Sam. 23:37; I Chron. 11:39).

NAHASH [Nā' hăsh]—SERPENT or ORACLE.
1. *An Amorite king* who besieged Jabesh-gilead and was defeated by Saul (I Sam. 11:1, 2; 12:12).
2. *The father of Shobi,* and another Ammonite king (II Sam. 10:2; 17:27; I Chron. 19:1, 2). Also the name of the mother of Abigail (II Sam. 17:25).

NAHATH [Nā' hăth]—DESCENT, LOWNESS or QUIET.
1. *A son of Reuel,* son of Esau (Gen. 36:13, 17; I Chron. 1:37).

2. *A son of Zophai* (I Chron. 6:26). Perhaps the Toah of I Chronicles 6:34.

3. *A Levite,* overseer of the offerings in the days of Hezekiah (II Chron. 31:13).

NAHBI [Näh' bī]—CONCEALED or JEHOVAH'S PROTECTION. *A prince of Naphtali,* and representative spy sent out by Moses (Num. 13:14).

NAHOR, NACHOR [Nā' hôr]—BREATHING HARD or SLAYER.
1. *A son of Serug* and grandfather of Abraham (Gen. 11:23–25; I Chron. 1:26).

2. *A son of Terah,* brother of Abraham, husband of Milcah, who bore him eight children (Gen. 11:26, 29).

NAHSHON, NAASSON [Näh' shŏn, Nā ăs' son]—ENCHANTING or OMINOUS. *Son of Amminadab* and prince of Judah in the days of Moses (Num. 1:7; 2:3). See Naashon.

NAHUM [Nā' hum]—COMPASSIONATE, COMFORTER or FULL OF COMFORT.
1. *The prophet who was born at Elkosh in Galilee,* and who prophesied against Nineveh (Nah. 1:1).

The Man Who Preached Doom

Nothing is known of this Minor Prophet outside of what we find in the opening of his small yet strong book. He was born at Elkosh, a village of Palestine. But although Nahum is among the notable unknown of the Bible, he was a student of the history of his time and was raised up to comfort God's people. He prophesied against Nineveh about 150 years after Jonah's revival there. At that time the city was still at the height of its glory (Nah. 3:16, 17). The empire was extremely cruel. The people gloated that "space failed for corpses of their enemies." They made "pyramids of human heads." Pillars were covered with the flayed skins of their rivals.

Nahum's mission was to declare the terrible doom of Nineveh and one hundred years later it fell. So great was the destruction of the city of the most ferocious, sensual, diabolically atrocious race of men that ever lived, that Alexander the Great marched by and did not know that a great city was under his feet. Lucian wrote, "Nineveh is perished and there is no trace left where once it was." Nahum, convinced that God was slow to anger but would yet take vengeance on His adversaries, "focusses the light of God's moral government upon wicked Nineveh and chants the death and dirge of the world's greatest oppressor."

The leading lessons to be gleaned from the Book of Nahum are encouraging to faith:

I. The goodness and unchangeableness of Jehovah.

II. The limits of divine forbearance.

III. Right prevails in the end.

IV. Darkness comes before the dawn.

V. The universality of God's government, its gracious purpose: its retributive character.

VI. Man's extremity is faith's hour and God's opportunity.

2. *Another Nahum.* In the A. V. Naum is mentioned as an ancestor of Jesus Christ (Luke 3:25).

NAPHISH, NEPHISH [Nā' phish, Nĕ' phish]—NUMEROUS or RESPIRATION. *A son of Ishmael,* son of Abraham and Hagar and founder of a clan who settled west of Jordan (Gen. 25:15; I Chron. 1:31; 5:19).

NAPHTALI, NEPHTHALIM [Năph' ta lī, Nĕph' tha lĭm]—OBTAINED BY WRESTLING. *The sixth son of Jacob* and second by Bilhah, Rachel's maid. Rachel gave her son his name because she had wrestled in prayer for God's favor and blessing (Gen. 30:8; 35:25). The tribe that descended from Naphtali bears his name (Num. 1:15, 42).

The Man Who Lacked Self-Control

In the last words of Jacob (Gen. 49:21), the patriarch speaks of Naphtali as "a hind let loose: he giveth goodly words"—a fluent orator but as erratic as the wild gazelle. Henry Thorne wrote of him,

> He is gifted undoubtedly, but he has no self-control. He will scamper through life aimlessly and without a goal. His uncontrolled energy may some day be his ruin. He may possibly leap over a fence, but he may also jump into a ditch. Byron was gifted, but of him it has been said —
>
> > He laid his hand upon the ocean's main,
> > And played familiar with his hoary locks.
>
> He was a man of brilliant talent and magnificent capacity, but he was also "a hind let loose." There was a wild extravagance in his career of wrong-doing that marred his influence and spoiled his life.

Nothing but divine grace can restrain those who are erratic. He who rebuked the rude tempest with a word (Job 38:11; Mark 4:39) and produced a great calm, can rebuke the turbulent and the reckless in any nature, and cause the energy that is wasted by folly to flow into channels of usefulness. God can make the rebel a priest and a king.

NARCISSUS [Năr' cĭs' sus]—FLOWER CAUSING LETHARGY or ASTONISHMENT. *A Roman* whose household Paul greeted. The apostle's salutation is not addressed to Narcissus himself but to the members of his household. He may have been the favorite freedman of Claudius the emperor (Rom. 16:11).

NATHAN [Nā' than]—HE HATH GIVEN.

1. *The third child of David,* born after he came to reign over Israel (II Sam. 5:14; I Chron. 3:5; 14:4).

2. *The distinguished prophet* during the reigns of David and Solomon, who brought home to David the enormity of his sin. What a piercing arrow from the divine bow that was — *Thou art the man*

(II Sam. 7:2–17; 12; I Kings 1; I Chron. 17). Although the confidential adviser of King David, Nathan was unsparing in his condemnation of his monarch's sin. Nathan also wrote a history (II Chron. 9:29).

3.   *The father of Igal,* one of David's heroes (II Sam. 23:36).

4.   *Father of Solomon's chief officer* (I Kings 4:5).

5.   *Son of Attai* and father of Zabad, of the tribe of Judah (I Chron. 2:36).

6.   *Brother of Joel,* one of David's heroes (I Chron. 11:38).

7.   *A chief man with Ezra* at the brook of Ahava (Ezra 8:16).

8.   *A son of Bani* who put away his foreign wife (Ezra 10:39).

9.   *A chief man in Israel* (Zech. 12:12).

10.   *An ancestor of Jesus Christ* (Luke 3:31).

NATHANAEL [Nā thăn' a el]—THE GIFT OF GOD. *A native of Cana in Galilee* whom Jesus called an Israelite in whom there was no guile (John 1:45–49; 21:2).

The Man Who Was Guileless

Nathanael is supposed to be the same as Bartholomew the Apostle. The name of Nathanael occurs in John but in none of the other gospels. He is introduced at the beginning and at the close of Christ's ministry. His doubt of Christ's Messiahship vanished when he met Him, and he was one of the seven to whom the risen Lord manifested Himself at the Lake of Galilee.

It may be that he bore a double name and is referred to as Bartholomew, whom John never mentions, just as the other evangelists never mention Nathanael. The name Bartholomew stands in conjunction with that of Philip. If the rule is accepted that Andrew and Simon are put together because the one led the other to Christ, there is a presumption in favor of Bartholomew of the first three gospels being the same as Nathanael of John's gospel, from the fact recorded by John only, that it was Philip who brought Nathanael to the Saviour. We reject the tradition that he was the bridegroom at the Cana marriage, or one of the two disciples on the Emmaus road.

Profitable aspects to be developed are these:

I.   Nathanael owed his introduction to Jesus to a friend. Have you introduced others to Him?

II.   Nathanael was prepared to listen to conversation about Christ. He readily received the witness of one who had found the Messiah. Have you found Him, and are you telling others the story?

III.   Nathanael's hopes were realized in an unexpected way. Often joy and rest come to us from the least expected quarter.

IV.   Nathanael accepted the sure test of truth and the sure cure of prejudice. "Come and see," "Taste and see."

V.   Nathanael's faith rejoiced the Master, and secured for him the promise of a growing blessing.

NATHAN-MELECH [Nā' than-mĕ' lech]—THE KING IS GIVER. *A*

eunuch or chamberlain who lived in Josiah's time and had a chamber
within the precincts of the Temple (II Kings 23:11).

NAUM [Nā um]—COMFORT. *An ancestor of Jesus Christ through
Mary.* See Nahum (Luke 3:25).

NEARIAH [Nē a rī' ah]—JEHOVAH HATH SHAKEN or DRIVES AWAY.
1. *Grandson of Shechaniah,* descendant of David (I Chron. 3:22, 23).
2. *A Simeonite captain* who assisted in the war against the Amalekites (I Chron. 4:42).

NEBAI [Nĕb' a ī]—NARROWING or PROJECTING. *A person who with
Nehemiah sealed the covenant* (Neh. 10:19).

NEBAJOTH, NEBAIOTH [Nē bā' joth, Nē bā' ioth]—HUSBANDRY.
The eldest son of Ishmael, son of Hagar (Gen. 25:13; 28:9; 36:3; I
Chron. 1:29), and founder of a tribal family (Isa. 60:7).

NEBAT [Nĕ' băt]—CULTIVATION. *Father of Jeroboam,* who rebelled
against Rehoboam and became the first king of the ten tribes of Israel
(I Kings 11:26; 12:2, 15). As Jeroboam I is always referred to as "the
son of Nebat," distinguishing him from Jeroboam II, one wonders
what influence father had over son.

NEBO [Nĕ' bō]—HEIGHT. *An ancestor of certain Jews* who had
taken foreign wives while in exile (Ezra 10:43). Also the name of
the mountain on which Moses died, and the name of a Chaldean idol
(Deut. 32:49; 34:1; Isa. 46:1).

NEBUCHADNEZZAR, NEBUCHADREZZAR, REZZAR [Nĕb u
chad nĕz' zar]—NEBO, DEFEND THE BOUNDARY. *Son of Nabopolassar and
king of Babylon,* who figures prominently as an enemy of God's people
(II Kings 24:1, 10, 11; Dan. 1-5).
The Man Whose Pride Turned Him Mad
This first Gentile monarch was the one who captured Jerusalem and
destroyed both city and temple. The inhabitants were carried into
Babylon as slaves. Nebuchadnezzar set up a golden image in Dura,
and the three Hebrew youths who refused to bow down to the image
were thrown into the fiery furnace but divinely preserved. Drunk
with pride, Nebuchadnezzar had dreams Daniel interpreted. Driven
out for a time from men, and living among oxen, he became a new
man and turned from his humiliation to honor God.
The encyclical letter written by the first head of Gentiles, for
Nebuchadnezzar was "a king of kings," reaches far and wide in the
lesson it teaches to all Gentile powers, until the times of the Gentiles
shall be fulfilled (Dan. 4: 34-37; Rev. 11:15-17). In this letter we
have:

I. The dream of a tree reaching in its height to heaven, and seen by all the world. This related to the king himself, who swayed the scepter of a universal empire, and whose power led to pride (Prov. 16:5–18).

II. The wise advice received from Spirit-anointed Daniel made clear how the king's error could be healed. God has been speaking to the Gentile nations ever since he gave them dominion, but a deaf ear has been turned to divine entreaties. In the face of appalling perils Gentile monarchy is crumbling today.

III. The patience of God is manifest in that twelve months have elapsed before the threatened judgment overtook the proud monarch. How long-suffering God is!

IV. Sore punishment led to deep humiliation and to a noble confusion in the presence of the world. God abased Nebuchadnezzar, and the day is coming when He will likewise abase the Gentile nations of earth. When the mightiest of all monarchs returns, He will lay hold of Gentile government and introduce His own world-kingdom and reign as the King of all Gentile kings. The scepter of universal dominion will rest in His pierced hands.

NEBUSHASBAN, NEBUSHAZBAN [Nĕb u shăs′ ban]—NEBO, SAVE ME. *A Babylonian prince* who held the office of Rab-saris under Nebuchadnezzar (Jer. 39:13).

NEBUZAR-ADAN [Nĕb′ u zär-ā′ dan]—NEBO HATH AN OFFSPRING. *The captain of the guard* left behind in Jerusalem after its capture (II Kings 25:8, 11, 20; Jer. 39:9, 10).

NECHO, NECO [Nĕ′ chō]—WHO WAS BEATEN. *The appellation given to the king of Egypt* (II Chron. 35:20, 22; 36:4). See Pharaoh.

NEDABIAH [Nĕd a bī′ ah]—JEHOVAH IS WILLING or BOUNTIFUL. *A son of king Jeconiah,* son of Jehoiakim, king of Judah (I Chron. 3:18).

NEHEMIAH [Nē he mī′ ah]—JEHOVAH HATH CONSOLED.
1. *A chief man who returned from exile* (Ezra 2:2; Neh. 7:7).
2. *The son of Hachaliah* and cup-bearer to king Artaxerxes (Neh. 1:1).

The Man Who Had a Mind to Work

Nehemiah and Hanani were the sons of Hachaliah (Neh. 1:1; 2:5; 7:2), and the references suggest that the family belonged to the capital. Nehemiah, although born in exile, grew up in the faith of Israel's God. Nehemiah's name appears as a prince, not as a priest (Neh. 9:38; 10:1), and he was perhaps the chief man who returned from Babylon with Zerubbabel (Ezra 2:2; Neh. 7:7). As the king's cup-bearer, he held a high place of honor in the palace of Shushan (Neh. 1:11), having confidential access to the king. His Persian name was Sheshbazzar (Ezra 1:8). He was one of the princes who signed the covenant (Neh. 9:38; 10:1). He became Governor of Jerusalem (Neh. 10:1). Josephus says that Nehemiah died of old age and that the repaired walls of the city constituted his best and most enduring monument.

For his patriotic task (Neh. 1:1-4), Nehemiah was well qualified. As a true Israelite, he labored for the purity of public worship, the integrity of family life, the sanctity of the sabbath. Ezra was the student and preacher; Nehemiah, the soldier and statesman. He was courageous and God-fearing, and brought to his labors a noble disinterestedness, and unblemished rectitude, a dauntless spirit and unswerving loyalty to God. Alexander Whyte in his helpful essay of Nehemiah speaks of him:

> As a self-contained man. A man of his own counsel. A man with the counsel of God alone in his mind and in his heart. A reserved and resolute man. A man to take command of other men. A man who will see things with his own eyes, and without all eyes seeing him. A man in no haste or hurry. He will not begin till he has counted the cost. And then he will not stop till he has finished the work.

While we are compelled to pass over a full exposition of the book of this patriotic Jew whose heart was stirred with sorrow over the derelict condition of Jerusalem, we must linger over some of its important aspects.

I. He illustrates the strength which comes from an inspiring purpose and definite aim. Open opposition and underhanded wiles had to be faced, but undauntedly Nehemiah persisted in his task (Neh. 6:3). Among the hostile methods directed against his noble mission were:

Ridicule (Neh. 2:19; 4:2). But Nehemiah prayed that such reproach might return to the reproachers which it did (Neh. 4:4-6).

Fear (Neh. 4:7-23). Enemies delivered an ultimatum but Nehemiah set a watch. Swords and trowels were united (Neh. 4:18).

Guile (Neh. 6:2-4). Nehemiah knew that conferences were useless, and so shunned them.

False accusation (Neh. 6:5-9). This patriot had no selfish motives behind his endeavors.

Temptation to tempt God (Neh. 6:10-13). Nehemiah refused to hide himself in the Temple as if he was doing wrong.

Corruption of friends and associates (Neh. 6:17-19). This was the meanest act of Nehemiah's foes.

II. He sets forth the strength that comes from humble dependence upon God. True to God and his principles, Nehemiah surmounted all his enemies and obstacles. His sterling character stood the acid test, for he was a man of dependence upon God (Neh. 1:5-11), single-hearted in his devotion to God and his work, wise in taking proper precautions against surprise attacks, ever encouraging to those who labored with him. Making his prayer to God, Nehemiah knew that God would fight for him (Neh. 4:9, 20).

III. He manifested the strength which comes from the sense of union and of fellowship. All classes of people, even the daughters, were ready to take their place around the damaged walls. High and low worked together for the accomplishment of a God-inspired task (Neh. 3:12). With scorn, Nehemiah rebuked the pride and negligence of the nobles "who put not their necks to the work of their Lord" (Neh. 3:5). Fulfilling their obligation by repairing "every man over against his house," the willing-heart with one mind to work illustrates the chain of living Christian fellowship set forth in Ecclesiastes 4:9. See I Corinthians 12:4–7.

3. *A son of Azbuk* and ruler of half the district of Jerusalem who repaired part of the wall—a common-sense enthusiast even as his illustrious namesake (Neh. 3:16).

NEHUM [Nē' hum]—CONSOLATION. *A chief man* who returned from exile with Zerubbabel (Neh. 7:7). Called Rehum in Ezra 2:2.

NEKODA [Nē kŏ' dă]—HERDSMAN or DISTINGUISHED.
1. *One of the Nethinims* whose descendants returned from exile (Ezra 2:48; Neh. 7:50).
2. *Another one of the above* whose descendants also returned from exile, but could not prove their genealogy (Ezra 2:60; Neh. 7:62).

NEMUEL [Nē mū' el]—GOD IS SPREADING.
1. *A Reubenite,* son of Eliab and brother of Dathan and Abiram, who strove against Moses (Num. 26:9).
2. *A son of Simeon,* second son of Jacob and Leah (Num. 26:12; I Chron. 4:24). Founder of a tribal family.

NEPHEG [Nē' pheg]—AN OFFSHOOT.
1. *A son of Izhar,* son of Kohath (Ex. 6:21).
2. *A son born to David after he became king of Israel* (II Sam. 5:15; I Chron. 3:7; 14:6).

NER [Nûr]—A LAMP or BRIGHTNESS. *A Benjamite,* son of Abiel and father of Abner, Saul's chief captain (I Sam. 14:50, 51).

NEREUS [Nē' re ŭs]—NAME OF A SEA GOD, WHO UNDER POSEDON OR NEPTUNE RULED THE MEDITERRANEAN SEA. *A Christian in Rome* to whom Paul sent a greeting (Rom. 16:15). Probably the son of Philologus. The phrase, "all the saints that are with them," indicates a community of believers accustomed to meet together for worship and fellowship.

NERGAL-SHAREZER [Nûr' gal-shā re' zer]—NERGAL, PROTECT THE KING.
1. *A prince of Nebuchadnezzar* (Jer. 39:3).

2. *Another prince* who held office in Jerusalem (Jer. 39:3, 13). Perhaps these two are the same person.

NERI [Nē' rī]—LIGHT OF THE LORD. *An ancestor of Christ* and somehow genealogically the father of Shealtiel (Luke 3:27).

NERIAH [Nē rī' ah]—LAMP OF JEHOVAH. *Son of Masseiah* and father of Baruch and Seraiah, scribe and messenger of Jeremiah (Jer. 32:12, 16).

NETHANEEL, NETHANEL [Nē thǎn' e el]—GOD GIVES or HATH GIVEN.
1. *A prince of the tribe of Issachar* in the early period of the wilderness wanderings (Num. 1:8; 2:5; 7:18, 23; 10:15).
2. *One of David's brothers,* fourth son of Jesse (I Chron. 2:14).
3. *A priest who blew a trumpet* when the Ark was brought back to the city of David (I Chron. 15:24).
4. *A Levite* whose son Shemaiah was employed by David for sanctuary service (I Chron. 24:6).
5. *A son of Obed-edom* appointed by David as gatekeeper for the Tabernacle (I Chron. 26:4).
6. *A prince of Judah* whom king Jehoshaphat sent to teach the people (II Chron. 17:7).
7. *A chief Levite* in Josiah's time (II Chron. 35:9).
8. *A son of Pashur* who had married a foreign wife (Ezra 10:22).
9. *A priest of the family of Jediah* who lived in the days of Joiakim (Neh. 12:21).
10. *An Aaronite musician* who assisted in the dedication of the wall (Neh. 12:36).

NETHANIAH [Nĕth a nī' ah]—JEHOVAH HATH GIVEN.
1. *Father of that Ishmael who slew Gedaliah,* whom Nebuchadnezzar had left governor in the land (II Kings 25:23, 25).
2. *A son of Asaph,* and chief singer in David's time (I Chron. 25:2, 12).
3. *A Levite* whom Jehoshaphat sent to teach the cities of Judah (II Chron. 17:8).
4. *The father of Jehudi* whom the princes of Judah sent to bring Baruch (Jer. 36:14).

NEZIAH [Nē zī' ah] —PRE-EMINENT or PURE. *One of the Nethinims,* the sacred official class, whose descendants returned from exile (Ezra 2:54; Neh. 7:56).

NICANOR [Nĭ cǎ' nor] —CONQUEROR, VICTORIOUS or I CONQUER. *One of the seven disciples* chosen by the Church at Jerusalem to look after Greek-speaking widows and the poor in general (Acts 6:5).

NICODEMUS [Nĭc o dē′ mus]—INNOCENT BLOOD or VICTOR OVER THE PEOPLE. *An elderly and somewhat wealthy Pharisee* and a member of the Sanhedrin (John 3:1–9; 7:50; 19:39).

The Man Who Came to Jesus by Night

Whenever Nicodemus is mentioned it is always with the label, "the same that came to Jesus by night." Why is this master in Israel always spoken of in this way? Was he a coward, afraid of what the fellow-members of the Sanhedrin would say if they saw him seeking out Jesus? We feel that he came by night because it was the best time for both Jesus and himself to have a quiet, uninterrupted conversation about spiritual matters. Nicodemus had been occupied all day with his teaching duties, and Jesus had been active in His out-of-door ministry. Now both could relax and talk through the night. It may be that Nicodemus had such a heart hunger that he could not wait until morning, and so came running to Jesus as soon as he could.

There had been no direct voice from God in Israel for a long time, and here was One whose message carried the stamp of divine authority. So Nicodemus, the cautious enquirer, but a man of spiritual perception (John 3:2), sought out Christ, and listened to one of His remarkable conversational sermons. Nicodemus figures three times in John's gospel:

He came to Christ (John 3:2). This master in Israel confessed Christ to be a Teacher sent from God and heard that in spite of his culture, position and religion, he needed to be born anew by the Spirit of God. His name, meaning "innocent blood," is suggestive. Nicodemus came to realize that his salvation was dependent upon the shedding of innocent blood (John 3:14, 16).

He spoke for Christ (John 7:45–52). As a fair-minded man, Nicodemus, although a disciple at heart and afraid to avow his faith, raised his voice on behalf of Christ as the Sanhedrin devised measures against Him. The rulers were His avowed enemies, and Nicodemus raised a point of order in favor of the One he had learned so much from. Perhaps he should have been more courageous and outspoken on Christ's behalf. When the Sanhedrin condemned Jesus to death, there was no protest from Nicodemus. It is likely that he absented himself from that fateful meeting.

He honored Christ (John 19:39, 40). After the death of Christ, ashamed of his cowardice, Nicodemus rendered loving though belated service to Christ. Openly he joined Joseph of Arimathaea, another secret disciple, in preparing Christ's body for a kingly burial. But the dead cannot appreciate our loving attention. Mary gave her spices to Jesus while He was alive. It is better to give flowers to the living than reserve them for their burial.

NICOLAS, NICOLAUS [Nĭc′ o las]—CONQUEROR OF THE PEOPLE. *A proselyte of Antioch,* one of the seven disciples selected by the apostles to care for widows and the poor (Acts 6:5).

NIGER [Nĭ' gûr]—BLACK. *The Latin surname of Simeon,* one of the prophets and teachers in Antioch. Simeon was the Jewish name, and Niger an assumed Gentile name (Acts 13:1).

NIMROD [Nĭm' rŏd]—VALIANT, STRONG or HE THAT RULES. *A son of Cush,* son of Ham. Nimrod was a mighty hunter and a potent monarch whose land bore his name (Gen. 10:8, 9; I Chron. 1:10; Micah 5:6).

NIMSHI [Nĭm' shĭ]—JEHOVAH REVEALS or DRAWN OUT. *An ancestor of Jehu,* and generally designated "son of Nimshi" (I Kings 19:16; II Kings 9:2, 20; II Chron. 22:7).

NOADIAH [Nō a dī' ah]—JEHOVAH HATH MET, ASSEMBLED or ORNAMENT OF THE LORD. *A son of Binnui,* who had charge of the gold and silver vessels brought back from captivity (Ezra 8:33). Also the name of the so-called prophetess whose evil pronouncements were intended to terrify Nehemiah (Neh. 6:14).

NOAH, NOE [Nō' ah]—REST.
1. *The son of Lamech* of the posterity of Seth—the tenth from Adam. He died at the age of 950 years (Gen. 5:29, 30, 32; 6:8). The LXX version says that the name is a play on the statement, "This same shall give us rest."

The Man Who Built the Ark

Nothing is known of the early life of Noah, who first appeared on the scene when he was five hundred years old. Evidently his father, Lamech, was a religious man and gave his son a fitting name, meaning *rest.* This much we do know about Noah, he lived in a time when men were universally corrupt, so much so that God said He would destroy the human race (Gen. 6:1-7).

In the midst of an age of moral darkness, Noah was perfect in his generation. He walked with God and had a life radiant with righteousness. Intimate with God, he learned of His purpose to destroy mankind (Heb. 11:7), and was given the strange and almost impossible task of building a vessel large enough to shelter his family and a pair of all the birds and the beasts of that time.

Noah set about the tremendous work of the Ark's construction. Daily he had to endure the ridicule of the godless. At last the waters of judgment covered the earth, but all within the Ark were safe and saved. What a striking illustration the Ark affords of Christ, who preserves us from the flood of divine judgment. Here is an outline for the pastor to extend:

I.   Noah walked with God in spite of surrounding iniquity (Gen. 6:8-12). There were saints in Caesar's household.

II. Noah was obedient when appointed to a difficult task (Gen. 6:14-21; 7:5).

III. Noah was remembered by God and delivered from death (Gen. 8:1). Romans 8:1 tells where we rest.

IV. Noah, by faith, worked out his salvation (Heb. 11:7). See Philippians 2:12.

V. Noah warned his neighbors of impending judgment. (II Peter 2:5). See Ezekiel 33:1–20.

VI. Noah built the first recorded altar (Gen. 8:20). See Hebrews 13:10.

VII. Noah was honored by God with an everlasting covenant (Gen. 9:12–17). See Hebrews 9:15.

2. *Also the name of a daughter of Zelophehad*, the grandson of Gilead (Num. 26:33).

NOBAH [Nō' bah]—BARKING. *A Manassite captain of Kenath* who gave the town his own name (Judg. 8:11).

NOBAI, NEBAI [Nĕb' a ī]—FRUIT OF THE LORD. *One of the chiefs* of the people who, with Nehemiah, sealed the covenant (Neh. 10:19). See Nebo.

NOGAH [Nō' gah]—BRILLIANCE or SHINING. *A son of David*, born after he became king of Israel (I Chron. 3:7; 14:6).

NOHAH [Nō' hah]—REST. *Fourth son of Benjamin* (I Chron. 8:2). Perhaps another name for Shephupham (Num. 26:39 R. V.).

NUN [Nŭn]—FISH or CONTINUATION. *An Ephraimite*, father of Joshua, Israel's great military leader (Ex. 33:11; Num. 11: 28). Joshua is always spoken of as "the son of Nun."

NYMPHAS [Nȳm' phas]—SACRED TO THE MUSES or BRIDEGROOM. *A believer of Laodicea* or Colosse to whom Paul sent a loving greeting. He was an influential person whose house was used as a meeting place for Christians (Col. 4:15).

O

OBADIAH [Ō ba dī' ah]—SERVANT or WORSHIPER OF JEHOVAH. Among the Semitic peoples many names, such as the one before us, were common, occurring frequently in the Old Testament. Little or nothing is known about the Obadiahs of the Bible, but the name has also been found on an ancient Hebrew seal.

1. *The pious governor of Ahab's palace* who hid one hundred of Jehovah's prophets (I Kings 18:3–16).

2. *The founder of a family of the lineage of David* (I Chron. 3:21).

3. *A man of Issachar* of the family of Tola (I Chron. 7:3).

4. *Son of Azel*, a descendant of king Saul (I Chron. 8:38; 9:44).

5. *Son of Shemaiah*, a Levite of Netophah (I Chron. 9:16).

6. *A Gadite* who joined David at Ziklag (I Chron. 12:9).

7. *Father of Ishmaiah*, prince of Zebulun in David's time (I Chron. 27:19).

8. *A prince of Judah*, sent by Jehoshaphat to teach the people (II Chron. 17:7).

9. *A Levite*, one of the overseers of the workmen who repaired the Temple in Josiah's time (II Chron. 34:12).

10. *Son of Jehiel*, a descendant of Joab who returned from exile with Ezra (Ezra 8:9).

11. *A priest* who, on behalf of his father's house, sealed the covenant (Neh. 10:5).

12. *A Levite*, founder of a family of sanctuary porters (Neh. 12:25).

13. *The prophet of Judah* who lived over 550 years before Christ (Obad. 1).

The Man Who Prophesied Disaster

This Minor Prophet cannot be identified. His book, the briefest in the Old Testament, gives his name, but there the record ends. Pusey says, "The silence of Scripture as to Obadiah stands in remarkable contrast with the anxiety of man to know something about him." His origin, age, life, country, parents and grave are all unknown. His is the voice of a stranger. He has been identified with the Levite of the same name sent by Jehoshaphat to teach in the cities of Judah (See No. 8). He has also been linked with the pious Obadiah of Ahab's house (See No. 1). Of the prophet's personal history not a single incident or even tradition has been preserved. The work is more important than the worker.

It would seem as if the prophet lived and labored between the taking of Jerusalem and the destruction of Idumea, since he speaks of "foreigners" entering Jerusalem and the day of Judah's destruction and distress (Obad. 11–14). Although his book is the shortest in the Hebrew Canon, consisting of only twenty-one verses, yet it demands more of our attention, proportionately, than any other book. Looking at it from the aspect of size, it is little, but weighty. *Multum in parvo*.

Obadiah's prophecy has always been a favorite one with the Jews. It is principally from Obadiah that they learned to apply the name Edom to Rome. "Edom" stands as the typical designation for all the deadliest foes of the House of Israel.

Edom was descended from Esau, the brother of Jacob, and thus the people were akin to the Children of Israel. Since the days of the Exodus there has been frequent conflict between the two races. The Edomites had shown themselves unfriendly to Moses and the Israelites, refusing them passage through their territory when marching towards Canaan, and this bitterness still continues, accounting for the present animosity of the Arab world toward the Jew.

Obadiah's style in writing is full of individuality. It is animated and vigorous, abounding in appeals and having the preponderance of interrogation of great point and vehemence. His language is simple and pure, with utterance often highly poetic.

The lessons to be gathered from Obadiah's description of the character and career, the downfall and doom of Edom; are clearly evident:

I. The similarity of sin and punishment.

II. God will not cast off His people forever.

III. Greed and cruelty are hateful to God.

IV. Pride goes before a fall.

V. The ultimate kingdom is the Lord's.

OBAL [Ō' bal]—BARE or INCONVENIENCE OF OLD AGE. *A son of Joktan* of the family of Shem (Gen. 10:28). Called Ebal in I Chronicles 1:22.

OBED [Ō' bed]—WORSHIPER or A SERVANT WHO WORSHIPS.

1. *Son of Boaz,* by Ruth, and better than ten sons to her, since through Obed she became an ancestress of Jesus Christ (Ruth 4:17–22; I Chron. 2:12; Matt. 1:5; Luke 3:32).

2. *Son of Ephlal,* descendant of Judah (I Chron. 2:37, 38).

3. *One of David's valiant men* (I Chron. 11:47).

4. *A son of Shemaiah,* a gatekeeper at the Tabernacle in David's time (I Chron. 26:7).

5. *Father of Azariah,* in the time of Athaliah (II Chron. 23:1).

OBED-EDOM [Ō' bed-ē' dom]—SERVANT OF EDOM or LABORER OF THE EARTH.

1. *A Levite,* one of David's bodyguard, in whose house the Ark was hid for three months. Its presence brought blessing to Obed-edom and all his family (II Sam. 6:10–12; I Chron. 13:13, 14; 15:25).

2. *A Levite,* gatekeeper of the Tabernacle, who marched before the Ark during its removal to Jerusalem (I Chron. 15:18–24; 26:4, 8, 15).

3. *A Levite* of the second degree who did regular duty at the tent erected for the Ark (I Chron. 16:5, 38).

4. *A son of Jeduthun,* who also served at the sanctuary. Perhaps Obed-edom the Korathite (I Chron. 16:38; II Chron. 25:24).

OBIL [Ō' bǐl]—DRIVER, LEADER or ONE WHO WEEPS. *An Ishmaelite camel keeper,* who had charge of David's camels (I Chron. 27:30).

OCRAN [Ŏc' ran]—TROUBLER. *Father of Pagiel,* chosen by Moses to number the people (Num. 1:13; 2:27; 7:72, 77; 10:26).

ODED [Ō' ded]—AIDING or HE HATH RESTORED.

1. *The father of the prophet Azariah* who encouraged Asa, king of Judah (II Chron. 15:1, 8).

2. *An Israelite prophet* in the reign of Pekah who successfully protested against the enslavement of the Judahites (II Chron. 28:9).

OG [Ŏg]—LONG-NECKED or BREAD BAKED IN ASHES. *The giant king of Bashan.* This man of huge stature, the last of the Rephaim, was slain at Edrei. The only big things of any note about this massive man, whose conquests lingered long in the imagination of the people (Ps. 135:11; 136:20), were his big body and his big bed (Num. 21:33; 32:33; Deut. 3:1–13).

OHAD [Ŏ′ hăd]—POWERFUL. *The third son of Simeon* (Gen. 46:10; Ex. 6:15).

OHEL [Ŏ′ hel]—BRIGHTNESS or A TENT. *A son of Zerubbabel,* descendant of King Jehoiakim (I Chron. 3:20).

OHOLIAB, AHOLIAB [Ŏ hŏ′ li ăb, Ā hŏ′ li ăb]—TENT OF THE FATHER. *The chief assistant of Bezaleel* (Ex. 31:6; 35:34; 36:1, 2; 38:23).

OLYMPAS [Ŏ lўm′ pas]—HEAVENLY. *A believer at Rome* to whom Paul sent a salutation (Rom. 16:15).

OMAR [Ŏ′ mar]—MOUNTAINEER, ELOQUENT or HE THAT SPEAKS. *A son of Eliphaz* and grandson of Esau. Chieftain of a tribe by the same name (Gen. 36:11, 15; I Chron. 1:36).

OMRI [Ŏm′ rī]—A BUNDLE OF CORN, IMPETUOUS or JEHOVAH APPORTIONS.
1. *Father of Ahab,* captain of the host, afterwards made king instead of Zimri who had slain Elah (I Kings 16:16–30; II Kings 8:26; II Chron. 22:2; Micah 6:16). Omri was one of the most important kings of Israel and the founder of a dynasty. He reigned for twelve years.
2. *A son of Becher,* son of Benjamin (I Chron. 7:8).
3. *A Judahite* of the family of Perez (I Chron. 9:4).
4. *Son of Michael* and a prince of the tribe of Issachar in David's time (I Chron. 27:18).

ON [Ŏn]—SUN or STRENGTH. *A Reubenite chief* who took part in the rebellion of Korah (Num. 16:1). Also the name of the capital of Lower Egypt (Gen. 41:45, 50).

ONAM [Ŏ′ nam]—WEALTHY or STRENGTH.
1. *Son of Shobal,* son of Seir (Gen. 36:23; I Chron. 1:40).
2. *A son of Jerahmeel,* a Judahite (I Chron. 2:26, 28).

ONAN [Ŏ' nan]—STRONG or PAIN. *Second son of Judah,* by the daughter of Shua the Canaanite. The method he adopted to evade the object of his marriage with his brother's widow was evil in God's sight, and He slew him (Gen. 38:4, 8, 9; 46:12; Num. 26:19; I Chron. 2:3).

ONESIMUS [Ŏ nĕs' Ĭ mŭs]—PROFITABLE. *The slave of Philemon,* Paul's convert (Col. 4:7–9; Philemon 10–19). Onesimus ran away from his master and came into contact with Paul, who led him to Christ after they met in Rome. Paul urged him to return to his master and entreated Philemon to receive Onesimus, not as a slave, but as a brother in the Lord. How the apostle approached Onesimus provides us with a beautiful exhibition of Christian courtesy.

ONESIPHORUS [Ŏn e sĭph' o rŭs]—BRINGING ADVANTAGE. *A believer in Ephesus* who befriended Paul (II Tim. 1:16; 4:19).

The Man Who Was Kind to His Friend

From the description Paul gives us of Onesiphorus, he must have been a lovely character. In his revealing essay of this rare character, Alexander Whyte speaks of him as "an elder in the Church of Ephesus, and a better elder there never was."

Much controversy has raged around Paul's cameo of Onesiphorus. Was he adorning the brow of a living man with a garland? Or was he placing a wreath upon the tomb of a saint? Some see in Paul's reference to "the house of Onesiphorus" a proof for the lawfulness of prayers for the dead. But Paul's language does not constitute a prayer, but only a wish or exclamation. The dead are beyond the influence of our intercessions.

There are several traits of the admirable life of Onesiphorus we can profitably meditate upon:

I.   He was repeatedly kind. "He *oft* refreshed me." In the overwhelming heat of his trials, Paul found himself revived when this dear saint came his way. What a blessed ministry it is to refresh the needy children of God!

II.   He associated himself with Paul's suffering. "He was not ashamed of my chain." Some of the apostle's friends did not like to own any connection with a chained man. But not so Onesiphorus. He had a big soul and brought consolation to the manacled prisoner. Many of God's best servants are harassed with chains of sorrow and of affliction. Let us not shrink from helping them.

III.   He made it his business to find Paul. "He sought me out." Matthew Henry says, "A good man will seek opportunities of doing good, and will not shun that offer." Is there someone you should hunt up and cheer?

IV.   He and his house were blessed for kindness shown. "The Lord give mercy to the house of Onesiphorus." Paul was not able to reward his friend for all his gracious solicitation, but the Lord could, and would. In ministering to Paul, Onesiphorous had ministered to the Lord, and of the Lord would be blessed.

OPHIR [Ō′ phûr]—FAT or RICH. *A son of Joktan,* a descendant of Shem (Gen. 10:29; I Chron. 1:23). Also the name of a place in South Arabia famous for gold and other products (I Kings 9.28; Ps. 45:9).

OPHRAH [Ŏph′ rah]—HAMLET or HIND. *A son of Meonothai,* of the tribe of Judah (I Chron. 4:14). Also the name of two different cities (Josh. 18:23; Judg. 6:11).

OREB [Ō′ reb]—A RAVEN or CAUTIOUS. *One of the two Midianite princes* defeated and put to death by Gibeon (Judg. 7:25; 8:3; Ps. 83:11). *Also the name of a rock near Beth-bareh,* whereon Oreb and Zeeb were slain (Judg. 7:25; Isa. 10:26).

OREN [Ō′ ren]—STRENGTH or FINE TREE. *Third son of Jerahmeel,* a Judahite (I Chron. 2:25).

ORNAN [Ŏr′nan]—STRONG or THAT REJOICES. *The Jebusite prince* whose threshing floor was purchased by David for an altar (I Chron. 21:15–25; II Chron. 3:1). Called Araunah in II Samuel 24:16.

OSEE [Ō′ zee]—SALVATION. *The Greek name of the prophet Hosea* (Rom. 9:25).

OSHEA [Ŏ shē′ ă]—GOD SAVES. The name of Joshua son of Nun, servant of Moses (Num. 13:8, 16).

OTHNI [Ŏth′ nī]—LION OF GOD or JEHOVAH IS FORCE. *A son of Shemaiah* and porter of the Tabernacle in David's time (I Chron. 26:7).

OTHNIEL [Ŏth′ nῐ el]—POWERFUL ONE or LION OF GOD. *A son of Kenaz,* younger brother of Caleb, who, after the death of Joshua, judged Israel for forty years. He is the first to be mentioned among the "Judges" (Josh. 15:17; Judg. 1:13; 3:9, 11: I Chron. 4:13). The Othniel mentioned in I Chronicles 27:15 is probably the same person.

Little is recorded of this saviour who came from the tribe of Judah. He followed the Lord with all his heart, and, Spirit-empowered, he fought for Israel and prevailed.

OZEM [Ō′ zem]—STRENGTH or THAT FASTS.
1. *The sixth son of Jesse,* and David's brother (I Chron. 2:15).
2. *A son of Jerahmeel,* son of Hezron (Chron. 2:25).

OZIAS [Ŏ zī' as]—STRENGTH FROM THE LORD. *An ancestor of Jesus Christ* (Matt. 1:8, 9). See Uzziah and Uzza (Ezra 2:49; Neh. 7:51).

OZNI [Ŏz' nī]—ATTENTIVE or JEHOVAH HEARS. *A son of Gad,* the seventh son of Jacob, and founder of the tribal family called Oznites (Num. 26:16). Perhaps the Ezbon of Genesis 46:16.

P

PAARAI [Pā' a raī]—REVELATION OF JEHOVAH or OPENING. *One of David's heroes,* from Aruboth in Judah (II Sam. 23:35). Called Naarai in I Chronicles 11:37.

PADON [Pā' don]—DELIVERANCES or REDEMPTION. *One of the family of Nethinims,* members of which returned from exile (Ezra 2:44; Neh. 7:47).

PAGIEL [Pā' ği el]—GOD MEETS or PREVENTION OF GOD. *A son of Ocran* and chief of the tribe of Issachar, chosen to take a census of the people (Num. 1:13; 2:27; 7:72, 77; 10:26).

PAHATH-MOAB [Pā' hath-mō' ab]—GOVERNOR OF MOAB.
1. *A person, part of whose clan returned from exile with Zerubbabel* (Ezra 2:6; 10:30; Neh. 3:11; 7:11).
2. *Another of the same clan* who returned from exile (Ezra 8:4). Also the name of a family sealing the covenant (Neh. 10:14).

PALAL [Pā' lal]—HE HATH JUDGED. *A son of Uzai,* who assisted in the repair of the city wall (Neh. 3:25).

PALLU, PHALLU [Păl' lū, Phăl' lū]—DISTINGUISHED or WONDERFUL. *The second son of Reuben* and founder of a tribal family (Gen. 46:9; Ex. 6:14; Num. 26:5, 8; I Chron. 5:3).

PALTI, PHALTI [Păl' tī, Phăl' tī]—DELIVERANCE BY GOD or BY RAPHU.
1. *A son of Raphu,* a Benjamite and representative spy (Num. 13:9).
2. *The son of Laish,* to whom Michal, David's wife, was given (I Sam. 25:44). See Paltiel.

PALTIEL, PHALTIEL [Păl' tĭ el, Phăl' tĭ el]—DELIVERER OF THE LORD.
1. *Son of Azzan* and prince of Issachar (Num. 34:26).

2. *Son of Laish* and the man to whom David's wife, Michal, was given (II Sam. 3:15). The same as Palti, No. 2.

PARMASHTA [Pär' mäsh' tä]—SUPERIOR. *A son of Haman, the Jews' enemy* (Esther 9:9).

PARMENAS [Pär' me näs]—FAITHFUL or I ABIDE. *One of the seven disciples* elected to care for Greek-speaking widows, the poor and the financial affairs generally of the Early Church (Acts 6:5).

PARNACH [Pär' näch]—VERY NIMBLE. *The father of Elizaphan,* a chief of Zebulun (Num. 34:25).

PAROSH, PHAROSH [Pä' rŏsh, Phä' rŏsh]—A FUGITIVE or FRUIT OF THE NORTH.
1. *One whose clan returned from exile with Zerubbabel* (Ezra 2:3; Neh. 7:8).
2. *Another whose descendants returned with Ezra* (Ezra 8:3).
3. *One whose descendants had married foreign wives* (Ezra 10:25).
4. *The father of Pedaiah* who helped to repair the city wall (Neh. 3:25).
Also the name of a family that, with Nehemiah, sealed the covenant (Neh. 10:14).

PARSHANDATHA [Pär shăn' da thä]—GIVEN TO PERSIA or DUNG OF IMPURITY. *A son of Haman the Agagite,* who was hanged with the rest of his brothers (Esther 9:7).

PARUAH [Pär ōō' ah]—FLOURISHING or INCREASE. *The father of Jehoshaphat,* one of Solomon's purveyors (I Kings 4:17).

PASACH [Pä' sach]—A DIVIDER or LIMPING. *A son of Japhlet,* an Asherite of the family of Beriah (I Chron. 7:33).

PASEAH, PHASEAH—[Pä sē' ah, Phä sē' ah]—LAME.
1. *A son of Eshton,* grandson of Chelub, a Judahite (I Chron. 4:12).
2. *One whose clan was reckoned among the Nethinims* (Ezra 2:49; Neh. 7:51).
3. *The father of Jehoiada* who helped rebuild the city wall (Neh. 3:6).

PASHUR, PASHHUR [Päsh' ŭr]—FREE or MULTIPLIES LIBERTY.
1. *A son of Malchijah* and head of a priestly family in Jerusalem (I Chron. 9:12; Ezra 2:38; 10:22; Neh. 7:41; 11:12).
2. *A son of Immer the priest,* who put Jeremiah in stocks because of his discouraging predictions (Jer. 20:1-6; 38:1).

3. *A priest who sealed the covenant* (Neh. 10:3).

4. *Son of Melchiah,* a prince of Judah in Jeremiah's day (Jer. 21:1; 38:1).

PATHRUSIM [Păth rōō' sĭm]—THE SOUTH LAND. *A descendant of the fifth son of Mizraim,* son of Ham (Gen. 10:14; I Chron. 1:12).

PATROBAS [Păt' ro băs]—ONE WHO PURSUES THE STEPS OF HIS FATHER. *A Christian in Rome* to whom Paul sent a greeting (Rom. 16:14).

PAUL [Pôul]—LITTLE. *The great apostle to the Gentiles,* whose original name was Saul, a grander title than that of Paul (Acts 13:9).

The Man Who Founded Churches

How impossible it is to sketch in a page or two the worth and work of the chief missionary of early Christianity! Whole volumes have been written on this expositor of a divine revelation, and the first and most prolific contributor to that marvel of literature, the New Testament. Dr. John Clifford suggests that the making of this remarkable man is revealed to us in six photographs, taken at different times, some by himself, others by the Evangelist Luke. They mark the successive stages of Paul's growth and suggest the formative energies operative at the chief epoch of his career. (See Acts 7:58; 22:3; 26:4, 5; Rom. 7; Gal. 1:13, 15; Phil. 3:5, for these epochs).

Here is a brief summary of this energetic, commanding, masterful man, who is one of the great characters, not only in the Bible, but in all history.

I. He was a native of Tarsus, and his father was a Roman—a fact significant in Paul's labors (Acts 21:39; 22:3, 25; 25:16).

II. He was a Pharisee Jew—a Pharisee by *birth,* son of Pharisees, and a Pharisee by *belief,* the hope and resurrection of the dead (Matt. 22:23; Acts 23:5, 6; Phil 3:5).

III. He was a freeborn citizen of Rome (Acts 22:25, 28).

IV. He had had a strict religious training. Circumcision admitted him to the covenant relation of his fathers (Phil. 3:5). As a Jewish boy, he would memorize Scripture (Deut. 6:4–9) and familiarize himself with Jewish history (Deut. 6:20–25).

V. He was a tent maker by trade (Acts 18:3). A Talmudic writer asks, "What is commanded of a father towards his son? To circumcise him, to teach him the law, to teach him a trade." (See I Cor. 4:12; I Thess. 2:9; II Thess. 3:8).

VI. He had received a good education, finishing up under the great philosopher, Gamaliel (Acts 22:3). As Paul quotes from the Greek poets, he must have been well acquainted with Greek philosophy and literature. Paul, however, studied not only in Jerusalem but also in "The College of Experience." Knowledge comes not only from books, but from the responsibility and experience of life (Phil. 4:11–13).

VII.   He had been a persecutor of Christ and of Christians (Acts 8:1–4). Enthusiastically Paul endeavored to stamp out the Christian faith. There is no evidence, however, that he himself killed anyone.

VIII.   He became a new creature in Christ Jesus. The persecutor became a believer (Acts 9:3–9; 22:6–11; 26:12–18). Paul never tired of telling the story of his striking conversion on that Damascus road.

IX.   He had ten years' training for his remarkable work. In Arabia, Damascus, Jerusalem, Syria and Cilicia, Paul spent much time in the study of Scripture and in prayer, knowing that God had called him to function as a witness and minister of the truth (Gal. 1:15–24).

X.   He was a great missionary and church builder. Paul undertook three fruitful missionary journeys, the influence of which cannot be overestimated (Acts 13:1; 28:31). In all his travels, trials and triumphs, Paul was borne along by the one incentive—"To do the will of Him that sent me" (John 6:38; Acts 21:13, 14).

XI.   He was a heart-stirring preacher. Three of his sermons are preserved for us in Acts and serve as models for preachers of all time. Paul relied upon Scripture and appealed to historical facts and prophecy. Ponder his sermon to Jews at Antioch (Acts 13:16–41); his sermon to Gentiles at Athens (Acts 17:22–31).

XII.   He was a most gifted writer. Of the twenty-seven books forming the New Testament, Paul was the author of fourteen of them, if we include Hebrews. How revealing are his valuable epistles! As Robert Speer puts it, "They show us his character with all its varied elements, his religious intensity, his originality, freshness and depth of thought, and his intellectual boldness and strength, while they reveal to us also his rich moral nature and his human heart enlarged by the grace of Christ."

Paul's bodily size and appearance may have been against him, judging from a second century apocryphal description of him: "He was a man little of stature, partly bald, with crooked legs, of vigorous physique, with eyes set close together and nose somewhat hooked." What he was in his appearance mattered little. Paul lived only to win others to Christ and to make Him known. If legend be true, at the end of his honored life, his foes led him out to the Appian Way where they severed his noble head from his frail body, and he died triumphantly for the Lord he dearly loved. To him life was Christ, and death a gain.

PAULUS [Pôu' lus]—LITTLE. *The surname of Sergius,* Roman deputy at Paphos who believed the Gospel when Elymas the sorcerer was struck blind (Acts 13:7, 12).

PEDAHEL [Pĕd' a hĕl]—GOD DELIVERS OT GOD HATH SAVED. *A prince of the tribe of Naphtali,* chosen to divide the land (Num. 34:28).

PEDAHZUR [Pē däh' zur]—THE ROCK DELIVERS or POWERFUL. *Father of Gamaliel*, the chief of Manasseh, chosen to help number the people (Num. 1:10; 2:20; 7:54, 59; 10:23).

PEDAIAH [Pē dā' iah]—JEHOVAH DELIVERS or REDEMPTION OF THE LORD.
1. *Grandfather of King Josiah* (II Kings 23:36).
2. *Son or grandson of Jeconiah* (I Chron. 3:18, 19).
3. *Father of Joel*, ruler of Manasseh in David's reign (I Chron. 27:20).
4. *A son of Parosh* who assisted in the repair of the city wall (Neh. 3:25).
5. *A prince or priest* who stood on Ezra's left hand as he read the Law to the people (Neh. 8:4; 13:13).
6. *A Benjamite of the family of Jeshiah* (Neh. 11:7).

PEKAH [Pě' kah]—OPENING OF THE EYES or WATCHFULNESS. *Son of Remaliah* and a captain under Pekahiah, against whom he conspired in order to reign in his stead. But he reaped as he sowed, for in turn he himself was slain by Hoshea the son of Elah (II Kings 15:25–37; 16:1, 5; II Chron. 28:6; Isa. 7:1).

PEKAHIAH [Pěk a hī' ah]—JEHOVAH HATH GIVEN SIGHT. *Son and successor of Menahem*, king of Israel, and slain by Pekah, after reigning two years (II Kings 15:22–26).

PELAIAH [Pěl a ī' ah]—JEHOVAH HATH MADE ILLUSTRIOUS.
1. *A son of Elioenai*, of the family of David (I Chron. 3:24).
2. *A priest* who explained the Law as Ezra read it (Neh. 8:7).
3. *A Levite* who, with others, sealed the covenant (Neh. 10:10).

PELALIAH [Pěl a lī' ah]—JEHOVAH JUDGES. *A priest* descended from Malchiah (Neh. 11:12).

PELATIAH [Pěl a tī' ah]—JEHOVAH DELIVERS or SETS FREE.
1. *A son of Hananiah* and grandson of Zerubbabel (I Chron. 3:21).
2. *A Simeonite captain*, successful in the war against Amalek (I Chron. 4:42).
3. *A son of Benaiah*, seen in vision by Ezekiel the prophet (Ezek. 11:1, 13). Also the name of a family sealing the covenant (Neh. 10:22).

PELEG [Pě' lěg]—DIVISION. *A son of Eber*, a Shemite, whose name indicates the time before the earth was divided (Gen. 10:25; 11:16–19; I Chron. 1:19, 25).

PELET [Pě' let]—ESCAPE or LIBERATION.

1. *A son of Jahdai* of the family of Caleb, son of Hezron (I Chron. 2:47).

2. *A son of Azmaveth*, one of David's captains (I Chron. 12:3).

PELETH [Pĕ′ leth]—SWIFTNESS or FLIGHT.

1. *A Reubenite* and father of On, who joined Korah, Dathan and Abiram in their revolt against Moses and Aaron (Num. 16:1).

2. *A son of Jonathan*, descendant of Pharez son of Judah (I Chron. 2:33).

PENUEL, PENIEL [Pĕ nū′ el, Pĕ nī′ el]—THE FACE OF GOD.

1. *A man of Judah* and the ancestor of the inhabitants of Gedor (I Chron. 4:4).

2. *A Benjamite of the family of Shashak* (I Chron. 8:25). Also the name of an encampment east of Jordan where Jacob wrestled with the angelic visitor (Gen. 32:30, 31; Judg. 8:8, 9, 17).

PERESH [Pĕ′ resh]—SEPARATE or DISTINCTION. *A son of Machir* son of Manasseh (I Chron. 7:16).

PEREZ, PHARES, PHAREZ [Pĕ′ rĕz, Phă′ rĕz, Phă′ rĕz]—BURSTING THROUGH, A BREACH. *A son of Judah* and one of the twins Tamar bore, who became the father of a tribal family and an ancestor of Jesus Christ (Gen. 38:29; Num. 26:20; Ruth 4:12, 18; I Chron. 27:3; Matt. 1:3).

PERIDA [Pĕ rī′ dă]—SEPARATION. *One of the servants of Solomon* whose descendants returned from exile with Zerubbabel (Neh. 7:57). Called Peruda in Ezra 2:55.

PERSIS [Pûr′ sis]—THAT WHICH DIVIDES. *A saint to whom Paul sent an affectionate greeting.* (Rom. 16:12).

PETER [Pĕ′ tûr]—A ROCK or STONE. *The Greek form of the Aramaic surname, Cephas.* Peter was the brother of Andrew and the son of Jona, or Johanan (Matt. 4:18; John 1:40; I Cor. 1:12).

The Man Who Fell but Rose Again

Peter is another of those outstanding characters in the Bible gallery of men, requiring a book all his own to fully expound his life and labors. From the many references to this *reed* transformed into a *rock*, we gather these facts and features of "The Big Fisherman."

He was a fisherman of Bethsaida, a name meaning "the house of fish." Afterwards he resided in Capernaum, where Jesus frequently lodged during His Galilean ministry.

His father was Jona, or Jonah, and Andrew was his brother. Both sons were fishermen on the Lake of Galilee and were evidently in partnership with Zebedee and his sons.

He first met Christ at Bethany beyond Jordan, where John the Baptist exercised his ministry. Both Peter and Andrew were disciples of the Baptist. It was Andrew who introduced Peter to Christ.

He received a triple call as friend, disciple and apostle. Through daily contact with Jesus, seeing and hearing His words and works, Peter's character was deepened and strengthened.

He was a man with many facets of character. His life can be approached from many angles. He was naturally impulsive (Matt. 14:28; 17:4; John 21:7); tenderhearted and affectionate (Matt. 26:75; John 13:9; 21:15–17); gifted with spiritual insight (John 6:68), yet sometimes slow to apprehend deeper truths (Matt. 15:15, 16); courageous in his confession of faith in Christ, yet guilty of a most cowardly denial (Matt. 16:16; John 6:69; Mark 14:67–71); self-sacrificing yet inclined towards self-seeking (Matt. 19:27), and presumption (Matt. 16:22; John 13:8; 18:10); immovable in his convictions (Acts 4:19, 20; 5:28, 29, 40, 42).

He became the leader and spokesman of the Apostolic Twelve and of the three privileged to witness the raising of Jairus' daughter, the Transfiguration, our Lord's agony in the Garden. He himself became a miracle worker, especially during the time portrayed in Acts.

He made a confession of Christ's deity which became the foundation of the Church, and was appointed steward with authority of the keys, meaning that his was to be the privilege of opening the door of salvation to the Jews.

He miserably failed his Lord in an hour of crisis, being the only disciple to deny Christ, yet he was restored and recommissioned by Jesus after His resurrection. He became the dauntless leader of the infant Church and was foremost to protest his loyalty to Christ. After Pentecost, Peter's ministry appears in four stages:

I.   Jerusalem activities, 29–35 A.D., when James eventually succeeded to leadership of the Church.

II.   Palestinean mission, 35–44 A.D., during which he remained for a while at Lydda and Joppa. He received a call to Caesarea, and in the house of Cornelius opened the door of privilege to the Gentiles.

III.   Syrian mission with Antioch as a center, 44–61 A.D., during which he was accompanied by his wife, who became the pioneer Zenana missionary.

IV.   Rome, 61 A.D. It would seem as if Peter reached here before Paul's release from his first imprisonment, and a few years later suffered martyrdom by crucifixion, as Christ prophesied he would. Legend has it that Peter deemed himself unworthy to die in exactly the same way as his Lord had, and so begged his crucifiers to crucify him upside down.

PETHAHIAH [Pĕth a hī′ ah]—JEHOVAH HATH SET FREE.

1.   *A priest* whose family was appointed by David to the nineteenth course (I Chron. 24:16).

274   ALL THE MEN OF THE BIBLE

2. *A Levite* who had married a foreign wife (Ezra 10:23).

3. *Another Levite* who regulated the devotions of the people (Neh. 9:5). Perhaps the same as No. 2.

4. *A son of Meshezabeel,* of the family of Zorah, and an official of the king of Persia for all matters concerning the returned exiles (Neh. 11:24).

PETHUEL [Pē thū' el]—GOD DELIVERS or THE NOBLE-MINDEDNESS OF GOD. *Father of Joel the prophet* (Joel 1:1).

PEULTHAI, PEULETHAI [Pē ŭl' thaī]—FULL OF WORK or JEHOVAH WORKS. *A Kohathite,* son of Obed-edom and a doorkeeper of the Tabernacle in David's time (I Chron. 26:5).

PHALEC [Phā' lec]—DIVISION. *The father of Ragau* and an ancestor of Jesus Christ. (Luke 3:35). See also Peleg.

PHALLU [Phăl' lū]—ADMIRABLE. *A son of Reuben* (Gen. 46:9).

PHALTI [Phăl' tī]—DELIVERANCE. *A son of Laish,* to whom Michal, David's wife, was given (I Sam. 25:44). See Palti.

PHANUEL [Phā nŭ' el]—VISION OF GOD. Of the tribe of Aser and *father of the prophetess, Anna,* who gave thanks in the Temple at seeing the child Jesus (Luke 2:36, 38).

PHARAOH [Phā' raōh]—SUN, GREAT HOUSE or THE DESTROYER. This was a title used as the general description of the sovereign of Egypt, both with and without the personal name attached. *Pharaoh* is an Egyptian term derived from *Phra,* meaning the sun, to which the Egyptians likened themselves. This is why we often see them represented with a disc or figure of the sun upon their heads. The Pharaohs of Bible times are as follows:

1. *The one who took Sarah from Abraham* (Gen. 12:15-20).

2. *The one who reigned when Joseph was prime minister* (Gen. 37:36; 40-50).

3. *The one who was king of Egypt when Moses was born* and in whose palace Moses was brought up (Ex. 1 and 2).

4. *The one who was king when Moses was fully grown* (Ex. 2:15).

5. *The one who persecuted the Israelites,* and whom Moses and Aaron challenged (Ex. 3:10, 11; 4:21, 22; 5-18).

6. *The one who reigned in the days of Solomon* and whose daughter Solomon married (I Kings 3:1; 7: 8).

7. *The one who was king in the days of Isaiah* (Isa 19:11; 30:2, 3; 36:6).

8. *The one who was father of Bithiah, wife of Mered,* of the tribe of Judah (I Chron. 4:18).

PHARAOH-HOPHRA [Phă' raōh-hŏph' rǎ]—PRIEST OF THE SUN. *Another king of Egypt* whose overthrow by Nebuchadnezzar was foretold by Jeremiah (Jer. 44:30).

PHARAOH-NECHO or NECHOH [Phă' raōh-nĕ' chō, Phă' raōh-nĕ' choh]—PHARAOH THE LAME. *A king of Egypt who fought against Nabopolassar,* king of Assyria, slew King Josiah at Megiddo, bound Jehoahaz at Riblah and made Eliakim his brother king in his stead (II Kings 23:29, 33–35; Jer. 37:5, 7; 46:2).

PHARES—[Phă ' rēz]—BREACH or RUPTURE. *Elder son of Judah by Tamar,* and father of Esrom (Matt. 1:3; Luke 3:33). See Pharez.

PHAREZ, PEREZ [Phă' rĕz, Pĕ' rĕz]—BREAK FORTH VIOLENTLY. *Elder son of Judah by Tamar his daughter-in-law,* and father of Hezron and Hamul. See Phares above (Gen. 38:29; 46:12; Num. 26:20, 21; Ruth 4:12, 18). For Pharzites see Numbers 26:20.

PHICHOL [Phĭ' chol]—GREAT, STRONG or MOUTH OF ALL. *Chief captain of Abimelech,* king of the Philistines in Abraham's time (Gen. 21:22, 32; 26:26).

PHILEMON [Phĭ lĕ' mon]—FRIENDLY or AFFECTIONATE. *A believer in Colossi* to whom Paul addressed a beautiful cameo of knightliness (Philemon 1).

The Man Whose Slave Came Back

Philemon, the rich, influential and pious Colossian was doubtless led to Christ by Paul, who therefore had power in his appeal for the return of Onesimus, Philemon's runaway slave, another convert of the apostle. The prayers, love, generosity, and hospitality of Philemon were ever in Paul's mind (Philemon 5, 7, 21, 22). His well-furnished home was the rendezvous of believers. "The church" met in his home, and, as the leader of the Christian congregation in Colosse, Philemon's influence must have been considerable. The close tie between Paul and Philemon is expressed in the phrase, "beloved and fellow worker."

Paul's approach to Philemon contained a sincere appraisal of character. With instinctive kindness and conscious diplomacy, the apostle praises Philemon for his Christian life and labors. From the lips of Onesimus he had heard often of Philemon's love, faith and liberality. The tired hearts of the poor or otherwise distressed and harassed saints had found in Philemon a pillar of comfort and strength, and Paul, without flattery, extols the one whose life was the fruit of a loving heart. Such a commendation of Philemon prepared his mind for the apostle's request on behalf of Onesimus. Purposely, Paul puts Philemon's love first, seeing it was an act of love he was to prompt him to manifest.

Philemon was urged to deal with Onesimus, not as chattel, but as a Christian. The kingly heart of Paul begged for the forgiveness of one who had sinned against his own name, for Onesimus means *profitable*. How could Philemon spurn such a gracious overture? Did he not owe all he was in grace to Paul? As Martin Luther put it, "Paul strips himself of his right and therefore compels Philemon to betake himself to his right."

Paul also urged that Philemon's forgiveness must be warm, full and free, "Receive him, that is, mine own bowels." The apostle's fervent plea did not fall upon deaf ears. Onesimus was met with the desired reception (Col. 4:9). Legend has it that Onesimus became the Bishop of Berea.

There is something touching in Paul's request to Philemon to pray that he might be liberated and then enjoy the loving hospitality of his home. Paul says that he wrote his letter with his own hand, and his signature eased the way for the return of Onesimus to his wronged master. It also shows us how to act in all graciousness to all men.

Of the Epistle to Philemon, "a little idyll of the progress of Christianity," as it has been called, much might be said. Bishop Handley Moule compares it with the admired letter of Pliny to his friend Sabinianus, to ask pardon for a young freedman who had offended Sabinianus. "It's [Pliny's letter] a graceful, kindly letter, written by a man whose character is the ideal of his age and class: the cultured and thoughtful Roman gentleman of the mildest period of the empire. . . . His heart has not the depth of Paul to clasp Onesimus in his arms and to commend him to Philemon as a friend in God for immortality." Nowhere in literature is there a gem so admirably adapted for the purpose on hand.

PHILETUS [Phĭ lē′ tus]—BELOVED, WORTHY OF LOVE or AMIABLE. *A heretic condemned,* along with Hymenaeus, for denials of the resurrection (II Tim. 2:17).

PHILIP [Phĭl′ ĭp]—WARRIOR or A LOVER OF HORSES.

1. *One of the twelve apostles,* a native of Bethsaida in Galilee (Matt. 10:3; Mark 3:18). Tradition has it that he was the one who requested of Jesus that he might first go and bury his father (Matt. 8:21, 22).

The Man of a Timid, Retiring Disposition

Unlike Andrew and John, Philip did not approach Jesus, but waited till He accosted him and invited him to join His company. Andrew and John found Jesus—Jesus found Philip, whose name is a Greek one both by custom and derivation. A Jewish name he must have had, since all the apostles were Jews, but what it was remains unknown.

In three lists Philip is bracketed with Nathanael as companion and fellow worker. Both were Galileans. This Philip must not be confused with Philip the Deacon, considered below. We never read of the later Philip before Pentecost, nor of Philip the Apostle after Pentecost.

The conversion and call of Philip are expressed simply: "Jesus . . . findeth Philip, and saith unto him, Follow me" (John 1:43). The call to faith and to follow came at once, and Philip was ready for both. The impressive feature of his conversion is that as soon as Christ found him, Philip sought to bring others to Christ. The convert became a soul winner. "Come and see," he said to Nathanael, and he won his friend.

When the hungry multitude gathered around Christ at the Sea of Galilee, Philip was tested by Christ (John 6: 5). Philip was singled out for a test of his faith, and for a great opportunity, which he lost, and with it lost a blessing. Instead of telling the Master that He was able to feed the hungry crowd, Philip made a mental calculation of how much food would be necessary to give each person a portion, and how much it would cost, and declared the project to be impossible. The seeking Greeks were led to Philip but although he sympathized with their request to see Christ, he was afraid and almost lost another opportunity (John 12:21). Yet Philip experienced familiar friendship with Jesus, for did He not call him by name? Slow to apprehend truth, he missed much, but Jesus had nothing but kind words for him (John 14:8). Tradition tells us that Philip died as a martyr at Heirapolis.

2. *A son of Herod the Great* and husband of Herodias. This was the royal Philip, who, disinherited by his father, lived a private life (Matt. 14:3; Mark 6:17; Luke 3:19).

3. *Another son of the above Herod* who was tetrarch of Iturea (Luke 3:1).

4. *One of the seven deacons of the Church at Jerusalem* who had four daughters (Acts 6:5; 8; 21:8).

The Man Who Loved to Evangelize

Philip was not content to serve tables, he loved to preach the Word, and was most successful in revival work. He was not a man to act on his own authority. He was a God-sent and Spirit-controlled evangelist (Acts 8:26–30). When the Spirit said, "Go," he obeyed with alacrity.

I. After the martyrdom of Stephen, Philip preached in Samaria with great success (Acts 8:4–8).

II. He led the Ethiopian to Christ and was the means of introducing Christianity to a heathen country (Acts 8:26–39).

III. He preached from city to city until he reached Caesarea (Acts 8:40).

IV. His four daughters were also preachers.

V. He had a godly home (Acts 21:8), in which Paul loved to stay, for he and Philip were like-minded.

PHILOLOGUS [Phĭ lol′ o gŭs]—A LOVER OF WORDS or OF LEARNING. *A believer in Rome* to whom Paul sent a salutation (Rom. 16:15).

PHINEHAS [Phĭn′ ĕ hăs]—FACE OF TRUST or MOUTH OF A SERPENT.
1. *A son of Eleazar,* one of Aaron's sons, who slew Zimri and Cozbi. He manifested great zeal, was the third high priest of the Jews and discharged his office most faithfully for nineteen years (Ex. 6:25; Num. 25:14, 15).
2. *The younger son of Eli,* the priest and judge of Israel. Phinehas, with his brother Hophni, disgraced the sacred office of priesthood and both were slain (I Sam. 1:3; 2:34; 4:4-19; 14:3).
3. *The father of Eleazar,* a priest who returned with Ezra (Ezra 8:33).

PHLEGON [Phlē′ gon] BURNING or ZEALOUS. *A believer in Rome* to whom Paul sent a loving greeting (Rom. 16:14).

PHURAH [Phū′ rah]—BEAUTY or BEARS FRUIT. *A servant of Gideon* who went down with him to visit the host of Midian (Judg. 7:10, 11). Also called Purah.

PHUT, PUT [Phŭt, Pŭt]—BROW or EXTENSION. *The third son of Ham,* Noah's son (Gen. 10:6; I Chron. 1:8), whose dwelling was in Lybia (Ezek. 27:10) and whose descendants became hired servants of the Syrians (Nah. 3:9).

PHUVAH, PUA, PUAH [Phū′ vah, Pū′ ă, Pū′ ah]—UTTERANCE.
1. *The second son of Issachar* (Gen. 46:13; Num. 26:23; I Chron. 7:1).
2. *The father of Tola* of the tribe of Issachar, who judged Israel after the death of Abimelech (Judg. 10:1).

PHYGELLUS, PHYGELUS [Phȳ jĕl′ lus]—FUGITIVE. *A believer in the province of Asia* who deserted Paul in the latter part of his labors (II Tim.1:15).

PILATE [Pī′ late]—ONE ARMED WITH A DART. *The surname of the fifth Roman procurator of Judea,* who was recalled by Tiberius and banished to Vienna, where tradition says he committed suicide in 41 A.D. (Matt. 27).

The Man Who Sinned Against Conscience

What a different story we would have had if Pilate had obeyed his own conscience and also had followed his wife's intuition and advice. Pilate held office for some twelve years, and by his covetous and cruel government caused himself to be hated both by the Jews and Samaritans. His first name, Pontius, means, "belonging to the sea."

What a man he was for shirking responsibilities! He turned Christ over to the Jewish authorities (John 18:31), and then to Herod (Luke 23:7). When Christ was returned to him, he proposed to inflict a minor penalty (Luke 23:22). When he could not silence the cry of the mob for the blood of Christ, he directed attention to Barabbas (Matt. 27:17), and when the die was cast, engaged in a hypocritical ceremony (Matt. 27:24).

Some authorities affirm that the name Pilate is from "Pilus," a felt cap which was worn by a slave as an emblem of liberty.

PILDASH [Pĭl' dăsh]—FLAME OF FIRE. *Sixth son of Nahor,* Abraham's brother (Gen. 22:22).

PILEHA, PILHA [Pĭl' e hă]—WORSHIP OR PLOWING. *One of those who, with Nehemiah, sealed the covenant* (Neh. 10:24).

PILTAI [Pĭl' taī]—JEHOVAH CAUSES TO ESCAPE. *A priest,* head of his father's house of Moadiah in the days of Joiakim Neh. 12:17).

PINON [Pī' non]—ORE, FIT OR PEARL. *A duke of Edom,* of the family of Esau, who gave his name to a town (Gen. 36:40, 41; I Chron. 1:52).

PIRAM [Pī' ram]—A WILD ASS OR SWIFT. *A Canaanite,* king of Jarmuth, and one of those slain by Joshua before Gideon (Josh. 10:3).

PISPAH [Pĭz' pah]—EXPANSION. *An Asherite,* a son of Jether (I Chron. 7:38).

PITHON [Pī' thon]—HARMLESS OR GIFT OF MOUTH. *A son of Micah* and descendant of King Saul (I Chron. 8:35; 9:41).

POCHERETH [Pŏch' e rĕth]—BINDING. *A servant of Solomon* whose descendants returned from exile with Zerubbabel (Ezra 2:57; Neh. 7:59).

PORATHA [Pŏr' a thă]—HAVING MANY CHARIOTS OR FRUITFUL. *One of the sons of Haman the Agagite.* He died with his brothers (Esther 9:8).

PORCIUS [Pôr'cĭ ŭs]—MEANING UNCERTAIN. *The procurator of the Jews who succeeded Felix* and who sent Paul to Rome. See Festus (Acts 24:27).

POTIPHAR [Pŏt' ĭ phar]—WHO IS OF THE SUN OR A FAT BULL. *The captain of Pharaoh's guard* to whom Joseph was sold by the Midianites. It was his wife who tried to seduce Joseph (Gen. 37:36; 39:1).

POTI-PHERAH, POTI-PHERA [Pŏt' ĭ-phē' rah]—BELONGING TO THE

SUN. *A priest of On and father of Asenath*, Joseph's wife (Gen. 41:45, 50; 46:20).

PROCHORUS [Prŏch' o rŭs]—LEADING IN A CHORUS, DANCE OF LEADER OF SINGERS. *One of the seven disciples chosen to care for widows and the poor* (Acts 6:5).

PUBLIUS [Pŭb' lǐ ŭs]—COMMON. *The chief man and landowner on the island of Melita* when Paul was shipwrecked (Acts 28:7, 8). Now Malta.

PUDENS [Pŭ' denz]—BASHFUL or SHAMEFACED. *A believer in Rome* who united with Paul in sending a greeting to Timothy (II Tim. 4:21).

PUL [Pŭl]—STRONG. *King of Assyria* who invaded Israel in the days of Menahim and was bribed to depart (II Kings 15:19; I Chron. 5:26). Also the name of a tribe or place in Africa (Isa. 66:19).

PUTIEL [Pŭ' tǐ el]—GOD ENLIGHTENS or AFFLICTED BY GOD. *Father-in-law of Eleazar*, son of Aaron (Ex. 6:25).

PYRRHUS [Pўr' rhŭs]—MEANING UNKNOWN. *The father of Sopater of Berea* (Acts 20:4 R.V.).

Q

Among the thousands of persons named in the Bible, there is only one under the letter Q, namely, Quartus, the Corinthian Christian whom Paul calls "a brother" and who joined the apostle in sending a salutation to the Church at Rome. Whether the apostle meant a brother of Erastus or a brother in the Lord is not clear (Rom. 16:23). Probably Quartus was among the seventy Jesus sent forth.

QUARTUS [Quär' tus]—THE FOURTH.
This name is associated with a quarternion of soldiers, that is, a file of four, the usual number for a night watch. Peter was placed under the guard of four quarternions of soldiers, or sixteen soldiers, in order that each might guard him three hours at a time (Acts 12:4).

It may be fitting at this point to discover the significance of the many friends Paul speaks of. Romans and Colossians are unique for their number of personal salutations. Paul himself was such a friendly person that friends gathered around him as moths do around a lighted lamp. In the majority of cases all we have is the mention of a name. Now and again Paul adds a brief, endearing term. But the fact that he mentions many by name, as in the case of Quartus, proves that he must have had some contact with them. Either he had met them on his journeys and they were blessed by his ministry, or they had ministered unto the apostle of their substance. By including their names in his letters, he gave them an imperishable memory.

There were multitudes of others who had labored with Paul in the Gospel, too numerous perhaps to be called by name. The apostle rejoiced, however, that their names, although not mentioned in his lists, were written in the Book of Life, and fully known of the Lord (Phil. 4:3). John also besought Demetrius to greet all his friends by name (III John 14).

R

RAAMAH, RAAMA [Rā′ a mah]—TREMBLING or GREATNESS. *The fourth son of Cush*, eldest son of Ham, and father of Sheba and Dedan (Gen. 10:7; I Chron. 1:9). Also the name of a place on the Persian Gulf and associated with Sheba as trading with Tyre (Ezek. 27:22).

RAAMIAH, REELAIAH [Rā a mī′ ah, Rē el ā′ iah]—JEHOVAH CAUSES TREMBLING. *One of the twelve chiefs* who returned with Zerubbabel (Ezra 2:2; Neh. 7:7).

RABMAG [Răb′ măg]—HEAD OF THE MAGI or CHIEF OF THE MAGICIANS. *The title of Nergal-sharezer, a Babylonian official* of Nebuchadnezzar present at the taking of Jerusalem (Jer. 39:3–13). Mag from magus (magi) might have been applied to a sacred caste in Babylon.

RABSARIS [Răb′ sa rĭs]—GRAND MASTER OF THE EUNUCHS.
1. *An officer under Nebuchadnezzar*, king of Babylon, and possibly the one who ordered the release of Jeremiah (Jer. 39:3–13).
2. *The title of an Assyrian official* sent by Sennacherib, king of Assyria, to Hezekiah to demand the surrender of Jerusalem (II Kings 18:17).

RABSHAKEH [Răb′ sha keh]—HEAD OF THE CUPBEARERS. *The title of the Assyrian military official under King Sennacherib*, who accompanied Rabsaris on the journey to Hezekiah to demand Jerusalem's surrender (II Kings 18:17–37; 19:4–8; Isa. 36:2–22; 37:4–8).

RADDAI [Răd′ da ī]—JEHOVAH SUBDUES or CUTTING UNDER. *The fifth son of Jesse*, the father of David (I Chron. 2:14).

RAGAU [Rā′ gôu]—A FRIEND. *Father of Saruch* and an ancestor of Christ (Luke 3:35). See Reu.

RAGUEL [Rā gū' el]—SHEPHERD, FRIEND OF GOD or JEHOVAH IS A FRIEND. *The father of Hobab* and father-in-law of Moses (Num. 10:29). Also called Jethro and Reuel.

RAHAM [Rā' hăm]—PITY, LOVE or AFFECTION. *The son of Shema,* the son of Hebron, descended from Caleb (I Chron. 2:44).

RAKEM, REKEM [Rā' kem, Rĕ' kem]—FRIENDSHIP or VARIEGATED. *Son of Sheresh,* grandson of Manasseh (I Chron. 7:16).

RAM [Răm]—HIGH or ELEVATED.
1. *Father of Amminadab* and son of Hezron and an ancestor of David and of Christ (Ruth 4:19; I Chron. 2:9, 10; Matt. 1:3, 4). He appears as Arni in Luke 3:33.
2. *Son of Jerahmeel,* brother of Ram, a man of Judah (I Chron. 2:25, 27).
3. *Head of the family to which Elihu belonged.* Also a descendant of Buz (Job 32:2).

RAMIAH [Rā mī' ah]—EXALTED IS JEHOVAH. *A son of Parosh* who had married a foreign wife (Ezra 10:25).

RAMOTH [Rā' moth]—HIGH PLACES or HEIGHTS. *A son of Bani* who put away his foreign wife (Ezra 10:29). Also the name of a Gershonite Levitical city in Issachar (I Chron. 6:73). Perhaps Jarmuth of Joshua 21:29, and Remath of Joshua 19:21. The name is likewise given to a Levitical city in Gilead in Had, and appears as Ramoth-gilead and Ramoth-mizpah (Deut. 4:43; Josh. 20:8; 21:38; I Chron. 6:80). See also south Ramoth (I Sam. 30:27).

RAPHA, RAPHAH [Rā' phă]—HE HAS HEALED, FEARFUL or RELAXATION.
1. *The fifth son of Benjamin* (I Chron. 8:2).
2. *A descendant of Jonathan,* Saul's son (I Chron. 8:37). Called Rephaiah in I Chronicles 9:43.
3. *An ancestor of certain Philistine warriors* slain in David's time and called "the giants" (II Sam. 21:16, 20, 21; I Chron. 20:4–8).

RAPHU [Rā'phu]—FEARED or HEALED. *A Benjamite,* father of Palti, and a spy sent out by Moses to report on Canaan (Num. 13:9).

REAIAH, REAIA [Rē a ī' ah, Rē a ī' ă]—JEHOVAH HAS SEEN or PROVIDED FOR.
1. *A son of Shobal,* son of Judah (I Chron. 4:2). Perhaps the Haroeh, meaning "the seeing one," of I Chronicles 2:52.
2. *Grandfather of Beerah,* prince of Reuben when Israel was carried away to Assyria (I Chron. 5:5).

3. *One of the family of Nethinims* whose descendants returned from exile with Zerubbabel (Ezra 2:47; Neh. 7:50).

REBA [Rē′ bă]—OFFSPRING, FOURTH PART or ONE WHO STOOPS. *One of the five Midianite kings* slain by Israel while they were in the plains of Moab (Num. 31:8; Josh. 13:21).

RECHAB [Rē′ chăb]—COMPANIONSHIP, A HORSEMAN or SQUARE.

1. *A son of Rimmon,* a Beerothite, captain of the band who slew Ish-bosheth in his bed, and who was put to death by David (II Sam. 4:2–9).

2. *Father of Jehonadab* and founder of a tribe known as the "Rechabites" (II Kings 10:15, 23).

The Man Who Vowed to Be Separate

This particular order had its rise in the religious revival that took place under Elijah and Elisha. The tenets of the followers of Rechab were a reaction and a protest against the luxury and license which under Jezebel and Ahab threatened to destroy the simplicity of the ancient nomadic life of Israel. Accordingly, the Rechabites vowed to drink no wine, nor build houses, nor sow seed, nor plant vineyards, but dwell in tents all their days. They were to remember they were strangers in the land. For 250 years they adhered faithfully to their rules but were driven from their tents when in 607 B.C. Nebuchadnezzar invaded Judah.

Of these noteworthy people, whose high moral example was specially commended by God, Dr. Dinsdale Young elaborates on these points:

I.   They honored the memory of the good.
II. They were marked by great simplicity of life.
III. They were worshipers of Jehovah.
IV. They maintained their integrity amid surrounding degeneracy.
V.   They had their principles severely tested.
VI. They received special blessing.

May all of us be found among God's true Rechabites!

3. *A descendant of Hemath a Kenite* (I Chron. 2:55).

4. *The father of Malchiah,* a chief man who, after his return from exile, helped to repair the wall of Jerusalem (Neh. 3:14).

REELAIAH [Rē el ā′ iah]—TREMBLING CAUSED BY JEHOVAH. *One of the principal men who returned from exile* with Zerubbabel (Ezra 2:2). Called Raamiah in Nehemiah 7:7.

REGEM [Rē′ ğĕm]—FRIENDSHIP or A FRIEND. *A son of Jahdai* of the family of Caleb, son of Jephunneh (I Chron. 2:47).

REGEM-MELECH [Rē′ ğem-mē′ lech]—FRIEND OF THE KING. *A man sent from Bethel* with a deputation to question the priest and prophets about a day of fasting and humiliation in memory of the Temple's destruction (Zech. 7:2).

REHABIAH [Rē ha bī′ ah]—JEHOVAH IS COMPREHENSIVE or GOD IS MY EXTENT. *The eldest son of Eliezer* and grandson of Moses (I Chron. 23:17; 24:21; 26:25).

REHOB [Rē′ hŏb]—WIDTH or AN OPEN SPACE.
1. *The father of Hadadezer,* king of Zobah in David's time (II Sam. 8:3, 12).
2. *A Levite* who with Nehemiah sealed the covenant (Neh. 10:11). Also the name of a Levitical town on the boundary line of the territory of Asher (Num. 13:21). Now called Hunin.

REHOBOAM, ROBOAM [Rē hō bō′ am, Rō bō′ am]—FREER OF THE PEOPLE or THE PEOPLE IS ENLARGED. *The son of Solomon by Naamah,* an Ammonitess (I Kings 11:43; 14:21).
At the revolt he was left with only two tribes.

The Man Who Scorned Good Advice

Although Rehoboam was the son of a wise father, he himself had a small mind. From the fifty references to this man, who scorned wise counsel, we can learn a great many facts. Although named as an ancestor of Christ (Matt. 1:7), he was unworthy of such an honor for three reasons.

I. He was dominated by a false principle. Rehoboam entertained an erroneous idea of the relation between a sovereign and his subjects. He was obsessed with the false premise that the subjects existed for the sovereign and not the sovereign for the subjects. Daily surrounded by unscrupulous flatterers who fed his self-importance, Rehoboam came to accept the nonsensical fiction of "the divine right of kings," that led him to treat his subjects as mere puppets to be manipulated for the benefit of his reigning house.

Whether this outlook was the result of a perverse disposition or wrong training may be hard to decide. Rehoboam had been brought up under the autocratic rule of his father, Solomon, to whom *subjects* were synonymous to *slaves.* When the people appealed, it was more against Solomon than Rehoboam, who had not had the opportunity of proving his quality as a king. So the first appeal to Rehoboam was, "Thy father made our yoke grievous," and the son sought to copy the defect of his father. Lamentable failure, however, overtook this feeble son of an illustrious father.

II. He followed the wrong advice. Alexander Whyte introduces his homily on *Rehoboam* with the sentence: "Just by one insolent and swaggering word, King Rehoboam lost for ever the ten tribes of Israel. And all Rehoboam's insane and suicidal history is written in our Bible for the admonition and instruction of all hot-blooded, ill-natured, and insolent-spoken men among ourselves."

What a different history of the Jews would have been written had Rehoboam not followed the advice of reckless counselors. When he went to Shechem, the rallying center of the northern tribes, to be formally crowned as king in succession to Solomon, the people were willing to accept Rehoboam on one condition, namely that he should lighten the burdens imposed upon them by Solomon. This reasonable request, which should have been acceded to without any hesitation, was met with the cautious reply: "Come again to me after three days." But Rehoboam lost a golden opportunity of healing the sores of fears and of preserving the unity of God's ancient people.

First of all, the king sought the advice of the old men who had been counselors of his father and whose ripe experience qualified them to guide Rehoboam. They urged the king to be kind and considerate. "Speak good words unto them, and they will be thy servants forever." But with his mind already made up, he rejected the counsel of the old men, and consulting the opinion of his young, rash companions who had always fed his vanity, he followed their advice and, assuming a haughty attitude, announced that he would add to the yoke of the people. "My father chastised you with whips, but I will chastise you with scorpions."

The effect was instantaneous, and a long-suffering people, smarting for so long under a sense of wrong, refused to be cowed, like the brave Hungarian people, by empty boastings. Thus the slumbering embers of revolt burst into a flame, and the kingdom was rent in twain and Israel's greatness destroyed.

III. He failed to give God the first place. If Rehoboam had consulted the Supreme King of Nations before seeking the advice of old and young men, how beneficial the monarchy would have been. While at the first he posed as the defender of the faith of his fathers and maintained the Temple services with signal fidelity, he failed to render God an undivided homage. The last years of Solomon's brilliant reign were darkened by the recognition of heathen gods and their degrading cults which, along with the fact that Rehoboam was the son of a heathen woman, helped to explain his apostasy. So attempting the impossible, he sought to please God and worship idols at the same time. But said Rehoboam's perfect Descendant: "No man can serve two masters."

At first pious (II Chron. 12:1) Rehoboam fell into such iniquity that an Egyptian scourge came upon the king and the two tribes he ruled. Brief penitence stayed vengeance, but the rot had set in (II Chron. 12: 5, 8). So we leave Rehoboam, who went astray in a threefold direction, ruining himself and the people he sought to govern. He lost the best part of his kingdom and reduced Israel as a whole to a subordinate rank among nations.

REHOBOTH [Rē hō' both]—WIDE SPACES. *The name of an Edomite king* (Gen. 36:37). Also the name of a well dug by the servants of Isaac (Gen. 26:22).

REHUM [Rē' hum]—PITY, BELOVED or MERCIFUL.

1. *One of the principal men who returned with Zerubbabel* (Ezra 2:23; Neh. 12:3). Called Nehum in Nehemiah 7:7.

2. *A Persian chancellor* under Artaxerxes (Ezra 4:8, 9, 17, 23).

3. *A Levite,* son of Bani, who helped to repair the wall at Jerusalem (Neh. 3:17).

4. *A member of the priestly family* that with Nehemiah sealed the covenant (Neh. 10:25).

REI [Rē' ī]—JEHOVAH IS A FRIEND, FRIENDLY or SOCIABLE. *David's friend* when Adonijah attempted to become king. He was likely an officer in the royal guard (I Kings 1:8).

REKEM (Rē' kem]—FRIENDSHIP or VARIEGATION.

1. *One of the five kings of Midian,* slain by Phinehas in the plains of Moab (Num. 31:8; Josh. 13:21).

2. *A son of Hebron* and father of Shammai (I Chron. 2:43, 44).

Also the name of a city in Benjamin, now called Ain-Karim (Josh. 18:27).

REMALIAH [Rĕm a lī' ah]—JEHOVAH INCREASES, JEHOVAH HATH ADORNED or EXALTATION OF THE LORD. *The father of Pekah,* who slew Pekahiah and reigned in his stead (II Kings 15:25–37; 16:1, 5; II Chron. 28:6; Isa. 7:1–9; 8:6).

REPHAEL [Rē' pha el]—GOD IS A HEALER, GOD HATH HEALED or MEDICINE OF GOD. *A Kohathite,* son of Shemaiah, the first-born of Obed-edom, and a member of a family of Tabernacle gatekeepers (I Chron. 26:7).

REPHAH [Rē' phah]—RICHES or HEALING. *A grandson of Ephraim,* through Beriah, and an ancestor of Joshua (I Chron. 7:25).

REPHAIAH [Rĕph a ī' ah]—JEHOVAH HEALS.

1. *A head of a family in David's house,* a Judahite (I Chron. 3:21).

2. *A Simeonite captain* who helped to lead the expedition into Edom (I Chron. 4:42).

3. *A son of Tola,* son of Issachar (I Chron. 7:2).

4. *A Benjamite* and descendant of Saul (I Chron. 9:43) and called Rapha in I Chronicles 8:37.

5. *One who helped Nehemiah* repair the wall (Neh. 3:9).

RESHEPH [Rē' sheph]—HASTE or A FLAME. *A son of Rephah,* grandson of Sarah the daughter of Ephraim (I Chron. 7:25).

REU, RAGAU [Rē' ū, Rā' gôu]—FRIEND or FRIENDSHIP. *A son of Peleg,* the fourth from Shem, and father of Shereg. An ancestor of

Abraham (Gen. 11:18–21; I Chron. 1:25). Like other men of that time, Reu was long-lived.

REUBEN [Reōō' ben]—BEHOLD A SON or VISION OF THE SON. *The first-born of Jacob by Leah* and founder of a tribal family (Gen. 29:32; 30:14).

The Man of Forfeited Privileges

In Jacob's dying blessing (Gen. 49:3, 4) are three circumstances concerning Reuben that seem to summarize his tragic story.

I. The privileges that should have been his. As the eldest son he was entitled to three portions above his brethren, namely, the priesthood, the birthright and the kingdom. But all three were forfeited and given to the others.

By right of birth, elevation to priestly eminence should have been Reuben's, but he proved himself unworthy of this "excellence of dignity." Impetuosity and instability totally unfitted him for the priesthood which went to Levi.

By right of birth, royal dignity should have been his as the first-born of his tribe, but Judah prevailed and the right of the scepter passed from Reuben to Judah.

By right of birth, Reuben should have been the head of the representative tribe. He was the beginning of his father's strength (Deut. 21:17), and though the eldest son, forfeited a double inheritance in the land. This right of the firstborn became Joseph's (Deut. 21:17). Reuben carried little importance in the history of Israel.

II. His irresolute and vacillating nature. Reuben revealed characteristics unbefitting one upon whom high responsibilities should have devolved. He lacked the tenacity and courage one expects to find in the eldest son of the family. He had none of his father's transformed nature after he became Israel.

Jacob described his son as being "unstable as water" (Gen. 49:4). Water is a suggestive symbol of instability. Think of the waterfall, as it splashes against the ledges of a rock! The rock abides; the fickle stream moves on in never-ceasing restlessness. Jacob saw in his firstborn son all the evidences of instability. Although a double excellency was within the reach of Reuben his father had to say of him, "Thou shalt not excel." The reward of unreliability and instability is inferiority. "Thou shalt not excel." The tribe of Reuben never rose to prominence and was among the first to be carried into captivity (I Chron. 5:26). In the blessing of Moses, Reuben's doom is sealed. Nothing but a depleted remnant would be his. "Let his men be very few" (Deut. 33:6). No judge, no prophet, no hero sprang from Reuben. By his sin Reuben had permanently impoverished his posterity.

III. His despicable crime. Reuben lost all the honors that should have been his because of his adulterous act with Bilhah, his father's concubine. Jacob, in his blessing, attributes Reuben's forfeited privileges to this heinous sin — a sin which brought a curse upon him.

This evil stream flowed on, for two Reubenites were ringleaders with Korah in assailing God's established order, and perished because of their defiance of God. Deborah, in her patriotic song, Judges 5, rebuked the children of Reuben for characteristic selfishness. Again the innate fickleness appeared.

Can it be that in spite of all his sad failures, there is a ray of hope for Reuben in the prophetic benediction of Moses, "Let Reuben live and not die" (Deut. 33:6)? Is this an evidence of divine grace—life for a sinner whose sin merited death? There is a gate of Reuben in the Golden City, and a tribe of Reuben in the Israel of God (Rev. 7:5). Reuben's name is *not first*, yet through grace it is there. "Let Reuben live and not die." Heaven will be full of Reubens who should have died but who live forevermore to sing the praises of God's redeeming grace.

REUEL [Reoo' el]—FRIEND OF GOD or GOD IS A FRIEND.

1. *A son of Esau* by Bashemath, daughter of Ishmael (Gen. 36:4–17; I Chron. 1:35, 37).

2. *The father-in-law of Moses* (Ex. 2:18). Called Jethro and Raguel (Num. 10:29).

3. *The father of Eliasaph,* and a Gadite (Num. 2:14). Called Deuel in Numbers 1:14.

4. *A Benjamite,* a son of Ibnijah, belonging to Jerusalem (I Chron. 9:8).

REZIA [Rē zī' ă]—JEHOVAH IS PLEASING. *An Asherite,* a son of Ulla (I Chron. 7:39). Also spelled Rizia.

REZIN [Rē' zin]—DOMINION or GOOD WILL.

1. *The last king of Damascus,* in the days of Jothan, king of Judah. He was slain by Tiglath-pileser (II Kings 15:37; 16:5–9; Isa. 7:1–8; 8:6; 9:11). Damascus sustained a siege of more than a year's duration, but was eventually taken and its king slain (II Kings 16:9).

2. *A founder of a family of Nethinims* whose descendants returned with Zerubbabel from captivity (Ezra 2:48; Neh. 7:50).

REZON [Rē' zŏn]—PRINCELINESS or NOBLE. *A son of Eliadah* and a subject of Hadadezer, king of Zobah. Although one of the king's military officers, he fled to Damascus, where he founded a kingdom and became a thorn in Solomon's side. His successors were bitter adversaries of Israel (I Kings 11:23).

RHESA [Rhē' să]—WILL or COURSE. *A descendant of Zerubbabel* and ancestor of Christ (Luke 3:27).

RIBAI [Rī' baī]—JEHOVAH CONTENDS or CONTENTIOUS. *The father of*

Ittai or Ithai, a Benjamite of Gibeah and one of David's valiant men (II Sam. 23:29; I Chron. 11:31).

RIMMON [Rĭm' mon]—A POMEGRANITE. *The father of two captains who served under King Ishbosheth* and became his murderers (II Sam. 4:2–9). Rimmon is also the name of a Syrian god, looked upon "as air-, weather-, and storm-god assimilated by popular etymology to the word for 'pomegranite,' " hence the meaning of the name. The symbol of the beneficent deity was the axe and a bundle of lightning-darts. It was in Rimmon's temple at Damascus that Naaman worshiped.

Rimmon is likewise the name of a city in Simeon now known as Um-er-Rumamin (Josh. 15:32; Zech. 14:10), and of a rock in Benjamin near Gibeah, now called Rummon or Rammun (Judg. 20:45, 47; 21:13), and of two cities, one in Simeon (I Chron. 4:32) and the other in Zebulon, spoken of in Hebrews as Rimmons (I Chron. 6:77).

RINNAH [Rĭn' nah]—A WILD CRY or STRENGTH. *A man of Judah,* a son of Shimon (I Chron. 4:20).

RIPHATH [Rĭ' phăth]—A CRUSHER OF ENEMIES. *One of the sons of Gomer,* son of Japheth (Gen. 10:3; I Chron. 1:6). Another reading is Diphath (I Chron. 1:6).

ROHGAH [Rōh' gah]—CLAMOR or ALARM. *A son of Shamer,* grandson of Beriah, son of Asher (I Chron. 7:34).

ROMAMTI-EZER [Rō măm' tĭ-ē' zûr]—HIGHEST HELP or I HAVE EXALTED HELP. *A son of Heman,* a singer in the Tabernacle in David's time, who was among the twenty-fourth course of singers (I Chron. 25:4, 31).

ROSH [Rŏsh]—A CHIEF, PRINCE or THE BEGINNING.
1. *A son of Benjamin* who went down to Egypt with Jacob and his sons (Gen. 46:21; Num. 26:38).
2. *The prince of northern people* mentioned along with Meshech and Tubal (Ezek. 38:1, 2; 39:1, R.V.).

The Man of the Northern Confederacy

It is not very difficult to prove that God, by His Spirit, gave to Ezekiel over twenty-five hundred years ago, a clear picture of the part Russia would play in the development and control of a Northern Confederacy of Nations. The R.V. of Ezekiel 38:2 reads: "Gog the land of Magog, the Prince of Rosh, Meshach and Tubal." Rosh, mentioned as a descendant of Benjamin (Gen. 46:21) means, "a prince over." The Araxes were called "Rhos."

That "the Prince of Rosh" is Asiatic Russia receives confirmation from the *Imperial Dictionary.* "Evidence exists of an ancient people called Rosh, or Rhos, supposed to be the original stem from which

the Russia or modern Russians have derived their race and name."
The saintly scholar, Bishop Lowther says: "Rosh, taken as a proper
name, in Ezekiel, signifies the inhabitants of Scythia, from whom
modern Russians derived their name." The Orientals called the
people who dwelt on the banks of the River Araxes "Rhos" or "Rosh,"
and the Arabic name for that river was also called "Rosh." Russia
was once known as Muscovy. It was Ivan IV, or "Ivan the Terrible,"
as he was called, who was the first to use the title, "Czar of Russia."

The discovery of Russia in Ezekiel's prophecy is not a fundamen-
talist invention of this mid-century. Prophetic students have been
accused of pressing Scripture interpretation beyond what is written
in this connection. But long before Russia became the threat to world
freedom, progress and peace she is today, Biblical scholars recognized
her portrayal in Ezekiel.

We must conclude therefore, that Ezekiel's "episode of Gog's invasion" (A. B. Davidson) points irrefutably and undeniably to the
Russians.

RUFUS [Roō' fus]—RED.
1. *A son of Simon the Cyrenian* who was compelled to bear the
Cross (Mark 15:21).
2. *A believer in Rome* greeted by Paul as "the chosen in the Lord"
together with "his mother and mine" (Rom. 16:13). Some writers feel
that these two may have been the same persons. "Simon's widow might
have emigrated to Rome with her two sons, where they became
people of eminence in the Church, and that this is the reason why
the brothers are mentioned by Mark (15:21), who probably wrote in
Rome" (*Hastings Dictionary*).

S

SABTA, SABTAH [Săb' tă, Săb' tah]—BREAKING THROUGH. *The third
son of Cush,* son of Ham, whose descendants dwell in the middle of
South Arabia (Gen. 10:7; I Chron. 1:9).

SABTECHA, SABTECHAH [Săb' te chă, Săb' te chah]—SURRENDER.
The youngest son of Cush, whose descendants dwelt on the east side of
the Persian Gulf (Gen. 10:7; I Chron. 1:9).

SACAR [Sā' cär]—HIRED or MERCHANDISE.
1. *Father of Ahiham,* one of David's heroes (I Chron. 11:35).
Called Sharar in II Samuel 23:33.
2. *A son of Obed-edom,* a Tabernacle gatekeeper in David's time
(I Chron. 26:4).

SADOC [Sā' dŏc]—RIGHTEOUS, JUST. *Son of Agor* and father of Achim, and an ancestor of Christ (Matt. 1:14). Called Zadoc in Ezra 7:2.

SALA, SALAH [Sā'lă, Sā' lah]—MEANING UNCERTAIN, PERHAPS FIRM. *Son of Arphaxad,* third son of Shem, and father of Eber (Gen. 10:24; 11:12-15; Luke 3:35).

SALATHIEL, SHEALTIEL [Sā' lă' thǐ el, Shē ăl' tǐ el]—ARK OF LOAN OF GOD. *Son or grandson of Jeconiah,* son of Jehoiakim, king of Judah (I Chron. 3:17; Ezra 3:2, 8; 5:2; Hag. 1:2, 12, 14; 2:2, 23). Ancestor of Christ (Matt. 1:12; Luke 3:27).

SALLAI [Săl' la ī]—EXALTED OF REJECTED.
1. *Son of Meshullam,* a chief of the family of Benjamites living in Jerusalem (Neh. 11:8).
2. *A priest* who returned from exile with Zerubbabel (Neh. 12:20). Also called Sallu in Nehemiah 11:7.

SALMA [Săl' mă]—STRENGTH, FIRMNESS. *A son of Caleb* son of Hur and father of Bethlehem (I Chron. 2:51, 54).

SALMON, SALMA, SALMAH [Săl' mŏn, Săl' mă]—PEACEABLE. *The father of Boaz,* Ruth's husband, and a man of Judah. Also an ancestor of Christ (Ruth 4:20, 21; I Chron. 2:11; Matt. 1:4, 5; Luke 3:32). Salmon is also the name of a mountain (Ps. 68:14).

SALU [Sā' lu]—UNFORTUNATE OF EXALTED. *A Simeonite,* father of Zimri whom Phinehas slew (Num. 25:14).

SAMGAR-NEBO [Săm' gär-nē' bō]—BE GRACIOUS, NEBO. *A prince of Nebuchadnezzar,* who sat in the gate at Jerusalem (Jer. 39:3).

SAMLAH [Săm' lah]—GARMENT OF ASTONISHMENT. *The fifth of the ancient kings of Edom,* a native of Masrekah (Gen. 36:36, 37; I Chron. 1:47, 48).

SAMSON [Săm' son]—DISTINGUISHED, STRONG OF SUN-MAN.
The Man of Contrasts
One of the most renowned of the Hebrew judges, Samson was a son of the Danite, Manoah, who judged Israel for twenty years. He was unique in that his birth and manner of life were foretold. Supernaturally endowed, he killed a lion, thirty Philistines and one thousand men. He broke the strongest bands, carried off the gates of Gaza and pulled down the Temple of Dagon (Judg. 13:24—16:30). He is found among the illustrious in Faith's Hall of Fame (Heb. 11:32).

As long as Samson remained a Nazarite he was unconquerable. He only of all the judges of whom we have any history, does everything single-handed and alone. Samson never called the armies of Israel together; he asked no assistance. What he did, he did alone in his own unconquerable strength. We are not told how he managed his court, nor about the wisdom of his judgments, nor about the manner of Israel's life for a whole generation under her gigantic judge.

The complex story of Samson teaches us the evils of mixed or foreign marriages (Judg. 14:3), the laxity of sexual relations and of playing with temptation. C. W. Emmet says that Samson "teaches us that bodily endowments, no less than spiritual, are a gift from God, however different may be our modern conception of the way in which they are bestowed, and that their retention depends on obedience to His laws."

But if Samson stands as an example "of impotence of mind in body strong," he also stands, in Milton's magnificent conception, as an example of patriotism and heroism in death, to all who "from his memory inflame their breast to matchless valour and adventures high."

The deadly results of Samson's self-indulgence after he broke his Nazarite vow, appear in their dark and ominous order:

Self-confidence: "I will go out" (Judg. 16:20).

Self-ignorance: "He wist not" (Judg. 16:20).

Self-weakness: "The Philistines laid hold on him" (Judg. 16:21).

Self-darkness: "They put out his eyes" (Judg. 16:21).

Self-degradation: "They brought him *down* to Gaza" (Judg. 16:1-3, 21).

Self-bondage: "They bound him with fetters" (Judg. 16:21).

Self-drudgery: "He did grind in the prison-house" (Judg. 16:21).

Self-humiliation: "Call for Samson, that he may make us sport" (Judg. 16:25, 27).

Samson stands out as a man of striking contrasts. He had a kind of Dr. Jekell and Mr. Hyde being.

I. He was separated as a Nazarite (Judg. 13:5), yet tampered with evil associations (Judg. 14:1-3).

II. He was occasionally Spirit-possessed (Judg. 13:25; 15:14), yet yielded to carnal appetites (Judg. 16:1-4).

III. He appeared childish in some of his plans (Judg. 15:4), yet was courageous in battle (Judg. 15:1-4).

IV. He was mighty in physical strength (Judg. 16:3, 9, 13, 14), yet weak in resisting temptation (Judg. 16:15-17).

V. He had a noble beginning but a sad end (Judg. 16:30).

SAMUEL [Săm' u el]—HEARD, ASKED OF GOD, OFFERING OF GOD or APPOINTED BY GOD.

The Man Who Had God's Ear

Samuel was the earliest of the Hebrew prophets after Moses and the last of the Judges. He was the son of Elkanah of Ephraim (I Sam.

1:1), and of Hannah, Elkanah's other wife. Samuel was her first-born and possibly saw the light of day at Ramah (I Sam. 2:11; 7:17). Hannah bore Elkanah five other children (I Sam. 2:21). There are many points of resemblance between Hannah and Mary, the mother of our Lord (I Sam. 2:1–11 with Luke 1:46–56).

Samuel was a Nazarite (I Sam. 1:11), the character of the vow being:

Abstinence from intoxicating drinks; self-denial and separation from sensual indulgence.

Free growth of hair, indicating the complete dedication of all the power of the head to God.

Avoidance of contact with a dead body as a token of absolute purity of life (Num. 6).

Samuel's call to service came when weaned and dedicated to God by his mother (I Sam. 1:24–28; 3:1–18). When Samuel was around twelve years of age he received his first revelation of the Lord, which was a clear message of doom against Eli's guilty house (I Sam. 3:11–14).

Samuel's ministry was of a fourfold nature. We see him:

I.   As a prophet. As a prophet of the Lord (I Sam. 2:27–35; 3:19–21; 8:22), his faithfulness was a rebuke to the unfaithfulness of Eli. To the end of his days Samuel exercised the office of prophet and his ministry was not in vain. Under the impact of his courageous pronouncements Israel renounced her idolatry and shook off the yoke of the Philistines.

II.   As an intercessor. Samuel was born in answer to prayer and his name constantly reminded him of the power of prayer and of the necessity of maintaining holy intimacy with God. Samuel deemed it a sin not to pray for others (I Sam. 7:5–8; 8:6; 12:17, 19, 23; 15:11).

III.   As a priest. Although Samuel was only a Levite and not a priest by descent, the words, "I will raise up," imply an extraordinary office (I Sam. 2:35; 7:9, 10; 13:8–10; Judg. 2:16). The exercises of priestly functions are proved by the following:

By intercession (I Sam. 7:9).

By offering sacrifices (I Sam. 7:9, 10).

By benediction (I Sam. 10:17, 25).

By anointing kings (I Sam. 10:1; 16:13).

IV.   As a judge. Of Samuel it is said that he "judged Israel all the days of his life." Even after the government of Israel had changed from that of a theocracy to a monarchy, Samuel still acted as a circuit judge, going from place to place giving divine judgment upon moral and spiritual questions, and maintaining in the hearts and lives of the people the law and authority of Jehovah (I Sam. 7:15–17). The appointment of his own sons as Judges to succeed him (I Sam. 8:1) was a parental mistake, for their wickedness gave the people reason for demanding a king (I Sam. 8:5).

The universal reverence and love the nation had for Samuel is proven by the grief manifested at his death. "All Israel lamented him" (I Sam. 25:1; 28:3). His passing as one of the great heroes of

Hebrew history makes impressive reading. Faith was the animating principle of his honored life and labors (Heb. 11:32).

SANBALLAT [Săn băl′ lat]—THE ENEMY IS SECRET. *A Horonite,* an enemy of the Jews. He opposed Nehemiah in the building of the wall (Neh. 2:10, 19; 4:1, 7; 6:1–14; 13:28). This most inveterate of Nehemiah's opponents derided the efforts of repair, and sought to hinder the work of the builders.

SAPH [Săph]—CONSUMMATION or PRESERVER. *One of the four Philistine giants slain by David's heroes* (II Sam. 21:18; I Chron. 20:4). Also called Sippai.

SARAPH [Sā′ raph]—BURNING. *A descendant of Shelah,* son of Judah, who exercised dominion in Moab (I Chron. 4:22).

SARGON [Sär′ gon]—THE CONSTITUTED KING or SNARES. *A king of Assyria* who succeeded the last Shalmaneser. He was a predecessor of Sennacherib (Isa. 20:1).

SARSECHIM [Sär sē′ chim]—CHIEF OF THE EUNUCHS. *A prince of Babylon* when Nebuchadnezzar took Jerusalem (Jer. 39:3).

SARUCH [Sā′ ruch] BRANCH—*Father of Nachor and son of Ragau,* and an ancestor of Christ (Luke 3:35).

SAUL, SHAUL [Sôul]—ASKED FOR or DEMANDED.
1. *The son of Kish,* and first king of Israel (I Sam. 9–11).
   A Man Who Lost His Kingdom
No man among Bible men had so many chances thrust upon him to make a success of life, and no man ever so missed them. Saul not only missed great opportunities, he deliberately abused them. His sun rose in splendor, but set in a tragic night. The downgrade of his life is the old familiar story of pride, egotism and the abuse of power leading to moral degradation and ruin. Here are the steps down the ladder:
He was a man anointed and filled with the Spirit. (I Sam. 11:6).
In his early years he was humble and practiced self-control (I Sam. 10:22; 10:27; 11:13).
Self-will restricted his influence (I Sam. 13:12, 13).
He became disobedient and was guilty of rash vows (I Sam. 15:11–23).
Jealousy prompted him to hunt and harm David (I Sam. 18:8; 19:1).
He patronized the superstition he had forbidden (I Sam. 28:7).
Wounded in battle, he ended up a suicide (I Sam. 31:4).
Having already destroyed his moral life, he ultimately destroyed his physical life. Saul's sad story is repeated almost daily.

2. *The sixth of the ancient kings of Edom,* from Rehoboth on the Euphrates (Gen. 36:37, 38).

3. *The original name of Paul,* a native of Tarsus (Acts 7:58). For fuller treatment see Paul.

SCEVA [Scē' vă]—I DISPOSE. *A member of one of the Jewish families* from which high priests were ordinarily chosen. His seven sons were exorcists, that is, they professed to have power over demons by naming over them the name of Jesus (Acts 19:14).

SEBA [Sē' bā]—OLD MAN. *The eldest son of Cush,* son of Ham (Gen. 10:7; I Chron. 1:9). Also the name of his land in northern Ethiopia (Ps. 72:10; Isa. 43:3).

SECUNDUS [Sē cŭn' dus]—SECONDARY OR FAVORABLE. *A believer of Thessalonica* who accompanied Paul from Macedonia to Asia Minor (Acts 20:4). Perhaps he carried alms from his city for needy saints.

SEGUB [Sē' gub]—EXALTED, PROTECTION OR FORTIFIED.

1. *The youngest son of Hiel the Benjamite* who rebuilt Jericho, and who was possibly sacrificed by his father when the gates were set up in defiance of a curse (I Kings 16:34).

2. *A son of Hezron,* grandson of Judah (I Chron. 2:21, 22).

SEIR [Sē' ûr]—ROUGH or WOODED. *The grandfather of Hori,* ancestor of the Horites (Gen. 36:20, 21; I Chron. 1:38). Also the name of a hilly region south of the Salt Sea (Gen. 14:6).

SELED [Sē' lĕd]—EXULTATION. *A man of Judah* of the family of Jerahmeel and grandson of Pharez, son of Judah (I Chron. 2:30).

SEMACHIAH [Sĕm a chī' ah]—JEHOVAH SUPPORTS or SUSTAINS. *A son of Shemaiah* and a Levite gatekeeper of the Tabernacle in David's time (I Chron. 26:7). Perhaps the same as Ismachiah (II Chron. 31:13).

SEMEI [Sĕm' e ī]—HEAR or OBEY. *An ancestor of Jesus Christ* (Luke 3:26), who lived after the exile. See Shimei.

SENNACHERIB [Sĕn năch' e rĭb]—THE MOON-GOD, SIN (the moon-god) HATH INCREASED THE BROTHERS or DESTRUCTION OF THE SWORD. *A son of Sargon* who succeeded to the throne after the murder of his father (II Kings 18:13; 19:16, 20, 36; II Chron. 32; Isa. 36:1; 37:17, 21, 37).

The Man Who Built Nineveh

This Assyrian king saw his boasted army destroyed in one night. He himself was slain by two of his sons in Nineveh in the Temple of Nisroch (II Kings 19:37). Sennacherib's great achievement in this area was the creation of Nineveh as a metropolis of the empire. It was he who built the wonderful palace of Konyungik and the great wall of Nineveh.

The Assyrian king's invading hosts marching through Judah leaving destruction behind them were vividly described by Byron in *The Destruction of Sennacherib:*

> The Assyrians came down like the wolf on the fold,
> And his cohorts were gleaming in purple and gold;
> And the sheen of their spears was like stars on the sea,
> When the blue wave rolls nightly on deep Galilee.

Fear seized the heart of Hezekiah as he faced the threats of Sennacherib and Rabshakeh, but the courage and faith of Isaiah were a strong tower to the troubled king and the inhabitants of Jerusalem. The prophet reminded Hezekiah that Jehovah, and not the horses, material force and human cleverness, was the hope of Judah. Jerusalem was God's city and He would preserve it (Isa. 37:33, 35). As we know, the city was saved by a remarkable providence. God commissioned one angel to slay one hundred eighty-five thousand Assyrians. If He can do that with one angel, what is He not able to do with a legion of the angelic army?

SENUAH [Sĕ nū' ah]—THE VIOLATED. *A Benjamite,* father of Judah who was second in charge over Jerusalem in Nehemiah's day (Neh. 11:9).

SEORIM [Sĕ ō' rim]—FEAR, DISTRESS. *A priest of David's time* to whom the fourth charge of the sanctuary was given by lot (I Chron. 24:8).

SERAIAH [Sĕr a ī' ah]—JEHOVAH IS PRINCE, THE LORD IS MY PRINCE, or SOLDIER OF THE LORD.

1. *One of king David's scribes* (II Sam. 8:17; see I Chron. 18:16 for Shavsha).

2. *The son of Azariah* and chief priest at Jerusalem when Nebuchadnezzar took it. This Seraiah, along with other renowned captives, was put to death at Riblah (II Kings 25:18; I Chron. 6:14; Ezra 7:1; Jer. 52:24).

3. *A son of Tanhumeth,* from Netophah, whom Gedaliah advised to submit to the Chaldeans. He was one of "the captains of the forces" (II Kings 25:23; Jer. 40:8).

4. *The second son of Kenez,* brother of Othniel and father of Joab (I Chron. 4:13, 14).

5. *A prince of Simeon,* son of Asiel and grandfather of Jehu, who drove furiously (I Chron. 4:35).

6. *One of the twelve leaders, a priest who returned from exile with Zerubbabel* (Ezra 2:2; Neh. 10:2; 12:1, 12).

7. *A priest, son of Hilkiah,* dwelling in Jerusalem after the exile and called "ruler of the house of God" (Neh. 11:11; 12:1).

8. *A chief man, son of Aziel,* and sent by Jehoiakim to apprehend Jeremiah and Baruch (Jer. 36:26).

9. *A son of Neriah and brother of Baruch,* a prince of Judah who went to Babylon with Zedekiah (Jer. 51:59, 61). For "quiet prince" the R.V. has "chief chamberlain."

SERED [Sē' red]—DELIVERENCE or FEAR. *The eldest son of Zebulun* and founder of a tribal family, the Seredites (Gen. 46:14; Num. 26:22, 26).

SERGIUS PAULUS [Sûr' jǐ ǔs Paōō' lus]—SMALL or LITTLE. *Proconsul or Roman deputy of Cyprus* when Paul and Barnabas visited it, and who was converted to God by Elymas or Bar-jesus being struck with blindness (Acts 13:7). It is said of Sergius that he:

Was a prudent man.

Desired to hear the word of God.

When he saw what was done, believed.

Was astonished at the doctrine of the Lord.

SERUG [Sē' rug]—SHOOT, BRANCH or FIRMNESS. *A son of Reu,* father of Nahor, father of Terah, and so an ancestor of Abraham (Gen. 11:20–23; I Chron. 1:26).

SETH, SHETH [Sĕth, Shĕth]—COMPENSATION, APPOINTED or SUBSTITUTED. *The third son of Adam and Eve,* born after the murder of Abel. Seth came as Abel's substitute (Gen. 4:25, 26; 5:3–8; I Chron. 1:1; Luke 3:38). Seth became the father of Enos, and died at the age of 912. When Eve said, "God hath set for me another seed instead of Abel," the word she used for "set" was *shāth* or *shĕth,* meaning "setting."

SETHUR [Sē' thur]—SECRETED, HIDDEN. *The son of Michael,* the representative spy sent from the tribe of Asher (Num. 13:13).

SHAAPH [Shā' ǎph]—UNION, FRIENDSHIP.

1. *A son of Jahdai,* son of Caleb, by his concubine Ephah (I Chron. 2:47).

2. *A son of Caleb,* son of Hezron, by his concubine Maachah (I Chron. 2:49).

SHAASHGAZ [Shā ǎsh' gǎz]—SERVANT OF THE BEAUTIFUL. *A chamberlain of King Ahasuerus,* who had charge of the king's concubines (Esther 2:14).

SHABBETHAI [Shăb' be thaī]—SABBATH BORN.

1. *A Levite* who assisted in the matter of those who had taken strange wives (Ezra 10:15).
2. *One who explained the law* read to the people by Ezra (Neh. 8:7).
3. *A chief Levite* in Jerusalem after the exile (Neh. 11:16).

SHACHIA [Shā chī' ă]—CAPTIVE OF THE LORD. *A Benjamite,* son of Shaharaim (I Chron. 8:10).

SHADRACH [Shā' drach]—DECREE OF MOON-GOD or SOFT, TENDER. The name given by the prince of the eunuchs at Babylon to *Hananiah, one of the three faithful Hebrew youths* (Dan. 1:7; 3:12–30). With his two companions, Meshach and Abednego, Shadrach was miraculously delivered from the burning fiery furnace.

SHAGE, SHAGEE [Shā' gē]—WANDERING or ERRING. *Father of Jonathan the Hararite,* one of David's mighty men (I Chron. 11:34). Some read Agee instead of Shagee on the authority of II Samuel 23:11.

SHAHARAIM [Shā ha rā' im]—DOUBLE DAWNING. *A Benjamite* who went to Moab and had numerous descendants of his two wives, Harhim and Baara (I Chron. 8:8).

SHALLUM, SHALLUN [Shăl' lum]—RECOMPENSE, RETRIBUTION or SPOILATION.
1. *A son of Jabesh,* who slew Zechariah, son of Jeroboam II. He became King of Israel for one month just before the near extinction of the nation, and was slain by Menahem, son of Gadi (II Kings 15:10, 13–15).
2. *A son of Tikvah* and husband of Huldah the prophetess in the days of Josiah (II Kings 22:14; II Chron. 34:22).
3. *A son of Sisamai* and father of Jakaniah, also a descendant of Judah (I Chron. 2:40, 41).
4. *The fourth son of king Josiah* (I Chron. 3:15).
5. *Grandson of Simeon,* second son of Jacob and a descendant of Shaul (I Chron. 4:25).
6. *The father of Hilkiah,* a member of the high priestly family of Zadok and an ancestor of Ezra (I Chron. 6:12, 13; Ezra 7:2). Called Meshullam in I Chronicles 9:11.
7. *The fourth son of Naphtali,* the second son of Bilhah, Rachel's handmaid (I Chron. 7:13). Called Shillem in Genesis 46:24.
8. *A son of Kore,* a Korhite and chief porter at the sanctuary (I Chron. 9:17, 19, 31; Ezra 2:42; Neh. 7:45).
9. *The father of Jehizkiah* who opposed the reduction of Jewish captives to slaves (II Chron. 28:12).
10. *A Tabernacle gatekeeper* whose foreign wife was put away (Ezra 10:24).

11. *One of the sons of Bani* who also had taken a foreign wife (Ezra 10:42).

12. *A son of Halohesh,* ruler of the half of Jerusalem, who with his daughters assisted in the repair of the wall (Neh. 3:12).

13. *A son of Col-hozeh,* ruler of part of Mizpah, who repaired the gate of the fountain (Neh. 3:15).

14. *The father of Hanameel,* uncle to the prophet Jeremiah (Jer. 32:7, 8).

15. *The father of Maaseiah,* an officer of the Temple in the time of Jehoiakim (Jer. 35:4).

SHALMAI [Shăl′ ma ī]—JEHOVAH IS RECOMPENSER. *One of the Nethinims* whose descendants returned with Zerubbabel from exile (Ezra 2:46; Neh. 7:48).

SHALMAN [Shăl′ man]—PEACEABLE. *An Assyrian king* who laid waste Beth-arbel. Sometimes identified with Shalmaneser (Hos. 10:14).

SHALMANESER [Shăl man ē zûr]—THE GOD SHALMANA IS CHIEF or PEACE TAKEN AWAY. *The name of several Assyrian kings.* This was Shalmaneser IV who succeeded Tiglath-pileser and who invaded Israel and carried off Hoshea and the ten tribes to Assyria (II Kings 17:3; 18:9).

SHAMA [Shā′ mă]—HEARER or HE HATH HEARD. *A son of Hothan,* the Aroerite, and one of David's mighty men (I Chron. 11:44).

SHAMED [Shā′ mĕd]—WATCHER, DESTROYER. *The third son of Elpaal* (I Chron. 8:12).

SHAMER [Shā′ mûr]—PRESERVER.
1. *Son of Mahli* and grandson of Merari (I Chron. 6:46).
2. *Son of Heber,* son of Beriah, son of Asher (I Chron. 7:34). Spelled Shomer in I Chronicles 7:32.

SHAMGAR [Shăm′ gär]—CUPBEARER or A SURPRISED STRANGER.
The Man Who Was Ready When Need Arose
Shamgar was the son of Anath, and third judge of Israel after the death of Joshua. His spectacular deliverance of Israel from the Philistines is suggestive (Judg. 3:31). Shamgar the son of Anath was ready to serve God in the common working day.

When he drove his oxen out that morning he did not dream that before nightfall he would accomplish a memorable deliverance for his land. But the call came and he was ready.

Another lesson to be learned from Shamgar is that God can be served with unlikely instruments. "What is that in thy hand?" In

Shamgar's hand was an oxgoad with which he slew six hundred Philistines.

We may not have genius, brilliance, gifts of speech or song, but if we are in the hand of Christ, He can take foolish things to confound the wise.

SHAMHUTH [Shăm' hŭth]—FAME, RENOWN or DESOLATION OF INIQUITY. *An Izrahite,* a captain of David's army who served in the fifth month (I Chron. 27:8). Perhaps Shammah.

SHAMIR [Shă' mĭr]—OPPRESSED, A PRISON or A THORN. *A son of Micah,* a Levite and descendant of Uzziel (I Chron. 24:24). Also the name of the hill country of Judah (Josh. 15:48), and of a city on Mount Ephraim, the home and burial place of Tola (Judg. 10:1, 2).

SHAMMA [Shăm' mă]—FAME, RENOWN or DESOLATION. *A son of Zophah* an Asherite (I Chron. 7:37).

SHAMMAH [Shăm' mah]—LOSS.
1. *A son of Reuel* and descendant of Esau and Ishmael, who became a duke of Edom (Gen. 36:13, 17; I Chron. 1:37).
2. *The third son of Jesse* and brother of David (I Sam. 16:9; 17:13).
3. *The son of Agee the Hararite,* and first of David's three mighty men (II Sam. 23:11).
4. *Another Hararite,* and one of David's heroes (II Sam. 23:33). Called Shammoth in I Chronicles 11:27, Shamhuth in I Chronicles 27:8.
5. *A Harodite,* also one of David's valiant men (II Sam. 23:25).

SHAMMAI [Shăm' ma ī]—CELEBRATED or WASTE.
1. *A son of Onam,* son of Jerahmeel, grandson of Judah (I Chron. 2:28, 32).
2. *The father of Maon* and son of Rekem of the house of Caleb son of Hezron (I Chron. 2:44, 45).
3. *A son or grandson of Ezra* registered with the tribe of Judah (I Chron. 4:17).

SHAMMOTH [Shăm' moth]—RENOWN. *A Harorite,* one of David's valiant men (I Chron. 11:27). See Shammah.

SHAMMUA, SHAMMUAH [Shăm mū' ă, Shăm mū' ah]—FAMOUS.
1. *A Reubenite,* son of Zaccur, sent by Moses to spy out the land of Canaan (Num. 13:4).
2. *A son of David by Bath-sheba,* born in Jerusalem (II Sam. 5:14; I Chron. 14:4). He bore his uncle's name (I Chron. 2:13), and is also called Shimea (I Chron. 3:5).
3. *A grandson of Juduthun* and father of Abda or Obadiah, a

Levite who led the Temple worship after the exile (Neh. 11:17). Called Shemaiah in I Chronicles 9:16.

4. *A priest in the family of Bilgah* in the days of Nehemiah, and head of his father's house (Neh. 12:18).

SHAMSHERAI [Shăm she rā' ī]—HEROIC. *A son of Jeroham,* a Benjamite (I Chron. 8:26).

SHAPHAM [Shā' pham]—YOUTHFUL, VIGOROUS. *A chief of Gad,* dwelling in Bashan, second in rank (I Chron. 5:12).

SHAPHAN [Shā' phan]—PRUDENT, SHY, ROCK BADGER or WILD RAT.
1. *A scribe,* son of Azaliah, father of Gemariah. It was this Shaphan who laid before King Josiah the law book discovered by Hilkiah in the temple (II Kings 22:3–14; II Chron. 34:8–20; Jer. 36:10–12) and who was the chief lay leader in the outworking of Josiah's reforms. For two generations his family played a worthy part as servants of Jehovah and as friends of Jeremiah.
2. *Father of Ahikam,* a chief officer in the court of Josiah (II Kings 22:12; 25:22; II Chron. 34:20; Jer. 26:24; 39:14; 40:5; 41:2; 43:6).
3. *A father of Elasah* by whom Jeremiah the prophet sent a letter to the exiles in Babylon (Jer. 29:3).
4. *The father of Jaaganiah* whom Ezekiel saw as enticing people to idolatry and whom he denounced as a ringleader (Ezek. 8:11).

SHAPHAT [Shā' phat]—JUDGE or HE HATH JUDGED.
1. *A Simeonite,* son of Hori, and tribe representative sent as a spy to Canaan (Num. 13:5).
2. *The father of Elisha the prophet* (I Kings 19:16, 19; II Kings 3:11; 6:31).
3. *A son of Shemaiah* included in the royal genealogy of Judah (I Chron. 3:22).
4. *A chief of Gadite in Bashan* (I Chron. 5:12).
5. *A son of Adlai* and David's overseer of cattle in the valley (I Chron. 27:29).

SHARAI [Shăr' a ī]—JEHOVAH IS DELIVERER, FREE or MY SON. *A son of Bani* induced to put away his foreign wife (Ezra 10:40).

SHARAR [Shā' rär]—FIRM or STRONG. *A Hararite,* father of one of David's mighty men (II Sam. 23:33). Called Sacar (I Chron. 11:35).

SHAREZER, SHEREZER [Sha rē'zẽr, She rē' zer]—PROTECT or PRESERVE THE KING.
1. *A son of Sennacherib,* king of Assyria, who with his brother Adrammelech killed their father in the temple of Nisroch at Nineveh (II Kings 19:37; Isa. 37:38).

2. *A man sent from Bethel* to consult the priests and prophets as to a day of humiliation (Zech. 7:2).

SHASHAI [Shăsh' a ī]—WHITE, PALE, NOBLE or FREE. *One of the sons of Bani* who married a foreign wife (Ezra 10:40).

SHASHAK [Shā' shăk]—ASSAULTER, RUNNER. *A son of Elpaal* a Benjamite (I Chron. 8:14, 25).

SHAUL [Shā' ul]—ASKED.
1. *A son of Simeon* by a Canaanitish woman (Gen. 46:10; Ex. 6:15; Num. 26:13; I Chron. 4:24).
2. *A king of Edom* from Rehoboth in the Euphrates (I Chron. 1:48, 49). Called Saul in Genesis 36:37.
3. *A son of Rohath,* son of Levi and founder of a tribal family (Num. 26:13; I Chron. 6:24).

SHAVSHA, SHISHA [Shăv' shă, Shī' shă]—NOBILITY or SPLENDOR. *A scribe in David's, time* and afterwards in Solomon's day (I Chron. 18:16). Perhaps identical with Seraiah the scribe (II Sam. 8:17); Sheva in II Samuel 20:25; Shisha in I Kings 4:3.

SHEAL [Shĕ' al]—REQUEST or AN ASKING. *A son of Bani* who put away his strange wife (Ezra 10:29).

SHEALTIEL [Shĕ ăl' tĭ el]—I HAVE ASKED OF GOD. *A son of Jeconiah,* and father of Zerubbabel who led the Jews back from the Babylonian exile (Ezra 3:2, 8; 5:2; Neh. 12:1; Hag. 1:1, 12, 14; 2:2). Also an ancestor of Christ (Matt. 1:12; Luke 3:27). Also called Salathiel.

SHEARIAH [Shĕ a rī' ah]—JEHOVAH IS DECIDER or HATH ESTEEMED. *A son of Azel,* a Benjamite and descendant of Jonathan of the family of Saul (I Chron. 8:38; 9:44).

SHEAR-JASHUB [Shĕ' är-jā' shŭb]—A REMNANT RETURNS. *A son of Isaiah the prophet,* whose name was designed to embody a prophecy (Isa. 7:3; 10:21).

SHEBA [Shĕ' bă]—SEVENTH, AN OATH or CAPTIVITY.
1. *Son of Raamah,* son of Cush, son of Ham (Gen. 10:7; I Chron. 1:9).
2. *Son of Joktan* of the family of Shem (Gen. 10:28; I Chron. 1:22).
3. *Son of Jokshan,* son of Abraham by Keturah (Gen. 25:3; I Chron. 1:32).
4. *A son of Bichri* who rebelled against David after Absalom's death. This worthless adventurer, who snatched at what he thought

was a chance of winning the sovereignty of northern Israel, had his head cut off by the people of Abel (II Sam. 20:1–22).

5. *A chief Gadite,* dwelling in Gibeah in Bashan (I Chron. 5:13, 16). Also the name of the Arabian home of the Queen of Sheba (1 Kings 10:1) and a city in Simeon (Josh. 19:2).

SHEBANIAH [Shĕb a nī' ah]—JEHOVAH IS POWERFUL, JEHOVAH HATH DEALT TENDERLY or THE LORD CONVERTS.

1. *A priest and trumpeter in David's time* who assisted in bringing up the ark from the house of Obed-edom (I Chron. 15:24).

2. *A Levite* who assisted in the services of the Tabernacle and who sealed the covenant on behalf of his family (Neh 9:4, 5; 10:10).

3. *Another priest* who with Nehemiah sealed the covenant (Neh. 10:4; 12:14).

4. *A Levite* who did the same (Neh. 10:12).

SHEBER [Shĕ' bûr]—BREAKING or FRACTURE. *A son of Caleb,* son of Jephunneh by his concubine (I Chron. 2:48).

SHEBNA, SHEBNAH [Shĕb ' nă]—YOUTHFULNESS, TENDERNESS or WHO RESTS HIMSELF.

1. *A scribe* or palace-governor of king Hezekiah (II Kings 18:18, 26, 37; 19:2; Isa. 36:3, 11, 22; 37:2).

2. *The treasurer over the king's house*—a man of great influence who was fond of display (Isa. 22:15–25) and against whom Isaiah directed one of his utterances.

SHEBUEL [Shĕb' u el]—GOD IS RENOWN or RETURN, O GOD.

1. *A son of Gershon,* son of Levi, grandson of Moses (I Chron. 23:16; 26:24).

2. *A son of Heman,* chief singer of the sanctuary in David's time (I Chron. 25:4). Also called Shubael.

SHECHANIAH [Shĕch a nī' ah]—JEHOVAH IS A NEIGHBOUR or JEHOVAH HATH DWELT.

1. *Head of a family of David's house,* but not in succession to the throne (I Chron. 3:21, 22).

2. *A descendant of a family that returned with Ezra from exile* (Ezra 8:3).

3. *Another whose descendants returned from exile* (Ezra 8:5).

4. *A son of Jehiel* who first confessed the trespass of taking strange, or non-Jewish wives (Ezra 10:2).

5. *Father of Shemaiah* who helped to repair the wall (Neh. 3:29).

6. *Father-in-law of Tobiah,* the Ammonite who opposed Nehemiah (Neh. 6:18).

7. *A priest* who returned with Zerubbabel (Neh. 12:3).

SHECHEM, SICHEM, SYCHEM, SYCHAR [Shě' chem]—SHOULDER.

1. *A son of Hamor,* a Hivite prince—"a prince of the country"—that is, of Shechem. It is not certain whether the Levitical city was named after the son of Hamor, or whether he was named after the city (Gen. 33:18, 19, 34; Josh. 24:32; Judg. 9:28).

The Man Who Disgraced His Princely Dignity

Shechem, a neighbor of Jacob, took advantage of his daughter's visit to the daughters of the Hivites. Doubtless Dinah was young and unaccustomed to the ways of the world, and taking advantage of her, Shechem proved himself unworthy of his high office. He was led into sin by what he saw, and while it is said that Shechem came to love the girl he had wronged and wanted to make her his wife, yet such a proposal was not possible, owing to God's command about His people marrying those of Gentile nations. The scheme of Jacob's sons need not be told. Suffice it to say that Simeon and Levi, Dinah's brothers, treacherously slew Shechem for his betrayal of their sister. To the credit of Shechem it is said that "he was more honourable than all the house of his father." As for Simeon and Levi, they earned a sad epitaph (Gen. 49:5–7).

2. *A son of Gilead,* son of Manasseh and founder of a tribal family (Num. 26:31; Josh. 17:2).

3. *A son of Shemidah,* a Manassite (I Chron. 7:19).

Shechem is also a name renowned in history. Jacob rested there (Gen. 33:18). Jesus met the woman of Samaria at the one-time city of refuge and the first residence of the kings of Israel (John 4:12). It is said that Justin Martyr was born here, about A.D. 100.

SHEDEUR [Shěd' e ur]—SHEDDING OF LIGHT or ALL MIGHTY. *Father of Elizur,* the Reubenite chief who assisted Moses in the wilderness (Num. 1:5; 2:10; 7:30, 35; 10:18).

SHEHARIAH [Shē ha rī' ah]—JEHOVAH IS THE DAWN or BROKEN FORTH AS THE DAWN. *A son of Jeroham,* a Benjamite (I Chron. 8:26).

SHELAH, SALAH, SALA [Shē' lah]—PEACE, PRAYER or THAT BREAKS.

1. *Youngest son of Judah,* by the daughter of Shuah the Canaanite, and founder of a tribal family (Gen. 38:5–26; 46:12; Num. 26:20; I Chron. 2:3; 4:21).

2. *A son of Arphaxad*—also called Salah (I Chron. 1:18, 24). Also the name used for the pool at Jerusalem (Neh. 3:15) and translated Siloah.

SHELEMIAH [Shěl e mī' ah]—JEHOVAH IS RECOMPENSE, RECOMPENSES or GOD IS MY PERFECTION.

1. *A Levite,* a doorkeeper of the Tabernacle in David's time (I Chron. 26:14).

2. *One of the sons of Bani* who put away his strange wife (Ezra 10:39).

3. *Another of the same family* who had done the same (Ezra 10:41).

4. *The father of the Hananiah* who helped to repair the wall (Neh. 3:30).

5. *A priest who had charge of the treasuries* and distributed money among the Levites (Neh. 13:13).

6. *A son of Cushi* and grandfather of Jehudi who brought Baruch before the princes of Judah (Jer. 36:14).

7. *The son of Abdeel* who was ordered by Jehoiakim to take Baruch the scribe and Jeremiah the prophet (Jer. 36:26).

8. *The father of Jehucal* who was sent by Zedekiah to Jeremiah in order to plead for his prayers (Jer. 37:3; 38:1).

9. *The father of Irijah,* captain of the guard, who arrested Jeremiah when he was about to leave Jerusalem (Jer. 37:13).

SHELEPH [Shē′ leph]—DRAWN OUT. *A son of Joktan* of the family of Shem in southern Arabia (Gen. 10:26; I Chron. 1:20).

SHELESH [Shē′ lesh]—MIGHT or TRIED. *An Asherite,* son of Helem and grandson of Beriah (I Chron. 7:35).

SHELOMI [Shĕl′ o mī]—JEHOVAH IS PEACE or PEACEFUL. *Father of Ahihud,* prince of Judah who lived during the latter part of the wilderness journey (Num. 34:27).

SHELOMITH [Shĕl′ o mĭth]—PEACEFULNESS.

1. *A son of Shimei,* a Gershonite Levite in David's time (I Chron. 23:9). The R.V. gives the name as Shelomoth.

2. *A son of Izhar,* of the Kohath family (I Chron. 23:18). Called Shelomoth in I Chronicles 24:22.

3. *A descendant of Moses* through Eliezer, set over David's dedicated treasures (I Chron. 26:25, 26, 28).

4. *A son or daughter of king Rehoboam* (II Chron. 11:20).

5. *An ancestor of a family that returned with Ezra* (Ezra 8:10). Shelomith is also the name of the daughter of Dibri (Lev. 24:11) and of the daughter of Zerubbabel (I Chron. 3:19).

SHELUMIEL [Shē lū′ mĭ el]—GOD'S PEACE or A FRIEND OF GOD. *The son of Zurishaddai* and a prince of the tribe of Simeon who assisted Moses in numbering the people (Num. 1:6; 2:12; 7:36, 41; 10:19).

SHEM, SEM [Shĕm, Sĕm]—RENOWN, or NAME. *A son of Noah,* and ancestor of Christ (Gen. 5:32).

From his name, it is to be inferred that Shem was a distinguished person. The men of Babel sought to make themselves a name (Gen. 11:4) and become, thereby, rivals of Shem. The greatness of Shem arose from the fact that he was a forerunner of Christ. Shem's name meaning "renown" foreshadowed the greater name "above every name" before which every knee shall bow (Luke 3:36). In offering praise to God, Noah said, "Blessed be the Lord God of Shem" (Gen. 9:26).

SHEMA [Shē′ mǎ]—REPUTE, FAME or RUMOR.

1. *A son of Hebron* and father of Raham (I Chron. 2:43, 44).
2. *A Reubenite,* a son of Joel and father of Azaz (I Chron. 5:4, 8).
3. *A Benjamite,* head of the inhabitants of Aijalon (I Chron. 8:13). Called Shimhi in verse twenty-one and Shimei in the R.V.
4. *A priest* who assisted Ezra in the public reading of the law (Neh. 8:4). Also the name of a city in Judah (Josh. 15:26).

SHEMAAH [Shē mā′ ah]—THE FAME. *A Benjamite of Gibeah* and father of two valiant men who joined David at Ziklag (I Chron. 12:3).

SHEMAIAH [Shĕm a ī′ ah]—JEHOVAH IS FAME, JEHOVAH HAS HEARD or OBEYS THE LORD.

Evidently this popular name was shared by many Bible men, and at times two of the following may be the same individual. It is not an easy matter to identify them exactly.

1. *A prophet sent by God* to prevent Rehoboam from warring against the house of Israel. His part in the revolution and history are clearly defined (I Kings 12:22; II Chron. 11:2; 12:5, 7, 15).
2. *Son of Shechaniah* and father of Hattush, descendant of Zerub-babel (I Chron. 3:22).
3. *Father of Shimri,* perhaps Shimei, and head of a family of Simeon (I Chron. 4:37). See verses twenty-six and twenty-seven.
4. *A son of Joel,* perhaps Shema of I Chronicles 5:8, and head of a family of Reuben (I Chron. 5:4).
5. *A Merarite Levite* dwelling in Jerusalem (I Chron. 9:14; Neh. 11:15).
6. *A Levite, father of Obadiah* (I Chron. 9:16). Called Shammua in Nehemiah 11:17.
7. *Head of the Levitical Kohath clan* who assisted in bringing the Ark from the house of Obed-edom (I Chron. 15:8, 11).
8. *The son of Nathaneel,* a Levite, who recorded the priestly office in David's time (I Chron. 24:6).
9. *Oldest son of Obed-edom,* a Korhite Levite and a gatekeeper of the Tabernacle in David's reign (I Chron. 26:4, 6, 7).
10. *A Levite,* commissioned by Jehoshaphat, to teach the people in Judah (II Chron. 17:8).
11. *A son of Jeduthun* who helped in the purification of the Temple under Hezekiah (II Chron. 29:14).
12. *A Levite in Hezekiah's time* who was over the freewill offerings of God (II Chron. 31:15).

13. *A chief Levite* in the days of Josiah (II Chron. 35:9).

14. *A son of Adonikam* who returned with Ezra from exile (Ezra 8:13).

15. *A chief man under Ezra* sent to Iddo to ask for ministers. (Ezra 8:16).

16. *A priest of the family of Harim* who married a foreign wife (Ezra 10:21).

17. *A person who helped to repair the wall* (Neh. 3:29).

18. *A son of Delaiah* hired by Sanballat and Tobiah to intimidate Nehemiah (Neh. 6:10).

19. *A priest,* one of the twenty-four courses of priests that with Nehemiah sealed the covenant (Neh. 10:8; 12:6, 18, 34, 35).

20. *A singer* who took part in the dedication of the wall (Neh. 12:36).

21. *Another, or perhaps the same person as the previous one,* who gave thanks at the dedication (Neh. 12:42).

22. *The father of Urijah the prophet* who was slain by Jehoiakim for prophesying against Jerusalem and Judah (Jer. 26:20).

23. *A prophet called "the Nehelamite"* who in captivity was actively engaged in reproving or opposing Jeremiah (Jer. 29:24–32).

24. *The father of Delaiah,* a prince of the Jews to whom Baruch read the roll he had written under Jeremiah's direction (Jer. 36:12).

SHEMARIAH, SHAMARIAH [Shĕm a rī' ah, Shăm a rī' ah]—GOD HATH KEPT or GOD IS MY GUARD.

1. *A mighty man,* a Benjamite who joined David at Ziklag (I Chron. 12:5).

2. *A son of Rehoboam,* son of Solomon (II Chron. 11:19).

3. *One of the family of Harim* who had married a foreign wife (Ezra 10:32).

4. *One of the family of Bani* who had done the same (Ezra 10:4).

SHEMEBER [Shĕm ē' ber]—SPLENDOR OF HEROISM. *The King of Zeboim* who defeated other kings in the cities of the plain (Gen. 14:2, 8, 10).

SHEMER [Shē' mûr]—ONE KEPT BY THE LORD or GUARDIAN. *Owner of a hill purchased by Omri* and on which he built Samaria (I Kings 16:24). Shomer in I Chronicles 7:32.
See others under Shamed and Shamer.

SHEMIDAH, SHEMIDA [Shē mī' dah, Shē mī' dă]—FAME OF KNOWING or SCIENCE OF THE HEAVENS. *A son of Gilead* and grandson of Manasseh (Num. 26:32; Josh. 17:2; I Chron. 7:19). Founder of a tribal family (Num. 26:32).

SHEMIRAMOTH [Shē mǐr' a mŏth]—FAME OF THE HIGHEST or HEIGHT OF THE HEAVENS.

1. *A Levite* responsible for the choral service of the Tabernacle (I Chron. 15:18, 20; 16:5).

2. *Another Levite,* whom Jehoshaphat sent to teach the people in Judah (II Chron. 17:8.)

SHEMUEL [Shē mū' el]—HEARD OF GOD.

1. *A Simeonite* appointed to assist in dividing the land west of Jordan (Num. 34:20). Perhaps the name is equivalent to Shelumiel.

2. *The father of Joel* (I Chron. 6:33).

3. *A grandson of Issachar* and head of a family (I Chron. 7:2).

SHENAZAR [Shē nā' zar]—LIGHT or SPLENDOR. *A son or grandson of Jecamiah,* son of Jehoiakim king of Judah (I Chron. 3:18). See Sheshbazzar.

SHEPHATIAH [Shĕph a tī' ah]—JEHOVAH IS JUDGE.

1. *The fifth son of David* by Abital (II Sam. 3:4; I Chron. 3:3).

2. *A Benjamite,* father of Meshullam whose home was in Jerusalem (I Chron. 9:8).

3. *A valiant man who came to David at Ziklag* (I Chron. 12:5).

4. *A prince of Simeon in David's reign* (I Chron. 27:16).

5. *A son of king Jehoshaphat* (II Chron. 21:2).

6. *A person whose many descendants returned from exile with Zerubbabel* (Ezra 2:4; Neh. 7:9).

7. *One of Solomon's servants* who also returned from exile (Ezra 2:57; Neh. 7:59).

8. *One whose descendant, Zebadiah, returned from exile* with eighty males (Ezra 8:8).

9. *A descendant of Pharez,* who dwelt in Jerusalem (Neh. 11:4).

10. *A son of Mattan,* a prince of Judah in Zedekiah's time (Jer. 38:1).

SHEPHO, SHEPHI [Shē' phō, Shē' phī]—UNCONCERN or SMOOTHNESS. *A son of Shobal* and a Horite chief (Gen. 36:23; I Chron. 1:40).

SHEPHUPHAM, SHEPHUPHAN [Shē phŭ' phan]—AN ADDER. *A son of Bela,* son of Benjamin and father of a tribal family (I Chron. 8:5). Called Muppim in Genesis 46:21 and Shuppim in I Chronicles 7:12, 15; 26:16.

SHEREBIAH [Shĕr e bī' ah]—JEHOVAH HATH MADE TO TREMBLE or JEHOVAH IS ORIGINATOR.

1. *A priest* with eighteen sons and brethren who returned with Ezra. Evidently a family of singers (Ezra 8:18, 24; Neh. 8:7; 9:4, 5).

2. *A Levite* who with Nehemiah sealed the covenant (Neh. 10:12; 12:8, 24).

SHERESH [Shĕ′resh]—UNION or ROOT. *A son of Machir* of the Manassite clan (I Chron. 7:16).

SHESHAI [Shĕ′shaī]—FREE, NOBLE or WHITISH. *A son of Anak,* who resided at Hebron, having been driven there by Caleb (Num. 13:22; Josh. 15:14; Judg. 1:10).

SHESHAN [Shĕ′shan]—FREE, NOBLE. *A Jerahmeelite,* grandson of Pharez son of Judah whose only daughter was given in marriage to an Egyptian slave (I Chron. 2:31, 34, 35).

SHESHBAZZAR [Shĕsh băz′zar]—O SUN-GOD PROTECT THE SON. *The prince of Judah made governor of Judah by Cyrus* (Ezra 1:8, 11; 5:14, 16). Elsewhere called Zerubbabel (Ezra 3:8).

SHETH [Shĕth]—COMPENSATION.
1. *A Moabite chief.* The Moabites were makers of war and tumult, and are named "sons of tumult" in the R.V. (Num. 24:17).
2. *A son of Adam* (I Chron. 1:1).

SHETHAR [Shĕ′thär]—STAR or COMMANDER. *One of the seven princes of Persia and Media* who had the right of access to the king's presence (Esther 1:14).

SHETHAR-BOZNAI [Shĕ′thär-bŏz′na ī]—STARRY SPLENDOR. *A Persian official* who with others attempted to prevent the returned Jewish exiles from rebuilding the Temple (Ezra 5:3, 6; 6:6, 13).

SHEVA, SHAVSHA [Shĕ′vă]—SELF-SATISFYING or VANITY.
1. *A scribe* or secretary of David (II Sam. 20:25).
2. *The father of Machbenah* and son of Maachah, concubine of Caleb son of Jephunneh (I Chron. 2:49).

SHILHI [Shĭl′hĭ]—ONE ARMED WITH DARTS. *Father of Azubah,* mother of King Jehoshaphat (I Kings 22:42; II Chron. 20:31).

SHILLEM [Shĭl′lem]—RETRIBUTION or RECOMPENSE. *The fourth son of Naphtali* and founder of a tribal family (Gen. 46:24; Num. 26:49). Called Shallum in I Chronicles 7:13.

SHILONI [Shī lō′nī]—SENT ONE. *Father of Zechariah,* of the sons of Parez or Pharez, son of Judah (Neh. 11:5). The R.V. says a Shilonite—see I Kings 11:29.

SHILSHAH [Shĭl′shah]—MIGHT, HEROISM or TRIAD. *The ninth son of Zophah,* an Asherite (I Chron. 7:37).

SHIMEAH, SHIMEA [Shĭm′ e ah, Shĭm′ e ă]—SPLENDOR or SOME-
THING HEARD.

1. *Son of Mikloth,* a Benjamite of the family of Saul (I Chron. 8:32).
2. *One of David's brothers* (II Sam. 13:3; 21:21). Appears as Shammah (I Sam. 16:9; 17:13). See II Samuel 21:21.
3. *A son of David* (I Chron. 3:5). See Shammuah.
4. *Father of Haggiah,* a Merarite (I Chron. 6:30).
5. *Father of Berachiah,* of the family of Gershon (I Chron. 6: 39).

SHIMEAM [Shĭm′ e ăm]—FAME or RUMOR. *A son of Mikloth,* a Benjamite resident in Jerusalem (I Chron. 9:38). Same as Shimeah in I Chronicles 8:32. Founder of a tribal family (I Chron. 2:55).

SHIMEI, SHIMI, SHIMHI [Shĭm′ e ī, Shī′ mī, Shĭm′ hī]—JEHOVAH IS FAME or FAMOUS.

Shimei, we are told, was a popular name among the Hebrews, being especially common in Levitical circles. But of the majority of men bearing it, little is known apart from the name.

1. *The Benjamite of the clan of Saul,* son of Gera who cursed David when he fled from Absalom (II Sam. 16:5, 7, 13; 19:16, 18, 21, 23). Although we have little knowledge of this most prominent Shimei, what we do know proves him to be, as Dr. Alexander Whyte expresses it, "A reptile of the royal house of Saul." This Shimei can be described as:

The Man Who Hated the Truth He Knew

This man who lived to curse knew only too well that David had never shed a single drop of Saul's blood, but it was not in his interest to admit the truth he knew. Because of his tribal and family connections it was natural for Shimei to be David's bitter enemy, and to heap his curses and insults upon the fugitive monarch.

When, however, David triumphantly returned after Absalom's tragic death, Shimei met the king with a hypocritical repentance. David accepted his apology and gave an oath that he would not put him to death. When further resistance was useless, Shimei feigned obedience to David, but in his heart was still bitterly opposed to him.

On his deathbed David's last words to Solomon about Shimei's blood being spilt, cause one to wonder whether David's long-suppressed revenge upon his enemy found utterance. Solomon would not allow Shimei to go beyond the walls of Jerusalem. All the time he remained in his city of refuge he was safe. If he passed without it, he would die. Shimei kept this arrangement for three years, then broke it on some trifling occasion and justly forfeited his life. At the command of Solomon he was executed by Benaiah. This was the last of those acts of justice on offenders against David which Solomon performed.

How do we act when men say all manner of evil against us falsely? Do we see the Lord in it all, and that He will work out our salvation in spite of adverse and sore criticisms and circumstances? Do we rest in the fact that the Lord will look upon our affliction and will requite us good for all evil, if only we wisely and silently and adoringly submit ourselves to it?

2. *A Courtier*, Shimei by name, an officer of David, remained true to the king when Adonijah sought to usurp the throne (I Kings 1:8).

3. *A son of Elah*, one of the twelve purveyors of Solomon, in Benjamin (I Kings 4:18). This Shimei has been identified as the one above in I Kings 1:8.

4. *A son of Gershon*, son of Levi, who founded a subdivision of the tribal family of Gershon (Ex. 6:17).

5. *A grandson of Jeconiah*, son of Jehoiakim king of Judah. A prince of the royal house (I Chron. 3:19).

6. *A son of Zacchur*, the Benjamite with sixteen sons and six daughters (I Chron. 4:26, 27).

7. *A Reubenite*, son of Gog (I Chron. 5:4).

8. *A Merarite*, son of Libni (I Chron. 6:29).

9. *Father of a chief family in Judah* (I Chron. 8:21).

10. *A Levite of the family of Laadan*—grandson of Levi (I Chron. 23:9).

11. *A Levite* to whom the tenth lot fell in the singing service of the Tabernacle during David's time. A son of Jeduthun (I Chron. 25:3, 17).

12. *A Ramathite* who was overseer in David's vineyards (I Chron. 27:27).

13. *A descendant of Heman*, who took part in the cleansing of the Temple in Hezekiah's time (II Chron. 29:14).

14. *A Levite* and brother of Conaniah, who had charge of the tithes (II Chron. 31:12, 13).

15. *A Levite* who had taken a strange wife (Ezra 10:23).

16. *One of the family of Hashum* who put away his wife (Ezra 10:33).

17. *A son of Bani*, who also put away his strange wife (Ezra 10:38).

18. *A Benjamite*, son of Kish and grandfather of Mordecai (Esther 2:5).

19. *A representative*, perhaps of the Gershonites who participated in mourning for national guilt (Zech. 12:13).

SHIMEON [Shĭm′ e on]—HEARING or AN ANSWERING OF PRAYER. *A son of Harim* who had married a foreign wife (Ezra 10:31).

SHIMMA [Shĭm′ mȧ]—FAME or RUMOR. *The third son of Jesse* and brother of David (I Chron. 2:13). Also called Shamma.

SHIMON [Shī′ mon]—TRIED or VALUER. *A descendant of Caleb son of Jephunneh*, registered with the tribes of Judah (I Chron. 4:20).

SHIMRATH [Shĭm' răth]— WATCH or GUARDING. *A son of Shimhi of Aijalon,* and descendant of Benjamin (I Chron. 8:21).

SHIMRI, SIMRI [Shĭm' rī, Sĭm' rī]—JEHOVAH IS WATCHING.
1. *A Simeonite* and head of a tribal family (I Chron. 4:37).
2. *Father of Jediael,* one of David's heroes (I Chron. 11:45).
3. *A son of Hosah* and Tabernacle gatekeeper (I Chron. 26:10).
4. *A son of Elizaphan* who assisted in Hezekiah's reformation (II Chron. 29:13).

SHIMRON, SHIMROM [Shĭm' rŏn, Shĭm' rŏm]—A GUARD or WATCH. *The fourth son of Issachar* and founder of a family. (Gen. 46:13; Num. 26:24; I Chron. 7:1). Also the name of a city of Zebulun whose kings Jabin called to his assistance (Josh. 11:1; 19:15). Also called Shimron-meron.

SHIMSHAI [Shĭm' shaī]—JEHOVAH IS SPLENDOR or SUNNY. *A scribe of Rehum* who complained to Artaxerxes about the Jews rebuilding the temple (Ezra 4:8, 9, 17, 23).

SHINAB [Shī' năb]—TOOTH OF THE FATHER. *The king of Admah* in Abraham's time (Gen. 14:2, 8–10), and defeated by Chedorlaomer.

SHIPHI [Shī' phī]—JEHOVAH IS FULNESS or ABOUNDING. *Father of Ziza,* a Simeonite prince (I Chron. 4:37).

SHIPHTAN [Shĭph' tan]—JUDGE or JUDICIAL. *Father of Kemuel,* an Ephraimite prince appointed to divide the land of Jordan (Num. 34:24).

SHISHA [Shī' shă]—DISTINCTION or NOBILITY. *Father of Elihoreph and Ahiah,* two of king Solomon's scribes (I Kings 4:3). See Shavsha.

SHISHAK [Shī' shăk]—MEANING OF NAME OBSCURE. *Sesconchis I,* founder of the twenty-second Bubastic dynasty, who reigned for twenty-one years. Jeroboam fled to him and was protected against Solomon. Shishak plundered Jerusalem in the fifth year of Rehoboam (I Kings 14:25; II Chron. 12:2–9). His name has been found on the Egyptian monuments in the form of Sheshnok. He might have been of Ethiopian origin. Tradition has it that with the aid of the military caste, he dethroned the Pharaoh who gave his daughter to Solomon.

SHITRAI [Shĭt' ra ī]—JEHOVAH IS DECIDING. *A Sharonite* who cared for David's herds in the plain of Sharon (I Chron. 27:29).

SHIZA [Shī' ză]—SPLENDOR or VEHEMENT LOVE. *The father of a Reubenite chief,* one of David's heroes. (I Chron. 11:42).

SHOBAB [Shō' bǎb]—RETURNING or RESTORED.
1. *A son of David born after he became king of Israel* (II Sam. 5:14; I Chron. 3:5; 14:4).
2. *A son of Caleb,* son of Hezron, whose mother's name was Azubah (I Chron. 2:18).

SHOBACH [Shō' bǎch]—EXPANSION, ONE WHO POURS OUT or CAPTIVITY. *A commander-in-chief under Hadarezer,* king of Zobal, defeated and slain by Joab (II Sam. 10:16, 18). Called Shophach in I Chronicles 19:16.

SHOBAI [Shō' ba ī]—JEHOVAH IS GLORIOUS or ONE WHO LEADS CAPTIVE. *A Levite and founder of a family of gatekeepers* whose descendants returned from exile with Zerubbabel (Ezra 2:42; Neh. 7:45).

SHOBAL [Shō' bal]—WANDERING or A TRAVELER.
1. *A son of Seir the Horite* and one of the dukes (Gen. 36:20, 23, 29; I Chron. 1:38, 40).
2. *A son of Caleb,* son of Hur (I Chron. 2:50, 52).
3. *A son of Judah* and father of Reaiah (I Chron. 4:1, 2).

SHOBEK [Shō' bek]—FREE or ONE WHO FORSAKES. *A Jewish chief* who with Nehemiah signed the covenant (Neh. 10:24).

SHOBI [Shō' bī]—JEHOVAH IS GLORIOUS or ONE WHO LEADS CAPTIVE. *A son of Nahash the king of Ammon,* who, with Machir of Lo-debar, showed kindness to David at the time of his flight from Absalom (II Sam. 17:27).

SHOHAM [Shō' hǎm]—BERYL or ONYX.—*A Levite,* a son of Jaaziah (I Chron. 24:27).

SHOMER [Shō' mûr]—KEEPER or WATCHMAN. *A son of Heber,* an Asherite (I Chron. 7:32). Also spelled Shamer in verse thirty-four. Shomer is likewise the name of the mother of Jehozabad (II Kings 12:21), and called Shimrith in II Chronicles 24:26.

SHOPHACH [Shō' phǎch]—EXTENSION. *The captain of the host of Hadarezer,* king of Zobah in David's time (I Chron. 19:16, 18). Called Shobach in II Samuel 10:16.

SHUA [Shōō' ǎ]—WEALTH. *The father of Judah's Canaanite wife* (Gen. 38:2, 12). Also the name of a daughter of Heber (I Chron. 7:32).

SHUAH [Shōō' ah]—PROSPERITY or DEPRESSION.
1. *A son of Keturah* by Abraham (Gen. 25:2; I Chron. 1:32). Probably Bildad the Shuhite belonged to this tribe (Job. 2:11).

2. *Brother of Chelub,* a descendant of Caleb son of Hur (I Chron. 4:11).

SHUAL [Shōō' al]—A FOX or A SMALL PET. *The third son of Zophah,* an Asherite (I Chron. 7:36). Also the name of a district in Benjamin (I Sam. 13:17). See Shalim and Hazar-shual.

SHUBAEL [Shōō' ba el]—MEANING OF NAME OBSCURE.
1. *A son or descendant of Amram,* grandson of Levi (I Chron. 24:20).
2. *A singer in the Tabernacle in David's time* (I Chron. 25:20). Perhaps the same as Shebuel in I Chronicles 25:4.

SHUHAM [Shōō' ham]—DEPRESSION. *A son of Dan* and founder of a tribal family (Num. 26:42, 43). Sometimes identified as Hushim in Genesis 46:23.

SHUNI [Shōō' nī]—FORTUNATE, CALM, QUIET. *The third son of Gad* and founder of a tribal family (Gen. 46:16; Num. 26:15).

SHUPHAM, SHUPPIM [Shōō' pham, Shŭp' pim)—SERPENT.
1. *A son of Benjamin* (Num. 26:39). Most likely the Shephuphan son of Bela (I Chron. 8:5).
2. *A Benjamite* (I Chron. 7:12, 15).
3. *A Levite gatekeeper* of the Tabernacle in David's time. (I Chron. 26:16).

SHUTHELAH [Shōō' the lah]—SETTING OF TELAH or A PLANT.
1. *A son of Ephraim* and founder of a tribal family (Num. 26: 35, 36; I Chron. 7:20).
2. *A son of Zabad,* a descendant of Ephraim (I Chron. 7:21).

SIAHA, SIA [Sī' a hȧ, Sī' ă]—CONGREGATION. *One of the Nethinims* who returned with Zerubbabel (Ezra 2:44; Neh. 7:47).

SIBBECHAI, SIBBECAI [Sĭb' be chaī, Sĭb' be caī]—JEHOVAH IS IN-TERVENING or ENTANGLING. *One of the family of Hushah* who slew Saph or Saffai, a Philistine giant in David's time (II Sam. 21:18; I Chron. 11:29; 20:4; 27:11). Called Mebunnai in II Samuel 23:27.

SIDON, ZIDON [Sī' dŏn]—FORTIFIED. *The eldest son of Canaan, son of Ham,* and founder of the tribal family, Sidonians (Gen. 10:15; Judg. 3:3). Also the name of the city now known as Saida.

SIHON [Sī' hŏn]—GREAT or SWEEPING OUT. *A king of the Amorites* at the time of Canaan's conquest. He refused to allow Israel to pass through his land and was defeated at Jahaz (Num. 21:21–33; Deut. 1:4; 3:2, 6; 4:46).

SILAS, SILVANUS [Sī' las, Sĭl vā' nus]—LOVER OF WORDS. *A distinguished member and prophet of the Apostolic Church at Jerusalem* who figures as the companion of Paul in his triumphs and trials. From the Book of Acts we learn that:

I.   He was one of the chief men among the brethren and therefore of Jewish birth (Acts 15:32).

II. He was sent as a delegate from the Apostolic Council with Paul and Barnabas to report the Council's decision (Acts 15:22).

III. He was probably a Roman citizen (Acts 16:37).

IV. His double qualification as a leading Jewish Christian and a Roman citizen eminently fitted him to take the place of Barnabas as Paul's companion (Acts 15:40).

V.   He suffered with Paul in prison (Acts 16:19, 25, 29), joining in the prayers and praises that midnight hour resulting in the conversion of the keeper of the prison.

VI. He was also associated with Peter, acting as bearer or scribe of Peter's first Epistle (I Pet. 5:12).

VII. He is probably the Silvanus who preached the Apostolic doctrine (II Cor. 1:19; see I Thess. 1:1; II Thess. 1:1).

SIMEON, SYMEON [Sĭm' e on]—HEARING, HEARS AND OBEYS or HEARING WITH ACCEPTANCE.

1. *The second son of Jacob by Leah* (Gen. 29:33).

The Man Who Was Self-Willed

It is not easy to deal with Simeon alone, since he is always associated with his brother, Levi. "Simeon and Levi are brethren" (Gen. 49:5). Of Simeon's personal history we know little. His name implies hearing with obedience, but Simeon was deaf in the day he should have heard, and disobedient and irresponsive when his lot hung in balance.

The first thing recorded about Simeon is that with Levi his brother, he drew the sword in treachery against the Shechemites and slew all the males. When rebuked by their father, they upheld indignantly their right to act as they did. Both acted "in their selfwill" (Gen. 49:6), which means they took malicious delight in their gross crime.

Simeon next appears in the story of Joseph, who felt it would be better to retain Simeon until Benjamin had been brought to the palace. Joseph felt with his father Jacob that Simeon and Levi would be best apart. In fact, Simeon had no blessing while joined with Levi and no prosperity while he was with Reuben. When separated, Simeon, at first, did not multiply (I Chron. 4:24–27). During the forty years in the wilderness the decrease of Simeon was remarkable. Because of the idolatry of the tribe, thousands were slain.

In the land of Canaan, Simeon joined with Judah, and this association marked a turning point in the history of the tribe. Judah and

Simeon went up together to Canaan (Judg. 1:1–3). Simeon means "obedient hearing," and Judah, "praise." The absorption of Simeon into the inheritance of Judah gave Simeon a place and work in Israel. In the final division of the land, foretold by Ezekiel, between Benjamin and Issachar, there is a portion for Simeon.

Over the gate to the Golden City, Simeon's name is inscribed—"Of the tribe of Simeon were sealed 12,000"—a way for even Simeon to enter the city of God above. From the time the Simeonites became aware of what God had done for them there was no more curse and no more captivity for them. Hitherto instruments of cruelty, they became instruments of warfare against the enemies of the Lord, ultimately earning the right to be included among the number eternally sealed (Rev. 7:7).

Self-will fittingly describes Simeon's career until he was separated from Levi. God hates self-will for He knows how it accounts for uncontrolled passions, and the failure to respond to higher appeals. Because of their self-will God, in His governmental dealings, scattered and impoverished the Simeonites. May we not come nigh their dwelling but ever seek to learn, prove and obey "that good and acceptable and perfect will of God."

2. *A just and devout man in Jerusalem who awaited the coming of Jesus, the Messiah* (Luke 2:25–34).

The Man Who Died Satisfied

The adoration and prophecy of Simeon, who waited for the consolation of Israel and blessed the Consoler when He appeared, is rich in spiritual suggestion. This spectator of the most significant birth of all history, endued with a prophetic spirit, kept the lamp of prophecy burning when religion was at a low ebb in Israel. Simeon means "one who hears and obeys" and this saintly Simeon knew the voice speaking in the prophets of old, and obeyed the light he saw. Coming into the Temple, he took the Babe in his arms and blessed God. What a wonderful benediction his was!

At last faith had been justified and Simeon could die without fear. Have our eyes seen the salvation of the Lord? Can we die in peace? In his swan song, Simeon was not ashamed to declare that the One born in the city of David was the Saviour of the world. This was more than the letter-learned scribes of his times had discerned. These were the men who looked upon Christ as a sign to be spoken against and to whom He would become a stone of stumbling and a rock of offense.

With godly Simeon it was different, for he was Spirit-taught and knew that Mary's Child was the One through whom the world was to be blessed. As he eagerly anticipated Christ's first advent, are we found patiently awaiting His second advent? When He does appear and we see Him as He is, ours will be the thrill Simeon experienced as He gazed upon the Lord's Christ.

3. *An ancestor of Jesus* (Luke 3:30).

4. *A disciple and prophet at Antioch,* surnamed Niger (Acts 13:1).

5. *The original name of a son of Jonas,* or John, and brother of Andrew an apostle of Christ. See Simon (Acts 15:14).

SIMON [Sī' mon]—HEARING.

1. *Simon Peter,* one time Galilean fisherman, an early disciple and apostle of Jesus Christ (Matt. 4:18; 10:2). For a brief outline of his life and labor, see material under Peter.

2. *Another of the Twelve Apostles,* called the "Canaanite," because of his connection with Cana in Galilea.

The Man Who Was Zealous

The Hebrew *canna* means, "zealous," thus the Greek Zelotes (Luke 6:15; Acts 1:13). As a Zealot, Simon belonged to the historical party which bore that name. This communion of noble-hearted men loved their own land and cherished their belief in its rightful independence, which made any foreign interference or dominion hateful. Their zeal for the laws of God which were their national laws, the guardian and source of their independence and liberty, attracted a lover of freedom such as Simon.

What we admire about this apostle is the fact that after he became Christ's follower, he never ceased to be known as the Zealot. What had attracted him as a man, he came to love as a Christian. In Christ's teaching the Zealot found the helper and handmaid of everything that he in his calmer moments could hope or look for. The lesson we gather for our own hearts is that we may carry our true and noblest selves into our following of Christ. Whatever hopes and aspirations we may have apart from Christ can find a true home in Christ. Simon, the Jewish patriot who chafed under the foreign yoke and sighed for emancipation, came to experience a sweeter yoke and a more blessed emancipation. May an increasing number of Christ's disciples strive to earn the honorable title, "zealous of spiritual gifts" (I Cor. 14:12).

3. *One of the brothers of our Lord* (Matt. 13:55; Mark 6:3).

4. *The one-time leper in Bethany,* in whose house the head of Jesus was anointed with oil (Matt. 26:6–13; Mark 14:3–9; John 12:1–8).

5. *A Cyrenian who was compelled to bear the cross* after Jesus and who was the father of Alexander and Rufus (Matt. 27:32). Shortly after, Jesus bore the cross, not only for Simon but for all men.

6. *A Pharisee* in whose house Jesus dined and had His feet washed with tears and anointed with ointment (Luke 7:40–44). This wealthy Simon or Simeon had every reason to be pleased with the banquet he provided, for he saw Jesus signally honored and the Pharisees, including himself, severely rebuked for their lack of forgiving love and grace. The woman's heart was as full of ointment as the box she carried. What sweet perfume filled the atmosphere as she stole to Christ's feet and washed them with her scalding tears, and then wiped those sacred feet with her long black hair! With the light of heaven in

318   ALL THE MEN OF THE BIBLE

her eyes and the blessed words of Jesus ringing in her ears, "Thy sins
are forgiven; go in peace," she left Simeon's house with all her sins
blotted out.

7. *The father of Judas Iscariot* (John 6:71; 12:4; 13:2, 26).

8. *A sorcerer* or magician in Samaria who sought to purchase the
gifts of the Spirit with money (Acts 8:9–24).

The Man Who Tried to Buy Power

The first glimpse we have of Simon Magus is that he paraded himself as "some great one," and is an exaggerated specimen of popularity
seekers among us today. This Samaritan mountebank, who carried
on his astounding impositions, was as bad as he was clever. He professed to be converted and was so deceitful that he completely deceived
Philip.

In Samaria, Philip was having tremendous success in his evangelistic
work, and Simon fell under the influence of his message, so much so
that he professed belief in Christ and was baptized. But when Peter
and John came on the scene to establish the work begun by Philip,
through the laying on of hands, miraculous gifts were imparted to
many of those Samaritan believers.

Simon, with his innate love of witchery, offered to buy from the
apostles the power of conferring spiritual gifts, and was rebuked in
language of such sternness as to lead him to beg of Peter to pray that
the severe judgment of God would not fall upon him because of his
sin. Peter detected that the thought of Simon's heart had not been
changed. Calvin says, "We may conjecture that Simon Magus repented." Scripture, however, is silent about his life after Peter's
rebuke. Ignatius, the earliest of the Fathers, calls Simon "the first
born of Satan." Irenaeus marks him out as the first of all heretics.
Because of his sin, the word simony came into being, a term meaning the effort to procure spiritual office by gifts. Simon Magus loved
the praises and adulations of men. How we have to guard against
the perils of popularity! Says Alexander Whyte, "Starve the self-seeking quack that is still within you. Beat him black and blue, as Paul
tells us he did."

9. *A tanner of Joppa*, with whom Simon Peter lodged when sent
for by Cornelius (Acts 9:43; 10:6, 27, 32). What precious fellowship
those two Simons must have had during those days! A tanner and a
fisherman! How they come to Jesus from every walk of life!

SIPPAI, SAPH [Sĭp paī, Săph]—JEHOVAH IS PRESERVER. *A son or a
descendant of Rapha*, the gigantic ancestor of the Rephaim, slain by
Sibbechai, the Hushathite in David's time (I Chron. 20:4). Called
Saph in II Samuel 21:18.

SISAMAI, SISMAI [Sĭ săm' a ī]—JEHOVAH IS DISTINGUISHED. *A son of
Eleasah* and father of Shallum, a Jerahmeelite (I Chron. 2:40).

SISERA [Sĭs' e rǎ]—MEDITATION, BATTLE ARRAY or SEES A HORSE.

1. *Commander of the Canaanite army* which held northern Israel in subjection. He was killed by Jael (Judg. 4:21, 22; I Sam. 12:9; Ps. 83:9). In his flight after battle with the Israelites under Barak, Sisera, overcome by fatigue, sought shelter in the tent of Jael, who treacherously slew him while asleep—the death prophesied by Deborah (Judg. 4:9). The most tragic aspect of the murder of Sisera is that of his anxious mother awaiting the return of her son. Jael's cruel act broke a mother's heart.

2. *One of the Nethinims* whose descendants returned with Zerubbabel (Ezra 2:53; Neh. 7:55).

SO [Sō]—LIFTED UP. *King of Egypt* of Ethiopian descent whose aid against Syria, Hoshea, the last king of Israel, endeavored to secure (II Kings 17:4).

SOCHO, SHOCO, SHOCHO [Sō' chō, Shō' cō, Shō' chō]—LEDGE or FORTIFICATION. *A son of Heber* (I Chron. 4:18). Also the name of a city in Judah rebuilt by Rehoboam (II Chron. 11:7; 28:18). Perhaps Socoh (Josh. 15:35).

SODI [Sō' dī]—JEHOVAH DETERMINES, A FAMILIAR ACQUAINTANCE or MY SECRET. *A Zebulunite,* father of Gaddiel, one of the twelve spies sent out to spy Canaan (Num. 13:10).

SOLOMON [Sŏl' o mon]—PEACE or PEACEABLE. *The tenth son of David,* and second by Bath-sheba, and the third king of Israel who reigned for forty years (II Sam. 5:14; 12:24). Solomon was also known as Jedidiah meaning, "beloved of the Lord."

The Man Who Was Full Yet Failed

We know little of the early life of Solomon. The name given him by Nathan, but not repeated because of its sacredness, implies David's restoration to divine favor (II Sam. 12:25). Loved of the Lord suggests the bestowal of unusual gifts (II Sam. 12:24, 25). It is also evident that young Solomon was greatly influenced both by his mother and Nathan (I Kings 1:11, 12).

With reference to the character and reign of Solomon, we cannot but agree with Alexander Whyte that, "The shipwreck of Solomon is surely the most terrible tragedy in all the world. For if ever there was a shining type of Christ in the Old Testament church, it was Solomon . . . but everyday sensuality made him in the end a castaway." Taking him all in all, Solomon stands out as a disappointing figure of Hebrew history. Think of the advantages he began with! There were the almost undisputed possession of David's throne, immense stores of wealth laid up by his father, exceptional divinely imparted mental abilities, the love and high hopes of the people. Solomon's start like the cloudless dawn of a summer's morning, might have been beautiful all his life through, but it ended in gloom because he wandered into God-forbidden paths. Thus a life beginning magnificently ended miserably. The man who penned and preached a thousand wise things failed to practice the wisdom he taught.

The work of Solomon was the development of his father's ideas of a consolidated kingdom, and what marvelous success crowned his efforts. Exercising the power of an oriental despot, he gave Israel a glory, prestige and splendor unsurpassed in the world's history. On the whole, however, Solomon seemed to rule for his own aggrandizement and not for the welfare of the people. Doubtless Solomon's artistic and literary gifts provided the masses with beneficial instruction, but the glory of Solomon brought the common people tears and groans. The great wealth provided by David for the building of a Temple speedily disappeared under Solomon's lavish spending, and the people had to pay heavily by taxation and poverty for his magnificent whims. Yet Jesus said that the lilies of the field had greater glory than all the gaudy pomp and pride of Solomon.

Solomon's ambition in the morning of his life was most commendable. His dream was a natural expression of this ambition, and his God-imparted wisdom an evidence of it (I Kings 3). Then his sacrifice at Gibeon indicates that Solomon desired religion to be associated with all external magnificence. Solomon's remarkable prayer also breathes the atmosphere of true piety and of his delight in the full recognition of God. Alas, however, Solomon came to the end of his days minus popularity and piety!

This first great naturalist the world ever saw, who wrote one thousand and five songs, three thousand proverbs and who had sagacity beyond compare, took his first step downward when he went to Egypt for his queen. A daughter of Pharaoh, sitting on the throne of David, must have shocked and saddened the godly elect of Israel. With this strange wife came her strange gods.

Then came the harem of outlandish women who caused Solomon to sin (Neh. 13:26). His wives—seven hundred of them and three hundred concubines—whom Solomon clave unto in love, turned him into an idolater (I Kings 11:1-8). Polygamy on such a vast scale and concession for his wives to worship their own heathen gods was bad enough, but to share in such sacrilegious worship in sight of the Temple Solomon himself had built, was nauseating to God.

Thus sensuality and pride of wealth brought about Solomon's deterioration. In the Book of Ecclesiastes which the king wrote, he surely depicted his own dissatisfaction with even life itself. All rivers ran into Solomon's sea: wisdom and knowledge, wine and women, wealth and fame, music and songs; he tried them all, but all was vanity and vexation of spirit simply because God had been left out.

Of Solomon's actual end little is known. He is described as an "old man" at sixty years of age. Whether Solomon repented and returned to God was a question warmly debated by the Early Fathers. There is no record of his repentance. He never wrote a penitential psalm like his father before him (Ps. 51). We have his remorse, discontent, disgust, self-contempt, "bitterer to drink than blood," but no sobs for his sin, no plea for pardon. Thus, with such a tragic failure before us, let us take to heart the fact that Solomon's wisdom did not teach him self-control, and that the only legacy of his violated home life was a son "ample in foolishness and lacking in understanding," as C. W. Emmet expresses it.

SOPATER, SOSIPATER [Sŏp' a tûr, Sō sĭp' a tûr]—OF GOOD PARENTAGE or DEFENDS HIS FATHER. *A Christian of Berea* who accompanied Paul from Greece to Asia on his way to Syria. Mention of his father's name, Pyrrhus, R.V., unusual in the New Testament, may suggest that he was of noble birth. As a kinsman or fellow countryman of Paul, Sopater joined him in sending salutations to the saints (Acts 20:4; Rom. 16:21).

SOPHERETH [Sŏph' e rĕth]—LEARNING. *A servant of Solomon,* of a family of Nethinims, whose descendants returned with Zerubbabel (Ezra 2:55; Neh. 7:57).

SOSTHENES [Sŏs' the nēs]—OF SOUND STRENGTH or SAVIOUR FROM "I SAVE."
1. *The chief ruler of the synagogue at Corinth* who suffered at the hands of the Hellenistic Greeks when Gallio dismissed the case against Paul (Acts 18:17 R.V.).
2. *The believer or "brother" whom Paul unites with himself in addressing the Corinthian Church* (I Cor. 1:1). Perhaps both references are to the same man, Sosthenes of Acts 18:17 becoming a Christian after the Gallio outburst.

SOTAI [Sō' ta ī]—JEHOVAH IS TURNING ASIDE or DEVIATOR. *Another of Solomon's servants* whose descendants returned with Zerubbabel (Ezra 2:55; Neh. 7:57).

STACHYS [Stă' chўs]—AN EAR OF CORN or YOKE. *A Christian in Rome* to whom Paul sent a greeting (Rom. 16:9).

STEPHANAS [Stĕph' a năs]—CROWNED. *A believer in Corinth* of some importance, whose household formed the first fruits of Paul's preaching in Achaia. With Fortunatus and Achaicus, Stephanas joined the apostle at Ephesus and was of great assistance to him there (I Cor. 1:16; 16:15, 17).

STEPHEN [Stē' phen]—WREATH or CROWN. *One of the seven primitive disciples chosen to serve tables.* Stephen was the most prominent of these. Although called to supervise benevolences, he overleaped the limitations of his task and became a powerful preacher. He was also the first martyr of the Christian Church, being stoned to death by the Jews (Acts 6:5–9; 7:59; 11:19; 22:20).

The Man with an Angel Face

The remarkable defense of Stephen in which he summarized Old Testament teachings provoked the Jewish leaders so much that they cast him out of the city and brutally stoned him to death. God, however, can make the wrath of man to praise Him, thus the prominent fruit of Stephen's martyrdom was the conviction and conversion of Saul of Tarsus, who witnessed Stephen's illegal murder, unsanctioned by Roman law. Stephen's character is worthy of emulation. He was a man:

Full of Faith—no room for doubt or fear in his heart (Acts 6:5).

Full of Grace—a gift from God proving itself in graciousness (Acts 6:8 R.V.).

Full of Power—the ability of God to do things (Acts 6:8).

Full of Light—the Holy Spirit within gave him the face of an angel (Acts 6:15).

Full of Scripture—Stephen covered history from Abraham to Christ (Acts 7).

Full of Wisdom (Acts 6:3, 10), wisdom from above (Jas. 1:5).

Full of Courage—the face and fear of man did not trouble Stephen (Acts 7:51–56).

Full of Love—the stones broke Stephen's head but not his heart. Grace was his to forgive his murderers (Acts 7:60).

SUAH [Sū' ah]—RICHES, DISTINCTION or SWEEPINGS. *An Asherite,* eldest son of Zophah (I Chron. 7:36).

SUSI [Sū'-sī]—JEHOVAH IS SWIFT, REJOICING or HORSEMAN. *A Manassite,* father of Gaddi, one of the twelve men sent to spy out the land (Num. 13:11).

T

TABBAOTH [Tăb' ba ŏth]—SPOTS. *A member of a family of Nethinims* who returned from exile with Zerubbabel (Ezra 2:43; Neh. 7:46).

TABEAL [Tā' be al]—GOD IS GOOD or NOT SCORNFUL. *Father of one of the allied kings* which Rezin of Damascus and Pekah of Israel attempted to make their puppet king of Judah (Isa. 7:6).

TABEEL [Tā' be el]—GOD IS GOOD. *A Persian official* in Samaria who complained to Artaxerxes about the activity of the Jews (Ezra 4:7).

TABRIMON, TABRIMMON [Tăb' rĭ mon]—RIMMON IS GOD. *A son of Hezion* and father of Ben-hadad, king of Syria in Asa's time (I Kings 15:18).

TAHAN [Tā' hăn]—PRECIOUSNESS or INCLINATION.
1. *A son of Ephraim* and founder of a tribal family (Num. 26:35).
2. *A descendant of the same family* in the fourth generation (I Chron. 7:25).

TAHATH—[Tā' hăth]—DEPRESSION or HUMILITY.
1. *A Kohathite Levite,* son of Assir and father of Uriel (I Chron. 6:24, 37).
2. *Son of Bered,* grandson of Shuthelah the son of Ephraim (I Chron. 7:20). Also the name of the twenty-fourth station of Israel from Egypt, and the eleventh from Sinai (Num. 33:26, 27).

TAHREA, TAREA [Täh' re ă, Tā' re ă]—FLIGHT or ADROITNESS. *A grandson of Mephibosheth,* son of Micah, and so a descendant of Saul through Jonathan (I Chron. 8:35; 9:41).

TALMAI [Tăl' maī]—BOLD, SPIRITED or MY FURROWS.
1. *A son of Anak* in Hebron and probably the founder of the family of Anakims, driven from Hebron by Caleb (Num. 13:22; Josh. 15:14; Judg. 1:10).
2. *A king of Geshur,* whose daughter Maacah was one of David's wives and Absalom's mother (II Sam. 3:3; 13:37; I Chron. 3:2).

TALMON [Tăl' mon]—OPPRESSOR or VIOLENT. *A Levite porter* and founder of a tribal family, members of which returned with Zerubbabel and served as porters in the new Temple (I Chron. 9:17; Ezra 2:42; Neh. 7:45; 11:19; 12:25).

TANHUMETH [Tăn' hu mĕth]—CONSOLATION. *A Netophathite* and one of the Hebrew captains who joined Gedaliah at Mizpah (II Kings 25:23; Jer. 40:8).

TAPPUAH [Tăp' pōō ah]—APPLE or HIGH PLACE. *A son of Hebron* (I Chron. 2:43). Also the name of a city near Hebron (Josh. 12:17; 15:34) and another in Ephraim, now known as Atuf (Josh. 16:8; 17:8).

TARSHISH, THARSHISH [Tär' shish, Thär' shish]—HARD or CONTEMPLATION. This name is frequently mentioned in the Old Testament, principally in connection with a place hard to identify. The navy and ships of Tarshish prove it to have been of maritime importance. Josephus, the Jewish historian, wrongly identified it with Tarsus (I Kings 10:22; II Chron. 9:21; Jonah 1:3; 4:2).

1. *A grandson of Javan,* grandson of Noah (Gen. 10:4, I Chron. 1:7).

2. *A Benjamite,* son of Bilhan, the grandson of Benjamin (I Chron. 7:10).

3. *One of the seven highest princes of Persia* who were privileged to enter the king's presence when they desired (Esther 1:14).

TARTAN [Tär' tan]—GREAT INCREASE. *The commander-in-chief of Sargon* and of Sennacherib, kings of Assyria, sent to Hezekiah (II Kings 18:17; Isa. 20:1).

TATNAI [Tăt' na ī]—OVERSEER OF GIFTS. *A Persian governor* west of the Euphrates river who opposed the rebuilding of the Temple, and wrote to Darius to prevent the same (Ezra 5:3, 6; 6:6, 13).

TEBAH [Tĕ' bah]—SLAUGHTER OF CATTLE, THICK, STRONG. *A son of Nahor* by Reumah his concubine and brother of Abraham. Also head of a tribal family (Gen. 22:24). See Tibhath the town (I Chron. 18:8).

TEBALIAH [Tĕb a lī' ah]—JEHOVAH IS PROTECTOR or JEHOVAH HATH PURIFIED. *A son of Hosah,* a Merarite gatekeeper at the Tabernacle in David's time (I Chron. 26:11).

TEHINNAH [Tĕ hĭn' nah]—ENTREATY or GRACE, SUPPLICATION. *A son of Eshton,* a descendant of Judah and father of Ir-nahash (I Chron. 4:12).

TEKOH, TEKOA [Tĕ kŏ' ă]—FIRM, SETTLEMENT. The name, not of an individual, but of *a family of Ashur,* a descendant of Hezron grandson of Judah (I Chron. 2:24; 4:5; 11:28).

TELAH [Tĕ' lah]—VIGOR or FRACTURE. *An Ephraimite,* father of Tahan, a descendant of Ephraim through Beriah (I Chron. 7:25).

TELEM [Tĕ' lem]—A LAMB or OPPRESSION. *A gatekeeper* of the sanctuary who, returning from exile, put away his foreign wife (Ezra 10:24). Also the name of a city in Judah (Josh. 15:24). See also Telaim of I Samuel 15:4. Perhaps the same as Talmon of Nehemiah 12:25.

TEMA [Tĕ' mă]—SUN BURNT or ADMIRATION. *A son of Ishmael* and founder of a tribal family that settled around the Persian Gulf (Gen. 25:15; I Chron. 1:30; Job 6:19; Isa. 21:14; Jer. 25:23). The modern Taima.

TEMAN, TEMANI [Tĕ' man]—PERFECT.
1. *A son of Eliphaz,* son of Esau (Gen. 36:11, 15; I Chron. 1:36).

2. *An Edomite chief* (Gen. 36:42; I Chron. 1:53). Also the name of a race and an Edomite city. Eliphaz is referred to as "the Temanite" (I Chron. 1:45; Job 2:11).

TEMENI [Těm′ e nī]—FORTUNATE. *A descendant of Ashur,* and descendant of Caleb son of Hur (I Chron. 4:6).

TERAH, TARAH, THARA [Tě′ rah, Tā′ ra, Thā′ rǎ]—WILD GOAT or TURNING, WANDERING. *A son of Nahor* and father of Abraham and ancestor of Christ (Gen. 11:24–32; Josh. 24:2; I Chron. 1:26; Luke 3:34). See Numbers 33:27, 28.

The Man Who Died Half Way

Along with his three sons, Abraham, Nahor and Haran, Terah migrated from Ur of the Chaldees to Haran, where he died. The reference to him serving other gods led some of the Jewish Fathers to think of Terah as a maker of idols (Josh. 24:2). Why did Terah die at Haran? Was it not his intention to go to Canaan (Gen. 11:31, 32)?

It was God's purpose to separate Abraham from his kindred (Gen. 12:1), but Terah and Lot left with him, an exodus, perhaps, Abraham could not prevent. Lot, although he reached Canaan, was a constant grief to his uncle. The death of Terah seems to suggest that complete separation unto God often means the severance of some of earth's dearest ties. Terah is also a type of many who step out for Christ but whose hopes of discipleship die half way. Beginning in the Spirit they end in the flesh. Halfway converts never make wholehearted saints. Are you at Haran, or is yours the joy of living in Canaan?

TERESH [Tě′ resh]—REVERENCE or AUSTERE. *A chamberlain* who kept the door of the palace, and who with Bigthana plotted to murder King Ahasuerus. Mordecai discovered the plot and Teresh was executed (Esther 2:21; 6:2).

TERTIUS [Tûr′ tius]—from the Latin, meaning, THE THIRD. *Paul's amanuensis,* who wrote at the apostle's dictation the Epistle to the Romans. Paul usually added his own autograph (Rom. 16:22, 25–27). Some writers have identified Tertius as Silas.

TERTULLUS [Tûr tŭl′ lus]—derived from Tertius, and meaning, LIAR or IMPOSTOR. *A Roman advocate* employed by the Jewish authorities to prosecute Paul before Felix, the Roman Governor or Procurator (Acts 24:1, 2; 25:8).

The style of his rhetorical address or brief was common to Roman advocates. With his power of glib eloquence as well as knowledge of Roman laws, the orator Tertullus sought to impress the mind of the judge. With the trick of his class, he began with flattery of the judge. All of the flattering epithets of the hired orator, however, stand out in striking contrast with "the righteousness, temperance, and judgment to come," Paul later spoke about to the same ruler.

From flattery of the judge, Tertullus passed to invective against the defendant, charging him with crimes he never committed. Paul in his defense presented a marked difference between his own frank manliness and the advocate's servile flattery. Tertullus could not rouse the conscience of Felix as Paul did. "Felix trembled," as Paul pressed home the truth of the Gospel and sent for him "the oftener," we read. What a tragedy it was that Felix did not follow his Spirit-impressed conscience!

THADDAEUS [Thăd dae′ us]—BREAST, ONE THAT PRAISES or MAN OF HEART. *One of the twelve apostles of Christ* (Matt. 10:3; Mark 3: 18), also called Labbeus, or Lebbeus, and sometimes identified as Jude, who wrote the epistle bearing his name. This apostle then, was known by three names, two of which were terms of endearment used toward him from early days. In this least known among the apostles, we have a man who discovered that love is the secret of obedience and that obedience is the secret of blessedness.

THAHASH [Thā′ hăsh]—KEEP SILENCE or REDDISH. *A son of Reumah,* concubine of Nahor, Abraham's brother (Gen. 22:24).

THAMAH, TAMAH, TEMAH [Thā′ mah]—COMBAT, LAUGHTER or SUPPRESSES. *A member of a family of the Nethinims* whose descendants returned from exile with Zerubbabel (Ezra 2:53; Neh. 7:55).

THEOPHILUS—[Thē ŏph′ ĭ lŭs]—LOVED BY GOD, LOVER OF GOD, or FRIEND OF GOD. *A Christian of high rank* for whose use Luke wrote his gospel and the Acts of the Apostles (Luke 1:3; Acts 1:1). The term "most excellent," used also of Felix and Festus (Acts 23:26; 24:3; 26:25), indicates that Theophilus was a Roman official to whom Luke paid due deference, even though he was on intimate terms with him. It has been suggested "Theophilus" was the name this Gentile nobleman chose at his conversion to Christianity. Evidently Luke had fully instructed him in the cardinal truths of the Gospel (Luke 1:3).

THEUDAS [Theū′ das]—FALSE TEACHER. *A Jewish impostor* mentioned by Gamaliel before the Sanhedrin as the leader of an unsuccessful rebellion of four hundred men, who were destroyed with him (Acts 5:36). The identity of Theudas has occupied the attention of scholars since the time of Josephus, who also mentions a leader of this name at the head of an insurrection. The description Gamaliel gives us of Theudas as "boasting himself to be somebody" that is, some great personage, may agree with the account given by Josephus that Theudas was the Simon, previously a slave of Herod's, who proclaimed himself king and burned Herod's palaces. Theudas was his alias to conceal his servile origin.

THOMAS [Thŏm' as]—TWIN. *One of the twelve apostles of Christ,* and called also Didymus (Matt. 10:3; Mark 3:18; Luke 6:15; John 11:16; 14:5; 20:24–29; 21-2; Acts 1:13).

The Man Who Doubted

Thomas, we are told, was not really a name but an epithet, meaning, like its Greek equivalent Didymus, "the twin." David Smith suggests that the apostle's name was Judas, but that he was named "the twin" to distinguish him from Judas, the son of James, and Judas Iscariot. Tradition credits him with the authorship of a gospel which is included in apocryphal literature.

Zealous, inquisitive and incredulous, he earned the title of "Thomas the Doubter." Because of his hesitancy in accepting the disciples' story of the Resurrection of Christ, Thomas has come down through the centuries as a typical pessimist and sceptic. But was he an habitual doubter? Some authorities suppose that the name Didymus alluded to his doubting propensities, since some versions render it as "double-minded."

Had we only the record of the first three gospels, Thomas would be to us simply a name, but John rescued him from oblivion, made him a reality to us and surrounded him with an undying interest. Tradition has it that he died a martyr.

Three traits seem to stand out in John's cameo of Thomas:

I. When he saw what he ought to do, nothing kept him back. When Jesus expressed his intention of going into Judea again, Thomas urged the disciples to accompany Christ even though it might mean death (John 11:16).

II. When he saw what he ought to do, he only wanted to see how he was to do it. At the Last Supper he acknowledged his ignorance of the place the Lord was going to and asked how he could know the way (John 14:5).

III. When he saw what it was he had to believe, he only wanted to see that it was right, and then to him there was no help for it. After our Lord's resurrection Thomas refused to believe in its reality except upon conditions which he himself laid down. How stirring was his confession of faith once convinced of the Resurrection (John 20:28; 21:2).

TIBERIUS [Tĭ bē' rĭ ŭs]—SON OF TIBER. *The stepson of Augustus* and third Emperor of Rome, A.D. 14–37 (Luke 3:1). His full name was Tiberius Caesar Augustus. A Souter reminds us that Tiberius was "an able general and a competent Emperor, but the unhappy experiences of his early life made him suspicious and timorous, and he put many of his rivals or supposed rivals to death. In his later years he was much under the influence of a villainous schemer, Sejamus."

TIBNI [Tĭb′ nĭ]—INTELLIGENT or STRAW. *A son of Ginath,* who disputed the throne for four years with Zimri or Omri (I Kings 16:21–23).

TIDAL [Tĭ′ dal]—BREAKS THE YOKE or RENOWN. *A king of Goüm or Goyim,* confederate with Chedorlaomer, Amraphel and Arioch, who invaded the cities of the plain in Abraham's time (Gen. 14:1–9). He is identified as Tudhal, king of Gutium.

TIGLATH-PILESER, TILGATH-PILNESER [Tĭg′ lath-pĭ lē′ zer, Tĭl′ gath-pĭl nē′ zer]—HINDERS, BINDS or MY STRENGTH IS THE GOD NINIB. *An Assyrian king* who reigned 745–727 B.C. Probably the Pul of II Kings 15:19, 29; 16:7, 10; I Chronicles 5:6, 26; II Chronicles 28:20. His reign was an active and important one, and his expeditions were most successful. He probably died when making one of them. The reader should consult both Biblical and secular history for a full account of this Babylonian monarch's exploits.

TIKVAH, TIKVATH [Tĭk′ vah, Tĭk′ văth]—STRENGTH or EXPECTATION.
1. *Father of Shallum,* husband of Huldah the prophetess (II Kings 22:14; II Chron. 34:22). Also called Tokhath.
2. *The father of Jahaziah* who recorded those who had married foreign wives (Ezra 10:15).

TILON [Tĭ′ lon] —SCORN. *A son of Shimon,* whose registry was with the tribe of Judah through Caleb the son of Jephunneh (I Chron. 4:20).

TIMAEUS [Tĭ mae′ us]—HIGHLY PRIZED. *Father of the blind beggar,* Bartimeus, who received his sight from Christ at Jericho (Mark 10:46).

TIMNA, TIMNAH [Tĭm′ nä, Tĭm′ nah]—RESTRAINING or INACCESSIBLE.
1. *A chief of Edom* descended from Esau (Gen. 36:40; I Chron. 1:51).
2. *A son of Eliphaz,* son of Esau (I Chron. 1:36). Also the name of a concubine of Eliphaz son of Esau (Gen. 36:12), and also of a daughter of Seir the Horite, and sister of Lotan (Gen. 36:22; I Chron. 1:39). Timnah is likewise the name of a city in Judah, now called Tibneh (Josh. 15:10, 57; II Chron. 28:18).

TIMON [Tĭ′ mon]—HONORABLE or DEEMED WORTHY. *One of the*

seven chosen to relieve the apostles of semi-secular work in the Early Church (Acts 6:5).

TIMOTHEUS, TIMOTHY [Tī mŏ′ the ŭs, Tĭm′ o thў]—HONORED OF GOD, WORSHIPING GOD or VALUED OF GOD. *A young man of Lystra,* son of Eunice, a Jewess, by a Greek father who was probably dead when Paul first visited the home (Acts 16:1).

The Man Who Confessed a Good Confession

As Paul contributes a full portrait of his spiritual son, many years his junior, let us string together the salient features of Timothy.

I. He was the child of godly heritage (II Tim. 1:5). His mother was a Christian Jewess and the daughter of another devout Jewess, Lois. His Greek father's name is unknown. It may be that Eunice became a Christian when Paul visited Lystra, a town not far from Paul's birthplace, Tarsus.

II. He was a youthful reader of Scripture (II Tim. 3:15). From a "babe" he had had knowledge of the Truth. How blessed children are if cradled in the things of God!

III. He was Paul's child in the faith (I Cor. 4:17; I Tim. 1:2; II Tim. 1:2). Probably Paul, a visitor of Timothy's house, led the young lad to Christ during his ministry in Iconium and Lystra since he refers to his persecutions there, which Timothy himself knew about (II Tim. 3:10, 11). One writer suggests that when Paul recovered from his stoning at Lystra it was in Timothy's home he found shelter and succor.

IV. He was ordained as a minister of the Gospel (I Tim. 4:14; II Tim. 1:6, 7). Conscious of Timothy's unique gifts, especially of evangelism (Rom. 16:21; II Tim. 4:5), it was fitting that Paul should choose him as a companion and fellow-worker. Faithfully he served Paul "as a son with his father," in the furtherance of the Gospel (Phil. 2:22). How indispensable he became to the apostle (Acts 17:14, 15; 18:5; 20:4)! Paul had no other companion so "like-minded" as Timothy, who enjoyed Paul's constant instruction (II Tim. 2:3; 3:14).

V. He was an ambassador charged with difficult tasks. The responsible and delicate mission of restoring a backsliding church required both gift and grace (I Cor. 14:17), as did the comfort of believers in the midst of tribulation (I Thess. 3:2).

VI. He was co-sufferer with Paul in the afflictions of the Gospel (II Tim. 1:8). Tradition says that Timothy died as a martyr for his faithfulness as a bishop in the reign of Domitian or Nerva. While attempting to stop an indecent heathen procession during the Festival of Diana, this God-honoring minister sealed his testimony with his blood. The two epistles Paul addressed to Timothy are rich in their pastoral counsel.

TIRAS [Tī′ ras]—DESIRE OF PARENTS. *A son of Japheth* and founder of a tribal family in Thracia (Gen. 10:2; I Chron. 1:5).

TIRHAKAH [Tûr' ha kah]—EXALTED. *A king of Cush,* the third and last king of the twentieth dynasty, and successor of Sevechus. Also known as Tarakos. He was contemporary with king Hezekiah (II Kings 19:9; Isa. 37:9).

TIRHANAH [Tûr' ha nah]—KINDNESS. *A son of Caleb,* brother of Jerahmeel, by Maacah his concubine (I Chron. 2:48).

TIRIA [Tûr' ĭ ă]—FOUNDATION. *A son of Jehaleleel,* a descendant of Judah through Caleb son of Jephunneh (I Chron. 4:16).

TIRSHATHA [Tûr' sha thă]—REVERENCE or BEHOLDING THE TIME. *The Persian title given to Zerubbabel* and Nehemiah as governors of Judah under the king of Persia. The Persian word means "His Excellency" or "His Reverence" (Ezra 2:63; Neh. 7:65, 70; 8:9; 10:1).

TITUS [Tī' tus]—HONORABLE FROM "I HONOR." *Titus was born of Gentile parents, and was a convert from heathenism.* It is more than likely that Paul led him to Christ (Gal. 2:3; Titus 1:4).

The Man Who Refreshed His Master

There seemed to have been a peculiar bond of affection between Paul and his Grecian convert. How Paul loved him and appreciated his trusted companionship (II Cor. 7:6, 13)! What an inspiration he was to Paul on several of his journeys (Gal. 2:1, 3)! In II Corinthians Paul mentions Titus some nine times. Paul sent Titus to Corinth as his delegate. Paul anxiously awaited the return of Titus, and he refreshed the spirit of the apostle both by his presence and the good news he brought from Corinth (II Cor. 2:12, 14).

In the precious epistle Paul sent to Titus, we learn more facts about the loving co-operation between these two noble men. When Paul was released from prison, Titus accompanied him on a visit to Crete, Paul leaving him there to assist the Church in a fourfold way:

I.   Set in order things that were wanting.
II. Ordain elders in every city.
III. Avoid unprofitable discussion.
IV. Duly assert his authority (Titus 1:5; 2:1; 3:9, 15).

It may be that Paul sent his epistle to Titus by the hands of Zenas and Apollos (3:13), to assist him in the difficult task at Crete.

Paul then wanted Titus to join him for the winter in Nicopolis (3:12). Titus was with the apostle during part of his second imprisonment in Rome (II Tim. 4:10). Both men were sustained in their arduous labors by "the blessed hope" (Titus 2:13).

A godly man of Corinth is spoken of as Titus Justus (Acts 18:7, R.V.). Titus himself is not mentioned directly in the Acts. Doubtless he was included in the "certain others" in Acts 15:2.

TOAH [Tō' ah]—DEPRESSION or HUMILITY. *A Kohathite Levite,*

father of Eliel and grandfather of Jeroham, who was the grandfather of the prophet Samuel (I Chron. 6:34). Called Tohu in I Samuel 1:1.

TOB-ADONIJAH [Tŏb'-ad o nī' jah]—GOOD IS MY LORD JEHOVAH or MY GOOD GOD. *One of the Levites sent by Jehoshaphat* to teach the law to the people in the cities of Judah (II Chron. 17:8).

TOBIAH, TOBIJAH [Tō bī' ah, Tō bī' jah]—JEHOVAH IS GOOD.
1. *A Levite* sent by Jehoshaphat to instruct the people of Judah (II Chron. 17:8).
2. *A founder* of a tribal family the descendants of which returned from exile but were unable to trace their genealogy (Ezra 2:60; Neh. 7:62).
3. *An Ammonite* who with Sanballat and others ridiculed the efforts of the Jews to rebuild the wall of Jerusalem (Neh. 2:10; 4:3, 7). This enemy of Nehemiah and of the Jews was silenced by the diligence of the people.
4. *A chief man* whose posterity returned from exile (Zech. 6:10, 14). He it was who obtained the gold and silver for Joshua's crown.

TOGARMAH [Tō gär' mah]—ALL BONE or STRONG. *The third son of Gomer,* son of Japheth, his brothers being Ashkenaz and Riphath (Gen. 10:3; I Chron. 1:6; Ezek. 27:14; 38:6).
Perhaps there is prophetic significance attached to Togarmah and "the house of Togarmah of the north quarters, and all his bands" (Ezek. 38:6). Jewish writers of the past usually wrote of the "Turks" as Togarmah, and the Armenians as "The House of Targon." It is not difficult, therefore, to identify Togarmah as Armenia or Turkey, the people of which assert their descendancy from Targon, or the Togarmah of Scripture.
The ultimate alliance of Turkey, according to prophecy, is with the Northern Confederacy Ezekiel defines. Dr. Sale-Harrison observes: "It is interesting to note that in Scripture "The King of the North" is called "The Old Assyrian" and apparently arises out of the present "Turkish territory." In the final alignment of the nations then, Togarmah will be allied with the north.

TOHU [Tō' hu]—HUMILITY, DEPRESSION or THAT LIVES. *A Kohathite,* a son of Zuph, ancestor of Samuel (I Sam. 1:1). Called Nahath in I Chronicles 6:26, and Toah in I Chronicles 6:34.

TOI, TOU [Tō' ī, Tō' ū]—WANDERING or ERROR. *A king of Hamath* on the Orontes in David's time, who congratulated David on his defeat of a common foe, Hadadezer (II Sam. 8:9, 10; I Chron. 18:9, 10).

TOLA [Tō' lă]—SCARLET, FROM THE COLOR OF A WORM.

1. *A son of Issachar* and founder of a tribal family (Gen. 46:13; Num. 26:23; I Chron. 7:1, 2).

2. *The son of Puah* of the tribe of Issachar. This Tola, sometimes identified with the first one, was the first of the five minor Judges, and judged Israel for twenty-three years. He lived and died at Shamar (Judg. 10:1, 2).

TROPHIMUS [Trŏph' Ĭ mŭs]—NOURISHING or WELL EDUCATED. *A believer living in Ephesus,* who with others accompanied Paul to Jerusalem (Acts 20:4; 21:29; II Tim. 4:20). Trophimus was falsely accused by the Jewish leaders who, seeing him with Paul, hastily concluded that he had brought his missionary companion into the inner court of the Temple which non-Jews were not allowed to enter. The last glimpse we have of Trophimus was when Paul left him at Miletus sick. The apostle who had the gift of healing could do nothing for his sick friend—a fact quack faith healers should note.

TUBAL [Too' bal]—WORLDLY POSSESSIONS or FLOWING FORTH. *A son of Japheth* (Gen. 10:2; I Chron. 1:5). Also the name of a country in Asia Minor mentioned in connection with Meshech (Isa. 66:19; Ezek. 27:13; 32:26; 38:2, 3; 39:1). This place is now identified as Tobolsk, capital of Asiatic Russia, and is therefore heavy with prophetic significance.

TUBAL-CAIN [Too' bal-cāin]—PRODUCTION OF FORGED WORK or FLOWING FORTH OF CAIN. *The son of Zillah,* one of Lamech's wives, of the race of Cain (Gen. 4:22).

The Man Who Invented Metal Tools

Tubal (or the Tibureni, noted for production of bronze articles, Ezek. 27:13) and Cain meaning "smith" marks Tubal-cain as "the father of every forger of copper and iron." In Ezekiel 27:13, Tubal is found bringing brass to the market of Tyre, and in Persian the word means copper. The alloy we call brass was absolutely unknown to the ancients. From the world's first coppersmith we learn that "metals and their use were kept a guarded secret in the possession of a single family, or clan, for many generations."

TYCHICUS [Tῐch' Ĭ cŭs]—FORTUNATE or FORTUITOUS. *A Christian in Asia Minor,* who traveled in advance of Paul as well as with him at times (Acts 20:4). Paul sent him to Ephesus where he delivered, and likely read, the circular letter, the Epistle to the Ephesians, to the Church there (Eph. 6:21). Then he went to Colosse and did the same with Colossians (Col. 4:7). He also had a mission to fulfill in Crete (II Tim. 4:12; Titus 3:12). Paul speaks of him in affectionate terms—"A brother beloved and faithful minister in the Lord," and able to "comfort your hearts."

TYRANNUS [Tī răn′ nus]—ABSOLUTE, SOVEREIGN or A TYRANT (from Tyrus, meaning strength). *A teacher* in a philosophical school in Ephesus in which Paul disputed daily for two years (Acts 19:9). Instructions in the Law were given in this school by Jewish scribes. Ellicott suggests that "Tyrannus was also a physician, and that, as such, he may have known Luke, or, possibly may have been among the Jews whom the decree of Claudius (Acts 18:2) had driven from Rome. An unconverted teacher of philosophy or rhetoric was not likely to have lent his class-room to a preacher of the new faith."

U

UCAL [Ū′ cal]—POWER. *An unknown person who is coupled by Agur with Ithiel* (Prov. 30:1).

UEL [Ū′ el]—WILL OF GOD. *A son of Bani* who married a strange, or foreign wife during the exile, and then put her away (Ezra 10:34).

ULAM [Ū′ lam]—SOLITARY, FRONT or THEIR FOLLY.
1. *A son of Sheresh,* grandson of Manasseh (I Chron. 7:16, 17).
2. *A son of Eshek,* a Benjamite of the family of Saul (I Chron. 8:39, 40). This Benjamite family was especially noted as archers (II Chron. 14:7, 8).

ULLA [Ŭl′ lă]—BURDEN, A YOKE or ELEVATION. *An Asherite,* probably descended from Helem (I Chron. 7:39).

UNNI, UNNO [Ŭn′ nī]—POOR, AFFLICTED or ANSWERING IS WITH JEHOVAH.
1. *A Levite* who was a contemporary of the high priest Jeshua (Neh. 12:9), and who returned with Zerubbabel.
2. *A Levite porter* over the choral services in the Tabernacle in David's time (I Chron. 15:18, 20). This Unni played a psaltery.

UR [Ŭr]—LIGHT, BRIGHTNESS or SETTLEMENT. *The father of Eliphal,* one of David's mighty men (I Chron. 11:35). Ur is also the name of the city where Abraham was born (Gen. 11:28, 31; 15:7; Neh. 9:7).

URBANE, URBANUS [Ŭr′ băne]—URBANE or POLITE. *This was a common name among slaves,* often found in inscriptions of the imperial household. Here it is the name of *a Christian to whom Paul* sent a greeting (Rom. 16:9).

URI [Ū′ rī]—LIGHT OF JEHOVAH or ENLIGHTENED. Sometimes this name was used as an abbreviation of Urijah.

1. *The father of Bezaleel,* the craftsman associated with the building of the Tabernacle (Ex. 31:2; 35:30; 38:22; I Chron. 2:20; II Chron. 1:5).

2. *The Father of Geber,* one of Solomon's taxgatherers (I Kings 4:19).

3. *A porter or gatekeeper* who put away his wife (Ezra 10:24).

URIAH, URIJAH, URIAS [Ū rī′ ah, U rī′ jah, U rī′ as]—JEHOVAH IS LIGHT.

1. *A high priest in Jerusalem,* who built an altar according to the pattern provided by King Ahaz (II Kings 16:10–16).

2. *A priest,* father of Meremoth, who helped rebuild the wall of Jerusalem (Ezra 8:33; Neh. 3:4, 21).

3. *A priest* who stood with Ezra as he read the law and addressed the people (Neh. 8:4).

4. *A priest* whom Isaiah deemed worthy to act as a witness. He is described as "a faithful witness" (Isa. 8:2). See Revelation 1:4; 2:13.

5. *A prophet,* the son of Shemaiah of Kirjath-jearim, whom Jehoiakin sent for into Egypt and slew him (Jer. 26:20–23).

6. *Uriah,* or Urias (Matt. 1:6) was also the name of the Hittite, husband of Bath-sheba, and one of David's thirty heroes (II Sam. 11; 12:9–15; 23:39; I Kings 15:5; I Chron. 11:41).

As David's general, Uriah distinguished himself by his loyalty and bravery in the army of the king. Alas, Uriah was barbarously, even murderously treated by the monarch he served! Failing to use Uriah as a shield for his sin against Uriah and Bath-sheba his wife, David had him killed in battle.

Thomas Goodwin points out that it was the "matter of Uriah," even more than the matter of Bath-sheba, that awakened the anger of the Lord against David. That is to say, it was David's sin of deliberation and determination, rather than his sin of sudden and intoxicating passion. But both sins matter and earn the judgment of God. Uriah had every right to disobey David in his deceitful commands. Through Nathan, the adulterer and murderer was brought back to God and wrote his confession in a penitential psalm (Ps. 51).

URIEL [Ū′ rǐ el]—A LIGHT, FLAME OF GOD or GOD IS MY LIGHT OR FIRE.

1. *A Levite of the family of Kohath,* son of Tahath, of the house of Izhar (I Chron. 6:24; 15:5, 11).

2. *A man of Gibeah,* father of Michaiah, one of Rehoboam's wives (II Chron. 13:2).

In the Apocrypha Uriel is one of four archangels responsible for the luminaries of heaven, and the angel with whom Jacob wrestled.

UTHAI [Ū′ tha ī]—JEHOVAH IS HELP.

1. *A son of Ammihud,* a man of Judah of the family of Perez or Pharez, who lived in Jerusalem (I Chron. 9:4).

2. *A son of Bigvai,* who returned with Ezra from exile to Jerusalem (Ezra 8:14).

UZ [Ūz]—FIRMNESS.
1. *A son of Aram* and grandson of Shem (Gen. 10:23; I Chron. 1:17).
2. *A son of Dishan,* a Horite in the land of Edom (Gen. 36:28; I Chron. 1:42). Uz is also the name of the land where Job was born and lived, and was part of the great Arabian desert running into Chaldea (Job 1:1; Jer. 25:20; Lam. 4:21).

UZAI [Ū′ za ī]—HOPED FOR. *Father of Palal* who helped to rebuild the damaged wall of Jerusalem (Neh. 3:25).

UZAL [Ū′ zal]—A WANDERER. *The sixth son of Joktan,* of the family of Shem, who settled in South Arabia, where the kings of Yemen dwelt (Gen. 10:27; I Chron. 1:21; Ezek. 27:19).

UZZA, UZZAH [Ŭz′ zȧ, Ŭz′ zah]—STRENGTH.
1. *A son of Abinadab* who died for touching the Ark (II Sam. 6:3–8; I Chron. 13:7–11). Perez-uzzah means "the breach of Uzzah."
2. *A son of Shimei,* a Merarite (I Chron. 6:29).
3. *A Benjamite,* brother of Ahihud, a son or descendant of Ehud (I Chron. 8:7).
4. *Founder of a family of Nethinims* who returned from exile with Zerubbabel (Ezra 2:49; Neh. 7:51).
5. *Owner of the garden in which Manasseh and Amon, kings of Judah,* were buried (II Kings 21:18, 26).

UZZI [Ŭz′ zī]—THE MIGHT OF JEHOVAH.
1. *A son of Bukki* and father of Zerahiah. Also a descendant of Aaron (I Chron. 6:5, 6, 51; Ezra 7:4).
2. *A grandson of Issachar* and father of Izrahiah, and head of his father's house (I Chron. 7:2, 3).
3. *A son of Bela,* Benjamin's son, and head of his house (I Chron. 7:7).
4. *The father of Elah,* a Benjamite (I Chron. 9:8).
5. *An overseer of the Levites* in Jerusalem after the exile (Neh. 11:22).
6. *A priest of the family of Jedaiah* in the days of the high priest Joiakim (Neh. 12:19, 42).

UZZIA [Ŭz zī′ ȧ]—MIGHT OF JEHOVAH. *An Asherite,* and one of David's mighty men (I Chron. 11:44).

UZZIAH [Ŭz zī′ ah]—STRENGTH OF THE LORD.
1. *A son of Uriel,* a Kohathite (I Chron. 6:24).

2. *The father of Jehonathan,* keeper of David's storehouses (I Chron. 27:25).

3. *A priest,* son of Harim, who put away his foreign wife (Ezra 10:21).

4. *The father of Athaniah,* who returned with other exiles to Jerusalem (Neh. 11:4).

5. *The son of Amaziah* and father of Jotham, king of Judah.

The Man Who Became a Leper through Pride

This renowned Uzziah, or Azariah, as he is sometimes called, demands more attention (II Kings 15:13, 30–34; II Chron. 26; 27:2; Isa. 1:1; 6:1; 7:1; Hos. 1:1; Amos 1:1; Zech. 14:5). His story can be gathered around three aspects:

I. His prosperity. Uzziah ascended the throne at the age of sixteen years, and it is said that "his mother's name also was Jecoliah of Jerusalem." These words, "his mother's name," are found about thirty times in Kings and Chronicles, and seem to indicate that the mother largely determined the character and conduct of the son. See II Kings 8:26; 12:1; 14:2.

Of Uzziah it is written that "as long as he sought the Lord, God made him to prosper" (see I Chron. 28:9; Ps. 69:32). As a king of Judah, Uzziah is remembered principally for the era of prosperity which prevailed during his reign. He reigned for fifty-two years, and a graphic account of what he accomplished for Judah has been preserved (II Chron. 26). Under Uzziah, Jerusalem was adorned with many and costly improvements, to which her citizens pointed with patriotic pride.

II. His pride. God finds it difficult to entrust prosperity to many of His people. It turns their heads and leads to pride as with Uzziah, of whom it is also said, "When he was strong, his heart was lifted up to his destruction." The king's special sin was a rash intrusion into the priest's office, and in this he was a type of the antichrist of the last days (Ex. 30:7, 8; Dan. 11:36, 37; II Thess. 2:3, 4). The king usurped the function of the chief priest and offered incense. Religiously, Uzziah is classed among the good kings (II Kings 15:1, 3), and had he been content to remain a good king, all would have been well.

III. His punishment. For his intrusion into the sacred duties of the priesthood, Uzziah was smitten with leprosy, and had to withdraw from public affairs, his son Jotham acting as his representative (II Kings 15:5). The leprous condition was an appropriate expression of God's indignation at Uzziah's presumption (see Ex. 4:6; Lev. 13:3, 12, 13, 25; Luke 4:27). Ultimately, he went to a leper's grave, but in the year the leper king died, Isaiah, who had looked upon Uzziah as his hero-king, had a vision that transformed his life and ministry (Isa. 6.).

Thus Uzziah is a blazing warning against the spiritual pride that brings presumption (II Chron. 26:16–21). Such a warning is needed today when the two chief snares of Satan for the servants of God seem to be spiritual pride and fleshly lust.

UZZIEL [Ŭz′ zĭ el]—GOD IS STRONG. There are six Bible men bearing this suggestive name.

1. *A son of Kohath,* son of Levi, kinsman of Aaron on his father's side (Ex. 6:18, 22; Lev. 10:4; Num. 3:19, 30; I Chron. 6:2; 15:10; 23:12, 20; 24:24).

2. *A Simeonite* who, in Hezekiah's reign, led a successful expedition against the Amalekites (I Chron. 4:42).

3. *A son of Bela,* son of Benjamin (I Chron. 7:7).

4. *A son of Heman,* an instrumentalist, set by David over the service of song (I Chron. 25:4).

5. *A Levite,* son of Jeduthun, who assisted Hezekiah in his work of reformation (II Chron. 29:14).

6. *The son of Harhaiah,* a goldsmith, who repaired a part of the wall of Jerusalem (Neh. 3:8).

Members of the tribal family of Uzziel are spoken of as Uzzielites (Num. 3:27; I Chron. 26:23).

V

VAJEZATHA, VAIZATHA [Vă jĕz′ a thă]—BORN OF IZED, STRONG AS THE WIND or SINCERE. *The tenth son of Haman* of Esther's time, who shared the fate of his brothers (Esther 9:9).

VANIAH [Vă nĭ′ ah]—GOD IS PRAISE or DISTRESS. *One of the sons of Bani* who married a foreign wife (Ezra 10:36).

VASHNI [Văsh′ nĭ]—GOD IS STRONG. *First-born of Samuel* the prophet (I Chron. 6:28). The prophet's oldest son is also named as Joel (I Sam. 8:2).

VOPHSI [Vŏph′ sĭ]—FRAGRANT or RICH. *The father of Nahbi* of the tribe of Judah who, with others, was sent to spy out the land (Num. 13:14).

Z

ZAAVAN, ZAVAN [Ză′ a văn, Ză′ van]—CONQUEST or CAUSING FEAR. *A son of Ezer,* a descendant of Seir the Horite (Gen. 36:27; I Chron. 1:42).

ZABAD [Zā' băd]—ENDOWER, HE HATH GIVEN or A GIFT. There are many names derived from this root in the Old Testament. It is associated with Zebulun (Gen. 30:20), and is found in fuller form in Zabdiel and Zebadiah (my gift is Jehovah).

1. *A son of Nathan* and grandson of Pharez, son of Judah (I Chron. 2:36, 37).

2. *A son of Tuhath*, father of Shuthelah, of Ephraim (I Chron. 7:21).

3. *A son of Ahlai*, one of David's mighty heroes (I Chron. 11:41).

4. *The son of Shimeath*, who assisted in the slaying of Joash, the king of Judah (II Chron. 24:26).

5. *A son of Zattu* who married a strange wife (Ezra 10:27).

6. *A son of Hashum who also put away his wife* (Ezra 10:33).

7. *A son of Nebo who likewise put away his wife* (Ezra 10:43).

ZABBAI [Zăb' baī]—ROVING ABOUT, HUMMING.

1. *One of the sons of Bebai* who married a foreign wife (Ezra 10:28).

2. *Father of Baruch* who helped to repair the wall of Jerusalem (Neh. 3:20).

ZABBUD [Zăb' bud]—WELL REMEMBERED, ENDOWED. *A son of Bigvai*, who returned with Ezra from exile (Ezra 8:14).

ZABDI [Zăb' dī]—THE GIFT OF JEHOVAH, JEHOVAH IS ENDOWER or DOWRY.

1. *The father of Carmi*, father of Achan. Also called Zimri (Josh. 7:1, 17, 18; I Chron. 2:6).

2. *A Benjamite*, son of Shimshi (I Chron. 8:19).

3. *A Shiphmite* from Shepham in Judah, and a storekeeper in David's time (I Chron. 27:27).

4. *A son of Asaph*, a Levite and father of Micha (Neh 11:17).

ZABDIEL [Zăb' dĭ el]— MY GIFT IS GOD or GOD IS ENDOWER.

1. *The father of Jashobeam*, one of David's officers, (I Chron. 27:2).

2. *A son of Haggedolim* and an overseer of priests in Jerusalem (Neh. 11:14).

ZABUD [Zā' bud]—ENDOWED or GIVER. *The son of Nathan*, a friend and chief minister of Solomon (I Kings 4:5 R.V.).

ZACCAI [Zăc' ca ī]—PURE, INNOCENT. *Founder of a family*, members of which returned from exile with Zerubbabel (Ezra 2:9; Neh. 7:14).

ZACCHAEUS [Zăc chae' us]—PURE or JUSTIFIED.
The Man Who Overcame Obstacles
Zacchaeus was the wealthy man of Jerusalem who gathered revenue

for the Roman government, but who became a disciple of Christ (Luke 19:1–10). A "chief publican," Zacchaeus might have been of a higher grade than Matthew.

Although not one of Christ's expected converts, Zacchaeus had heard much about Christ and was determined to see Him for himself. When ultimately Christ came his way there were two obstacles in his way—the crowd, and his own short stature. But he quickly overcame both hindrances.

I.   The crowd. It is strange that those who were enthusiastic about Christ were the very people blocking Zacchaeus' view. What a lesson for our hearts can be gleaned from this fact!

II.   The short stature. The other difficulty was Zacchaeus himself. His native hindrance was his small stature, which he quickly overcame. Up the tree he climbed and had the best view of Jesus that day. If we would see Jesus we too must scramble higher than ourselves.

III.   The call to discipleship. Our Lord called Zacchaeus down and invited Himself to his house. Zacchaeus was a sinner and Christ saved him. Quickly Zacchaeus revealed the depth of his surrender to his newly found Master. There came an immediate and generous restitution.

ZACCUR, ZACCHUR [Zăc′cur, Zăc′chur]—WELL REMEMBERED, PURE.

1.   A Reubenite, father of Shammua, one of the spies sent out by Moses (Num. 13:4).

2.   A Simeonite, son of Hamuel and father of Shimei (I Chron. 4:26).

3.   A Merarite Levite, a son of Jaaziah (I Chron. 24:27).

4.   A son of Asaph and father of Michaiah. Also head of a course of musicians set up by David (I Chron. 25:2, 10; Neh. 12:35).

5.   A son of Imri, who rebuilt part of the wall after Nehemiah came from Shushan (Neh. 3:2).

6.   A Levite who sealed the covenant (Neh. 10:12).

7.   A son of Mattaniah and father of Hanan (Neh. 13:13).

ZACHARIAH [Zăch a rī′ ah]—JEHOVAH IS RENOWNED.

1.   Son of Jeroboam II, king of Israel (II Kings 14:29; 15:8, 11).

2.   Father of Abi or Abijah, wife of Ahaz and mother of Hezekiah (II Kings 18:2; II Chron. 29:1).

ZACHARIAS [Zăch a rī as]—JEHOVAH IS RENOWNED.

1.   The son of Barachias, or Jehoiada (II Chron. 24:20–22). This Zacharias is the martyr mentioned by Christ (Matt. 23:35; Luke 11:51) who was the righteous man murdered by the Jews in the court of the Temple, between the sanctuary and the house.

2.   The father of John the Baptist (Luke 1:5–67; 3:2).

The Man Who Was Stricken Dumb

The priest of the eighth course of Abia was visited by the angel Gabriel as he was ministering in his turn in the Temple. The revelation came to him about the birth of a son in his old age, and of his name and mission. His disbelief of the divine message was punished by dumbness, an affliction which vanished when John was circumcised and named.

In obedience to Gabriel's command, the babe was named John, and upon his presentation to God, Zacharias, by the Spirit, composed his magnificent Benediction. After this he vanishes from Holy Writ.

3. *The name suggested for John the Baptist* by his friends (Luke 1:59).

ZACHER [Zā′ chûr]—FAME. *A son of Jeiel, father of Gibeon,* a Benjamite—also called Zechariah (I Chron. 8:31; 9:37).

ZADOK [Zā′ dŏk]—RIGHTEOUS, JUSTIFIED.

The Man Who Remained Loyal

1. *The son of Ahitub* and father of Ahimaaz, a priest in David's time (II Sam. 8:17; 15:24–36; 17:15; 18:19, 27; 19:11; 20:25). Other references may be found in I Kings, I, II Chronicles, Ezra and Ezekiel.

This Zadok was appointed priest by Solomon in the place of Abiathar, because of his own loyalty (I Kings 1:8), and the disloyalty of Abiathar (1 Kings 1:7).

Zadok was the founder of an important part of the priesthood and from Solomon's time his descendants constituted the most prominent family among the order of priests.

As a young man, he was mighty of valor (I Chron. 12:27, 28).

As a friend of David, Zadok remained true to him during Absalom's rebellion (II Sam. 15:24–29).

As a priest he remained faithful to David although his colleague deserted the king (I Kings 1:7, 8). For his loyalty he retained his high and holy office till his death (I Kings 2:26, 27).

2. *The father of Jerusha,* wife of Uzziah and mother of Jotham, king of Judah (II Kings 15:33; II Chron. 27:1).

3. *Son of Ahitub,* grandson of Azariah, high priest in Solomon's great Temple (I Chron. 6:12; 9:11).

4. *The son of Baana* who shared in the repair of the wall of Jerusalem (Neh. 3:4).

5. *A priest,* son of Immer (Neh. 3:29).

6. *One of the chiefs of the people* who sealed the covenant (Neh. 10:21).

7. *A son of Meraioth,* of priestly ancestry (Neh. 11:11).

8. *The scribe or priest* appointed by Nehemiah to take charge of the treasuries of the Lord's house (Neh. 13:13). He may have been the same Zadok of Nehemiah 3:29.

ZAHAM [Zā' ham]—FATNESS or LOATHING. *A son of Rehoboam,* Solomon's son (II Chron. 11:19).

ZALAPH [Zā' laph]—PURIFICATION or FRACTURE. *The father of a certain Hanun* who repaired a part of the wall of Jerusalem (Neh. 3:30).

ZALMON, SALMON [Zăl' mŏn, Săl' mŏn]—SHADY or ASCENT. *An Ahohite,* one of David's mighty men (II Sam. 23:28), who is also called Ilai in I Chronicles 11:29. Zalmon is likewise the name of a wooded mountain area near Shechem (Judg. 9:48; Ps. 68:14).

ZALMUNNA [Zăl mŭn' nă]—SHELTER IS DENIED or WITHDRAWN FROM PROTECTION. *One of the two kings of Midian* slain by Gideon (Judg. 8:5–21; Ps. 83:11).

ZANOAH [Zā nŏ' ah]—BROKEN DISTRICT. *One of the family of Caleb,* son of Jephunneh (I Chron. 4:18). Also the name of two cities (Josh. 15:34, 56; Neh. 3:13; 11:30).

ZAPHNATH-PAANEAH [Zăph' nath-pā a nē' ah]—SAVIOR OF THE WORLD or GIVER OF THE NOURISHMENT OF LIFE. *This common type of an Egyptian name* given to Joseph by Pharaoh came from a root meaning "God hath said he liveth" (Gen. 41:45). From the sound of the name the Jews felt it meant the revealer of secrets, or one discovering hidden things. How typical Joseph is of Jesus, who came as the true Saviour of the world (I John 4:14). See Joseph.

ZARA, ZARAH, ZERAH [Zā' ră, Zā' rah, Zē' rah]—SPROUT or BRIGHTNESS. *The son of Judah* by his daughter-in-law Tamar or Thamar (Gen. 38:30; 46:12; Num. 26:20; Josh. 7:1, 24; 22:20; I Chron. 2:4–6; 9:6; Neh. 11:24; Matt. 1:3).

ZATTU, ZATTHU [Zăt' tu, Zăt' thu]—LOVELY, PLEASANT.
1. *Founder of a family* whose descendants returned with Zerubbabel from captivity (Ezra 2:8; 10:27; Neh. 7:13).
2. *A member of the family who put away his strange wife and sealed the covenant* (Neh. 10:14).

ZAZA [Zā' ză]—ABUNDANCE or PROJECTION. *A son of Jonathan,* a Jerahmeelite (I Chron. 2:33).

ZEBADIAH [Zĕb a dī' ah]—JEHOVAH HATH ENDOWED, or THE LORD IS MY PORTION.
1. *A grandson of Elpaal,* a Benjamite of the house of Beriah (I Chron. 8:15).
2. *A son of Elpaal,* also a Benjamite (I Chron. 8:17, 18).

3. *A son of Jeroham of Geder,* who joined David at Ziklag (I Chron. 12:7).

4. *A son of Meshelemiah,* a Korhite Levite in David's reign (I Chron. 26:1, 2).

5. *A son of Asahel,* son of Zeruiah and Joab's brother (I Chron. 27:7).

6. *One of the Levites sent forth by Jehoshaphat to teach* the people the law (II Chron. 17:8).

7. *The son of Ishmael,* a prince of Judah, who judged cases in the court established by Jehoshaphat (II Chron. 19:11).

8. *The son of Shephatiah* and head of a tribal family (Ezra 8:8).

9. *A priest of the house of Immer* who put away his strange wife (Ezra 10:20).

ZEBAH [Zĕ′ bah]—VICTIM or SACRIFICE. *This Midianite king* defeated and slain by Gideon is always mentioned along with Zalmunna (Judg. 8; Ps. 83:11). The death of these two kings meant a turning point in the struggle of the Israelites against their Midianite oppressors. For this reason their slaughter is graphically described, and was commemorated long after as a crisis in the nation's history (Ps. 83:11; Isa. 9:4; 10:26).

ZEBEDEE [Zĕb′ e dee]—JEHOVAH IS GIFT or THE GIFT OF GOD. *The husband of Salome* and father of James and John, two of the apostles. Since he is referred to as having "hired servants," he must have been comparatively rich (Matt. 4:21; 10:2; 20:20; 26:37; 27:56; Mark 1:19, 20; 3:17; 10:35; Luke 5:10; John 21:2). A fisherman by trade, it was only natural that his sons followed the same occupation.

ZEBINA [Ze bĭ′ nă]—ONE WHO IS BOUGHT. *One of the sons of Nebo* who put away his foreign wife (Ezra 10:43).

ZEBUL [Zĕ′ bul]—AN HABITATION. *An officer of Abimelech* and governor of Shechem (Judg. 9:28, 41). Zebul was a strategist. With no forces at his command, he was obliged to use craft, which he did most effectively, in the suppression of the revolt of Gaal.

ZEBULUN, ZABULON [Zĕb′ u lŭn, Zăb′ u lŏn]—DWELLING or WISHED FOR HABITATION.

The Man of the Open Door

The tenth son of Jacob and the sixth of Leah (Gen. 30:20). He was progenitor of three tribal families through his three sons, Sered, Elon and Jahleel, who went down into Egypt with the other sons and grandsons of Jacob (Gen. 46:14; 49:13; Josh. 19:10; Rev. 7:8). Zebulun became the commercial tribe, and one of the few tribes from which there was an opening by way of the sea to the vast world beyond. By maintaining this open door, the people were able to bring in the treasures of the deep (Deut. 33:19).

This mercantile tribe had the opportunity of being a missionary tribe. It may be that such an open door for usefulness was in the mind of Moses when he said of Zebulun, and her neighbor Issachar, "They shall call the people unto the mountain; there shall they offer sacrifices of righteousness" (Deut. 33:19). The Bible speaks of other open doors (I Cor. 16:9; Rev. 3:8).

The suggestive name of Zebulun meaning "to dwell," may have come about through Leah saying, "Now will my husband dwell with me." Is not the Lord Himself a place for the saint to dwell (I Kings 8:13)? Zebulun became the earthly habitation for the Lord of Glory as prophesied by Isaiah of old (Isa. 9:1–7). Zebul is used of God's dwelling in the Temple (II Chron. 6:2) and of heaven (Isa. 63:15).

ZECHARIAH, ZECHER [Zĕch a rī'ah]—JEHOVAH REMEMBERS or JEHOVAH IS RENOWNED.

The Man Who Preached Hope and Mercy

1. *The prophet in Judah,* whose Spirit-inspired book is the eleventh among the Minor Prophets (Ezra 5:1; 6:14; Zech. 1:1; 7:1; 7:8).

Among the many bearing the name of Zechariah, the one who wrote the Book of Zechariah, was, like Haggai, a prophet of the Restoration. As a son of the priest named Iddo (Neh. 12:4), Zechariah was of priestly descent, and likely a priest himself. Doubtless he was born in Babylon and exercised his ministry in times of political turbulence and great unrest. His call was one for righteousness in home life, in the political arena and in worship.

Zechariah's mission was of a varied nature. He had to:

    I.   Arouse the people to activity in rebuilding the Temple.

    II.   Restore the theocratic spirit or recognition of God-government.

    III.   Rekindle the nation's faith and hope during the coming desolation.

    IV.   Reorganize the true worship of God.

    V.   Remove idolatry from the nation.

As "the prophet of hope and mercy" Zechariah has given us a series of eight night visions which portrayed the final restoration of Israel and the security and blessing which will be their portion when the Lord reigns in their midst. The prophet uses the personal pronoun freely and is always careful to date his oracles. Note:

The scouts of Jehovah; He watches over His own (Zech. 1:7–17).

The four horns; enemies are destroyed (Zech. 1:18–21).

God is surveyor; enlargement and security (Zech. 2:1–8).

Joshua consecrated; righteousness restored (Zech. 3).

The lampstand; the sufficiency of grace (Zech. 4).

The flying roll; sinners judged (Zech. 5:1–4).

The woman; sin removed (Zech. 5–11).

The four chariots; judgment begins (Zech. 6:1–8).

One or two unique features of the Book of Zechariah are worthy of mention. His references to Christ are numerous and detailed. Next to Isaiah, Zechariah carries the most frequent prophecies of the Messiah, especially to Him as the suffering King. The prophet depicts Him as:

The meek King (Zech. 9:9 with Matt. 21:5; John 12:13).

The One sold for thirty pieces of silver (Zech. 11:13 with Matt. 26:15).

The pierced Saviour (Zech. 12:10 with John 19:37).

The smitten Shepherd (Zech. 13:7 with Matt. 26:31; Mark 14:27).

Zechariah is the first of the prophets to mention Satan. He recognized sin as an independent working power and personifies sin in the woman of his vision.

Numerous lessons can be gleaned from this Old Testament prophet who saw Christ's day and rejoiced.

Calamity should not create despondency but inspire wisdom.

A lost vocation can be restored.

All past guilt can be atoned for.

The will of God abides and prevails.

The servant dies but the Master lives and His work continues.

The supplies of divine grace are continuous and abundant.

Fasting and feasting are nothing in themselves.

Faith and faithfulness are everything.

The key to the eastern situation is the Jew.

Many other Zechariahs are to be found in the Bible's vast portrait gallery of men.

2. *A chief Reubenite* when genealogies were prepared (I Chron. 5:7).

3. *A son of Meshelemiah,* a Levite, a gatekeeper of the Tabernacle in David's time (I Chron. 9:21; 26:2, 14).

4. *A brother of Ner* and uncle of Saul (I Chron. 9:37), also called Zacher (I Chron. 8:31).

5. *A Levite musician* in David's reign (I Chron. 15:18, 20; 16:5).

6. *A Tabernacle priest* in David's time (I Chron. 15:24).

7. *A son of Isshiah,* a Levite of the family of Kohath (I Chron. 24:25).

8. *A son of Hosah,* a gatekeeper of the Tabernacle (I Chron. 26:11).

9. *The father of Iddo* and chief of the half tribe of Manasseh (I Chron. 27:21).

10. *A prince of Judah* used by Jehoshaphat to teach the law (II Chron. 17:7).

11. *The father of Jahaziel,* who encouraged the king's army against Moab (II Chron. 20:14).

12. *The third son of Jehoshaphat* (II Chron. 21:2).

13. *Son of Jehoiada the priest,* who was stoned to death for rebuking the people for their idolatry. Announcement of divine judgment was more than the idolaters could stand, so at the bidding of the king in the court of the Lord's house he died a death similar to that of Stephen. His dying words, "The Lord look upon it, and require it," were long remembered (II Chron. 24:20, 21).

14. *A person who understood the visions of God* (II Chron. 26:5).

15. *A son of Asaph,* a Levite who helped to cleanse the Temple (II Chron. 29:13).

16. *A son of Kohath,* a Levite, and overseer of temple repairs (II Chron. 34:12).

17. *A prince of Judah* in the days of Josiah (II Chron. 35:8).

18. *A chief man* who returned with Ezra from exile (Ezra 8:3).

19. *A son of Bebai* who also returned (Ezra 8:11, 16).

20. *A returned captive* who put away his wife (Ezra 10:26).

21. *A prince* who stood beside Ezra (Neh. 8:4).

22. *The son of Amariah,* a descendant of Pharez (Neh. 11:4).

23. *A Shilonite* (Neh. 11:5).

24. *Son of Pashur,* a priest (Neh. 11:12).

25. *A priest of Joiakim's time* (Neh. 12:16).

26. *An Asaphite,* who helped in the purification of the wall of Jerusalem (Neh. 12:35, 41).

27. *A witness Isaiah used.* Perhaps the same Zechariah of II Chronicles 26:5 and Isaiah 8:2.

ZEDEKIAH [Zĕd e kī′ ah]—JEHOVAH IS MIGHT or JEHOVAH IS RIGHTEOUS.

The Man Who Vacillated

1. *The last king of Judah* before its fall at the hands of the Babylonians. Zedekiah is classed among the evil kings. He was the third son of Josiah to become king. Mattaniah was his original name, but upon his succession to Jehoiachin, Nebuchadnezzar named him Zedekiah. What we know of him can be found in II Kings 24, 25; I Chronicles 3:15; II Chronicles 36:10, 11, as well as in almost fifty references in Jeremiah. (See 1:3; 21:1, 3, 7, 8). Jeremiah prophesied during the whole of the reign of Zedekiah.

As a ruler, Zedekiah lacked the three indispensable qualifications for leadership, namely, poise, vision, resolution. He came to a disrupted kingdom, and while he meant well, Zedekiah could not keep his head amid confusion. Vacillating, he lacked the courage to labor on with a resolute heart. He was easily persuaded to rebel against the Chaldeans (II Kings 25), and under Jeremiah's advice surrendered the city to the Chaldeans (Jer. 21:9, 10).

This troubled reign ended tragically. Zedekiah attempted to escape from the disaster Jeremiah had predicted, but was overtaken and brought to Nebuchadnezzar, who slew the captive king's children before his eyes, then blinded the king himself and sent him in chains to Babylon. Zedekiah, however, died on the way.

The Man Who Was Rude

2. *A son of Chenaanah,* a false prophet who encouraged Ahab to attack the Syrians at Ramoth-gilead (I Kings 22:11, 24; II Chron. 18:10, 23). When Micaiah, a true prophet of God, contradicted Zedekiah's prediction, he struck the man of God upon the cheek and insulted him. Micaiah did not retaliate, but warned Zedekiah that he would come to regret his action (I Kings 22:11–25), which he did. Along with other political agitators, Zedekiah brought on himself the cruel punishment of being roasted in the fire by the order of Nebuchadnezzar.

3. *A son or successor of Jeconiah* (I Chron. 3:16).

4. *A son of Maaseiah,* a false and immoral prophet (Jer. 29:21).

5. *The son of Hananiah,* a prince in the reign of Jehoiakim (Jer. 36:12).

ZEEB [Zē′ eb]—WOLF. *A prince of Midian* defeated and slain by Gideon at the winepress, and afterwards named Zeeb (Judg 7:25; 8:3; Ps. 83:11).

ZELEK [Zē′ lek]—RENT or A SHADOW. *An Ammonite,* one of David's valiant captains (II Sam. 23:37; I Chron. 11:39).

ZELOPHEHAD [Zē lō′ phe hăd]—THE FIRST-BORN. *The son of Hepher* and grandson of Gilead, who died during the wilderness wanderings, leaving no male issue, but only five daughters. This lack of issue meant the enacting of a law whereby an inheritance could pass to a daughter (Num. 17:1–8: 26:33). Thus the five daughters of Zelophehad successfully asserted their claim to their father's inheritance (Josh. 17:3; I Chron. 7:15).

ZELOTES [Zē lō′ tēs]—ZEALOUS or FULL OF ZEAL. *The surname of Simon,* one of the Twelve, also called "The Canaanite" from being a native of Cana (Matt. 10:4; Mark 3:18; Luke 6:15; Acts 1:13). By this epithet he is distinguished from Simon Peter. See Simon Zelotes.

ZEMIRA, ZEMIRAH [Ze mī′ ră , Ze mī′ rah]—A MELODY or A SONG. *A son of Becher,* a Benjamite (I Chron. 7:8).

ZENAS [Zē′ nas]—THE GIFT OF ZEUS. *A Christian lawyer,* skilled in Jewish law, whom Paul asks Titus to bring or send to him from Crete, with Apollos (Titus 3:13).

Have you ever thought what occupations are represented by many of the men of the Bible?

ZEPHANIAH [Zĕph a nī′ ah]—JEHOVAH IS DARKNESS or GOD HIDES.

The Man of Moral Earnestness

1. *A son of Cushi,* who prophesied in the days of Josiah (Zeph 1:1). The prophet Zephaniah gives us a most minute account of his genealogy—a rare thing for a prophet! Possibly he pursued this course for two reasons:

To distinguish himself from three others of the same name, mentioned below.

To point out his relation to the great monarch, Hezekiah. The Hizkiah of Zephaniah 1:1 is identical with King Hezekiah. Zephaniah was therefore of royal descent.

The prophecy of Zephaniah, ninth among the Minor Prophets, is one of reproof and judgment. George Adam Smith said of it, "No hotter book lies in all the Old Testament." What a graphic picture of Judah's spiritual pride this prophet of judgment paints! Worshippers of God were found sprawled on their housetops worshiping the moon and stars (Zeph. 1:4, 5). The spirit of practical atheism had possessed the people (Zeph. 1:12), and their religious leaders had lost their moral seriousness (Zeph. 3:4).

Zephaniah sees no way out of such departure from God but judgment, so he announces the day of the Lord, denounces idolaters, waverers and apostates and pronounces doom on wrongdoers (Zeph. 1:7, 8). Much that he predicted has been partially fulfilled, but ultimate fulfillment is still future.

The Lord is "in the midst" for judgment (Zeph. 1–3:8).

The Lord is "in the midst" for salvation (Zeph. 3:9–20).

The present value of the Book of Zephaniah must not be lost sight of. We have:

    I.   The revelation of social and moral conditions.

    II.   An earnest moral tone and deep sense of sin.

    III.   The disciplinary value of suffering (Zeph. 3:7, 11, 13).

    IV.   The comforting doctrine of Providence.

    V.   Are we God's Zephaniahs—His sheltered ones (Ps. 17:8; 27:5, 7)?

Other men with the name of Zephaniah are:

2. *A Levite of the family of Kohath* and of the house of Izhar, who is mentioned among the ancestors of Heman the singer (I Chron. 6:36–38).

3. *A priest,* the son of Maaseiah, who ministered in Jerusalem in the reign of King Hezekiah and the prophet Jeremiah. This Zephaniah had the oversight of the Temple and was put to death at Riblah (II Kings 25:18–30; Jer. 21:1; 29:25–29; 37:3; 52:24–29).

4. *The father of one Josiah* who lived in the day of Zerubbabel and the prophet Zechariah, and into whose house in Jerusalem the messenger from the Jews went (Zech. 6:10–14).

ZEPHO, ZEPHI [Zē′ phō, Zē′ phī]—WATCH or THAT SEES. *A son of*

Eliphaz, grandson of Esau and one of the "dukes" of Edom (Gen. 36:11, 15; I Chron. 1:36).

ZEPHON, ZAPHON [Zē′ phon]—DARK, WINTRY or EXPECTATION. *A son of Gad* who founded a tribal family (Num. 26:15). Called Ziphion in Genesis 46:16. The Zephonites were descendants of Zephon (Num. 26:15).

ZERAH, ZARAH, ZARA [Zē′ rah, Zā′ rah]—SPROUT or SPRINGING UP OF LIGHT.
1. *A son of Reuel,* son of Esau. One of the "dukes" (Gen. 36:13, 17; I Chron. 1:37).
2. *The father of Jobab,* second of the early kings of Edom (Gen. 36:33; I Chron. 1:44).
3. *One of the twins born to Judah* by his daughter-in-law, Tamar (Gen. 38:30; Num. 26:20; Josh. 7:1, 24; I Chron. 2:4).
4. *A son of Simeon,* of a tribal family (Num. 26:13; I Chron. 4:24). Called Zohar, meaning "dazzling whiteness" (Gen. 46:10; Ex. 6:15).
5. *A Levite of the family of Gershon* (I Chron. 6:21).
6. *The father of Ethni,* a Levite (I Chron. 6:41).
7. *The Ethiopian king* who led an army against Asa but suffered a great slaughter at Mareshah (II Chron. 14:9–15).

ZERAHIAH [Zĕr a hī′ ah]—THE LORD IS RISEN or JEHOVAH IS APPEARING.
1. *A priest,* son of Uzzi, an ancestor of Ezra (I Chron. 6:6, 51; Ezra 7:4).
2. *The father of Elihoenai,* a descendant of Pahath-moab (Ezra 8:4).

ZERETH [Zē′ reth]—BRIGHTNESS, SPLENDOR. *A son of Helah,* descendant of Judah through Caleb, son of Hur (I Chron. 4:7).

ZERI, IZRI [Zē′ rī]—BALM. *A son of Jeduthun* responsible for the service of song in David's time (I Chron. 25:3).

ZEROR [Zē′ rôr]—A BUNDLE or THAT STRAITENS. *Father of Abiel,* a Benjamite and an ancestor of Saul (I Sam. 9:1).

ZERUBBABEL, ZOROBABEL [Zē rŭb′ ba bĕl, Zō rŏb′ a bĕl]—AN OFFSPRING OF BABEL or BEGOTTEN IN BABYLON.
The Man with a Purpose
A son of Shealtiel, related to David and heir to the throne of Judah (I Chron. 3:19). He is also spoken of as a son of Pedaiah, brother of Shealtiel, who doubtless died childless, and made his nephew his legal heir, calling him his son (Ex. 2:10; Ezra 3.2, 8; Neh. 12:1). He repre-

sented the Davidic monarchy (Hag. 2:20–23) and was an ancestor of our Lord (Matt. 1:12, 13; Luke 3:27). Sheshbazzar was perhaps the name given to Zerubbabel by the Babylonians (Ezra 1:8, 11; 5:14).

Exiles, returning from captivity, were led by Zerubbabel and others (Ezra 2:1–64; Neh. 7:5–7; 12:1–9). In the ruined city of Jerusalem he acted along with the high priest Jeshua in the restoration of Temple services (Ezra 3:1–9). Ultimately Zerubbabel became Persian governor under Darius, and after much delay succeeded in rebuilding the Temple (Zech. 4:1–14). There were those who looked upon Zerubbabel as the coming Messiah (Zech. 3:1, 8–10). Because of the deep personal interest he took in the Temple it was often called Zerubbabel's Temple.

ZETHAM [Zē' tham]—SHINING or PLACE OF OLIVES. *A son or grandson of Jehieli*, a Gershonite (I Chron. 23:8; 26:22).

ZETHAN [Zē' than]—SHINING or PLACE OF OLIVES. *A son of Bilhan*, grandson of Benjamin (I Chron. 7:10).

ZETHAR [Zē' thär]—SACRIFICE or HE THAT EXAMINES. *A eunuch*, one of the seven chamberlains of King Ahasuerus (Esther 1:10).

ZIA [Zī' ă]—TERROR or TERRIFIED. *A Gadite* and probably head of his father's house (I Chron. 5:13).

ZIBA [Zī' bă]—PLANTATION or STRENGTH. *One of Saul's servants* who served Mephibosheth, but who falsely obtained half of his master's property from David (II Sam. 9:2–12; 16:1–4; 19:17, 29). Mephibosheth cleared himself of Ziba's treachery (II Sam. 19:24–30).

ZIBEON [Zĭb' e on]—WILD ROBBER or SEIZING PREY.
1. *A Hivite*, grandfather of Adah, one of Esau's wives (Gen. 36:2, 14).
2. *A son of Seir the Horite* (Gen. 36:20, 24, 29; I Chron. 1:38, 40).

ZIBIA [Zĭb' Ĭ ă]—STRENGTH or A FEMALE GAZELLE. *A Benjamite*, son of Hodesh (I Chron. 8:9).

ZICHRI [Zĭch' rĭ]—FAMOUS, RENOWNED.
1. *A son of Izhar*, grandson of Levi (Ex. 6:21). Also known as Zithri.
2. *A Benjamite, son of Shimhi* (I Chron. 8:19).
3. *A Benjamite, son of Shashak* (I Chron. 8:23)
4. *A Benjamite, son of Jeroham* (I Chron. 8:27).
5. *A Levite, son of Asaph* (I Chron. 9:15). Likely the same person as Zaccur (I Chron. 25:2, 10; Neh. 12:35).
6. *A descendant of Eliezer, son of Moses* (I Chron. 26·°5)

7. *Father of Eliezer,* a chief Reubenite in David's time (I Chron. 27:16).

8. *Father of Amasiah,* a captain of Jehoshaphat (II Chron. 17:16).

9. *Father of Elishaphat* and captain in Jehoshaphat's army who helped to make Joash king of Israel (II Chron. 23:1).

10. *A valiant Ephraimite* who slew the son of Ahaz, king of Judah (II Chron. 28:7).

11. *Father of Joel,* a Benjamite and overseer of the Benjamites after the exile (Neh. 11:9).

12. *A priest of the sons of Abijah* who lived in the days of Nehemiah and the high priest Joiakim (Neh. 12:17).

ZIDKIJAH [Zĭd kĭ′ jah]—JEHOVAH IS MIGHT. *A chief prince of the Jews* who sealed the covenant (Neh. 10:1).

ZIDON, SIDON [Zĭ′ dŏn, Sĭ′ dŏn]—FORTRESS. *Eldest son of Canaan,* son of Ham (Gen. 10:15; I Chron. 1:13).
Also the name of a famous city in Asher, now called Saida (Gen. 10:19).

ZIHA [Zĭ′ hă]—SUNNINESS.
1. *Founder and head of a family of Nethinims* who returned from exile with Zerubbabel (Ezra 2:43; Neh. 7:46). It may be that Ziha is the same person of Nehemiah 11:21.

2. *A ruler of the Nethinims* in Jerusalem (Neh. 11:21).
The Nethinim or Nethinims, meaning "men who are given," were the servants or slaves of the Temple and given for the service of the Levites (Ezra 8:20). Originally they were assigned to lowly duties (Josh. 9:23) but gradually rose to superior positions (Ezra 8:24) becoming, in prestige, equivalent to the Levites.

ZILTHAI, ZILLETHAI [Zĭl′ thaī]—SHADOW OF THE LORD.
1. *A Benjamite,* son of Shimhi (I Chron. 8:20).

2. *A Manassite,* captain of one thousand, who joined David at Ziklag (I Chron. 12:20).

ZIMMAH [Zĭm′ mah]—COUNSEL, CONSIDERATION.
1. *A son of Jahath,* a Gershonite Levite (I Chron. 6:20).

2. *Another Gershonite Levite* of the fourth degree (I Chron. 6:42).

3. *Father of Joah* who assisted in Hezekiah's reform (II Chron. 29:12).

ZIMRAN [Zĭm′ ran]—CELEBRATED OT THE SINGER. *A son of Abraham by Keturah* (Gen. 25:2; I Chron. 1:32).

ZIMRI [Zĭm′ rī]—CELEBRATED OT VINE.
1. *A prince of the tribe of Simeon,* slain by Phinehas (Num. 25:14).

2. *A captain who slew Elah,* and who in turn was slain by Omri (I Kings 16:9–20; II Kings 9:31). He seized the throne of his king, Elah, but only held it for seven days. He encouraged Israel to sin after the ways of Jeroboam (I Kings 16:9–20).

3. *A son of Zerah,* son of Judah (I Chron. 2:6).

4. *A Benjamite,* descendant of Jonathan, Saul's son (I Chron. 8:36; 9:42).

Also the name of an unknown place (Jer. 25:25).

ZINA [Zī′ nă]—BORROWED. *A son of Shimei, a Gershonite* (I Chron. 23:10). Also called Zizah in verse eleven.

ZIPH [Zĭph]—REFINING PLACE.

1. *A grandson of Caleb,* son of Hezron (I Chron. 2:42).

2. *A son of Jehaleleel,* son of Caleb, son of Jephunneh (I Chron. 4:16).

ZIPHAH [Zī′ phah]—LENT. *A son of Jehaleleel,* a descendant of Caleb (I Chron. 4:16).

ZIPHION [Zĭph′ Ĭ on]—LOOKING OUT or SERPENT. *A son of Gad,* also called Zephon (Gen. 46:16; Num. 26:15).

ZIPPOR [Zĭp′ por]—A SPARROW or EARLY IN THE MORNING. *Father of Balak,* king of Moab, who hired Balaam to curse Israel (Num. 22:2–18; Josh. 24:9; Judg. 11:25).

ZITHRI [Zĭth′ rĭ]—JEHOVAH IS PROTECTION, TO HIDE or OVERTURN. *A son of Uzziel,* son of Kohath (Ex. 6:22).

ZIZA, ZIZAH [Zī′ ză, Zī′ zah]—FERTILITY or BRIGHTNESS.

1. *A Simeonite,* son of Shiphi, descendant of Shemaiah (I Chron. 4:37).

2. *A Levite* of the family of Gershon (I Chron. 23:11). Spelled Zina in verse ten.

3. *A son of Rehoboam* by his queen Maachah (II Chron. 11:20).

ZOHAR [Zō′ här]—WHITE, SHINING or DISTINCTION.

1. *Father of Ephron,* from whom Abraham bought the cave of Machpelah (Gen. 23:8; 25:9).

2. *A son of Simeon,* second son of Judah (Gen. 46:10; Ex. 6:15).

ZOHETH [Zō′ heth]—CORPULENT, STRONG. *A son of Ishi,* registered with the tribe of Judah (I Chron. 4:20).

ZOPHAH [Zō′ phah]—WATCH or EXPANSE. *A son of Helem,* grandson of Beriah, son of Asher (I Chron. 7:35, 36).

ZOPHAI [Zō′ phaï]—WATCHER. *A son of Elkanah,* father of the prophet Samuel (I Chron. 6:26). Called Zuph in I Samuel 1:1.

ZOPHAR [Zō′ phar]—HAIRY, EXPANSE or PLEASANT ABODE.

The Man Who Boasted of His Knowledge of God

A Naamathite, third in order of Job's friends (Job 2:11; 11:1; 20:1; 42:9).

Described in the Septuagint as "King of the Minaeans."

The three friends of Job represent three ways of solving the mysterious problems of divine government in the affairs of men. Eliphaz the Temanite is the symbol of human experience or history. Bildad the Shuhite is the symbol of human tradition or philosophy. Zophar the Naamathite is the symbol of human merit or moral law. Zophar of Naamah (Josh. 15:41) had a name suggestive of his manner. It comes from a root meaning "to twitter," and one of his faults was he dealt with profound things in a more lighthearted, flippant way than his two companions.

Zophar was a religious dogmatist, resorting to rigorous legal and religious methods (Job 11:3–20). His dogmatism, however, rested upon what he thought he knew. He advocated good living. If Job would only turn from his sin and sincerely repent, then God would pardon and restore him. With forcible language, Zophar declared that suffering is judgment warning the sinner to repent and escape heavier punishment.

Zophar himself erred in that he presumed to know all about God and pleaded the worth of human merit in His sight. So he called on poor Job to prepare his heart (Job 11:13). Dr. C. I. Scofield says that "Zophar was a religious dogmatist who assumes to know all about God: what God will do in any given case, why He will do it, and all His thoughts about it. Of all forms of dogmatism this is most irreverent, and least open to reason." Self-effort or human merit can never satisfy God or produce a rightousness pleasing to Him.

ZUAR [Zū′ ar]—LITTLE, SMALLNESS. *Father of Nethaneel,* a chief of Issachar (Num. 1:8; 2:5; 7:18, 23; 10:15).

ZUPH [Zŭph]—HONEYCOMB. *A Kohathite,* an ancestor of the prophet Samuel (I Sam. 1:1; I Chron. 6:35). Also the name of a place (I Sam. 9:5). See Zophai (I Chron. 6:26).

ZUR [Zûr]—ROCK.

1. *A prince of Midian* and father of Cozbi (Num. 25:15; 31:8; Josh. 13:21).

2. *A son of Jehiel,* a Benjamite (I Chron. 8:30; 9:36).

ZURIEL [Zū′ rï el]—GOD IS A ROCK. *A Merarite chief,* son of Abihail (Num. 3:35 R.V.).

ZURISHADDAI [Zŭ rĭ shăd′ da ĭ]—THE ALMIGHTY IS A ROCK. Father *of Shelumiel,* the chief of the tribe of Simeon, chosen to help Moses number the people (Num. 1:6; 2:12; 7:36, 41; 10:19).

The Great Host of Unnamed Bible Men

III

The Great Host of Unnamed Bible Men

Did you know that there are thousands upon thousands of unnamed men in the Bible? Many of them can be called "God's Anonymous Men." Too often we fix our attention exclusively on the greater characters of the Book, yet the vast host of the inconspicuous and unnamed has been preserved by the pen of inspiration as being worthy of our meditation. The unknown saints — unknown, that is, to human fame—must not be passed by. While full consideration must be given to those God called into the limelight, we dare not ignore others who remain in the shadow of obscurity or anonymity. So let us think of many Bible men whose deeds are recorded, but not their names. The following list is by no means complete.

While three of Adam's sons are named, others born of him and Eve are not named (Gen. 5:4). Were they among the many who perished in the Flood?

None of the carpenters who assisted in the building of the Ark are mentioned, neither are several of those who labored in the preparation of the Tabernacle. The same is true of the overseers of the Temple repairs in the reign of Jehoash, whose honesty was such that their superiors had no need to scrutinize their accounts.

Gideon's three hundred men, valiant heroes all, deserve to be named but appear among the unknown servants of the Lord.

The three valiant men who at the risk of life brought water from the well of Bethlehem are not named. These anonymous heroes, however, left behind a stirring example of courage and of love for their leader.

Also among the unnamed of the Bible we have the seven thousand who refused to bow to Baal. God knew them but Elijah was not aware of them. If only the members of this host had openly declared themselves as being on God's side, how they would have cheered the lonely heart of Elijah.

The nameless prophet who has been referred to as, "this great man of God who comes out of a cloud, shines for a splendid moment before all men's eyes, and then dies under a cloud," is another unknown man. Heroic, he was yet human, an unnamed man whose fascinating story lies in its mixture of courage and weakness (I Kings 13:1-3).

The New Testament abounds in its anonymous characters, historical and literary. By the latter, we mean those employed in parabolic form, which our Lord freely used. Those He portrays might have been in-

357

dividuals He had observed. Many of these literary characters are as forceful as many of the historical ones. Think of:

The Hypocrites — (Matt. 6:2, 16; 7:5).
The Wise Men — (Matt. 2:1).
The Sower — (Matt. 13:3, 24).
The Shepherd — (Matt. 18:12).
The Brother — (Matt. 18:15).
The King — (Matt. 18:23).
The Householder — (Matt. 20:1).
The Man with Two Sons — (Matt. 21:28).
The King — (Matt. 22:2, 12).
The Servant — (Matt. 24:46).
The Bridegroom — (Matt. 25:1).
The Traveler — (Matt. 25:14).
The Strong Man — (Mark 3:27).
The Rich Man — (Mark 10:25).
The Man Journeying — (Mark 13:34).
The Creditor — (Luke 7:41).
The Good Samaritan — (Luke 10:36).
The Friend — (Luke 11:5, 11).
The Rich Fool — (Luke 12:16).
The Wise Steward — (Luke 12:42).
The Guest — (Luke 14:7).
The Builder — (Luke 14:28).
The King — (Luke 14:31).
The Loving Father and His Sons — (Luke 15).
The Shrewd Steward — (Luke 16:1-13).
The Snobbish Pharisees — (Luke 18:9-14).

The historical unnamed characters of the New Testament are far more numerous than all the named men of the Bible put together. Here is a galaxy of these anonymous men, famous or infamous as the case may be, although unknown by name:

The Wise Men from the East — (Matt. 2:1, 2).
The Sick and Lunatic Men — (Matt. 4:23, 24).
The Leper — (Matt. 8:2).
The Centurion and His Servant — (Matt. 8:5, 9).
The Certain Scribe — (Matt. 8:19).
The Two Demon-Possessed Men — (Matt. 8:28).
The Palsied Man and His Four Bearers — (Matt. 9:2).
The Two Blind Men — (Matt. 9:27).
The Man with a Withered Arm — (Matt. 12:10).
The Demoniac — (Matt. 12:22).
The Four Thousand Men — (Matt. 15:38).
The Lunatic — (Matt. 17:15).
The Young Child — (Matt. 18:2; 19:13).
The Rich Young Ruler — (Matt. 19:16).
The Blind Men — (Matt. 20:34).
The Man Who Owned an Ass — (Matt. 21:3).

The Lawyer — (Matt. 22:35).
The Man Who had a Chamber — (Matt. 26:18).
The Two False Witnesses — (Matt. 26:60).
The Soldiers Who Stripped Christ — (Matt. 27:27).
The Two Thieves — (Matt. 27:38).
The One Who Offered the Sponge — (Matt. 27:48).
The Saints Who Were Raised — (Matt. 27:52).
The Centurion — (Matt. 27:54).
The Man with an Unclean Spirit — (Mark 1:23).
The Maniac of the Tombs — (Mark 5:2).
The Executioner of John — (Mark 6:27).
The Lad Who Gave His Lunch — (Mark 6:38).
The Five Thousand Men — (Mark 6:44).
The Deaf and Dumb Man — (Mark 7:32).
The One Who Cast Out Devils — (Mark 9:38).
The Young Men — (Mark 14:51; 16:5).
The Shepherds — (Luke 2:8).
The Widow's Son — (Luke 7:12).
The Seventy Disciples — (Luke 10:1).
The Questioners — (Luke 12:13; 13:23).
The Man with Dropsy — (Luke 14:2).
The Ten Lepers — (Luke 17:12).
The Pharisee and the Publican — (Luke 18:10).
The Nobleman — (Luke 19:12).
The Unnamed Disciple — (Luke 24:13).
The Ruler of the Feast — (John 2:9).
The Samaritans — (John 4:40).
The Nobleman — (John 4:46).
The Infirm Man — (John 5:5).
The Man Born Blind — (John 9:1).
The Greeks — (John 12:20).
The Unnamed among the 120 — (Acts 1:15).
The Men Among the Three Thousand — (Acts 2:41).
The Lame Man — (Acts 3:2).
The Five Thousand Men — (Acts 4:4; 5:14).
The Eunuch — (Acts 8:37).
The Cripple — (Acts 14:8).
The Jailer — (Acts 16:27).

Paul in his Epistles sent personal greetings to many of his fellow laborers whom he knew and named. But think of those who are summarized as "the brethren" or referred to as "other fellow labourers, whose names are in the book of life." Glance over the unnamed men referred to in the following passages: Acts 17:34; 19:10, 14; 21:33; 22:25; 23:16, 18; 27:11; 28:8, 16; I Corinthians 5:1; 6:1; II Corinthians 11:32; 12:2; Philippians 4:3; II Thessalonians 3:11, 14; Jude 4.

Many heroes of the faith are named by the sacred writer (Heb. 11), but what about the others equally faithful and sacrificial, about whom the historian did not write (Heb. 11:32, 36)? Space prevents us from enumerating all the men symbolized in the Book of Revelation.

We cannot but wonder why there are so many anonymous servants. Tradition has given names to several of them such as the Wise Men, the Rich Ruler and the Two Thieves, but Scripture is silent as to their identity. Is there a lesson to be learned from such obscurity? We praise famous men, but what can we do about those who pass away with no memorial, who die as though they have never been?

It is comforting to realize that although multitudes of workers are "unknown" they are "yet well known." They are "manifest unto God," who sees that which is hidden from the human eye, and whose approval is the highest reward. Their abiding influence cannot be hid. Of the unknown, who are in the majority, J. I. Hasler says:

> Though such unknown ones may not be lights in the world which "cannot be hid," as are their more famous counterparts, yet they are like salt mingling with the mass to stay corruption, or like the leaven which works obscurely. The "Elijahs" because of their very prominence, cannot escape commemoration; the "anonymous servants" need special commemoration because of the less prominent nature of what they do. Their value lies in the silent witness of sheer goodness, integrity of character, and their faith in GOD. In their ministry in the home circle or in the Church, and in their helpful influence on other lives with which they come into contact they truly serve God. In a Kentish churchyard one such found a resting-place and on his tombstone is this significant inscription, "He encouraged others in doing good."

For ourselves, it is sufficient to know that, whether our names are blazoned abroad or unknown, easy or difficult to pronounce, short or long, full of meaning or unattractive, they are written upon God's palms and in heaven every child of His is to have a new name (Isa. 49:16; Rev. 2:17).

The Greatest of All Bible Men

IV

The Greatest of All Bible Men

Because Christ is the light, lighting every man that cometh into the world (John 1:4, 9), all the men of the Bible, and all men of all ages for that matter, are related to the Man Christ Jesus, either directly or indirectly. In this alphabetical treatment of Bible men, we purposely omitted any specific reference to Him who was found in fashion as a Man so that we could devote an entire chapter to His descent and designations.

It must be understood that it is not our purpose to give a study in *Christology*. Professor Alexander Stewart says, "He who would worthily write the life of Christ must have a pen dipped in the imaginative sympathy of a poet, in the prophet's fire, in the artist's charm and grace and in the reverence and purity of the saint." Our endeavor is to show His relation to men. Thomas Dekker wrote of Christ in 1570:

> The best of man
> That e'er wore earth about Him as a sufferer:
> A soft, meek, patient, humble, tranquil spirit,
> The first true Gentleman that ever breathed.

In the days of His flesh, Christ constantly asserted His own superior greatness among men. No man dared make the same claim. Familiar as He was with the great saints in God's portrait gallery, He could say of Himself, "Behold a greater is here" (Matt. 12; John 4:10–18; 8: 53–58).

He was greater than Abraham in the pre-eminence of His rank. The Jews boasted that Abraham was the head and founder of their race. Christ is the Head of the Church.

He was greater than the Temple in the magnificence of His glory. The Temple was the center and expression of worship. Now we gather in His name whether it be in cabin or cathedral.

He was greater than Solomon in the excellence of His wisdom. Israel's illustrious king was the richest and wisest of the kings, but both his wealth and wisdom were derived from Him who was made unto our *wisdom*.

He was greater than Jonah in the beneficence of His mission. The runaway prophet was against God blessing Gentiles as well as Jews. Christ came not to call the righteous, but sinners to repentance.

He was greater than Jacob in the munificence of His gift. Jacob gave his people a well (John 4:12). Christ provided, for all who are His, rivers of living water (John 7:37–39).

Christ came into the world of men as the holiest Man ever born. In human form, He was the same as other Bible men but unique in character. All the men of the Bible, with the sole exception of Adam, were born with inherent evil (Ps. 51:5). Christ was born sinless (Heb. 4:15). He was separate from sinners in that He was without inherent or practiced sin. No man could convince or convict this Man among men of sin.

His Genealogies

Both Matthew and Luke set forth the genealogies of Christ. The Old Testament opens with the thought, "Behold, I make all things." The New Testament begins with the promise, "Behold, I make all things new." This is why it introduces us right away to the Second Man, the Lord from Heaven. The inspired historian begins with Christ's historic genealogy, for it must be made clear that He is bone of our bone and flesh of our flesh.

Matthew, especially interested in the Jew, sets forth Christ as "the son of David" and traces His lineage back two thousand years to Abraham. As the rightful Heir to the Kingdom, Matthew proclaims Christ as the King of Israel.

Luke, writing for the Gentiles, gives a careful outline of natural descendants and proves that Christ sprang from the first man, Adam. Step by step, he carries us back to the father of the human race. Prominence is given to Christ in Luke's gospel as the Son of Man. As the Son of God, He became the Son of Man, that He might make the sons of men the sons of God.

As it was common for the Jews to distribute genealogies into divisions containing some mystical number, some generations were repeated or omitted. Three great epochs are covered by these genealogical trees, representing three great stages in the development of Old Testament promises in relation to men.

Abraham to David

To Abraham and his seed were promises made, and in his seed all nations are to be blessed.

David to Captivity in Babylon

Blessings to nations should come through a king of the Davidic line.

The Captivity to Christ

As the result of their bondage, the people were cured of their idolatry. Israel was more spiritual after the Dispersion. Only a small remnant returned to Palestine. The rest remained in Babylon or were scattered abroad (Jas. 1:1).

In the fulness of time Christ came to realize all the promises made to Abraham and David and to the people scattered abroad through the prophets. The heavenly descent of Christ is told with exquisite simplicity and delicacy.

Since the first promise that the Messiah would come as "the seed of the woman" (Gen. 3:15), generation after generation looked forward to the coming of the great Deliverer. Such a Monarch was to come in the direct line of descent from certain ancient sovereigns and saints, and every Jewish mother had hopes of bearing such a Saviour. This was why barrenness produced unutterable sorrow, as the distress of Hannah reveals. Jewish mothers hoped that out of the number of their children, God might raise up one to sit on David's throne. At last, Mary was the one to be favored above all women.

The genealogies of Old and New Testaments alike then are signposts pointing to Christ as the end of the old dispensation and the beginning of the new. Specimens of depravity are dragged from the long-forgotten past to take their places among the lineal ancestors of Jesus to prove that the glory of the line is not in the line itself but in Him in whom the genealogies end.

His Names

We distinguish between the explicit names and the titles of respect, dignity or office used of our Lord. As this volume is taken up with all the men of the Bible and their names, with their meanings, it is our purpose in this chapter to indicate the expressed names of Him who spake as no man spake. The manifold designations and titles used to describe His Person, Power and Position show a fascinating aspect fully dealt with in that most useful handbook, *Titles of The Triune God* by Herbert F. Stevenson.

Jesus

We place this peerless name first because it is the ineffable name of Him who wrapped Himself around with the garment of our humanity. Other names are dear, but His is dearer. *Jesus* was the name divinely given before His birth. "Thou shalt call His name Jesus" (Matt. 1:21). This familiar name, so sweet in a believer's ear, occurs some seven hundred times in the New Testament.

The name *Joshua* is equivalent to *Jesus*, and the Old Testament warrior is a fitting type of our Lord. Joshua saved the people of Israel by leading them through the River Jordan, He fought their battles and was steadfast in his allegiance to God and His people. Jesus is our heavenly Joshua, who fought the grim battle on our behalf at Calvary, providing thereby a blood-bought deliverance for sin-bound souls. He is now our Leader, our Protector, and will never cease in His care of us until He has us safely in the sheepfold on the other side.

Among English-speaking peoples the names of Jehovah and Jesus are considered too sacred for sinful human beings to adopt, but in Spain, Portugal and South America, the people have no qualms about using Jesus as a Christian name. Among the Greeks and Scandinavians, there is no hesitancy about using Christ as a Christian name.

Christ

Pilate asked, "What then shall I do with Jesus who is called Christ?" By divine revelation Peter recognized Jesus as the Christ (Matt. 16:16). Although referred to as a title by many, Christ is a definite name used over three hundred times in the New Testament and means "The Anointed One." Prophets had foretold His coming as the Messiah and now His kingly authority is recorded. Our Lord used the name Jesus of Himself (Acts 9:5), but never the name Christ.

From Christ comes "Christian" and from "Christian," "Christianity." The Gospel we preach to a needy world is the Gospel of Christ (Rom. 1:16). As the Christ-ones we can only honor Christ by having the same power resting upon us as we seek to serve Him.

Both Jesus and Christ are combined and used as "Jesus Christ" some one hundred times in the New Testament (Matt. 16:20; Acts 2:36). Taken together, these two names imply the mystic union existing in Him as the God-Man. His work and worth are one, even as His name and nature are.

Lord

In announcing His birth to the shepherds, the angel spoke of Him as "Christ the Lord" (Luke 2:11). It is somewhat remarkable to observe that the word Lord comes into prominence after the resurrection when God "made that same Jesus...both Lord and Christ." Before His resurrection we read of "the body of Jesus" and afterwards, "the body of the Lord Jesus." Lord is a name expressing His sovereignty and majesty and no man can own Him as Lord but by the Holy Spirit (I Cor. 12:3; I Pet. 3:15 R.V.).

Among the ancients a name not only summed up a man's history but represented his personality with which it was almost identical. Hence "in My name," that is, His full name, "The Lord Jesus Christ," there is the suggestion of actual incorporation with the divine speaker.

Shiloh

The name of a revered city (Josh. 18:1), Shiloh is also a name used prophetically of Christ (Gen. 49:10). Meaning "one who pacifies," this name speaks of Christ as the Peacemaker. Christ not only provided peace by His cross and proclaimed peace, He is peace personified. *He* is our peace. Peace then, is not something but Someone.

A few writers suggest that Shiloh means, "He whose right it is." Such an interpretation, however, is not far removed from the above meaning since the right or prerogative to usher in a reign of peace is Christ's (Ezek. 21:27). During His millennial reign, the name of Christ will be as ointment poured forth.

Emmanuel

The true believer has no difficulty in accepting Isaiah's prophecy of Christ who was virgin-born. "They shall call His name Emmanuel" (Isa. 7:14; Matt. 1:23). This further name meaning "God with us" indicates a progressive revelation of the Lord. In the Old Testament, it is "God *for* us." As the result of the Incarnation it is "God *with* us," for Christ came as God manifest in flesh. He came and dwelt among men (John 1:14). Through the advent of the Holy Spirit it is now "God *in* us." "*Christ in you,* the hope of glory" (Col. 1:27).

The prophet Isaiah also gives us a plurality of names under the singular form, "His *name*" (Isa. 9:6). Actually there are five names mentioned, although Isaiah says, "His name shall be called..." We have another instance of the use of the singular form to describe a plurality of persons in our Lord's commission, in which we are instructed to baptize all believers, "In the *name* of the Father, and of the Son, and of the Holy Spirit" (Matt. 28:19). One name — three Persons. A proof, surely, of the unity of the Godhead. Isaiah's names of Christ emanating from "His name," speak of the unity of His transcendent attributes. They are the various facets of the same brilliant diamond.

Wonderful

That this word is a name can be proved by the reply of the angel of the Lord to Manoah who had asked his name, "Why askest thou thus after my name, seeing it is secret" (Judg. 13:18)? The word for secret is "wonderful," and the same word in the next verse, "wonderously."

Is not Christ wonderful in all His works, ways and words? As we meditate upon His wonderful grace and contemplate His wonderful government we can truly say, "The world has never seen His like — and never will!"

Counselor

Some expositors bring these first two names together and refer to Christ as "The Wonderful Counselor" or "The Wonder of a Counselor." The One who could speak with authority came as the Embodiment of perfect wisdom and knowledge (Prov. 8:14). How tragic it is when men fail to ask counsel at His mouth (Josh. 9:14; II Chron. 25:16)! These are days when godless rulers take counsel together to destroy God's cause (Ps. 2:1; Neh. 6:7), but His counsel ever prevails. The life of a person or of a people is enriched when His name is joyfully and triumphantly accepted as "Counselor."

The Mighty God

Faith and fear can never exist together. If Christ is received and revered as "The Mighty God," doubts disappear. No foe is dreaded when this One, whom the winds and the waves obeyed, is at hand to preserve and bless. How can we yield to worry or unbelieving anxiety if we believe that all the power of the Godhead is at our disposal?

The Everlasting Father

What grief a father's death can cause! How we feel the loss of his transient guidance and provision! But the One born in Bethlehem was named "The Everlasting Father." In His everlasting love, within His everlasting arms, within His Father's heart which pitieth His own, we have safety, rest and comfort.

"The Father of Eternity" is given as the literal meaning of this expressive name. The attribute of everlastingness is His. He is from everlasting to everlasting and He permits us to share in His abiding and undecaying life.

The Prince of Peace

Loyal hearts live on His legacy of peace. "My peace I leave with you." Christ breathes an assured tranquility into our hearts. He makes us the recipients of a peace passing all understanding — and *misunderstanding* as well! Through His finished work at Calvary He provided peace for troubled hearts. We cannot *make* our peace with God. Through the blood of the Cross peace has been made. All the sinner can do is to accept this peace.

The royal day is coming when Christ will return to earth as the Prince of Peace. When He comes to usher in His reign there will be no frontiers to His kingdom of peace and righteousness (Zech. 4:5-9).

The Branch

Zechariah had a vision of the Lord when he wrote of Him, "Behold, the man whose name is The BRANCH" (Zech. 6:12). Just as the branch is the dependent part of a tree, so while on earth Christ thought of Himself as a Branch. "The Son can do nothing of Himself." In true humility He expressed His utter dependence upon the Father.

What are we but branches (John 15:5)? As such we have nothing and can do nothing apart from Christ. The function of the branch is to bear fruit. As the "Branch" Christ brought to fruition all the promises given to prophets and kings of old.

The Last Adam

Christ is not spoken of as "the *second* Adam" but as "the *last* Adam." No further federal Head is to come. Adam was the head of the human race. Christ is the Head of the spiritual race. Mankind is divided into those who are "in Adam" or "in Christ." The first Adam was created out of the dust of the earth. The last Adam was conceived of the Holy Spirit. The first Adam was born innocent and became a sinner. The last Adam was born holy and remained sinless. The first Adam was a man and remained a man, developing human frailties. The last Adam was made a quickening spirit — a life-giving Saviour. The first Adam was of the earth, earthy and natural. The last Adam was from heaven and spiritual (I Cor. 15:45-47).

The Word of God

John alone uses the glorious name. Describing Christ's return in power and glory, he says, "His name is called The Word of God" (Rev. 19:13). It is beyond the mind of men to conceive all that is embodied in this name of His. John elsewhere speaks of Him as being the Word from the dateless past (John 1:1).

As words are the expression of thought, so Christ came as the expression or revealer of the Father. He appeared as the culmination of the revelation of the Father (John 1:18; 14:9).

How one wishes it could have been possible within the scope of this book on Bible men to have dealt with the manifold titles and designations of Christ, as well as His explicit names! One writer has suggested that there are 365 names and titles given to Him, whose name is above every name, that is, an inspiring revelation of Him for each day of the year. If, however, we could bring them all together what else could we do but sing with Charles Wesley?

> Join all the glorious names
>   Of wisdom, love, and power,
> That ever mortals knew,
>   That angels ever bore:
> *All* are too mean to speak His worth,
>   Too mean to set my Saviour forth.

Bibliography

Bibliography

Bible Character Studies

Biblical Character Studies (London: James Nisbet and Co.).

Cumming, Elder, *Spiritual Photography* (Scotland: Drummonds Tract Society).

Mackay, W. Mackintosh, *Bible Types of Modern Men* (New York: George H. Doran Co.).

———, *The Men Whom Jesus Made* (New York: George H. Doran Co.).

Matheson, George, *Representative Men of the Bible* (London: Hodder and Stoughton).

Men of the Old Testament (Manchester: James Robins).

Moody, Talmadge and Parker, *Bible Characters* (Grand Rapids: Zondervan Publishing House).

Sell, Henry T., *Studies of Great Bible Men* (New York: Fleming H. Revell).

Waller, C. H., *The Names on the Gates of Pearl* (Sampson Low, Marston, Searle & Rivington).

White, W. W., *Studies in Old Testament Characters* (New York: International YMCA).

Whyte, Alexander, *Bible Characters* (Grand Rapids: Zondervan Publishing House).

Young, Dinsdale T., *Neglected People of the Bible* (London: Hodder and Stoughton).

Studies on the Twelve Apostles

Cumming, Elder, *He Chose Twelve* (Scotland: Drummonds Tract Society).

Edwards, F., *These Twelve* (London: Alexander and Shepheard).

Greenhough, J. G., *The Apostles of Our Lord* (London: Hodder and Stoughton).

Jones, J. D., *The Glorious Company of the Apostles* (London: James Clarke).

Lord, F. Townley, *The Master and His Men* (London: Carey Press).

M'Lean, Daniel, *Studies of the Apostles* (Edinburgh: John Menzies Co.).

Smith, Elsdon C., *The Study of Our Names* (New York: Harper Brothers).

Stevenson, Herbert F., *Titles of the Triune God* (London: Marshall, Morgan & Scott; New York: Fleming H. Revell).

Concordances and Commentaries

Baxter, J. Sidlow, *Explore the Book* (London: Marshall, Morgan & Scott).

Cruden, Alexander, *Cruden's Complete Concordance* (Grand Rapids: Zondervan Publishing House).

Davis, John, *A Dictionary of the Bible* (Philadelphia: Wilde and Co.).

Ellicott's Commentary of the Whole Bible (Grand Rapids: Zondervan Publishing House).

Fausset's Bible Encyclopaedia and Dictionary (Grand Rapids: Zondervan Publishing House).

Hastings, James, *The Dictionary of the Bible* (London: Hodder and Stoughton).

————, *The Greater Men and Women of the Bible* (London: Hodder and Stoughton).

The Scofield Reference Bible (New York: Oxford Press).

The Student's Bible Companion (London: Pickering and Inglis).

Young's Analytical Concordance (London: Lutterworth Press; New York: Funk & Wagnalls).

Index of Major Characters

Index of Major Characters

This is a partial index of the more familiar male characters in the Bible. Not designed to be complete, it will, nevertheless, serve to guide the reader quickly to the listing of the character in which he is interested.

We want to hear from you. Please send your comments about this book to us in care of the address below. Thank you.

ZONDERVAN™

GRAND RAPIDS, MICHIGAN 49530 USA

WWW.ZONDERVAN.COM